D0322894

Theoretical Aspects of
Reasoning About Knowledge
PROCEEDINGS OF THE 1986 CONFERENCE

Edited by
JOSEPH Y. HALPERN
IBM Almaden Research Center

MARCH 19–22, 1986
MONTEREY, CALIFORNIA

Cosponsored By
IBM
AMERICAN ASSOCIATION OF ARTIFICIAL INTELLIGENCE
and the
OFFICE OF NAVAL RESEARCH
In Cooperation With
ASSOCIATION FOR COMPUTING MACHINERY

Library of Congress Cataloging-in-Publication Data

Theoretical aspects of reasoning about knowledge :
    proceedings of the 1986 conference, March 19–22,
    1986, Monterey, California.

    Includes bibliographies and index.
    1. Artificial intelligence—Congresses.   2. Knowledge,
Theory of—Congresses.   3. Logic, Symbolic and Mathemati-
cal—Congresses.   4. Reasoning—Congresses.   I. Halpern,
Joseph Y., 1953–   . II. International Business
Machines Corporation.   III. American Association of
Artificial Intelligence.   IV. United States. Office
of Naval Research.   V. Association for Computing
Machinery.
Q334.T47   1986   006.3   86-2755
ISBN 0-934613-04-4

Morgan Kaufmann Publishers, Inc.
95 First Street
Los Altos, California 94022
© 1986 by Morgan Kaufmann Publishers, Inc.
All rights reserved.

90 89 88 87 86   5 4 3 2 1

TABLE OF CONTENTS

Foreword

Foreword

Work on reasoning about knowledge has been carried out by researchers in a number of different fields: philosophy, linguistics, artificial intelligence, economics, and theoretical computer science, among others. This conference represents the first attempt to bring together researchers from all these areas to discuss issues of mutual interest. In order to maintain a small workshop-like atmosphere, we decided to hold the conference at the Asilomar Conference Center in Monterey, California, and limit the number of attendees to a few invited people and authors of accepted papers.

Interest in the conference far exceeded all my expectations. I was deluged by requests for further information from all parts of the world. Ninety-eight papers were submitted in response to a call for papers. The program committee members - Michael Fischer, Joe Halpern, Hector Levesque, Robert Moore, Rohit Parikh, Robert Stalnaker, Richmond Thomason, and Moshe Vardi - considered all the papers carefully. At least three and usually four members of the committee read each one. In the end only nineteen of these papers were selected. There were two reasons for choosing so few. One, of course, was to make sure that only papers of the highest quality appeared. But, just as important, we wanted to make sure that the available time at the conference was not completely taken up by presentations; we hoped to allow participants at the conference plenty of time to exchange ideas.

This volume consists of those nineteen papers together with a few invited papers intended to provide an overview of the state of the art of the field. None of the final submissions was formally refereed, and many of them represent preliminary reports on continuing research. It is anticipated that most of these papers will appear, in more polished and complete form, in scientific journals. Nevertheless, I believe that anyone interested in the field of reasoning about knowledge will find this to be a useful volume of extremely high-quality papers.

There are a number of people and organizations that I would like to acknowledge at this point. First of all, the members of the program committee deserve special thanks for all their efforts in helping to bring about the conference. Besides reading papers, they had to help formulate guidelines for a first-ever conference of this type. Ron Fagin and Yoram Moses provided frequent suggestions and encouragement, while Suzette Bartz gave invaluable secretarial support. The conference was held in cooperation with the Association for Computing Machinery, and was made possible by the generous support of IBM, the American Association of Artificial Intelligence (AAAI), and the Office of Naval Research (under grant N00014-85-G-0244). Thanks again to everyone!

Joe Halpern

REASONING ABOUT KNOWLEDGE: AN OVERVIEW

Joseph Y. Halpern
IBM Research Laboratory
Almaden, CA 95193

Abstract: In this overview paper, I will attempt to identify and describe some of the common threads that tie together work in reasoning about knowledge in such diverse fields as philosophy, economics, linguistics, artificial intelligence, and theoretical computer science. I will briefly discuss some of the more recent work, particularly in computer science, and suggest some lines for future research.

1. Introduction

Although *epistemology*, the study of knowledge, has a long and honorable tradition in philosophy, starting with the Greeks, the idea of a formal logical analysis of reasoning about knowledge is somewhat more recent, going back to at least von Wright ([Wr]). The first book-length treatment of epistemic logic is Hintikka's seminal work, *Knowledge and Belief* [Hi1]. The 1960's saw a flourishing of interest in this area in the philosophy community. Axioms for knowledge were suggested, attacked, and defended. Models for the various axiomatizations were proposed, mainly in terms of possible-worlds semantics, and then again attacked and defended (see, for example, [Ge,Len,BP]).

More recently, reasoning about knowledge has found applications in such diverse fields as economics, linguistics, artificial intelligence, and computer science. While researchers in these areas have tended to look to philosophy for their initial inspiration, it has also been the case that their more pragmatic concerns, which often centered around more computational issues such as the difficulty of computing knowledge, have not been treated in the philosophical literature. The commonality of concerns of researchers in all these areas has been quite remarkable. Unfortunately, lack of communication between researchers in the various fields, while perhaps not as remarkable, has also been rather noticeable.

In this overview paper, I will attempt to identify and describe some of the common threads that tie together research in reasoning about knowledge in all the areas mentioned above. I will also briefly discuss some of the more recent work, particularly in computer science, and suggest some lines for future research. This should by no means be viewed as a comprehensive survey. The topics covered clearly reflect my own biases.

2. The "classical" model

We'll begin by reviewing the "classical" model for knowledge and belief (now over 25 years old!), the so-called *possible-worlds* model. The intuitive idea here is that besides the true state of affairs, there are a number of other possible states of affairs, or possible worlds. Some of these possible worlds may be indistinguishable to an agent from the true world. An agent is then said to *know* a fact φ if φ is true in all the worlds he thinks possible. For example, an agent may think that two states of the world are possible: in one it is sunny in London, while in the other it is raining in London. However, in both these states it is sunny in San Francisco. Thus, this agent knows that it is sunny in San Francisco, but does not know whether it is sunny in London.

The philosophical literature has tended to concentrate on the one-agent case, in order to emphasize the properties of knowledge. However, many applications of interest involve multiple agents. Then it becomes important to consider not only what an agent knows about "nature", but also what he knows about what the other agents know and don't know. It should be clear that this kind of reasoning is crucial in bargaining and economic decision making. As we shall see, it is also relevant in analyzing protocols in distributed computing systems (in this context, of course, the "agents" are the processors in the system). Such reasoning can get very complicated. Most people quickly lose the thread of such nested sentences as "Dean doesn't know whether Nixon knows that Dean knows that Nixon knows about the Watergate break-in"; (this example comes from [ClM], where the point is investigated further). But this is precisely the type of reasoning that goes on in proving lower bounds for certain distributed protocols (cf. [HM,DM]).

In order to formalize this situation, we first need a language. The language I'll consider here is a propositional modal logic for m agents. Starting with primitive propositions p, q, r, ..., more complicated formulas are formed by closing off under negation, conjunction, and the modal operators K_1, ..., K_m. Thus, if φ and ψ are formulas, then so are $\sim\varphi$, $\varphi \wedge \psi$, and $K_i\varphi$, $i = 1,...,m$. This last formula is read "agent i knows φ". The K_i's are called modal operators; hence the name modal logic. We could also consider a first-order modal logic that allows quantification, but the propositional case is somewhat simpler and has all the ingredients we need for our discussion.

Kripke structures [Kr] provide a useful formal tool for giving semantics to this language. A Kripke structure M is a tuple $(S, \pi, \mathscr{P}_1, ..., \mathscr{P}_m)$, where S is a set of *states* or *possible worlds*, π is an assignment of truth values to the primitive propositions for each state $s \in S$ (so that $\pi(s,p) \in \{\text{true}, \text{false}\}$ for each state s and primitive proposition p), and $\mathscr{P}_i$ is an equivalence relation on S for $i = 1,...,m$ (recall that an equivalence relation is a binary relation which is reflexive, symmetric, and transitive). $\mathscr{P}_i$ is agent i's *possibility relation*. Intuitively, $(s,t) \in \mathscr{P}_i$ if agent i cannot distinguish state s from state t (so that if s is the actual state of the world, agent i would consider t a possible state of the world).

We now define a relation $\models$, where $M, s \models \varphi$ is read "φ is true, or *satisfied*, in state s of model M":

$M, s \models p$ for a primitive proposition p if $\pi(p,s) = \text{true}$

$M, s \models \sim\varphi$ if $M, s \not\models \varphi$

$M, s \models \varphi \wedge \psi$ if $M, s \models \varphi$ and $M, s \models \psi$

$M, s \models K_i\varphi$ if $M, t \models \varphi$ for all t such that $(s,t) \in \mathscr{P}_i$.

The last clause is designed to capture the intuition that agent i knows φ exactly if φ is true in all the worlds that i thinks are possible.

These ideas are perhaps best illustrated by an example. One advantage of Kripke structures is that we can easily represent them as labelled directed graphs, where the nodes are exactly the states in S and two nodes s and t are connected by an edge labelled i exactly if $(s,t) \in \mathscr{P}_i$. Consider the graph below, where $S = \{s_1, s_2, s_3\}$ and there are two agents, Alice and Bob. Assume for simplicity there are only one primitive proposition in the language, say p. We can think of p as standing for "it is sunny in San Francisco". Thus, in state s_1, it is sunny

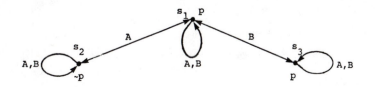

in San Francisco, but Alice doesn't know it (since she considers both s_1 and s_2 possible). On the other hand, she does know that Bob knows whether or not it is sunny in San Francisco (since in both states she considers possible, Bob knows the weather at that state). Bob knows that it is sunny in San Francisco, but he doesn't know that Alice doesn't know this fact (since he considers s_3 possible, and in s_3 Alice does know it!). Formally, we have

$$M, s_1 \models p \wedge \sim K_A p \wedge K_A (K_B p \vee K_B \sim p) \wedge K_B p \wedge \sim K_B \sim K_A p.$$

Note that in both s_1 and s_3, the primitive proposition p gets the same truth value. One might think that in some sense, therefore, s_1 and s_3 are the same, and one of them can be eliminated. This is not true! A state is not completely characterized by the truth values that the primitive propositions get there. The possibility relation is also crucial. For example, at s_1, Alice doesn't know p, while at s_3 she does. Even with only one primitive proposition, there are non-trivial models with infinitely many states.

The notion of knowledge defined here has a number of interesting technical properties. It can be shown that if a formula φ is satisfiable in some model, it is satisfiable in a model with at most 2^n states, where n is the length of φ viewed as a string of symbols. From this result, it follows that the logic is decidable: there is an algorithm that, given a formula φ, can tell whether or not it is *valid* (i.e., true in every state of every model). However, deciding validity is not easy. Any algorithm that does so requires space polynomial in the size of the input formula ([HM2]). Since we believe polynomial space corresponds to exponential time, this would suggest it would also require time exponential in the size of the formula, a quite unreasonable requirement in practice. The one-agent case is somewhat simpler. As shown by Ladner [La], a satisfiable formula in the one-agent case can in fact always be satisfied in a model with at most n states. As a consequence, the decision procedure in the one-agent case in NP-complete. However, we also believe that NP-complete problems require exponential time in practice, so even the one-agent case is quite difficult. (See [HU] for an introduction to complexity theory.)

The notion of knowledge we have been considering can be completely characterized by the following *sound* and *complete* axiom system, due to Hintikka ([Hi1]); i.e., all the axioms are valid and every valid formula can be proved from these axioms.

A1. All instances of propositional tautologies.

A2. $K_i \varphi \wedge K_i (\varphi \Rightarrow \psi) \Rightarrow K_i \psi$

A3. $K_i \varphi \Rightarrow \varphi$

A4. $K_i \varphi \Rightarrow K_i K_i \varphi$

A5. $\sim K_i \varphi \Rightarrow K_i \sim K_i \varphi$

R1. $\dfrac{\varphi, \ \varphi \Rightarrow \psi}{\psi}$ (modus ponens)

R2. $\dfrac{\varphi}{K_i \varphi}$

A1 and R1, of course, are holdovers from propositional logic. A2 says that an agent's knowledge is closed under implication, A3 says that an agent only knows things that are true. This is the axiom that is usually taken to distinguish *knowledge* from *belief*. You cannot know a fact that is false, although you may believe it. A4 and A5 are axioms of introspection. Intuitively, they say that an agent is introspective: he can look at his knowledge base and will know what he knows and doesn't know. There are numerous papers in the philosophical literature discussing the appropriateness of these axioms (cf. [Len]). Philosophers have tended to reject both of the introspection axioms for various reasons.

The validity of A3, A4, and A5 is due to the fact that we have taken the $\mathcal{P}_i$'s to be equivalence relations. In a precise sense, A3 follows from the fact that $\mathcal{P}_i$ is reflexive, A4 from the fact that it is transitive, and A5 from the fact that it is symmetric and transitive. By modifying the properties of the $\mathcal{P}_i$ relations, we can get notions of knowledge that satisfy different axioms. For example, by taking $\mathcal{P}_i$ to be reflexive and transitive, but not necessarily symmetric, we retain A3 and A4, but lose A5; similar modifications give us a notion that corresponds to belief, and does not satisfy A3. (See [HM2] for a survey of these issues, as well as a review of the standard techniques of modal logic which give completeness proofs in all these cases.)

However, the possible-worlds approach seems to commit us to A2 and R2. This forces us to a view of our agents as "ideal knowers", ones that know all valid formulas as well as all logical consequences of their knowledge. This certainly doesn't seem to be a realistic model for human agents (although it might perhaps be acceptable as a first approximation). Nor does it seem to even be an adequate model for a knowledge base which is bounded in terms of the computation time and space in memory that it can use. We discuss some approaches to this problem of *logical omniscience* in Section 5 below.

3. A concrete interpretation: distributed systems

While it is not clear whether or not the model presented above is appropriate for human reasoning, it can capture quite well much of the reasoning that goes on in analyzing distributed systems. Indeed, the distributed systems point of view allows us to give quite a concrete interpretation to states in a Kripke structure.

A distributed system consists of a collection of processors, say $1, ..., m$, connected by a communication network. The processors communicate with each other over the links in the network. Each processor is a state machine, which at all times is in some state. This state is a function of its initial state, the messages it has received, and possibly some internal events (such as the ticking of a clock). The *global state* of the system is just a description of each processor's state. We can associate a Kripke structure with a distributed system by taking the states in the structure to be all the possible global states of the system over time. The $\mathcal{P}_i$ relations are defined by $(s, t) \in \mathcal{P}_i$ if processor i has the same state in global states s and t. Note that this definition makes $\mathcal{P}_i$ an equivalence relation. The primitive propositions in this setting would be statements like "the value of processor i's local variable x is 0" or "processor j's current state is σ".

This model, or slight variants of it, has appeared in many recent papers in distributed systems (cf. [HM1,PR,HF,ChM,DM,FI,LR,FV2]). Note that in this model, knowledge is an "external" notion. We don't imagine a processor scratching its head wondering whether or not it knows a certain fact φ. Rather, a programmer reasoning about a particular protocol would say, from the outside, that the processor knows φ because in all global states consistent with its current state (intuitively, all the global states that the processor could be in, for all it knows) φ is true.

This notion of knowledge is information based, and does *not* take into account, for example, the difficulty involved in computing knowledge. Nor could a processor necessarily answer questions based on its knowledge, with respect to this definition of knowledge. So on what basis can we even view this as knowledge? When trying to prove properties such as lower bounds on the number of rounds required to complete a given protocol, the kinds of arguments that one often hears have the form "We can't stop after only three rounds, because processor 1 might not know that processor 2 knows that processor 3 is faulty." Now this informal use of the word "know" is exactly captured by the definition above. Let φ state that processor 2 knows that processor 3 is faulty. Then processor 1 doesn't know φ exactly if there is a global state of the system that it cannot distinguish from the actual state where φ does not hold; i.e., where processor 2 doesn't know that processor 3 is faulty.

It is interesting to note that essentially the identical notion of knowledge was developed independently by Rosenschein and his coworkers (cf. [Ro,RK]) and used for describing and analyzing situated automata in AI applications.

4. Some variants of the "classical" model

While we can give states in a Kripke structure a clear interpretation when we are considering distributed systems, their interpretation is not so clear when we try to model human reasoning, even assuming we are dealing with "ideal knowers". Recall that a state cannot be characterized simply by the primitive propositions that are true in that state. A better characterization of a state would consist of the primitive propositions that are true there, together with the set of states that each agent cannot distinguish from that state (this, after all, is the information carried by the edges of the graph corresponding to the Kripke structure). But this is circular: we are characterizing a state in terms of other states!

The circularity can be broken by taking the knowledge structures approach described in [FHV]. A *knowledge structure* is constructed inductively as follows. A depth 0 world is just a truth assignment to the primitive propositions. A depth 1 world essentially consists of a set of depth 0 worlds for each agent, intuitively, all those depth 0 worlds that the agent thinks possible; a depth 2 world essentially consists of a set of depth 1 worlds for each agent, etc. (There are also some consistency conditions that these worlds must satisfy, but we omit them here.) The limit of this construction is a knowledge structure.

There is a very close relationship between knowledge structures and Kripke structures. Every state in a Kripke structure corresponds to a knowledge structure where the same formulas are true, and every knowledge structure corresponds to a state in some Kripke structure. Thus the same axioms characterize knowledge structures and Kripke structures. By modifying the consistency conditions that worlds must satisfy, we can get knowledge structures that do not necessarily satisfy A3, A4, and A5 ([FHV,FV1,Va1]). However, just as for Kripke structures, we do seem to be committed to A2 and R2.

Interestingly, a parallel development is apparent in the economics literature on knowledge. The first economics paper to give a formal model for knowledge is that of Aumann [Au]; his model is essentially identical to a Kripke structure, but with the added feature of a probability measure on the set of states.[1] Then Mertens and Zamir constructed a model that is essentially a knowledge structure, carrying along the probability at each level (cf. [MZ]). By including probability in the picture in this way, we can reason about the probability an agent assigns to another agent assigning a certainly probability that certain propositions are true, and so on. Such an analysis is critical in, for example, game-theoretic arguments.

5. The problem of logical omniscience

As we mentioned above, all the models that have been described so far assume that agents are ideal knowers, who know all valid formulas and all logical consequences of their knowledge. Clearly this is not a realistic view of human agents; it is also an inappropriate model for a number of other applications. What features an appropriate model should have may depend on the application.

One approach that has frequently been suggested is the syntactic approach: what an agent knows is simply represented by a set of formulas (cf. [Eb,MoH]). Of course, this set need not be constrained to be closed under logical consequence or to contain all instances of a given axiom scheme. While this approach does allow us to define a notion of knowledge that doesn't suffer from the logical omniscience problem, it is a notion that is extremely difficult to analyze. If knowledge is represented by an arbitrary set of formulas, we have no principles to guide a knowledge-based analysis. A somewhat more sophisticated approach is taken by Konolige ([Ko]), who considers starting with a set of base facts, and then closing off under a (possibly incomplete) set of deduction rules.

One semantic approach that has been taken is to augment the standard possible worlds by "impossible" worlds, where the customary rules of logic do not hold (cf. [Cr1,Ra,RB]). However, these impossible worlds have not been very well motivated (although see [Hi2] for motivation for one of these models). More recently, Levesque ([Lev2]) has given a more

---

1 Actually, instead of considering equivalence relations, Aumann viewed the $\mathscr{P}_i$'s as *partitions* of S, where a partition is a set of disjoint subsets whose union is all of S. But a partition is just another way of looking at an equivalence relation. More formally, given a partition $\mathscr{P}$ of S, we can construct the equivalence relation $\mathscr{P}'$ where $(s,t) \in \mathscr{P}'$ iff s and t are in the same subset of $\mathscr{P}$. Conversely, given an equivalence relation $\mathscr{P}'$, we can construct the partition $\mathscr{P}$ whose subsets consist of the equivalence classes of $\mathscr{P}'$.

intuitively plausible semantic approach. He distinguishes between *implicit* knowledge and *explicit* knowledge, where explicit knowledge consists of those facts that you are explicitly aware of, while implicit knowledge consists, intuitively, of all the logical consequences of explicit knowledge. Of course, an agent may not be aware of all his implicit knowledge. It is implicit knowledge that satisfies all the axioms we discussed above. Levesque considers a possible-worlds model where, in a given state, a primitive proposition may be either true, false, both (so that the state is inconsistent), or neither.[2] He then develops a logic of implicit and explicit belief based on this approach. (Although Levesque considers belief rather than knowledge, his results can easily be extended to the case of knowledge.) Explicit belief implies implicit belief, but not conversely. It turns out that $B\varphi \Rightarrow B\psi$ holds in Levesque's logic for propositional formulas φ and ψ exactly if φ *entails* ψ in *relevance logic*,[3] where B is the modal operator for explicit belief (Levesque only considers the one-agent case, so the B is not subscripted). Levesque's logic avoids the logical omniscience problem, in that it is not the case that if φ is a tautology, then $B\varphi$ holds. However, an agent in Levesque's logic is still a perfect reasoner as far as relevance logic may be concerned. While it is not clear that humans are any better at relevance logic than propositional logic, there may still be some interesting applications to Levesque's ideas. For example, Levesque has shown that for an interesting subclass of formulas in his logic (namely, those of the form $B\varphi \Rightarrow B\psi$, where φ and ψ are propositional formulas in conjunctive normal form), the validity problem can be decided in polynomial time. Such results indicate that this may be a useful logic for a knowledge base to use. An efficient algorithm could be written which would allow a knowledge base to answer questions based on what it knows, with respect to this notion of knowledge.

Levesque's polynomial time results do not seem to extend once we allow meta-reasoning (i.e., an agent reasoning about his own knowledge) or consider several agents. We remark, though, that by extending Levesque's ideas, Patel-Schneider ([Pa]) and Lakemeyer ([Lak]) have designed semantics for a first-order logic of knowledge which has an interesting decidable fragment.

Fagin and Halpern have taken a slightly different approach to this issue ([FH]). Their *logic of general awareness* is essentially a mixture of syntax and semantics. It starts with a standard Kripke structure, and adds to each state a set of formulas that the agent is "aware" of at that state. Implicit knowledge is defined just as knowledge was before. Explicit knowledge consists of implicit knowledge plus awareness. Thus an agent explicitly knows φ if φ is true in all the worlds an agent considers possible and φ is in the awareness set for

---

2   Levesque calls his states *situations*, and they are essentially the situations of *situation semantics* (cf. [BP]). For further details on the situation semantics approach to modelling knowledge and belief, the interested reader is encouraged to consult [BP].

3   Relevance logic is a weakening of propositional logic that uses a notion of entailment rather than implication. It was motivated by a desire to avoid some of the well-known paradoxes of implication in propositional logic, such as the fact that $(\varphi \Rightarrow \psi) \vee (\psi \Rightarrow \varphi)$ is a tautology for any formulas φ and ψ. See [AB] for further discussion.

that agent.   We can give these models a concrete interpretation along the lines of the distributed system interpretation described above by imagining that each processor is running some algorithm to compute what it knows, given the information it has received.   The awareness set is just the set of formulas it can figure out the truth of, using this algorithm, in some prespecified time or space bound.

Let me mention one final approach to the problem of logical omniscience, this one inspired by work of Montague. Montague gives a possible-worlds semantics to epistemic logic (in that formulas are still associated with sets of possible worlds), but knowledge is not modelled as a relation between possible worlds; i.e., there is no $\mathcal{P}_i$ relation ([Mon]; see also [Va2]). By doing this we lose the intuition that an agent knows φ exactly if φ is true in all worlds that agent considers possible. But this approach does provide a handle to getting around the logical omniscience problem.   One deficiency in Montague's semantics is that, while agents need not know all logical consequences of their knowledge, they are unable to distinguish between logically equivalent formulas. To solve this, Thomason went a step further by supplying a model-theoretic semantics that does not use possible worlds [Th] (see also [Cr2]).

6. Common knowledge

A persistent theme in almost every discipline that has considered knowledge at all is the study of *common knowledge* and its cousins, such as *mutual belief*. There are many approaches to defining common knowledge (see [Ba] for a discussion). For our purposes, we can take it to be the case that when a group has common knowledge of φ, then not only does everyone in the group know that φ is true, but everyone knows that everyone knows, everyone knows that everyone knows that everyone knows, etc.   Note that if we take $E\varphi$ to represent "everyone knows φ" and $C\varphi$ to represent "φ is common knowledge", then it is straightforward to give semantics to these formulas in Kripke structures:

$M, s \models E\varphi$ if $M, t \models \varphi$ for all t such that $(s, t) \in \mathcal{P}_1 \cup ... \cup \mathcal{P}_m$

(so that $M, s \models E\varphi$ iff $M, s \models K_1\varphi \wedge ... \wedge K_m\varphi$)

$M, s \models C\varphi$ if $M, s \models E^k\varphi$ for $k = 1, 2, ...$, where $E^1\varphi = E\varphi$ and $E^{k+1}\varphi = EE^k\varphi$.

This key notion was first studied by David Lewis, in the context of conventions ([Lew]). Lewis points out that in order for something to be a convention, it must be common knowledge among the members of the group. It also arises in discourse understanding. If Ann asks Bob "Have you ever seen the movie playing at the Roxy tonight?", then in order for this question to be interpreted appropriately, not only must Ann and Bob know what movie is playing tonight, but Ann must know that Bob knows, Bob must know that Ann knows that Bob knows, etc. (this is discussed in great detail in [ClM], although see [PC] for a slightly dissenting view).

Interest in common knowledge in the economics community was inspired by Aumann's seminal result [Au]. Aumann showed that if two people have the same priors, and their posteriors for a given event are common knowledge, then these posteriors must be equal. This result says that people with the same priors *cannot agree to disagree*. Since then, common knowledge has received a great deal of attention in the economics literature, with issues such as complete axiomatizations ([Mi]) and the number of rounds of communication information required before the posteriors for an event become common knowledge ([GP]) being examined. (Further results and references can be found in [MS,Ca,TW].)

The questions that have arisen in distributed systems work on knowledge are surprisingly similar to those of economics. Again the key observation is that agreement implies common knowledge of the agreement, so that common knowledge becomes an important tool in analyzing protocols for agreement. To help illustrate this point, consider the *coordinated attack problem* from the distributed systems folklore ([Gr]):[4]

Two divisions of an army are camped on two hilltops overlooking a common valley. In the valley awaits the enemy. It is clear that if both divisions attack the enemy simultaneously they will win the battle, whereas if only one division attacks it will be defeated. The divisions do not initially have plans for launching an attack on the enemy, and the commanding general of the first division wishes to coordinate a simultaneous attack (at some time the next day). Neither general will decide to attack unless he is sure that the other will attack with him. The generals can only communicate by means of a messenger. Normally, it takes the messenger one hour to get from one encampment to the other. However, it is possible that he will get lost in the dark or, worse yet, be captured by the enemy. Fortunately, on this particular night, everything goes smoothly. How long will it take them to coordinate an attack?

Suppose the messenger sent by general A makes it to general B with a message saying "Let's attack at dawn". Will general B attack? Of course not, since general A does not know he got the message, and thus may not attack. So general B sends the messenger back with an acknowledgement. Suppose the messenger makes it. Will general A attack? No, because now general B does not know he got the message, so he thinks general A may think that he (B) didn't get the original message, and thus not attack. So A sends the messenger back with an acknowledgement. But of course, this is not enough either. I will leave it to the reader to convince himself that no amount of acknowledgements sent back and forth will ever guarantee agreement. Note that this is true even if the messenger succeeds in delivering the message every time. All that is required in this reasoning is the *possibility* that the messenger doesn't succeed.

This rather convoluted reasoning can easily be expressed in terms of knowledge. Each time the messenger makes a transit, the depth of the generals' knowledge increases by one, so it goes from "B knows" to "A knows that B knows" to "A knows that B knows that A

---

4   The following discussion is taken from [HM1].

knows" (that the attack is to be held at dawn), and so on. However, they never attain common knowledge that the attack is to be held at dawn by this protocol. Indeed, it can be shown (see [HM1]), that in any system where communication is not guaranteed, common knowledge is not attainable. Since it can also be shown that in a precise sense agreement implies common knowledge, it follows as a corollary that the generals cannot agree to a coordinated attack *in any run of any protocol.* (Of course, this does not rule out the possibility of a probabilistic notion of agreement, so that with high probability they both attack.)

Interestingly, Halpern and Moses show that not only is common knowledge not attainable in systems where communication is not guaranteed, it is also not attainable in systems where communication *is* guaranteed, as long as there is some uncertainty in message delivery time. Thus, in practical distributed systems, common knowledge is not attainable. This remark holds for systems of communicating humans as well as processors. What is going on here? After all, we often do reach agreement (or seem to!). Common knowledge is attainable in "idealized" models of reality where we assume, for example, events can be guaranteed to happen simultaneously. Even if we cannot always make this assumption in practice, it turns out that there are some variants of common knowledge that are attainable under more reasonable assumptions, and these variants are indistinguishable in certain cases from true common knowledge (see [HM1]). Such variants may prove a useful tool for specifying and analyzing different assumptions on communication in distributed systems (see also [FI] for further discussion along these lines).

7. Knowledge, communication, and action

Implicit in much of the previous discussion has been the strong relationship between knowledge, communication, and action. Indeed, much of the motivation for studying knowledge by researchers in all areas has been that of understanding the knowledge required to perform certain actions, and how that knowledge can be acquired through communication. I will just briefly touch on some of the more recent trends in this area.

Early work of McCarthy and Hayes [McH] argued that a planning program needs to explicitly reason about its ability to perform an action. Moore [Mo] took this one step further by emphasizing the crucial relationship between knowledge and action. Knowledge is necessary to perform actions, and new knowledge is gained as a result of performing actions. Moore went on to construct a logic with possible-worlds semantics that allowed explicit reasoning about knowledge and action, and then considered the problem of automatically generating deductions within the logic. This work has recently been extended by Morgenstern [Mor]; she views "know" as a syntactic predicate on formulas rather than a modal operator.

Another issue that has received a lot of attention recently is the relationship between knowledge and communication. Levesque considered this from the point of view of a knowledge base that could interact with its domain via *TELL* and *ASK* operations ([Lev1]). He showed, somewhat surprisingly, that the result of *TELL*ing a knowledge base an arbitrary sentence in a first-order logic of knowledge is always equivalent to the result of *TELL*ing it a purely first-order sentence (i.e. one without any occurrences of K). It is worth remarking here that it is crucial to Levesque's result that there is only one knowledge base, i.e. one agent, in the picture.

Characterizing the states of knowledge that result after communication is also surprisingly subtle. One might think, for example, that after telling someone a fact p they will know p (at least, if it is common knowledge that the teller is honest). But this is not true. For example, consider the sentence "p is true but you don't know it". When told to agent i, this would be represented as $p \wedge \sim K_i p$. Now this sentence might be perfectly true when it is said. But after i is told this fact, it is not the case that $K_i(p \wedge \sim K_i p)$ holds. In fact, this latter formula is provably inconsistent! It is the case, though, that i knows that $p \wedge \sim K_i p$ was true before, although it is no longer true now.

Even if we do not allow formulas that refer to knowledge, consider the difficulty of characterizing the knowledge of an agent Alice that has been told only one fact: the primitive proposition p. Intuitively, all she knows is p. Since we are assuming ideal agents, Alice also knows all the logical consequence of p. But is this all she knows? Suppose q is another primitive proposition. Surely Alice doesn't know q, i.e. $\sim K_A q$ holds. But we assume Alice can do perfect introspection, so that she knows about her lack of knowledge of q. Thus $K_A \sim K_A q$ holds. But this means that even if "all Alice knows is p", then she also knows $\sim K_A q$, which is surely not a logical consequence of p! The situation can get even more complicated if we let Bob into the picture. For then Alice knows that Bob doesn't know that Alice knows q (how can he, since in fact she doesn't know q, and Bob does not know false facts). And knowing that Bob can also do perfect introspection, Alice knows that Bob knows this fact; i.e., $K_A K_B \sim K_B K_A p$ holds! Thus, despite her limited knowledge, Alice knows a nontrivial fact about Bob's knowledge (see [FHV,HM3] for further discussion of these points). Part of the difficulty here is due to *negative introspection*, i.e., the fact that one has knowledge about one's own lack of knowledge. If we remove this feature from our model (i.e., discard axiom A5), things become much easier (cf. [Va1]).

A related issue is characterizing what states of knowledge are attainable as a function of the communication medium. [HM1] already shows that while common knowledge is a perfectly consistent state of knowledge, it is not attainable if communication is not guaranteed or even if it is guaranteed and there is uncertainty about the message transmission time (see [ChM,FI] for related results). [FV2] provides a complete characterization of the states of knowledge of the current world attainable in a synchronous system where communication is not guaranteed. However, many open questions still remain in this area. Typical examples include: characterizing asynchronous systems, proving bounds on the number of messages required to attain certain attainable states of knowledge (cf. the results of [GP]), and dealing with knowledge about the past and future.

Most of the work discussed above has implicitly or explicitly assumed that the messages received are consistent. The situation gets much more complicated if messages may be inconsistent. This quickly leads into a whole complex of issues involving belief revision and reasoning in the presence of inconsistency. Although I won't attempt to open this can of worms here, these are issues that must eventually be considered in designing a knowledge base, for example, since there is always the possibility of getting inconsistent information from a user (see [Be] for some further discussion on this topic).

8. Areas for Further Research

I will conclude now with what I consider to be a number of hard problems for further research. Although they are listed separately below, it should be clear that there is a lot of overlap among them. Many of these problems have already been mentioned in this overview. Of course, these are only *some* of the important problems in the field; the list is by no means an exhaustive.

1. *Models for resource-bounded reasoning.* Find models appropriate to capture resource-bounded reasoners, particularly models that incorporate time. Another desideratum for such models is that they be powerful and flexible enough to capture various theories of learning. There have actually been a number of papers that have considered logics of knowledge and time (cf. [Sa,Leh,LR,HV]). Fagin and Halpern [FH] show that interesting properties of bounded reasoning can be captured by letting the awareness set vary over time. However, no attempt has been made to systematically study and model situations where such change occurs.

2. *Models that take into account the cost of acquiring knowledge.* These may very well end up being special cases of models that model resource-bounded reasoning, but the idea of cost of knowledge is so important that I include it as a special case here. Cost of acquiring knowledge is particularly relevant in such areas as cryptography and economics. Goldwasser, Micali, and Rackoff's work on *knolwedge complexity* ([GMR]), which attempts to quantify the amount of information released during an interaction in terms of computational complexity theory, may provide the right approach to tackling this problem. The idea here is that you gain extra information as a result of an interaction exactly if you can perform a computation using your limited (polynomial-time) resources that you could not perform before the interaction.

3. *Logics of knowledge with easy decision procedures.* Find well-motivated sublanguages that are simple enough to allow a computer to completely carry out all reasoning in that sublanguage, yet powerful enough to capture many features of interest. (See [Lev2,Pa,Lak] for some steps in this direction.) These logics should allow meta-reasoning (reasoning about one's own knowledge) and reasoning about the knowledge of other agents if at all possible.

4. *Knowledge, action, and communication.* Find good models for the interaction between knowledge and action, especially when the knowledge is partial. Characterize the states of knowledge attainable under different assumptions on the communication medium.

5. *Knowledge and cryptography.* Relate some of these models to work going on in understanding cryptographic protocols. The idea is to formally analyze, for example, *public key*

cryptosystems such as that of [RSA]. Here all the information required to break the code is known in principle (since the encoding key is published publicly, say in a telephone book), but the code is still hard to break since (we believe) it is very hard to compute the decoding key from the encoding key. Some preliminary steps have already been taken (see, for example, [Me,GMR]), but much work remains to be done. Note that the cost of computing knowledge becomes particularly important here, as well as analyzing probabilistic knowledge. Being able to break the code with high probability is essentially as good as knowing how to break the code.

The problems listed above are far from completely specified. Indeed, a large part of the difficulty of the problem lies in finding a precise formulation of it amenable to attack. And, at least as important, is the problem of finding a formulation that is intuitively natural, and can really be used to clarify the analysis of important problems in areas such as economics, linguistics, or distributed computation. Further experience with using knowledge to specify and reason about distributed systems and AI systems should help to enhance our understanding as well as guiding further research. Indeed, by focussing in on such applications we can often get a much better grasp of how to handle more general problems. I am optimistic that major advances can be made on a number of fronts in the near future.

Because reasoning about knowledge is an area that lies at the intersection of a number of fields, any advances made could have wide-spread impact. But in order for this to be true, researchers in the relevant communities need to be more aware of each other's work. I hope that this paper will help open the lines of communication.

Acknowledgements: I'd like to thank Ron Fagin, Hector Levesque, Yoram Moses, and Moshe Vardi for their useful comments on an earlier draft of this paper.

References

[AB]   A. R. Anderson and N.D. Belnap, *Entailment, the Logic of Relevance and Necessity*, Princeton University Press, 1975.

[Au]   R.J. Aumann, Agreeing to disagree, *Annals of Statistics*, 1976, pp. 1236-1239.

[Ba]   J. Barwise, Modelling shared understanding, unpublished manuscript, 1985.

[BP]   J. Barwise and J. Perry, *Situations and Attitudes*, Bradford Books, MIT Press, 1983.

[Be]   N.D. Belnap, A useful four-valued logic, in *Modern Uses of Multiple-Valued Logic* (eds. G. Epstein and J.M. Dunn), Reidel, 1977.

[Ca]   J.A.K. Cave, Learning to agree, *Economics Letters* **12**, 1983, pp. 147-152.

[ChM]   M. Chandy and J. Misra, How processes learn, *Proceedings of the 4th ACM Symposium on Principles of Distributed Computing*, 1985, pp. 204-214.

[CM]   H.H. Clark and C.R. Marshall, Definite reference and mutual knowledge, in *Elements of Discourse Understanding* (eds. A.K. Joshi, B.L. Webber, and I.A. Sag), Cambridge University Press, 1981.

[Cr1]   M.J. Cresswell, *Logics and Languages*, Methuen and Co., 1973.

[Cr2]   M.J. Cresswell, *Structured Meanings*, MIT Press, 1985.

[DM]   C. Dwork and Y. Moses, Knowledge and common knowledge in a Byzantine environment I: crash failures, to appear in *Proceedings of the Conference on Theoretical Aspects of Reasoning About Knowledge* (ed. J.Y. Halpern), Morgan Kaufmann, 1986.

[Eb]   R. A. Eberle, A logic of believing, knowing and inferring, *Synthese* 26, 1974, pp. 356-382.

[FH]   R. Fagin and J.Y. Halpern, Belief, awareness, and limited reasoning, *Proceedings of the Ninth International Joint Conference on Artificial Intelligence*, 1985, pp. 491-501.

[FHV]   R. Fagin, J.Y. Halpern, and M.Y. Vardi, A model-theoretic analysis of knowledge, *Proceedings of the 25th Annual IEEE Symposium on Foundations of Computer Science*, 1984, pp. 268-278.

[FV1]   R. Fagin and M. Y. Vardi, An internal semantics for modal logic, *Proceedings of the 17th ACM Symposium on Theory of Computing*, 1985, pp. 305-315.

[FV2]   R. Fagin and M.Y. Vardi, Knowledge and implicit knowledge in a distributed environment, *Proceedings of the Conference on Theoretical Aspects of Reasoning About Knowledge* (ed. J.Y. Halpern), Morgan Kaufmann, 1986.

[FI]   M.J. Fischer and N. Immerman, Foundations of knowledge for distributed systems, *Proceedings of the Conference on Theoretical Aspects of Reasoning About Knowledge* (ed. J.Y. Halpern), Morgan Kaufmann, 1986.

[GP]   J. Geanokoplos and H. Polemarchakis, We can't disagree forever, *Journal of Economic Theory* 28:1, 1982, pp. 192-200.

[Ge]   E. Gettier, Is justified true belief knowledge?, *Analysis* 23, 1963, pp. 121-123

[GMR]   S. Goldwasser, S. Micali, and C. Rackoff, The knowledge complexity of interactive proof-systems, *Proceedings of the 17th Symposium on Theory of Computing* 1985, pp. 291-304.

[Gr]   J. Gray, Notes on data base operating systems, IBM Research Report RJ 2188, 1978.

[HF]   J.Y. Halpern and R. Fagin, A formal model of knowledge, action, and communication in distributed systems: preliminary report, *Proceedings of the 4th ACM Symposium on the Principles of Distributed Computing*, 1985, pp. 224-236.

[HM1]   J.Y. Halpern and Y.O. Moses, Knowledge and common knowledge in a distributed environment, *Proceedings of the 3rd ACM Conference on Principles of Distributed Computing*, 1984, pp. 50-61; revised version to appear as IBM Research Report, Jan. 1986.

[HM2]   J.Y. Halpern and Y.O. Moses, A guide to the modal logics of knowledge and belief: preliminary report, *Proceedings of the Ninth International Joint Conference on Artificial Intelligence*, pp. 480-490, 1985.

[HM3]   J.Y. Halpern and Y.O. Moses, Towards a theory of knowledge and ignorance, in *Proceedings of the Workshop on Non-Monotonic Reasoning*, AAAI, 1984; also reprinted in *Logics and Models of Concurrent Systems* (ed. K. Apt), Springer-Verlag, 1985, pp. 459-476.

[HV]   J.Y. Halpern and M.Y. Vardi, The complexity of reasoning about knowledge and time, unpublished manuscript, 1985.

[Hi1]   J. Hintikka, *Knowledge and belief*, Cornell University Press, 1962.

[Hi2]   J. Hintikka, Impossible possible worlds vindicated, *Journal of Philosophical Logic* **4** 1975, pp. 475-484.

[HU]   J.E. Hopcroft and J.D. Ullman, *Introduction to Automata Theory, Languages, and Computation*, Addison-Wesley, 1979.

[Ko]   K. Konolige, Belief and incompleteness, SRI Artificial Intelligence Note 319, SRI International, Menlo Park, 1984.

[Kr]   S. Kripke, Semantical analysis of modal logic, *Zeitschrift fur Mathematische Logik und Grundlagen der Mathematik* **9**, 1963, pp. 67-96.

[Lad]   R.E. Ladner, The computational complexity of provability in systems of modal propositional logic, *SIAM Journal on Computing* **6**:3, 1977, pp. 467-480.

[LR]   R. Ladner and J.H. Reif, The logic of distributed protocols, *Proceedings of the Conference on Theoretical Aspects of Reasoning About Knowledge* (ed. J.Y. Halpern), Morgan Kaufmann, 1986.

[Lak]   G. Lakemeyer, Steps towards a first-order logic of explicit and implicit belief, *Proceedings of the Conference on Theoretical Aspects of Reasoning About Knowledge* (ed. J.Y. Halpern), Morgan Kaufmann, 1986.

[Leh]   D.J. Lehmann, Knowledge, common knowledge, and related puzzles, *Proceedings of the Third Annual ACM Conference on Principles of Distributed Computing*, 1984, pp. 62-67.

[Len]   W. Lenzen, Recent work in epistemic logic, *Acta Philosophica Fennica* **30**, 1978, pp. 1-219.

[Lev1]   H.J. Levesque, Foundations of a functional approach to knowledge representation, *Artificial Intelligence* **23**, 1984, pp. 155-212.

[Lev2]   H. J. Levesque, A logic of implicit and explicit belief, *Proceedings of the National Conference on Artificial Intelligence*, 1984, pp. 198-202; a revised and expanded version appears as FLAIR Technical Report #32, 1984.

[Lew]   D. Lewis, *Convention, A Philosophical Study*, Harvard University Press, 1969.

[McH]   J. McCarthy and P.J. Hayes, Some philosophical problems form the standpoint of artificial intelligence, in *Machine Intelligence* **4** (eds. B. Meltzer and D. Michie), Edinburgh University Press, 1969, pp. 463-502

[Me]   M. J. Merritt, *Cryptographic Protocols*, Ph.D. Thesis, Georgia Institute of Technology, 1983.

[MZ]   J.F. Mertens and S. Zamir, Formalization of Harsanyi's notion of "type" and "consistency" in games with incomplete information, C.O.R.E. Discussion Paper, Universite Catholique de Louvain, 1982.

[Mi]   P. Milgrom, An axiomatic characterization of common knowledge, *Econometrica*, **49**:1, 1981, pp. 219-222.

[MS]   P. Milgrom and N. Stokey, Information, trade, and common knowledge, *Journal of Economic Theory* **26**:1, 1982, pp. 17-26.

[Mon]   R. Montague, Universal grammar, *Theoria* **36**, 1970, pp. 373-398.

[Mo]   R.C. Moore, Reasoning about knowledge and action, Technical Note 191, Artificial Intelligence Center, SRI International, 1980.

[MoH]   R. C. Moore and G. Hendrix, Computational models of beliefs and the semantics of belief sentences, Technical Note 187, SRI International, Menlo Park, 1979.

[Mor]   L. Morgenstern, A first-order theory of planning, knowledge and action, *Proceedings of the Conference on Theoretical Aspects of Reasoning About Knowledge* (ed. J.Y. Halpern), Morgan Kaufmann, 1986.

[PR]   R. Parikh and R. Ramanujam, Distributed processing and the logic of knowledge, *Proceedings of the Brooklyn College Workshop on Logics of Programs* (ed. R. Parikh), 1985, pp. 256-268.

[Pa]   P.F. Patel-Schneider, A decidable first-order logic for knowledge representation, *Proceedings of the Ninth International Joint Conference on Artificial Intelligence*, 1985, pp. 455-458.

[PC]   C.R. Perrault and P.R. Cohen, It's for your own good: a note on inaccurate reference, in *Elements of Discourse Understanding* (eds. A.K. Joshi, B.L. Webber, I.A. Sag), Cambridge University Press, 1981.

[Ra]   V. Rantala, Impossible worlds semantics and logical omniscience, *Acta Philosophica Fennica* **35** 1982, pp. 106-115.

[RB]   N. Rescher and R. Brandom, *The Logic of Inconsistency*, Rowman and Littlefield, 1979.

[RSA]   R. Rivest, A. Shamir, and L. Adleman, A method for obtaining digital signatures and public-key cryptosystems, *Communications of the ACM*, 21:2, 1978, pp. 120-126.

[Ro]   S.J. Rosenschein, Formal theories of knowledge in AI and robotics, *Proceedings of Workshop on Intelligent Robots: Achievements and Issues*, SRI International, 1984, pp. 237-252.

[RK]   S.J. Rosenchein and L.P. Kaelbling, The synthesis of digital machines with provable epistemic properties, *Proceedings of the Conference on Theoretical Aspects of Reasoning About Knoweldge* (ed. J.Y. Halpern), Morgan Kaufmann, 1986.

[Sa]   M. Sato, A study of Kripke-style methods of some modal logics by Gentzen's sequential method, *Publications of the Research Institute for Mathematical Sciences, Kyoto University*, 13:2 1977.

[TW]   T.C. Tan and S.R. Werlang, On Aumann's notion of common knowledge - an alternative approach, *Proceedings of the Conference on Theoretical Aspects of Reasoning About Knowledge* (ed. J.Y. Halpern), Morgan Kaufmann, 1986.

[Th]   R.H. Thomason, A model theory for propositional attitudes, *Linguistics and Philosophy* **4**, 1980, pp. 47-70.

[Va1]   M.Y. Vardi, A model-theoretic analysis of monotonic logic, *Proceedings of the Ninth International Joint Conference on Artificial Intelligence*, 1985, pp. 509-512.

[Va2]   M. Y. Vardi, On epistemic logic and logical omniscience, *Proceedings of the Conference on Theoretical Aspects of Reasoning About Knowledge* (ed. J.Y. Halpern), Morgan Kaufmann, 1986.

[Wr]   G.H. von Wright, *An Essay in Modal Logic*, North-Holland, Amsterdam, 1951.

VARIETIES OF SELF-REFERENCE

Brian Cantwell Smith

Intelligent Systems Laboratory, Xerox PARC
3333 Coyote Hill Road, Palo Alto, California 94304; and
Center for the Study of Language and Information
Stanford University, Stanford, California 94305

ABSTRACT

The significance of any system of explicit representation depends not only on the immediate properties of its representational structures, but also on two aspects of the attendant circumstances: implicit relations among, and processes defined over, those individual representations, and larger circumstances in the world in which the whole representational system is embedded. This relativity of representation to circumstance facilitates local inference, and enables representation to connect with action, but it also limits expressive power, blocks generalisation, and inhibits communication. Thus there seems to be an inherent tension between the effectiveness of located action and the detachment of general-purpose reasoning.

It is argued that various mechanisms of causally-connected self-reference enable a system to transcend the apparent tension, and partially escape the confines of circumstantial relativity. As well as examining self-reference in general, the paper shows how a variety of particular self-referential mechanisms — autonymy, introspection, and reflection — provide the means to overcome specific kinds of implicit relativity. These mechanisms are based on distinct notions of self: self as unity, self as complex system, self as independent agent. Their power derives from their ability to render explicit what would otherwise be implicit, and implicit what would otherwise be explicit, all the while maintaining causal connection between the two. Without this causal connection, a system would either be inexorably parochial, or else remain entirely disconnected from its subject matter. When appropriately connected, however, a self-referential system can move plastically back and forth between local effectiveness and detached generality.

19

1. INTRODUCTION

"If I had more time, I would write you more briefly." So, according to legend, said Cicero, thereby making reference to himself in three different ways at once. First, he quite explicitly referred to himself, in the sense of naming himself as part of his subject matter. Second, his sentence has content, or conveys information, only when understood "with reference to him" — specifically, with reference to the circumstances of his utterance. To see this, note that if I were to use the same sentence right now I would say something quite different (something, for example, that might lead you to wonder whether this paper might not have been shorter). Similarly, the pronoun 'you' picks someone out only relative to Cicero's speech act; the present tense aspect of 'had' gets at a time two millenia ago; and so on and so forth. Third, as well as referring to himself in these elementary ways, he also said something that reflected a certain understanding of himself and of his writing, enabling him to make a claim about how he would have behaved, had his circumstances been different.

In spite of all these self-directed properties, though, there's something universal about Cicero's statement, transcending what was particular to his situation. It is exactly this universality that has led the statement to survive. So we might say in summary that Cicero *referred to himself*, that the content of his statement was *self-relative*, that he expressed or manifested *self-understanding*, and yet that, in spite of all of these things, he managed to say something that didn't, ultimately, have much to do with himself at all.

Or we might like to say such things, if only we knew what those phrases meant. One problem is that thay all talk about the familiar, but not very well-understood, notion of 'self'. Perry [1983] has claimed that the self is so "burdened by the history of philosophy" as to almost have been abandoned by that tradition (though his own work, on which I will depend in the first two sections, is a notable exception). AI researchers, however, have rushed in with characteristic fearlessness and tackled self-reference head-on. AI's interest in the self isn't new: dreams of self-understanding systems have permeated the field since its earliest days. Only recently, however, has this general interest given way to specific analyses and proposals. Technical reports have begun to appear in what we can informally divide into three traditions. The first, which (following Moore) I'll call the *autoepistemic* tradition, has emerged as part of a more general investigation into reasoning about knowledge and belief (the theme of this conference). A second more procedural tradition, focusing on so-called meta-level reasoning and inference about control, is illustrated by such systems as FOL and 3-Lisp; for discussion I'll call this the *control* camp. Finally, in collaboration with the philosophical and linguistic communities, what I'll call the *circumstantial* tradition in AI has increasing come to recognise the pervasiveness of the self-relativity of thought and language (self-reference in the sense of "with reference to self").[1]

In spite of all this burgeoning activity, two problems haven't been adequately addressed. The first is obvious, though difficult: while many particular mechanisms have been proposed, no clear, single concept of the self has emerged, capable of unifying all the disparate efforts. Technical results in the three traditions overlap suprisingly little, for example, in spite of their apparently common concern. Nor has the general enterprise been properly located in the wider intellectual context. For example, as well as exploring the *self*, we should understand what sort of *reference* self-reference involves, and how it relates to reference more generally. Also, it hasn't been made clear how the inquiries just cited relate to the self-referential puzzles and paradoxes of logic (which, for discussion, I'll call *narrow* self-reference). At first glance the two seem rather different: AI is apparently concerned with reference to agents, not sentences, for starters, and with whole, complex selves, not individual utterances or even beliefs. We're interested in something like the lay, intuitive notion of "self" that we use in explaining someone's actions by saying that they lack self-knowledge. It isn't obvious that there is anything even circular, let alone paradoxical, about this familiar notion (folk psychology doesn't go into any infinite loops over it). And yet we will uncover important similarities having to do with limits.

The second problem is more pointed: there seems to be a contradiction lurking behind all this interest in self-reference. The real goal of AI, after all, is to design or understand systems that can reason about the *world*, not about *themselves*. Who cares, really, about a computer's sitting in the corner referring to itself? Like people, computers are presumably useful to the extent that they participate with us in our common environment: help us with finances, control medical systems, etc. Introspection, reflection, and self-reference may be intriguing and incestuous puzzles, but AI is a pragmatic enterprise. Somehow — in ways that no one has yet adequately explained — self-reference must have some connection with full participation in the world.

In this paper I will attempt to address both problems at once, claiming that the deep regularities underlying self-reference arise from necessary architectural aspects of any embedded system. Both cited problems arise from our failure to understand this — a failure attributable in part to our reliance on restricted semantical techniques, particularly techniques borrowed from traditional mathematical logic, that ignore circumstantial relativity. Once we can see what problem the self is "designed to solve", we'll be able to integrate the separate traditions, and explain the apparent contradiction.

The analysis will proceed in three parts. First, in section 2 I will assemble a framework in terms of which to understand both self and self-reference, motivated in part by the technical proposals just cited. The major insights of the circumstantial tradition will be particularly relevant here. Second, in section 3, I'll sketch a tentative analysis of the structure of the circumstantial relativity of any representational system. This specificity will be necessary in order to ground the third, more particular analysis, presented in section 4, of a spectrum of self-referential mechanisms. Starting with the simple indexical pronoun 'I', and with unique identifiers, I will examine assumptions underlying the autoepistemic tradition, moving finally to canvass various models of introspection and reflection that have developed within the control camp.

The way I will resolve the contradiction is actually quite simple. It is suggested by my inclusion of self-*relativity* right alongside genuine self-*reference*. Some readers (semanticists, especially) may suspect that this is a pun, or even a use/mention mistake. But in fact almost exactly the opposite is true — the two notions are intimately related, forming something of a complementary pair. Time and again we'll see how an increase in the latter enables a decrease in the former. For fundamental reasons of efficiency, all organisms must at the ground level be tremendously self-relative. On the other hand, although it enables action, this self-relativity inhibits cognitive expressiveness, proscribes communication, restricts awareness of higher level generalisations, and generally interferes with the agent's attaining a variety of otherwise desirable states. The role of self-reference is to compensate for this parochial self-relativity, while retaining the ability to act.

Explicit self-reference, that is, can provide an escape from implicit self-relativity.

Intuitively, it's easy to see why. Suppose, upon hearing a twig break in the woods, I shout "There's a bear on the right!" My meaning would be perfectly clear, but I have explicitly mentioned only one of the four arguments involved in the *to-the-right-of* relation;[2] the other three remain implicit and self-relative, determined by circumstance. However I can lessen the degree of implicit self-relativity by mentioning some of the other arguments explicitly. Look at this as a two stage process: one to get rid of the implicitness, one to get rid of the self-relativity (implicitness and self-relativity, that is, are distinct; *both* characterise ground-level action). In particular, the first move is to shift from the original statement to another that has roughly the same content, but that makes another argument explicit: "There's someone to the right *of me*." This latter statement is still self-relative, of course, but in a different, explicit, way. Now that I have a place for another argument, I can make the second move, and use a different expression to refer to someone else: "There's someone to the right *of you*", or "There's someone to the right *of us all*."

Thus the self provides a fulcrum, allowing a system to shift in and out of the particularities of its local situation. Both directions of mediation are necessary: neither totally local relativity, nor completely detached generality, would be adequate on its own. Roughly, the first would enable you to act, but thoughtlessly; the second, to think, but ineffectively.

So there is really no contradiction, after all. There is some irony, though: the self is the source of the problem, as well as being an ingredient in the solution. The overall goal in attaining detached general-purpose reasoning is to flush the self from the wings. However, the way to do that is first to drag it onto center stage. If you were to stop there, then you really would be stuck with a contradiction — or at least with a system so self-involved it couldn't reason about the world at all. Fortunately, however, once the self is brought into explicit view, it can then be summarily dismissed.

2. CIRCUMSTANCE, SELF, AND CAUSAL CONNECTION

2.A. ASSUMPTIONS

I'll focus on *representational* systems — without defining them, though I'll assume they include both people and computers, at least with respect to what we would intuitively call their linguistic, logical, or rational properties. For a variety of reasons I won't insist that representational systems be 'syntactic' or 'formal' (although what I have to say would equally well apply under what people take to be that conception).[3] Several other assumptions, however, will be important.

First, I take it that systems don't represent as indivisible wholes, in single representational acts, but in some sense have representational parts, each of which can be said to have content at least somewhat independently (*what* content a part has, however, will often depend on all the other parts — i.e., the parts don't need to be *semantically* independent). I take this notion of "part" very broadly: parts might be internal structures (tokens of mentalese, data structures, whatever), distinct utterances or discourse fragments issued over time, or even different aspects or dimensions of a complex mental state (what Perry has informally called mental "counties"). I will use 'agent' or 'system' to refer to a representational system as a whole, and 'representational structure' to refer to ingredients. When I specifically want to focus on the internal structures that are causally responsible for an agent's or system's actions, however, I will talk of *impressions* (as opposed to expressions, which I take to be tokens or utterances, external to an agent, in a consensual language). Impressions are meant to include data structures, elements of a knowledge representation system, or aspects of a total mental state. Such structures are sometimes classified abstractly (particularly in the "abstract data type" tradition), or identified with other abstract things to which they are thought to be isomorphic (like *beliefs*), but I will refer to them directly, because of my architectural bias and interest in causal role.

Second, representational structures are themselves likely to be compositionally constituted, which just means that they too may have parts (nothing is being said about compositional semantics, at least not yet). Again, the notion of part is rough; imagine something like a grammatical structure, or set of partially independent properties or elements, each of which contributes to the meaning of the whole. Utterances constituted of words according to the dictates of grammar are one example; composite structures in a data or 'knowledge' base are another. Thus the words 'I', 'would', 'have', and so on, are components of Cicero's claim (at least in its English translation). Since the term 'element' is biased towards ingredient objects and away from features or characteristics, and 'property' is biased the other way, I will refer to such parts as *aspects* of a structure or impression.

Finally, each constituent will be assumed to have what philosophers would call a *meaning*, which is something, probably abstract, that indicates just what and how it contributes to the content of the composite wholes in which it participates (i.e., I'm now adopting just about the weakest form of compositional semantics I can imagine). Meaning is not, typically, the same as content; rather, it's something that plays a role in giving a representation, or a use of a representation, whatever content it has. So the meaning of the word 'Katlyn' might be something like a relation between speakers and the world, a relation that enables those speakers, when they use the word, thereby to refer to whoever has that particular name in the overall situation being described. Though it's ultimately untenable, one can think of meaning as something a representational structure has, so to speak, *on its own*; the content arises only when it is used, in a full set of circumstances. So 'I' means the same thing when different people use it, but those uses have different contents.

As well as distinguishing meaning and content, we need to distinguish the latter — roughly, what a representation or statement is about — from an even more general notion of semantical *significance*, where the latter is taken to include not only the content but the full conceptual or functional role that the representational structure can play in and for the agent.[4] So for example in a computer implementation of a natural deduction system for traditional logic, a formula's content might be taken to be its standard (model-theoretic) interpretation, whereas its full significance would include its proof-theoretic role as well. It is distinctive of standard logical systems to view a sentence's meaning as the sole determiner of its content, and to take content as independent of any other aspect of significance. Situation theory [Barwise & Perry 1983] distinguishes meaning and content, and admits the dependence of the latter on circumstance, but takes both as specifiable independent of conceptual or functional role. In some of the cases we will look at, however, such as the use of inheritance mechanisms to implement default reasoning, all three will be inextricably intertwined.

2.B. CIRCUMSTANTIAL RELATIVITY

Given these distinctions, the most important observation for our purposes is that a great deal of the full significance of a representational system will not, in general, be directly or explicitly represented by any of the representational structures of which it is composed. Instead, it will be contributed by the attendant circumstances. Section 3 will be devoted to saying what "attendant circumstances" might mean, but some familiar examples will illustrate the basic intuition. As we've already seen, who the word 'I' refers to isn't indicated on the word itself, nor is it part of the word's meaning; rather, the meaning of 'I' is merely that it refers *to whoever says it*. Similarly, the referent of a pronoun may be determined by the structure and circumstances of the conversation in which it is used. If I say "solar tax credits have been extended for a year", the year in question, and the temporal constraints I place on it by using the past tense, emerge from the time of my utterance, not from anything explicit in the words. And, to take perhaps the ultimate example, whether what I say is *true* — which is, after all, part of its significance — is determined by the world, not (at least typically) by anything about the sentence itself.

Similarly, as the Carroll paradoxes show, the fundamental rules of inference can't themselves emerge in virtue of being explicitly represented, because further or deeper rules of inference would be required in order to use them. Nor do even the so-called "eternal" sentences of mathematics and logic carry all of their significance on their sleeve. That a predicate letter is a predicate letter, which is important to the interpretation of a formula in logic, is true in, but isn't represented by, that formula. Similarly, Lisp's being dynamically scoped isn't explicitly represented in Lisp. Or take the inheritance example suggested above: suppose you implement a representation system where a (representation of a) property attached to a node in a taxonomic lattice is taken to mean "an object of this type should be taken to have this property unless there is more specific evidence to the contrary". Thus, to use the standard example, if an impression of FLIES(X) is attached to the BIRD node, then the system is wired to believe that a particular bird will fly so long as there isn't an impression of ¬FLIES(X) attached in the lattice between the BIRD node and the individual node representing the bird in question. In such a system the content of the "so long as there isn't ..." part of the impression's meaning is architecturally determined: it is an implicit part of the overall system's structure, not explicitly represented, and it depends on the surrounding circumstances that obtain throughout the rest of the system, not on anything local to the particular structure under consideration.

This last example is intended to suggest why I am not distinguishing internal circumstance (whether there are other impressions standing in certain relational properties with a given one, say) and external circumstance (who is talking, where the agent is located, etc.). An informal division between the two will be introduced in section 3, but the similarities are more important than the differences, as evidenced in the similarities of mechanisms to cope with them. For one thing, since activity has to arise, ultimately, from the local interaction of parts, it may not matter whether a part's relational partner is somewhere across the system, or outside in the world; what will matter is that it's not right here. Also, the internal/external distinction isn't clean: since agents are part of the world in which they are embedded, some properties cross the boundary. For example, the passage of so-called 'real time' is often as crucial for internal mechanism as for overall agent.

2.C. EFFICIENCY

Before trying to carve circumstantial relativity into some coherent substructure, it's worth understanding why it's so pervasive. The answer has to do with efficiency, in a broad sense of that term. Specifically, in order for a finite agent to survive in an indefinitely variable world, it is important that multiple uses of its parts or aspects have different consequences, each appropriate to how the world is at that particular moment. Partly this enables a system to avoid drowning in details; any facts that are persistent across its experience can be "designed out", so to speak, and carried by the environment (as gravity carries the orientation argument for the human notion of to-the-right-of). But efficiency goes deeper, having also to do with how to cope with genuinely different situations.

The point is easiest to see in the case of action, where in fact it's so obvious as to be almost banal. Specifically, different occurences of what we take to be the same action have different consequences, depending on the circumstances of the world in which they take place. So if take a scoop with my back-hoe, what I get in the shovel will depend not on my action as such, but on the ground behind my tractor. Thus I can perfectly coherently say things like "after doing the same thing over and over, I suddenly cut the telephone cable." I.e., one can imagine viewing an action (read: meaning) as a relation between a local flexing of appendages and the situation in which that flexing takes place. The consequences of the action in a given situation (read: content) can be determined by applying the relation to the situation itself.

Action works this way because any other way of doing it would be horribly inefficient. Each day we want our actions to have different consequences (eating new meals, for example); it would be a terrible strain if we had to be structured differently for each one. As it is, we can have a finite and relatively stable structure, which can locally repeat doing the same things; the circumstantial relativity of perception and action will take care of providing the new consequences. The result is an efficient solution to what Perry characterises as a fundamental design problem:

> Imagine you want to populate the world with animals that will act effectively to meet their needs.
>
> There is one fundamental problem. Since these organisms will be scattered about in different locations, what they should do to meet their needs will depend on where they are and what things are like *around them*. This seems to present a problem. You can't just make them all the same, for you don't want them to do the same thing. You want those in front of nuts to lunge and gobble, and those who aren't to wander around until they are. (I have Grice's squarrels in mind.)
>
> You decide to make them each different. ... But then it strikes you that there is a more efficient way to do it. You can make them all the same, as long as you are a bit more abstract about it. You can make them all the same, [in the sense of having] their action controlling states depend on where they are. And you can do that, by giving them perception, as long as it is perception of the things about them. That is, you can make their internal states work in terms of what we have called subject relative conditions and abilities. You make them each go into state G when they are hungry and there are nuts in front of them, and each lunge forward and gobble when they are in state G.
>
> This way of solving a design problem, we call efficiency. [Perry 1983]

Like eating, representation needs to be efficient, and for similar reasons. First, actions are required in order to use and profit from the internal impressions: what page a least-recently-used virtual memory system discards, for example, will depend on circumstances. Second, impressions can themselves be circumstantially relative (what Perry calls "subject-relative") as both the pronoun and inheritance examples show. Finally, you would expect *ground-level* representations — representations connected directly with action and perception — to have the same (efficient) relativity as the actions and perceptions with which they are connected. Only in this way is there any hope of giving the connection between representation and action the requisite integrity. It is plausible to imagine a signal on the optic nerve directly engendering a rough impression of THERE'S-SOMETHING-TO-THE-RIGHT, but implausible to imagine its producing (and even this, of course, is still earth-relative):

RIGHT(SOMETHING, 38°N/120°W, 187°N, GRAVITY-NORMAL, 3-JAN-86/12:40:04)

Similarly, the stomach must first create the grounded impression "HUNGRY!"; it would take inference to turn this into "Won't you have some more pie?"

2.D. THE ROLE OF THE SELF

Circumstantial relativity isn't something an agent should expect to get over, but it has a down side. First, it doesn't lend itself to communication, if the relevant circumstances of the two communicators differ. If some agent A were simply to give agent B a copy of one of its representations, and B were to incorporate it bodily, the result might have completely different significance (and possibly even meaning) from the original. Information would not have been conveyed. If you're facing me, hear me say "there's a bear on the right!", take the sentence as your own, and then leap to *your* left, you would land in trouble.

Second, one of representation's great virtues is that it can empower a system with respect to situations remote in space or time, outside the system's own local circumstances. However, in order to represent those situations using impressions connected to those it uses to control action, the system must at least represent its own relativity, in order to be able to mediate between those less self-relative generalisations and more familiar implicit ones. I.e., to the extent that the content of its representational structures arise from implicit factors, it is impossible for a system to modify, discriminate with respect to, or make different use of any of the implicitly represented aspects of those representations' contents. If "HUNGRY!", without any argument, is the system's only means of representing the property of hunger, then it won't be able to represent any generalisation involving anyone else (such as that the bear on the right is hungry), or anything generic, such as that hunger sharpens the mind.

The third limit arising from circumstantial relativity depends on another fundamental fact about representation: its ability to represent situations in ways other than how they are. I will call this property of representation its partial *disconnection* (thus tree rings, under normal conditions of rainfall, don't quite qualify as representations because they are so nomically locked in to what they purportedly represent that they can't be wrong). A particular case of internal disconnection illustrates the third limit of circumstantial relativity. Typically, as long as some aspect of internal architecture isn't represented, the system will behave in the "standard" way with respect to that aspect. So, to consider the inheritance example again, the default $FLIES(X)$ will always be interpreted by the underlying architecture in the "so long as there isn't ... " way. Suppose, however, that you want a variant on this behaviour: say, that the default should be over-ridden only if information to the contrary has been obtained from a reliable external source. Being implicit, however, the default way of doing things isn't available for this kind of modification. But if the internal dependence had been explicitly represented, then (as a consequence of the generative power of representation generally) the appropriate modified behaviour could probably be represented as well. In this way (under some constraints we'll get to in a moment) a system could alter its behaviour appropriately. In sum, explicit representation of circumstantial relativity paves the way for more flexible behaviour; without it, a system is locked into its primitive ways of doing things.

The representation of circumstantial relativity requires, among other things, the representation of one's self, because that self is the source of the relativity. There are of course different aspects of self, corresponding to different aspects of relativity: the self as a unity (such as for the *to-the-right-of* case), the self as a complex organization (for the inheritance example), the self as an agent (in generalising about the consequences of hunger).

Note that merely giving a system an impression that refers to it doesn't automatically solve the problem of circumstantial relativity. To see this, imagine installing within a system, as if by surgery, some impressions less self-relative than usual. For example, one might imagine providing a three-place representation RIGHT$_3$(X,Y,Z), and a distinguished token — say, $ME — to use as its own name. Chances are such representations would be conceptually possible, in the sense of not being architecturally precluded. They might enable an agent to reason (rather like a theorem-proving system) about some world. The problem would be that there would be no way for that system to act in that world, were it to find itself suddenly located there (no way for it to connect RIGHT$_3$ with the grounded THERE'S-SOMETHING-TO-THE-RIGHT!). The experience for the system might be a little like that of students who learn mathematics in a totally formal way (in the derogative sense), being able to manipulate formulae of various shapes around in prescribed ways, with no real sense of what they mean. Such a solution wouldn't make the representations *matter* to the system; they wouldn't connect with the agent's life. Furthermore, in a more realistic case where surgery is precluded (say, ours), there's no way to see how such representations could arise, given that they would have no direct tie to action or perception.

There's a problem, in other words: you've got to connect your explicit representations of circumstantial relativity with your grounded, circumstantially relative representations, which in turn connect with action. I will call this the problem of *appropriately connected detachment*. Entirely *disconnected* detachment, as the surgery example shows, is probably easy enough to obtain (at least in some sense), but it wouldn't be significant. Totally *connected* detachment is a bit of a contradiction in terms, but one can imagine an explicit representation so locked into the default circumstances that it wouldn't give you any power above and beyond what the grounded default case provided in the first place.

What is wanted is a mechanism that will continually mediate between the two kinds of representation — that will enable a system to shift, smoothly and flexibly, between indexical and implicit representations that can engender action, and generic and more explicit representations that enable it to communicate with others and in general have a certain detachment from its circumstances. The problem is to provide something like an ability to "translate" between the two kinds (or, rather, among elements arranged along a continuum, or even throughout a space — as we've seen, this is no simple dichotomy), just often enough to maintain the appropriate *causal connection* between located action and detached reasoning, but not so often as to lock them together. The right degree of causally connected self-reference, in other words, is our candidate for solving the problem of connected detachment. It enables a system to extricate itself from the limits of its its own indexicality, and yet at the very same moment to remain causally connected to its own ability to act.

There is one final thing to be said about self-reference mechanisms in general, before turning to particular varieties. In any representational system, the subject matter is represented in terms of what we might call a theory or conceptual scheme that identifies the salient objects, properties, relations, etc., in terms of which the terms and claims of the representation are stated. Except for some limiting simple cases, that is, representation is *theory-relative*. By this I don't mean so much relative to an explicit account, in the sense of a theory viewed as a set of sentences, but relative to a way of carving the world up, a way of finding oneself coherent, a scheme of individuation.

Granting this theory-relativity, we can see that causally connected self-reference requires the following three things:

1. A theory of the self, in terms of which the system's behaviour, structure, or significance can be found coherent. There is no *particular* aspect of the self that needs to be made explicit by this theory: we will see examples ranging from almost content-free sets of names, to complex accounts of internal properties and external relations.

2. An encoding of this theory within the system, so that representations or impressions formulated in its terms can play a causal role in guiding the behaviour of the system.

3. A mechanism of connection that enables smooth shifting back and forth between direct thinking about, and acting in, the world, and detached reasoning about one's self and one's embedding situation. The only example we have seen so far is a mechanism that mediates between K-ary representations of N-ary relations and K + 1-ary representations, as in the *to-the-right-of* case; more complex examples will emerge.

The first two alone aren't sufficient because they don't address the problem of causal connection. Thus the so-called 'meta-circular interpreters' of Lisp, as presented for example in [Steele & Sussman and 1978], meet the first two requirements, but there is no connection between them and the underlying system they are disconnected models of.

3. THE STRUCTURE OF CIRCUMSTANCE

I said earlier that particular mechanisms of self-reference can be understood as responses to different aspects of circumstantial relativity, which depend in turn on different aspects of circumstance itself. This means that, in order to understand these different mechanisms, we need an account of how circumstance is structured. This is a problem, for several reasons. First, there is probably no more problematic area of semantics. Second, we need a general account, since the whole point is to unify different proposals; nothing would be served by an account of how circumstance is treated by, say, semantic net impressions of a first-order language. Third, we *especially* can't assume the circumstantial structure of traditional first-order logic, since the whole attempt to make logical and mathematical language "eternal" can be viewed as an attempt to rid such systems of as much circumstantial relativity as possible. Although that goal isn't entirely met, as the Carroll paradoxes show, the formulae of logical systems certainly lack some of the important kinds of relativity that characterise embedded systems.

My strategy, given these difficulties, will be to give a rough sketch of the structure of circumstance. All I will ask of it is that it support the demands of the next section. Since my basic point is to show *how* the structure of self-reference reflects the structure of circumstantial relativity, any particular analysis of circumstance — including this one — can be taken as somewhat of an example.

By the *immediate* aspects or properties of a representational structure or impression I will mean those properties that can play a direct causal role in engendering any computational regimen defined over them. As such, they must not be relational — especially not to distal objects — but instead be locally and directly determinable, in such a way that a process interacting with or using the representation can "read off" the property without further ado (i.e., without inference). They must, that is, be immediately causally effective, in the sense that processes interacting with the structures can act differentially depending on their presence or absence.

For example, the (type) identity of tokens of a representational code (i.e., whether a given structure is a token of the word "elaborate" or not), how many elements a composite structure has, etc., would be counted as immediate. Non-immediate properties would include truth, being my favourite representation, and whether there is another type-identical representation elsewhere in a larger composite structure or system of which this particular representational structure is a part. This last example suggests that immediacy, which otherwise sounds like Fodor's notion of a *formal* property, is more locally restrictive, since all 'internal' properties of a computational system, it seems, count as formal to him.[5] Positive existence will count as immediate, but negative existence not, since there is nothing for the latter property to be an immediate property of.

Although it's tempting to compare the notion of an immediate property with apparently more familiar notions, such as of a syntactic, intrinsic, or non-relational property, such comparisons would involve us in more complexity than they're worth. The important point is merely that I mean to get at those aspects of a representational structure that affect or engender processes that use it; just what those properties *are*, especially in any given case, is less important.

In the last section I distinguished a system as a whole, its ingredient structures, and those structure's aspects or parts. With that set of distinctions, plus our semantic notions of meaning, content, and significance, plus the current notion of immediacy, we can define everything else we need. Specifically, I will say that something is *explicitly represented* by a structure or impression if it is represented by an immediate aspect of that structure. In contrast, something is *implicit* (with respect to an action or representation) if it is part of the circumstances that determine the content or significance of the representation or action, but is not explicitly represented. For example, I am explicitly represented by the sentence 'I am now writing section 3', since 'I' is a grammatical constituent of the sentence I use, and constituent identity is immediate. On the other hand, if I continue by saying 'but I should stop because it's after midnight', and the word 'midnight' represents the time in the Pacific Time Zone, then the Pacific Time Zone is an implicit part of the relevant circumstances. Similarly, if I say "there's a bear to the right", I am implicitly involved, but not explicitly represented.

There are shades of a use/mention distinction in the way I am characterising the implicit/explicit distinction: things are explicitly represented (nothing, yet, is explicit on its own) only if they are out there in the content, so to speak — part of the described situation, or referents. Something is explicitly represented, that is, only if it is mentioned, whereas something can be implicit either if it is used, or if it plays a middle role, not part of the sign itself, nor of the content or significance, but of the surrounding circumstance that mediates between the two. Thus the words of an utterance, on this view, are an implicit part of the circumstances that determine that utterance's content, since they are not themselves explicitly represented by the utterance (i.e, I am explicitly represented by 'I am writing', but 'I' plays only an implicit role). Where it won't cause confusion, however, I will also talk about explicit or implicit representations of things, as shorthand for representations that represent those things explicitly or implicitly.

Finally, by extension, I will say that something is explicit (*simpliciter*) only if it meets two criteria: it is explicitly represented, and it plays the role it plays in virtue of that explicit representation. So someone would be said to be an explicit part of a conversation only if they were explicitly refered to, and had whatever influence they had in virtue of that explicit representation. From this definition it follows that to *make something explicit* is to represent it explicitly in a causally connected way. Being implicit and explicit thus end up rather on a par, in the sense that both have to do with playing a role: to be *implicit* is to play a role directly; to be explicit is to play a role in virtue of being explicitly represented — which is to say, being represented by an immediate property.

We need to define one further notion, and then we are done. I have already called representational structures *self-relative* if different occurences of them (or things of which those occurences are a part) are part of the circumstances that determine their content. As pointed out above, however, there is more than one notion of part: part of the whole, and part of part of the whole. Rather than proliferating a raft of different notions of self-relativity, it will be convenient merely to separate the facts and situations of the overall circumstances into three broad categories: *external* circumstances, having to do with parts of the world in which the overall system is not a participant; *indexical* circumstances, including those situations in the world at large in which the system is a constituent, and *internal* circumstances, including both the ingredient impressions, processes defined over them, relations among them, etc. Thus who is President, and whether Shakespeare wrote the sonnet discovered in the Bodleian Library, would be paradigmatically external; where an agent was, and whom it was talking to, would be indexical. Internal circumstances would include whether a represented formula's negation is also represented; what inference rules can be, or are being, applied; how often this impression has been used since the system's last cup of coffee; etc. Finally, representations will derivatively be called *external, indexical,* or *internal* (or a mixture) depending on whether their content depends on the corresponding kind of circumstance.

This typology allows us to say all sorts of natural things: that the agent plays an implicit role in the significance of THERE'S-SOMETHING-TO-THE-RIGHT!; that 'I' is an explicit, indexical representation of an agent; that a truly unique identifier would be an explicit, non-indexical name; etc. Note also that a formula in a system of first order logic, at least in terms of its standard model-theoretic interpretation, has no implicit relativity to external or indexical circumstance (other than to the described situation itself), and no relativity to internal circumstance "outside" the formula, but aspects of it are nonetheless relative to the (implicit) internal structure of the formula itself (whether a variable is free, or what quantifier binds it, is implicitly determined by the structure of the expression containing it). Prolog impressions, however, are implicitly relative to internal circumstances of the beyond-formula variety (because of CUT, etc.), and are often used indexically. For example, the Prolog term RIGHT(JOHN,MARY), if it meant that Mary was to the right of John *from the system's perspective*, would be indexical.

4. VARIETIES OF SELF-REFERENCE

We can now show how various mechanisms of self-reference facilitate connected detachment.

4.A. AUTONYMY

I will call a system *autonymic* just in case it is capable of using a name for itself in a causally connected way. Just using a name that refers to itself doesn't make a system autonymic, even if that use affects the system in some way. What matters is that the name connect up, for the system, with its underlying, grounded, indexical architecture. To see this, imagine an expert system designed to diagnose possible hardware faults based on statistical analyses of reports of recoverable errors. Such a system might be given the data on its own recoverable errors, filed under a name known by its users to refer to it. The system's running this particular data set, furthermore, might eventually affect its very own existence (leading to board replacement, say). Even so, the system's behaviour wouldn't be any different in this case: it would yield up its conclusions entirely unaffected by the self-referential character of this externally provided name. When a system or agent reponds differentially, however — as for example do most electronic mail systems, which recognise and deal specially with messages addressed to their own users, forwarding other messages along to neighbouring machines — it will merit the label.

As we have already seen, two ingredients are required for autonymy. The first is a mechanism to convert K-ary impressions (of N-ary relations[6]) to K+1-ary impressions. For example, from the 0-ary HUNGRY! and unary RIGHT(SOMEONE), we need to produce HUNGRY( ), and RIGHT(SOMEONE,). Second, we need a term, or name, to use so that the new, more explicit, version has the same content as the prior, implicit version. This is required because, on the story we're telling, it is this particular explicit version that, in virtue of being directly connected to the perceptual and action-engendering version, gives any more general versions their semantic integrity.

As the mail example suggests, something like a unique identifier can play this role. This is common in computational cases: designers of autonymic systems typically provide a way in which each system, though initially cast from the same mold, can be individually modified to react to its own unique name before being brought into service (a chore the system operators would do in "initialising" the system). As Perry suggests, however, this isn't efficient: it requires that each system be structured somewhat differently. What is distinctive about the pronoun 'I', in contrast, is that it gives exactly (type-)identical systems a way of explicitly referring to themselves. 'I', in other words, is an indexical term allowing explicit, but self-relative (hence efficient) self-reference. It doesn't on its own help a system to escape from its indexicality, but, because it makes that indexicality explicit, it is the minimal step away from fully implicit indexicality.

Causal connections to implement autonymy are so simple as to seem trivial, but their importance outstrips their simple structure. The mail systems provide a good example: that each mail host recognise its own name, and attach its own name to messages headed out into the external world, is a simple enough task, but crucial to the functioning of the electronic mail community.

4.B. INTROSPECTION

Purely autonymic mechanisms, in virtue of the inherent simplicity of names, are almost completely theory-neutral. By *introspective* systems, in contrast, I will refer to systems with causally connected self-referential mechanisms that render explicit, in some substantial way, some of their otherwise implicit internal structure. Since most of the self-referential mechanisms that have actually been proposed fall in this class, this variety of self-reference will occupy most of our remaining attention.

The first step, in analysing introspective systems, is to distinguish our own theoretical commitments from the theoretical commitments we attribute to the agents we study. The difference can be seen by comparing Levesque's [1984] logic of "explicit" and "implicit" belief (his terms, not ours, though the meanings are similar) with Fagin & Halpern's [1985] logics of belief and awareness. Levesque's use of B and L for explicit and implicit belief are predicates of the theorist; nothing in his account — as he himself notes — commits him to the view that the agents he describes parse the world in terms of anything like the belief predicate (i.e., in Fagin & Halpern's phrase, they need not be "aware" of the belief predicate). Fagin and Halpern, on the other hand, when they use such axioms as

$B\varphi \Rightarrow BB\varphi$, thereby commit the agents to an awareness of the same belief predicate they themselves use. I.e., for us to say "A believes φ" is for us to adopt the notion of belief; for us to say "A believes that it believes φ" commits A to the notion as well. Iterated epistemic axioms like $B\varphi \Rightarrow BB\varphi$ can therefore be misleading, since the inner B's represents the agents' views; the outer ones the theorists'.

In the self-referential models typical of the autoepistemic tradition, the correspondence between explicit representation and belief is so close that this identification of agent's and theorist's commitment seems harmless, but when we deal with more complex introspective theories we will have to allocate theoretical commitments more carefully. For example, some theories that are straightforward, from a theorist's point of view, may be difficult or impossible for introspective systems to use, if they assume a perspective necessarily external to the agents they are theories of. Furthermore, different introspective theories require different primitive ("wired-in") support, whereas we, as external theorists, can use any theory we like, without fear of architectural consequence. For example, it is only a small move for a theorist to change from a theory of a programming languge that objectifies only the environment, to one that also objectifies the continuation. On the other hand, programming systems that can introspect using continuations are an order of magnitude more subtle than ones that introspect solely in terms of environments (we'll see why in a moment).

Keeping these cautions in mind, consider, as a first introspective example, an almost trivial autoepistemic computational agent comprising a set of base level representations, whose content, though perhaps self-relative, has primarily to do with facts about the world external to the system. As is usual in such cases, we will presume that the representation of each fact engenders the system's belief in that fact — we'll adopt, that is, the *Knowledge Representation Hypothesis* [Smith 1985] — so for familiarity we will call these representations *beliefs*, rather than impressions. Ignore reasoning entirely, for the moment, and assume that the agent believes only what has somehow been stored in its memory. For introspective capability, augment the base set of beliefs with a set of sentences formulated in terms of what Levesque calls an explicit belief predicate. So, for example, as well as containing the "belief" MARRIED(JOHN), imagine the system also being able to represent B(MARRIED(JOHN)).[7] We will call the whole system $, and its simple introspective representations B-sentences. (Note: In this and subsequent discussion I am representing impressions within $, not giving theoretical statements in a logic about $, so sentences of the form φ represent beliefs $ already has, and B-sentences represent introspective beliefs. All occurences of B, in other words, represent theoretical commitments on $'s part.)

$'s B-sentences, though introspective, are still implicit and indexical, in several ways. First, the agent doing the believing — i.e., $ itself — remains implicitly (and efficiently) determined by internal circumstance, as does the current belief set with respect to which the B-sentence derives its truth conditions. I.e., $B\alpha$ is true just in case α is one of the base-level sentences, meaning that it is explicitly represented in $'s general internal store, which will presumably change over time. Furthemore, by hypothesis, any implicitness or indexicality of $'s base-level beliefs is inherited by the B-sentences: B(RIGHT(X)) is no more explicit about RIGHT's other three arguments than is the simpler RIGHT(X).

Given that $ is so simple, do the B-sentences do any useful work? Since we have claimed that introspective representations render explicit what was otherwise implicit, it is natural to wonder what otherwise implicit aspect of $'s base-level beliefs these B-sentences represent. The answer requires a simple typology of "relations of structured correspondence". In particular, I will call a representation *iconic* (what is sometimes called *analogue*) if it represents each object, property, and relation in the represented domain with a corresponding object, property, and relation in the representation (iconic representations are thus fully explicit). Similarly, I'll say that a representation *objectifies* any property or relation that it represents with an object. Thus for example the sentence MARRIED(JOHN,MARY) objectifies marriage, since it uses (an instance of) the object 'MARRIED' to signify (an instance of) the relation of marriage that connects John and Mary. A representation *absorbs* any object, property, or relation that it represents with itself (thus the grammar rule EXP → OP(EXP,EXP) absorbs left-to-right adjacency). Finally, I will say that a representation is *polar* just in case it represents an absence with a presence, or vice versa (positive polarity in the first case, negative in the second). For example, the absence of a key in a hotel mail slot is often taken to signify the presence of the tenant in the hotel, making mail slots a negatively polar iconic representation of occupancy.

If all *B*-sentences were positive, then $\mathfrak{S}$'s introspective representations would be a partial, non-polar, iconic representation of its base level beliefs (partial because we're not necessarily assuming $B\alpha$ for all α). Since such representations objectify nothing, and therefore doesn't increase the explicitness of the base level, they aren't much use on their own. Causal connection for them is also obviously trivial. Negative *B*-sentences, however, of the form $\neg B\alpha$, make the introspective representations positively polar, thereby objectifying an otherwise implicit property of base level representations: namely, the property of negative existence (we have already seen that negative existence isn't immediate, which forces it to be implicit, unless explicitly represented as in this case). Thus $\neg B\alpha$ makes explicit one of the simplest imagineable implicit properties of a set of internal representations. No slight on importance is suggested, but it is noteworthy how close the correspondence between introspective impression and base-level impression remains: the objects of the introspective level correspond one-to-one with the objects of the base level; only a single, unary property is objectified (no relations); etc. Nonetheless, that one "rendering explicit" can have substantial computational consequences, because (once causal connection is solved) it makes immediate what wasn't otherwise immediate, with the effect that computational consequence can depend directly on the absence of a belief, which it couldn't do in the non-introspective version.

Causal connection, even with the positive polarity, is still relatively simple. $B\alpha$ will be true just in case α is an element of the set of representations, and although negative existence is not an immediate property of the belief set, constituent identity in a finite set is, so that it can be computed with only a moderate amount of inference — just a membership check on the base level belief set. Thus returning 'yes' or 'no' upon being *asked* $\neg B\alpha$ is relatively straightforward; it is perhaps less clear what should happen if $\neg B\alpha$ were *asserted*, although one can easily imagine a system in which this would either trigger a complaint, if α were already in the base set, or else perhaps cause its removal.

This example illustrates what will become an increasingly common theme: causal connection is typically easy or hard depending on two things:

1. The explicitness of the introspective representation (that is, the closeness of correspondence between the immediate properties of the introspective representation and its content); and

2. The immediacy of the aspects of self thereby explicitly represented.

An explicit representation of immediate properties of base-level beliefs, that is (which we have in this case), sustains relatively straightforward causal connection (this is really the point made in [Konolige

1985]). This equation — immediacy on both ends, simply connected — is hardly surprising, since immediacy is what engenders computational effect, and computational effect is required at both ends of causal connection. To the extent that immediacy on either end is lessened, or the connection becomes more complex, causal connection typically becomes that much more difficult.

Examples of such difficulty aren't hard to come by. They arise as soon as we complicate the example and consider introspective impressions that represent more complex internal properties — particularly relational ones. Curiously, in these more realistic cases introspective relativity itself tends to rise, as well as the non-immediacy of what is represented. Thus consider Moore's [1983] interpretation of $M\alpha$ as "α is consistent". This introspective representation is locally indexical because it is relative to the entire base-level set of representations, which isn't explicitly represented with its own parameter. Moore himself points out this relativity:

> "The operator M changes its meaning with context just as do indexical words in natural language, such as 'I', 'here', and 'now'. ... Whereas default reasoning is nonmonotonic because it is defeasible, autoepistemic reasoning is nonmonotonic because it is indexical."[8]

As it happens, however, this indexicality isn't what makes the causal connection of consistency difficult; rather, the problem stems from the fact that consistency itself isn't an immediate property, but a (computationally expensive) relational property of the entire base-level set. Similarly, when interpreted as "implied (or entailed) by the base level set", as in both Konolige and Fagin & Halpern, B is a relational, not immediate property (though again it is circumstantially relative), and causal connection consequently becomes problematic.

The environment and continuation aspects of the control structure of Lisp programs, made explicit in the introspective 3-Lisp, are also implicit, but not relational, and therefore more computationally tractable than consistency. 3-Lisp is so designed that causal connection is supported in both directions (see below); as well as obtaining a representation of what the continuation was, you can also cause the continuation to be as represented. So in 3-Lisp you can *assert* the introspective representation (whereas it is not clear what that would mean under the consistency reading of $M\alpha$, for example). Similarly, various different aspects of the Prolog proof procedure — goal set, control strategy, output — are made introspectively explicit in Bowen & Kowalski's amalgamated logic programming proposals. Again, the consistent assumption sets in a truth-maintenance system, typically implicit, are made explicit in deKleer's [1986] ATMS.

Since it would be hopeless to delve into these or any other introspective proposal in depth, I will devote the remainder of this section to three broad problems they all must deal with. First, however, it's important to note that the introspective models that typify the autoepistemic tradition represent an extremely constrained conception of introspective possibility. Admittedly, that tradition doesn't limit introspective beliefs to $B\alpha$ or $\neg B\alpha$, with B meaning "is immediately represented in the base level set", as our initial example suggests: the consistency reading of M, as Moore's example shows, and readings of B (or L) as "is implied by the rest of the belief set" are much more complex, as the discussion of causal connection makes clear. Nonetheless, such accounts can still largely be viewed as positively polar, iconic representations of derivable extensions of the base set. There is no inherent reason, however, to limit introspective deliberations to such one- or two-predicate vocabularies: one can easily imagine systems with introspective access to proof mechanisms and the state of proof procedures (as is typical in proposals from the control camp), or theories of self that deal with whether ground-level beliefs are chauvinist, creative, or largely derived from children's books. The kinds of meta-level reasoning that prompted AI's interest in self, cited for example in [Collins 1975], aren't limited to knowing *what* one believes, but having some understanding of it. The potential subject matter of introspection, in other words, is at least as broad as clinical psychology. In sum, whereas one can agree with Konolige's [1985] opening statement that "introspection is a general term covering the ability of an agent to reflect upon the workings of his own cognitive functions", there is no reason to limit those reflections as drastically as he does in constraining his "ideal introspective agents" to think nothing more interesting than "do I or don't I believe α?"

Introspective Integrity

The three issues that must be faced by any model of introspection are largely independent of basic cognitive architecture or theory of self. The first I call introspective *integrity*: it includes all questions of whether introspective representations are true, but extends as well to questions of whether any other significant properties they have (truth is only one) mesh appropriately with their content. In $\oplus$'s case integrity is relatively simple: $B\alpha$ should be represented just in case α is, and $\neg B\alpha$ just in case α is not. This simplicity depends partly on the simplicity of the introspective representational language, but also on another property of $\oplus$ we haven't yet mentioned: the truth of $\oplus$'s introspective structures depends only on facts about the base-level representations, independent of introspective commentary. For an example where this doesn't hold, imagine a system where any impression (base-level or otherwise) is believed unless there is introspective annotation stating otherwise. Such a system would probably profit from an explicit representation of the truth and belief predicates, so that statements like "I should probably believe this, even though Mary doubts it", and "this can't be true, because it conflicts with something else I believe" could be represented (truth-maintenance systems are not unlike this). In such a case it would be natural to ask of any given base-level impression whether it is believed, but this can't be settled by inspecting only the base-level impressions. It would depend both on the state of the base level memory and on *implications* of the introspective commentary, and might therefore be arbitrarily difficult to decide. The truth-functional integrity of such a system would thus be inextricably relational.

Integrity is not offered as a property an introspective system must achieve, but rather as a notion with which to categorise and understand particular introspective axioms and mechanisms. For example, all of Konolige's notions of "ideality", "faithfulness", and "fulfillment" can be viewed as proposals for kinds of partial integrity. Similarly, Fagin and Halpern's $A_i\varphi \Rightarrow A_iA_i\varphi$ axiom for self-reflective systems is an axiom that ensures introspective integrity for their notion of awareness. In a particular case even outright introspective falsehoods could be licensed.

Truth isn't the only significant property, and therefore isn't the only aspect of integrity that matters, as we can see by looking at Bowen & Kowalski's DEMO predicate. According to the standard story, logic programs have both a declarative reading, under which clauses can be taken as formulae in a first-order language, and a procedural reading, under which they (implicitly) specify a particular control sequence, which implements a particular instance of the proof (derivability) relation. It follows that the *declarative* reading of DEMO should signify an abstraction over the (implicit) *procedural* regimen (i.e., $[\![\text{DEMO}]\!] = \vdash$, to be a little cavalier about notation). But this is not all that is required, if DEMO is to play the role they imagine: it must also be the case that the *procedural* reading of DEMO — i.e., the control sequence engendered by an instance of DEMO(PROG,GOALS) — must also lead to GOALS's being derived from PROG. Similarly, in 3-Lisp, where 'Φ' was used to signify content (i.e., roughly $[\![...]\!]$), and 'Ψ' to indicate procedural consequence (roughly, $\vdash$), and where Ψ (actually called NORMALISE) was the internal impression representing procedural consequence, it was necessary to show not only that $\Phi(\Psi') = \Psi$, but also, very roughly, that $\Psi(\Psi') \approx \Psi$. The general point is the following: suppose you have an impression A of some aspect P of the internal state (i.e., such that $[\![A]\!] = P$). In order for this to count as having *rendered P explicit* (rather than just as representing P explicitly), a use of this representation A of P must also *engender P* (remember, we said that something is rendered explicit only if it subsequently participates in the circumstances in virtue of that representation).

Intuitively, what this all means is that, in order to count as having introspective access to some aspect of your self, you must not only be able to represent that aspect, but you must be able to use that representation — step through it, so to speak, in what we informally call "problem-solving mode" — in such a way that this introspective deliberations *can serve as one way of doing what is being introspected about.* This might seem like a luxury, since after all there are things we can think about (such as how we ride a bicycle) that we can't simulate in virtue of reasoning with those thoughts. But one of the advertised powers of introspection is its ability to enable us to do things differently from how our underlying architecture would have done them. If we can't do them (introspectively) in the same way the architecture would have done them (non-introspectively), there seems little chance that we will be able to move beyond our base level capabilities. This is part of what causal connection demands. Thus, according to our account, although I can think about how I ride a bicycle, since I can't ride a bicycle by thinking about it, I can't call those thoughts causally-connected introspection.

Introspective Force

The second major issue, once again having to do with causal connection, is what I call introspective *force*. It has to do not with the causal efficacy of the introspective structures themselves, but with the causal connection between those structures and the aspects of self they represent. This is the problem addressed by what have been called 'linking rules', 'reflection principles', 'semantic attachment', 'level-shifting', etc.,[9] although simple quotation and disquotation operators are even simpler examples — e.g., InterLisp's KWOTE and (some of its uses of) EVAL; 3-Lisp's ↑ and ↓. In the discussion so far, I have characterised causal connection rather symmetrically, as a relation between representations and actual aspects of self. As the sophistication of introspection increases, however, the relation between self and self-representation not only grows more complex, but the two directions of connection — from self to representation (I'll call this "upwards"), and from representation to self ("downwards") — take on rather different properties. The differences are at least analogous to (what current ideology takes as) the distinction between beliefs and goals.

Imagine, to borrow an example from [Smith 1984], paddling a canoe through whitewater, exiting an eddy leaning upstream rather than downstream, and dunking. If, sitting on the bank a few moments later, you were to think about how to do better, you would first have to obtain an explicit representation of what you were doing just a moment earlier (this is the "belief" case: how do you go from a fact to a true belief about it?). It's no good to think "Ah, yes, the 20th century is drawing to a close"; you want to represent the very local situation that led you to fall into the river. This is the connection from reality (i.e., self) to representation. But similarly, after analysing the affair, and concluding that things would have gone better if you had leaned the other way, you don't want merely to sit on the bank, fatuously contemplating an improved self: the idea is to get back in the water and do better. You need, that is, a connection from representation to reality (more like what is called a "goal": you've got the representation; you want the facts to fit it). Both kinds of connection are germane even for as simple a self-referential representation as $\neg B\alpha$: the system might need to know whether $\neg B\alpha$ is true, or it might want to make it true. On $\mathcal{S}$'s reading of B as "is explicitly represented" neither is too hard; if B means "consistent", the story, as we have already noted, would be very different.

As McDermott and Doyle [1980] discovered, it is easy to motivate perfectly determinate readings for introspective predicates where the causal connection isn't computable, even upwards. In the downwards case, moreover, if the property represented is a relational one, there may be no unique determinate solution (lots of things, typically, could make $\neg M\alpha$ true). It is thus a substantial problem, in actually designing an effective introspective architecture, to put in place sufficient mechanism to mediate between general introspectively represented goals and the specific actions on the self that have the dual properties of being causally connected (so that they can be put into effect) and satisfying the goal in question. This problem, however, is simply a particular case of the general issue of designing and planning action; since it isn't specific to the introspective case, it needn't concern us here.

Introspective Overlap

The third issue that must be faced by introspective systems is what I will call the problem of *introspective overlap*, which arises when the implicit circumstances of introspective impression coincide with, or include, what has been rendered explicit. The issue arises because the introspective representations are themselves part of what constitutes the agent. As such, any claims they make that involve, explicitly or implicitly, properties of the whole state of the agent, will be claims that they are likely, in virtue of their own existence or treatment, to affect. Introspective representations of relational properties that obtain between a particular impression and the whole set are obvious candidates for this difficulty. For example, if six beliefs were represented, one could not truthfully add the impression TOTAL-NUMBER-OF-BELIEFS(6); one would have to add TOTAL-NUMBER-OF-BELIEFS(7).

This overlap between content and circumstance is what opens the way for the puzzles and paradoxes of narrow self-reference. It is a more general notion than strict "circularity", since the problems can arise even if the representational structure itself is not part of its own content. An early but familiar example in computer science arose in the case of debugging systems for programming languages with substantial interpreter state, when written in the same language as the programs they were used to debug. These debugging systems, introspective by our account, rendered explicit the otherwise implicit parts of the control state of some other fragment of the overall system. The problem was that they too engendered control state (used global variables, occupied stack space, etc.), thereby introducing a variety of confusions because of unwanted conflict. These confusions often occasioned extraordinarily intricate code to sidestep the most serious problems, sometimes with only partial success. The fundamental problem, however, is easily described in our present terminology: the implicit aspect of the system that was rendered explicit remained the implicit aspect of the explicit rendering. There was no circularity involved, but there was overlap, with concommitant problems.

Overlap isn't necessarily a mistake: the indexicality that 'I' renders explicit is the same indexicality that implicitly gives the pronoun its content (similarly for 'here' and 'now'). Problems seem to arise only when negatives or activity affect what would otherwise be the case. It is typically necessary, in such cases, to give an introspective mechanism an appropriate *vantage point*, analogous to that provided by type hierarchies in logic, so that it can muck about with its subject matter without affecting the circumstances that make that subject matter its content.

Overlap only arises when the introspective machinery makes some implicit aspect of the internal circumstances explicit; it isn't a problem when what is implicit to the base-level is also implicit for the introspective machinery. Thus various systems, such as MRS and Soar, apparently don't make explicit any otherwise implicit state (everything that can be seen, self-referentially, is *already* explicit; what is implicit remains so), so the problem of overlap doesn't arise. In some other cases, such as in BROWN [Friedman and Wand 1984], overlap would occur, but the power of the introspective machinery is curtailed in advance to avoid contradiction. Handling overlap coherently was one of the problems that 3-Lisp was designed to solve: its purpose was to demonstrate the compatibility, in a theory-relative introspective procedural system, of detached vantage point, substantial implicit state, and complete causal connection (at the time I called 3-Lisp 'reflective', not 'introspective', but I now think this was a mistake: reflection — see below — was what I wanted; introspection was what I had). The continuation structures of 3-Lisp, representing the dynamic state of the overlapping processor, were what made it interesting. The other two aspects that were made explicit — structural identity, roughly, and lexical environment — didn't overlap (this is why, as we said earlier, an introspective variant of 3-Lisp that only rendered these two aspects explicit would be essentially trivial).

3-Lisp's particular solution to the problem of overlap was to provide what amounted to a type hierarchy for control, and in terms of that to provide, as a primitive part of the underlying architecture, mechanisms that always maintained the integrity of the connection between self-representation and facts thereby represented. So tight a connection was possible in 3-Lisp — because, as stated, continuations aren't relational — that it could be defined as equivalent (in an important sense) to the infinite idealisation in which all of its internal aspects (relative to its highly constrained theory) were always explicitly represented to itself. As a consequence, both external theorist and internal program could pretend, even with respect to recursively specified higher ranks of introspection, that it was indefinitely introspective with perfect causal connection. This particular architecture, however, clearly won't generalise to more comprehensive introspective theories, such as those involving consistency.

There is obviously no limit to the expressiveness of introspective representation, or intricacy of causal connection, though there are very real limits on the total combination of introspective expressiveness, integrity, and force. In the human case it seems clear that causal connection is the practical problem, especially in the "downwards" direction from representation to fact: though it's not exactly easy to come by psychological self-knowledge, it seems much harder, given such knowledge, to become the person you can so easily represent yourself to be.

The real challenge to self-reference, however, stems not from the limits on introspection, where after all one has, at least in some sense, access to everything being theorised about, but from the difficulty of obtaining a non-indexical representation of one's participation in the external world.

4.C. REFLECTION

In the last section a point was made that we need to go back to, because within it lie the seeds of the limits of introspective self-reference. In particular, it was pointed out, in connection with the move from the base-level RIGHT(X) to the introspective B(RIGHT(X)), that all of the implicitness of the former is inherited by the latter. The self-relativity of RIGHT — the fact that three of its four arguments get filled in by the indexical circumstances of the agent — is left implicit even in the introspective version. By a *reflective* system, in contrast, I will mean any system that is not only introspective, but that is also able to represent the external world, including its own self and circumstances, in such a way as to render explicit, among other things, the indexicality of its own embeddedness. This representational capacity, however, is (as usual) insufficient on its own; the system must at the same time retain causal connection between this detached representation, and its basic, indexical, non-explicit representations, which enable it to act in that external world.

Like substantial introspection, reflection is thus something we can only approximate; complete detachment is presumably impossible, both because no one knows to what extent properties that seem universal are in fact local but just happen to hold throughout our limited experience, and because it is very likely, for reasons of efficiency, that we won't ever have represented them. Reflection is also hard to attain, because of the requirement of causal connection. Finally, in order to obtain a representation of oneself that is truly external — i.e., that would hold from an external agent's perspective — one must first represent to oneself everything implicit about one's internal structure and state that isn't universally shared. Without this kind of self-knowledge, what one takes to be a detached representation of the world will still be implicitly self-relative, in ways one presumably won't realise. Introspection is therefore a prerequisite for substantial reflection (self-knowledge is a precursor of detachment). Yet in spite of these difficulties, reflection is necessary if one is to escape from the confines of self-relativity.

What then can we say about reflection, if it is so important? No very much, at least yet. Of the three self-referential traditions we've been tracking, neither the autoepistemic nor the control has addressed relativity to the external world. In both cases the self-referential focus has remained internal, though for different reasons. In the autoepistemic case, the "language" typically used for external representation either has either been, or been closely based on, mathematical logic, which, as Barwise and Perry have repeatedly emphasized, doesn't admit, in its foundations, of external relativity to circumstance. Hence logic's focus on sentences, rather than on statements, and its semantic models of mathematical structures, not situations in the world. In spite of all this, however, as pointed out earlier, even purely mathematical systems are permeated with internal implicitness: with questions of consistency, truth, etc. It is this internal relativity on which autoepistemic models of self-reference have therefore concentrated.

The control tradition stems more directly from computer science and programming language semantics, which have by and large trafficked in internal accounts. Its failure to deal with external relativity is roughly the dual of the autoepistemic's: whereas the autoepistemic tradition has dealt with external content, but not with relativity, computer science has focused on complex relativity, but not on the external world. Hence computer science's self-referential tradition — the control camp — has also dealt only with internal introspection. Programs, in particular, are typically viewed as (procedural) specifications of how a system should behave; as a result their subject matter is taken to be the internal world of the resulting system: its structures, operations, behaviour. Although one can (and I do) argue that the resulting computational systems are themselves representational, therefore bearing a "content" relation to the world in which they are ultimately deployed, that system–world relation isn't addressed by traditional programming language analyses. As a result, the implicitness represented by such self-referential models as metacircular interpreters [Steele & Sussman 1978], BROWN [Friedman and Wand 1984], MRS [Genesereth et al 1983], etc., is also primarily internal.[10]

Thus there is somewhat of a gap between the self-referential mechanisms that have so far been proposed (which are primarily introspective), and the accounts of external relativity offered by the circumstantial camp. What we need are mechanisms for rendering that external implicitness explicit. As usual, causal connection will be the difficult problem — more difficult than for introspection, since internal circumstance is always within the causal reach of the agent. The consistency of a set of first-order sentences may be difficult or impossible for a formal system to ascertain, but that isn't because there is crucial information somehow beyond the reach of that system, remote in time and space, to which other systems might have better access. Determining consistency is hard *all by itself.* The external circumstantial dependencies of ordinary language and thinking, however, are different: who is the right person to perform some particular function, for example, is something that only the world can ever know for sure. The best reflective agent will have direct causal access — and probably only partial access at that — to only one potential candidate.

This doesn't mean that serious reflection is impossible, however, partly because of our three-way, rather than two-way, categorisation of circumstance into external, indexical, and internal. The truth of whether Shakespeare wrote the sonnet is external; the implicitness motivated by efficiency, however, is typically indexical, not external, and indexicality has to do with the circumstances in which the agent participates — with circumstances, some of which, at least, should be relatively *nearby*. If there is any locality in this world, there seems more hope of an agent's knowing about local circumstances than about situations arbitrarily remote in space and time. What's enduringly difficult, of course, is that even those circumstances must be represented as if by another.

5. THE LIMITS OF SELF REFERENCE

Perfect self-knowledge is obviously impossible, for at least three reasons: because of the complexity of the calculations involved (such as those illustrated by consistency); because of the theory-relativity (no theory can render *everything* explicit); and because some circumstantial relativity — particularly indexical and external — is simply beyond the causal reach of the agent. But there are other limits as well. An important one stems from the fact that it is, ultimately, the same self that one is representing, and as such certain possibilities are physically excluded. The self can never be viewed in its entirety, because there is no place to stand — no vantage point from which to look.

Another limit — more a danger than a constraint — was intimated at the outset: although introspection (and self-knowledge) is a prerequisite to substantial reflection, it remains true that the power of all of these mechanisms derives ultimately from their ability to support more general, more detached, more communicable reasoning. It is a danger, however, that a system, in climbing up out of its embedded position, will end up thinking solely about its self, rather than using its self to get outside itself. This would lead to a self-involved — ultimately autistic — sort of system, of no use whatsoever.

These limits notwithstanding, self-reference and self-understanding are important. One can look out, see three people around the table, and represent the situation with "there are four people at this dinner party". One may also notice, perhaps with only introspective capability, that one is repeating oneself. But then one goes on to observe that, by doing so, one is acting inappropriately: that from the other three's perspective one looks like a fool. And then — here's where causal connection gets its bite — as soon as one has achieved this detached view of the situation, this representation from the outside, one scurries back into the introspective state, replaces the designator of that fourth person with 'I', recognises its special self-referential role, collapses back down to the fully implicit structures that engender talking, cuts them off, and thereby shuts up.

That's almost as good as writing more briefly.

ACKNOWLEDGEMENTS

I am indebted to everyone involved in AI's inquiry into self-reference, for their participation in what I take to be a collaborative inquiry. Particular recognition goes to Jim des Rivières, fellow traveller in the upper reaches of 3-Lisp, and to all other members of the Knights of the Lambda Calculus. Finally, a special debt is owed to John Perry: although most of the analysis in section 4 precedes his influence, much of the framework in which it is presented here, especially the emphasis on indexical relativity, is due to him. My thanks.

NOTES

1. For examples of the autoepistemic tradition, see for example [Fagin & Halpern 1985], [Konolige 1985], [Levesque 1984], [Moore 1983], and [Perlis 1985]. For the control tradition, see [Batali 1983], [Bowen & Kowalski 1982], [Davis 1976], [Davis 1980], [de Kleer et al 1979], [des Rivières and Smith 1984], [Doyle 1980], [Friedman & Wand 1984], [Genesereth & Smith 1982], [Hayes 1973], [Laird & Newell 1983], [Laird et al. forthcoming], [Smith 1982], [Smith 1984], and [Weyhrauch 1980]. For the circumstantial tradition, see [Kaplan 1979], [Barwise & Perry 1983], [Perry 1985a], [Perry 1985b], [Perry forthcoming], and [Rosenschein 1985]. Finally, I should mention those who have studied self-reference in specific cognitive tasks: for example [Collins 1975] and [Lenat & Brown 1984].

2. The fourth is orientation. Even if you and I are in the same place, and if A is to the right of B from my point of view, A will nonetheless be to the left of B from your point of view, if you happen to be standing on your head. Gravity establishes such a universal orientation that we rarely need to make this circumstantially determined argument position explicit.

3. Primarily because I don't think the notion of 'formality', as applied to computation, is coherent. See [Smith forthcoming (a)].

4. The term "conceptual role" is associated with Harman; see [Harman 1982], and [Smith 1984] for a computational account treating both content and conceptual role simultaneously.

5. However immediacy can also be less restrictive, since I will countenance some semantic properties as immediate, such as direct quotation, small arithmetic properties exemplified by immediate structures, etc. See [Fodor 1980], and [Smith forthcoming (a)]

6. For reasons that will be obvious, I don't think there is ever any reason — or need — to presume there is a final "fact of the matter" regarding how many arguments relations *really* have (or even that relations, as opposed to representations of them, *have* an arity). What is needed (for example in a scientific account) is a representation that makes explicit enough of the arguments so as to be able to convey, as widely as possible, insight, understanding, truth, whatever. If the universe were in fact an ordered progression of big bangs, numbered 1–..., with the relevant forces proportional to $1/k$ in each case (i.e., we're currently in the second round), all the relations of physics would turn out to have another parameter. That would be ok.

7. Or, if you prefer, *B*('MARRIED(JOHN)'). For purposes of this paper I don't need to take a stand on the question of the semantic or syntactic nature of believe objects, which is fortunate, because I no longer think it is a well-formed question. See [Smith forthcoming (b)].

8. [Moore 1983] pp. 6–7. By 'meaning' he means what we call content, and by 'indexical' he means what we mean by 'internally relative', but his point of course is valid.

9. 'Linking rule' is used in [Bowen & Kowalski 1982], 'semantic attachment' in [Weyhrauch 1980], 'level-shifting' in [des Rivières and Smith 1984], 'reflection principles' in [Weyhrauch 1980].

10. Not realising this fully at the time, I didn't initially describe 3-Lisp [Smith 1982, 1984] in a way that was very accessible to the programming language community. 3-Lisp's semantical model, in particular, was based on a conception of computation where the subject matter of a program was taken to include not only the system whose behaviour was being engendered, but also the subject matter of the resulting system. I still believe that this is often how programming is *understood*, even if implicitly, by a large number of programmers; my analysis, however, would have been more accessible had this non-standard semantic conception been treated more explicitly. Ironically, however, in spite of this semantical orientation, the only "external" world 3-Lisp was able to deal with was that of pure (and simple) mathematics, so it didn't really live up to its own semantical mandate.

REFERENCES

Barwise, Jon, and Perry, John (1983): *Situations and Attitudes*, Cambridge: Bradford Books.

Batali, John (1983): "Computational Introspection", M.I.T. A.I. Laboratory Memo AIM–701, Cambridge Mass.

Bowen, Kenneth A., and Kowalski, Robert A. (1982): "Amalgamating Language and Metalanguage in Logic Programming", in *Logic Programming*, ed. K. L. Clark and S.-A Tarlund, New York: Academic Press.

Collins, A. M., Warnock, E., Aiello, N, and Miller, M (1975): "Reasoning from Incomplete Knowledge", in *Representation and Understanding*, Bobrow, D. G., and Collins, A., eds., New York: Academic Press.

Davis, Randall (1976): "Applications of meta level knowledge to the construction, maintenance, and use of large knowledge bases", Stanford AI Memo 283 (July 1976), reprinted in Davis, R., and Lenta, D. B. (eds.) *Knowledge-Based Systems in Artificial Intelligence*, New York: McGraw-Hill.

———— (1980): "Meta-Rules: Reasoning About Control", *Artificial Intelligence* 15: 3, pp. 179–222.

de Kleer, John, Doyle, Jon, Steele, Guy L., and Sussman, Gerry J. (1979): "Explicit Control of Reasoning", in *Artificial Intelligence: An MIT Perspective*, ed. P. H. Winston and R. H. Brown, Cambridge: MIT Press.

de Kleer, Johan (1986): "An Assumption-Based TMS", *Artificial Intelligence*, to appear 1986.

des Rivières, James and Smith, Brian C. (1984): "The Implementation of Procedurally Reflective Langauges", *Proc. Conference on LISP and Functional Programming*, pp. 331–347, Austin Texas. Also available as Xerox PARC Intelligent Systems Laboratory Technical Report ISL–4, Palo Alto, California, 1984.

Doyle, Jon (1980): "A Model for Deliberation, Action, and Introspection", M.I.T. Artificial Intelligence Laboratory Memo AIM–TR–581, Cambridge Mass.

Fagin, Ronald, and Halpern, Joseph Y. (1985): "Belief, Awareness, and Limited Reasoning: Preliminary Report", *Proceedings of IJCAI-85*, pp. 491–501, Los Angeles, California.

Fodor, Jerry (1980): "Methodological Solipsism Considered as a Research Strategy in Cognitive Psychology", *The Behavioural and Brain Sciences*, 3: 1, pp. 63–73. Reprinted in Fodor, J. *RePresentations*, Cambridge: Bradford 1981.

Friedman, Daniel P., and Wand, Mitchell (1984): "Reification: Reflection without Metaphysics", *Proc. Conference on LISP and Functional Programming*, pp. 348–355, Austin Texas.

Genesereth, Michael R., and Smith, David E. (1982): "Meta-Level Architecture", Stanford Heuristic Programming Project Technical Report HPP–81–6, version of December 1982, Stanford California.

Genesereth, Michael R., Greiner, Richard, and Smith, David E. (1983): "MRS – A Meta-Level Representation System", Stanford Heuristic Programming Project Technical Report HPP–83–27, Stanford California.

Halpern, Joseph Y., and Moses, Yoram (1985): "A Guide to the Modal Logics of Knowledge and Belief: Preliminary Draft", *Proceedings of IJCAI-85*, pp. 480–490, Los Angeles, California.

Harman, Gilbert (1982): "Conceptual Role Semantics", *Notre Dame Journal of Formal Logic*, 23, pp. 242–256.

Hayes, Patrick J. (1973): "Computation and Deduction", Proceedings of 1973 Mathematical Foundations of Computer Science (MFCS) Symposium, Czechoslovakian Academy of Sciences.

Kaplan, David (1979): "On the Logic of Demonstratives", in *Perspectives in the Philosophy of Language*, ed. P. A. French, T. E. Uehling, Jr., and H. K. Wettstein, Minneaspolis, pp 383–412.

Konolige, Kurt (1985): "A Computational Theory of Belief Introspection", *Proceedings of IJCAI-85*, pp. 502–508, Los Angeles, California.

Kowalski, Robert. (1979): "Algorithm = Logic + Control", *CACM* 22, pp. 424–436.

Laird, John E., and Newell, Allen (1983): "A Universal Weak Method: Summary of Results", in *Proceedings of IJCAI-83*, pp. 771–773, Karlsruhe, West Germany

Laird, John E., Newell, Allen, and Rosenbloom, Paul S. (forthcoming): "Soar: An Architecture for General Intelligence", forthcoming.

Lenat, Douglas B., and Brown, John Seely (1984): "Why AM and EURISKO Appear to Work", *Artificial Intelligence* 23, pp. 269–294.

Levesque, Hector J. (1984): "A Logic of Implicit and Explicit Belief", *Proceedings of the AAAI-84 Conference*, pp. 198–202, Austin, Texas. A revised and expanded version available as FLAIR Technical Report 32, Fairchild Artificial Intelligence Laboratory, Palo Alto, California, 1984.

McDermott, Drew, and Doyle, Jon (1980): "Non-Monotonic Logic I", *Artificial Intelligence* 13:1&2, pp. 41–72.

Moore, Robert C. (1983): "Semantical Considerations on Nonmonotonic Logic", Artificial Intelligence Center Technical Note 284, SRI International, Menlo Park, California.

Perlis, Donald (1985): "Languages with Self-Reference I: Foundations", *Artificial Intelligence* 25, pp. 301–322.

Perry, John (1983): "Unburdening the Self", unpublished manuscript, presented at the Conference on Individualism, Center for the Humanities, Stanford University, Stanford California.

———— (1985a): "Self-Knowledge and Self-Representation", in *Proceedings of IJCAI-85*, pp. 1238–1242, Los Angeles, California.

———— (1985b): "Perception, Action, and the Structure of Believing", in Grandy & Warner, eds: *Philosophical Grounds of Rationality*, Oxford: Oxford University Press, pp. 330–359.

———— (forthcoming): "Thought Without Representation", to be presented at a Joint Symposium of the Mind Association and the Aristotelian Society, London, July 1986.

Rosenschein, Stanley J. (1985): "Formal Theories of Knowledge in AI and Robotics," in *Proceedings of Workshop on Intelligent Robots: Achievements and Issues*, David Nitzan, ed., SRI International, Menlo Park, California.

Smith, Brian Cantwell (1982): "Reflection and Semantics in a Procedural Language", M.I.T. Laboratory for Computer Science Technical Report MIT–TR–272.

———— (1984): "Reflection and Semantics in Lisp", Conference Record of 11th POPL, pp. 23–35, Salt Lake City, Utah. Also available as Xerox PARC Intelligent Systems Laboratory Technical Report ISL–5, Palo Alto, California, 1984.

———— (1985), "Prologue to 'Reflection and Semantics in a Procedural Language' ", reprinted in R. Brachman and H. Levesque, eds., *Readings in Knowledge Representation*, Los Altos, CA: Morgan Kaufman, pp. 31–39.

———— (forthcoming a): "Is Computation Formal?", Stanford University CSLI Technical Report.

———— (forthcoming b): "Categories of Correspondence", Stanford CSLI Technical Report.

Steele, Guy L. Jr, and Sussman, Gerry J. (1978): "The Art of the Interpreter, or, the Modularity Complex (Parts Zero, One and Two)", M.I.T. Artificial Intelligence Laboratory Memo No 453, Cambridge, Mass.

Weyhrauch, Richard W. (1980): "Prolegomena to a Theory of Mechanized Formal Reasoning", *Artificial Intelligence* 13: 1&2, pp. 133–170.

PEGS AND ALECS

Fred Landman
Department of Philosophy
University of Amsterdam

ABSTRACT

A major problem in semantics is the question how identity statements can be informative. To answer this question we have to determine what the status is of the objects that language users talk about when they exchange information. It is argued that the assumption of discourse representation theory, that these objects are variables in some representation, leads to problems. To cope with these problems, a theory of pegs is developed, partial objects at an intermediate level of information, to which the partial information states of language users ascribe properties, and that language users can keep track of in the process of information growth. This theory is applied to notorious problems of identity, like the morningstar-paradox, Kripke's puzzle about belief, and the paradox of the hooded man. Within the theory of pegs, an analysis of donkey-sentences is given, that resembles the analysis of discourse representation theory, except that it is not based on variables. To this end, alecs are introduced, pegs which, relative to some information state, can play the role of all pegs with certain properties.

1. Partial objects and identity

This paper is concerned with the analysis of identity statements in frameworks of partial information, and with the status of partial objects. More in particular, it contains a comparison between discourse representation theory and data semantics on these issues, and it develops a theory of partial objects within the latter framework.

The main problem it addresses is the proper treatment of epistemic puzzles of identity, like the well-known Hesperus-Phosphorus puzzle. The problem can be formulated in general as follows: what and where are the objects we talk about? The Babylonians talk about Hesperus and Phosphorus, and agree that they talk about two things, i.e. they talk as if there are two. Yet, if the objects they talk about are private representations of real objects in their minds, then there are four objects (two for each speaker). On the other hand, if they are real objects in the world, there is only one object. What is the level of objects talked about, where there are two? Further, our information about the objects we talk about may grow, but we assume that they are the same objects, before and after our conversation: we can keep track of the objects we talk about in the process of information growth. Finally, the Babylonians are not aware of the identity of Hesperus and Phosphorus, and they regard the information that this is the case as completely new to them, as epistemically contingent.

It is notoriously hard for theories to capture all these things at the same time.

Discourse representation theory is a collective name for two formally equivalent theories, that of Kamp [1981] and that of Heim [1982].

On Kamp's view, language users make representations of the utterances they hear and add these to representations of earlier discourse. These representations contain discourse markers, marking the objects talked about; predicates, marking the properties ascribed to them; and logical structure. Representations get a semantics because language users, so to say, compare these representations with the world: embedding functions map discourse markers onto objects in the world, satisfying recursive embedding conditions.

Heim's theory distinguishes a level of discourse syntax, containing discourse markers (which are variables), and a level of discourse semantics, containing discourse referents ('file cards'). The embedding conditions are here part of the discourse semantics: the interpretation of a (discourse-) syntactic representation is a file, a set of discourse referents and a set of embedding conditions.

The theories are equivalent, because, for Heim, discourse markers are *variables*, and discourse referents are (classical) *variable meaning*. As in classical logic, a variable meaning (be it the index of the variable, or that function that assigns to every assignment function the value of that variable for it) can, without problems, be identified with the variable itself, and from that the equivalence follows.

So, in discourse representation theory, the objects talked about are variables, linked through embedding conditions to real objects in the world (the model). There are two ways that identity conditions can be dealt with: either—as one would expect—through the embedding conditions, or directly at the level of representation. However, there are problems with both.

As for the first strategy, though the Babylonians are not aware of the identity, they do point at an object in the sky. The embedding conditions of their discourse should map both Hesperus and Phosporus on what they point at. But then, adding an identity condition to the discourse will not reduce the set of embedding conditions, and will provide no new information. (Note that it does not help to replace the world in which their discourse is embedded by a set of possible worlds or a situation (a chunk of the world), since what they point at twice will be in that chunk of the world every time they point at it, and it will be constant through that set of possible worlds.)

The second strategy runs into different problems. Variables are syntactic expressions, symbols. In that, they are like words. But symbols have trivial identity conditions: a symbol is identical to itself and to nothing else (that is, *as* a symbol). You cannot make two symbols into one, and hence you cannot identify Hesperus and Phosphorus.

I will argue that, in order to make the identity conditions epistemically contingent, we cannot regard the objects we talk about as real objects in the world, nor can we take them to be symbols in some representation; they are semantic objects with non-trivial identity conditions, at an intermediate level of information, that language users postulate and share: *partial objects* that can merge in the process of information growth.

In agreement with Heim, I will defend the view that the objects we talk about are ingredients of a level of discourse semantics, and that, as such, they should be understood as 'real objects in disguise'. But they are not variables or variable meanings, but partial objects.

I will very shortly discuss two approaches to partial objects.

Parsons [1981] takes them to be sets of properties. Hesperus is a set of properties that Hesperus has, Phosphorus a set of properties that Phosphorus has; the two need not be the same. However, Parsons combines this with a classical analysis of identity. This has the consequence that, if the information grows, we cannot say that we get better informed about Hesperus and Phosphorus. We can only say that the old objects Hesperus and Phosphorus are replaced by new ones. We cannot keep track of Hesperus and Phosphorus in the process of information growth and in the end, the discovery that Hesperus is Phosphorus is turned into the linguistic decision to choose new referents for the names Hesperus and Phosphorus, like choosing a penname.

Scott [1980]'s domain theory is somewhat similar to Parsons' theory: partial objects are constructed as proper filters of properties, or propositions, in an information system. An *information system* is a structure of propositions (also called possible facts) based on two informational notions: that of information containment and that of incompatibility of information. Both are relations between propositions. Formally, we take an information system to be a meet-semilattice, a set partially ordered by information containment and closed under combination of information, with a minimal element: the impossible proposition, containing incompatible information. Two propositions are incompatible if their combination is the impossible proposition.

The advantage over Parsons' theory is that the information perspective allows a non-classical, monotonic analysis of identity, like: two objects (proper filters) are identical if they can only grow towards one and the same total object (ultrafilter). Such a non-classical analysis of identity is essential for a theory that takes partial objects seriously: it is classical identity that makes an object identical to itself and to nothing else, that makes an object total. On Parsons's approach, information growth comes down to replacing total objects by larger total objects: hence, Hesperus on one stage of the information is a different object from Hesperus at some other stage, and if Hesperus and Phosphorus are different sets of properties, they are non-identical. The present, non-classical, analysis makes the identity of Hesperus and Phosphorus contingent: they can be identical even if they are different partial objects (if only they grow towards the same total object). In this respect, we have gained some advantage. But not enough. We still cannot keep track of Hesperus in the process of information growth. As long as Hesperus can grow towards different total objects, it is a different object at different stages of the information. And this has the unfortunate consequence that it is not only the identity of Hesperus and Phosphorus that is contingent, but that of Hesperus and Hesperus itself as well: as long as Hesperus can grow towards different total objects, the statement that Hesperus is Hesperus is undefined.

2. Data semantics

In the next section I will discuss the analysis of these problems in data semantics. Here I will very shortly introduce the basic principles of that theory.

On the ontological side, we assume a set of 'objects' D, an information system of propositions $\mathfrak{I}$, a set of properties $\mathcal{P}$, and an interpretation function ι, interpreting constants directly as objects, and predicates as properties. Properties are certain functions mapping n-tuples of objects onto propositions.

Information states are defined as sets (proper filters) of propositions. This gives us notions like 'extension of inmformation', 'total information' (relative to the model), etc.

The main partiality comes in with the semantics: instead of a recursive definition of truth conditions, the semantics gives a recursive specification of conditions for truth ($\Vdash$) and falsity ($\dashv\!\vert$) *on the basis of* an information state **s** (verification/falsification conditions, assertability conditions, or conditions of evidence). Since properties map objects onto propositions, atomic formulas can be interpreted as propositions. The semantic behaviour of modals and conditionals is defined in terms of possible extensions of information states. Examples of clauses are:

$s \Vdash P(c) \text{ iff } \iota(P)(\iota(c)) \in s$

$s \dashv P(c) \text{ iff } \iota(P)(\iota(c)) \text{ is incompatible with some proposition in } s$

$s \Vdash \mathbf{may}\varphi \text{ iff for some } s' \supseteq s \; s' \Vdash \varphi$

$s \Vdash \mathbf{must}\varphi \text{ iff for all } s' \supseteq s \text{ there is an } s'' \supseteq s \text{ such that } s'' \Vdash \varphi$

For reasons given in Landman [1986], these clauses for modals are too simple, but they suffice for our purposes here. Unfortunately, this is not so for the conditional: later in this paper I will use the rather involved analysis of conditionals that was developed in Landman [1986]. However, I cannot here give all the definitions that it uses, so I will describe the semantics of the conditional informally here, and refer to Landman [1986] for the formalization:

$s \Vdash (\varphi \to \psi)$ iff for every way of extending s, if the first thing that happens to the antecedent φ there is that it becomes true, then right after that has happened, the consequent ψ must be true

A crucial consequence of adopting assertability instead of truth as the basis of the recursion is that modals (like **may**) can be instable under extension of information (true on the basis of limited evidence, false later on).

The main concern of the present paper is: what are these 'objects'? They are to be partial objects, but in what respects? If we don't assume them to be real objects in the world, nor private objects in our minds, then what are they? It is time to introduce the heroes of this paper: they are pegs.

3. Pegs

What are pegs?

Pegs are things to hang your coat on. Or your hat. They change their appearance, if you do that. But we find no reason in that to say that it is not the same peg. Of course, real pegs are physical objects, and we hang hardly anything on them but cloths. Our pegs are informational objects, and the things we hang on them are properties.

As always there has to be someone who hangs the cloths on the peg, or takes them off again. Pegs are not made with the hats already on them, nor is it impossible to take the hats off them, or else they would be worseless pegs, that's simply not what they are for. It is essential for being a peg that you can hang coats on them, and someone has to do it. In our case, it is the information available to us that hangs the properties on the pegs: our cloak-room attendants are the information states.

Properties map pegs on facts; information states contain facts. Suppose we have a peg p and a property P. If our information state does not yet contain the fact $P(p)$ then it has not yet hung the property on the peg. It has, if it grows into a state that does contain that fact. They are not very special pegs, actually, except that you can hang a lot on them. Our cloak-room attendent is of the old-fashioned kind, however. It abhors to hang two coats on one peg of which the colours clash, and so it refuses to do that. We will see that it has other peculiar character traits, in due course.

Now what about the following questions:

When does a peg have a certain property?

Do pegs exist?

How many pegs are there?

It is important to realize that—even if we want to make ourselves feel liberal—these questions are *completely irrelevant*. I tend to be less liberal in this matter, and think that they are not just irrelevant, but *nonsensical*. It is a nonsensical question to ask whether a peg has a certain property: pegs don't *have* properties; properties are *ascribed* to them by information states. But don't we say that an object in the world has a certain property and couldn't that object be a peg? To say that an object in the world is a peg which has a certain property should be interpreted as to say that the complete information state which we assume to be the best possible approximation of the real world *ascribes* that property to that object. It is a nonsensical question to ask, out of the blue, whether a peg exists; information states ascribe existence to pegs. Similarly, it is nonsensical to ask for the cardinality of the set of pegs, *because pegs do not have identity conditions*, identity conditions are no better than properties, they are ascribed to pegs by information states; pegs can be identified by information states. If we want to ask how many objects there are according to a certain information state, then we should count the number of distinct sets of pegs that are identified by that information state. But the cardinality of that domain changes in the course of information growth. But of course, interpreted in this way, it is a legitimate question to ask, say, how many objects there are in the world, because—as we will see—on total information all identity conditions are fixed, and we ask for the number of *distinctions* that this information state makes, that is, the number of equivalence classes of pegs under identity.

To formulate this matter somewhat differently: I refuse and reject it as nonsensical to regard pegs as classical, static objects, that have properties, that do or do not exist, and that are identical with themselves only; *by squeezing them into the armour of classical logic in this way, we try to understand a dynamic process as a static one.* Compare it with a movie. A movie is a dynamic entity which gains its sense by the things happening in it. We can stop the movie at a certain point, freeze the action at a certain scene; that can even help us to understand the movie better. But taking a classical view on the movie, is taking an *external* view on it, regard it as an ordered set of distinct images. Doing that might serve some purposes, but we cannot understand the *meaning* of the movie in that way, because its meaning lies in the action, in the things that are happening in it. It is impossible to understand a movie if, while watching it, you seriously regard it as a long sequence of distinct pictures. It is only by ignoring that aspect of the movie, by stepping in it, that is, by taking an *internal* view, that we can make sense of it.

Information exchange is a dynamic process. In modelling it, we make a classical reconstruction of it, we use sets, classical model-structures, as the marble out of which we sculpt our reconstruction of this process, the statue which depicts the process. We can try to understand the depicted process completely in terms of the pieces of marble used, the material used to model the process, but we shouldn't; it may give us a better understanding of our reconstruction of the process, but not of the process itself.

Information states hang properties on pegs. They refuse to hang incompatible properties on one peg. Being partial objects themselves, they can be very short-sighted, in fact, they can only distinguish one peg from another by the properties that hang on them: they can tell them apart if one of them has a property incompatible with some property that the other one has. So there can be lots of pegs that an information state cannot tell apart. One might think that the customers will complain about that, and say that they don't get the right hat, because it comes from a different peg, but properties are very special hats, even if they come from different pegs, they are the same hat, so most customers don't complain. In fact, the only trouble makers are the classical logicians: they are the ones who insist to get their hat from the same peg, and in that they rudely force our information state to strain its eyes more than is justified.

For us, on the other hand, precisely the fact that sometimes pegs cannot be told apart on the basis of an information state forms the *key* to their nature: *the essence of partial information is that it cannot justify certain distinctions, and the decision about the identity of certain pegs is a prime example of that.*

Let us give some definitions:

d_1 is **discernable from** d_2 **on the basis of** information state s iff there is a property P such that:
either $P(d_1) \in$ s while $P(d_2)$ is incompatible with some fact $f \in$ s
or $P(d_2) \in$ s while $P(d_1)$ is incompatible with some fact $f \in$ s

Actually, we should generalize this to n-place properties where d_1 and d_2 are among the arguments, but this is straightforward, and we won't bother.

d_1 and d_2 are **indiscernable on the basis of** s iff they are not discernable on the basis of s

So d_1 and d_2 are indiscernable on the basis of the information if they don't have incompatible properties. We can also give a stronger notion of indiscernability: d_1 and d_2 are strongly indiscernable on the basis of the information if they have the same properties on that basis. We can distinguish various degrees of strength here. We can let d_1 and d_2 be indiscernable only with respect to the properties involved in the information, or let them be indiscernable also with respect to those properties that they *must* and *may* have on the basis of the information. It is the latter notion that we will define and use here:

d_1 and d_2 are **strongly indiscernable on the basis of s** iff for all properties P : $\text{s} \Vdash P(d_1)$ iff $\text{s} \Vdash P(d_2)$ and $\text{s} \dashv\vert P(d_1)$ iff $\text{s} \dashv\vert P(d_2)$ and

$\text{s} \Vdash \textbf{must}\, P(d_1)$ iff $\text{s} \Vdash \textbf{must}\, P(d_2)$ and $\text{s} \Vdash \textbf{may}\, P(d_1)$ iff $\text{s} \Vdash \textbf{may}\, P(d_2)$

Note that the fact that on the basis of our information they *can* have property P, does not necessarily mean that they will have P in the *same* extensions of the information, that would again be a stronger notion of indiscernability. Here we will be satisfied with calling d_1 and d_2 strongly indiscernable if our information ascribes the same properties to them; further if the properties that they must have on the basis of our information are the same, and similarly for the properties that they may have.

For later use we will also introduce a *one way* version of the latter notion:

d_1 is an **indiscernable approximation of** d_2 **in s** iff for all properties P : if $\text{s} \Vdash P(d_1)$ then $\text{s} \Vdash P(d_2)$ and if $\text{s} \dashv\vert P(d_1)$ then $\text{s} \dashv\vert P(d_2)$ and

if $\text{s} \Vdash \textbf{must}\, P(d_1)$ then $\text{s} \Vdash \textbf{must}\, P(d_2)$ and if $\text{s} \Vdash \textbf{may}\, P(d_1)$ then

$\text{s} \Vdash \textbf{may}\, P(d_2)$

Now we can see why indiscernability contains the key to the proper understanding of pegs. Suppose that you don't have information at all, that $\text{s} = \emptyset$. *Then all pegs are indiscernable.* Pegs get discernable only through information growth. So pegs can also be called *indiscernable objects*, because in the beginning, there were indiscernables.

So for some pegs your information may contain enough facts to tell them apart, but there can be lots of pegs, which are indistinguishable as far as your information is concerned. If we think about what it means for an identity statement to be true or false on the basis of an information state, we see that the *falsification* condition is straightforward:

$\text{s} \dashv\vert (c_1 = c_2)$ iff $\iota(c_1)$ and $\iota(c_2)$ are *discernable* on the basis of s

We will, of course, *not* define $(c_1 = c_2)$ to be true on the basis of s if their interpretations are indiscernable: though s does not contain enough information to distinguish between those two, it can very well be that s admits the possibility that it grows into an information state that *does* contain enough information to distinguish between them. However, as soon as *that* possibility is eliminated, we *can* say that we have enough information to regard them as identical:

$\text{s} \Vdash (c_1 = c_2)$ iff for no $\text{s}' \supseteq \text{s}$ it holds that $\iota(c_1)$ and $\iota(c_2)$ are discernable on the basis of s'

We will also call two *pegs* identical on the basis of s if they are indiscernable on the basis of every extension of s.

Before we go on, let us briefly return to the question: 'how many objects are there in the world?' and a related question: 'to which real object in the world does a peg refer?'.

Let w be a total information state, a maximal approximation of a possible world. The following holds for w:

If d_1 and d_2 are indiscernable on the basis of w then they are identical on the basis of w.

If a total information state does not contain a property that can distinguish between d_1 and d_2 then of course there is also no extension of it which does.

We call **the referent of d in w** the equivalence class:

$$\{d' : d' \text{ and } d \text{ are identical on the basis of } \text{w}\}$$

The **real objects** in the world w are the equivalence classes under identity on the basis of w. So d_1 and d_2 refer to the same object in the world if they have the same referent in it. Also, the number of real objects in the world is the cardinality of the set of objects in the world. So we can have objects in our theory who behave like 'the real guys': they are constructions out of pegs under the assumption that our information is total.

We will put this notion of object to use later.

Note that we will often be in an information state s such that $\text{s} \Vdash \textbf{may}\,(a = b)$ and $\text{s} \Vdash \textbf{may}\,(a \neq b)$. Of course, once s has grown into an information state s' where $\text{s}' \Vdash (a = b)$ it also holds that $\text{s}' \dashv\vert (a \neq b)$

This, basically, is what pegs are. They are the objects we assume in conversation, and which we follow through information growth. On very partial information they are indiscernable from other objects to which they may be identical, but also from which they may be discernable in the end. Even though we may ascribe wrong properties to them, it is an *objective* matter to which object in the real world they refer and also what properties they have there: if our information state ascribes to something we point at a property which, after some consideration, we agree it doesn't have, we don't substitute a different object for it, we don't pretend that we were pointing at something different, but we change our information state to a state which ascribes different properties to it; we *correct* our information, that is, we transcend from an information state that was not part of the total information state w_0 which approximates the real world, to one that is.

I assume with Heim that there is a level of discourse semantics in between the level of discourse syntax and the real world, in fact that intersubjective level is our main level of interpretation, the real world plays hardly a semantic role at all, it is there as a regulative idea which sets our standard of correctness. In conversation we build up a structure or sequence of logical forms. These contain markers and predicates which are interpreted as pegs, the objects we talk about, and properties. Two different markers, distinct symbols, can be interpreted as the same peg, if our conversation assumes that we talk about only one object (as I argue in Landman [1986], there can be syntactic reasons for introducing distinct markers in the discourse, even if there is only one object talked about). Logical forms are evaluated with respect to an information state, the direct context, containing the information we agree upon. This information state is a set of facts, pegs are not in it, but each information state uniquely determines the domain of those pegs about which it contains information. Accepting new information leads to extension of the structure of logical forms and update of the information state, a transition from one information state to another. The new information state can contain more facts about pegs which were already in the domain of the old information state, as well as contain facts about a larger domain of pegs, introduce new objects to be talked about. The main difference between Heim's theory and mine lies in the relation between discourse syntax and discourse semantics (an embedding versus just a homomorphism) and in the nature of discourse referents (variables versus indiscernables). We will see later in this paper that this invites a difference in the analysis of complex discourses as well.

4. Strangers and acquaintances

We will now discuss some wellknown semantic puzzles.

Let us first return to Babylonia. We said that three things were very clear: the Babylonians talked about the same thing, when they pointed at Hesperus; the thing they talked about is the same thing before and after their conversation; and they are not aware that Hesperus is the same heavenly body as Phosporus. It is clear that if we assume Hesperus and Phosphorus to be pegs, that get their disguises through the information state that the Babylonians share, we can account for these three things. Though there may be four objects in their heads altogether and though there is only one object in the world, their information state ascribes properties to two pegs. And even if they have different information, even if there is not an information state (or part of it) which they share, their information states ascribe properties to those two pegs, in the situation described it ascribes the property of being visible at the evening sky to Hesperus and the property of being visible at the morning sky to Phosporus. Similarly, through information growth during the conversation, more properties are ascribed to both these pegs, but they stay the same peg: pegs are not locked in information states in the sense that every new information state is a new slide with new objects in it; we can follow pegs through information growth (and information change).

It is precisely this that distinguishes the present theory from those that identify partial objects with sets of properties: sets of properties *are* locked in information states: either you follow a particular set of properties in larger information, and you regard that particular set as an object distinguishable from its supersets, or you follow larger and larger sets of properties, but then you have no way along those paths to choose one way rather than another, i.e. to identify it with the one possible extension rather than another. Pegs don't have that problem because they choose their own way. If there are two possible sets of properties which a peg may adopt, it will choose one information state to adopt the one set, and another to adopt the other; *within* an information state a peg always makes a decision on which properties it adopts. If it chooses the one set, there may be other pegs from which it is indiscernable that take the other choice, but it can also very well be that no such pegs exist.

Thirdly, it can certainly be the case that our Babylonians have no opinion about the identity or non-identity of Hesperus and Phosphorus, their information state may be one on the basis of which both **may**$(h = p)$ and **may**$(h \neq p)$ is true. They may be forced to add the empirical evidence provided by new astronomical discoveries to their information state, and in that way they will adopt an information state on the basis of which $(h = p)$ is true, there is no reason why they would not be astonished by this evidence. The identity of Hesperus and Phosphorus may be an ontological necessity, but that is an external perspective on their identity conditions. Within the Babylonian perspective the identity of Hesperus and Phosphorus is contingent. The situation is different for an identity statement like $(h = h)$. No information state is able to distinguish the peg Hesperus from itself. $(h = h)$ is certainly true on the basis of the Babylonian information state. Note further that, though identity conditions depend on information states, we can still say that the pegs Hesperus and Phosphorus, *as they are used* by the Babylonians, even if their information state is one on the basis of which Hesperus and Phosphorus are not identical, still refer to one and the same object in the world, the planet Venus. *We* are fully justified to say that the planet Venus was already discovered in Babylonian times, we don't have to say that the Babylonians only discovered two things they pointed at. Even if they believed that the things they were pointing at were the chariots of the evening god and the morning god, respectively, it still is the case that *those things* in fact are the planet Venus. They themselves would accept that, if only they were presented with the right evidence.

Other famous deixis cases, like John Perry, looking in the mirror, saying to himself: "where have I seen that face before?" and David Kaplan, saying while pointing over his shoulder at a picture of Spiro Agnew, which occupies the place of his beloved portrait of Rudolf Carnap: "that is the most important twentieth century philosopher." are analyzed in the same vein.

Let us turn to Kripke's puzzle (Kripke [1979]).
Kripke tells the story of Pierre, a French boy, who during his youth in France hears those fascinating stories about this beautiful town London—in French, of course, so he knows it by the name of 'Londres', but that is no reason for us to deny that on the basis of what he has heard he thinks that London must be beautiful. Then, on a bad day, he is brought to an ugly and dirty suburb of London, to start a new life. He never leaves this suburb and has to learn English the hard way, because none of his neighbours knows even a single word of French. He finds out, of course, that the town he is living in is called 'London', and in days of depression he curses his miserable life, screaming out his sincere belief that London is the ugliest town he knows. Often he sighs in his native tongue: "Que je habitais à jolie Londres!", "If only I lived in beautiful London!"

Kripke's puzzle is interesting, because, unlike most mistaken identity puzzles, the contradiction in his belief does not depend on a clear mistake that he made, on the contrary, he has quite good reasons to believe that the town he was told about is beautiful, and equally good reasons to believe that the town he is living in is ugly (of course, once he recognizes the identity, something has to go). Moreover—as Kripke says—the problem does not make use of dubious principles of substitution, but only of plausible principles of translation (for *us* in describing Pierre's belief).

We can assume that the logical form that Pierre assigns to the sentence-pair **London is ugly. Londres est Jolie.** is the same as we do: $< l_1, U(l_1), l_2, J(l_2) >$. It is very obvious that Pierre's information state is different from ours. We can put the whole problem there, and then there is no difference at all between this case and the Hesperus-Phosphorus case: our information state provides evidence that $(h_1 = h_2)$, Pierre's doesn't.

If we do that, we miss one aspect of the puzzle, namely, that *we* are justified to apply to plausible principles of translation *because* for us h_1 and h_2 are markers for one and the same peg: we can translate because we assume that there is only one object we talk about, whether we talk about it in French, or in English. Obviously, here Pierre's *linguistic* assumptions differ from ours: Pierre clearly talks as if there are two objects. We have to assume that our mapping from discourse syntax to discourse semantics differs from Pierre's mapping. When talking about London, we share the convention that our discourse markers are mapped on the same peg. (This convention can be broken, when two people, after their holydays have so different experiences of the city of London, that one says: "It seems as if we've been to a completely different town. I don't know about *your* London, but *my* London was beautiful.") But Pierre does not share this convention, his discourse markers are mapped onto distinct pegs.

But we should ask: how can this be? Clearly, when in France he was told about Londres, he and his educators talked about the same peg. Now in England, he and his neighbours also talk about the same peg. But would not his neighbours and his educators agree that there is only one peg *they* talk about (assuming that his educators do know that Londres id London)? And if that is so, how can his French peg be different from his English peg? The explanation is that this takes a more rigid view on pegs than is justified.

Perhaps his neighbours and his educators *would* agree *if they were engaged in a conversation*, but they were not. When we start a conversation, we make some assumptions about the things we talk about, these assumptions belong to the initial conditions which are reset every time we start a new conversation. We agree to talk about London. We know that lots of people have talked about London before, and we know they talked about the same thing. That means that if we talk about their conversations about London, we will use the peg we have agreed upon for that. It does not mean that it is essential for the success of our conversation that we *literally* make sure that we use no other peg than they did, that we use exactly the same thing. We just take the model too serious if we do.

We can say that they talked about the same thing as we do, and they could have said that we would talk about the same thing as they did, and we can say that the peg London plays the same role in our context as the peg London did in their context, but to check whether those objects are literally the same, through contexts which are not part of one conversation, is to take a classical step out of the context. When someone starts a conversation with: "As I said yesterday about London,. . ." the step to conversational success is not to retrieve from your memory the information about which was the exact peg that was used yesterday, but to agree upon a peg now, and ascribe to it the properties that were mentioned yesterday. If we draw the track of London through our increasing information over the years, we may use a different coloured pen from time to time, as long as we make sure that as far as we are concerned it is the same track. When we start a conversation, we agree upon the pegs, like we synchronize our watches. Within the conversation we even assume that they are the same pegs as used in earlier conversation, but we're not going to be bothered about that: if they're not, we identify them. If these French educators of Pierre have set their assumptions on a literally different peg than his English neighbours, then noboby bothers, as long as they are willing to reset these assumptions in a joint conversation.

But that is of course Pierre's problem. He lacks precisely the vital information to reset his French peg in talks to his English neighbours. In that way, he *can* share the same assumptions with his educators *and* with his neighbours. If he would join a French-English dialogue then his problem would soon be discovered, because he will find out that the other participants have reset their pegs, while he hasn't. His discovery then that London is Londres is partly a *linguistic* discovery. It might take place by showing him a French and English map of England.

But apart from that, though he thinks that they don't, in a conversation, his two pegs for London and Londres refer to the same real object, the city of London, and the other participants can show him that they do. In this respect the puzzle is similar to the Hesperus-Phosphorus case.

A third puzzle goes back to Eubulides, Aristotle's famous critic, to whom also the Liar Paradox and the Sorites Paradox are credited. It is called the Paradox of the Hooded Man: You say you know who your brother is. But that man who came in just now with his head covered is your brother. And you said you did not know who he was.

The paradox is discussed as a problem for possible world semantics in Groenendijk and Stokhof [1982]. If my information is represented as the set of epistemic alternatives that I cannot exclude, then I can be said to know who the winner of the 1984-*Tour de France-Feminin* is, if in every alternative that is admitted for me, the one who won the Tour *there* is the one who *in fact* (that is, in the real world) won the Tour. So, to know who is the winner is to have the *specific* information that one and the same individual has won the Tour in all my epistemic alternatives and in fact.

Now consider the following example. We are at a party, and I say to you, pointing at a woman on the other side of the room: "Do you know who that is?" And you answer me: "No, I haven't the faintest idea." The problem now is that, given the justified trust you have in your perceptual capacities, in all your epistemic alternatives that woman is standing on the other side of the room, and so by definition you know who she is. But yet, you don't. Now I point at a man, next to her, and you say: "I know him alright, he's my brother." For the possible world analysis, the situation is the same, but this time I have no problem in accepting that you indeed know who that is. To pinpoint with somewhat more precision what the problem is, let us make the following additional assumption: at the party there is also a man whom we both cannot tell apart from his twinbrother, although we know them both. Again I ask you who that man is, and you say: "I don't know, I can't tell them apart." Again, I accept what you say as true, without problem: I, as well, cannot tell them apart.

Why do you know who your brother is, and not who the others are? Not because your brother is the same object in all your epistemic alternatives, since the others are as well. You know who your brother is, because you are *acquainted* to him in a way you are not acquainted with the others. In what sense are you acquainted with your brother that you are not with the twins? Both twins are acquaintences of yours. What is crucial for acquaintance as meant here, is that those objects you are acquainted with are the objects that you can tell apart on the basis of your information. But can you not distinguish between all persons at the party, and hence can you not tell them all apart? No, because, though the domain of discussion may be limited to persons present at the party, *we always assume that there are others besides that, who we do not care to distinguish from each other.* The difference is that you are acquainted with your brother in this sense *that you can distinguish him from these others as well.* And that is precisely what you cannot do for the others: you always take into account some, or lots cf people outside this room from which you could not tell them apart. For one thing, you may know who has won the 1984-*Tour de France-Feminin*, without being able to distinguish her from the woman at the other side of the room, while you certainly know that your brother didn't.

Being acquainted with your brother in this way, does not imply that you are completely informed about him, acquainted objects need not be total objects: to know who he is you need not know all his properties, it only means that *on the basis of your present information, and in the present context* you can distinguish him from other persons.

We see that if we assume all characters introduced here to be pegs, we can use the definitions of indiscernability and identity on the basis of the information easily to define the notion of acquaintance. But there is a problem here. I said above, that you can be regarded to be acquainted with your brother, even though you don't know all his properties. But then there can always be those nasty pegs that only have properties of which you don't know whether your brother has them or not, and you cannot tell your brother apart from those pegs, so you never know who your brother is. Take the hooded man. Your information tells you only a few things about him: he is a man, he just came in, and he has his head covered. All of them are properties that your information either ascribes to your brother, or about which it is silent. So for all you know this man *could be* your brother. But then your information does not distinguish between the two, and your brother is as much a stranger to you as is the hooded man. And still, when asked, after your brother's identity has been revealed, whether you did know who you brother was and who the hooded man was, you are tempted to say that the hooded man was a stranger for you, but of course in your acquaintance with your brother nothing really has changed. In fact, on thinking about it, this is typically the kind of joke he would enjoy.

The point about acquaintance is not that you can distinguish your brother from any peg whatsoever, because some pegs are so much strangers to you, have so few properties that they can be anyone. Precisely because *they* are complete strangers, you don't take their indiscernability with your acquaintances as an argument that you don't have acquaintances. You don't have to distinguish your brother from all those strangers that you assume to exist, but that you really don't know anything about. *What is crucial about knowing who your brother is, is that you can distinguish him from those pegs about which you know at least as much as you do about your brother.* Your information provides you with a lot of facts about your brother. If all these facts could, as far as your information is concerned, fit different pegs, one of which your brother, then indeed you don't know who your brother is. The basis of acquaintance is not solely the weak notion of indiscernability, which says that two pegs are indiscernable on the basis of the information if they don't have incompatible properties, but it involves the notion of *strong indiscernability* as well: two pegs are strongly indiscernable on the basis of the information if they have the same properties in it and if the same properties are incompatible with them.

This is how we determine whether we know who your brother is: we compare your brother with all the pegs that are weakly indiscernable from him on the basis of the information, the hooded man being one of them. And then we ask: suppose we add to such a peg all the properties that we know your brother has (we talk about basic properties, of course, and not about logically complex properties like being identical to your brother, in other words, we talk about pegs as if they are pegs and not as if they are classical objects), and similarly, we add to your brother all the properties that this peg has. In other words, suppose we make your brother and this peg strongly indiscernable. Then you are acquainted with your brother if doing that brings you in an information state on the basis of which they are *identical*. You are not acquainted with a peg, if there is a peg indiscernable with it, such that if you make the two strongly indiscernable it is *then* still possible to find new evidence that tells them apart after all.

Take two pegs, of one you only know that he is a young man, of the other you only know that he is a fat man; you can extend your information to a state where you know that both are young and fat men, where they are strongly indiscernable. They are not acquaintances to you, because it is very well possible for your information to grow into a state that tells them apart after all. The same for the hooded man: there can be lots of hooded men, which on some extension of your information are strongly indiscernable from this one, but that in general won't be enough information to regard them as identical. Your brother is a different case: you are so well informed about him that you know that if you gradually find out of a stranger that he has a remarkable resemblance to your brother, there is a stage where this resemblance can no longer be a coincidence, where you find out that he cannot be anyone else but your brother. And if it's not your brother, you will have found that out long before you could have reached the stage where they would have precisely the same properties.

This leads to the folowing definition:

d_1 is **acquainted on the basis of s** iff for all d_2 such that d_1 and d_2 are weakly indiscernable on the basis of **s** it holds that for all $s' \supseteq s$: if d_1 and d_2 are strongly indiscernable on the basis of s' then d_1 and d_2 are identical on the basis of s'

On this definition it is possible to say that you don't know who the hooded man is, but that you do know who your brother is, although you don't have enough information to strictly tell them apart. The same holds for the twin brothers at the party. That case involves three pegs: the twin brothers Bruce and Brian, and the peg you are pointing at. The question asked is: is this Bruce or Brian? Both Bruce and Brian can be acquainted objects for you, there is also no reason why they themselves should be indiscernable: you can very well know that their characters are completely different. But you know far less about the peg standing at the party, he is indiscernable with both of them, and there is no reason to be found in your information to suppose that another peg with the same properties has to be the same object.

Of course, acquaintedness comes in degrees: this peg is far less a stranger to you than is the hooded man. If you know that a peg is strongly indiscernable from the hooded man, then still you have no idea at all who he might be, he may be identified with any man whatsoever. If a peg has the same properties as the peg at the party then the admissible extensions of your information state are narrowed down to four kinds: they can both be identified with Brian, both with Bruce, and one with Brian and the other with Bruce. *Given the present definition of acquaintedness* we can also state the difference between the hooded man and the man at the party without talking about other strongly indiscernable pegs (which sounds more intuitive): the hooded man is highly unacquainted, because there can be lots of acquainted objects it can be identified with. The man at the party is only slightly unacquainted, because we do know that in whatever way our information may grow, it will always be identified with one of the acquainted objects Bruce or Brian. Acquainted objects themselves won't be identified with other acquainted objects than themselves.

Of course, there is a large influence of context (that is, background context) here. You are acquainted with someone only relative to a certain standard of precision. That holds for your brother, it even holds for yourself. You may be acquainted with your brother in the present context, but he may become more of a stranger to you if the context is changed and a different standard of precision is imposed. For instance, in the present context you can disregard the possibility that, unknown to you, your brother is one of a twin, which in the past changed places every week. If someone, or some evidence, forces you to regard that as a possibility, or even as the fact of the matter, you are forced into a context in which different standards hold: facts which before you did not even have to consider to reject them, suddenly destroy your certainty and you do have to admit to yourself: if I accept those facts, and I reconsider things in this light, then I don't know who my brother is, after all. Dr. Jekyll may change into Mr. Hyde each night without knowing it, he may even hear so much about Mr. Hyde that he can regard himself as acquainted with him. In that context, the question whether he is Mr. Hyde has the same answer for him, as it has for us: of course he is not. Only when faced with the dreadful truth, he has to ask himself seriously who he is.

One might think that the case of the hooded man is a highly constructed one, which we don't often find in real life. Nothing could be more of an illusion than that. In the paper you see a picture of a huge demo which you attended, and you know you must be somewhere in that crowd, but of course you couldn't tell which of those persons is you, you can see the faces of those in the front of the picture, and you know you're not among them, but the rest of them swim in a sea of indiscernability. But it is not *that* that makes you wonder who you really are.

5: Kind hearts and coronets

Kind Hearts and Coronets is a filmcomedy about a man who marries a noblewoman that is eighth in line for an important heritage. Not having patience enough to wait till all these seven relatives have died, he decides to murder them all, and so he does. Towards the end he is arrested for the only murder in the whole movie that he did not commit. A most remarkable aspect of the movie is that all seven noble victims are played by Alec Guinness.

There is something fascinating about that. Suppose you're watching that movie and you see Alec Guinness come in, what do you know about that situation? Well, since Alec Guinness plays all (noble) victims you know that *a victim comes in*. You certainly don't know that all victims come in, even though he plays them all, you even needn't know which one of them comes in. Now suppose that you know that this is the kind of movie where, if Alec Guinness comes in, he wears a hat. What is it that you know about this movie then? Since Alec Guinness plays all victims, you know that *if a victim comes in, he wears a hat*, and that means that *every victim who comes in, wears a hat*.

We see that Alec Guinness is a remarkable actor indeed. If we know that he comes in, we have existential information about the movie. If we know that if he comes in he wears a hat, we suddenly have universal information about the movie.

The sentences

A victim comes in
If a victim comes in he wears a hat

form, of course, part of the Case of the Beaten Donkey(s). I find the analogue persuasive: if we can invite Alec Guinness to live in our model, it seems that we have the right person to be the interpretation of the existential term **a victim**.

The analysis of donkey sentences is the most impressive aspect of discourse representation theory. The elegance of the analysis is most clear in Heim's perspicuous presentation. It comes down to the following ideas:

1. Existential terms are *variables* and not quantifiers.
2. Quantifiers are *nonselective*, they bind every variable in their scope. This amounts to the slight revision of the classical notion of variable binding, by replacing the notion: 'assignment g is identical to assignment f with the possible exception of the value of the variable x' by the notion: 'assignment g agrees with assignment f at least on the values for the variables in set X'.
3. *Existential closure* instead of univeral closure: a formula $\varphi(x_n)$ with free variable x_n is regarded as equivalent to $\exists x_n \varphi(x_n)$ instead of (as usual) to $\forall x_n \varphi(x_n)$: a discourse is true if there is *some* faithful embedding of it in the world (instead of: every embedding in the world is faithful).

4. Conditionals introduce a two-place *universal discourse quantifier*, relating the variables in an antecedent discourse to those in a consequent discourse. This quantifier has the following semantics: for every variable assignment that makes the antecedent discourse true, there is a variable assignment that makes the consequent discourse true and that does not assign different values to the variables of the antecedent discourse.

Given that existential terms are variables, the peculiar behaviour of existential terms in donkey sentences follows immediately: **a victim comes in** has logical form x_1 *is a victim and* x_1 *comes in*, which is interpreted existentially by existential closure; **if a victim comes is he wears a hat** has logical form *(x_1 is a victim and x_1 comes in) → x_1 wears a hat)*, where → is a universal discourse quantifier that binds x_1.

Pronouns are chameleontic. Sometimes they are very much like proper names, constants, sometimes they are more like variables. A theory that does not want to treat them as ambiguous has to make a choice. Either it reduces constants to variables, while allowing for some rather constant variables, or it reduces variables to constants, claiming that variables are names as well, but—of course—names for rather variable objects. (For an extensive discussion of these alternatives in relation to the semantics of pronouns, see Partee [1984].)

Discourse representation theory is a prime example of the first approach, an example of the second approach is Kit Fine's theory of arbitrary objects (Fine [1984]). I think that the question whether pronouns are variables or constants is not a trivial matter to be settled by taste, but is one of the main intriguing questions in semantics, namely the question how to draw the borderline between syntax and semantics. In fact, it is no other question than the one that was posed before: what is the meaning of a variable?

In what follows, I will choose the side (though not the theory) of Fine in this matter: the meanings of variables are alecs.

6. Alecs

What are alecs?
The answer suggested by the last section is: alecs are actors who play several characters in a play or movie. Of course, real actors are also human beings, like the characters they play: Alecs, similarly, are pegs. In the domain of pegs, we will find alecs and the characters they play.

The hard question then is: what makes a peg into an alec? What properties should pegs have to become alecs? Since pegs don't have properties, this has to mean: what should an information state be like for a peg to be an alec?

We are right in the middle of the movie. We see Alec Guinness come in. He plays the role of a victim. He is not identical to that victim: he plays him, he mimicks his behaviour. At the end of the movie, Alec will have played all victims. One of the victims is already dead, he certainly doesn't come in in this scene, but if Alec has the property of coming in at the basis of our information, Alec will keep that property till the end of the movie, when we have complete information. Then apparently at the end of the movie, we only see Alec in one particular role, apparently, he can't play that role there. Given this perspective, it seems plausible to describe the special nature of Alec as follows:

a is an alec, with respect to being a victim, on the basis of **s** iff for all *d* **s** contains the information that *if d* is a victim, then *d* maybe identical to *a*.

This is nothing but the skolem-function approach to donkey sentences: you associate with *a* for every branch extending **s** the role that *a* plays there. And we know also that this won't work, because it makes alecs existential, also when they are embedded in conditionals.

Another alternative is to impose a partial order of specificity on the domain of pegs, and let the characters be the maximally specific objects, and let Alec be an object that can grow into every victim on every information state; then at the end of the movie, Alec still can grow into every victim, plays all roles.

This is basically Kit Fine's theory of arbitrary objects: Alec is the arbitrary victim. This also won't work, because it makes alecs universal also when they are not embedded: if the arbitrary victim comes in, then every victim comes in.

If we try to identify Alec with one victim in each possible outcome, or with all victims in some, or all victims in all, then we will unavoidably collaps into one of these alternatives. Also, what do we do with those victims who are already dead? Alec *has* played them, but the present stage of the movie will not be one in which he still can play them, and that is also a factor that will spoil the universal behaviour in conditional contexts, if alecs are existential in non-conditional contexts, and vice versa. The fact that there is a persuasive analogy between existential terms and certain actors does not imply that we should not be very careful in deciding which aspects of the metaphor should be formalized and how: like most analogies, it breaks down at certain points, and it is unadvisable to impose it by brute force.

Let me try to present a slightly different picture.

Let us assume that language users take their present information state **s** to be part of a conversational play, which they assume has a beginning point s_0, where $s_0 \subseteq s$. s_0 contains the initial conditions of the conversation. The possible courses of the whole play, then are the branches (maximal chains) in the set $\mathcal{B}_s$ of extensions of s_0, the possible end-scenes are the total elements of those branches. If b is a branch, I will use t_b for its endpoint.

If we want to impose the requirement that Alec plays all roles, then that does not imply that he is identical to any of the roles he plays. I take it to mean that for every character there is a stage in which Alec mimicks the behaviour of that character, there is a stage where Alec's properties and the properties that are added to him there are the same as the properties of that character. We can also say it as follows: there is a stage where Alec and that character are *strongly indiscernable*. However, this cannot be exactly what we want. If we already know of two characters that one wears a red beard and the other a brown beard then Alec can't play both, because each of them will have that beard during all stages, so he can't be strongly indiscernable from both. So Alec does what every actor does if he doesn't have the right outfit: he plays without and lets the audience imagine the beard itself. Alec can't be strongly indiscernable from both, *but he can be an indiscernable approximation of both*: at least the properties that *he* has will be properties that the characters he plays will have as well. Alec has the capacity to *imitate* every character up to a certain stage. Of course, there is always a moment where the imitation becomes obvious, in the end, there is only one real role that Alec can play, namely himself, but as long as we haven't reached that stage, the imitation can be persuasive.

I use this formulation to bring us in the right direction. Taken literally it is far from a solution. For, it has all the problems we could think of for the old alternatives. Take a branch and consider Alec and one of his roles. For some time they act the same. But at the same time, a different role is there that develops in a different direction. How can Alec ever play that role? Should we allow Alec to *change* its role at a branch? But then it has to change its properties at that branch, the properties which according to the information states there it certainly has. If Alec can be non-monotonic in that sense, then he won't be a peg. And in this respect the interpretations of existential terms should not be like actors who change their properties radically in the course of the film, by playing a different role: if we get the information that a victim comes in who wears a hat, we are not going to suppose that we can continue that discourse with: "He doesn't come in", because we mean a different role. That is one point where the metaphor breaks down.

A second point where that is the case is, that if we get the information that a is a victim and a comes in, the requirement that a is an Alec will not mean that he plays the role of all victims (though that can be an initial requirement), but what is relevant for us is, that he plays the role of all victims that come in. In evaluating the existential sentence **a man comes in** on an information state, the property of being an alec will be a three place relation between a peg, the property of being a man that comes in, and an information state. That is, if we say: "A victim comes in", without saying who we mean, we don't have to take into account those victims of which we know that they don't come in.

An alec has to play in some way or other several roles in the play, since at the end of the play he has played them. The fact that this alec has played a certain role, means that between the beginning and the end of the play, he somewhere played that part, somewhere was an indiscernable approximation of that character. Consider a branch b, with beginning point s_0 and endpoint t_b. That branch is the story of the play which ends in t_b, but there are many alternative ways of telling the same story: there are many branches which start in s_0 and end in t_b (they are not different stories, but different orders in which the same information can be obtained). That an alec plays a particular character in that play means that there is a particular way of telling that story in which he plays that character, a way of following that alec in a particular role. If we say that in that play he plays different characters, we mean that there are different ways we can follow him through the same play. We can regard those branches as providing the different roles that an alec plays, and if we say that after the play is over he has played several characters, we do not take that to mean that on a particular branch with that endpoint he showed the same behaviour as all those characters, but rather that for each of those characters there is a such a branch where he showed the behaviour of that character.

We will call the branches that have the same beginning and endpoint as a branch b **the alternatives of** b.

This gives us a way of formalizing the notion of an alec as we intend it here:

$Alec(a, \mathcal{P}, s)$, peg a is an **alec** with respect to set of properties $\mathcal{P}$ in s, iff for every branch $b \in \mathcal{B}_s$ and every peg d which at some stage of that branch has the properties in $\mathcal{P}$, there is an alternative b' for b where at some stage a has the properties in $\mathcal{P}$ and a is an indiscernable approximation of d.

The best way of understanding the particularities of this definition, is to see what this notion can do for us in the case of existential terms.

In the course of a conversation someone utters the sentence **a victim comes in**. We change the information state we were in, to a state s on the basis of which that sentence is true. We do that by choosing a peg a to which s ascribes the properties of being a victim and coming in, where a is an alec in s with respect to these properties, i.e.

$alec(a, \lfloor victim, come\ in \rfloor, s)$ and s $\Vdash victim(a) \wedge come\ in(a)$

So on the basis of s, a is a victim that comes in. The fact that it is an alec tells you that for every branch, extending s and every object that at some stage of that branch is a victim that comes in, there is an alternative for that branch where a is an indiscernable approximation of it for some time. This gives you existential information: you know that on every way your information can be extended you will find *some* object (namely a) which is a victim that comes in (you do not have to know *which* victim comes in). It does not give you universal information, there is no reason why it would imply that every victim comes in.

Now consider the conditional sentence **If a victim comes in he wears a hat**. To add this to your information you also go to an information state where you have chosen an alec a such that it holds that if a comes in, a wears a hat.

$alec(a, \lfloor victim, come\ in \rfloor, s)$ and s $\Vdash (victim(a) \wedge come\ in(a)) \rightarrow wear\ a\ hat(a)$

The conditional part of this means, on the definition introduced in the section on data semantics: for every branch extending s if the first thing that happens with respect to $victim(a) \wedge come\ in(a)$ is that it becomes true there then $wear\ a\ hat(a)$ must be true there. (Note that, in the universal case, a need not, and normally will not, have properties *in* s itself, even though it is an alec in it. This corresponds to Heim's condition that indefinites introduce new markers. We can say that a is only introduced as an object in s if it has properties in s.)

Now take any branch where some object d is a victim and comes in somewhere. Then you know that there is an alternative for that branch where a is a victim and comes in and is an indiscernable approximation of d at some stage. But, given the conditional, that means that a must wear a hat there, and since it is an indiscernable approximation of d there, d must wear a hat there as well. This means that every branch where some object d is a victim that comes in, has an alternative where d wears a hat as well. Since the alternatives have the same endpoint as that branch, the fact that d wears a hat will reach that endpoint (which means that in one stage or other it also has to reach that point on the other branch), and we see that on every way our information can be extended with an object that is a victim and comes in, we will find out that it wears a hat as well: in the context of the antecedent of a conditional, the existential term is interpreted universally (see also figure 1).

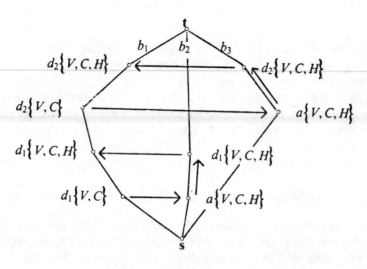

figure 1

These examples use only one existential term. An extension of the notion of an alec with respect to a set of properties, to an alec-pair (*n*-tuple) with respect to a set of properties and relations is straightforward.

Alecs are pegs, partial objects, which you can follow through your information, about which you can be deadly wrong, which you can mistake for others, and which can turn out to be identical to others. With alecs, it is no mistery any longer how in uttering a hob-nob sentence:

Hob believes that a witch poisoned his cow and Nob believes that she killed his sow

we talk about one object that doesn't exist, that Both Hob and Nob believe to be the same, although none of them believes a particular witch to have done those deeds: because she is an alec, and as an alec she is a peg.

Discourse semantics is the level of objects we talk about, partial objects, that we can learn to distinguish from each other, but objects that we can also learn to identify with each other. As far as this epistemic contingency is concerned the referents of existential terms are not different from those of other terms: we can discover that they are the same or distinct. This is hard to understand, if we are forced to assume that they are variables, symbols. Fortunately, we don't have to. We can use the partiality of pegs to introduce alecs, objects that express their variability in their behaviour in information growth.

Epilogue

What is the moral of this paper?

It has never failed to be perplexing that people are able to make sense out of the words of others in this jungle of uncertainty, indeterminacy, unspecificity, vagueness, indefiniteness, and indiscernability. Some believe that we can rely on the context to solve all these things for us. Indeed, I would say, the context of shared assumptions of the language users is an important source of efficiency in our information exchange, but not in the sense that it resolves indiscernability. At the contrary. We want to talk about some issues, be it pizza toppings or the meaning of life, but if we had to wait till the context had resolved the vagueness in that, we'd better do something else. But we are impatient. Instead, we let the context set a few pegs for these things, *accept* that we really don't know enough about them, that there can be lots of others, which are more or less indiscernable from them, and start talking about them. The real trick is that we don't care about our lack of knowledge, that we even exploit it: pegs are the trick that partial information has found to express itself, and indiscernability is the basis of their success, their efficiency. Alecs are so useful because you can let them play the role of practically anything, without having to be over-precise. They would be useless, if our information were complete, maximally precise, etc.: the real world makes too many distinctions to be managable.

Alecs are indefinite objects. But they are *potentially* definite. If you want to talk about something, and you introduce an alec for it, then *by the very nature of an alec* you deliver yourself to the assumption that, how indefinite it may be, how indiscernable on the basis of your present information it may be, you know what it would take in principle to make it definite, *and* you know that in principle it *can* be made definite. You know that *because* you know what it would take for your information to grow and you know that your information can grow. Since pegs and alecs are objects whose indiscernability is determined by your information, the assumption that your information can be made total, and the assumption that you know what it would be if your information were total, has the consequence that they are potentially discernable, potentially specific, potentially definite. Of course, it can be in practice hard to figure out what would make them definite, and that will certainly influence judgements about the acceptability of anaphora in particular cases. But the assumption that we talk about pegs *is* the assumption that exchange of information is about things that, if only we were better informed, we could tell apart. We cannot talk about that of which we have to assume that it is indiscernable in principle. Even if the world were so, that there *are* things that are principally indiscernable, when we talk about them, we introduce pegs for them and therewith pretend that they are not. Where we give up the assumption that we can get better informed, our words lose their intersubjective meaning and are reduced to their form and subjective appearance.

Note

This paper is an abridged version of the paper 'Pegs and alecs' in Landman [1986]. It appears here with permission from Foris Publications, Dordrecht-Cinnaminsion, which is gratefully acknowledged. The research for this paper was financially supported by the Netherlands Organization for the Advancement of Pure Research (Z.W.O.) and by Barbara Partee's grant from the System Development Foundation.

This paper would have been impossible for me to write without the help and stimulation of Emmon Bach, Renate Bartsch, Jeroen Groenendijk, Nirit Kadmon, Barbara Partee, Craige Roberts, Martin Stokhof, Ray Turner, and Frank Veltman.

References

Fine, K.,1984, 'A defense of arbitrary objects', in: Landman and Veltman (eds.), *Varieties of Formal Semantics,* GRASS 3, Foris, Dordrecht

Groenendijk, J. and M. Stokhof,1982, 'Formal and acquainted objects in the theory of information', paper presented at the *Groningen Workshop on Interrogative Quantification.*

Heim, I.,1982, *The Semantics of Definite and Indefinite Noun Phrases,* Diss., UMass., Amherst

Kamp, H.,1981,'A theory of truth and semantic representation', in: Groenendijk, Janssen and Stokhof (eds.), *Formal Methods in the Study of Language,* Mathematical Centre Tracts, Amsterdam. Reprinted in: Groenendijk, Janssen and Stokhof (eds.),1983, *Truth, Interpretation, Information,* GRASS 2, Foris, Dordrecht

Kripke, S.,1979, 'A puzzle about belief', in: Margalit (ed.), *Meaning and Use,* Reidel, Dordrecht

Landman, F.,1986, *Towards a Theory of Information. The Status of Partial Objects in Semantics,* GRASS 6, Foris, Dordrecht

Parsons, T.,1981, *Non-existent Objects,* Yale UP, New Yersey

Partee, B.,1984, 'Compositionality', in: Landman and Veltman (eds.), *Varieties of Formal Semantics,* GRASS 3, Foris, Dordrecht

Scott, D.,1980, *Lectures on a Mathematical Theory of Computation,* Oxford University Computer laboratory. Technical Monograph PRG-19

REASONING ABOUT KNOWLEDGE IN PHILOSOPHY:
THE PARADIGM OF EPISTEMIC LOGIC

Jaakko Hintikka
Department of Philosophy
Florida State University
Tallahassee, FL 32306

ABSTRACT

Theories of knowledge representation and reasoning about knowledge in philosophy are considered from the vantage point of epistemic logic. This logic is primarily a logic of knowing that, and its semantics can be considered an explication of the well-known idea that "information means elimination of uncertainty". A number of other theories are discussed as further developments of epistemic logic. They include:

(1) theory of questions and answers.

(2) interplay of quantifiers and epistemic concepts.

(3) representations of other kinds of knowledge than knowing that, especially those expressed by knows + an indirect wh-question and by knows + direct grammatical object.

(4) the problem of cross-identification; the coexistence of different cross-identification methods.

(5) the problem of logical omniscience.

(6) informational independence in epistemic logic and its manifestations, including the de dicto - de re contrast and wh-questions with outside quantifiers.

(7) an interrogative model of inquiry and its applications, especially the conceptualization of tacit knowledge and of range of attention.

Epistemic logic as a vehicle of knowledge representation

The main vehicle of speaking and reasoning about knowledge in philosophy has recently been epistemic logic.[1] Even though epistemic logic is not the only relevant language-game in town, it offers a useful perspective here, for certain other approaches can be thought of as improvements on epistemic logic. In its axiomatic-deductive forms, epistemic logic is normally considered a branch of modal logic, and its semantics is usually subsumed under the misleading heading of "possible-worlds semantics".[2] I will not attempt here a survey of the existing literature on epistemic logic. Most of this literature is focused on syntactical (e.g., deductive and axiomatic) methods of dealing with knowledge representation and reasoning about knowledge. This is in my view a serious defect in much of the current work on epistemic logic. For typically the most interesting problems and solutions are found by considering the model-theoretical (semantical) situation. For this reason, I will not attempt here a survey of existing literature, but a review of some of the central conceptual problems arising in epistemic logic.

The basic laws of epistemic logic are in fact easily obtained on a basis of a simple semantical idea. It is that all talk about knowledge (in the sense of knowing that) presupposes a set (space) W of models (a.k.a. scenarios, worlds or situations) and a knower b who has so much information that he or she can restrict his or her attention to a subset W_1 of the space W. Since W_1 is relative not only to b but also to the scenario $w_0 \in W$ in which b's knowledge is being considered, the obvious implementation of this intuitive idea, which of course is but a form of the old adage "information is elimination of uncertainty", is to assume that a two-place relation R is defined on W for each b. The members of W_1 are the worlds compatible with what b knows in w_0. Then W_1 is the set of all scenarios to which w_0 bears this relation. The relation will be called an epistemic alternativeness relation, and the members of W_1 are called the epistemic b-alternatives to w_0. Thus "b knows that S" is true in w_0 iff S is true in all the epistemic b-alternatives to w_0.

Each such alternativeness relation must be assumed to be reflexive (what is known is true) and transitive. (If b is in a position to rule out all scenarios in $W-W_1$, b is ipso facto in a position to rule out the claim that he or

---

[1]The idea of epistemic logic goes back at least to G.H. von Wright, An Essay in Modal Logic, North-Holland, Amsterdam, 1951. The first book-length treatment was my Knowledge and Belief: An Introduction to the Logic of the Two Notions, Cornell U.P., Ithaca, 1962.
[2]For a partial survey of earlier work, see Wolfgang Lenzen, Recent Work in Epistemic Logic (Acta Philosophica Fennica vol. 30, no. 1) Societas Philosophica Fennica, Helsinki, 1978.

she is not in such a position.)   These definitions and stipulations (combined with a suitable semantics for the usual quantification theory) specify the semantics of a system of epistemic logic, and hence its deductive-axiomatic treatment, subject to the qualifications to be discussed below.

The resulting logic turns out not to be devoid of interest.   Its propositional part (restricted to one knower) is the logic of the topological closure operation.   Hence epistemic logic is related to the logic of topology. Its laws are in effect those of intuitionistic logic.   There are also close relations[3] between the semantics of epistemic logic and the technique of forcing.[3]   However, in order to reach this connection, the semantics of negation and conditional have to be modified somewhat.

Many of the further developments in epistemic logic can be thought of as solutions to problems concerning the epistemic logic so far set up.   One of the first problems is to represent the other kinds of knowledge for instance, the kinds of knowledge expressed by knows + indirect wh-questions and by knows + a direct grammatical object, by starting from the knows that construction. This basic construction (b knows that S) in my notation by " {b} K S".[4]

Two comments are in order here.

(a) The propositional alternatives I have called "scenarios" or "models" can be states of affairs, situations, courses of events, or entire world histories. The last of these applications is highlighted by philosophers' misleading term "possible-worlds semantics".   This term is misleading, because applications to entire universes are scarcely found outside philosophers' speculations.[5]   The primary intended applications are to scenarios covering relatively small pieces of space-time.   Thus the label "situation semantics",[6] which has recently been applied to a study of additional relations between what I have called scenarios, does not mark any sharp contrast to rightly understood possible-worlds semantics.

3See here, e.g., Melvin Fitting, Intuitionistic Logic, Model Theory, and Forcing, North-Holland, Amsterdam, 1969; Kenneth A. Bowen, Model Theory for Modal Logic, D. Reidel, Dordrecht, 1979.   These treatises are not addressed to the specific problems of epistemic logic, however.
4In the earlier literature, the knower used to be indicated by a subscript. This is misleading, however, for the term referring to the knower is not within the scope of the epistemic operator.
5Some philosophers have tried to find a difference in principle between the two kinds of applications.   It is nevertheless clearer in epistemic logic than in some of the parallel theories that the intended applications have always been to "small worlds", to use L.J. Savage's phrase.
6See Jon Barwise and John Perry, Situations and Attitudes, MIT Press, Cambridge, Mass., 1983.

(b) The most important application of epistemic logic is to the theory of questions and answers.[7]   No separate treatment is needed, however, for a direct question like

(1.1)   Who's living here?

can be construed as a request of information which might as well be expressed by

(1.2)   Bring it about that I know who is living here.

Here the subordinate clause is an indirect question with "knows" as its main verb.   I have called it the desideratum of the question (1.1).   It fells within the purview of epistemic logic (see sec. 2 below).   And obviously the logical study of direct questions like (1.1) reduces largely to the study of their desiderata.

The first and foremost problem is the theory of questions and answers concerns the relation of a question ot its (conclusive) answers.   When does a reply, say "d" to a wh-question like (1.1) do its job?   Obviously when it makes the desideratum

(1.3)   I know who lives here

true.   But what does the reply "d" in fact accomplish?   Obviously, the truth of

(1.4)   I know that d lives here.

Hence the problem of answerhood is the question as to when (1.4) implies (1.3).   Now the logical forms of (1.3) and (1.4) are, fairly obviously (but see sec. 4 below),

(1.5) $(\exists x) \{I\} K$ (x lives here)

and

(1.6) $\{I\} K$ (d lives here)

---

[7] See here Jaakko Hintikka, The Semantics of Questions and the Questions of Semantics (Acta Philosophica Fennica, vol. 28, no. 4), Societas Philosophica Fennica, Helsinki, 1976.

Hence the operative problem is when (1.6) implies (1.5).   This is a question concerning the interplay of quantifiers and epistemic operators.   This interplay will be discussed in section 2 below.[8]

Quantifiers in epistemic logic.   Knowing + indirect wh-questions

The first conceptual problem I shall analyze is the representation of other kinds of knowledge than knowing that.[9]   They include the kind of knowledge expressed linguistically by the constructions knows + indirect wh-question and knows + a direct grammatical object object.   Here philosophers' preoccupation with the surface phenomena of ordinary usage has seriously hampered their theorizing.   In fact, the right treatment is nevertheless not hard to find.   It can be presented as a succession of steps.

(i) In order ot use quantifiers in context which, like epistemic contexts involve a multitude of scenarios, it must be assumed that criteria of identity for individuals across worlds have been given.   In order to have a vivid vocabularly, I shall speak of the imaginary lines connecting the counterparts of the same individual in different model or scenarios as "world lines".

Once a warp of world lines connecting the members of W is given (for each relevant knower), truth conditions for quantified sentences in a (first order) epistemic language.   Such truth-conditions solve all the conceptual problems Quine and others have raised or, rather, transform them into problems concerning the way world lines are drawn.

(ii) It cannot be assumed that the same individuals exist in all models.   Then the basic laws of quantification theory have to be revised by changing some of the instantiation rules.   For instance, the law of universal instantiation might be changed so as to read:

(UI)   If "x" occurs in S[x] outside the scopes of all epistemic operators,

$$(2.1) \quad \frac{(\forall x)S[x] \quad \& \quad (\exists y)(z=y)}{S[z]}$$

In other words, when we speak of z as a member of the actual world, we have to assume that it exists in that world in order for it to be a bona fide value of quantifiers pertaining inter alia to the actual world.[10]

_____

8The question here is under what conditions existential generalization is valid in epistemic logic.   The conditions are of course the same as the conditions on valid universal instantiation dealt with in sec. 2, part ii, below.
9Cf. here chapter 1 of my book, The Intentions of Intentionality, D. Reidel, Dordrecht, 1974.
10I am assuming that a distinction is made between those name-like free singular terms which pick out the same individual from different worlds and

(iii) The obvious formal counterpart of a <u>knows</u> + an indirect wh-question, e.g., of

(2.2)   <u>b</u> knows who (say, x) is such that S[x]

is

(2.3) $(\exists x)$ $\{\underline{b}\}$ K S[x].

This paraphrase amounts to saying that <u>b</u> knows who (x) is such that S[x] is there to be a world line which in all of <u>b</u>'s knowledge worlds picks out an individual x satisfying in that world the condition S[x].

The best proof of the aptness of this rational reconstruction of "knowing + wh-construction" sentences is that it leads into an elegant and powerful analysis of the relation of a (direct) wh-question to its (conclusive) answers.

(iv) In order for this idea to work, we nevertheless must allow world lines to break down in a more radical sense than the failure of an individual to exist in a given "world". We must allow a world line of x to break down in a world w_1 in the strong sense that it does not even make sense to ask whether x exists in w_1 or not.[11] For otherwise (if all world lines could be extended <u>ad libitum</u>) everybody would know the identity of every individual (under some <u>guise</u> or other, so to speak), on the basis of the paraphrase of constructions of the form <u>knowing</u> + indirect wh-question agreed on in (iii).

In other words, the natural model-theoretical counterpart of <u>b</u>'s knowing the identity of x is that some world line passing through x (considered as a member of the actual world) spans all of <u>b</u>'s knowledge worlds.

How is the well-definedness of x in a world w_1 (i.e., the extendibility of the world line of x to w_1) to be expressed in a formal language? The obvious candidate is the truth of "x=x" in w_1. This simple idea yields the first fully satisfactory treatment of quantification in epistemic contexts. This treatment has not been worked out in the literature, but the main points are nevertheless clear. Since the truth of $(\exists z)(x=z)$ implies that of x=x, no changes are needed in the quantifier rules. Instead, we need a three-value logic with different kinds of negations, forced on us by the idea that if x is undefined in a world w_1, any atomic sentence containing "x" does not have either of the two usual truth-values "true" and "false" in w_1.

(v) Essentially the same treatment can be extended to higher-order logic. (Such a treatment is needed, among other purposes, for applications of epistemic logic to the theory of questions and answers.) There is one

---

those that might refer to different individuals in different worlds. Here "z" is assumed to be of the former kind.
11This matter will be dealt with in a greater detail in a projected monograph of mine.

difference, however. In the case of higher-order entities, existence is not needed as a condition of being a value of a quantified variable. (It is not clear what existence might mean here.) But well-definedness is still required. Hence the counterpart to (UI) for, e.g., one-place second-order quantifier is

$$(UI)' \qquad \frac{(\forall X)S[X] \quad \varepsilon \quad (Y = Y)}{S[Y]}$$

where (Y = Y) is to be taken to same as

(2.4) $(\forall x)(Y(x) \Leftrightarrow Y(x))$

(vi) There is another crucially important feature of the conceptual situation here which has been obscured by the surface phenomena of ordinary language and therefore neglected by philosophers. This is the fact that that in certain situations there are two systems of world lines in operation.[12]   A knower's (say, b's) cognitive relations to his or her environment (including past situations in which b was directly involved) span a framework which can be used for the purpose of drawing world lines. Such a world line connects such (scenario-bound) individuals as play the same role in these first-hand cognitive relations to b from b's perspective. The simplest example is visual perception (visual knowledge). There the relevant framework is b's visual space and the world lines perspectively drawn connect the individuals occupying the same slot in b's visual geometry. (If b does not see who or what they are, they are not the same absolutely or descriptively identified entities). In other words, b's perspectively identified objects are his or her visual objects. This can be extended to other kinds of knowledge in a fairly straightforward way.

Because of the presence of two systems of world lines, we must have two pairs of quantifiers corresponding to (relying on) them. Success in the perspectival cross-identification will then be expressed in the same way as with the other (public, descriptive) mode of identification, but with a different kind of quantifiers, say (ax) and (ex), instead of $(\forall x)$ and $(\exists x)$. Then

(2.5)   (ex) $\{\underline{b}\} K(\underline{d} = x)$

will say, assuming a case of visual knowledge situation, that b can find a niche for d among b's visual objects. In other words, (2.5) says that b sees (and recognizes) d. More generally speaking, (2.5) says that b is acquainted with d, i.e., knows d. Here we thus have an analysis of the knows + a direct grammatical object construction. This construction can be analyzed in terms of knowing that plus perspectival (contextual) quantifiers.

In intuitive terms, the contrast between the two different cross-identification methods has variously been described as putting a name to

---

12See here chapters 3-4 of my book The Intentions of Intentionality, D. Reidel, Dordrecht, 1974.

a face vs. putting a face to a name, answering what-questions vs. answering a where-question, etc. These explanations are only partial ones, however, and do not bring out fully the underlying model-theoretical situation. Hence they (like the terms "visual object" and "object of acquaintance") have to be taken with a pinch of salt.

Even though most philosophical logicians have chosen to disregard this duality of quantifiers and modes of cross-identification, it is one of the most important phenomena in the field of knowledge representation, important both epistemologically and psychologically. In epistemology, the distinction has in effect figured as Bertrand Russell's contrast between knowledge by description and knowledge by acquaintance.[13] In psychology, the same distinction is manifested[14] as the contrast between what are called semantical and episodic memory[14] as well as a distinction between two kinds of visual systems.[15]

The problem of "logical omniscience"

The model-theoretical treatment of epistemic logic so far outlined leads to a paradoxical result. Suppose that $\vdash (S_1 \supset S_2)$, i.e., that all models of S_1 are models of S_2. Then all the epistemic alternatives in which S_1 are true are also alternatives in which S_2 is true. From this it follows that the following will be true for any $\underline{b}$ and in any scenario:

$$(3.1) \quad \{b\}K\, S_1 \quad \supset \quad \{b\}K\, S_2$$

In brief, everybody always knows all the logical consequences of what he or she knows. This is obviously an unacceptable result, and in certain quarters it is still considered a sufficient reason for rejecting a model-theoretic analysis of epistemic concepts.[16]

This follows only if the paradox, known naturally as the paradox of logical omniscience, is unavoidable. And it has been known for quite a while that it is not. In fact, we have have one of the several unmistakable but unheralded triumphs of epistemic logic. There are in fact two equivalent ways of

---

13Bertrand Russell, "Knowledge by Acquaintance and Knowledge by Description", in Mysticism and Logic, George Allen & Unwin, London, 1917; chapter 5 of The Problems of Philosophy, Home University Library, London, 1912; and cf. Jaakko Hintikka, Knowledge by Acquaintance - Individuation by Acquaintance, in D.F. Pears, editor, Bertrand Russell (Modern Studies in Philosophy), Doubleday, Garden City, N.J., 1972, pp. 52-79.
14See Endel Tulving. Elements of Episodic Memory, Clarendon Press, Oxford, 1983.
15See Lucia Vaina, From Vision to Cognition: A Computational Theory of Higher-Level Visual Functions, D. Reidel, Dordrecht, 1986.
16Cf., e.g., Noam Chomsky, The Generative Enterprise, Foris, Dordrecht, 1982. From what is reported in the rest of this section, this objection against possible-worlds analysis of knowledge was effectively disposed of more than ten years ago.

delineating the subclass of logical consequences $\vdash (S_1 \supset S_2)$ for which (3.1) holds.

(i) This set can be defined by putting syntactical restrictions on the deductive argument which leads from S_1 to S_2. This argument can of course be of many different kinds. It turns out, however, that for all the half-way natural ones, the same heuristic idea works and gives the same result. In an easily appreciated sense, the number of free individual symbols together with the number of layers of quantifiers determine how many individuals are considered in a given sentence S (or in a given argument). The natural restriction on the argument from S_1 to S_2 now is that this parameter should never be larger at any stage of the argument than it is in S_1 or S_2.[17]

Even though this basic idea is thus easy to understand and to implement, no simple axiomatic-deductive system codifying it has been presented in the literature.

This way of defining knowledge-preserving logical inferences is connected, via the idea of so many individuals considered in their relation to each other in an argument with a wealth of traditional philosophical issues in the philosophy of logic and mathematics.[18] The same idea also promises connections with the psychology of deductive reasoning.[19]

(ii) This syntactical (deductive-axiomatic) restriction on "logical omniscience" yield the same result as a different and apparently completely unlike line of thought. This line begins with an interesting generalization of the concept of model (world, scenario). Unlike its rivals as a candidate for the role of a logically nonstandard world (semantical bases of so-called paraconsistent logics),[20] this generalization is completely realistic. Indeed, this generalization is but a variant of the notion of urn model in probability theory, and is referred to by the same term.[21] In an obvious sense, nested quantifiers can be thought of as representing successive "draws" of individuals from an "urn", i.e. from the domain of a model, or (perhaps a little more

17See Jaakko Hintikka, "Knowledge, Belief, and Logical Consequence" in Hintikka, The Intentions of Intentionality, D. Reidel, Dordrecht, 1975.

18See Jaakko Hintikka, Logic, Language-Games, and Information, Clarendon Press, Oxford, 1973.

19See Jaakko Hintikka, "Mental Models, Semantical Games, and Varieties of Intelligence", in Lucia Vaina, ed., Varieties of Intelligence, D. Reidel, Dordrecht, 1986.

20The so-called paraconsistent logics have never been any realistic model-theoretical and pragmatic interpretation, and hence have in their present form little interest. Cf. here Nicholas Rescher and Robert Brandom The Logic of Inconsistency, Basil Blackwell, Oxford, 1979.

21See Veikko Rantala, "Urn Models: A New Kind of Non-Standard Model for First-Order Logic", Journal of Philosophical Logic, vol. 4 (1975), pp. 455-474, reprinted in Esa Saarinen, Game-Theoretical Semantics, D. Reidel, Dordrecht, 1979.

vividly) as a series successful searches of individuals from the model. The concept of urn model is obtained by letting the set of available individuals change between successive "draws". (The world, in other words, is run by a malicious demon who can restrict the set of available individuals in tandem with our examination of te world (via successive searches or "draws").

Actually, not all and sundry urn models are natural candidates for the role of epistemically possible but (classically speaking) logically impossible worlds which are the model-theoretical codification of the failure of logical omniscience. For that role, only those urn models (changing models) are acceptable which vary so subtly that they cannot be told apart from the invariant (classical) models by means of sequences of draws as long as those involved in a given sentence.[22] It turns out that the conditionals $(S_1 \supset S_2)$ which are true in all such "almost invariant" urn models (at the length of sequence of draws envisaged in the conditional) are precisely the same as those for which the step from $\vdash (S_1 \supset S_2)$ to (3.1) is authorized by the syntactical restriction.

Epistemic logic and informational independence

One of the most characteristic features of epistemic logic has barely been mentioned in the existing literature.[23] In order to see what is involved, let us consider the familiar distinction between

(4.1)   b knows that there is an individual x such that S[x]

and

(4.2)   b knows of some individual x that S[x].

Usually, it is said that these two are to be represented in the language of epistemic logic by

(4.3)   {b} K (∃x) S[x]

and

(4.4)   (∃x) {b} K S[x],

respectively. Here the latter has roughly the force

22See Jaakko Hintikka, "Impossible Possible Worlds Vindicated", Journal of Philosophical Logic vol. 4 (1975), pp. 475-484, reprinted ibid.
23The first time this interesting phenomenon was pointed out in the literature is in Lauri Carlson and Alice ter Meulen, "Informational Independence in Intensional Context", in Esa Saarinen et al., eds., Essays in Honour of Jaakko Hintikka, D. Reidel, Dordrecht, 1979, pp. 61-72.

(4.5)   <u>b</u> knows who (what), say x, is such that S[x].

Hence the contrast in question is roughly that between "knowing that there is" and "knowing who or what".

I am not questioning the status of (4.4) as being logically equivalent with (4.2), i.e., as a possible translation of (4.2). What I am asking is how this translation comes about, i.e., what the mechanism is that leads us from (4.2) to (4.4). It is usually assumed, as the rendering (4.4) of (4.2) shows, that the mechanism in question is the relative order (relative scopes) of K and ($\exists$x). The linguistic evidence for this idea is unconvincing, however. It is much more natural to assume that in epistemic context like (4.2), the choice of the individual we are talking about is independent of epistemic considerations, i.e., that the quantifier somehow ranges over just the actually existing individuals. This independence can be captured by the two-dimensional expression

(4.6) $(\exists x)$
            $\{\underline{b}\} K$ S[x]

Even though the meaning of (4.6) is intuitively obvious, further explanations are needed here to incorporate expressions like (4.6) in our formal language. In order to spell out the semantics of expressions like (4.6) we must combine possible-worlds analysis of epistemic concepts (as sketched ever so briefly in section 1 above) with what has been called game-theoretical semantics (GTS).[24] Very briefly, in GTS the truth of a sentence S in a model M is explicated as the existence of a winning strategy in a certain verification game (semantical game G(S) played with S on M for one of the players, called Myself (or the Verifier) against an opponent called Nature (or the Falsifier). Most of the rules of these games can be anticipated on the basis of the verification idea. The following are cases in point:

(G.E)   If the game has reached the sentence ($\exists$x) S[x]

and M, Myself chooses an individual from the domain do(M) of M. Then the game is continued with respect to S[b] and M.

(G.U)   Similarly except that Nature chooses b.

(G.v)   G(S_1 v S_2) (played on M) begins with Myself's choice of S_i (i = 1 or 2) The rest of the game is G(S_i)(played on the same model M).

24See here Esa Saarinen, ed., <u>Game-Theoretical Semantics</u>, D. Reidel, Dordrecht, 1979, and Jaakko Hintikka and Jack Kulas, <u>The Game of Language</u>, D. Reidel, Dordrecht, 1983.

(G. ε) Similarly, except that Nature chooses S_i.

(G.~) G(~S) is like G(S) except that the roles of the two players are reversed.

(G.K) If the game has reached the sentence $\{b\} K S$ and the model (world) M_0, Nature chooses an epistemic b-alternative M_1 to M_0. The game is continued with respect to S and M_1.

In terms of GTS, the semantics of branching formulas like (4.6) can be dealt with explicitly.[25]   What they instantiate is the well-known game-theoretical phenomenon of informational independence. In (4.6), the moves connected with "$(\exists x)$" and "$\{b\} K$" are each made without knowledge of the other move. More generally, each move is associated with an information set including those other moves which are known to the player making the move. Hence the operator structure of a sentence need not always be partly even partially ordered.

We can sometimes linearize the branching notation used in (4.6) by attaching to each quantifier an indication which shows which of the earlier epistemic operators (if any) it is informationally independent of. Thus (4.6) can be written, in a self-explanatory notation, as

(4.7) $\{b\} K (\exists x / \{b\} K) S[x]$

which is of course logically equivalent with (4.6) and (4.4).

It is a most important general fact about the logic of epistemic concepts that when they mix with quantifiers, these quantifiers frequently have to be taken to be independent of some of the epistemic operators present. For instance, the so-called de re reading of quantifiers is in reality precisely the reading obtained by taking the quantifier in question to be informationally independent of an epistemic (or other intentional) operator.

GTS shows that (and how) other primitives of one's language, not just the quantifiers, can be independent of epistemic operators. For instance, an atomic predicate A(x) or a proper name a may be evaluated in M_0 independently of an epistemic operator; say "$\{b\} K$". This may be indicated by writing A(x/$\{b\}$K) or a/$\{b\}$K. Since the epistemic operator governs the choice of an alternative world M_1, this means evaluating these primitive in the pre-epistemic-move-model M_0. And since in the winning strategy they clearly have to be evaluated so as to assign to them their actual references, such

_____

25For branching quantifier structures, there exists a growing body of studies. For references, see the bibliography of Jaakko Hintikka and Jack Kulas, The Game of Language, D. Reidel, Dordrecht, 1983. Independences between other kinds of concepts have scarcely been studied, except for the papers referred to here.

expressions as $A(x/\{\underline{b}\}K)$ and $a/\{\underline{b}\}K$ in effect pick out the actual references in M_o.

As the equivalence of (4.6) and (4.4) illustrates, in the simplest cases sentences containing informationally independent quantifiers have non-independent equivalents. But even in such cases, a notation which spells out the independence can bring out the intended logical form of our epistemic statements more clearly than the dependent (linear) notation. For instance, natural-language statements of the form

(4.8)   <u>b</u> knows who (say, x) is such that A(x)

(where A is an atomic predicate) have normally two readings, which in the linear traditional notation are expressed as follows:

(4.9) $(\exists x) \{\underline{b}\} K \quad A(x)$

(4.10) $(\forall x)(A(x) \supset (\exists z)(y=z \; \& \; \{\underline{b}\}K \; A(x)))$.

The parallelism of the two is not obvious in (4.9)-(4.10) but is brought out much more clearly in an independence-friendly notation as follows:

(4.11) $\{\underline{b}\} K \; (\exists x/\{\underline{b}\}K) \; (A(x/\{\underline{b}\}K) \; \& \; A(x))$

(4.12) $\{\underline{b}\} K \; (\forall x/\{\underline{b}\}K)(A(x/\{\underline{b}\}K) \supset A(x))$.

However, in other cases the independence notation can be indispensable.[26] For instance,

(4.13)   <u>b</u> knows whom everybody adores

cannot be expressed (on the reading according to which different persons may have different idols) by

(4.14) $(\forall x)(\exists y)(\exists z) \; (x = z \; \& \; \{b\} K \; (z \text{ admires } y))$,

for (4.14) implies (as you can easily see) that <u>b</u> knows the identity of each person and of his or her admireree. In fact, the force of (4.13) can only be expressed (unless we resort to higher-order quantifiers) by something like

(4.15) $\{\underline{b}\}K(\forall x)(\exists y/\{\underline{b}\}K) \; (x \text{ admires } y)$.

Indeed, (4.15) (unlike (4.14)) is logically equivalent with

---

[26] See here Jaakko Hintikka, "Questions with Outside Quantifiers", in R. Schneider, K. Tuite and R. Chametzky, eds., Papers from the Parasession on Nondeclaratives, Chicago Linguistics Society, Chicago, 1982, pp. 83-92.

(4.16) $(\exists f) \{\underline{b}\} K (\forall x) (x \text{ admires } f(x))$

which neatly brings out the obviously intended force of (4.13). For what (4.13) says is, obviously, that $\underline{b}$ knows how to find, for a given x, whom x admires, i.e., knows a function which takes in from any person to someone she or he admires. And this is precisely what (4.16) says.

Notice that the informational dependence of the different operators $\{\underline{b}\} K$, $(\forall x)$, and $(\exists y)$ in (4.15) is not even partially ordered, but exhibit a loop structure:

(4.17)

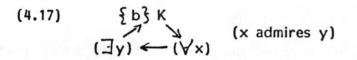

         (x admires y)

This is logically equivalent with (4.15). A semantical game connected with (4.17) is hard to implement in the usual move-by-move form. It is easy to "play" in what game theorists call the normal form of a game: Both players choose a strategy, which jointly determine the course of the game, including its outcome. This observation is connected with the equivalence of (4.16) with (4.17). It has some general interest as an illustration of what different kinds of games (in the sense of game theory) can be like.

Thus the independence notation sometimes lends added power to epistemic logic. How much more? It is known that the force of quantification theory with branching quantifiers is extremely strong, coming close to that of the entire second-order logic.[27] Hence no complete axiomatization of quantified epistemic logic with unlimited independence is possible. However, for a variety of simpler cases, for instance, when all the cases of independence pertain to ignorance of a move connected with a single unnegated epistemic operator $\{\underline{b}\} K$, an explicit formal treatment may very well be possible, even though it has not been presented in the literature.

Knowledge acquisition by questioning

So far, I have been concerned with problems of knowledge representation and only indirectly with reasoning about knowledge. Of course, the representation problem has to be solved before problems about reasoning are tackled. But what is represented is already acquired and already available knowledge, whereas much of the actual reasoning about knowledge is also concerned with the step-by-step processes of knowledge acquisition. For instance, in the well-known puzzle variously known as the case of cheating

---

27See here Jaakko Hintikka, "Quantifiers vs. Quantification Theory", Linguistic Inquiry, vol. 5 (1974), pp. 153-177, reprinted in Esa Saarinen, editor, Game-Theoretical Semantics, D. Reidel, Dordrecht, 1979.

husbands or of the wise men,[28] the reasoning of the participants depends essentially on their knowing what the others knew or did not know at the preceding stage of their synchronized reasoning processes.

One way of modelling knowledge acquisition is to conceptualize it as a series of questions a reasoner, here termed the Inquirer, addresses to a source of information, to be called the Oracle (in some applications, more naturally called Nature).[29]   The answers, when available, may be used by the Inquirer as premises for the purpose of deriving a given conclusion C (or, in an alternative version of the model) for the purpose of answering the question "C or not-C"?   In this process, steps of deduction may alternate with each other, and the Inquirer may have a fixed initial premise T (called the theoretical premise) available for the purpose.[30]   The deductive rules to be used are restricted to those that satisfy the subformula principle. Before a question may be asked by the Inquirer, its presupposition must have been established.[31]

In this way we obtain what I have called the interrogative game or the interrogative model of inquiry. Since the logic of questions and answers is in effect (as was pointed in section 1 above, part (b)) a branch of epistemic logic, the interrogative model can also be thought of as another outgrowth of epistemic logic. One of the main advantages of the interrogative model is that

28See, e.g., Danny Dolev, Joseph Y. Halpern and Yoram Moses, "Cheating Husbands and Other Stories: A Case Study of Knowledge, Action and Communication", preprint, 1985.

29The model sketched here has been studied in a number of papers of mine. See, e.g., Jaakko Hintikka and Merrill B. Hintikka, "Sherlock Holmes Encounters Modern Logic: Towards a Theory of Information-Seeking by Questioning", in E.M. Barth and J.L. Martens, Argumentation: Approaches to Theory Formation, John Benjamins, Amsterdam, 1982, pp. 55-76; "The Logic of Science as a Model-Oriented Logic", in P.D. Asquith and P. Kitcher, eds., PSA 1984, vol. 1, Philosophy of Science of Association, East Lansing, MI, 1984, pp. 177-185.

30As a book-keeping device we can use a Beth-type semantical tableau. (For them, see W.W. Beth, "Semantic Entailment and Formal Derivability", Mededelingen van de Koninklijke Nederlandse Akademie van Wetenschappen, Afd. Letterkunde, N.R. vol. 18, no. 13, Amsterdam, 1955, pp. 309-342.) Then we can use all the usual terminology of the tableau method, and the deductive "moves" will be simply tableau-building rules. (We shall minimize movements between the left and the right column, however, and restrict the rules to those in keeping with the subformula principle.) Each application of the game rules is then relative to a given stage of some one subtableau. As is well known, the tableau method is simply the mirror image of a Gentzen-type sequent calculus. The only novelty here is that Nature's answers are entered into the left column of a subtableau as additional premises.

31For the concept of presupposition presupposed here, see Jaakko Hintikka The Semantics of Questions and the Questions of Semantics (Acta Philosophica Fennica, vol. 28, no. 4), Societas Philosophica Fennica, Helsinki, 1976.

it enables us to discuss cognitive strategies and not only static cognitive situations. This possibility can be realized in many different ways. The Oracle can be literally nature, and nature's answers can then be scientific experiments. In a simpler case, the source of information is one's environment, and the answers the Inquirer can hope to obtain are perceptual observations. But in other cases, the available answers can be items of information stored in the database of a computer, which will then play the role of the Oracle. In still other applications, the computer is the Inquirer's own brain, and the totality of available answers define's the Inquirer's tacit knowledge. The most natural application is undoubtedly one in which the answerer (the Oracle) is another human being, with whom the Inquirer is engaged in a dialogue. We can also allow for the interrogation "game" to be a symmetrical n-person game in which at each interrogative move each player can address a question to each of the other players. Some of the most intriguing types of reasoning about knowledge can be dealt with by means of such games, for instance, the "case of the cheating husbands". Such applications and extensions can be thought of as belonging to the logical theory of dialogues (discourse).[32]

I shall not discuss the details of any of these applications detail. It is in order, however, to locate some of the crucial parameters which play a role in these different interrogative games and distinguish them from each other.

(i) In different applications, different kinds of questions are answered by the Oracle. The most clear-cut restraints here are those that depend on the logical complexity, especially the quantifier prefix structure of the available answers. For instance, sense-perception can only answer yer-or-no questions concerning particular matters of fact of one's environment. For a logician, these are yes-or-no questions concerning atomic sentences.

(b) In contrast, controlled experiments can yield answers which codify functional dependencies. Such answers must have an AE quantifier prefix (i.e. a prefix of the form $(\forall x)(\exists y)$).[33]

(c) Again the information stored in the memory of a human being or of a computer can logically speaking be of arbitrarily high complexity.

There are of course but special cases of a long spectrum of different kinds of interrogative procedures, distinguished from each other by the quantificational complexity of available answers. This spectrum ranges from

---

[32]An excellent example of what can be done in this direction is Lauri Carlson, Dialogue Games, D. Reidel, Dordrecht, 1982.

[33]This observation has important consequences for the contemporary philosophy of science, where it has generally been assumed that only questions concerning the truth or falsity of atomic sentences are answerable by Nature. In reality, the logic of experimental inquiry is an AE logic, not the logic of the atomistic case.

case (a) via the different AEA... prefixes to the unlimited case (c). This hierarchy turns out to be highly important for many purposes, especially in the philosophy of science.

There of course are normally other kinds of limitations on available answers. In all these cases, it obviously makes a difference to the strategy selection of the Inquirer what (partial or total) knowledge he or she has of the limitations on available answers. This is illustrated by the knowledge which the user of a database may have as to what information is or is not stored in it.

(ii) In many applications of the interrogative model and indeed in many applications of epistemic logic, it makes a crucial difference what kind of knowledge we are dealing with. For instance, tacit knowledge must fairly obviously be modelled by a sub-oracle. The list of propositions stored in the "memory" of this sub-oracle defines the extent of the Inquirer's tacit knowledge by delimiting the set of available answers this sub-oracle can answer. (I am speaking of sub-oracle here because in realistic uses of my model the Inquirer can of course consult other sources of information than her or his tacit knowledge.)

At the other extreme there is the completely activated knowledge the Inquirer has. This is naturally modelled by the set of those sentences which have been put forward by the Inquirer as outcomes of interrogative or deductive moves (or which have the status of explicit initial premises of the interrogative process). This might be called the Inquirer's active knowledge.

Active knowledge, unlike tacit knowledge, is relative to a stage of the interrogative game. Dealing with such vital for reasoning about knowledge, for it is a speaker's active knowledge that he or she is aware of and can report to others.

But neither tacit knowledge nor active knowledge obeys the laws of epistemic logic. For instance, neither is closed with respect to logical consequence, not even if relations of logical consequence are restrained as indicated in section 3 above. In order to be able to develop satisfactory ways of reasoning about knowledge, we consider other kinds of knowledge. Among the most important ones there are the following:

The Inquirer's potential knowledge consists of all the conclusions C the Inquirer can establish by means of the interrogative process.

The Inquirer's virtual knowledge consists of all the conclusions C the Inquirer can establish by means of the interrogative process without introducing new "auxiliary" individuals into the argument in the sense of sec. 2 (i).

By limiting the Inquirer's moves to deductive ones we can similarly define potential deductive knowledge and virtual deductive knowledge.

(iii) The purely logical properties of the interrogative games are also of considerable interest. Let us denote the interrogative derivability of C from T in a model M by $T \Vdash_M C$. This relation depends of course on whatever restrictions there may be on available answers. It turns out that this relation depends also on the set RA of available tautological premises of the form

(5.1) $(S_i \lor \sim S_i)$

where $i \in$ ra.   The reason is that in interrogative processes one cannot always restrict one's methods to those satisfying the subformula principle.[34]   In other words, metalogical results analogous to Gentzen's first Hauptsatz, which implies the eliminability of premises of the form (5.1), of the cut rule, of unrestricted modus ponens, etc.

There is a sense in which the notion of interrogative derivability is between the relations of logical consequence $T \vdash C$ and the truth of C in M, i.e., $M \models C$.   For if no questions are allowed, $T \Vdash_M C$ obviously reduces to $T \vdash C$.   On the other hand, if no restrictions are imposed on available answers or on available tautological premises RA, it can be shown that $\phi \Vdash_M C$ iff $M \models C$ (ϕ = the empty set).

The set RA has an intuitive interpretation which is worth noting here. What the set RA codifies is essentially the totality of yes-or-no questions which the Inquirer is prepared to ask (independently of the initial premise T). A restriction on RA is therefore very much like a restriction on the Inquirer's range of attention, primarily in the sense of a restriction on the range of questions the Inquirer is prepared to raise, secondarily in the sense of a restriction on the items of tacit knowledge the Inquirer can activate.   This is because the activation of such knowledge can only happen by means of questions whose presuppositions have to be available to the Inquirer.   Thus the concept of range of attention is not purely subjective and psychological but has an objective logical and epistemological counterpart.

This is but an example of the many possibilities of analyzing - and synthesizing - interesting epistemic concepts by means of the interrogative model.   Most of the work in utilizing these possibilities still remains to be done.

Acknowledgement: The research reported here was made possible by NSF Grant # IST-8310936 (Information Science and Technology).

---

[34]The notions of subformula principle, cut elimination, Gentzen's Hauptsatz, etc. are explained in any decent introduction to proof theory.   For Gentzen's classical papers, see M.E.Szabo, ed., The Collected Papers of Gerhard Gentzen, North-Holland, Amsterdam, 1969.

REASONING ABOUT KNOWLEDGE IN ARTIFICIAL INTELLIGENCE

Robert C. Moore
SRI International
Menlo Park, California, and Cambridge, England

SUMMARY

This talk looks at work on reasoning about knowledge within what might be termed "classical" AI. That is, it is assumed that the information contained in an intelligent system is for the most part embodied in data structures that explicitly represent the propositions that the system knows or believes, and that queries to this "knowledge base" are handled by applying inference rules in a way that amounts to searching for a derivation of an answer to the query.

Given this point of view, the first question that comes up in reasoning about knowledge in AI is how to *represent* information about what someone knows. The fact that this is not altogether obvious has been a prime motivation for work in AI on reasoning about knowledge. Another motivation comes from AI work on planning. In trying to formulate a plan of action to achieve some goal, an agent may not have enough information. It is often necessary to reason about what knowledge is needed to carry out a plan and how that knowledge can be obtained. A third motivation is found in recent work in natural-language processing that tries to take into account the mental state of the person that the system is communicating with in interpreting and generating utterances. This usually requires reasoning about what that person knows. Finally, there are connections to work on nonmonotonic reasoning -- most nonmonotonic reasoning systems have special inference rules that do not apply if their conclusions are known to be false, and in some systems this involves explicit reasoning about what the system itself knows.

A number of different techniques have been used or proposed for reasoning about knowledge in AI systems. Several different attempts have been made to face the problems head on, reasoning explicitly in a first-order way, treating propositions as objects and knowing as a binary relation. Another approach that has been extensively explored is to axiomatize within first-order logic the possible-world semantics of some variant of Hintikka's modal epistemic logic. A third approach uses the idea of *semantic attachment* to simulate other agents' reasoning from their knowledge.

Two particular issues deserve special comment. One is the question of why the application of the known decision procedures for various modal epistemic logics is not among the list of commonly used techinques for reasoning about knowledge in AI. The principal answer is that decision procedures generally exist only for *propositional* modal epistemic logics, and many AI applications seem to require quantification. Secondly, the straightforward application of these decision procedures in many cases would require treating the system's entire knowledge base as the antecedent of the formula to be decided. Practical application of such decision procedures would thus require that only the *relevant* information in the knowledge base be taken into account, and determining relevance is a notoriously unsolved problem.

Perhaps the most hotly contested issue in this field, however, is the issue of logical omniscience. Most approaches based on modal epistemic logic or possible worlds have built into them the assumption that agents know all the logical consequences of their knowledge. This assumption, though enormously simplifying, is generally regarded to be clearly false. Nevertheless, it is an assumption that is frequently made for lack of an alternative that permits a system to conclude that other agents will make all the inferences that seem to be obvious.

THE SYNTHESIS OF DIGITAL MACHINES
WITH PROVABLE EPISTEMIC PROPERTIES

Stanley J. Rosenschein
Artificial Intelligence Center
SRI International
Center for the Study of
Language and Information
Stanford University

Leslie Pack Kaelbling
Artificial Intelligence Center
SRI International
Center for the Study of
Language and Information
Stanford University

ABSTRACT

Researchers using epistemic logic as a formal framework for studying knowledge properties of AI systems often interpret the knowledge formula $K(x, \varphi)$ to mean that machine x encodes φ in its state as a syntactic formula or can derive it inferentially. By defining $K(x, \varphi)$, instead, in terms of the correlation between the state of the machine and that of its environment, the formal properties of modal system S5 can be satisfied without having to store representations of formulas as data structures. In this paper, we apply the correlational definition of knowledge to machines with composite structure. In particular, we describe how epistemic properties of synchronous digital machines can be analyzed, starting at the level of gates and delays, by modeling the machine's components as agents in a multi-agent system and reasoning about the flow of information among them. We also introduce Rex, a language for recursively computing machine descriptions, and illustrate how it can be used to construct machines with provable knowledge properties.

Introduction

Many important computer applications, such as process control, avionics, robotics, and artificial intelligence, involve the design of hardware and software that are part of a larger system embedded in a physical environment. In typical applications of this kind, the computer's principal task is to track and react to conditions in the environment. As more open-ended environments are considered and as the conditions to be recognized and the responses to be generated become more complex, the designer's task becomes correspondingly more difficult. One useful abstraction in the design of such systems is the concept of *knowledge*. The statement "system *x knows* φ" provides a compact description of the *propositional content* of information encoded in x's state without specifying the details of the encoding.

Much of the work on formalizing knowledge that has been done in philosophy [3,7], theoretical computer science [2], and AI [12,9,6] has focused on abstract properties and has not been concerned with concrete physical or computational interpretations of the central concept of "knowledge." When such interpretations have been given for AI systems, they have typically involved encoding sentences of a formal language as data structures in the machine. For instance, a system might be regarded as knowing φ if its knowledge base contained a sentence expressing φ, or if such a sentence could be computationally derived from other sentences in the knowledge base. One important advantage of this approach is the ease with which the designer can attribute propositional interpretations to the machine's states. However, there are disadvantages as well, notably in the area of computational complexity.

The situated-automata approach [13], in contrast, takes as its point of departure a concrete computational model for epistemic logic that is compatible with, but does not depend on, viewing the system as manipulating sentences of a logic. In the situated-automata framework, the concept of knowledge is analyzed in terms of logical relationships between the state of a process (e.g., a machine) and that of its surrounding world. Because of constraints between a process and its environment, not every state of the process-environment pair is possible, in general. A process x is said to know a proposition φ (written $K(x,\varphi)$) in a situation where its internal state is v if φ holds in all possible situations in which x is in state v. This definition of knowledge satisfies the axioms of modal system S5, including consequential closure and positive and negative introspection.

In its original formulation, situated-automata theory dealt with the state of a system as an unanalyzed whole. Since machines designed for complex applications ordinarily take on too many states to enumerate explicitly, these machines must be built hierarchically, with the size of the state set growing as the product of the sizes of the state sets of the component machines. This paper extends situated-automata theory to such hierarchically constructed machines. In particular, we use the situated-automata model of knowledge to analyze synchronous digital machines by viewing their components as elements of a multi-agent system and reasoning about the flow of information among these components.

On the practical level, the situated-automata approach has led to the development of Rex, a set of tools for constructing complex machines with rigorously definable epistemic properties. Instead of writing a program that defines the target machine directly, the designer writes a program that, when run, computes a logical description of the machine. This description is then effectively realized either as circuitry, as code for a parallel machine, or as a program that simulates the machine on a sequential computer. Since synchronization with the environment lies at the heart of our definition of knowledge, the Rex tools have been designed to guarantee real-time interaction between the target machine and the environment. Of course, the Rex system need not be real-time since it is not itself intended to be coupled to the physical environment.

Theoretical Background

A theory of intelligent embedded systems must be capable of describing how states of the system encode information about other parts of the world over time. Thus the logic must, at the very least, deal with processes, their states, time, and knowledge. Our approach is to use a propositional language that is enriched with terms for processes and the values they can take on (i.e., states they can be in) and is closed under various temporal and epistemic operators. The semantic interpretation for this language is given in terms of times, locations, and possible worlds. Processes are modeled as spatial "trajectories" with cross-world identity, i.e., they are identified with functions from world-time pairs to complex spatial locations. Knowledge is modeled in terms of the relationship between the states of a process and states of the environment. Before defining the semantics, we specify the formal language.

Language

We begin by defining the symbols of the language:

$Symbols:$ $P = \{start, p_1, p_2, \ldots\}$ (atomic formulas),
$A = \{[\,], a_1, a_2, \ldots\}$ (process constants),
$C = \{\langle\,\rangle, c_1, c_2, \ldots\}$ (value constants),
$F = \{f_1, f_2, \ldots\}$ (function symbols),
$\{\Delta_c\}_{c \in C}$ (delay-element predicates),
$\{\Pi_f\}_{f \in F}$ (function-element predicates),
$=$ (equality symbol)
$[\,|\,], \langle\,|\,\rangle$ (pairing functions),
$\wedge, \neg$ (Boolean connectives),
$K, \Box_W, \Box_T, \bigcirc$ (modalities),
$*, \circ$ (term operators).

Next, we give the formation rules:

Terms:
1. If e is a *process* (resp. *value*) *constant*, then e is a *process* (resp. *value*) *term*.
2. If e_1, e_2 are *process* (resp. *value*) *terms*, then so is $[e_1 \mid e_2]$ (resp. $\langle e_1 \mid e_2 \rangle$).
3. If x is a *process term*, then $*x$ is a *value term*.

4. If u is a *value term* and f is a *function symbol*, then $f(u)$ is a *value term*.
5. If e is a *term*, then so is $\circ e$.
6. Nothing else is a *term*.

Formulas:
1. If p is an *atomic formula*, then p is a *formula*.
2. If e_1, e_2 are *terms*, then $e_1 = e_2$ is a *formula*.
3. If c is a *value constant*, f is a *function symbol*, and x, y are *process terms*, then $\Delta_c(x, y)$ and $\Pi_f(x, y)$ are *formulas*.
4. If φ and ψ are *formulas*, then so are $(\varphi \wedge \psi)$, $\neg \varphi$, $\Box_W \varphi$, $\Box_T \varphi$, and $\bigcirc \varphi$.
5. If x is a *process term* and φ is a *formula*, then $K(x, \varphi)$ is a *formula*.
6. Nothing else is a *formula*.

The connectives $\vee, \rightarrow, \leftrightarrow$ are defined as follows: $\varphi \vee \psi = \neg(\neg \varphi \wedge \neg \psi)$, $\varphi \rightarrow \psi = \neg \varphi \vee \psi$, and $\varphi \leftrightarrow \psi = \varphi \rightarrow \psi \wedge \psi \rightarrow \varphi$. A combined necessity operator can be formed from the time and world modalities: $\Box \varphi = \Box_W \Box_T \varphi$. Dual modal operators can also be defined: $\Diamond \varphi = \neg \ Box \neg \varphi$, etc. We abbreviate $\langle u_1 \mid \langle u_2 \mid \cdots \langle\rangle \cdots \rangle\rangle$ as $\langle u_1, u_2, \cdots \rangle$ and $[x_1 \mid [x_2 \mid \cdots [\ ] \cdots]]$ as $[x_1, x_2, \cdots]$. We sometimes take integers to be value constants and lower case letters early in the alphabet to be process constants. We also omit parentheses according to the usual conventions.

Semantics

The semantics of our logic is given with respect to a model of space, time, possibility and state. Possibility is modeled using the standard techniques of possible-worlds semantics. For each possible world and instant of time, the model assigns an atomic state to every atomic location. Processes occupy collections of atomic locations; these collections vary with time and possible world. In order to conveniently name subprocesses, we structure space and state by closing the set of locations and the set of states under *pairing* operations. Formally, if A is a set, we define $pairs(A)$ to be the least set that contains A, includes the distinguished element nil_A, and is closed under pairing: $x, y \in pairs(A)$ implies $(x, y) \in pairs(A)$.

Models: $\mathcal{M} = (W, T, L, Q, q, I = (I_P, I_A, I_C, I_F))$, where
1. W is a nonempty set of *possible worlds*.
2. T is a nonempty set of *time instants* isomorphic to the natural numbers.
3. L is a nonempty set of *atomic locations*.
4. Q is a nonempty set of *atomic states*.
5. $q : L \times W \times T \rightarrow Q$ assigns atomic states to atomic locations at every world-time pair.
6. $I_P : P \rightarrow 2^{W \times T}$ interprets atomic formulas as sets of world-time pairs.
7. $I_A : A \rightarrow ((W \times T) \rightarrow pairs(L))$ interprets process constants as processes.
8. $I_C : C \rightarrow pairs(Q)$ interprets value constants as value structures.
9. $I_F : F \rightarrow pairs(Q) \rightarrow pairs(Q)$ interprets function symbols as functions on value structures.

We extend the function q to pairs by defining $\hat{q} : pairs(L) \times W \times T \to pairs(Q)$ as follows:

$$\hat{q}(nil_L, w, t) = nil_Q,$$
$$\hat{q}(\ell, w, t) = q(w, t, \ell) \text{ for } \ell \in L,$$
$$\hat{q}((s_1, s_2), w, t) = (\hat{q}(s_1, w, t), \hat{q}(s_2, w, t))$$

The denotation of a term e relative to a model and a world-time pair, written $[\![e]\!]_t^{M,w}$, is defined as follows (reference to the model is supressed):

1. $[\![a]\!]_t^w = I_A(a)(w, t)$ if a is a *process constant*.
2. $[\![c]\!]_t^w = I_C(a)$ if c is a *value constant*.
3. $[\![[x \mid y]]\!]_t^w = ([\![x]\!]_t^w, [\![y]\!]_t^w)$.
4. $[\![\langle u \mid v \rangle]\!]_t^w = ([\![u]\!]_t^w, [\![v]\!]_t^w)$.
5. $[\![*x]\!]_t^w = \hat{q}([\![x]\!]_t^w, w, t)$, where
6. $[\![f(u)]\!]_t^w = I_F(f)([\![u]\!]_t^w)$.
7. $[\![\circ e]\!]_t^w = [\![e]\!]_{t+1}^w$.

Satisfaction of formulas is defined relative to a model M and a world-time pair w, t (again we supress reference to the model):

1. $w, t \models p$ if $\langle w, t \rangle \in I_P(p)$, for $p \in P$.
2. $w, t \models e_1 = e_2$ if $[\![e_1]\!]_t^w = [\![e_2]\!]_t^w$.
3. $w, t \models \Delta_c(x, y)$ if $\hat{q}([\![y]\!]_t^w, w, 0) = I_C(c)$ and $\hat{q}([\![y]\!]_t^w, w, t+1) = \hat{q}([\![x]\!]_t^w, w, t)$
4. $w, t \models \Pi_f(x, y)$ if $\hat{q}([\![y]\!]_t^w, w, t) = I_F(f)(\hat{q}([\![x]\!]_t^w, w, t))$
5. $w, t \models (\varphi \wedge \psi)$ if $w, t \models \varphi$ and $w, t \models \psi$.
6. $w, t \models \neg\varphi$ if $w, t \not\models \varphi$.
7. $w, t \models \Box_W \varphi$ if $w', t \models \varphi$ for all $w' \in W$.
8. $w, t \models \Box_T \varphi$ if $w, t' \models \varphi$ for all $t' \in T$.
9. $w, t \models \bigcirc\varphi$ if $w, t+1 \models \varphi$.
10. $w, t \models K(x, \varphi)$ iff $w', t' \models \varphi$ for all w', t' such that $\hat{q}([\![x]\!]_{t'}^{w'}, w', t') = \hat{q}([\![x]\!]_t^w, w, t)$.

A model M is said to simply *satisfy* a formula iff $M, w, t \models \varphi$ for all $w \in W, t \in T$. A formula is *valid* if it is satisfied by every model. A set of formulas Γ *entails* a formula φ (written $\Gamma \models \varphi$) iff every model that satisfies each sentence of Γ also satisfies φ.

We do not present a axiomatic treatment of the logic; the interested reader is referred to standard treatments of modal logic [4], logics of time and knowledge [10,8], and their application to AI [12,13]. In a later section we present informal proofs in the logical language and appeal to valid formulas and entailments involving K and other modal operators. Some of these are listed here.

1. Theorems of propositional logic and temporal logic [10,1].

2. $\models K(x, \varphi) \rightarrow \varphi$ (truth).

3. $\models K(x, \varphi \rightarrow \psi) \rightarrow (K(x, \varphi) \rightarrow K(x, \psi)))$ (consequential closure).

4. $\models K(x, \varphi) \rightarrow K(x, K(x, \varphi))$ (positive introspection).

5. $\models \neg K(x, \varphi) \rightarrow K(x, \neg K(x, \varphi))$ (negative introspection).

6. $\models *X = v \rightarrow K(X, *X = v)$ (self-awareness).

7. $\models \Box_W \varphi \rightarrow \varphi$

8. $\models \Box_T \varphi \rightarrow \varphi$

9. $\models \Delta_c(x, y) \rightarrow \Box_T(start \rightarrow *y = c \wedge \circ *y = *x)$

10. $\models \Pi_f(x, y) \rightarrow \Box_T(*y = f(*x))$

11. $\varphi, \varphi \rightarrow \psi \models \psi$ (modus ponens).

12. $\varphi \models K(x, \varphi)$ (epistemic necessitation).

13. $\varphi \models \Box_W \varphi$ (alethic necessitation).

14. $\varphi \models \Box_T \varphi$ (temporal necessitation).

15. $\varphi \models \bigcirc_T \varphi$ (succedent necessitation).

Modeling Machines in the Logic

Physical processes (of which the processes in the logic are idealizations) can be described in many different ways. One class of descriptions specifies permanent *structural* relationships among processes and their subparts. *Behavioral* descriptions, on the other hand, specify how the states of processes vary over time. *Epistemic* descriptions form yet another class, specifying the information carried by processes. These descriptions may be interrelated; for instance, a structural constraint may entail certain behavioral properties, which, in turn, have epistemic correlates.

We use the logic to model a *machine* as a collection of (possibly complex) processes related by various constraints of the types discussed above. The physical components of a digital computer may be modeled as processes. When we wish to be concrete, we refer to these processes as *storage locations*. The physical state of a storage location, x, can then be modeled in the logic as the value, $*x$, of that process.

Just as complex physical machines are built up from primitive components of a few basic types, complex machine descriptions are made up of primitive contraints corresponding to the basic component types. Pure functional machines (e.g., logic gates), are modeled in the logic by function-element predicates Π_f, and delay components are modeled by delay-element predicates, Δ_c. The component modeled by Π_f "instantaneously" computes the primitive function f; the delay component modeled by Δ_c initially emits the constant c, followed by the stream of its input values, displaced in time by one unit.

Rex : A Framework for Hierarchical Machine Specification

Rex is a language for the hierarchical specification of complex machines made up of the primitive types discussed in the previous section. From the Rex specification of a machine, a low-level machine description is computed. This machine description, which stipulates how the value of each atomic storage location is to be computed over time, may then be instantiated in a variety of media (software, physical circuitry), making an actual machine that satisfies the initial specification.

Description of Rex

The Rex language is most easily seen as an extension of the Lisp language [11] to include forms that incrementally calculate the low level description of a machine. This section will provide a formal description of a simple subset of Rex, which, although it has the full power of Rex, is somewhat more tedious to program in than the full language. A more practical introduction to the full language is given in a separate reference manual [5].

Rex extends Lisp through the addition of a number of forms which compute machine descriptions. There are two types of Lisp value that we will use to represent these machine descriptions. They are *constraints* and *constrained storage terms*. A constraint represents a conjunction of wffs that describe the behavior of storage locations with respect to one another. Within a constraint, storage locations are named by *storage terms*, which are typically represented by Lisp atoms. A wff may specify the way in which the value of one location is to be computed from the values of other locations or require that a pair of (possibly complex) storage locations be *behaviorally equivalent*. Two storage locations are behaviorally equivalent if, at every point in time, each contains the same value as the other; behaviorally equivalent storage locations may be conveniently realized as the same physical storage location. Constrained storage terms are made up of a distinguished storage term and a wff which specifies the behavior of the location named by that storage term in terms of other storage locations.

We will give the semantics of the Rex forms by defining them in Lisp. Before we do this, however, we must describe some Lisp functions for manipulating the special Rex types discussed above.

(make-cst *st c*) This function takes *st*, a storage term, and *c*, a constraint, and returns the constrained storage term made up of *st* and *c*.

(storage-term *cst*) This is a simple selector function, returning the storage term associated with the constrained storage term *cst*.

(constraint *cst*) This selector returns the constraint associated with constrained storage term *cst*.

(make-delta *init next result*) This function creates a wff that specifies the initial value of the storage location denoted by *result* to be *init*, and the rest of its values to be those of the storage location denoted by *next*, delayed by one time unit. *init* must be a value of the type that may be contained in an atomic storage location (in all of our examples we will use integers as the basic value type); *next* and *result* are both storage terms. This function returns the list (DELTA *init next result*), which is expressed in the logic by $\Delta_{init}(next, result)$.

(make-pi *fcn* (*arg₁ ... argₙ*) *result*) This function creates a wff that specifies that the contents of the storage location denoted by *result* be the result of applying *fcn* to the contents of the storage locations of $arg_1 \ldots arg_n$. The returned value is (PI *fcn* ($arg_1 \ldots arg_n$) *result*) which is equivalent to $\Pi_{fcn}([arg_1, \ldots, arg_n], result)$ in the logic.

(make-equiv st_1 st_2) This function creates a wff that requires that the storage locations referred to by st_1 and st_2 are behaviorally equivalent. The returned value is (== st_1 st_2) which is expressed in the logic by $\Box(*st_1 = *st_2)$.

(null-stg) This function, returns the null storage term.

(make-stg-pair st_1 st_2) This function performs the pairing operation on storage locations. It returns a storage term which is the pair of storage terms st_1 and st_2.

(conjoin $c_1 \ldots c_n$) This function takes an arbitrary number of constraints and returns a constraint which their conjunction.

In addition, we assume the existence of a set of standard Lisp functions, including **gensym**, which returns a new, distinct atom each time it is called.

The following table has the Rex forms in the left column, with the corresponding Lisp definitions in the right column.

```
(storage name)                (make-cst name ())

(plusm [cst₁ cst₂] result)    (conjoin (make-pi 'plus
                                        (list (storage-term cst₁) (storage-term cst₂))
                                        (storage-term result))
                                       (constraint cst₁) (constraint cst₂)
                                       (constraint result))

(init-next init next result)  (conjoin (make-delta init (storage-term next)
                                                (storage-term result))
                                       (constraint next) (constraint result))

[]                            (null-stg)

[cst₁ | cst₂]                 (make-cst (make-stg-pair (storage-term cst₁)
                                                (storage-term cst₂))
                                        (conjoin (constraint cst₁)
                                                (constraint cst₂)))

(== cst₁ cst₂)                (conjoin (make-equiv (storage-term cst₁)
                                                (storage-term cst₂))
                                       (constraint cst₁)
                                       (constraint cst₂))

(some (v₁...vₙ) c₁...cₘ)       ((lambda (v₁ ... vₙ) (conjoin c₁ ... cₘ))
```

```
(gensym) ... (gensym))
```

In the definitions above, `plusm` is just one example of a number of standard arithmetic and logical primitives available to the programmer. Primitive functional machines follow the convention of being named by the name of the function they compute with an 'm' appended to the end.

It is important to note that the Rex primitive forms define the way values are to be computed when the machine being specified is ultimately run. It is also necessary, however, to have be able to dynamically control the specification of machines at compile time. We use the Lisp form `if` to create machine specifications which are conditional on the values of Lisp expressions at compile time. Arguments which are not constrained storage terms, are referred to as *value parameters*, and are also used in the compile-time control of machine specification.

Complex functions returning constraints or constrained storage terms may be built up out of the Rex forms, and defined using the Lisp **defun** form. Once such functions are defined, a low-level machine description is calculated in two steps. The first step consists of evaluating a Rex form or function that returns a constraint. This constraint is a machine description, but is not yet in conveniently usable form, since there are typically a large number of equivalence wffs, making it difficult to see which storage terms are distinct from one another. The function makem takes a constraint as input and *canonicalizes* it, returning a useful low-level machine description.

The wffs in a non-canonical constraint can be separated into two types: equivalence constraints and pi or delta constraints. From the equivalence constraints it is possible to compute equivalence classes of storage terms using the unification algorithm. A canonical member can then be chosen from each equivalence class; this is said to be the canonical name of the storage location represented by that equivalence class. Canonicalization is the process of computing the equivalence relation on storage terms, and substituting canonical names for non-canonical names of storage locations into the rest of the wffs of the constraint. This process is illustrated by an example in the next section.

A Simple Example of Rex

In this section we present a simple Rex program and illustrate the process of computing a low-level machine description from the high-level specification. The example will be a machine with one input and one output. The input can range over integers; the output will always be zero or one. The output will be one if the machine has ever (since it was started) had one, two, or three as its input. Following are the function definitions that make up the specification of the machine.

```
(defun ever-a-one-two-three? (input output)
  (some (member? const1 const2 const3)
```

```
                    (constant 1 const1)
                    (constant 2 const2)
                    (constant 3 const3)
                    (memberm 3 [const1 const2 const3] input member?)
                    (everm member? output)))

(defun everm (input ever?)
  (some (this-time-or-last)
    (orm [input ever?] this-time-or-last)
    (init-next 0 this-time-or-last ever?)))

(defun memberm (length list item member?)
  (if (= length 0)
      (constant 0 member?)
      (some (head tail equal-head? member-tail?)
        (== list [head | tail])
        (equalm [item head] equal-head?)
        (memberm (- length 1) tail item member-tail?)
        (orm [equal-head? member-tail?] member?))))

(defun constant (value const)
  (init-next value const const))
```

The constant function returns a wff term that requires the storage location of const
to always contain the value value. The memberm function is a recursive specification of the
standard member function. length is an integer specifying the length of list, which is list
of constrained storage terms, and item is a simple constrained storage term. The storage
location of the result is constraint to always will contain a 1 if the the contents of item is
equal to the contents of one of the elements of list, otherwise it will contain 0. The if is
used at compile time to control the layout of the runtime computation structure. Note also
the use of == to structurally decompose list in the case that we know that it is at least
one element long. The everm function returns a constraint that requires the storage location
ever? to contain 1 if the contents of input have ever been 1, else to contain 0.

Our top level function ever-a-one-two-three? returns a constraint relating the behavior
of the storage locations of input and output. If the contents of the storage location of input
have ever been a member of the list whose elements are the constants 1, 2, and 3, the contents
of the storage location of output will be 1, else 0.

The first step in creating a low-level description of a machine satisfying this specification
is to evaluate the form

                    (ever-a-one-two-three (storage 'input) (storage 'output))

which will calculate a non-canonical constraint. The left column of the following figure contains a listing of part of the non-canonical constraint. The symbols with numeric suffixes were
generated by gensym. Since there are 76 equational wffs, we only exhibit a few of them. The
right column contains the entire constraint after it has been canonicalized.

```
((PI EQUAL (ITEM1023 HEAD1027) EQUAL1029)        ((PI EQUAL (INPUT HEAD1027) EQUAL1029)
 (PI OR (EQUAL1029 RESULT10301031) OR1048)        (PI OR (EQUAL1029 DELAY1047) OR1048)
 (PI EQUAL (ITEM1012 HEAD1016) EQUAL1018)         (PI EQUAL (INPUT HEAD1016) EQUAL1018)
 (PI OR (EQUAL1018 RESULT10191020) OR1049)        (PI OR (EQUAL1018 OR1048) OR1049)
 (PI EQUAL (ITEM1001 HEAD1005) EQUAL1007)         (PI EQUAL (INPUT HEAD1005) EQUAL1007)
 (PI OR (EQUAL1007 RESULT10081009) OR1050)        (PI OR (EQUAL1007 OR1049) OR1050)
 (PI OR (INPUT1053 RESULT1055) OR1056)            (PI OR (OR1050 OUTPUT) UPDATE1059)
 (DELTA 1 DELAY976 UPDATE973)                     (DELTA 1 HEAD1005 HEAD1005)
 (DELTA 2 DELAY986 UPDATE983)                     (DELTA 2 HEAD1016 HEAD1016)
 (DELTA 3 DELAY996 UPDATE993)                     (DELTA 3 HEAD1027 HEAD1027)
 (DELTA 0 DELAY1047 UPDATE1044)                   (DELTA 0 DELAY1047 DELAY1047)
 (DELTA 0 UPDATE1059 DELAY1062)                   (DELTA 0 UPDATE1059 OUTPUT))
 (== INPUT INPUT966)
 (== OUTPUT OUTPUT965)
 (== (RESULT387967 RESULT387977 RESULT387987)
    LIST1000)
 (== LIST1000 (HEAD1005 . TAIL1006))
 (== TAIL1006 LIST1011)
 (== LIST1011 (HEAD1016 . TAIL1017))
 ... )
```

This can be interpreted as a linear description of the wiring diagram of the "circuit" diagrammed below.

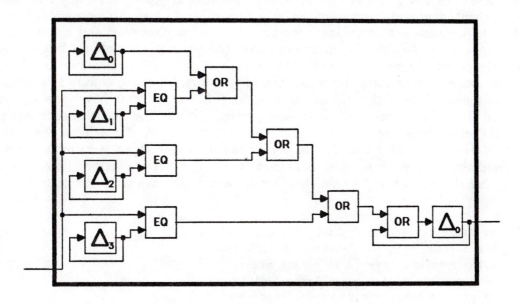

Example

In this section we present the Rex specification of a robot that intermittently senses the location of a moving object in its environment and tries to keep track of whether the object is within *shouting distance* (a certain radius) of the robot. Due to the degradation of information over time and motion of the robot, sometimes the machine will *know* that the object is within shouting distance, sometimes it will *know* that the object is *not* within shouting distance, and sometimes it will not know either proposition. We characterize the epistemic properties of the outputs of this machine in terms of the epistemic properties of its inputs and sketch a proof of this characterization.

Description of the shoutm Machine

The machine has three inputs, which we will refer to as x, y, and action. The values of x and y encode the cartesian coordinates of the object detected by the sensor in the robot's current frame of reference; if no object is sensed, the values of x and y are equal to the distiguished constant BOTTOM. The values of action encode the robot's last action; it can take on four possible values: MOVE means that the robot moved one unit in the direction it was facing; RTURN means that the robot turned 90 degrees to the right; LTURN means that the robot turned 90 degrees to the left; NOOP means that the robot did nothing.

The machine has two output lines, K-shout-dist and K-not-shout-dist. We show that K-shout-dist *knows* that the object is within shouting distance whenever its value is 1, and that K-not-shout-dist knows that the object is *not* within shouting distance whenever its value is 1.

The top-level Rex function specifies the relation between x, y, and action, on the one hand, and K-shout-dist and K-not-shout-dist, on the other, by introducing complex inter-mediate locations, queue, K-shout-dist-vec and K-not-shout-dist-vec, and constraining them with respect to the top-level inputs and outputs. The queue will contain the last several sightings of the object; the number of such sightings is specified by the value parameter size. Each sighting carries some information about the current location of the object. In general, the older the sighting, the weaker the information, since the object may have moved since it was sighted (it can move one unit of distance per unit time). The queue of sightings is mapped into K-shout-dist-vec, a vector of boolean values, the ith of which has the value 1 if the information in the ith element of the queue entails that the object is within shouting distance. Similarly, the queue is mapped into K-not-shout-dist-vec, a vector with elements that signify that the object is not within shouting distance when they carry the value 1.

```
(defun shoutm (size x y action K-shout-dist K-not-shout-dist)
  (some (queue K-shout-dist-vec K-not-shout-dist-vec)
    (queue-with-transform size [x y] action queue)
    (mapfn 'K-shoutable 0 size queue K-shout-dist-vec)
    (mapfn 'K-not-shoutable 0 size queue K-not-shout-dist-vec)
    (morm size K-shout-dist-vec K-shout-dist)
    (morm size K-not-shout-dist-vec K-not-shout-dist)))
```

To illustrate the flexibility of Rex, we parameterize the specification of the vectors K-shout-dist-vec and K-not-shout-dist-vec and their connection to queue not only by size, but by the functional value parameters K-shoutable and K-not-shoutable which are applied to queue by mapfn.

Epistemic Properties of the shoutm Machine

The formal property we wish to prove of the **shoutm** machine specification is

$$\Gamma, \text{shoutm}(n, X, Y, A, S, Ns), InputAxioms(X, Y, A) \models *S = 1 \rightarrow K(S, wsd)$$

where Γ is a *background theory*, i.e., a collection of wffs embodying general facts about the robot world; $\text{shoutm}(n, X, Y, A, S, Ns)$ is the wff computed by Rex that describes the **shoutm** machine; and $InputAxioms(X, Y, A)$ are all the instances of the following schema:

$$(*[X, Y] = \langle x, y \rangle \wedge x \neq \perp \wedge y \neq \perp \rightarrow locf(\langle x, y \rangle, 0)) \wedge (*A = a \rightarrow doing(a)),$$

where $x, y \in \mathbf{N}$ and $a \in \{\texttt{MOVE}, \texttt{LTURN}, \texttt{RTURN}, \texttt{NOOP}\}$. The atomic formula *wsd* designates the proposition "the object is within shouting distance". The formula designated by $locf(\langle x_i, y_i \rangle, i)$ expresses the fact that i time units ago the object was at what is location x_i, y_i in the current frame of reference. $doing(a)$ expresses the proposition that the robot is doing the action referred to by a. We assume that Γ contains, among other things, axioms relating *locf* to *doing*.

The truth of the epistemic specification of **shoutm** follows directly from three lemmas that characterize the constraints imposed by **queue-with-transform**, **mapfn**, **K-shoutable**, and **morm**. Only the proof of the third lemma will be presented; the proofs of the other two lemmas are similar in structure. We also prove an auxiliary fact relating states of processes and knowledge.

Lemma 1 $\Gamma, \texttt{queue-with-transform}(n, [X, Y], A, [E_1, \ldots, E_n]), InputAxioms(X, Y, A) \models$

$$\bigvee_{i=1}^{n} (*E_i = \langle x_i, y_i \rangle \rightarrow K(E_i, locf(\langle x_i, y_i \rangle, i)))$$

This result relates the values, $\langle x_i, y_i \rangle$, of each element, E_i, of the queue to $locf(\langle x_i, y_i \rangle, i)$, taking into account the fact that the values $\langle x_i, y_i \rangle$ are interpreted relative to the robot's current frame of reference and are updated at each step depending on the the value of A.

Lemma 2 $\Gamma, \texttt{mapfn}(\texttt{K-shoutable}, 0, n, [E_1, \ldots, E_n], [F_1, \ldots, F_n]),$

$$\bigvee_{i=1}^{n} (*E_i = \langle x_i, y_i \rangle \rightarrow K(E_i, locf(\langle x_i, y_i \rangle, i))) \models \bigwedge_{i=1}^{n} (*F_i = 1 \rightarrow K(F_i, wsd))$$

The definition of **mapfn** is such that **K-shoutable** will be applied to each of the E_i, yielding F_i. This lemma asserts that if the inputs to the **K-shoutable** machines always encode the uncertain location of the object, then when any of the outputs has the value 1, it carries the information that the object is within shouting distance.

Lemma 3

$$\text{morm}(n, [F_1, \ldots, F_n], R), \bigwedge_{i=1}^{n} (*F_i = 1 \rightarrow K(F_i, \varphi)) \models \Box (*R = 1 \rightarrow K(R, \varphi))$$

If each input to the morm machine knows the proposition φ when it has the value 1, then the output knows φ when it has the value 1.

Proof of Lemma 3

The following Rex definition is the specification of the morm (morm stands for "multiple or machine"). It builds the definition of a machine that computes the n-ary or function by accumulating $n - 1$ binary orm constraints, where n is the value parameter length.

```
(defun morm (length vector result)
  (if (= length 0)
      (constant 0 result)
      (some (head tail result1)
        (== vector [head | tail])
        (morm (- length 1) tail result1)
        (orm [head result1] result))))
```

The proof of Lemma 3 requires the following fact about morm,

$$\text{morm}(n, [F_1, \ldots, F_n], R) \models \Box ([*F_1 = 1 \lor \ldots \lor *F_n = 1] \leftrightarrow *R = 1),$$

which can be easily proved by induction on the size of the input vector, length.

By propositional reasoning,

$$\bigwedge_{i=1}^{n} (*F_i = 1 \rightarrow K(F_i, \varphi)) \models \bigvee_{i=1}^{n} *F_i = 1 \rightarrow \bigvee_{i=1}^{n} K(F_i, \varphi).$$

Combining this with the previous fact about the values of morm, and substituting $*R = 1$ for $(*F_1 = 1 \lor \ldots \lor *F_n = 1)$, we derive

$$\text{morm}(n, [F_1, \ldots, F_n], R), \bigwedge_{i=1}^{n} (*F_i = 1 \rightarrow K(F_i, \varphi)) \models *R = 1 \rightarrow \bigvee_{i=1}^{n} K(F_i, \varphi)$$

It follows from the epistemic axiom of truth and the properties of disjunction that $K(F_1, \varphi) \lor \ldots \lor K(F_n, \varphi) \rightarrow \varphi$, so we can derive

$$\text{morm}(n, [F_1, \ldots, F_n], R), \bigwedge_{i=1}^{n} (*F_i = 1 \rightarrow K(F_i, \varphi)) \models (*R = 1 \rightarrow \varphi).$$

Since $P \models \Box P$ and $\Box(*x = v \rightarrow \varphi) \rightarrow (*x = v \rightarrow K(x, \varphi))$ is valid (see proof below),

$$\texttt{morm}(n, [F_1, \ldots, F_n], R), \bigwedge_{i=1}^{n}(*F_i = 1 \rightarrow K(F_i, \varphi)) \models (*R = 1 \rightarrow K(R, \varphi)).$$

All that remains is to verify the validity of

$$\Box(*x = v \rightarrow \varphi) \rightarrow (*x = v \rightarrow K(x, \varphi)).$$

We begin by observing a fact about the epistemic properties of machines that is an instance of the more general fact that all agents know necessary truths.

$$\Box(*x = v \rightarrow \varphi) \rightarrow K(x, *x = v \rightarrow \varphi)$$

This fact, together with the self-awareness axiom,

$$*x = v \rightarrow K(x, *x = v),$$

implies that

$$\Box(*x = v \rightarrow \varphi) \wedge *x = v \rightarrow K(x, *x = v \rightarrow \varphi) \wedge K(x, *x = v).$$

As an instance of consequential closure axiom schema of epistemic logic, we have

$$K(x, *x = v \rightarrow \varphi) \wedge K(x, *x = v) \rightarrow K(x, \varphi).$$

Chaining the two preceding statements, we have

$$\Box(*x = v \rightarrow \varphi) \wedge *x = v \rightarrow K(x, \varphi),$$

which directly implies the result:

$$\Box(*x = v \rightarrow \varphi) \rightarrow (*x = v \rightarrow K(x, \varphi)).$$

Application

The software tools and analytic techniques described in this paper are currently being applied to SRI's mobile robot. An implementation of Rex exists that generates sequential code for controlling the robot. Since the machine descriptions computed by Rex are similar to circuit diagrams, more direct realizations in hardware are being considered. Two of the challenges in robot analysis and synthesis are: (1) how to relate the representations used in perceptual processing to the representations involved in higher-level reasoning and planning, and (2) how to process information from the environment in real time. The framework presented in this paper appears to offer advantages in both areas. Since the attribution of knowledge is based on objective behavioral properties of the machine, the propositional content of different representational structures can be more easily compared. Furthermore, since the attribution of content does not depend on general-purpose deduction mechanisms, much of the permanent knowledge of the system can be compiled into the structure of the machine, decreasing the amount of computation required at runtime.

Acknowledgments

This work was supported in part by a gift from the Systems Development Foundation, in part by FMC Corporation under contract 147466 (SRI Project 7390), and in part by General Motors Research Laboratories under contract 50-13 (SRI Project 8662).

We have profited greatly from discussions with David Chapman and from comments by Fernando Pereira on a previous draft.

References

[1] Gabbay, Dov, Amir Pnueli, Saharon Shelah, and Jonathan Stavi. "On the Temporal Analysis of Fairness." Conference Record of the Seventh Annual ACM Symposium on Principles of Programming Languages, 1980, pp. 163-173.

[2] Halpern, Joseph and Y.O. Moses. "Knowledge and Common Knowledge in a Distributed Environment." Proceedings of the 3rd ACM Conference on Principles of Distributed Computing, 1984, pp. 50-61; a revised version appears as IBM RJ 4421, 1984.

[3] Hintikka, J. *Knowledge and Belief.* Cornell University Press, Ithaca, 1962.

[4] Hughes, G. E. and M. J. Cresswell. *An Introduction to Modal Logic.* Methuen and Co. Ltd., London, 1968.

[5] Kaelbling, Leslie Pack. *Programming in Rex.* Technical Note, Artificial Intelligence Center, SRI International, Menlo Park, CA, (forthcoming.)

[6] Konolige, Kurt. *A Deduction Model of Belief and its Logics.* Technical Note No. 326, Artificial Intelligence Center, SRI International, Menlo Park, CA, August, 1984.

[7] Kripke, Saul. "Semantical Analysis of Modal Logic." *Zeitschrift fur Mathematische Logik und Grundlagen der Mathematik* 9, 1963, pp. 67-96.

[8] Lehmann, Daniel. "Knowledge, Common Knowledge and Related Puzzles." Proceedings of the 3rd Annual ACM Conference on Principles of Distributed Computing, 1984, pp. 62-67.

[9] Levesque, Hector J. "A Logic of Implicit and Explicit Belief." Proceedings of the National Conference on Artificial Intelligence, 1984, pp. 198-202.

[10] Manna, Zohar and Amir Pnueli, "Verification of Concurrent Programs: the Temporal Framework," *The Correctness Problem in Computer Science* (R. S. Boyer and J. S. Moore, eds.), International Lecture Series in Computer Science, Academic Press, London, 1981.

[11] McCarthy, John, P. W. Abrams, D. J. Edwards, T. P. Hart, and M. I. Levin. *Lisp 1.5 Programmer's Manual,* second edition. MIT Press, Cambridge, Mass, 1965.

[12] Moore, Robert C. "A Formal Theory of Knowledge and Action." In *Formal Theories of the Commonsense World,* Jerry R. Hobbs and Robert C. Moore (eds.), Ablex Publishing Company, Norwood, New Jersey, 1985.

[13] Rosenschein, Stanley J. "Formal Theories of Knowledge in AI and Robotics." *New Generation Computing* Vol. 3, No. 4 (in press). Ohmsha, Ltd. Tokyo, Japan.

A First Order Theory of Planning, Knowledge, and Action

Leora Morgenstern

New York University

Department of Computer Science

New York, N.Y. 10012

ABSTRACT

Most AI planners work on the assumption that they have complete knowledge of their problem domain and situation so that planning an action consists of searching for an action sequence that achieves some desired goal. In actual planning situations, we rarely know enough to map out a detailed plan of action when we start out. Instead, we initially draw up a sketchy plan and fill in details as we proceed. This paper presents a formalism based upon a syntactic logic of knowledge which is expressive enough to describe this flexible planning process.

1. Introduction

Most AI planners work on the assumption that they have complete knowledge of their problem domain and situation, so that planning an action consists of searching through a pre-packaged list of action operators for an action sequence that achieves some desired goal. Real life planning rarely works this way, because we usually don't have enough information to map out a detailed plan of action when we start out. Instead we initially draw up a sketchy plan and fill in details as we gain more exact information about the world.

A robust planning system must have similar capabilities if it is to work in a complex domain. In particular, it needs a solid theory of knowledge, action, and communication, so that it can produce a coherent plan even when its knowledge of the problem domain and problem situation is incomplete. Some work has already been done in this field, most notably by Robert Moore [Moore 1980], who has developed a theory of knowledge and action in which it is possible, for example, for an agent who knows the combination of a safe to reason that he knows how to open the safe. Due to the inherent limitations of Moore's formalism, however, Moore cannot attack the problems of knowledge, action, and communication in their full generality.

This paper presents a logic that is expressive enough to deal with the problems that faced Moore's system. In the next section of this paper, we review Moore's work on knowledge and action and demonstrate its logical limitations. Afterwards, we present an alternate approach, discuss its power, and show how it can be integrated with Moore's work on knowledge and action. Finally, we show how this logic of knowledge and action can be extended to a more robust theory of planning, and demonstrate solutions to a number of problems that cannot be handled by current theories of knowledge and action.

2. Moore's Logic of Knowledge and Action

The bulk of Moore's work on knowledge and action is directed towards explaining how knowledge affects action. Prior to Moore's pioneering work, researchers such as McCarthy and Hayes [1969] had argued that a planning program needs to explicitly reason about its ability to perform an action. These researchers suggested writing down explicit knowledge precondition axioms for each action, so that a planning program could reason that it knew how to do an action if the relevant knowledge precondition axioms were true. Unfortunately, this approach leads to an explosion of knowledge precondition axioms and unacceptably long proofs. This problem, which we will call the problem of knowledge preconditions, is the one that Moore's system seeks to solve.

Moore uses a standard S4 modal logic of knowledge, with the following axiom schemata:

M1: Axioms of ordinary propositional logic
M2: Know(A,P) => P (veridicality)
M3: Know(A,P) => Know(A,Know(A,P)) (positive introspection)
M4: Know(A,P=>Q) => (Know(A,P) => Know(A,Q)) (consequential closure)
M5: If P is an axiom, then Know(A,P) is an axiom (necessitation)

The semantics for 'know' are given in terms of a Kripkean possible worlds semantics [Kripke 1963a&b, Hintikka 1962 & 1969]: an agent knows p in a particular world if and only if p is true in all worlds that are knowledge equivalent to his world. By positing that 'know' is a reflexive and transitive relation, we get the effect of M1-M5.

The notion of a rigid designator - something that denotes the same individual in all possible worlds [Kripke 1972] - plays an important role in Moore's theory of knowledge and action. According to Moore, we can in general say that we know who somebody is or what something is if we know a rigid designator for that person or object. Similarly, says Moore, we know what an action description is, and thus how to do the action, if we know of a rigid designator for that action. Moreover, we know how to do an action if we know of an executable description of that action. Moore thus argues that a rigid designator for an action must be its executable description.

In practice, continues Moore, most action types are rigid functions which map rigid designators onto rigid designators, or are axiomatically defined in terms of other rigid functions. Thus if an agent knows rigid designators for the parameters of such an action, he knows a rigid designator for the action itself, and thus knows how to do the action.

Moore has thus characterized the knowledge preconditions for all actions with one principle. He has effectively dealt with the problem of knowledge preconditions while presenting a cogent explanation of what it means for an agent to know how to do an action.

2.1. Criticisms of Moore's System

Unfortunately, Moore's system is beset by a host of problems. In the first place, it is intuitively implausible that an executable description of an action can serve as a rigid designator for that action. Rather, an executable description of an action seems to be a property of that action that varies among different possible worlds. For example, in 1950 the executable description of dial(911) was a sequence of rotate-dial movements, while in 2050, if dial phones will be obsolete, the executable description of that same action might be a sequence of push-button movements. Given any executable description of an action, we can imagine some possible world in which that executable description would not work.

Secondly, Moore's assumptions regarding an agent's knowledge seem excessively strong. In his system all agents know all axioms. This implies that all agents have the same level of procedural knowledge, so that all an agent might not know is some of the slot fillers in some action. Yet there are clearly many situations in which an agent cannot do an action because he has no idea how to do the general procedure. Moore's system admits of no such possibility, since all general procedures for action are known. Moreover, it is impossible in Moore's system to relax the requirement that all axioms are known by all agents; this is a direct consequence of the possible worlds semantics on 'know.'

Thirdly, Moore's system is simply not expressive enough to handle a lot of our statements about knowledge. This criticism in fact applies to any standard first order modal logic of knowledge. Because we cannot quantify over sentences, we cannot formulate such sentences as 'John knows that Bill knows something that he doesn't know.' Assuming that knowledge about actions is in the form of statements, we also cannot express 'John knows that Bill knows how to fire a gun' unless John himself knows how to fire a gun.

Finally, we note that Moore's system deals with only one of the many issues that must be addressed by a complete theory of knowledge and action. An agent must not only be able to reason about whether he knows how to do an action at a particular time, but should also be able to reason about whether he might eventually know how to do that action, how he can learn to do the action, and whether he can delegate the action to some subordinate agent.

3. An Alternate Approach: 'Know' as a Syntactic Predicate

Our first task in developing a theory of knowledge and action is choosing a formalism for our theory. We reject first order modal logic, since that turns out to be insufficiently expressive for our needs. A move to a higher order modal logic [e.g., Gallin 1975] is likewise rejected because we would no longer have a complete proof procedure, and a higher order modal logic with possible worlds semantics would still entail that all agents know all axioms. Instead, we turn to a first order predicate logic with quotation, where 'know' is a syntactic predicate that ranges over names of sentences. Such an approach allows us to formulate the examples of the last section that gave Moore's system so much trouble. For example, 'John knows that Bill knows something that he doesn't know' can be formulated as

Know(John,'Exists x (Know(Bill,x) and ~Know(John,x))'). Although we are effectively quantifying over sentences, our system remains first order because we are really quantifying over *names* of sentences, which are just strings or numbers.

Unfortunately, treating 'know' as a syntactic predicate leads to severe difficulties [Montague 1963]. In their simplest form, these difficulties manifest themselves as the

Knower Paradox [Montague and Kaplan 1960]: If 'know' is a syntactic predicate, we can construct a sentence S such that S iff Know(a, "S'). Assuming veridicality, consequential closure, and necessitation on these two principles, S is inconsistent.

Providing some resolution to the Knower Paradox is thus a prerequisite to any syntactic theory of knowledge. We first observe that the Knower Paradox is just a variant of the Liar Paradox: if we allow 'true' to be a syntactic predicate in a classical logical language, we can construct a sentence such as P iff ˜True('P'), which is of course inconsistent. To avoid this paradox, Tarski suggested that we have a hierarchy of languages and a hierarchy of truth predicates, one truth predicate per language. In no case is a language allowed to contain its own truth predicate, so we cannot construct paradoxical statements. Konolige [1981] has suggested constructing a hierarchy of know predicates to avoid the Knower Paradox, but we reject this approach because of various unsatisfying features of Tarski's hierarchy of predicates [Kripke 1975]: In the first place, it is implausible that people are consciously aware of using different truth predicates when they speak. Secondly, we often do not know which truth predicate to use when we utter a particular statement. Finally, it is impossible, in Tarski's approach to construct a pair of sentences, each of which refers to the truth value of the other, although such sentences may make perfect sense. Suppose, for example, that John Dean says 'All of Nixon's utterances about Watergate are false' and that Nixon says 'Everything Dean says about Watergate is false.' If both Dean and Nixon have made some trivial but true statement about Watergate, both statements will be false, but will certainly make sense. Moreover, the truth values of statements such as these often depend on empirical facts about the world, not on the syntactic structure of the statements.

These problems have led Kripke [1975] to develop a theory of truth which avoids both the Liar Paradox and the unattractive features of Tarski's approach. Our strategy will be to examine Kripke's construction and adapt it to a theory of knowledge which avoids the Knower Paradox.

Kripke's basic idea is that not every sentence is assigned a value of true or false;

viciously self-referential statements whether paradoxical or non-paradoxical get an indeterminate truth value, the third value in a three valued logic. Kripke's three valued logic is based on Kleene's [1952]: a or b is true if a is true or b is true, false if both a and b are false, of indeterminate value otherwise; forall x P(x) is true if P(x) is true for all x, false if P is false for at least one x, and undetermined otherwise.

Like Tarski, Kripke considers a hierarchy of languages, but only one truth predicate $T(x)$. He starts out with a language L_0 which contains only sentences that do not involve the concept of truth. The language at the next level L_1 contains all the sentences of L_0, plus those sentences which talk about the truth or falsity of sentences in L_0. This process continues as we ascend the hierarchy and is defined for every L_α where α is an ordinal. In general, at successor levels we take the truth predicates over the previous level; at limit levels we take the union of all sentences declared true or false at previous levels. At some level L_σ we will no longer be able to assign truth values to any more statements no matter how much higher we ascend the hierarchy. We call those statements that have been assigned a truth value in L_σ grounded; all other statements are called ungrounded and take on the third, indeterminate truth value of the three valued logic. Moreover, we can show that viciously self referential statements such as the Liar Sentence are ungrounded in such a construction.

3.1. Relevance of Kripke's Work to a Logic of Knowledge

Our strategy for avoiding the Knower Paradox will be to construct a language in which sentences like S iff Know(a,"S") as well as the Liar and Truthteller sentences are not grounded. Like Kripke, we will construct a hierarchy of languages, building up towards a language which contains its own truth and knowledge predicates. We will be explaining knowledge as true belief, though for the purposes of this construction we could as well have taken knowledge to be justified true belief; the former strategy is adopted purely for reasons of simplicity. We start off with a classical first order language L, which comes with a fixed set of predicates and relations, including the relation Believe(a,p). Believe(a,p) is a well defined function on all strings p.[1] Our first language L_0 contains only sentences that do not involve the concepts of truth or knowledge. As we ascend the hierarchy, more and more of these sentences will get truth values. In general, at any (successor) level i, we say that Know(a,p) is true in L_i if p has a positive truth value in L_{i-1} and a believes p; Know(a,p) is false if p has a negative truth value in L_{i-1}, *or* if p is true in L_{i-1} but a does not believe p; and that Know(a,p) is undefined otherwise. T(x) and Know(a,x) have truth values at a limit level iff they have truth values at a lower level. We can show that this construction is monotonic: that as we ascend the hierarchy the extensions of T(x) and Know(a,x) increase, and that we eventually reach a fixed point L_σ such that the extension of T(x) and $\bigcup_a$ Know(a,x) remain the same for L_σ and $L_{\sigma+1}$. As before, we call a sentence grounded if it has been assigned a truth value at L_σ; otherwise it is ungrounded. It is easy to see that sentences like the Knower sentence as well as the Liar and Truthteller sentences are ungrounded in such a construction. We have thus successfully resolved the Knower Paradox and have dealt with the primary objection to a logic that treats 'know' as a syntactic predicate.[2]

4. Planning, Knowledge, and Action

We can now proceed to develop our theory of knowledge and action. In this section, we expand Moore's solution to the problem of knowledge preconditions and integrate it with a first order theory of knowledge and action. The resulting theory can handle Moore's benchmark problems: agents can reason that they know how to perform an action or sequence of actions, and they can obtain knowledge as the result of an action. We then extend our theory so that we can deal with more complex planning problems. We show that

---

1-To avoid the Believer Paradox that such a move entails, we reject the 'assumption of arrogance': Believe(a,'Believe(a,p) => p').

2-It should be noted that this logic is not classical. In particular the law of the excluded middle does not hold for ungrounded sentences. Thus the axiom schemata T('x') => x, x =>T('x'), Know(a,'x') => x do not hold for ungrounded sentences. We do however, have the classical inference rules T('x')/x, x/T('x'), Know(a,'x')/x, and can demonstrate that classical logic does hold for grounded statements. For attempts to resolve the paradoxes within classical two valued logic, see Perlis 1981, Gupta 1982, Herzberger 1982, Asher & Kamp, 1986. (These systems all lose the classical inference rules.)

we can deal with an agent who plans to learn how to cook by enrolling in cooking classes, and an agent who accomplishes a task that he is incapable of doing by assigning it to subordinate agents.

4.1. The Basic Theory

We start by giving a brief description of our language. We will be using a first order language L and a temporal logic which is loosely based on the work of McDermott [1982]. L comes with a set of (possibly partially) interpreted predicates, functions, constants, and variables. The distinguished variable s ranges over situations. A collection of consecutive situations is known as an interval. Actions and events are collections of intervals; an action and an agent map onto an event. All predicates are qualified by a situation or interval. Well formed formulas are built up in the usual way out of the basic building blocks of L using the standard logical connectives v and ˜ and the universal quantifier forall. Given a wff x, we can apply the godelization function G to obtain the string that represents x. In general, we write G(x) as 'x'. G is invertible; given any string we can recover the formula it represents. Assuming a model M, we now give the semantics for True and Know:

(1) $M \models T(p)$ iff $M \models G^{-1}(p)$

(2) $M \models Know(a,p,s)$ iff $M \models T(p)$ and $M \models Believe(a,p,s)$

Note that (1) implies that T(a v b) iff T(a) v T(b) and T(˜a) iff ˜T(a).

We note that the quoting mechanism is *opaque* in many respects so that saying things correctly becomes quite complicated. To facilitate writing down axioms, we introduce two syntactic abbreviations: a name-of operator @, where @ applied to an object yields the name of that object, and an antiquote operator ˆˆ, where ˆˆ applied to a string variable p yields the string that p stands for.

We are now ready to present some axiom schemata that capture our basic intuitions on knowledge. Not surprisingly, these schemata are rather similar to Moore's M1-M5; whether we treat 'know' as a modal operator or as a syntactic predicate, our basic intuitions on knowledge remain the same. It should be noted that the schemata below, particularly K2-K4, hold only for grounded statements.

K1: Axioms of ordinary predicate logic   (see [Mendelson 1964], Section 2.3)
K2: Know(a,p,s) => p (veridicality)
K3: Know(a,p,s) => Know(a,'Know(@a,^p^,@s)',s)) (positive introspection)
K4: Agents know the rules of inference:
   (i) Know(a,'implies(^p^,^q^)',s) and Know(a,p,s) => Know(a,q,s)
   (Modus Ponens)
   (ii) Know(a,'p',s) => Know(a,'Forall x (p)',s)
   (Generalization)
K5a:If p is an axiom of predicate logic then Know(a,p,s) for any s
K5b:Know(a,K1-K5b,s) for any s

It will be noticed that K1-K5 differ from M1-M5 in two important ways:

(1) K1 and K4 are quite a bit stronger than their counterparts, M1-M4. M1 and M4 just specify that all axioms of propositional logic are in the system and that agents can and do use the rule of inference Modus Ponens. Thus, the system supports only inferences made via the rules of propositional logic, and assumes that agents are limited to these inferences as well. In contrast, K1 specifies that all axioms of predicate logic are in the system, and K4 posits that agents can and do reason with the rules of inference of predicate logic. [3] Our system is thus considerably more powerful. Traditionally, modal logic has restricted itself to the propositional calculus since the introduction of quantifiers poses so many problems ([Marcus 1971], [Kaplan 1971], [Hughes and Cresswell 1968]). Of course, not much can be said without predicate calculus; Moore's system, however, lets in predicate calculus through the back door since the actual proofs of theorems are carried out in the first order theory of possible worlds. We, on the other hand, have to explicitly assert all the axioms of predicate calculus and assume that all agents can and do reason with these principles. These axioms are strong enough to prove that all agents know all logical consequences of their knowledge, and that they thus behave like 'perfect reasoners.'

(2) On the other hand, K5 is a good deal weaker than M5. As we have said previously,

---

3- Of course, the axioms and inference rules are not fixed; we may decide to use a different set, such as is presented in [Kleene 1955], or choose a natural deduction system, as in [Mates 1972], where there are no logical axioms, but more rules of inference. For ease of presentation, we have chosen a system with the minimal number of inference rules.

we do not wish to assume that all agents know all axioms, since there are many axioms on the world that agents simply aren't aware of. We do, however, wish to assume that all agents know all axioms of logic and the basic axioms of knowledge. K5a and K5b capture these constraints, thus avoiding the overly strong assumptions on knowledge that modal logics and possible worlds semantics entail.

As the first step in an integrated theory of knowledge and action, we must provide a solution to Moore's problem: when can we say that an agent knows how to do an action?

Much of Moore's work on this subject is insightful, and it plays a major role in our theory. It is indeed true that an agent knows how to do an action if he knows an executable description for that action. It also seems clear that if an agent knows the general procedure for some parameterized action type and knows in a particular case what the parameters of the action are, that he knows an executable description for that particular action. We contend, however, that it is not in general true that agents know the general procedures for all action types. Instead, we divide the class of actions into *primitive* action types, which are very basic actions such as Put-on and Lift, and *complex* action types such as Bake-Cake and Drive, which are themselves axiomatically defined in terms of primitive actions. We argue that all agents do know the general procedures for the primitive action types. However, because agents in our system do not necessarily know how complex action types are composed out of primitive actions, an agent knows the process for a complex action type only if he knows how that action type is composed out of primitive action types.

We thus say an agent knows how to do an action if

a) the action type is primitive and he knows what the parameters of the action are (knows constants for those parameters) *or* if

b) he knows how the action is built up out of simpler actions and he knows how to perform those simpler actions.

In particular, an agent knows how to do a sequence of actions t1,...,tn if he knows how to do t1 and completing any action ti in the sequence results in his knowing how to perform the next action. Thus in our system, as in Moore's, an agent need not be able to perform an entire action sequence when he starts to do the action.

It is useful to distinguish between the concepts of *knowing how* to perform an action and *being able* to perform that action. An agent who knows how to perform an action in a particular situation may still be unable to actually perform that action in that situation, because certain other conditions are not satisfied. For example, an agent who knows how to drive a car in S1 may be unable to drive in S1 if no car is available or if the roads are icy. In general, we say that an agent can-perform an action in a situation if he knows how to perform the action, if the physical preconditions for the action are satisfied, and - in the case of an action which involves more than one agent - if certain social protocols governing the behavior of agents are satisfied.

Often, an agent is more interested in being able to achieve some goal than in being able to perform a particular action. For such situations, we introduce the predicate know-how-to-achieve. We say that an agent knows-how-to-achieve a situation with a desired property if he knows of some action that will achieve the desired situation and he can-perform that action.

These three concepts - know-how-to-perform, can-perform, and know-how-to-achieve - are the building blocks of our theory of knowledge and action. Using them, we can solve all of the benchmark problems that Moore's system solved. But these problems - which involved a single agent reasoning about his ability to do an action or sequence of actions, and which demonstrated the knowledge an agent might obtain by performing an action - represent only a small portion of the problems that a robust theory of planning should handle. In a real world situation, agents who do not know how to perform some action do not simply give up, but reason about whether they can obtain the information they need from some other agent, or delegate the action to other more knowledgeable agents. Moore's system could not describe such scenarios since the logic he used was not expressive enough to describe an agent's partial knowledge of another agent's knowledge. Our theory, on the other hand, is sufficiently expressive for these needs, and we can thus apply ourselves to developing a theory which can handle the aforementioned problems.

4.2. Extensions to Planning

We begin by formally introducing the concept of a plan. Typically, AI planning theories (e.g. [Sacerdoti 1977, McDermott 1985]) have considered only plans constructed out of actions done by a single agent. This concept of planning suffices for simple blocks-world type planning domains, and for restricted classes of problems in simplified multi-agent domains. It does not, however, work well in reasonably complex multi-agent domains in which agents rely upon other agents' actions as they plan. Consider, for example, my plan to get to the airport: Do(I, hail(taxi)) ; Do(driver(taxi),drive(taxi,airport)) ; Do(I, pay(driver(taxi)). The taxi driver's action is an essential part of my plan. We thus define a plan as a structure of events constructed according to specified formation rules, where an event can be any action done by an agent or an 'actorless' event such as a thunderstorm or tornado, and the formation rules correspond to the control structures given in standard real time concurrent programming languages, such as described in [Davis 1984].

Analogous to the concept of can-perform for actions, we introduce the notion of can-execute for plans. An agent a can execute plan p in situation s if he knows in s that he will be able to perform all the actions in the plan for which he is an agent, and can predict that all other events in the plan occur in their proper order. [4] Using this concept, we can now say that an agent can-plan-to-perform an action if he knows of some plan that he can execute which will bring him to a state where he can perform that action. This terminology allows us to describe a situation where, for example, John can plan to call Mary on the phone by asking his friend Bill to tell him her phone number. Likewise, an agent can plan to learn how to make a souffle by registering for classes in a cooking school. Again, an essential part of the agent's plan is his ability to predict the occurrence of the cooking lessons.

4- Note that according to this broad definition, agents can-execute plans that are independently predictable events, such as the sun rising each morning or the president's annual State of the Union address.

Often, an agent who does not know how to do a particular action will be able to delegate the action to another subordinate agent. To formalize this concept, we introduce the predicate 'control', where control(a,b,t) means that agent a controls agent b with respect to a task, or action, t. The control predicate introduces a rather intricate structure on the relationships among agents. To visualize this structure, we can construct a graph by assigning a unique node to each agent, a unique color to each task, and drawing a directed edge of a particular color between two nodes if one agent controls the other with respect to that particular task. Note that while the complete graph is quite complex, the structure that we obtain by considering edges of only one color is simply a forest of trees: a purely hierarchical structure.

We now posit that an agent who controls another agent with respect to a particular task can delegate that task to the controlled agent, and furthermore, that an agent who has been delegated a task will do the task if he possibly can. We can now describe a situation where a supervisor can plan to get an action done by delegating it to his subordinates. Note that he need not know how to do the task that he delegates; he merely must be able to reason that his subordinates know how to do the task. Finally, to integrate the concept of delegation with our theory of planning, we say that an agent can-plan to get an action performed if he either can plan to perform the action himself, or can plan to delegate the action to another agent.

5. Conclusion

We have thus far constructed the foundations for a logic of planning, knowledge, and action. We have demonstrated that our theory solves Moore's benchmark problems (see [Morgenstern 1986] for details) and have begun to extend our theory so that it can deal with more complex planning problems. Although we are still a long way from completing work on a robust theory of knowledge, action, and communication, we believe that our current logic is flexible and expressive enough to provide the basis for such a theory. There are several reasons to believe this to be true:

[1]   Agents in our theory have genuinely differing levels of procedural knowledge.

[2]   Agents in our theory can reason about other agents' knowledge. This is true even when an agent has only a vague idea of what the more knowledgeable agent knows.

[3]   Strings are a natural and important part of our theory. This will prove useful in developing any theory of communication, since so many communicative actions operate primarily on strings. Moreover, since an agent's knowledge about actions is in the form of strings, it should be easy to describe how an agent teaches another agent to do an action.

In sum, our observations suggest that we will be able to extend our current theory to one that is considerably more complex.

Acknowledgements: I'd like to thank Ernie Davis for his ideas, suggestions, and guidance, and for all the weekly discussions that led up to this paper. Thanks also to Phil Cohen, Jeff Finger, Jerry Hobbs, David Israel, Kurt Konolige, Bob Moore, Stan Rosenschein, and Moshe Vardi for helpful discussions and criticisms.

BIBLIOGRAPHY

Appelt, Douglas: *Planning Natural Language Utterances to Satisfy Multiple Goals,* SRI International Technical Note 259, 1982

Asher, Nicholas and Hans Kamp: 'The Knower Paradox and the Logic of Attitudes,' *Proc. Conf. on Theoretical Aspects of Reasoning about Knowledge,* Monterey, 1986 (this volume)

Davis, Ernest: 'A High Level Real-Time Programming Language,' NYU Technical Report, 1984

Fikes, R.E. and Nils Nilsson: 'STRIPS: a New Approach to the Application of Theorem Proving to Problem Solving,' *Artificial Intelligence,* Vol 2, 1971

Gallin, Daniel: *Intensional and Higher Order Modal Logics,* American Elsevier, New York, 1975

Gupta, Anil: 'Truth and Paradox,' *Journal of Philosophical Logic* Vol. 11, No. 1, 1982

Herzberger, Hans: 'Notes on Naive Semantics,' *Journal of Philosophical Logic* Vol. 11, No. 1, 1982

Hintikka, Jaakko: *Knowledge and Belief,* Cornell University Press, Ithica 1962

Hintikka, Jaakko: 'Semantics for Propositional Attitudes,' in Leonard Linsky, ed. *Reference and Modality,* 1971

Hobbs, Jerry and Robert Moore: *Formal Theories of the Commonsense World,* Ablex Publishing Co., Norwood, 1985

Hughes, G.E. and M.J. Cresswell: *An Introduction to Modal Logic,* Methuen, London, 1968

Kaplan, David and Richard Montague: 'A Paradox Regained,' Notre Dame Journal of Formal Logic, vol.1 no.3, pp.79-90, 1960. Also Chapter 9 in **Richmond Thomason, ed:** *Formal Philosophy*

Kaplan, David: 'Quantifying In,' in **Leonard Linsky, ed.** *Reference and Modality*

Kleene, Stephen C.: *Introduction to Metamathematics,* Van Nostrand, New York, 1952

Konolige, Kurt: 'A First Order Formalization of Knowledge and Action for a Multi-agent Planning System' in J.E.Hays and D.Michie, eds. *Machine Intelligence 10,* 1982

Kripke, Saul: *Naming and Necessity,* Harvard University Press, Cambridge, 1972

Kripke, Saul: 'Outline of a Theory of Truth,' Journal of Philosophy, Vol 72, pp. 690-716, 1975.

Kripke, Saul: 'Semantical Analysis of Modal Logic,' *Zeitschrift fur Mathematische Logik und Grundlagen der Mathematik,* Vol. 9, 1963

Kripke, Saul: 'Semantical Considerations on Modal Logic,' *Acta Philosophica Fennica,* fasc. 16, pp.83-94, 1963. Also in **Leonard Linsky, ed:** *Reference and Modality*

Linsky, Leonard, ed: *Reference and Modality,* Oxford University Press, London 1971

Marcus, Ruth Barcan: 'Extensionality' in **Leonard Linsky, ed.** *Reference and Modality*

Mates, Benson: *Elementary Logic,* Oxford University Press, 1972

McCarthy, John and Patrick Hayes: 'Some Philosophical Problems from the Standpoint of Artificial Intelligence' in Bernard Meltzer, ed: *Machine Intelligence 4,* 1969

McDermott, Drew: 'A Temporal Logic for Reasoning About Processes and Plans,' *Cognitive Science,* 1982

McDermott, Drew: 'Reasoning About Plans' in Hobbs and Moore, eds. *Formal Theories of the Commonsense World,* 1985

Mendelson, Eliot: *Introduction to Mathematical Logic,* Van Nostrand, Princeton, 1964

Montague, Richard: 'Syntactical Treatments of Modality with Corollaries on Reflexion Principles and Finite Axiomatizability' in *Acta Philosophica Fennica,* fasc. 16, pp. 153-167 1963. Also in **Richmond Thomason, ed:** *Formal Philosophy*

Moore, Robert: *Reasoning About Knowledge and Action,* SRI Technical Note 191, 1980

Morgenstern, Leora: 'Preliminary Studies Toward a Logic of Knowledge, Action, and Communication,' NYU Technical Note, 1986

Perlis, Don: *Language, Computation, and Reality,* unpublished manuscript, 1981

Sacerdoti, Earl: *A Structure for Plans and Behavior,* American Elsevier, New York 1977

Thomason, Richmond, ed: *Formal Philosophy: Selected Papers of Richard Montague,* Yale University Press, New Haven 1974

The Consistency of Syntactical Treatments of Knowledge

Jim des Rivières

Department of Computer Science
University of Toronto
Toronto, Canada   M5S 1A4

Hector J. Levesque

Department of Computer Science
University of Toronto and
The Canadian Institute for Advanced Research

Abstract

The relative expressive power of a sentential operator $\Box\alpha$ is compared to that of a syntactical predicate $L(`\alpha')$ in the setting of first-order logics. Despite results by Montague and by Thomason that claim otherwise, any of the so-called "modal" logics of knowledge and belief can be translated into classical first-order logics that have a corresponding predicate on sentences.

¡Modality, SI; Modal Logic, NO!
— *John McCarthy*

In most logics of knowledge and belief there is a symbol in the language that is intended to be interpreted as "knows" (or "believes"). In first-order logics there is some flexibility regarding the syntactic type of this symbol, namely the choice between a sentential operator symbol, say **K**, which would be used like the negation operator ¬ to prefix a *formula* (e.g., **K**($P \supset Q$)), and a predicate symbol Know, which would be used in the standard first-order manner to prefix a *term* that is the name of a formula (e.g., Know('$P \supset Q$')). We would like to report on our findings concerning the relative expressive power of sentential operators *versus* these so-called syntactical predicates and the apparent difficulties in consistently formalizing the predicate approach.

A glimpse at the literature on logics of knowledge and belief reveals a diversity of approaches, with the expected split between operators and predicates: Hintikka [2], Levesque [6,7], and Konolige [4] are among those who have put forward first-order logics extended with sentential operators for knowledge and belief; McCarthy [8], Creary [1], Moore [11], Konolige [3], and Perlis [14], are just some who have proposed first-order logics of knowledge and belief that employ one or more predicates on sentences (sometimes in the guise of *concepts* as pointed out by McCarthy in [8]). Although this is not the place to delve into the reasons for the split, we note that the issues touched on in this paper may have been contributing factors.[1]

When discussing the translation (or conversion, or reduction) of a sentential operator to a syntactical predicate, it is not immediately clear what properties must be preserved. In the context of the modality of necessity, where the symbol □ is the usual necessity operator, Quine has stated that

> there would be comfort in being able to regard '□' as mere shorthand for 'Nec' and a pair of quotation marks — thus '□(9 is odd)' for 'Nec '9 is odd''. (Quine, [16, p. 268])

This is completely analogous to the way a sentence involving the connective ≡ can be understood, *macro*-style, as shorthand for one expressed entirely in terms of the connective symbols ⊃ and ∧. Implicit in Quine's desideratum is the property that iterated necessity operators should be read in a like fashion — thus □□(9 is odd) would be short not for Nec('□(9 is odd)'), but rather Nec('Nec('9 is odd')').

Let us tentatively adopt just such a reading of □ and see how the modal laws should be reinterpreted. For simplicity, we will refer to the language with the □ symbol as the "modal" language, and the other one as the "classical" language. Further, we will use L as the name for the unary predicate symbol that appears in the classical language but not in the modal one, chiefly because what we have to say has nothing to do with necessity or any other specific modality.[2]

One of the axiom schemata of the standard epistemic and alethic modal logics is

---

[1]Moore certainly thought so: "The main reason that modal logics are generally favored over syntactic methods, however, is that there are severe difficulties in formalizing the syntactic approach." [11, p. 216]

[2]In fact, the main application in AI of our results will be for knowledge and belief.

$$\Box\alpha \supset \alpha,$$

where α is a schematic letter ranging over all sentences in the modal language. For example, if P and Q are nullary predicate letters in the modal language, the sentence

$$\Box(P \wedge \Box Q) \supset (P \wedge \Box Q)$$

is an instance of that axiom schema. When, following Quine, we reinterpret this as shorthand, we see it as an abbreviation for the sentence

$$L(`P \wedge L(`Q')') \supset (P \wedge L(`Q')).$$

Using Quine's quasi-quotation to more correctly reflect the fact that α is being used as a schematic sentence letter, we can re-express the above schema as

$$L(\ulcorner\alpha\urcorner) \supset \alpha.$$

But the key question here is: Over which sentences should α range? The modal language? The entire classical language? Or perhaps just a subset thereof?

A sentence schema is best viewed as an abbreviation for a set of sentences in a language; convenience aside, it is the set that matters, nothing else. When trying to translate a schema in one language into one in another language, the schema should first be expanded into the set of sentences that it describes, then each of these sentences should be translated individually, and finally one can try to find a convenient schematic description of that resulting set. The other way of approaching it — simply translate the non-schematic portion of the schema and consider all schematic letters as ranging over sentences in the target language — need not always lead to the correct result.

If we carefully follow the steps mentioned above, the schema in the modal language expands to a particular (infinite) set of sentences in the modal language, and then each of these sentences is seen to be shorthand for some sentence in the classical language. The corresponding classical schema must cover all and only the sentences in this set. Note, however, there are some sentences in the classical language that have no shorthand equivalent in the modal language. For example, $\exists x\, L(x)$ has no short form, because of the occurrence of a variable in the argument position of an L predication.[3] In other words, our re-reading of sentences in the modal language only yields a subset of the classical language. Call a sentence *regular* if it belongs to this subset. Since the regular sentences are a proper subset of the classical language, and since every sentence described by a modal schema will correspond to a regular one, the correct re-interpretation of any modal schema will necessarily be a schema whose schematic letters range over just the regular sentences in the classical language. The correct re-reading of the schema:

$$\Box\alpha \supset \alpha \quad \text{for all sentences } \alpha \text{ in the modal language,}$$

---

[3] Recall that modal sentences may not use L (it's not a symbol in the modal language) and, as will be seen later, even formulas like $\exists x\, \Box\alpha$ will never give rise to formulas that have x in the initial argument position of L.

is, therefore, the schema:

$$L(\ulcorner\alpha\urcorner) \supset \alpha \quad \text{for all } regular \text{ sentences } \alpha \text{ in the classical language.}$$

With this as our basis, we will show that there can be syntactical treatments of modal operators of the form Quine has wished for all along.

The remainder of this paper is organized as follows. After laying down our background assumptions in the next section, we review Montague's and Thomason's results. The matter of making precise our notational games is taken up in the section following that, along with proof that the simple way of deriving syntactical treatments of arbitrary sentential operators is consistent. We are then in a position to apply this technique to the standard modal logics to obtain classical first-order logics with all of the properties one might reasonably expect. Montague's and Thomason's negative results will be seen to apply only if the modal axiom schemata are inappropriately translated into ones in which the schematic sentence letters range over the *entire* classical language. We conclude with some suggested directions for future research.

Terminology and Notation

We assume throughout that the common base language will be a first-order logical language $\mathcal{L}$ with logical symbols $\neg$, $\supset$, and $\forall$, and replete with predicate, function and constant symbols.[4] The Greek letters α, β, and γ will be used for open formulas; ϕ, ψ, and σ will stand for sentences (closed formulas); S and T will stand for sets of sentences.

$\mathcal{L}(\Box)$ will be the "modal" language obtained by augmenting $\mathcal{L}$ with the unary sentential operator $\Box$, and $\mathcal{L}(L)$ will be the classical language obtained from $\mathcal{L}$ by adding the family of $(n+1)$-ary predicate symbols L_n, for each natural number n.[5] When we aren't concerned with quantifying into modal contexts, we'll often use the symbol L as a synonym for L_0. (In a later section we will suggest how to get by with a single 2-place predicate symbol.)

For the sake of brevity, we have focussed our attention on languages with one extra unary sentential operator. There is no difficulty in adapting our techniques to sets of operators of arbitrary arities.

Because we will be considering syntactical treatments of sentential operators, we need to be precise about what this involves. As we understand Quine and Montague, such a treatment necessarily involves a predicate of sentences as notational forms. These *syntactical* predicates would be prefixed to a term that serves to name some formula (or term) in some (perhaps different) language. The only syntactical predicates that we will encounter are the L_i, which are found only in the language $\mathcal{L}(L)$. We will require that our languages have a collection of closed terms that serve as names for each of the formulas and terms of $\mathcal{L}(L)$. These terms are called the *encoding terms* for $\mathcal{L}(L)$; the encoding term corresponding to the formula α will be written $\ulcorner\alpha\urcorner$. Distinct formulas will have distinct encoding terms. Although

---

[4]Other logical symbols like $\vee$ and $\exists$ can be introduced as abbreviations in the customary manner.

[5]Quine [16] calls L a *multigrade* predicate symbol.

we place no other constraints on the encoding scheme, we do wish to point out that the kind we have in mind would *not* employ an infinite number of distinct function and constant *symbols*. This is because we wish our systems to be able to express the standard notions of *elementary syntax* [10], including the functions for forming, dissecting, and categorizing the formulas of the language being encoded.[6] The encoding scheme plays only a background role, remaining invariant throughout the presentation.

Translation functions that map formulas of one language into formulas of another play a key role in this investigation. Embeddings are one kind of translation function that are of fundamental importance.

Definition   Let $\mathcal{L}_1$ and $\mathcal{L}_2$ be languages, both of which use at least the connectives of first-order logic. A translation function $^\circ: \mathcal{L}_1 \to \mathcal{L}_2$ is an *embedding of $\mathcal{L}_1$ in $\mathcal{L}_2$* iff

(i) $^\circ$ maps atomic formulas to themselves; i.e., $\alpha^\circ = \alpha$.

(ii) $^\circ$ distributes over the connectives of first-order logic; i.e., $(\neg\alpha)^\circ = \neg\alpha^\circ$, $(\alpha \supset \beta)^\circ = \alpha^\circ \supset \beta^\circ$, and $(\forall x\, \alpha)^\circ = \forall x\, \alpha^\circ$.

(iii) α° has the same free variables as α.

In other words, an embedding is a homomorphism from $\mathcal{L}_1$ to $\mathcal{L}_2$ except that it is almost entirely unrestricted in its treatment of non-standard symbols of $\mathcal{L}_1$, such as the operator $\Box$.

The generalization of theoremhood to include modal languages is defined in terms of embeddings. For the remainder of this section, unless otherwise indicated, the source language $\mathcal{L}_1$ can be either $\mathcal{L}(\Box)$ or $\mathcal{L}(L)$, with $\phi \in \mathcal{L}_1$ and $S \subseteq \mathcal{L}_1$; the target language $\mathcal{L}_2$ will always be $\mathcal{L}(L)$.

Definition ϕ is an *extended theorem* iff for every embedding $^\circ$ of $\mathcal{L}_1$ in $\mathcal{L}(L)$, ϕ° is a theorem of first-order logic.

Clearly, if $\mathcal{L}_1$ does not contain any non-standard symbols, the only embedding possible is the identity function. The extended theorems of $\mathcal{L}(L)$ are, therefore, precisely the theorems of first-order logic.

On the other hand, ϕ is an extended theorem of the modal language $\mathcal{L}(\Box)$ iff ϕ with every subformula $\Box\beta$ replaced by any formula γ of $\mathcal{L}(L)$ with the same free variables is a theorem of first-order logic. Note, however, that not all substitution instances of theorems of first-order logic will be extended theorems. For example, while $(\forall x\, \alpha \supset \alpha(x/t))$ is a theorem of first-order logic for any α, a substitution instance of it,

$$\forall x\, \Box P(x) \supset \Box P(t),$$

---

[6]The reader will not be lead astray if he thinks of $\mathcal{L}$ as being the language of elementary number theory, $\mathcal{A}$, with non-logical symbols $=$, s (successor), $+$, $\cdot$, and 0. For a particular theory, take Robinson's finitely-axiomatized arithmetic theory **Q** [18], and understand the encoding terms to be a subset of the numerals 0, $s0$, $ss0$, etc., set in correspondence with the terms and formulas of $\mathcal{A}(L)$ via some sort of Gödel numbering scheme.

is not a theorem of quantified modal S4. Fortunately, it is not an extended theorem according to the above definition.

The notions of derivability and consistency can also be defined in a way that is compatible with first-order logic while, at the same time, being applicable to modal languages as well.

Definition ϕ is *derivable* from S (written $S \vdash \phi$) iff ϕ follows from S and the extended theorems of $\mathcal{L}_1$ by *modus ponens* alone.

Since the set of extended theorems is itself closed under *modus ponens*, $\vdash \phi$ iff ϕ is an extended theorem. Moreover, since *modus ponens* is the only rule of inference, the Deduction Theorem holds.

Definition S is *inconsistent* iff $S \vdash \phi$ for every ϕ in $\mathcal{L}_1$.

When $\mathcal{L}_1 = \mathcal{L}(L)$, these definitions coincide with the usual ones. For $\mathcal{L}(\Box)$, the above definitions automatically restrict our attention to modal systems that are "upward compatible" with first-order predicate calculus. While this immediately rules out some systems, such as intuitionistic and relevance logics, it sanctions the usual modal theories. For example, the set of theorems of quantified modal logic S5 is consistent according to the above definition. In addition, we are allowing for *very* different sorts of modal theories. Although air-tight constraints are imposed on the interpretation of the connective symbols occurring outside the scope of a $\Box$ operator, the interpretation of the $\Box$ operator itself and, therefore, everything within its scope is almost totally unconstrained. The $\Box$ operator can be made as referentially opaque as desired. For example,

$$\{\forall x \, \Box P(x), \neg \forall y \, \Box P(y)\}$$

is consistent. In this case the '$\Box$' could be read as "uses the variable 'x' freely".

Review of Montague and Thomason

The first result, due to Montague [9], sets its sights on syntactical treatments of the standard modal logics that include the axiom of necessity, such as **T**, **S4**, and **S5**. In this theorem, and the one following it, the open formula α with free variable x should be viewed as a generalization of the atomic formula $L(x)$.

Theorem 1 (Montague, Theorem 1)   Let $\mathcal{A}^+$ be a first-order language that contains at least the non-logical symbols of elementary number theory. Let T be a set of sentences of $\mathcal{A}^+$ and α a formula of $\mathcal{A}^+$ with one free variable. Suppose that the following conditions are met, for all sentences ϕ and ψ of $\mathcal{A}^+$.

  (i) $T \vdash Q$, where Q is the single axiom for Robinson's arithmetic system **Q**,

 (ii) $T \vdash \alpha(\ulcorner\phi\urcorner) \supset \phi$,

(iii) $T \vdash \alpha(\ulcorner\alpha(\ulcorner\phi\urcorner) \supset \phi\urcorner)$,

(iv) $T \vdash \alpha(\ulcorner\phi \supset \psi\urcorner) \supset (\alpha(\ulcorner\phi\urcorner) \supset \alpha(\ulcorner\psi\urcorner))$,

(v) $T \vdash \alpha(\ulcorner \phi \urcorner)$, if ϕ is a logical axiom.

Then T is inconsistent.

Proof: The proof involves a "self-referential" sentence of the form $\sigma \equiv \alpha(\ulcorner Q \supset \neg \sigma \urcorner)$, which is shown to be paradoxical. Refer to the original paper for details. ∎

From this result Montague reasons as follows:

> Now what general conclusions can be drawn from Theorems 1–4? In the first place, observe that the schemata in conditions (ii)–(v) of Theorem 1 are provable in the well-known systems of first-order modal logic with identity.... These schemata would, moreover, be provable in any reasonable extension of predicate logic of S1, the weakest of the Lewis modal calculi. Further, it is not unnatural to impose condition (i): modal logic, like ordinary logic, ought to be applicable to an arbitrary subject matter, including arithmetic....
>
> *Thus if necessity is to be treated syntactically, that is, as a predicate of sentences, as Carnap and Quine have urged, then virtually all of modal logic, even the weak system S1, must be sacrificed.* (Montague, [9, p. 294]; Italics added)

Theorem 1 obviously applies to standard approaches to idealized knowledge (e.g., Hintikka [2]), since they share the same basic axiom schemata with the modal logics. But logics of idealized belief, for which the axiom schema corresponding to condition (ii) is inappropriate, are not covered. With the close ties between knowledge and truth, and given Tarski's famous theorem [17] on the non-definability of a truth predicate,[7] one might always hope that belief predicates would not be susceptible to paradoxes of self-reference. However, as the next theorem due to Thomason [19] shows, logics of idealized belief — notably weak S5 — are also in jeopardy.

Theorem 2 (Thomason, Theorem 2)[8] Let $\mathcal{A}^+$ be a first-order language that contains at least the non-logical symbols of elementary number theory. Let T be a set of sentences of $\mathcal{A}^+$ and α a formula of $\mathcal{A}^+$ with one free variable. Suppose that the following conditions are met, for all sentences ϕ and ψ of $\mathcal{A}^+$.

(i) $T \vdash \alpha(\ulcorner \phi \urcorner) \supset \alpha(\ulcorner \alpha(\ulcorner \phi \urcorner) \urcorner)$,

(ii) $T \vdash \alpha(\ulcorner \alpha(\ulcorner \phi \urcorner) \supset \phi \urcorner)$,

(iii) $T \vdash \alpha(\ulcorner \phi \urcorner)$, if ϕ is a logical axiom,

(iv) $T \vdash \alpha(\ulcorner \phi \supset \psi \urcorner) \supset (\alpha(\ulcorner \phi \urcorner) \supset \alpha(\ulcorner \psi \urcorner))$.

Then for all sentences $\psi \in \mathcal{A}^+$,

(v) $T \vdash \alpha(\ulcorner Q \urcorner) \supset \alpha(\ulcorner \psi \urcorner)$

where Q is the single axiom for **Q**.

---

[7] In fact, Montague considered his result to be a refinement of Tarski's.

[8] With some minor changes: no relativization, sentences in place of arbitrary formulas, and a bug fix.

Proof: Similar to the proof of Montague's theorem, this proof involves a paradoxical sentence of the form $\sigma \equiv (Q \supset \alpha(\ulcorner \neg\sigma \urcorner))$. Refer to the original paper for details.   ∎

Thomason concludes:

> Though this theorem does not show T to be inconsistent, it does establish that T would become inconsistent upon the addition of $[\alpha(\ulcorner Q \urcorner)]$ and $\neg\alpha(\ulcorner \psi \urcorner)$, for any formula ψ. This seems to show a coherent theory of idealized belief as a syntactical predicate to be problematic. (Thomason, [19, p. 393])

Thus the syntactical predicate approach to knowledge and belief appears to be seriously flawed — and in a way that the operator approach is not. In what follows, we will show that these appearances are indeed deceiving and are based on a misconception of what should be required of a syntactical treatment of modality.

A Translation-Based Syntactical Treatment

In this section we will define a particular embedding * from formulas of $\mathcal{L}(\square)$ to formulas of $\mathcal{L}(L)$ and show that this mapping preserves the important property of derivability. That is, for all $T \subseteq \mathcal{L}(\square)$ and $\sigma \in \mathcal{L}(\square)$, $T \vdash \sigma$ iff $T^* \vdash \sigma^*$. We will see that * maps $\mathcal{L}(\square)$ to a subset of $\mathcal{L}(L)$. Consequently, sets of sentences arising from the proper translation of sets of modal sentences will only dictate how the predicate L should treat a subset of $\mathcal{L}(L)$, while remaining completely neutral on the rest.

The Translation Function *

We introduce a translation function from the modal language to the classical one in order to make precise the idea of reading $\square$ as shorthand for L and a pair of quotation marks.

Definition   The translation function * is defined to be the embedding of $\mathcal{L}(\square)$ in $\mathcal{L}(L)$ with the property

$$(\square\alpha)^* = L_n(\ulcorner \alpha^* \urcorner, x_1, x_2, \ldots, x_n)$$

where $x_1, x_2, \ldots x_n$ are the free variables of the formula α, listed in some predetermined, fixed order.

* is clearly 1–1, since $L_n \notin \mathcal{L}(\square)$ and distinct formulas have distinct encoding terms.

Definition $\alpha \in \mathcal{L}(L)$ is *regular* iff $\alpha = \gamma^*$ for some $\gamma \in \mathcal{L}(\square)$. In other words, the set of regular formulas is just $\mathcal{L}(\square)^*$ (see Figure 1).

Reductions

For a mapping such as * to be considered to be a reduction of the modal *operator* to a syntactical predicate, it must, at the very least, preserve derivability.

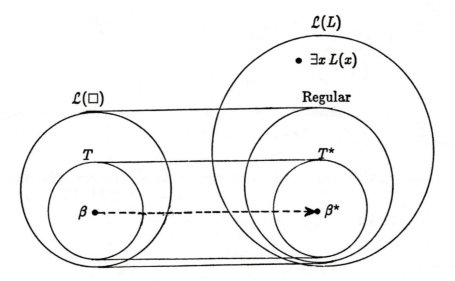

Figure 1: The Regular Formulas of $\mathcal{L}(L)$.

Definition   A translation function $^\diamond\colon \mathcal{L}_1 \to \mathcal{L}_2$ is said to be a *reduction* of $S \subseteq \mathcal{L}_1$ to $T \subseteq \mathcal{L}_2$ if, for all $\phi \in \mathcal{L}_1$,

$$S \vdash \phi \iff T \vdash \phi^\diamond.$$

Morgan's syntactic approach [12] provides a good example of how to reduce arbitrary logics to classical first-order ones. Note, however, that a reduction need not preserve any aspect of a sentence's structure. On the other hand, we are interested in the *embedding* *, which observes all of the normal connectives, mapping $\neg$ to $\neg$, $\supset$ to $\supset$, etc., and also preserves all atomic formulas. This is because, following Quine, we wish to re-interpret the $\square$ operator somehow as a predicate, but leave the rest of the modal sentence unchanged.

More generally, we are also interested in translation functions that can be used to reduce not just a single set of sentences but all such sets.

Definition   A translation function $^\diamond\colon \mathcal{L}_1 \to \mathcal{L}_2$ is said to be a *general reduction* of $\mathcal{L}_1$ to $\mathcal{L}_2$ if for every $T \subseteq \mathcal{L}_1$, $^\diamond$ is a reduction of T to $T^\diamond = \{\phi^\diamond \mid \phi \in T\}$.

Lemma 3 General reductions preserve consistency. That is, if $^\diamond$ is a general reduction of $\mathcal{L}_1$ to $\mathcal{L}_2$, then for all $T \subseteq \mathcal{L}_1$, T is consistent iff $T^\diamond$ is consistent.

Proof: $T \subseteq \mathcal{L}_1$ inconsistent $\iff U \vdash \phi$ for all $\phi \in \mathcal{L}_1 \iff T^\diamond \vdash \phi^\diamond \iff T^\diamond \vdash (\sigma \wedge \neg\sigma)^\diamond$ for all $\sigma \iff T^\diamond \vdash \sigma^\diamond \wedge \neg\sigma^\diamond \iff T^\diamond$ inconsistent.   ∎

Properties of *

Lemma 4 For any $\phi \in \mathcal{L}(\square)$, if ϕ° is satisfiable for some embedding $^\circ$ of $\mathcal{L}(\square)$ in $\mathcal{L}(L)$, then ϕ^* is also satisfiable.

Proof: If ϕ° is satisfiable, then it is satisfiable in a term model $M = (\mathcal{T}, I)$ whose domain $\mathcal{T}$ includes all of the closed terms of $\mathcal{L}(L)$. Define $M^* = (\mathcal{T}, I^*)$ be the first-order model structure for $\mathcal{L}(L)$ with domain of interpretation $\mathcal{T}$ and agreeing with M on the interpretation of all non-logical symbols except $\{L_0, L_1, \ldots\}$; i.e, let $I^*(P) = I(P)$ for each predicate symbol P of $\mathcal{L}$. For each $n \geq 0$, define

$$I^*(L_n) = \{(\ulcorner \alpha^* \urcorner, t_1, \ldots, t_n) \in \mathcal{T}^{n+1} \mid \begin{array}{l} \alpha \in \mathcal{L}(\square) \text{ with free variables } x_1, \ldots, x_n \\ \text{and } M, \nu^{x_1,\ldots,x_n}_{t_1,\ldots,t_n} \models (\square\alpha)^\circ\}\end{array}$$

We show by induction on the structure of any formula $\alpha \in \mathcal{L}(\square)$ that, for all variable assignments ν,

$$M, \nu \models \alpha^\circ \iff M^*, \nu \models \alpha^*.$$

There are five cases:

(1) α is atomic. It follows immediately from the fact that $\alpha^\circ = \alpha^*$ and that M and M^* agree on the interpretation of all predicate symbols and terms of $\mathcal{L}$ (i.e., exclusive of the L_i predicates).

(2) $\alpha = \square\beta$. Let $x_1, \ldots, x_n$ be the free variables of β.

$$\begin{aligned} M, \nu \models (\square\beta)^\circ &\iff (\ulcorner \beta^* \urcorner, \nu(x_1), \ldots, \nu(x_n)) \in I^*(L_n) \quad (\text{since } \gamma^* = \beta^* \text{ iff } \gamma = \beta) \\ &\iff M^*, \nu \models L_n(\ulcorner \beta^* \urcorner, x_1, \ldots, x_n) \\ &\iff M^*, \nu \models (\square\beta)^*. \end{aligned}$$

(3) $\alpha = \neg\beta$.

$$\begin{aligned} M, \nu \models (\neg\beta)^\circ &\iff M, \nu \models \neg\beta^\circ \\ &\iff M, \nu \not\models \beta^\circ \\ &\iff M^*, \nu \not\models \beta^* \quad \text{(by the induction hypothesis)} \\ &\iff M^*, \nu \models \neg\beta^* (= (\neg\beta)^*). \end{aligned}$$

(4) $\alpha = \beta \supset \gamma$. Similar to the preceding case.

(5) $\alpha = \forall x \beta$.

$$\begin{aligned} M, \nu \models (\forall x \beta)^\circ &\iff M, \nu \models \forall x \beta^\circ \\ &\iff M, \nu^x_t \models \beta^\circ \text{ for all } t \in \mathcal{T} \\ &\iff M^*, \nu^x_t \models \beta^* \text{ for all } t \in \mathcal{T} \quad \text{(by the induction hypothesis)} \\ &\iff M^*, \nu \models \forall x \beta^* (= (\forall x \beta)^*). \end{aligned}$$

Thus, for all $\alpha \in \mathcal{L}(\square)$ and all assignments ν,

$$M, \nu \models \alpha^\circ \iff M^*, \nu \models \alpha^*.$$

∎

Lemma 5 For all $\phi \in \mathcal{L}(\square), \vdash \phi \Longleftrightarrow \vdash \phi^\star$.

Proof: ($\Rightarrow$) If $\vdash \phi$ then ϕ is an extended theorem of $\mathcal{L}(\square)$. Therefore, by the definition of extended theorem, $\vdash \phi^\circ$ for every embedding $^\circ$ of $\mathcal{L}(\square)$ in $\mathcal{L}(L)$, of which $\star$ is included.
($\Leftarrow$) If $\nvdash \phi$ then ϕ is not an extended theorem. So, $\nvdash \phi^\circ$ for some embedding $^\circ$. By first-order completeness, $\neg\phi^\circ$ is satisfiable. By Lemma 4, $\neg\phi^\star$ must also be satisfiable. Therefore $\nvdash \phi^\star$ by first-order soundness.   ∎

Theorem 6 $\star$ is a general embedding reduction of $\mathcal{L}(\square)$ to $\mathcal{L}(L)$.

Proof: Take any $T \subseteq \mathcal{L}(\square)$ and any $\phi \in \mathcal{L}(\square)$. Then

$$
\begin{aligned}
T \vdash \phi \quad &\Longleftrightarrow \quad \vdash \sigma_1 \supset \cdots \supset \sigma_k \supset \phi \text{ for some } \sigma_1, \ldots, \sigma_k \in T \\
&\Longleftrightarrow \quad \vdash (\sigma_1 \supset \sigma_2 \supset \cdots \supset \sigma_k \supset \phi)^\star \qquad \text{(by Lemma 5)} \\
&\Longleftrightarrow \quad \vdash \sigma_1^\star \supset \sigma_2^\star \supset \cdots \supset \sigma_k^\star \supset \phi^\star \\
&\Longleftrightarrow \quad T^\star \vdash \phi^\star.
\end{aligned}
$$

Hence $\star$ is a general reduction of $\mathcal{L}(\square)$ to $\mathcal{L}(L)$.   ∎

Montague and Thomason Revisited

By Theorem 6, given any consistent set of sentences over the modal language $\mathcal{L}(\square)$ one can always reduce it using $\star$ to a consistent set of sentences of $\mathcal{L}(L)$ in which the role of the extra sentential operator is played instead by a syntactical predicate. This treatment is entirely consonant with the systematic reading of the operator $\square$ as shorthand for the multigrade predicate L and a pair of quotation marks that Quine has countenanced. Applied to a genuine modal theory such as S5, one obtains a classical first-order system that rightfully deserves to be considered as *a syntactical treatment of modality*.

But how, then, are we to reconcile this with Montague's result, which seemed to show that syntactical treatments of modality are not possible? The answer is quite simple. Notice that in conditions (ii)–(v) of Theorem 1, which are supposed to be the predicate counterparts of the modal theorem schemata $(\square\phi \supset \phi)$, $\square(\square\phi \supset \phi)$, etc., respectively, are schemata with ϕ and ψ ranging over the *entire* classical language. These conditions are overly stringent. As mentioned earlier, the correct predicate counterparts of the modal schemata are the classical schemata (ii)–(v) with ϕ and ψ ranging over *just the regular subset* of the classical language. As the following result illustrates, by restricting ϕ and ψ in conditions (ii)–(v) to be regular, the claim of inconsistency no longer follows. This means that the irregular sentences are indeed the source of any inconsistencies (a stronger claim than the simple observation that Montague's *proof* employs irregular sentences).

Non-Theorem 7 (cf. Theorem 1)   Let $\mathcal{A}^+$ be a first-order language that contains at least the non-logical symbols of elementary number theory. Let T be a set of sentences of $\mathcal{A}^+$ and α a formula of $\mathcal{A}^+$ with one free variable. Suppose that the following conditions are met, for all <u>*regular*</u> sentences ϕ and ψ of $\mathcal{A}^+$.

(i) $T \vdash Q$, where Q is the single axiom for Robinson's arithmetic system $\mathbf{Q}$,

(ii) $T \vdash \alpha(\ulcorner \phi \urcorner) \supset \phi$,

(iii) $T \vdash \alpha(\ulcorner \alpha(\ulcorner \phi \urcorner) \supset \phi \urcorner)$,

(iv) $T \vdash \alpha(\ulcorner \phi \supset \psi \urcorner) \supset (\alpha(\ulcorner \phi \urcorner) \supset \alpha(\ulcorner \psi \urcorner))$,

(v) $T \vdash \alpha(\ulcorner \phi \urcorner)$, if ϕ is a logical axiom.

Then T is inconsistent.

Counterexample: Let $S \subseteq \mathcal{A}(\square)$ consist of the theorems of the modal system **S5** together with the single axiom Q of Robinson's arithmetic. S is consistent since it is satisfiable in a suitable Kripke model with arithmetic. For $\mathcal{A}^+$ use $\mathcal{A}(L)$, for α use the open formula $L_0(\dot{x})$, and let $T = S^*$. Condition (i) holds since $Q = Q^*$ and $Q \in S$. $(\square \sigma \supset \sigma) \in S$ for every $\sigma \in \mathcal{A}(\square)$, because this is a theorem schema for **S5**. Hence $S^* \vdash L_0(\ulcorner \sigma^* \urcorner) \supset \sigma^*$ for every $\sigma \in \mathcal{A}(\square)$; i.e., $S^* \vdash \alpha(\ulcorner \phi \urcorner) \supset \phi$ for every *regular* $\phi \in \mathcal{A}(L)$. Similarly, conditions (iii)–(v) follows in virtue of the corresponding properties of **S5**. By Theorem 6, * is a general reduction, which are always consistency preserving by Lemma 3. So S^* is consistent, providing a counterexample to this slightly modified statement of Montague's theorem.   ∎

Similar considerations apply equally well to Thomason's result.

Non-Theorem 8 (cf. Theorem 2)   Let $\mathcal{A}^+$ be a first-order language that contains at least the non-logical symbols of elementary number theory. Let T be a set of sentences of $\mathcal{A}^+$ and α a formula of $\mathcal{A}^+$ with one free variable. Suppose that the following conditions are met, for all *regular* sentences ϕ and ψ of $\mathcal{A}^+$.

(i) $T \vdash \alpha(\ulcorner \phi \urcorner) \supset \alpha(\ulcorner \alpha(\ulcorner \phi \urcorner)\urcorner)$,

(ii) $T \vdash \alpha(\ulcorner \alpha(\ulcorner \phi \urcorner) \supset \phi \urcorner)$,

(iii) $T \vdash \alpha(\ulcorner \phi \urcorner)$, if ϕ is a logical axiom,

(iv) $T \vdash \alpha(\ulcorner \phi \supset \psi \urcorner) \supset (\alpha(\ulcorner \phi \urcorner) \supset \alpha(\ulcorner \psi \urcorner))$.

Then for all sentences $\psi \in \mathcal{A}^+$,

(v) $T \vdash \alpha(\ulcorner Q \urcorner) \supset \alpha(\ulcorner \psi \urcorner)$

where Q is the single axiom for $\mathbf{Q}$.

Counterexample: Use the same counterexample as in the preceding non-theorem.   ∎

Why it Works

Non-Theorems 7 and 8 indicate quite clearly that the restriction to regular sentences makes a significant difference. What is happening is this. Both Montague's and Thomason's proofs rely on the existence of fixed points for certain formulas in the language. In particular, Montague's proof requires that there be a sentence ϕ satisfying $T \vdash \phi \equiv \alpha(\ulcorner Q \supset \neg \phi \urcorner)$. The existence of such a *fixed-point* sentence ϕ follows from the Fixed-Point Theorem (a proof appears in [10]). The particular fixed point ϕ whose construction is given in his proof has the form

$$\forall x \left(x = \ulcorner \forall y \left(\delta(x,y) \supset \alpha(y) \right) \urcorner \supset \forall y \left(\delta(x,y) \supset \alpha(y) \right) \right)$$

where δ is a (regular) formula with two free variables. The important thing to note is that this ϕ is *not* a regular sentence because it contains the subformula $L(y)$ $(= \alpha(y))$. Similarly, Thomason's Theorem 2 relies on a fixed point ϕ such that $T \vdash \phi \equiv (Q \supset \alpha(\ulcorner \neg \phi \urcorner))$, and, again, the ϕ constructed would not be regular. Furthermore, *no regular sentence could be used in place of these ϕ sentences*. By restricting our attention to the regular sentences we are failing to provide axioms that apply to those fixed point sentences upon which their results hinge.

Other Considerations

Compatibility with First-Order Theories with Equality

Note that if T is a modal theory with a built-in equality predicate, it need not be the case that T^* be compatible with first-order predicate calculus with equality. In particular, T might confuse the encoding terms; e.g., $T \vdash \ulcorner \sigma^* \urcorner = \ulcorner \neg \sigma^* \urcorner$ for some σ. Then, even though $\ulcorner \sigma^* \urcorner$ and $\ulcorner \neg \sigma^* \urcorner$ are distinct encoding terms and the sentence $(\Box \sigma \wedge \neg \Box \neg \sigma)$ is consistent, T^* would be inconsistent with the full set of theorems of $=$ applied to L because $T^* \vdash L(\ulcorner \sigma^* \urcorner) \wedge \neg L(\ulcorner \neg \sigma^* \urcorner)$. To guarantee that such difficulties do not arise, a restriction must be placed on T to ensure that distinct encoding terms cannot be conflated.

Assume that the notion of extended theorem is redefined in terms of embeddings into first-order predicate calculus *with equality*, and that derivability, consistency, etc. are reinterpreted accordingly.

Definition T is *adequate* iff $T \not\vdash s = t$ for all distinct encoding terms s and t.

Robinson's arithmetic system $\mathbf{Q}$ is adequate for encoding expressions using a subset of the numerals, since $Q \vdash s \neq t$ for all distinct closed terms s and t.

Theorem 9   When restricted to adequate sets of sentences, $*$ is a general embedding reduction of $\mathcal{L}(\Box)$ to $\mathcal{L}(L)$.

Proof: A variation of Lemma 4 must be shown to hold. The restiction that ϕ be adequate is needed to ensure the existence of a model for $\phi^\diamond$ that interprets distinct encoding terms as distinct domain elements (being equivalence classes defined over the terms). Then Lemma 5 and Theorem 6 go through, *mutatis mutandis*. We will not repeat the proofs here; instead, we leave them as an exercise for the obsessed reader.   ∎

Comparison to Perlis' Truth Schema

This work has a definite tie-in to the recent work on limited truth predicates. We will discuss this briefly and mention how that has a bearing on the finite axiomatizability of syntactical treatments of knowledge and belief.

Perlis has recently argued [13] that it is overly restrictive to work within a representational framework that precludes any chance of even *expressing* a statement that is potentially paradoxical. After all, we routinely make statements about our own statments, reason about the our own reasoning and our relationship with the external world, and so forth. On occasion we may stumble into a paradox, but we usually react to it more with amusement than anything else.

Perlis has advocated working in classical first-order logic containing a syntactical predicate for truth with the ability to explicitly refer to any formula in the language. Beginning with a theory T over a language $\mathcal{L}$, he shows how to extend it to another classical first-order theory $P(T)$ over the extended language $\mathcal{L}(\text{True})$, True being the suitably-limited truth predicate for the full language $\mathcal{L}(\text{True})$. The axiom schema that is used to extend T to $P(T)$ is

$$\text{True}(\ulcorner \phi \urcorner) \equiv \phi^\circ \quad \text{for all sentences } \phi \in \mathcal{L}(\text{True}), \tag{1}$$

where ϕ° is a variant of ϕ obtained by performing certain, straightforward transformations on some of its subformulas (we need not be concerned with the details here).

Our work relates to his in the following manner. Extend Perlis' base theory T over $\mathcal{L}$ to $R(T)$ over the language $\mathcal{L}(\square)$ by adjoining all instances of the axiom schema

$$\square \phi \equiv \phi \quad \text{for all sentences } \phi \in \mathcal{L}(\square).$$

This axiom schema is obviously consistent; all it says is that $\square$ is a logical *no-op*. We can now translate $\mathcal{L}(\square)$ to $\mathcal{L}(\text{True})$ with the embedding that satisfies $(\square \phi)^\bullet$ to $\text{True}(\ulcorner \phi^\bullet \urcorner)$; i.e., $\bullet$ is a minor variation on our $*$ that assumes that there is no quantification into modal contexts. It can be shown that $R(T)^\bullet$ is a proper subtheory of $P(T)$. That is, Perlis' limited truth schema (1) includes all of the sentences that a translation-based schema would contain (i.e., all of the regular ones). Indeed, any useful truth schema should handle the regular sentences at the very least. In a sense, $R(T)^\bullet$ is a *minimal* theory, a standard by which the adequacy of other proposals such as Perlis' can be gauged. This is just as one might have expected: whereas our concern was to provide a syntactical treatment of modality without falling prey to the paradoxes of self-reference, Perlis was going after a limited form of self-reference.

Finite Axiomatizability

As Quine has pointed out in [16], a family of predicate symbols like L_i can always be reduced to a single 2-place predicate symbol L_ϵ that takes a finite sequence of variable-value pairings (i.e., an environment/a-list) as its second argument. We would revamp $*$ so that

$$(\square \alpha)^* = L_\epsilon(\ulcorner \alpha^* \urcorner, \langle \langle \ulcorner x_1 \urcorner, x_1 \rangle, \langle \ulcorner x_2 \urcorner, x_2 \rangle, \ldots, \langle \ulcorner x_n \urcorner, x_n \rangle \rangle),$$

where $x_1, x_2, \ldots x_n$ are the free variables of α.

Having a finite language is a necessary start if you are to construct a finite axiomatization, but it is clearly not sufficient. For people interested in translating standard modal theories, one must also attend to problems concerning axiom schemata. Under what circumstances can an axiom schema be replaced by a finite set of axioms? We do not have the full answer yet. However, it does appear that many of the common axiom schemata can be collapsed into single axioms. For example, the schema $\Box(\phi \supset \phi)$, when translated, could be rendered

$$\forall x \, \forall e \, \texttt{regular}(x) \supset L_e(\texttt{implies}(x,x),e),$$

where `regular` and `implies` are predicates and functions defined over sentence encodings (and easily finitely axiomatized).[9] Unfortunately, a schema like $(\Box\phi \supset \phi)$ cannot be handled exactly as above because a schematic variable appears outside the scope of any $\Box$. It would appear, however, that such schemata can be handled indirectly via a limited truth predicate, like the ones discussed above, in addition to the syntactical predicate being axiomatized. Truth predicates, as it happens, *do* have finite axiomatizations. We hope to be able to report on this at a later date.

Concluding Remarks

The spectre of inconsistency has always loomed over those research programmes which (for good reasons and bad) have attempted to formalize modalities in first-order terms. McCarthy expressed the fear as follows:

> We have not yet investigated the matter, but plausible axioms for necessity or knowledge expressed in terms of concepts may lead to the paradoxes discussed in Kaplan and Montague (1960) and Montague (1963). Our intention is that the paradoxes can be avoided by restricting the axioms concerning knowledge, and necessity of statements about necessity. The restrictions will be somewhat unintuitive as are the restrictions necessary to avoid the paradoxes of naive set theory. (McCarthy, [8, p. 146])

This research has attempted to allay these fears. It shows that any intensional operator governed by a reasonable modal theory, that is, a theory containing all the extended theorems and closed under *modus ponens*, can be treated syntactically in a simple and intuitive way. This certainly applies to (more or less) conventional logics of knowledge such as [7], but also to non-standard ones such as [4] and [5]. There is no danger of introducing inconsistency as long as the treatment does not explicitly insist on more than its modal logic counterpart. It is only those that go beyond this, for example to deal with self-reference directly, that are at risk. This, we feel, vindicates Quine and should help to dispel the erroneous impression suggested by the results of Montague and Thomason to the effect that classical first-order languages were unable to serve as the basis for logics of the modalities and the propositional attitudes, in effect *forcing* one to employ intensional logics. As our results show, predicate approaches are the more expressive of the two (or, at any rate, *not* the *less* expressive). Clearly more care is required with them in order to avoid inconsistencies, but perhaps this is a direct consequence of their greater expressive power.

---

[9]However, such sentences may not themselves be regular, and, for that reason, need not be among the sentences that are explicitly believed (or known, or whatever other propositional attitude the logic might be formalizing). An interesting open problem is to identify whether or not these irregular sentences can also be made objects of belief without causing problems.

Acknowledgements

We would like especially to thank Calvin Ostrum for bringing several relevant papers to our attention, and for making helpful suggestions on the overall structure of the paper, many of which have been adopted. Wilf LaLonde and Dave Etherington also gave us invaluable feedback on an earlier draft. This research has been supported in part by the Natural Sciences and Engineering Research Council of Canada.

References

[1] Creary, Lewis G., "Propositional Attitudes: Fregean Representations and Simulative Reasoning," *Proceedings of IJCAI-6*, Volume 1, Tokyo, 1979, 176–181.

[2] Hintikka, Jaakko, *Knowledge and Belief*, Ithaca: Cornell University Press, 1962.

[3] Konolige, Kurt, "A First-Order Formalisation of Knowledge and Action for a Multi-Agent Planning System," J.E. Hayes, D. Michie, and Y.-H. Pao (Eds.) *Machine Intelligence* **10**, Chichester: Ellis Horwood and New York: Halstead Press, 1982, 41–72.

[4] Konolige, Kurt, *A Deduction Model of Belief and its Logics*, Stanford Computer Science Report STAN-CS-84-1022, Stanford, June 1984.

[5] Lakemeyer, Gerhard, "Steps Towards a First-Order Logic of Explicit Knowledge and Belief," *these proceedings*.

[6] Levesque, Hector, "A Formal Treatment of Incomplete Knowledge Bases," FLAIR Technical Report No. 3, Fairchild, Palo Alto, 1982.

[7] Levesque, Hector, "Foundations of a Functional Approach to Knowledge Representation," *Artificial Intelligence* **23**, 1984, 155–215.

[8] McCarthy, John, "First-Order Theories of Individual Concepts and Propositions," in J.E. Hayes, D. Michie, and L.I. Mikulick (eds.), *Machine Intelligence* **9**, Chichester: Ellis Horwood and New York: Halstead Press, 1979, 129–147.

[9] Montague, Richard, "Syntactical Treatment of Modality, with Corollaries on Reflexion Principles and Finite Axiomatizability," *Acta Philosophica Fennica* **16**, 1963, 153–167. Reprinted in R. Montague, *Formal Philosophy*, New Haven: Yale University Press, 1974, 286–302.

[10] Montague, Richard, "Theories Incomparable with Respect to Relative Interpretability," *Journal of Symbolic Logic* **27**, 1962, 195–211.

[11] Moore, Robert C., "Reasoning about Knowledge and Action," SRI Technical Note 191, Menlo Park, October 1980.

[12] Morgan, Charles G., "Methods for Automated Theorem Proving in Nonclassical Logics," IEEE *Transactions on Computers* **C-25**, 8, August 1976, 852–862.

[13] Perlis, Donald, "Languages with Self-Reference I: Foundations," *Artificial Intelligence* **25**, 1985, 301–322.

[14] Perlis, Donald, *Language, Computation, and Reality*, Ph.D. dissertation, Department of Computer Science, University of Rochester, Rochester, NY, 1981. (Manuscript received from author.)

[15] Quine, Willard V.O., "Three Grades of Modal Involvement," *Proceedings of the XIth International Congress of Philosophy*, Volume 14, North-Holland, Amsterdam, 1953. Reprinted in W.V.O. Quine, *The Ways of Paradox and Other Essays, Revised and Enlarged Edition*, 158–176. *[Not referenced.]*

[16] Quine, Willard V.O., "Intensions Revisited", in P.A. French, T.E. Uehling Jr., H.K. Wettstein (eds.) *Contemporary Perspectives in the Philosophy of Language*, Minneapolis: University of Minnesota Press, 1979, 268–274.

[17] Tarski, Alfred, "Der Wahrheitsbegriff in den formalisierten Sprachen," *Studia Philosophia* **1**, 1936, 261–405. English translation: "The Concept of Truth in Formalized Languages" appears in A. Tarski, *Logic, Semantics, and Metamathematics*, Oxford, 1956.

[18] Tarski, Alfred, A. Mostowski, and R. Robinson, *Undecidable Theories*, Amsterdam, 1953.

[19] Thomason, Richmond H., "A Note on Syntactical Treatments of Modality," *Synthese* **44**, 1980, 391–395.

THE KNOWER'S PARADOX AND
REPRESENTATIONAL THEORIES OF ATTITUDES

Nicholas M. Asher
Dept. of Philosophy
Center for Cognitive
 Science
University of Texas
Austin, TX 78712

Johan A. W. Kamp
Dept. of Philosophy
Center for Cognitive
 Science
University of Texas
Austin, TX 78712

ABSTRACT

This paper is about a well-known problem concerning the treatment of propositional attitudes. Results obtained by Kaplan and Montague in the early sixties imply that certain propositional attitude theories are threatened with inconsistency. How large the variety of such theories really is has been stressed by Thomason (1980). It includes all those attitude accounts that are often referred to as "representational." We show that many non-representational theories avoid those paradoxes only so long as they refrain from incorporating certain further notions which seem as worthy of formalization as those they contain. In view of these artificial limitations that must be imposed to keep the paradoxes out, such non-representational theories offer no genuine advantage over representational alternatives. The Kaplan-Montague results therefore require a different response than has often been thought appropriate. Rather than taking refuge in a non-representational theory one should adapt the representational approach in such a way that the threat of inconsistency disappears. The paper ends with a sketch of how this might be accomplished.

INTRODUCTION

This paper is about a well-known problem concerning the treatment of propositional attitudes. Results obtained by Kaplan and Montague in the early sixties imply that certain propositional attitude theories are threatened with inconsistency. Thomason (1980) has stressed just how large the variety of such theories really is. It includes all those attitude accounts that are often referred to as "representational." The reason these results are so problematic is that representational theories of attitudes seem to enjoy some well-known advantages over non-representational accounts. We ourselves are committed to a particular type of representational theory, and so the Kaplan-Montague-Thomason results have a special urgency for us. We are unwilling to give up the advantages of a representational account, even though that might seem to be the obvious solution to the problem. We will instead make a case for a different response. That case involves two separate considerations. First, we will argue that most non-representational theories themselves do not embody a really satisfactory response to the paradoxes, since they avoid these paradoxes only so long as they refrain from incorporating certain further notions which seem as worthy of formalization as those they contain. Thus, non-representational theories offer no genuine advantage over representational alternatives. Second, we will indicate one way in which a representational account might be altered so that the threat of inconsistency is removed. We will end by showing how this alteration affects the logic of the attitudes and how it permits the study of self-referential and even paradoxical attitudes-- yielding an additional advantage for our approach.

THE KNOWER'S PARADOX AND NON REPRESENTATIONAL THEORIES

We begin by reviewing how and why the problems that Kaplan and Montague brought to light arise. The difficulty is most easily exposed -- and in fact it was first noted -- in relation to one type of representational theory, that which takes the objects of the attitudes to be sentences of its own language. That attitudes such as belief and knowledge are to be analyzed as predicates of sentences is a view which has been put forward by a number of eminent philosophers, among them Carnap and Quine. In 1963 Montague reached the surprising conclusion that this proposal has paradoxical consequences.

One of the results Montague obtained was the following. Let T be an extension of Q^{∂} (Robinson arithmetic relativized to the formula ∂ whose only free variable is u), and for any sentence ψ let $\langle\psi\rangle$ be the numeral denoting the goedel number of ψ. Suppose that for any sentences ψ, φ and some one place predicate of expressions K: (K1) $\vdash_T K(\langle\psi\rangle) \to \psi$, (K2) if ψ is a theorem of logic then $\vdash_T K(\langle\psi\rangle)$, (K3) $\vdash_T (K(\langle\psi\rangle)\ \&\ K(\langle\psi \to \varphi\rangle)) \to K(\langle\varphi\rangle)$, (K4) $\vdash_T K(\langle K(\langle\psi\rangle)\to\psi\rangle)$. Then T is inconsistent. So intuitively valid principles of epistemic logic yield a contradiction when knowledge is represented as a predicate of sentences in a language with sufficient syntactic resources. This surprising result has come to be known as the Knower Paradox.

Thomason (1980) shows that commonly accepted principles of doxastic logic lead to similar paradoxes in theories which contain a sentence predicate representing belief.[1] He also argues that

---

[1] Let $\langle\varphi\rangle$ be the standard name of φ and let 'B' be a 1 place predicate. Intuitively 'B(x)' means that A (some fixed believer) believes that x. Then the following are commonly accepted principles of doxastic logic: (B1) $B(\langle\varphi \to \psi\rangle)\ \&\ B(\langle\varphi\rangle) \to B(\langle\psi\rangle)$, (B2) if φ is a theorem of logic then $B(\langle\varphi\rangle)$, (B3) $B(\langle\varphi\rangle) \to B(\langle B(\langle\varphi\rangle)\rangle)$, (B4) $B(\langle B(\langle\varphi\rangle) \to \varphi\rangle)$. If the theory, besides containing (B1) - (B4) also contains enough machinery for talking about its own syntax, then, Thomason shows, the belief of some intuitively harmless tautologies entails the belief of any sentence whatsoever.

Montague's results not only affect those representational theories which identify the objects of the attitudes with sentences of their own language, but that they pose a threat to all representational theories. He reasons as follows: Suppose that a certain attitude, say belief, is treated as a property of "proposition-like" objects -- let us call them 'propositions' -- which are built up from atomic constituents in much the same way that sentences are. Then, Thomason observes, with enough arithmetic at our disposal we can associate in the familiar way a "goedel number" with each such object and we can mimic the relevant structural properties of and relations between such objects by explicitly defined arithmetical predicates of their goedel numbers. This goedelization of propositions can then be exploited, he argues, to derive a contradiction in much the same way as it was obtained by Montague.

Thomason stresses the importance of what he refers to as the "recursive" character of the representational objects -- by which we take him to mean the principle that propositions are built up by certain combinatorial principles from basic constituents.   From one perspective, the perspective of the believer reflecting upon the nature of his beliefs, this emphasis seems appropriate. Suppose that a person's beliefs involve representations that he himself sees as built up recursively from constituents in much the same way that sentences are. Further, suppose that he has some means for thinking about the constituent structure of representations in a sufficiently systematic and detailed way. Suppose finally that the inferences he is prepared to acknowledge as valid (and which he is consequently prepared to use in forming new beliefs from beliefs he already has) include the schemata (B1)-(B4) as well as those of classical logic.   Then he will be able to go from any apparently harmless belief to an explicitly contradictory one by faultlessly reasoning in a way that parallels the Montague-Thomason argument. At this point, such a person should feel perplexed-- no less so, in fact, than the philosopher who sets out with the idea that belief must be analyzable as a predicate of sentences and that (B1)-(B4) are valid principles for such a predicate but who then, perhaps by reading Thomason, discovers to his surprise that things just cannot be that way.

If we focus on ascriptions of belief to sentient beings from an external prespective, however, the relevance of the recursive character of representations is less obvious. In fact the implications of Montague's original results are even more damaging than Thomason's argument suggests. To derive a paradox along the lines Montague and Kaplan discovered, it suffices to exploit a belief or knowledge predicate of propositions (whatever one takes propositions to be) to define a related predicate, satisfying the same familiar epistemic or doxastic principles, on goedel numbers of sentences. There are a number of different situations in which this is possible.   Relevant factors are: (i) what machinery the theory contains for talking about the structure of its propositions and what assumptions about propositional structure it makes; (ii) the precise form in which the theory expresses the problematic epistemic or doxastic principles; and (iii) whether the theory has the means of formally representing the expression relation between sentences and propositions (i.e. the relation which holds between a proposition p and a sentence φ expressing p).   Only in rather special cases have we been able to verify that something like Thomason's 'recursiveness' assumption is essential to the argument. On the other hand, there are many situations in which the knower paradox causes trouble independently of any assumption about the recursive or compositional structure of the attitudinal objects.

This last point is related to an observation we wish to make about a familiar non-representational framework for the analysis of propositional attitudes. This is the framework provided by Montague's system of Intensional Logic, or IL, in which propositions are treated as sets of possible worlds. IL is known to be immune against the epistemic and doxastic paradoxes, and for that very reason has been thought preferable as a framework for attitude analysis. But suppose IL is enriched with enough arithmetic to permit goedelization (e.g. we add the axioms of Q to the valid sentences of the theory). Let H be some particular goedelization relation -- i.e. n stands in the relation H to the sentence φ if n is the goedel number, according to some chosen goedelization scheme, of ψ. This relation determines a second relation G between numbers and propositions, which holds between n and p if n is the goedel number of a sentence which expresses p. Semantically this relation is completely defined; i.e., its extension is fully determined in each of the models of this extended system of IL. It might therefore seem harmless to add to the given system a binary predicate to represent this relation; and to adopt as new axioms such intuitively valid sentences as a) $G(\underline{n},^\wedge\psi)$, where $\underline{n}$ is the n-th numeral and n the goedel number of ψ, b) $(\forall u)$ $(Sen(u) \rightarrow (\exists!p)$ $G(u,p))$, where 'Sen' is the arithmetical predicate which is satisfied by just those numbers which are goedel numbers of sentences, and c) $\forall p(G(\underline{n},p) \rightarrow (\check{} p \leftrightarrow \psi))$, where $\underline{n}$ and ψ are as under a). However, this addition renders the system inconsistent; for we can now define a 'truth' predicate T of goedel numbers $(T(u) = (\exists p)$ $(G(u,p)$ & $\check{} p))$ for which we can easily show that $T(\underline{n}) \leftrightarrow \psi$ is valid whenever n is the goedel number of ψ. The inconsistency then follows in the usual way.

The fact that certain semantically well-defined relations cannot be incorporated into IL shows it to be unsuitable as a general framework for philosophical analysis. Thus, it is unsuitable, in particular, as a framework for an analysis of the attitudes. This conclusion should be especially disturbing to those who favor such a theory, as the advantages it is supposed to have depend crucially on the artificial limitations to which the expressive power of IL is subject.

The impossibility of representing in IL the expression relation between propositions and the goedel numbers of the sentences expressing them has, we saw, nothing to do with the presence or absence of attitudinal predicates but arises independently, because the language contains the sentence forming operator $\check{}$. But in certain weaker systems which lack this operator, it may be precisely the presence of an attitudinal predicate, together with the familiar epistemic or doxastic principles that govern its behavior, which prevents the addition of the predicate G. In these cases G could be used to define a corresponding attitudinal predicate of numbers $(K'(n) = (\exists p)$ $(G(n,p)$ & $K(p)))$; and under suitable conditions one could show that the principles governing K also hold for K'. The contradiction then follows as in Montague (1963) or Thomason (1980).

We have argued that the emphasis on the recursive character of representational structure is appropriate when we consider the attitudinal paradoxes from the perspective of somebody who reasons about his own knowledge or beliefs. But we have also emphasized that, when we focus on certain formal theories of attitude attribution, representational structure need not be very significant, since the paradoxical results will ensue in any case as long as the theory has the means of relating the syntactic structure of its own sentences to the attitudinal objects it posits. There are, however, some theories of attitude attribution in which representational structure is a crucial ingredient in the derivation of the paradox. Consider for instance a theory containing predicates expressing structural properties and relations of the representations it posits as attitudinal objects. Thus, for instance, it might contain a 3-place predicate which holds between representations p, q and r iff r has the structure of a conjunction of p and q. Suppose that the theory contains enough set theory to guarantee the existence of arbitrary finite sequences of whatever objects are included in its universe of discourse, as well as the mathematics needed for arithmetization of syntax. Suppose further that the theory states that each representation is built up recursively from atomic constituents (i.e. that for each representation there is a sequence of representations which gives a decomposition of the representation into its constituents). Then it will be possible to give an explicit definition of the relation J which holds between a number n and a representation r iff n is the goedel number of r. In other words there will be a definable predicate $J(x, y)$ which, in any intended model for the theory, will be satisfied by n and r iff n is the goedel number of r. Using J we can explicitly define K' from K: $(\forall x)$ $(K'(x) \leftrightarrow (\exists y)$ $(J(x,y)$ & $K(y)))$. Again, if the theory already contained the principles (K1) – (K4) it will also contain the corresponding sentences with K' instead of K (this is not entirely trivial, and in fact it is not even quite correctly stated; but the claim can be substantiated). So inconsistency arises in such a theory in any case.

It should be stressed that a theory in which representational structure is able to cause this kind of havoc must contain a non trivial amount of additional machinery. It is not obvious that every representational theory should come so heavily equipped.

This is not to say of course that the "representationalists" that Thomason takes to task in his article should not be criticized. Probably most of those who have advocated a representational theory of propositional attitudes have been unaware that the seemingly innocuous machinery needed to derive the paradoxes causes the troubles that it does. Some might still happily accept this machinery as a useful component or addition to their representational views. Nevertheless, the possibility of representational theorires that are weak enough to escape the paradox should not be dismissed out of hand. Precisely what scope remains for such theories is a matter that needs further investigation.

These remarks provide a far from complete picture of what the full spectrum of attitudinal theories that succumb to the knower paradox is like. But we hope they indicate that the Knower Paradox is not confined to those representational theories that Thomason seems to have had primarily in mind. It equally affects theories that do not attribute much structure to their attitudinal objects, but which are able to express a good deal about the connection between propositions and the sentences expressing them. Only the familiar systems of epistemic and doxastic logic, in which knowledge and belief are treated as sentential operators, and which do not treat propositions as objects, seem solidly protected from the problems we have touched upon. But those systems are so weak that they can hardly serve as adequate frameworks for analyzing the attitudes. For instance there does not seem to be any plausible way of representing within such a system statements like 'Bill knows everything that Sue knows'.

If the only drawback of intensional systems were that one cannot augment them with certain intuitively well-defined predicates such as G, this by itself might not be a good enough reason for abandoning the intensional framework. However, the framework is unsatisfactory for quite different reasons as well. First, sentences which identify the objects of the attitudes with sets of possible worlds cannot be prevented (in any natural way) from entailing that replacement of the complement of an attitude attribution by a sentence logically equivalent to it always preserves correctness of the attribution. This substitution principle goes counter to some of our most deeply rooted intuitions about such attitudes as belief. Also, the way in which attitudes have thus far been formalized within IL seems fundamentally unsuitable for attitudinal and pseudo-attitudinal notions whose objects are unequivocally sentences. 'x is justified in asserting the sentence s', for instance, is intuitively as clear a concept as 'x knows that s' and as much deserving of analysis. But it can hardly be interpreted as a relation between persons and propositions; its only plausible formalization is as a relation between individuals and sentences. As the notion intuitively satisfies the principles **(K1) - (K4)**, its representation as a sentence predicate will introduce the familiar difficulties, irrespective of how other attitudes are handled. At this point the advantage IL once seemed to have over representational theories-- that of treating knowledge and belief in such a way that the familiar principles of doxastic and epistemic logic can be vindicated -- would be very much reduced if not altogether lost.

REPRESENTATIONAL THEORIES

Representational theories do not suffer from some of the drawbacks of the intensional approach. They do not, for instance, imply that attitudes are invariant under logical equivalence. But they need to find some alternative answer to the problems Montague and Thomason have pointed out.

SEMANTICS

There is, as Montague's work made plain, an intimate connection between the Knower Paradox and the Liar Paradox -- in fact both are instances of some more general pattern. In the light of this it is worth noting that the two paradoxes have led to rather different responses. In principle it is possible to deal with the Liar Paradox by treating truth as a sentential operator, or, alternatively, as a property of sets of possible worlds. Such a treatment would be the natural analogue of the operator approach and the intensional approach to knowledge and belief, but it is completely trivial and consequently has had few if any serious proponents. Instead, the Liar Paradox has led to developments in quite different directions. Tarski proposed as a remedy an infinite hierarchy of increasingly powerful languages, each next one containing a truth predicate for its predecessor, while none contains such a predicate for itself. This move blocks the semantic paradoxes; but it has been felt to be unduly restrictive as it also eliminates the possibility of forming any sentences that speak about their own truth or falsity. A reluctance to throw out all sorts of "semantic" self-reference for the sake of consistency has led more recently to a very different approach, that of Kripke (1975), Gupta (1982), and Herzberger (1982) among others. This approach treats truth as a predicate of sentences and freely permits self reference; but its semantics is partial. The effect is that all the 'good' sentences, including the sound self-referential ones, end up with a definite truth value, while the Liar Sentence and other truly paradoxical sentences do not. This approach has proved fruitful and illuminating in connection with truth. We believe that it also holds considerable promise in relation to the attitudes.

A parallel treatment of the attitudes, however, is considerably more complicated. While truth is an extensional notion -- in the sense that the truth value of 'it is true that φ' is determined by the truth value of φ -- knowledge and belief are not. In fact we have argued these attitudes are not even intensional: φ and ψ may have the same intension while 'x believes that φ' and 'x believes that ψ' differ in truth value. This is one of the reasons for abandoning efforts to analyze the attitudes in strictly intensional terms.

Indeed the kind of analysis we prefer uses the framework of discourse representation theory. It would be free of the inadequacies of intensional semantics.[2] But to develop that analysis here would require far more explanation and justification than we have room for. We have therefore adopted a more traditional framework, familiar since the work of Hintikka (1962), in which knowledge and belief are characterized in terms of possible worlds. In this approach the knowledge (beliefs) of a person a at a world w is (are) represented by a set $W_{K,a}(w)$ ($W_{B,a}(w)$) of possible worlds, the set of all worlds compatible with the totality of a's knowledge (beliefs) in w. In the extant versions of this analysis, the sets $W_{K,a}(w)$ and $W_{B,a}(w)$ determine the truth values of knowledge and belief reports at w in a way familiar from modal logic; for instance, 'a knows that φ' is true at w iff φ is true in all worlds in $W_{K,a}(w)$.

Once the object language countenances self-referential reports, however, the formula for determining the truth values of attitude reports ceases to be self-evident. Just as there is a problem about the truth value of the liar sentence even when all the relevant facts are established, so there remains a problem about the truth values of some knowledge and belief reports, even after all facts, including those about the subject's knowledge and beliefs, have been determined. So, if we think of

---

[2]For a discussion of some of these issues, see Kamp (1985), Asher (forthcoming).

$W_{B,a}(w)$ as determining all the facts about a's beliefs at w, there will still be a problem about which self-referential belief reports about a are true at w. Our problem, then, will be to determine, for any possible world structure W with alternativeness relations for knowledge and belief, what in each world of W are the extensions for the knowledge and belief predicates, K and B.

As in similar analyses of the concept of truth that have inspired our work, we must expect the extensions of K and B to be essentially partial. In particular, the truly paradoxical attitude reports, such as the "knower sentence" which says of itself that its negation is known, should come out as neither definitely true nor definitely false. A judicious analysis, however, will succeed in assigning many other sentences, including some that contain elements of self-reference a truth value. There exist two quite different ways for arriving at such partial extensions: the first due to Kripke (1975), the second due to Herzberger (1982) and Gupta (1982). We will follow here the Herzberger-Gupta method. This method uses only classical, bivalent extensions but incorporates a process of repeated revision. Only the elements which from some point in the sequence of revisions onwards remain inside the predicate's extension count as definitely in the extension of the predicate. We have no absolutely compelling argument for our choice of the Herzberger Gupta strategy, but we think it has a number of advantages, some already discussed in Gupta and some others which we will detail below.

From these informal remarks, it ought to be fairly clear what our semantics for knowledge and belief will be like. So the formal definitions below will hold few surprises. We follow the familiar practice of representing the worlds compatible with all of a's knowledge in w by means of an "alternativeness" relation $R_{K,a}$; $w R_{K,a} w'$ iff w' is compatible with the totality of a's knowledge in w. We shall write '[wR]' to denote the set of all w' such that wRw'. Our object language will be a first order language L which contains two two-place predicates K and B. $K(x,y)$ is to be read as 'x knows that y' and $B(x,y)$ as 'x believes that y'. Our models for L are of the form $\langle W, D, [\![ ]\!], \{R_{K,a}\}_{a \in A}, \{R_{B,a}\}_{a \in A}\rangle$, where: (i) W is a set of worlds; (ii) D is a function that assigns to each $w \in W$ a non empty set; D_w is called the *universe* of w; (iii) $\mathfrak{M}$ has a *fixed universe*, i.e., for all $w, w' \in W$, $D_w = D_{w'}$; (iv) $A \subseteq D_w$; (v) $[\![ ]\!]$ is a function which assigns to each non logical constant of L a classical extension at each world; thus if c is an individual constant of L, $[\![c]\!]_w$ is a member of D_w, and if Q is an n-ary predicate $[\![Q]\!]_w \subseteq D_w^n$; (vi) each individual constant c is *rigid* in $\mathfrak{M}$; i.e., for all $w, w' \in W$ in $\mathfrak{M}$, $[\![c]\!]_w = [\![c]\!]_{w'}$; (vii) $\mathfrak{M}$ is *sentence complete*; i.e., every sentence of L is included in the fixed universe of $\mathfrak{M}$.

Such models appear to provide two different means for determining, at any world w, the truth value of sentences of the forms $K(a, \varphi)$ and $B(a, \varphi)$. On the one hand, the model theory for predicate logic implies that $B(a, \varphi)$ is true in $\mathfrak{M}$ at w iff $\langle a, \varphi \rangle \in [\![B]\!]_{\mathfrak{M},w}$. On the other hand, given that $B(a, \varphi)$ is intended as 'a believes that φ', the sentence should be true just in case φ is true at all $w' \in [wR_{B,a}]$. Ideally it should not matter which means we choose; the extension of B should correctly reflect the beliefs a has at w, as determined via the relations $R_{B,a}$. So it ought to be that

(1) For every sentence ψ and world w $\langle a, \psi \rangle \in [\![B]\!]_{\mathfrak{M},w}$ iff ψ is true at all $w' \in [wR_{\mathfrak{M},B,a}]$.

We shall call L-models *doxastically coherent* iff (1) holds. Similarly, we shall say that a model $\mathfrak{M}$ is *epistemically coherent* iff (2) holds in M:

(2) For every sentence ψ and world w $\langle a, \psi \rangle \in [\![K]\!]_{\mathfrak{M},w}$ iff ψ is true at all $w' \in [wR_{\mathfrak{M},K,a}]$.

In general, coherence is more than we can hope for. There are many models in which we find worlds w such that $[\![B]\!]_w$ and $[\![K]\!]_w$ conflict with what is true at the members of $[wR_{K,a}]$ and $[wR_{B,a}]$.

For instance, it can happen that for some sentence φ of L $\langle a, \varphi \rangle \in \llbracket B \rrbracket_w$ but that for some w' such that $wR_{B,a}w'$, φ is false at w'. What are we to say in this situation about the truth or falsity at w of the report 'a believes that φ'?

Before we discuss this question, let us simplify matters by considering the special case where the set A consists of a single agent a. We assume that in each model $\mathfrak{M}$ we consider, a is named by the constant $\underline{a}$ ($a = \llbracket \underline{a} \rrbracket$ in $\mathfrak{M}$), and we shall abbreviate 'K($\underline{a}$, φ)' and 'B($\underline{a}$, φ)' to 'K(φ)' and 'B(φ)'.[3] Moreover, we will confine our attention in what follows to the predicate B and ignore K and the corresponding alternativeness relation $R_{K,a}$. We will denote the alternativeness relation $R_{B,a}$ simply by 'R'. All that we will say from here on about belief also applies to knowledge.

To return to the situation just described, it evidently does not involve a doxastically coherent model, and there is no one unequivocally right answer to the question we have asked. The answer we shall give stems in part from the motivation we gave for our models $\mathfrak{M}$. We already adopted the view that the alternativeness relations determine whatever facts there are about a's beliefs. So if there is a conflict between $\llbracket B \rrbracket$ and R, it is the former we should regard as misrepresenting the true state of affairs and thus in need of adjustment. The obvious formula for this is,

(3) $\llbracket B \rrbracket_w = \{ \varphi : (\forall w' \in [wR]) \, \varphi \text{ is true in } w' \}$.

But (3) only brings us back to the original question: if φ is of the form 'B(c)', what is it for φ to be true at w'? The seemingly sensible suggestion that the R alternatives of w' provide the answer leads to an infinite regress for precisely the sentences that we are most interested in here. Suppose for instance that the constant b denotes in $\mathfrak{M}$ the sentence $\neg$B(b); b says that a does not believe it. Let us call such a sentence the "believer sentence." Should b $\in \llbracket B \rrbracket_w$? According to R, that will be so just in case b-- that is $\neg$B(b)-- holds in every w' $\in [wR]$. But whether b is true in w' reduces to the question of whether b fails in some w'' $\in [w'R]$, and so on. Evidently, this strategy for evaluation leads nowhere in such cases. The policy we will adopt instead, a direct analogue of that followed by Herzberger and Gupta, is to evaluate sentences at a world using the extension of the belief predicate.

The effect of this decision may be, of course, that the adjustment given by (3) will not be definitive. For instance, it may alter the extension of B, and with it the truth value of φ, at worlds w' $\in [wR]$; consequently, the extension of B at w may be out of sync once again. One might hope that further adjustments will lead eventually to coherence. But, as with truth, there are situations in which such harmony is never achieved. As we will see shortly, this is so in particular for truly paradoxical sentences such as the sentence b above. Another, weaker hope one might have is that those sentences that get "settled," i.e., which do not move in and out of the extension of B any more once a certain number of adjustments have occurred, get settled already after a finite number of adjustments. This would make our task easier, since we would not have to contemplate transfinite sequences of corrections. But, again as with the parallel theories of truth, there are ways of carrying the adjustment procedure past limit ordinals, and when those are added one finds that certain sentences only get settled at some transfinite stage.

Unfortunately, there are different ways of carrying the adjustment process past limit ordinals which lead to different continuations at subsequent ordinals but between which it is difficult to choose. We have adopted a clause that minimizes the positive extension of B at limit ordinals; it is in essence the intensional analogue of the clause adopted by Herzberger (1982). This clause will prevent all

---

[3]We will almost always ignore the distinction between objects and the constants denoting them. In the last sentence above this would have meant using the metalinguistic symbol 'a' to refer to the agent a and to the constant $\underline{a}$ of L that denotes a. No confusion should, we hope, arise from this practice.

paradoxical sentences, such as the believer sentence, from being stably true (i.e. true at a world w in $\mathfrak{M}$ for all γ in excess of some ordinal β).[4]

We thus arrive at the following definition. Given any model $\mathfrak{M}$ we define for each ordinal α the model $\mathfrak{M}^\alpha$, where $\mathfrak{M}^\alpha = \langle W_\mathfrak{M}, D_\mathfrak{M}, R_\mathfrak{M}, [\![\,]\!]^\alpha \rangle$, $[\![Q]\!]^\alpha = [\![Q]\!]_\mathfrak{M}$ for all nonlogical constants Q other than B, and $[\![B]\!]^\alpha$ is defined as follows:

i) $[\![B]\!]^0_w = [\![B]\!]_w$

ii) $[\![B]\!]_w{}^{\alpha+1} = \{\varphi: \forall w'(wRw' \to [\![\varphi]\!]_{\mathfrak{M}^\alpha,w'} = 1)\}$

iii) For limit ordinal α, $[\![B]\!]_w{}^\alpha = \{\varphi: (\exists\beta{<}\alpha)(\forall\gamma)(\beta{\leq}\gamma{<}\alpha \to \varphi \in [\![B]\!]_w{}^\gamma)\}$

The adjustment procedure defined above for $[\![B]\!]_w$ reflects the idea that the (initial) extensions of B should be seen as secondary. From this perspective it is natural to consider, besides models for L, what we shall call *model structures*. Model structures are like models except that they do not assign extensions to the predicate B. Thus, a model structure $\mathcal{M}$ can be turned into a model by extending $[\![\,]\!]_\mathcal{M}$ so that it interprets B as well. In general there is more than one way of turning a model structure into a model. We say that a model structure is *essentially incoherent* if every model that can be obtained from it is incoherent.

So far we have not given any of our reasons for adopting the revision method of Herzberger and Gupta rather than the substantially different strategy of Kripke (1975). Some of these have to do with formal advantages that we see in the Herzberger-Gupta approach, w;hich we do not yet have the technical tools to describe. But there is also a conceptual motive that underlies our choice, and this seems a good place to explain what it is.

Until now we have spoken of the problem how the truth values of self-referential sentences should be determined from what might be called an external perspective. We assumed that there was a determinate set of facts concerning the subject's beliefs and asked what, in the light of those facts, could be said about the truth values of certain self-referential belief to that subject. But besides this external point of view there is also an internal perspective on the issue, and it is from that perspective, we feel, that some of the puzzling features of paradoxical self-reference are most clearly visible. The internal perspective is that of a subject who wonders whether he should regard a certain self-referential sentence as true or should regard himself as knowing or believing it. In reflecting upon such a question, the subject is easily led to engage in hypothetical reasoning of the form: 'suppose φ were true. Then that would mean...' Sometimes the outcome of such a deduction is a conclusion that contradicts the assumption from which it starts and this conclusion can then serve as the point of departure for a similar bout of reasoning that produces a new conclusion that contradicts the first and so on. In this way the subject finds himself driven from one answer to the question he posed himself to the opposite answer, and back again. The conclusion that he is likely to draw from all this-- that

---

[4]A perhaps more plausible alternative, given the lack of arguments pointing towards one of these possibilities for revision at limit ordinals, is to allow all of them. Each of these schemes is available at each limit ordinal. In this way we get, starting from a given model $\mathfrak{M}$, not a linear hierarchy of models $\mathfrak{M}^\alpha$ but a branching structure. The definitely believed sentences, according to such a model, would then be those which settle into the extension of B along every branch of the structure, and the definitely not believed sentences those that fall outside the extension of B along every branch. We will, however, refrain from working out that alternative here.

there really is no definite answer to be found-- derives from his awareness that every answer one might want to give would lead to its contradictory and thus be inherently unstable.

We see this process of rationally driven revision as a crucial feature of paradoxical self-reference. For this reason we prefer the method of Gupta and Herzberger, which we believe captures some of the essential features of this process. Kripke's method, in contrast, offers no explication of this aspect of self-referential sentences at all. At best it can be said to offer a plausible account of the way in which we settle the truth values of what Kripke himself has called the *grounded* sentences, sentences which do contain occurrences of the relevant predicate (for Kripke this is of course the truth predicate) but which are not self-referential that their evaluation never leads us back to the question of their own truth or falsity.

TYPES OF MODEL COHERENCE AND SELF-REFERENCE

While some models become coherent after one or more revisions, others do not. For the remainder of this paper, we will look into some of the questions relating to coherence. Which models can be turned into coherent ones? How many iterations are necessary before coherence is reached? Which sentences get settled and which do not? And finally what are the "logics" of knowledge and belief that coherent and incoherent models determine?

There are three distinct factors that determine whether a model $\mathfrak{M}$ becomes coherent after revision (i.e., whether $\mathfrak{M}^\alpha$ is coherent for some ordinal α): (i) the forms of self-reference that are realized in $\mathfrak{M}$, (ii) the constraints on the alternativeness relation $R_{\mathfrak{M}}$ (i.e., whether $R_{\mathfrak{M}}$ is transitive, etc.), (iii) the initial intension $[\![B]\!]^0$. The role of each of these factors will become clear as we look in detail at the effects of the revision in some particular cases.

But first a general remark about forms of self-reference. There are essentially two semantic mechanisms by means of which self-reference can arise, naming and quantification. Quantification always produces self-reference in our models. For every quantifier includes in its range the set of all sentences, and thus in particular the sentence in which it occurs. Consequently, there exist model structures that are essentially incoherent. For we can always select certain predicates of L to play the role of those syntactic predicates that are sufficient for the construction along Goedelian lines of sentences, which on the intended interpretation of their predicates can be paradoxical. In this way, we could, for instance, formulate a version φ of the believer sentence. If M is a model structure in which the syntactic predicates get their intended interpretations and in which some reasonable conditions are placed on the alternativeness relation, then in no model $\mathfrak{M}$ obtainable from M will φ ever settle at any world w-- i.e., for every ordinal α there are $\beta, \gamma > \alpha$ such that $\varphi \in [\![B]\!]_w^\beta$ iff $\varphi \notin [\![B]\!]_w^\gamma$. Thus, $\mathfrak{M}$ is essentially incoherent.

Quantificational self-reference is a subject about which we have little of importance to say in this paper. It is an extremely important topic but much too complex to handle here. We do want to look closely into the other variety of self-reference which arises through naming. But to study this other kind of self-reference, we must eliminate all possible interference from self-reference of the quantificational sort. There are several ways in which this can be done. Given our aims, it is immaterial which we choose. The one we have adopted is to restrict attention to those sentences of L in which all quantifiers are restricted by the formula $\neg S(u)$, and to those model structures and models in which for all w $[\![S]\!]_w$ is the set of L sentences and $[\![B]\!]_w \subseteq [\![S]\!]_w$.

As Kripke (1975) was the first to make fully explicit, self-reference may arise because a certain name designates a sentence in which it itself occurs. The model theoretic counterpart of this situation is that where a certain constant c denotes in a given model $\mathfrak{M}$ a sentence that contains c. We will refer to this type of reference as *designative* self-reference, and we will concentrate for most of the remainder of this section on models in which such self-reference arises. We will be largely preoccupied, moreover, with looking at one particular instance of designative self-reference, that of the believer sentence, in the form in which it was first given on p. 9 above. Although the results we will obtain for this sentence depend to some extent on special properties that it has, we hope they will give the reader some idea of what may be expected in connection wih other cases of designative self-reference.

Two very simple examples of designative self-reference in a model $\mathfrak{M}$ are exhibited by the following assignments to the constants b and c: (i) $[b]_{\mathfrak{M}} = \neg B(b)$ (i.e., b denotes the believer sentence), (ii) $[c]_{\mathfrak{M}} = B(c)$. To get an impression of how such sentences fare under iterated revision, let us consider models in which they constitute the only cases of designative self-reference. We shall first concentrate just on the believer sentence. Let M be a model structure such that (a) (i) holds, (b) for every individual constant $d \neq b$, $[d]_M$ is not a sentence of L. Given what b denotes in M we might expect that M cannot be turned into a coherent model. Propositions (1) – (3) show that this is generally, though not invariably, true.

<u>Proposition 1</u>: Suppose R_M is transitive and (ii) $(\exists w \in W_M)$ $([wR_M] \neq \emptyset$ & $(\forall w' \in [wR_M])$ $[w'R_M] \neq \emptyset$. Then M is essentially incoherent.

The proof, though simple, is instructive in that one can see how b behaves under revision. Suppose $\mathfrak{M}$ is any model obtained from M, and suppose that $\mathfrak{M}$ is coherent. Let w be a world such that ($[wR_M]$ $\neq \emptyset$ & $(\forall w' \in [wR_M])$ $[w'R_M] \neq \emptyset$. There are two possibilities. a) $b \in [B]_{\mathfrak{M},w}$. Then $\forall w' \in [wR]$ $\mathfrak{M} \vDash_{w'} b$. So since b is the sentence $\neg B(b)$, $\forall w' \in [wR]$ $b \notin [B]_{w'}$. $[wR] \neq \emptyset$. So let $w' \in [wR]$. Since $b \notin [B]_{w'}$ there is a $w'' \in [w'R]$ such that it is not the case that $\mathfrak{M} \vDash_{w''} b$. So $b \in [B]_{w''}$. Since R is transitive, $w'' \in [wR]$, which contradicts that $b \in [B]_{w''}$. b) Now suppose that $b \notin [B]_{w}$. Then there is a $w' \in [wR]$ such that it is not the case that $\mathfrak{M} \vDash_{w'} b$. So $b \in [B]_{w'}$. So $(\forall w'' \in [w'R])$ $\mathfrak{M} \vDash_{w''} b$. $[w'R] \neq \emptyset$, so let $w'' \in [w'R]$. Then $\mathfrak{M} \vDash_{w''} b$, and so $b \notin [B]_{w''}$. So there is a $w''' \in [w''R]$ such that it is not the case that $\mathfrak{M} \vDash_{w'''} b$. But since R is transitive, $w''' \in [w'R]$ and so $\mathfrak{M} \vDash_{w'''} b$, which is a contradiction.

<u>Proposition 2</u>: Suppose M is essentially incoherent. Then condition (ii) of proposition 1 holds.

Since the transitivity of the alternativeness relation is standardly assumed in semantics for doxastic logic, there is a point to combining propositions 1 and 2:[5]

Proposition 3: Suppose R is transitive. Then M is essentially incoherent iff M satisfies the condition (ii) of proposition 1.

We need just a little more machinery to state some results concerning how the believer sentence and other paradoxical sentences drift in and out of the extensions of B. These results are interesting, at least in part because they do not depend on the initial extensions of B. Define the *b-profile at a world w in* M to be the set of ordinals Γ such that for each $\alpha \in \Gamma$, $b \in [\![B]\!]^\alpha_{M,w}$. Similarly, for any set of ordinals β, the *b-profile at w in* M *on* β is the intersection of the b-profile at w in M and β. We also need to define more precisely certain forms of designative self-reference. Let $<_M$ be the transitive closure of the relation that holds between two constants c and d iff c names in M a sentence containing d. We will define M to be *non-self-referential* iff $<_M$ is well founded. Otherwise, M is *self-referential*. Moreover if C is a set of individual constants and $<_M\upharpoonright C$ is not well founded, then we say C is *self-referential in* M. A set of sentences S is *self-referential in* M iff there is a set of individual constants C such that: (i) C is self-referential in M, (ii) each member of C denotes in M a member of S, and (iii) C contains a designator for each sentence in S.

We can predict the character of some models for L without reference to either the initial intension of B or the alternativeness relation: we can extend the main proof in Gupta (1982) to show that every non-self-referential model M is coherent. This is true regardless of the type of alternativeness relation or initial intension for B in M.

For self-reflexive models even of a very simple kind, however, we need to have at least some information concerning the character of the alternativeness relation to make some concrete predictions.

Proposition 4: Suppose that M is a model such that: (i) $[\![b]\!]_M = \neg B(b)$; (ii) no constant other than b denotes a sentence in M; (iii) R_M is transitive. Then for any $w \in W_M$ the b-profile at w in M on ω is one of the following: (i) $\varnothing$, (ii) the even natural numbers, (iii) the odd natural numbers, and (iv) ω. Moreover, (iv) arises only if $[wR] = \varnothing$.

---

[5] We have not at this point been able to supply a condition on R which is both necessary and sufficient for the essential incoherence of M. A necessary condition for essential incoherence that is relevant to cases where R is not transitive as well as to cases where it is, is that the inverse of R_M be not well-founded. But this condition is not sufficient as the following model structure in which R is indeed not-well-founded shows. Let M be a model structure with the properties (a) and (b) and which is such that $W_M = \{w_0, w_1\}$ and R_M is the relation $\{\langle w_0, w_1\rangle, \langle w_1, w_0\rangle\}$. Let M be a model obtained from M by adding $[\![B]\!]_{w_0}$ and $[\![B]\!]_{w_1}$ such that $b \in [\![B]\!]_{w_0}{}^0$ and $b \notin [\![B]\!]_{w_1}{}^0$ or $b \notin [\![B]\!]_{w_0}{}^0$ and $b \in [\![B]\!]_{w_1}{}^0$. Then M will be coherent and thus M not essentially incoherent. When we generalize from this last example, we come to appreciate that a condition on R that is both necessary and sufficient for essential incoherence could not be very simple. To appreciate this observe that while the model structure we just defined is not essentially incoherent, a similar model structure with three worlds w_1, w_2, w_3 and an alternativeness relation consisting of the pairs $\langle w_1, w_2\rangle$, $\langle w_2, w_3\rangle$, $\langle w_3, w_1\rangle$ is essentially incoherent. This oddity generalizes to all odd and even loops: if R_M contains a loop with an odd number of elements then it is essentially incoherent; on the other hand, if R_M consists only of loops with even number of elements then M is not.

Proof: Assume first that R is serial-- i.e., $\forall w\ [wR] \neq \varnothing$. Suppose $w \in W$. We distinguish the following cases.

$\quad$ (a) $(\forall w_1 \in [wR])(\exists w_2 \in [w_1R])\ b \in [\![B]\!]_{w_2}{}^0$.

Then $b \notin [\![B]\!]_{w'}{}^1$ for all $w' \in [wR] \cup \{w\}$. From this and the seriality of R, it follows that for $n \geq 2$ and $w' \in [wR]\ b \in [\![B]\!]_{w'}{}^n$ iff n is even. So in particular the b-profile at w on ω is the set of even numbers.

$\quad$ (b) $(\exists w_1 \in [wR])(\forall w_2 \in [w_1R])\ b \notin [\![B]\!]_{w_2}{}^0$.

Let w_1 be such a member of $[wR]$. Then for each $w' \in [w_1R] \cup \{w_1\}$, $b \in [\![B]\!]_{w'}{}^1$. By an argument similar to that in (a), $b \in [\![B]\!]_{w'}{}^n$ iff n is odd. Since $w_1 \in [wR]$, this implies that if n is even, $b \notin [\![B]\!]_w{}^n$. To make further progress, we divide (b) into two subcases:

$\quad$ (b.1) $(\exists w_1 \in [wR])(\forall w_2 \in [w_1R])\ b \in [\![B]\!]_{w_2}{}^0$.

Let w_1 be as assumed. Then $(\forall w_2 \in [w_1R] \cup \{w_1\})\ (b \in [\![B]\!]_{w_2}{}^n \leftrightarrow n$ is even$)$. Again because $w_1 \in [wR]$, $b \notin [\![B]\!]_w{}^n$, if n is odd. By what we have already seen under (b), this implies that the b-profile on ω at w in $\mathfrak{M}$ is $\varnothing$.

$\quad$ (b.2) $(\forall w_1 \in [wR])(\exists w_2 \in [w_1R])\ b \notin [\![B]\!]_{w_2}{}^0$.

This case requires yet another bifurcation.

$\quad$ (b.2.i) $(\exists w_1 \in [wR])(\forall w_2 \in [w_1R])\exists w_3 \in [w_2R])\ b \in [\![B]\!]_{w_3}{}^0$.

Then if w_1 is as assumed, we conclude as under (a) that for each $w' \in [w_1R] \cup \{w_1\}$ $(b \in [\![B]\!]_{w'}{}^n$ iff n is even$)$. This holds in particular for w_1, and as $w_1 \in [wR]$, we conclude that b cannot belong to $[\![B]\!]_w{}^n$ when n is odd. So in this case the b-profile at w on ω is again $\varnothing$.

$\quad$ (b.2.ii) $(\forall w_1 \in [wR])(\exists w_2 \in [w_1R])(\forall w_3 \in [w_2R])\ b \notin [\![B]\!]_{w_3}{}^0$.

Then for each $w_1 \in [wR]$ there is a w_1' such that for all $w'' \in [w_1'R] \cup \{w_1'\}$ $(b \in [\![B]\!]_{w''}{}^n$ iff n is odd$)$. Consequently, for every $w_1 \in [wR]\ b \notin [\![B]\!]_{w_1}{}^n$ for even n, and so $b \in [\![B]\!]_w{}^n$ when n is odd. So the b-profile at w on ω consists of all the odd natural numbers.

If we drop the assumption that R is serial on W, we must also consider w such that $[wR] = \varnothing$ and w such that $(\exists w' \in [wR])\ w'R = \varnothing$. These give us $\varnothing$ and ω as b-profiles. This completes the proof.

It is not difficult to extend the result of proposition 4 so that it covers the full b-profile. Because of our clause for limit ordinals b (and any other paradoxical sentence) is never in $[\![B]\!]_w{}^\lambda$ for λ a limit ordinal and for all $w \in W$. So we immediately conclude that for any limit ordinal λ, the b-profile at w in $\mathfrak{M}$ on $(\lambda + \omega) \setminus \lambda$ is one of the sets: $\varnothing$, $(\lambda + \omega) \setminus \lambda$, $\{\lambda + 2n + 1 : n \in \omega\}$. Indeed, we have:

Proposition 5: Suppose that $\mathfrak{M}$ is as in proposition 4. Then for any limit ordinal λ and natural number n:

$\quad$ (i) if $[wR] = \varnothing$, then $b \in [\![B]\!]_w{}^{\lambda + n}$

$\quad$ (ii) if $(\exists w_1 \in [wR])\ [w_1R] = \varnothing$, then $b \notin [\![B]\!]_w{}^{\lambda + n}$

$\quad$ (iii) if $[wR] \neq \varnothing$ and $\neg(\exists w_1 \in [wR])\ [w_1R] = \varnothing$, then $b \in [\![B]\!]_w{}^{\lambda + n}$ iff n is even.[6]

---

[6] When R is not transitive, the b-profiles cannot be described in nearly such simple terms.

It is instructive to compare the behavior of the paradoxical believer sentence with the harmlessly self-referential c. Suppose that M is a model structure in which $[\![c]\!]_M = B(c)$ and all other constants denote non-sentences in M. Then if R is transitive, any model $\mathfrak{m}$ obtained from M will be coherent after one revision-- i.e., the coherent model will be $\mathfrak{m}^1$. If R is not transitive, there is no guarantee that coherence will be achieved that quickly; but it will be reached eventually. It should be noted that although c is not paradoxical, it is not a *grounded* sentence either in the sense of Kripke (1975). This implies that c's truth value cannot be determined without reference to the initial extensions of B. Indeed we find that in all but a few marginal cases, the model structure M does not determine the truth value of c: we can always turn M into two different models $\mathfrak{m}_1$ and $\mathfrak{m}_2$ for each w, so that in $\mathfrak{m}_1$ c is true at w while in $\mathfrak{m}_2$ it is false at w.

The results obtained in this section so far are all quite easily established. It appears to be much more difficult to arrive at an equally detailed understanding of the behavior under revision of more complicated cases of designative self-reference. The only general result we are in a position to state as a theorem here uses rather strong constraints on the alternativeness relation. Before we can state this result, however, we must introduce a few more concepts. Suppose that $\mathfrak{m}$ is a model and that the set C of constants is self-referential in $\mathfrak{m}$. We say that C *is simply self-referential* in $\mathfrak{m}$ iff each c ∈ C denotes in $\mathfrak{m}$ a boolean combination of sentences each one of which either (a) is of the form B(d) with d ∈ C or (b) does not contain B. For any set of constants C of L, model $\mathfrak{m}$ and w ∈ $W_\mathfrak{m}$, the *C-characteristic of* w *in* $\mathfrak{m}$ is the function f: C → {0,1} such that for c ∈ C f(c) = 1 iff c ∈ $[\![B]\!]_{\mathfrak{m}, w}$. By the C-*profile at* w *in* $\mathfrak{m}$ we understand the function defined on the class of all ordinals which maps each ordinal α onto the C-characteristic of w in $\mathfrak{m}^\alpha$. Similarly, if β is a set of ordinals then the C-*profile at* w *on* β *in* $\mathfrak{m}$ is the restriction to β of the C-profile at w in $\mathfrak{m}$.

Proposition 6: Suppose that $\mathfrak{m}$ is a model, C a finite set of constants that is simply referential in $\mathfrak{m}$ and that $R_\mathfrak{m}$ is transitive, serial and euclidean (i.e., $(\forall w_1, w_2, w_3)((w_1Rw_2 \& w_1Rw_3) \to w_2Rw_3)$). Then there are natural numbers n and m such that for each w ∈ $W_\mathfrak{m}$ the C-profile at w on ω in $\mathfrak{m}$ is *cyclical after* n *with period* m; that is, if r ≥ n and s = k.m + r then the C-characteristic at w in $\mathfrak{m}^s$ equals the C-characteristic at w in $\mathfrak{m}^r$.
It is straightfoward to extend this result to a similar one about full C-profiles.

The constraints we have imposed on R in proposition 6 are such as to make the proof almost trivial. But they are also quite strong; in particular the euclidean property can hardly be justified on the strength of our intuitions about belief. One might conjecture that the conclusion of proposition 6 also follows when the serial and the euclidean constraint are dropped. But a proof for this claim would be much more difficult.

We conclude this section with a result that is, like proposition 4, a special case of the conjecture we have juist made, and which concerns an instance of self-reference that has been discussed elsewhere in the literature on this topic (see e.g. Herzberger (1982)).
Proposition 7: Suppose $\mathfrak{m}$ is a model such that (i) $[\![b]\!]_\mathfrak{m} = \neg B(c)$, (ii) $[\![c]\!]_\mathfrak{m} = B(b)$, (iii) all other constants of L do not denote sentences (iv) $R_\mathfrak{m}$ is transitive. Then for each w ∈ $W_\mathfrak{m}$ the {b,c}-profile at w on ω in $\mathfrak{m}$ is cyclical after 4 with period 4.

LOGIC OF THE ATTITUDES

The paradox Montague and Kaplan discovered was that languages capable of expressing enough about their own syntax cannot contain sentence predicates for concepts like belief that satisfy the intuitively valid and commonly accepted logical principles ascribed to them.   The point of this paper has been to explore an as yet scarcely investigated way out of this difficulty, which sacrifices as little as possible from the totality of logical and semantical intuitions that their work shows to be incompatible. Of course, in a straightforward sense their results are definitive: any consistent, formal theory which treats belief as a predicate of sentences must give up something.   In approaches of the sort we have advocated what has to go is part of the concept specific logical principles (such as, e.g., (B1) - (B4) for a predicate of belief) by which we would like to see these predicates governed, but which they cannot obey without exception.   In this respect, the familiar and prima facie desirable doxastic logics are in the same position as is the Tarski T-schema in the work on truth on which we have built here. In particular, at least one of the axioms (B1) - (B4) will have to give up its absolute validity, if the semantic analysis we have offered is viable at all.[8]

It should not be surprising that (B4) is prominent among the principles that will be so affected. Propositions 10 and 11 below make this explicit. But it should be noted that it is only in the presence of truly paradoxical sentences that there is a need for giving up anything at all, as is evident from propositions 8 and 9.

Proposition 8: Suppose M is a designatively non-self-referential model structure (i.e. $<_M$ is well founded). Then (a) there is an intension $[\![B]\!]$ such that the model $\mathfrak{m}$ obtained by adding $[\![B]\!]$ to M is coherent; (b) for any model $\mathfrak{m}$ obtained from M by adding intensions for B there is an α such that $\mathfrak{m}^\alpha$ is coherent.

Proposition 9: Suppose $\mathfrak{m}$ is coherent and that (i)R is transitive and (ii) reflexive on its range (i.e., $(\forall w\, w' \in W_{\mathfrak{m}})(wRw' \to w'Rw')$). Then all instances of (B1)-(B4) are true in $\mathfrak{m}$ at all worlds.

These two propositions suggest that it is legitimate to take the logic of belief sentences that are free of self-reference to contain all these axioms. In fact it may be appropriate to extend this claim to a somewhat larger domain, which also includes some self-referential sentences. As we have seen, there are self-referential sentences which admit of coherent models. For instance, every model structure M, in which the only instance of self-reference is the sentence c, where $[\![c]\!]_M = B(c)$, can be turned into a coherent model with the appropriate choice for $[\![B]\!]$. Moreover, if R_M is transitive and reflexive on its range, then _any_ model $\mathfrak{m}$ obtained from M will coherent after one revision (i.e. $\mathfrak{m}^1$ is coherent).

What are we to make of the suggestions made in propositions 8 and 9 and the ensuing remarks? Evidently to turn them into arguments, we need an antecedent account of what would qualify as logically valid, given the kind of model theory we have developed. To get such an account we cannot simply extrapolate from the well understood and straightforward relationship between logic and semantics that is found in classical logic, exemplified by the familiar syntax and semanics of first order predicate logic. For like many other alternatives to the classical case, the model theory of the

---

[8]We again in this section continue as we have talking solely of belief. The parallel remarks to be made about knowledge are, we hope, an easy extrapolation.

previous section offers a number of different options for defining an associated logic, between which it is quite difficult if not impossible to make a well motivated choice. Suppose for instance we want to define what it is for a sentence to be logically valid. Presumably we want to say that the valid sentences are those that are invariably true. But how should we interpret this in the context of the model theory of this paper? What is it for a sentence to be "invariably true"? True at which worlds in which models? Here we face a number of different options, no one of which stands out unequivocally as the right one. Should we , for instance, include only coherent models, or should the truth values in non coherent models also count? If we go for the second option, should we consider all of them or only some distinguished subclass? These are only some of the questions that an account of validity must answer. Others, familiar from the literature on modal logic pertain to the constraints that should be imposed on the alternativeness relation. As we shall see below, there are further questions as well. Not until all these questions are settled will it be possible to assess the tentative claims about the logic of the non-self-referential and of the "harmlessly" self-referential sentences of L.

It is with similar caution that the reader should interpret the next two propositions which concern the logic of arbitrary designative self-refernce. When self-reference is not of the harmless variety exemplified by c, models as a rule start out incoherent and cannot be made coherent upon revision. Even such models, however, reach a certain kind of stability after enough revisions.

Proposition 10 : For each L model $\mathfrak{m}$ there is a least ordinal α_0, such that: (i) for each $w \in W_{\mathfrak{m}}$ and each sentence φ $\varphi \in [\![B]\!]_{\mathfrak{m}, w}{}^{\alpha_0}$ iff $(\forall \beta \geq \alpha)$ $\varphi \in [\![B]\!]_{\mathfrak{m}, w}{}^{\beta}$, (ii) after α_0 the revision process goes through a fixed cycle-- i.e. there is an ordinal γ such that for any $\beta_1, \beta_2 > \alpha_0$ if there is a $\partial < \gamma$ such that $\beta_1 = \gamma \pi_1 + \partial$ and $\beta_2 = \gamma \pi_2 + \partial$, then for all $w \in W_{\mathfrak{m}}$ $[\![B]\!]_{w}{}^{\beta_1} = [\![B]\!]_{w}{}^{\beta_2}$.

We shall call such an ordinal as α_0 a *minimization ordinal* for $\mathfrak{m}$ and $\mathfrak{m}^{\alpha_0}$ a *metastable model*. It follows from our definitions that if $\mathfrak{m}$ is coherent then the minimization ordinal for $\mathfrak{m}$ is 0 and the smallest γ satisfying (ii) in proposition 10 is 1.

One way of defining the logic of designative self-refernce would be to identify the valid sentences as those which come out true throughout all metastable models. On this assumption and given the appropriate choice of constraints for R, the schemata (B1) - (B3) will still come out valid, in the sense that all their instances are valid. But (B4) will now have false instances and so lose its validity as a schema.

Proposition 11 : Suppose $\mathfrak{m}^{\alpha}$ is a metastable model and suppose R is transitive in $\mathfrak{m}^{\alpha}$. Then every instance of (B1) –(B3) is true at every world in $W_{\mathfrak{m}^{\alpha}}$. Further, as long as R satisfies condition (ii) of Proposition 1, $\mathfrak{m}^{\alpha}$ will yield counterinstances to (B4) at some world.

Of course, this is not surprising; something had to give. However, within our framework, even (B4) retains a weaker kind of validity. To explain this, we should note that when $\mathfrak{m}^{\alpha}$ is metastable, the sentences that are not in $[\![B]\!]_{\mathfrak{m}, w}{}^{\alpha}$ fall into two natural classes-- those that remain outside $[\![B]\!]_{\mathfrak{m}, w}{}^{\beta}$ for all $\beta \geq \alpha$ and those that continue to move in and out of $[\![B]\!]_{w}$. The first might be naturally regarded as the *antiextension* of B at w-- the set of sentences that are definitely not believed at w. The second consists of sentences whose status as beliefs is forever in doubt. We can use the extension and antiextension of B in $\mathfrak{m}^{\alpha}$ to construct a partial model $\mathfrak{m}$. In any of the familiar valuation schemes for partial models-- the Kleene valuations or supervaluation schemes, certain sentences will not get a truth value. With reference to (B4), we now find that, on any of these valuation schemes, none of its instances come out false at any world of $\mathfrak{m}$. So if we were to identify the valid sentences as those which never come out false in any of the partial models associated with metastable models, the schema (B4) gets reinstated as valid.

One must not forget, however, that this rehabilitation of (B4) is something of a sham. For example, the instance of (B4) which we get by replacing φ in it with the paradoxical believer sentence will lack a truth value at each partial model, and so it will never actually come out false. But it certainly will never come out true either. Thus, it would be unwise to rely upon such instances of the principle when engaging in doxastic reasoning.

This last observation leads us back into not only questions about choices between valuation schemes but also fundamental issues of logic and its relation to semantics. Since we have already said we cannot deal adequately with these questions here, better to stop now and save a fuller treatment of these issues for another occasion.

References

N. Asher: 1985, 'Belief in Discourse Representation Theory,' forthcoming in *Journal of Philosophical Logic.*

A. Gupta: 1982, 'Truth and Paradox,' *Journal of Philosophical Logic* 11, pp. 1-60.

H. Herzberger: 1982, 'Notes on Naive Semantics,' *Journal of Philosophical Logic* 11, pp. 61-102.

H. Herzberger: 1982, 'Naive Semantics and the Liar Paradox,' *Journal of Philosophy* 79, pp. 479-497.

H. Kamp: 1985, 'Context Thought and Communication,' *Proceedings of the Aristotelian Society,* 1984-85.

D. Kaplan & R. Montague: 1960, 'A Paradox Regained,' *Notre Dame Journal of Formal Logic* 1, pp. 79-90.

S. Kripke: 1975, 'Outline of a New Theory of Truth,' *Journal of Philosophy* 72, pp. 690-715.

R. Montague: 1963, 'Syntactical Treatments of Modality, with Corollaries on Reflexion Principles and Finite Axiomatizability,' *Acta Philosophica Fennica* 16, pp. 153-167.

R. Thomason: 1980, 'A Note on Syntactical Treatments of Modality,' *Synthese* 44, pp. 391-395.

Knowledge and Common Knowledge in a
Byzantine Environment I: Crash failures

(Extended Abstract)

Cynthia Dwork
IBM Almaden Research Center,
San Jose, CA 95193

Yoram Moses
MIT Laboratory for Computer Science,
Cambridge, MA 02139

ABSTRACT

By analyzing the states of knowledge that the processors attain in an unreliable system of a simple type, we capture some of the basic underlying structure of such systems. The analysis provides us with a better understanding of existing protocols for problems such as Byzantine agreement, generalizes them considerably, and facilitates the design of improved protocols for many related problems.

1. Introduction

The problem of designing effective protocols for distributed systems whose components are unreliable is both important and difficult. In general, a protocol for a distributed system in which all components are liable to fail cannot unconditionally guarantee to achieve non-trivial goals. In particular, if all processors in the system fail at an early stage of an execution of the protocol, then fairly little will be achieved regardless of what actions the protocol intended for the processors to perform. However, such universal failures are not very common in practice, and we are often faced with the problem of seeking protocols that will function correctly so long as the number, type, and pattern of failures during the execution of the protocol are reasonably limited. A requirement that is often made of such protocols is *t-resiliency* — that they be guaranteed to achieve a particular goal so long as no more than t processors fail.

A good example of a desirable goal for a protocol in an unreliable system is called *Simultaneous Byzantine Agreement* (SBA), a variant of the Byzantine agreement problem introduced in [PSL]:

Given are n processors, at most t of which might be faulty. Each processor p_i has an initial value $x_i \in \{0, 1\}$. Required is a protocol with the following properties:

1. Every non-faulty processor p_i irreversibly "decides" on a value $y_i \in \{0, 1\}$.

2. The non-faulty processors all decide on the same value.

3. The non-faulty processors all decide simultaneously, i.e., in the same round of computation.

4. If all initial bits x_i are identical, then all non-faulty processors decide x_i.

A related problem, in which condition 4 is modified to require that the non-faulty processors decide x_i only in case all processors start with x_i and no failures occur, is called *Weak Simultaneous Byzantine Agreement* (WSBA). Throughout the paper we will use t to denote an upper bound on the number of faulty processors. We call a distributed system whose processors are unreliable a *Byzantine environment*.

The Byzantine agreement problem embodies some of the fundamental issues involved in the design of effective protocols for unreliable systems, and has been studied extensively in the literature (see [F] for a survey). Interestingly, although many researchers have obtained a good intuition for the Byzantine agreement problem, many aspects of this problem still seem to be mysterious in many ways, and the general rules underlying some of the phenomena related to it are still unclear.

A number of recent papers have looked at the role of knowledge in distributed computing (cf. [CM], [HM], [PR]). They suggest that knowledge is an important conceptual abstraction in distributed systems, and that the design and analysis of distributed protocols may benefit from explicitly reasoning about the states of knowledge that the system goes through during an execution of the protocol. In [HM], special attention is given to states of knowledge of *groups* of processors, with the states of *common knowledge* and *implicit knowledge* singled out as states of knowledge that are of particular interest. As we will see, in order to be able to reach SBA on a decision value v, the non-faulty processors must attain common knowledge that conditions that allow deciding v hold. In fact, the problem of attaining common knowledge of a given fact in a Byzantine environment turns out to be a direct generalization of the SBA problem.

We wish to investigate the states of knowledge that can be attained by the group of non-faulty processors in a Byzantine environment. In particular, we are interested in determining what facts become common knowledge at the various stages of the execution of a particular protocol. In this paper we restrict our attention to systems in which communication is synchronous and reliable, and the only type of processor faults possible are *crash failures*: a faulty processor might crash at some point, after which it sends no messages at all. Despite the fact that crash failures are relatively benign, and dealing with arbitrary possibly malicious failures is often more complicated, work on the Byzantine agreement problem has shown that many of the difficulties of working in a Byzantine environment are already exhibited in this model. By analyzing the states of knowledge that processors can attain as a function of the pattern of messages in a given protocol, we can characterize the types of coordinated simultaneous actions that can be performed at various points in the execution of the protocol. The results of this analysis directly apply to the design of protocols for SBA, WSBA, and other problems.

The main contribution of this paper is to illustrate how a knowledge-based analysis of protocols in a Byzantine environment can provide insight into the fundamental properties of such systems. This insight can be used to help us design improved t-resilient protocols for Byzantine agreement and related problems. We perform a careful analysis of the upper and lower bound proofs on the number of rounds necessary to reach common knowledge of facts in a Byzantine system. Our lower bound proofs generalize and simplify the proof of the $t+1$ round worst-case lower bound for SBA (cf. [DLM], [DS], [CD], [FL], [H], [LF]), and characterize for the first time exactly which patterns of failures require the protocol to run for $t+1$ rounds. We similarly characterize the failure patterns that allow attaining SBA in k rounds of communication, for all $k \leq t+1$, and construct a simple protocol for SBA that always halts at the earliest possible round, given the pattern in which processors fail during a given run of the protocol. In many cases, this turns out to be much earlier than in any protocol previously known.

The analysis also provides some insight into how assumptions about the reliability of the system affect the states of knowledge attainable in the system. We briefly consider some other reliability assumptions and apply our analysis to them.

Section 2 contains the basic definitions and some of the fundamental properties of our model of a distributed system and of knowledge in a distributed system. Section 3 investigates the states of knowledge attainable in a particular fairly general protocol. Section 4 contains an analysis of the lower bounds corresponding to the analysis of Section 3, simplifying and generalizing the well-known $t+1$ round worst-case lower bound for reaching SBA. Section 5 discusses some applications of our analysis to problems related to SBA, and Section 6 includes some concluding remarks.

2. Definitions and preliminary results

In this section we present a number of basic definitions that will be used in the rest of the paper, and discuss some of their implications. Our treatment will generally follow along the lines of [HM], simplified and modified for our purposes.

We consider a synchronous distributed system consisting of a finite collection of $n \geq 2$ processors (automata) $\{p_1, p_2, \ldots, p_n\}$, each pair of which are connected by a two-way communication link. The processors share a discrete global clock that starts out at time 0 and advances by increments of one. Communication in the system proceeds in a sequence of *rounds*, with round k taking place between time $k-1$ and time k. In each round, every processor first sends the messages it needs to send to other processors, and then it receives the messages that were sent to it by other processors in the same round. The identity of the sender and destination of each message, as well as the round in which it is sent, are assumed to be part of the message. At any given time, a processor's *message history* consists of the set of messages it has sent and received. Every processor p starts out with some *initial state* σ. A processor's *view* at any given time consists of its initial state, message history, and the time on the global clock. We think of the processors as following a *protocol*, which specifies exactly what messages each processor is required to send (and what other actions the processor should take) at each round, as a *deterministic* function of the processor's view. However, a processor might be *faulty*, in which case it might commit a stopping failure at an arbitrary round $k > 0$. If a processor *commits a stopping failure* at round k (or simply *fails* at round k), then it obeys its protocol in all rounds preceding round k, it does not send any messages in the rounds following k, and in round k it sends an arbitrary (not necessarily strict) subset of the messages it is required by its protocol to send. (Since a failed processor sends no further messages, we need not make any assumptions regarding what messages it receives in its failing round and in later rounds.) For technical reasons, we assume that once a processor fails, its view becomes a distinguished *failed* view. The set A of *active* processors at time k consists of all of the processors that did not fail in the first k rounds.

A *run* ρ of such a system is a complete history of its behavior, from time 0 until the end of time. This includes each processor's initial state, message history, and, if the processor fails, the round in which it fails. An *execution* is a pair (ρ, k), where ρ is a run and k is a natural number. We will use (ρ, k) to refer to the state of ρ after its first k rounds. Two executions (ρ, k) and (ρ', k) will be considered equal if all processors start in the same initial states and display the same behavior in the first k rounds of ρ and ρ'. The list of the processors' initial states is called the system's *initial configuration*. We denote processor p's view at (ρ, k) by $v(p, \rho, k)$. Furthermore, we will sometimes parameterize the set A of active processors by the particular execution, denoted $A(\rho, k)$.

Following [HM], we identify a distributed system with the set S of the possible runs of a particular fixed protocol $P = (P(1), \ldots, P(n))$, where $P(i)$ is the part of the protocol followed by processor p_i. This set essentially encodes all of the relevant information about the execution of the protocol in the system. In analyzing the properties of t-resilient protocols, the system we are interested in is the set of all possible runs of the protocol in which the system starts in one of a set of possible initial configurations, and no more than

t processors fail. Such a set will be called a *t-uniform* system for P. A given protocol is a t-resilient protocol for SBA if all runs of the t-uniform system in which the set of possible initial configurations is $\{0,1\}^n$ satisfy the requirements of SBA.

We assume the existence of an underlying logical language for representing *ground* facts about the system. By ground we mean facts about the state of the system that do not explicitly mention processors' knowledge. Formally, a ground fact φ will be identified with a set of executions $\tau(\varphi) \subseteq S \times N$, where N is the set of natural numbers. Given a run $\rho \in S$ of the system and a time k, we will say that φ holds at (ρ, k), denoted $(S, \rho, k) \models \varphi$, iff $(\rho, k) \in \tau(\varphi)$. We will define various ground facts as we go along. The set of executions corresponding to these facts will be clear from the context.

Given a system S, we now formally define what facts a processor is said to "know" at any given point (ρ, k) for $\rho \in S$. (Our definition will correspond to [HM]'s "total view" interpretation of knowledge). We say that a processor p_i *knows* a fact ψ in S at (ρ, k), denoted $(S, \rho, k) \models K_i\psi$, if for all executions $(\rho', k) \in S \times \{k\}$ satisfying $v(p_i, \rho, k) = v(p_i, \rho', k)$ it is the case that $(S, \rho', k) \models \psi$. Roughly speaking, p_i knows ψ if ψ is guaranteed to hold, given p_i's view of the run. Notice that this definition guarantees that the "knowledge axiom" $K_i\varphi \supset \varphi$ is valid[1] (see [HM], [HM2] for other properties of K_i under this definition).

Having defined knowledge for individual processors, we now extend this definition to states of group knowledge. Given a group $G \subseteq \{p_1, \ldots, p_n\}$, we first define G's *view* at (ρ, k), denoted $v(G, \rho, k)$:

$$v(G, \rho, k) = \{\langle p, v(p, \rho, k)\rangle : p \in G\}.$$

Thus, roughly speaking, G's view is simply the joint view of its members. Extending our definition for individuals' knowledge, we say that *the group G has implicit knowledge* of φ at (ρ, k), denoted $(S, \rho, k) \models I_G\varphi$, if for all runs $\rho' \in S$ satisfying $v(G, \rho, k) = v(G, \rho', k)$ it is the case that $(S, \rho', k) \models \varphi$. Intuitively, G has implicit knowledge of φ if the joint view of G's members guarantees that φ holds. Notice that if processor p knows φ and processor q knows $\varphi \supset \psi$, then together they have implicit knowledge of ψ, even if neither of them knows ψ individually. We refer the reader to [HM] and [HM2] for a discussion and a formal treatment of I_G. In this paper we are mainly interested in states of knowledge of the group A of active processors. The set of active processors is said to implicitly know φ, denoted $I_A\varphi$, exactly if $I_G\varphi$ holds for the set $G = A$. Stated more formally,

$$(S, \rho, k) \models I_A\varphi \text{ iff } (S, \rho, k) \models I_G\varphi \text{ for } G = A(\rho, k).$$

Although $I_A\varphi$ is defined in terms of $I_G\varphi$, it is not the case that I_A and I_G have the same properties. The reason for this is that whereas G is a fixed set, membership in A may vary over time and differs from one run to another. Thus, for example, it is often the case that for $G = A(\rho, k)$ we have $(S, \rho, k) \not\models I_G(A = G)$, because there is some run $\rho' \in S$ such that $v(G, \rho, k) = v(G, \rho', k)$ and where G is a strict subset of $A(\rho', k)$. Consequently, whereas the formula $\neg I_G\varphi \supset I_G\neg I_G\varphi$ is valid, the corresponding formula $\neg I_A\varphi \supset I_A\neg I_A\varphi$ is not

---

[1]   A formula is said to be *valid* if it is true of all executions in all systems.

valid! (Notice, however, that $I_A(G \subseteq A)$ holds whenever $G \subseteq A$.)[2] Since the form of implicit knowledge that concerns us most is I_A, we will call it simply *implicit knowledge*, and denote it by I.

We now show that, roughly speaking, in t-uniform systems once a fact about the past is not implicitly known it is lost forever; it will not become implicit knowledge at a later time. We say that a fact ψ is *about the first k rounds* if for all runs $\rho \in S$ it is the case that $(S, \rho, k) \models \psi$ iff $(S, \rho, \ell) \models \psi$ for all $\ell \geq k$. In particular, facts about the first 0 rounds are facts about the initial configuration. We now have:

Theorem 1:   Let S be a t-uniform system, let ψ be a fact about the first k rounds, and let $\ell > k$.   If $(S, \rho, k) \not\models I\psi$ then $(S, \rho, \ell) \not\models I\psi$.

Proof: Let $\ell > k$, and let ρ and ψ be such that ψ is about the first k rounds and $(S, \rho, k) \not\models I\psi$. Let $G = A(\rho, k)$. It follows that there exists a run $\rho' \in S$ such that $v(G, \rho, k) = v(G, \rho', k)$, and $(S, \rho', k) \not\models \psi$. Let ρ'' be a run with the following properties: (i) $(\rho'', k) = (\rho', k)$; (ii) All processors in $A(\rho', k) - G$ fail in round $k+1$ of ρ'' before sending any messages; and (iii) From round $k + 1$ on all processors in G behave in ρ'' exactly as they do in ρ. Notice that $\rho'' \in S$ since all of the processors follow the same protocol in ρ'' and in ρ, and no more processors fail in ρ'' than do in ρ. By construction of ρ'' we have that $A(\rho'', \ell) = A(\rho, \ell)$ and that the active processors have identical views in (ρ'', ℓ) and in (ρ, ℓ). It follows that $(S, \rho'', \ell) \models I\psi$ iff $(S, \rho, \ell) \models I\psi$. Since ψ is a fact about the first k rounds and $(\rho'', k) = (\rho', k)$, we have that $(S, \rho'', \ell) \not\models \psi$ because $(S, \rho', k) \not\models \psi$. Thus, in particular, $(S, \rho'', \ell) \not\models I\psi$ and it follows that $(S, \rho, \ell) \not\models I\psi$ and we are done. $\bowtie$

Fagin and Vardi perform an interesting analysis of implicit knowledge in reliable systems (cf. [FV]). Among other things, they prove that the set of facts that are implicit knowledge about the initial configuration does not change with time. I.e., in reliable systems the implication in the statement of the Theorem 1 becomes an equivalence. However, in t-uniform Byzantine systems it is clearly the case that implicit knowledge can be "lost". For example, if processor p_i may start in initial states σ and σ', and in a particular run of the system p_i starts in state σ and fails in the first round before sending any messages, then whereas $I("p_i$ started in state $\sigma")$ holds at time 0, it does not hold at any later time.

We now introduce the two other states of group knowledge that are central to our analysis. Given a group of processors G, $E_G\varphi$ (read "everyone in G knows φ") and $C_G\varphi$ ("φ is common knowledge in G") are defined as follows (cf. [HM]):

$$E_G^1\varphi = E_G\varphi = \bigwedge_{p_i \in G} K_i\varphi,$$

$$E_G^{m+1}\varphi = E_G(E_G^m\varphi), \quad m \geq 1, \quad \text{and}$$

$$C_G\varphi = \varphi \wedge E_G\varphi \wedge E_G^2\varphi \wedge \cdots \wedge E_G^m\varphi \wedge \cdots.$$

----

[2] Whereas I_G satisfies the axioms of the logical system S5, it is easy to show that I_A satisfies the axioms of S4 (cf. [HM2]).

The states E_A and C_A, in which we will be most interested, are defined in the same way as E_G and C_G. Because membership in A is not explicitly given, it is sometimes useful to think of $E_A\varphi$ in the following equivalent form:

$$E_A\varphi = \bigwedge_{1 \leq i \leq n} (p_i \in A \supset K_i\varphi),$$

It is interesting to note that in contrast to the case of implicit knowledge, the basic properties of E_A and C_A are the same as those of E_G and C_G, stated in [HM]. In particular, C_A satisfies the axioms of S5 (cf. [HM2]). Thus, in particular, C_A satisfies the "consequence closure" axiom:

CONSEQUENCE CLOSURE: $(C_A\varphi \wedge C_A(\varphi \supset \psi)) \supset C_A\psi.$

A fact that is crucial in our proofs is that C_A satisfies the "induction" axiom:

INDUCTION AXIOM: $C_A(\varphi \supset E_A\varphi) \supset (\varphi \supset C_A\varphi).$

In the remainder of this paper, we will use I, E, and C as shorthand for I_A, E_A, and C_A.

Two executions (ρ, k) and (ρ', k) are said to be *directly similar*, denoted $(\rho, k) \approx (\rho', k)$, if for some processor p active in ρ at time k it is the case that $v(p, \rho, k) = v(p, \rho', k)$. Thus, two executions are directly similar if some active processor cannot distinguish between them. As an immediate consequence of our the definitions, we have:

$$(S, \rho, k) \models E\varphi \text{ iff } (S, \rho', k) \models \varphi \text{ for all } \rho' \in S \text{ such that } (\rho, k) \approx (\rho', k)$$

Notice that the $\approx$ relation is reflexive and symmetric, but not transitive. We say that (ρ, k) and (ρ', k) are *similar*, denoted $(\rho, k) \sim (\rho', k)$, if for some finite m there are runs $\rho_1, \rho_2, \ldots, \rho_m \in S$ such that

$$(\rho, k) \approx (\rho_1, k) \approx (\rho_2, k) \approx \cdots \approx (\rho_m, k) \approx (\rho', k).$$

The similarity relation $\sim$ is simply the transitive closure of the $\approx$ relation, and thus is an equivalence relation.

We can now show:

Theorem 2:

a) $(S, \rho, k) \models C\varphi$ iff $(S, \rho', k) \models \varphi$ for all $\rho' \in S$ such that $(\rho, k) \sim (\rho', k)$.

b) If $(S, \rho, k) \models \varphi$ for all $\rho \in S$, then $(S, \rho, k) \models C\varphi$ for all $\rho \in S$.

Proof: (a) follows by a straightforward induction on m showing that $(S, \rho, k) \models E^m\varphi$ iff $(S, \rho', k) \models \varphi$ for all ρ' such that there exist $\rho_1, \ldots, \rho_{m-1}$ with $(\rho, k) \approx (\rho_1, k) \approx \cdots \approx (\rho_{m-1}, k) \approx (\rho', k)$. Part (b) follows directly from (a).   ▱

Theorem 2 is very useful in relating common knowledge and actions that are guaranteed to be performed simultaneously. For example, we can use Theorem 2(b) and the "induction axiom" in order to relate the ability or inability to attain common knowledge of certain facts with the possibility or impossibility of reaching simultaneous Byzantine agreement. We model a processor's "deciding v" by the processor sending the message "the decision value is v" to itself, and have:

Corollary 3:   Let S be a system in which the processors follow a protocol for SBA. If the active processors decide on a value v at (ρ, k), then

a) $(S, \rho, k) \models C($ "All processors are deciding v"), and

b) $(S, \rho, k) \models C($"At least one processor had v as its initial value").

Proof: Let φ be the fact "all processors are deciding v". Given that the protocol guarantees that SBA is attained in S, it is the case that whenever some processor decides v all active processors do, and thus the formula $\varphi \supset E\varphi$ is valid in S (i.e., for all $\rho \in S$ and $k \geq 0$ we have $(S, \rho, k) \models \varphi \supset E\varphi$). Thus, by Theorem 2(b) it follows that $C(\varphi \supset E\varphi)$ is also valid. The "induction axiom" states that $C(\varphi \supset E\varphi) \supset (\varphi \supset C\varphi)$. Combining these two facts we have that $\varphi \supset C\varphi$ is valid, and thus if $(S, \rho, k) \models \varphi$ then $(S, \rho, k) \models C\varphi$ and we are done with part (a). For (b), let ψ be "at least one processor had v as its initial value", and notice SBA guarantees that $\varphi \supset \psi$ is valid in S. Thus, by Theorem 2(b), so is $C(\varphi \supset \psi)$. The "consequence closure" axiom states that $(C\varphi \wedge C(\varphi \supset \psi)) \supset C\psi$ is valid, and we conclude that $C\varphi \supset C\psi$ is valid. By part (a) we have that $(S, \rho, k) \models \varphi$ implies that $(S, \rho, k) \models C(\varphi)$, from which we can now conclude that $(S, \rho, k) \models C\psi$ and we are done.   ⋈

3.   Analysis of a simple protocol

In this section we take a close look at t-uniform systems $S_\hat{P}$ in which all processors follow a simple and fairly general protocol $\hat{P}$: For $k \geq 0$, in round $k + 1$ each processor *sends its view at time k (i.e., after k rounds) to all other processors.*

We are interested in the states of knowledge about the initial configuration that the set of active processors attains at different stages of the execution of this protocol. Intuitively, the protocol $\hat{P}$ should provide the processors with "as much knowledge as possible" about the initial configuration, and facilitate the ability of the system to perform actions that depend on the initial configuration.

A fact φ is called *stable* if once it becomes true it remains true forever (cf. [HM]). For example, facts about the first k rounds, and in particular facts about the system's initial configuration, are stable. Since a processor's knowledge is based on a processor's view, and an active processor's view grows monotonically with time, it is the case that if φ is stable then so are $E\varphi$ and $C\varphi$ (although, as we have seen, this is not true for $I\varphi$).

A round in which no processor fails is called a *clean* round. Similarly, a round that is not clean is called *dirty*. If, for some k, round k of a run in which the processors all follow $\hat{P}$ is clean, then every active processor's view at the end of round k includes the view of the active processors at time $k - 1$. In particular it follows that any stable fact that is implicit knowledge at time $k - 1$ is known to everyone at time k. Consequently, at time k all processors know exactly the same facts about the initial configuration. Furthermore, Theorem 1 together with the fact that $E\varphi$ is stable when φ is, imply that at any point after a clean round, all of the processors have identical knowledge about the initial configuration. Therefore, once it is common knowledge that there was a clean round, it is common knowledge that the processors have an identical view of the initial configuration. Recall that any property that holds at all points (ρ, k) is common knowledge at all points (ρ, k).

In particular, it is common knowledge no more than t processors can fail in any run of the system, and that all processors are following the protocol $\hat{P}$. We can now show:

Theorem 4:   Let φ be a fact about the initial configuration.

a) $(S_\rho, \rho, t+1) \models I\varphi$ iff $(S_\rho, \rho, t+1) \models C\varphi$.

b) $(S_\rho, \rho, n-1) \models I\varphi$ iff $(S_\rho, \rho, n-1) \models C\varphi$.

Proof: Notice that the "if" direction in both cases is immediate, since $C\psi \supset I\psi$ is valid for all facts ψ. We now show the other direction. Let φ be a fact about the initial configuration. Since at most t processors fail in any run of S_ρ, it follows by the pigeonhole principle that at least one of the first $t+1$ rounds of every run is clean. By Theorem 1 and the discussion above we have that at any point following a clean round it is the case that $I\varphi$ holds iff $E\varphi$ does. In particular, this means that in all runs of S_ρ it is the case that after $t+1$ rounds $I\varphi$ holds iff $E\varphi$ does. Notice also that $E\varphi \equiv E(I\varphi)$ is valid (since $K_i\varphi \supset I\varphi$ is). Now by Theorem 2(b) and the "induction axiom" we are done. For part (b), notice that in all runs of S_ρ one of the following two possibilities holds: either there is a clean round by time $n-1$, or there is at most one active processor at time $n-1$. In the first case we can argue as in (a) that $I\varphi$ holds at time $n-1$ iff $E(I\varphi)$ does. However, this is also true in the second case, since when there is at most one active processor p_i it is the case that $K_i\psi \equiv I\psi \equiv E\psi$. And since $K_i\psi \supset K_i(I\psi)$ is valid, for all facts ψ we have that $I\psi \equiv E(I\psi)$. Thus, again by Theorem 2(b) and the "induction axiom" we are done.   ⋈

As a consequence of Theorem 4 and the discussion preceding it we have that any action that depends on the system's initial configuration can be carried out simultaneously in a consistent way by the set of active processors at any time $k \geq \min\{t+1, n-1\}$. This is consistent with the fact that there are simple t-resilient protocols for SBA that attain SBA in $t+1$ rounds. Interestingly, none of the known protocols for SBA attain SBA in less than $t+1$ rounds in *any* run. It is therefore natural to ask whether a protocol for SBA can ever attain SBA in less than $t+1$ rounds. Clearly, once it is common knowledge that a clean round has occurred, SBA can be attained. And as we shall see, there are cases in which the existence of a clean round becomes common knowledge before time $t+1$. *When* the existence of a clean round becomes common knowledge depends crucially on the pattern of failures, and on the time in which failures become implicitly known to the group of active processors. For example, if a processor p detects t failures in the first round of a run of $\hat{P}$, then the second round of the run will be clean, and at the end of the second round all active processors will know that p detected t failures in round 1. It follows from the induction axiom and Theorem 2(b) that at the end of round 2 it will be *common knowledge* that all processors have an identical view of the initial configuration (check!). Clearly, the processors can then perform any action that depends on the initial configuration (e.g., SBA) in a consistent way. In the remainder of this section we show a class of runs of S_ρ in which the processors attain common knowledge of an identical view of the initial configuration at time k, for every k between 2 and $t+1$. In the next section, we will prove that this is in fact a precise classification of the runs according to the time in which common knowledge of an identical view of the initial configuration is attained.

Intuitively, if there are more than k failures by the end of round k, then from the point of view of the ability to delay the first clean round, failures have been "wasted". In particular, if for some k it is the case that there are $k + j$ failures by the end of round k, then there must be a clean round before time $t + 1 - j$ (in fact, between round $k + 1$ and round $t + 1 - j$). This motivates the following definitions: We denote the number of processors that fail by the end of round k in ρ by $N(\rho, k)$. We define the *difference at* (ρ, k), denoted $d(\rho, k)$, by

$$d(\rho, k) \overset{\text{def}}{=} N(\rho, k) - k.$$

We also define the *maximal difference in* (ρ, ℓ), denoted $D(\rho, \ell)$, by

$$D(\rho, \ell) \overset{\text{def}}{=} \max_{k \leq \ell} d(\rho, k).$$

Observe that $d(\rho, 0) = 0$ for all runs ρ, since $N(\rho, 0) = 0$. Furthermore, in a t-uniform system it is always the case that $d(\rho, k) \leq t - k$, since $N(\rho, k) \leq t$. Let D be a variable whose value at a point (ρ, k) is $D(\rho, k)$. Similarly, let $d(k)$ be a variable whose value at any point in ρ is $d(\rho, k)$. An important observation is that if at time $t + 1 - j$ it is common knowledge that $D \geq j$, then it is common knowledge that a clean round has occurred, and that all processors have an identical view of the initial configuration. As we will see, the protocol $\hat{P}$ has the property that if it ever becomes implicit knowledge that $D \geq j$ then at time $t + 1 - j$ it is common knowledge that $D \geq j$. This leads us to the following definition: Given a system S, the *wastefulness* of (ρ, ℓ) with respect to S, denoted $\mathcal{W}(S, \rho, \ell)$, is defined by:

$$\mathcal{W}(S, \rho, \ell) \overset{\text{def}}{=} \max\{j : (S, \rho, \ell) \models I(D \geq j)\}.$$

In words, the wastefulness of (ρ, ℓ) is the maximal value that the difference $d(\rho, \cdot)$ is implicitly known to have assumed by time ℓ. We now formally prove the claims informally stated above. We start with a somewhat technical lemma discussing the properties of wastefulness in the case of S_ρ:

Lemma 5:   Let $\rho \in S_\rho$.

  a) If $\mathcal{W}(S_\rho, \rho, \ell) = j$ then there is a particular $k \leq \ell$ such that $(S_\rho, \rho, \ell) \models I(d(k) \geq j)$.

  b) If $I(d(k) \geq j)$ holds at time k then at time $k + 1$ either $E(d(k) \geq j)$ holds, or $I(d(k + 1) \geq j)$ does.

  c) $\mathcal{W}(S_\rho, \rho, k + 1) \geq \mathcal{W}(S_\rho, \rho, k)$ for all $k \geq 0$.

Proof: For part (a), let $\rho \in S_\rho$ satisfy $(S_\rho, \rho, \ell) \models I(D \geq j)$, and assume that for no k is it the case that $(S_\rho, \rho, \ell) \models I(d(k) \geq j))$. Let ρ' be a run of $\hat{P}$ such that $(\rho', 0) = (\rho, 0)$, and in which the only messages not to be delivered are those that are implicitly known at (ρ, ℓ) not to have been delivered. It is easy to check that $\rho' \in S_\rho$, since no more than t processors fail in it, and processor failures are crash failures. Because it is not implicit knowledge at (ρ, ℓ) that $d(k) \geq j$ for any k, it follows that $D(\rho', \ell) < j$. If we show that the group $G = A(\rho, \ell)$ has exactly the same view in (ρ, ℓ) and in (ρ', ℓ) we will be done, since this will contradict the assumption that $(S_\rho, \rho, \ell) \models I(D \geq j)$. We now prove that $A(\rho, \ell)$ has the same view in (ρ, ℓ) and in (ρ', ℓ). Define $G(\ell) = A(\rho, \ell)$. For $k < \ell$, assume inductively that $G(k+1)$ is defined, and for all processors $p_i \in G(k+1)$ let $g(p_i, k)$ be the set of processors from which p_i receives a message in round $k+1$ of ρ. Define

$$G(k) \stackrel{\text{def}}{=} \bigcup_{p_i \in G(k+1)} g(p_i, k).$$

Let $G'(\ell) = G(\ell)$, and for $k < \ell$ define $g'(p_i, k)$ and $G'(k)$ from $G'(k+1)$ in an analogous fashion (substituting G, g, and ρ by G', g', and ρ'). We now show by induction on $\ell - k$ that if $k < \ell$ then for all $p_i \in G(k+1)$ we have that $g(p_i, k) = g'(p_i, k)$ and that $G(k) = G'(k)$. Let $k < \ell$ and assume inductively that $G(k+1) = G'(k+1)$. (Notice that we have defined $G(\ell) = G'(\ell)$.) Let $p_i \in G(k+1)$. The protocol $\hat{P}$ guarantees that the precise identity of $g(p_i, k)$ for $p_i \in G(k+1)$ is implicitly known at (ρ, ℓ). It follows that processor p_j sends a message to p_i in round $k+1$ of ρ iff p_j sends p_i a round $k+1$ message in ρ'. It thus follows that $g(p_i, k) = g'(p_i, k)$. Since this is true for all $p_i \in G(k+1)$, we have that $G(k) = G'(k)$, and the claim is proven. Notice that $G(k) \supseteq G(k+1)$. We now show by induction on k that for all $p_i \in G(k)$ it is the case that $v(p_i, \rho, k) = v(p_i, \rho', k)$. The case $k = 0$ follows from the fact that $(\rho, 0) = (\rho', 0)$ and $G(0) = G'(0)$. Assume inductively the claim holds for $k - 1$, and we prove it for k. Observe that $v(p_i, \rho, k)$ for $p_i \in G(k)$ is determined by $v(p_i, \rho, k-1)$ and by $v(g(p_i, k-1), \rho, k-1)$. Since by the inductive hypothesis we have that $g(p_i, k-1) = g'(p_i, k-1)$, and that $v(g(p_i, k-1), \rho, k-1) = v(g'(p_i, \rho', k-1))$, and that $v(p_i, \rho, k-1) = v(p_i, \rho', k-1)$, it follows that $v(p_i, \rho, k) = v(p_i, \rho', k)$. It now follows that $v(G(\ell), \rho, \ell) = v(G(\ell), \rho', \ell)$, and we are done with part (a).

For part (b), assume that $(S_\rho, \rho, k) \models I(d(k) \geq j)$. If $d(k) \geq j$ is not known to everyone at $(\rho, k+1)$ then there must be (at least one) processor, say q, that fails in round $k+1$ by not sending a message to at least one processor, say p, that is active at time $k+1$. Thus, in particular, p knows at time $k+1$ that q has failed. Now, $\hat{P}$ ensures that all processors that fail by (ρ, k) are known by everyone at $(\rho, k+1)$ to have failed. It follows that if $d(k) \geq j$ is not known to everyone at time $k+1$ then $d(k+1) \geq j$ is implicit knowledge at that time. For (c), assume that $\mathcal{W}(\rho, k) = j$. Then by part (a) there is some $k' \leq k$ such that $(S_\rho, \rho, k) \models I(d(k') \geq j)$. Without loss of generality let k' be the largest such number. If $k' < k$ then by (b) we have that at time $k' + 1 \leq k$ everyone knows that $d(k') \geq j$. But $E(d(k') \geq j)$ is a stable fact because $d(k') \geq j$ is, and in this case $\mathcal{W}(\rho, k+1) \geq j$, and the claim of (c) holds. If $k' = k$ then part (b) implies that at time $k+1$ either everyone will know that $d(k) \geq j$ or it will be implicit knowledge that $d(k+1) \geq j$. In both cases we will have $\mathcal{W}(\rho, k+1) \geq j$, and we are done. $\bowtie$

Lemma 5(c) suggests that we define the *wastefulness* of a run ρ, denoted $\mathcal{W}(S, \rho)$, to be the maximal value that $\mathcal{W}(S, \rho, k)$ assumes. We now have:

Theorem 6:

a) $\mathcal{W}(S_\rho, \rho) = j$ iff $(S_\rho, \rho, t + 1 - j) \models E(\mathcal{W}(S_\rho, \text{"the current run"}) = j)$.

b) Let φ be a fact about the initial configuration. If $\mathcal{W}(S_\rho, \rho) = j$ then $(S_\rho, \rho, t + 1 - j) \models I\varphi$ iff $(S_\rho, \rho, t + 1 - j) \models C\varphi$.

Sketch of Proof: For (a), Notice that if $\mathcal{W}(S_\rho, \rho) = j$ for some $k \leq t + 1 - j$ it is the case that $(S_\rho, \rho, k) \models I(D \geq j)$, and at least one of the rounds $k + 1, \ldots, t - j$ is clean. Lemma 5(a) and (b) imply that $I(D \geq j)$ is a stable fact in S_ρ. The claim of part(a) now follows. For (b), use part (a) to show that at $t + 1 - j$ the existence of a clean round is common knowledge, and follow the proof of Theorem 4. $\bowtie$

Thus, certain patterns of failures help the processors to reach common knowledge of an identical view of the initial configuration early. As a consequence of Theorem 6 we have:

Corollary 7:   There is a t-resilient protocol for SBA that reaches SBA in $t + 1 - \mathcal{W}(S_\rho, \rho)$ rounds in all runs ρ of the protocol in which at most t processors fail.

Proof: The protocol (identical for all processors p_i) is:

> **for** $\ell \geq 0$ *perform the following at time* ℓ:
>   **if** $K_i(D \geq t + 1 - \ell)$
>   **then**   *halt (and send no messages in the following rounds);*
>   *decide 0 if* K_i(*"some initial value* x_j *was 0"*);
>   *decide 1 otherwise.*
>   **else**   *send* p_i*'s current view to all processors in round* $\ell + 1$.

By Theorem 6(a) all correct processors halt after $t + 1 - \mathcal{W}(S_\rho, \rho)$ rounds. By Theorem 6(b) the active processors have common knowledge of the fact that they have an identical view of the initial configuration. Thus, their decisions are identical. The decision function clearly satisfies the requirements of SBA. $\bowtie$

Notice that in runs in which many failures become visible early it is the case that SBA is attained by this protocol significantly earlier than time $t + 1$. We are aware of no other protocol for SBA that stops before time $t + 1$ in some cases. In the next section we will show that the protocol of Corollary 7 is optimal in the sense that for any given pattern of failures, it attains SBA no later than any other protocol for SBA does.

The number of bits of information required to describe a processor's view at round k is exponential in k. Thus, messages in the above protocol might be too long to be practical. By modifying the protocol slightly so that messages specify only the sender's view of the initial configuration and of the failure pattern, we get a protocol for SBA with the same properties in which the length of each message is $O(n + t \log n)$.

4.   Lower bounds

We are about to show that the only non-trivial facts that can become common knowledge in a run ρ of a t-uniform system S before time $t + 1 - \mathcal{W}(S, \rho)$ are facts about the wastefulness of the run. We do this by showing that all executions (ρ, ℓ) with $\mathcal{W}(S, \rho, \ell) \leq t - \ell$ are similar. However, we first need a lemma that, roughly speaking, says that if $D(\rho, \ell) \leq t - \ell$ then (ρ, ℓ) is similar to an execution that looks just like (ρ, ℓ) (in terms of the initial configuration and the pattern of failures), except that the last processor to fail in (ρ, ℓ) never fails. More formally:

Lemma 8:   Let $t \le n-2$, and let S be a t-uniform system. Let $k \le \ell$, let $(\rho, \ell) \in S \times \{\ell\}$ be an execution such that $D(\rho, \ell) \le t - \ell$ and no processor fails in (ρ, ℓ) after round k. If p fails in round k of (ρ, ℓ), then there exists a run $\hat{\rho} \in S$ such that $(\rho, \ell) \sim (\hat{\rho}, \ell)$, where $(\rho, k-1) = (\hat{\rho}, k-1)$, the kth-round behavior of all processors $p' \ne p$ is identical in ρ and in $\hat{\rho}$, processor p does not fail in $(\hat{\rho}, \ell)$, and no processor fails in $(\hat{\rho}, \ell)$ after round k.

Proof: We will prove the claim by induction on $j = \ell - k$.

Case $j = 0$ (i.e., $k = \ell$):   Let $Q = \{q_1, \ldots, q_s\}$ be the set of processors active at (ρ, ℓ) to whom p fails to send a message in round k of ρ. If $s = 0$ then no processor active at (ρ, ℓ) can distinguish (ρ, ℓ) from an execution $(\hat{\rho}, \ell)$ that differs from (ρ, ℓ) only in that p does not fail in $(\hat{\rho}, \ell)$. Assume that $s > 0$. Since $t \le n - 2$, there must be some processor $p_i \in A(\rho, \ell) - \{q_s\}$. Clearly, p_i's view at (ρ, ℓ) is independent of whether or not p sent a message to q_s in round ℓ. Thus, $(\rho, \ell) \sim (\rho', \ell)$, where (ρ', ℓ) differs from (ρ, ℓ) only in that p does send a message to q_s in round ℓ of (ρ', ℓ). Now, since q_s is active at (ρ', ℓ), and p does send q_s a message in round ℓ of (ρ', ℓ), processor q_s's view at (ρ', ℓ) is independent of whether p fails in (ρ', ℓ), and thus $(\rho', \ell) \sim (\hat{\rho}, \ell)$, where $(\hat{\rho}, \ell)$ has the desired properties. By transitivity of $\sim$ we also have that $(\rho, \ell) \sim (\hat{\rho}, \ell)$.

Case $j > 0$ (i.e., $k < \ell$):   Assume inductively that the claim holds for $j - 1$. Again, let $Q = \{q_1, \ldots, q_s\}$ be the set of processors active at (ρ, ℓ) to whom p fails to send a message in round k of (ρ, ℓ). We prove our claim by induction on s. If $s = 0$ then no processor active in (ρ, ℓ) can distinguish whether p failed in round k or in round $k+1$. Thus, $(\rho, \ell) \sim (\rho', \ell)$, where (ρ', ℓ) differs from (ρ, ℓ) only in that rather than failing in round k, processor p fails in round $k+1$ of (ρ', ℓ) before sending any messages. Since $\ell - (k+1) = j - 1$, we have by the inductive hypothesis that $(\rho', \ell) \sim (\hat{\rho}, \ell)$, where $(\hat{\rho}, \ell)$ has the desired properties. By transitivity of $\sim$ we have that $(\rho, \ell) \sim (\hat{\rho}, \ell)$. Now assume that $s > 0$ and that the claim is true for $s - 1$. Let (ρ_s, ℓ) be an execution such that $(\rho_s, k) = (\rho, k)$, processor q_s fails in round $k+1$ of ρ_s before sending any messages, and no other processor fails in ρ_s after round k. Clearly $D(\rho_s, \ell) \le t - \ell$, since $d(\rho_s, k') = d(\rho, k') \le t - \ell$ for all $k' \le k$, and $d(\rho_s, k+1) = N(\rho_s, k+1) - (k+1) = N(\rho, k) + 1 - (k+1) = d(\rho, k) \le t - \ell$. Notice also that no processor fails in (ρ_s, ℓ) after round $k + 1$. Thus, by the inductive assumption on $j - 1$, we have that $(\rho_s, \ell) \sim (\rho, \ell)$. Let $p_i \in A(\rho_s, \ell)$. Clearly p_i's view at (ρ_s, ℓ) is independent of whether p sent a message to q_s in round k of (ρ_s, ℓ). Thus, $(\rho_s, \ell) \sim (\rho'_s, \ell)$, where ρ'_s differs from ρ_s in that p does send a message to q_s in round k of ρ'_s. Again by the inductive hypothesis for $j - 1$ we have that $(\rho'_s, \ell) \sim (\rho', \ell)$, where $(\rho'_s, k) = (\rho', k)$ and no processor fails in (ρ', ℓ) after round k. Processor p fails to send round k messages only to $s - 1$ processors in ρ', and thus by the inductive hypothesis for $s - 1$ we have that $(\rho', \ell) \sim (\hat{\rho}, \ell)$, where $(\hat{\rho}, \ell)$ has the desired properties. By the symmetry and transitivity of $\sim$, we have that $(\rho, \ell) \sim (\hat{\rho}, \ell)$, and we are done. $\bowtie$

Recall that a t-resilient protocol for SBA is required to attain SBA in all runs of the protocol in which the initial configuration is in $\{0,1\}^n$ and there are no more than t failures. Notice that in this set the initial states of the different processors are independent. We say that a t-uniform system is *independent* if the set of initial configurations possible in the system is of the form $\Sigma_1 \times \Sigma_2 \times \cdots \times \Sigma_n$, for fixed sets Σ_i. That is, there is no necessary dependence between the initial states of the different processors. We can now use Lemma 8 to show:

Theorem 9:   Let $t \leq n - 2$ and let S be an independent t-uniform system.

a) If $\ell \leq t$ then all failure-free executions $(\rho, \ell) \in S \times \{\ell\}$ are similar.

b) If $\mathcal{W}(S, \rho, \ell) \leq t - \ell$ and $\mathcal{W}(S, \rho', \ell) \leq t - \ell$, then $(\rho, \ell) \sim (\rho', \ell)$.

Proof: (a) Assume that $\ell \leq t$ and let (ρ, ℓ) and $(\hat{\rho}, \ell)$ be failure-free executions. We wish to show that $(\rho, \ell) \sim (\hat{\rho}, \ell)$. Let $Q = \{q_1, \ldots, q_s\}$ be the set of processors whose initial states in ρ and $\hat{\rho}$ differ. We prove by induction on s that $(\rho, \ell) \sim (\hat{\rho}, \ell)$. If $s = 0$ then $(\rho, \ell) = (\hat{\rho}, \ell)$ and we are done. Let $s > 0$ and assume inductively that all failure-free executions that differ from $(\hat{\rho}, \ell)$ in the initial state of no more than $s - 1$ processors are similar to it. Let (ρ_s, ℓ) be an execution such that $(\rho, 0) = (\rho_s, 0)$, in which q_s fails in the first round without sending any messages, and no other processor fails. Clearly $D(\rho_s, \ell) = 0 \leq t - \ell$, and by Lemma 8 we have that $(\rho_s, \ell) \sim (\rho, \ell)$. Let $p_i \in A(\rho_s, \ell)$. Given that S is an independent t-uniform system, processor p_i's view at (ρ_s, ℓ) is independent of whether the initial state of q_s is as in ρ or as in $\hat{\rho}$. Thus, $(\rho_s, \ell) \sim (\rho'_s, \ell)$, where ρ'_s differs from ρ_s only in that the initial state of q_s in ρ'_s is as in $\hat{\rho}$. Again by Lemma 8 we have that $(\rho'_s, \ell) \sim (\rho', \ell)$, where $(\rho'_s, 0) = (\rho', 0)$, and (ρ', ℓ) is failure-free. Since (ρ', ℓ) differs from $(\hat{\rho}, \ell)$ only on the initial states of $s - 1$ processors, by the inductive assumption we have that $(\rho', \ell) \sim (\hat{\rho}, \ell)$, and by the symmetry and transitivity of $\sim$ we have $(\rho, \ell) \sim (\hat{\rho}, \ell)$, and we are done with part (a).

(b)   If $\mathcal{W}(S, \rho, \ell) \leq t - \ell$ then in particular it is not implicit knowledge at (ρ, ℓ) that $d(k) > t - \ell$ for some $k \leq \ell$. It follows that $(\rho, \ell) \sim (\bar{\rho}, \ell)$, for some $\bar{\rho} \in S$ satisfying $D(\bar{\rho}, \ell) \leq t - \ell$. Using Lemma 8, a straightforward induction on the number of processors that fail in $(\bar{\rho}, \ell)$ shows that $(\bar{\rho}, \ell) \sim (\hat{\rho}, \ell)$, where $(\hat{\rho}, \ell)$ is failure-free. By transitivity of $\sim$ we have that $(\rho, \ell) \sim (\hat{\rho}, \ell)$. The same argument applies to (ρ', ℓ), and the claim now follows from part (a).   ⋈

Observe that the assumption of independence of the initial configurations is essential to this lower bound. Lemma 8 can also be used to characterize non-independent systems. Lemma 8 and Theorem 9(a) generalize and somewhat simplify the $t + 1$ round lower bound on the worst-case behavior of SBA in our model (see [DLM], [DS], [FL], [H], [CD]). As we will see in the sequel, Theorem 9(b) allows us to completely characterize the runs in which $t + 1$ rounds are necessary for attaining SBA, as well as those that require k rounds, for all k. More generally, Theorem 2(a) and Theorem 9(b) provide us with a lower bound on the time by which facts can become common knowledge in t-uniform systems. Formally, we have:

Theorem 10:   Let $t \leq n - 2$, let S be an independent t-uniform system, and let $\rho' \in S$ satisfy $\mathcal{W}(S, \rho') \leq t - \ell$. If $(S, \rho', \ell) \not\models \varphi$, then $(S, \rho, \ell) \not\models C\varphi$ for all $\rho \in S$ satisfying $\mathcal{W}(S, \rho) \leq t - \ell$.   ⋈

Theorem 10 and Theorem 6(b) completely characterize when non-trivial facts about the initial configuration become common knowledge in the runs of S_ρ. In a precise sense, they imply that the only fact that is common knowledge at (ρ, k), for $k \leq t - \mathcal{W}(S_\rho, \rho)$, is that the wastefulness is less than $t + 1 - k$. Formally, we have:

Corollary 11: Let $t \leq n-2$, let $S_{\hat{P}}$ be an independent t-uniform system for $\hat{P}$, and let $\mathcal{W}(S_{\hat{P}}, \rho) \leq t - \ell$. Then $(S_{\hat{P}}, \rho, \ell) \models C\varphi$ iff for all $\rho' \in S_{\hat{P}}$ such that $\mathcal{W}(S_{\hat{P}}, \rho', \ell) \leq t - \ell$ it is the case that $(S_{\hat{P}}, \rho', \ell) \models \varphi$. ⋈

Furthermore, Corollary 3 and Theorem 10 immediately imply:

Corollary 12: Let $t \leq n-2$, let $\mathcal{P}$ be a t-resilient protocol for SBA, and let S be a t-uniform system for $\mathcal{P}$, with $\rho \in S$. Then SBA is not attained in ρ in fewer than $t + 1 - \mathcal{W}(S, \rho)$ rounds. ⋈

Corollary 12 proves that SBA cannot be attained in the runs of $\hat{P}$ any earlier than it is attained by the protocol of Corollary 7. However, it still seems possible that using another protocol SBA will be attainable in fewer rounds than in the protocol of Corollary 7. We now show that this protocol is optimal in a rather strong sense: given an initial configuration and the pattern in which failures occur, no protocol protocol attains SBA in fewer rounds than the protocol of Corollary 7. In order to state this claim rigorously and prove it, we need to make a few definitions.

We denote the initial configuration of the system by $\bar{\sigma}$. A *failure pattern* is a list π of faulty processors, and for each faulty processor p_i a specification of a round r_i in which it fails and a "forbidden" subset Q_i of the processors to whom it necessarily does not send messages in its failing round. Notice that given a protocol $\mathcal{P}$, the initial configuration and failure pattern uniquely determine a run of the protocol. (However, a run of the protocol may be the result of more than one failure pattern in protocols that don't require all processors to send messages to all other processors in every round.) Thus, we can represent a run by a triple $\langle \mathcal{P}, \bar{\sigma}, \pi \rangle$. We are now ready to show that the wastefulness of a run resulting from a given initial configuration and failure pattern is no greater than its wastefulness in $S_{\hat{P}}$. Given Corollary 12, this will imply that the protocol of Corollary 7 always attains SBA at the earliest possible time, given the initial configuration and failure pattern.

Theorem 13: Let S be a t-uniform system for a protocol $\mathcal{P}$, and let $\rho = \langle \mathcal{P}, \bar{\sigma}, \pi \rangle$, and let $\hat{\rho} = \langle \hat{\mathcal{P}}, \bar{\sigma}, \pi \rangle$. Then $\mathcal{W}(S, \rho) \leq \mathcal{W}(S_{\hat{P}}, \hat{\rho})$.

Proof: We will show a more general fact from which the theorem will follow. Given an initial configuration $\bar{\sigma}'$, and a failure pattern π', let $\rho' = \langle \mathcal{P}, \bar{\sigma}', \pi' \rangle$ and $\hat{\rho}' = \langle \hat{\mathcal{P}}, \bar{\sigma}', \pi' \rangle$. Notice that $A(\rho, k') = A(\hat{\rho}, k')$ for all k'. We claim that for all k and all $p_i \in A(\rho, k)$ it is the case that if $v(p_i, \hat{\rho}, k) = v(p_i, \hat{\rho}', k)$ then $v(p_i, \rho, k) = v(p_i, \rho', k)$. We argue by induction on k. The case $k = 0$ is immediate. Let $k > 0$ and assume inductively that the claim holds for all processors in $A(\rho, k-1)$ at time $k-1$. Thus, if $v(p_i, \hat{\rho}, k) = v(p_i, \hat{\rho}', k)$ and p_j sends a round k message to p_i in $\hat{\rho}$, then p_j has the same view at $(\hat{\rho}, k-1)$ and $(\hat{\rho}', k-1)$, and p_j also sends p_i a round k message in $\hat{\rho}'$. In this case both π and π' determine that round k messages from p_j to p_i are delivered. By the inductive assumption p_j also has the same view in $(\rho, k-1)$ and in $(\rho', k-1)$. It follows that $\mathcal{P}$ requires p_j to act identically in round k of both ρ and ρ'. And if p_j is required to send p_i a round k message in ρ then it is required to send p_i the same message in round k of ρ'. Processor p_j does not send a round k message to p_i in $\hat{\rho}$ only if π determines that p_j cannot send p_i such a message. But then for similar reasons π' must also determine that p_j does not send p_i a round k message.

It follows that in this case p_j does not send p_i a round k message in ρ or in ρ'. Thus, for all processors p_j it is the case that p_i receives a round k message from p_j in ρ iff p_i receives an identical message from p_j in round k of ρ'. The inductive assumption also implies that $v(p_i, \rho, k-1) = v(p_i, \rho', k-1)$, and it now follows that $v(p_i, \rho, k) = v(p_i, \rho', k)$ and we are done with the claim. We now show how the theorem follows from this claim. Assume that $\mathcal{W}(S, \rho) = j$ and that $\mathcal{W}(S_\rho, \hat{\rho}) < j$. Then there is a time k such that $(S, \rho, k) \models I(D \geq j)$, and $(S_\rho, \hat{\rho}, k) \not\models I(D \geq j)$. Let $G = A(\hat{\rho}, k)$ (notice that $G = A(\rho, k)$ as well). It follows that there is a run $\hat{\rho}' \in S_\rho$ such that $v(G, \hat{\rho}, k) = v(G, \hat{\rho}', k)$ and $D(\hat{\rho}', k) < j$. Let $\bar{\sigma}'$ and π' be the initial configuration and failure pattern in $\hat{\rho}'$. Let ρ' be the run of $\mathcal{P}$ corresponding to $\bar{\sigma}'$ and π'. Since $v(G, \hat{\rho}, k) = v(G, \hat{\rho}', k)$, our claim implies that $v(G, \rho, k) = v(G, \rho', k)$. But since $D(\rho', k) = D(\hat{\rho}', k) < j$ and $A(\rho, k) = G$, we have that $(S, \rho, k) \not\models I(D \geq j)$, contradicting our original assumption. $\bowtie$

Theorem 13 and Corollary 12 now imply that the protocol of Corollary 7 is indeed optimal in the strong sense we intended: given any initial configuration and failure pattern, it attains SBA as early as any t-resilient protocol for SBA can. In light of Theorem 13, we can talk about the inherent *wastefulness* $w(\pi)$ of a failure pattern π, defined to be $\mathcal{W}(S_\rho, \langle \hat{P}, \bar{\sigma}, \pi \rangle)$. That $w(\pi)$ is well defined follows from the fact that runs ρ of S_ρ have the property that $\mathcal{W}(S_\rho, \rho, k)$ depends only on the pattern of failures and is independent of the initial configuration. This can be proved by a straightforward induction on k, and is left to the reader. Lemma 8 through Corollary 12 can now be viewed as statements about the effect of the failure pattern on the similarity of executions and on what facts can become common knowledge at various times in the execution of an arbitrary t-resilient protocol. Corollaries 7 and 12 tell us that exactly $t + 1 - w(\pi)$ rounds are necessary to attain SBA in runs of any t-resilient protocol for SBA that have pattern failure π (in the rest of the paper we will use π to refer to the failure pattern of the run in question). This provides a complete characterization of the number of rounds required to reach SBA in a run, given the pattern in which failures occur.

We have seen that the only facts that become common knowledge before time $t + 1 - w(\pi)$ are facts about the wastefulness of the run. In the previous section we saw that in runs of S_ρ the processors attain common knowledge of an identical view of the initial configuration at time $t + 1 - w(\pi)$. Thus, we have a complete description of when facts about the initial configuration become common knowledge. It is interesting to ask the more general question of when arbitrary facts become common knowledge. Using Lemma 5 it is possible to show that at time $t + 1 - w(\pi)$ in a run of S_ρ it is not only common knowledge that there was a clean round, but there is a particular round that is commonly known to have appeared clean to all active processors. Let $k(\pi)$ denote the latest such round. Thus, at time $t + 1 - w(\pi)$ it is common knowledge that the processors have an identical view of the first $k(\pi) - 1$ rounds. There is some number, say f of processors that are commonly known at time $t + 1 - w(\pi)$ to have failed by time $k(\pi) - 1$. Let $t' = t - f$. Roughly speaking, time $k(\pi)$ can now be regarded as the start of a new run, and for appropriate definitions of $d'(k)$ and $w'(\pi)$, we get that at time $k(\pi) + t' + 1 - w'(\pi)$ the system will attain common knowledge of a common view of the state of the system at time $k(\pi)$. Interestingly, it can be shown that $k(\pi) + t' + 1 - w'(\pi) = t + 2 - w(\pi)$. That is, one round after the processors attain common knowledge of (a common view of) the state of the run at time $k(\pi) - 1$, they attain common knowledge of the state of the run at time $k(\pi)$. In fact, at the end of each round following time $t + 1 - w(\pi)$ the active processors attain common knowledge of a common view of at least one (sometimes more) additional past round. Again, the techniques of Sections 3 and 4 can be used to show that the pattern of failures determines when an arbitrary fact about the first k rounds may become common knowledge, and the simple protocol $\hat{P}$ of Section 3 is in a precise sense the fastest to attain common knowledge of such facts. Details are left to the reader.

5. Applications

Throughout the paper we have shown how our results regarding when common knowledge of various facts is attained in a Byzantine system affect the SBA problem. In this section we discuss some further consequences of the analysis presented in the previous sections. This is intended to illustrate the types of applications that the analysis can be used for. We start by considering some problems that are closely related to SBA.

The problem of *Weak* SBA (WSBA) mentioned in the introduction, which differs from SBA in that clause (4) is changed so that the active processors are required to decide on a value v only if all initial values were v and *no processor fails* was introduced by Lamport as a weakening of SBA. However, Theorem 9(b) immediately implies that the active processors do not have common knowledge of whether any processors failed before time $t + 1 - w(\pi)$, in any run of a t-resilient protocol for WSBA with failure pattern π. And since SBA can already be performed at time $t + 1 - w(\pi)$, we have that t-resilient protocols cannot attain WSBA any earlier than they can SBA. Theorem 9 also describes why the variant of SBA used in this paper (which was introduced by [FL]) is essentially equivalent to the original version of the *Byzantine Generals* problem of [PSL], in which only one processor initially has a value, and the processors need to decide on this value if the processor does not fail, and on a consistent value otherwise.

It has been a folk conjecture that a t-resilient protocol that guarantees to perform any non-trivial action simultaneously requires $t + 1$ rounds in the worst case. We will now show that this is not the case. Let *Bivalent Agreement* be defined by clauses (1)–(3) of SBA, and replacing clause (4) by:

4'. At least one run of the protocol decides 0, and at least one run decides 1.

Thus, so long as no more than t processors fail, all processors must decide on the same value simultaneously, and both 0 and 1 must be attainable values. Theorem 2 implies that any action that is guaranteed to be performed simultaneously requires some fact to become common knowledge before the action can be performed. Theorem 6(b) implies that at the end of round 2 of S_ρ it is common knowledge whether or not the wastefulness of the run is $t - 1$ (i.e., whether t processors were seen to have failed in the first round). Thus, we can easily derive a t-resilient protocol for Bivalent agreement: Each processor follows $\hat{P}$ for the first two rounds, and then decides 0 if it knows that t processors failed in the first round, and 1 otherwise. This protocol attains Bivalent agreement in two rounds, and Theorem 10 implies that there is no faster protocol for Bivalent agreement so long as $t \leq n - 2$. Furthermore, it implies that in a precise sense this is the only two-round protocol for Bivalent agreement. We leave it to the reader to check that if $t \geq n - 1$ then there is a protocol for Bivalent agreement that requires only one round. Thus, Bivalent agreement is a truly easier problem than SBA. We note that [FLP] and [DDS] prove that in an asynchronous system there is no 1-resilient protocol for an even weaker variant of Bivalent agreement.

We have stressed the connection between common knowledge and simultaneous actions. Interestingly, the lower bounds on the time required for attaining common knowledge imply worst-case bounds on the behavior of t-resilient protocols that perform coordinated actions that are not required to be performed simultaneously. For example, *Eventual Byzantine Agreement* (EBA) is defined by clauses (1), (2), and (4) of SBA: the processors' decisions need not be simultaneous (cf. [DRS]). There are well-known protocols that attain EBA after two rounds in failure-free runs (for which $w(\pi) = 0$). However, using Theorems 2, 10, and 13 it is not hard to show that a t-resilient protocol for EBA must require $t + 1$ rounds in some runs with $w(\pi) = 0$. More generally, these theorems show that such a protocol must require $t + 1 - j$ rounds in some runs with $w(\pi) = j$. This is a slight refinement of the well-known fact that EBA requires $t + 1$ rounds in the worst case (cf. [DRS]). Many very relevant and interesting aspects of EBA are not covered by our analysis. We believe that an analysis of EBA should involve a study of when the states of ϵ-common knowledge and eventual common knowledge (cf. [HM]) are attained in a Byzantine environment. This is an interesting open problem.

As our investigation centered around t-resilient protocols, we now briefly discuss some other possible reliability assumptions. Recall that Theorem 4 states that all active processors are guaranteed to have an identical view of the system's initial configuration at time $t + 1$ in every run of a t-uniform system for $\hat{P}$. This follows simply from the fact that at time $t + 1$ it is common knowledge that one of the previous rounds was clean. Instead of t-resiliency, we could require that a protocol for SBA be guaranteed to attain SBA so long as no more than k consecutive rounds are dirty. In the system corresponding to all the runs of $\hat{P}$ in which at most k consecutive rounds are dirty, it is common knowledge at time $k + 1$ that a clean round has occurred, and $\hat{P}$ can be converted in to a protocol for SBA that is guaranteed to attain SBA in no more than $k + 1$ rounds. This means, for example, that if processors in a Byzantine system are known to fail at least two at a time, SBA can be achieved in $t/2 + 1$ rounds. Having a bound of k consecutive dirty rounds seems in many cases to be a more appropriate assumption about a system than having a bound of t on the total number of failures possible, since the latter is not a local assumption. Of course, these two assumptions are not mutually exclusive, and we may often have a small bound on the possible number of consecutive dirty rounds, when only a much larger bound holds for the total number of failures. The bound on the number of consecutive dirty rounds implies a good upper bound on SBA in the case of crash failures.

Another way we can consider varying the reliability assumptions about the system is by restricting the number of possible processor failures that can occur in a round. For example, let us consider the assumption that at most one processor can fail in any given round of the computation, and at most t processors might fail overall. We are interested in the question of whether such assumptions allow us to attain SBA quickly. Unfortunately, the lower bound proofs of Lemma 8 and Theorem 9 work very well for this reliability model. In fact, since all of the runs of such a system are guaranteed to have wastefulness 0, even Bivalent agreement cannot be attained in any run of the system in less than $t + 1$ rounds! SBA and WSBA clearly require $t + 1$ rounds in *all* runs of the system. We now present a somewhat artificial variant of this assumption that provides us with a non-uniform reliability assumption whose behavior is interesting and somewhat counter-intuitive: We say that a protocol for SBA is *one visible failure resistant* (1-VFR) if it is guaranteed to attain SBA so long as no more than one processor failure becomes visible to the active processors in any given round. The set of possible runs of a protocol P that display such behavior will be called a *visibly restrained* system for P. It is possible to show that in the visibly restrained system for the simple protocol $\hat{P}$ of Section 3 it is common knowledge at time 2 whether round 1 is clean, and therefore WSBA can be attained in two rounds. However, SBA can be shown to require $n - 1$ rounds in runs of $\hat{P}$ in which one processor fails in every round except possibly the $(n - 1)$st round. (If one adds a bound of $t \leq n - 2$ on the total number of failures possible, $n - 1$ is replaced by $t + 1$.) Interestingly, there is a 1-VFR protocol for SBA that is guaranteed to attain SBA in three rounds (in all runs)! Thus, for the 1-VFR reliability model, our simple protocol is no longer a most general protocol. The reason for the odd behavior of 1-VFR protocols is that the patterns of failures of the runs that satisfy 1-VFR are intimately related to the structure of the protocol. Thus, the protocol can restrict the patterns of failures possible and make effective use of the 1-VFR assumption. Details and further discussion are given in the full paper.

6. Conclusions

This paper analyzes the states of knowledge attainable in the course of the execution of various protocols in the system, for the case of a particular simple model of unreliable distributed systems that is fairly popular in the literature. Motivated by the work of [HM], the analysis focused mainly on when facts that are implicitly known become common knowledge in systems in which there is an upper bound of t on the number of possible faulty processors. This problem was shown to be a direct generalization of problems such as Simultaneous Byzantine Agreement, in which it is required that consistent actions be performed simultaneously at all non-faulty sites of the system. By deriving exact bounds on the question of when facts become common knowledge, we immediately got exact bounds for SBA and many other problems. An interesting fact that came out of the analysis was that the pattern in which processors fail in a given run determines a lower bound on the time in which facts about the system's initial configuration become common knowledge, with different patterns determining different bounds. Ironically, facts become common knowledge faster in cases when many processors fail early in the run. The somewhat paradoxical argument for this is that, given an upper bound on the total number of failures possible, if many processors fail early then only few can fail later. The protocol can make use of the fact that the rest of the run is relatively free of failures. As a by-product of the analysis, we were able to derive a simple improved protocol for SBA that is optimal in *all* runs.

Our analysis shows that the essential driving force behind many of the phenomena in unreliable systems seems to be the inherent uncertainty that a particular site in such a system has about the global state of the system. We come to grips with this uncertainty by performing a knowledge-based analysis of such a system. We stress that our analysis was by and large restricted to protocols for simultaneous actions in a rather clean and simple model of unreliable systems: synchronous systems with global clocks and crash failures. We believe that performing similar analyses for nastier models of failures will prove very exciting, and will provide a much better understanding of the true structure underlying the richer failure models, and of the differences between the failure models. The ideas and techniques developed in this paper should provide a sound basis on which to build such an analysis, although it is clear that a number of additional ideas would be required.

In summary, the treatment in this paper differs from the usual approach to Byzantine agreement type problems in that we make explicit and essential use of reasoning about knowledge in order to reach conclusions about the possibility or impossibility of carrying out certain desired actions in a distributed environment. The generality and applicability of our results suggest that this is a promising approach.

Acknowledgements: We wish to thank Brian Coan, Ron Fagin, Joe Halpern, Nancy Lynch, and Moshe Vardi for stimulating discussions. The work of the second author was supported in part by an IBM Post-doctoral fellowship. Some of the work was done while he was at Stanford University, supported by DARPA contract N00039-82-C-0250, and by an IBM Research Student Associateship.

References

[CD]   B. Coan and C. Dwork, Simultaneity is harder than agreement, To appear, *Proceedings of the Fifth Symposium on Reliability in Distributed Software and Database Systems*, 1986.

[CM]   K. M. Chandy and J. Misra, How processes learn, *Proceedings of the Fourth ACM Symposium on the Principles of Distributed Computing*, 1985, pp. 204-214.

[DLM]   R. DeMillo, N. A. Lynch, and M. Merritt, Cryptographic Protocols, *Proceedings of the Fourteenth Annual ACM Symposium on the Theory of Computing*, 1982, pp. 383-400.

[DDS]   D. Dolev, C. Dwork, and L. Stockmeyer, On the minimal synchronization needed for distributed consensus, *Proceedings of the 24th Annual Symposium on Foundations of Computer Science*, 1983, pp. 369-397.

[DRS]   D. Dolev, R. Reischuk, and H. R. Strong, Eventual is earlier than immediate, *Proceedings of the 23th Annual Symposium on Foundations of Computer Science*, 1982, pp. 196-203.

[DS]   D. Dolev H. R. Strong, Polynomial algorithms for multiple processor agreement, *Proceedings of the Fourteenth Annual ACM Symposium on the Theory of Computing*, 1982, pp. 401-407.

[FV]   R. Fagin and M. Y. Vardi, Knowledge and implicit knowledge in a distributed environment, *Proceedings of the Conference on Theoretical Aspects of Reasoning About Knowledge*, Monterey, 1986.

[F]   M. J. Fischer, The consensus problem in unreliable distributed systems (A brief survey), *Yale University Technical Report YALEU/DCS/RR-273*, 1983.

[FL]   M. J. Fischer and N. A. Lynch, A lower bound for the time to assure interactive consistency, *Information Processing Letters*, 14:4, 1982, pp. 183-186.

[FLP] M. J. Fischer, N. A. Lynch, and M. Paterson, Impossibility of distributed consensus with one faulty process, *Proceedings of the second Symposium on Principles of Database Systems*, 1983.

[H]   V. Hadzilacos, A lower bound for Byzantine agreement with fail-stop processors, *Harvard University Technical Report TR-21-83*.

[HM]   J. Y. Halpern and Y. Moses, Knowledge and common knowledge in a distributed environment, Version of December 1985 is available as an IBM RJ. Early versions appeared in *Proceedings of the Third ACM Symposium on the Principles of Distributed Computing*, 1984, pp. 50–61; revised as IBM research report *RJ 4421*, 1984.

[HM2] J. Y. Halpern and Y. Moses, A guide to the modal logic of knowledge and belief, *Proceedings of the Ninth International Joint Conference on Artificial Intelligence*, 1985, pp. 480-490.

[LF]   L. Lamport and M. J. Fischer, Byzantine grenerals and transaction commit protocols, *SRI Technical Report Op.62*, 1982.

[PR]   R. Parikh and R. Ramanujam, Distributed processes and the logic of knowledge (preliminary report), *Proceedings of the Workshop on Logics of Programs*, 1985, pp. 256-268.

[PSL] M. Pease, R. Shostak, and L. Lamport, Reaching agreement in the presence of faults, *JACM*, 27:2, 1980, pp. 228-234.

FOUNDATIONS OF KNOWLEDGE FOR DISTRIBUTED SYSTEMS

Michael J. Fischer* and Neil Immerman[†]

Computer Science Department
Yale University
New Haven, CT 06520

Abstract

We give a simple, yet very general definition for distributed protocols. We then define notions of knowledge and common knowledge appropriate for these protocols. We study how changes in the states of knowledge relate to more standard notions of computation. We find that by restricting our formulas to certain sets of global states we can realize different, appropriate definitions of knowledge with fundamentally different properties.

---

*Research supported in part by the National Science Foundation under Grant Number DCR-8405478 and by the Office of Naval Research under Contract Number N00014-82-K-0154.

[†]Research supported by an NSF postdoctoral fellowship and the Mathematical Sciences Research Insitute, Berkeley.

1   Introduction

Knowledge and common knowledge are intuitive concepts that help us reason about ordinary everyday situations in which we have only partial information. They become more complicated when other agents in the situation are intelligent and have reasoning power, for then our state of knowledge contains not only facts about the world but also facts about the state of knowledge of others, and how these states change over time depends on the agents' reasoning ability as well as on the occurrence of external events. (Cf. the "muddy children's problem" in [HM84].) It is appealing to use these concepts to reason about distributed protocols, for processors of a distributed system can be thought of as independent agents with only partial information about the global state of the system. To be sure our reasoning is correct, it is necessary to have rigorous and precise definitions of the intuitive concepts underlying such terms as "global state", "time", "knowledge", "message", etc. Only then can we be sure to avoid the circularities and inconsistencies that are all too common in informal reasoning.

Halpern and Moses informally define various notions of "knowledge" and "common knowledge" in the context of a particular model of distributed systems in which every processor has a clock and stores in its state the entire history of messages sent to it [HM84]. They argue that while common knowledge is desirable, it is unattainable in many realistic settings. They suggest a hierarchy of weakened versions of common knowledge and discuss conditions under which these can be achieved.

We find the assertion that "common knowledge is not attainable in real world systems"[1] to be at variance with our intuition, for it seems clear that "common knowledge" in the intuitive sense *is* attained in the real world. To understand this disparity between the formal model and our intuition, we examine, simplify, and make more precise the informal definitions given in [HM84].

We first give quite general and simple definitions of distributed protocol, knowledge and common knowledge. Under these simplified definitions, the arguments of [HM84], suitably formalized, still apply to show the impossibility of attaining common knowledge in systems without globally simultaneous transitions. We then show that it is not necessary to discard the notions of knowledge and common knowledge in favor of weaker ones in order to obtain realistic and useful definitions; rather, one can discard the assumption that formulas be interpretable at every global state and instead interpret them only at a subset of "safe" states. This is analogous to notions of database consistency in which the database is only required to be consistent at times when no transaction is in the middle of execution. Using the same definitions as before but restricted to safe states, we get a new and different notion of common knowledge which *can* be attained in situations where Halpern-Moses common knowledge cannot.

We conclude that formalizing these concepts is subtle, and seemingly innocuous assumptions can lead to unexpected results. Our desire is to formalize concepts of knowledge so that they may aid the design of distributed algorithms and clear proofs of their properties. We believe we have provided a solid base for future work in this area.

---

[1][HM84], Conclusions.

2   Distibuted Protocols

2.1   A General Model

Definition 2.1 *A* distributed protocol,

$$\mathcal{P} = \langle n, Q, I, \tau \rangle,$$

consists of a number n of participants, a set Q of local states, a set $I \subseteq Q^n$ of initial global states, and a next move relation $\tau \subseteq Q^n \times Q^n$ on global states.

For any protocol $\mathcal{P}$, let $R_\mathcal{P}$ be the τ-reachable global states of $\mathcal{P}$, that is, the set of all global states we can reach by starting in I and taking any number of τ steps. By definition, only the reachable global states can occur in a run of $\mathcal{P}$. In general it may be a complex task to tell if a given element of Q^n is in $R_\mathcal{P}$; however, in this paper we will only be concerned with the reachable global states. For $p \in Q^n$ a global state and i a participant, we write $(p)_i$ to denote the ith component of p. We will also use the notation $p \overset{i}{\sim} q$ to mean that $p, q \in R_\mathcal{P}$ and $(p)_i = (q)_i$, i.e. they are indistinguishable from i's point of view. Obviously each $\overset{i}{\sim}$ is an equivalence relation.[2]

Our definition of protocol is certainly simple and precise. Let us argue that it is also sufficiently general. Anything we would be willing to call a distributed system can be broken up into a finite number of logical entities which we call "participants". A participant may be any component of a system: a processor, a buffer, a clock, etc.[3] Each participant has some total configuration that we are calling its (local) state. Furthermore, the states of all the participants combined should determine the entire state of the system and thus which global states can next be entered.

It is easy to see for example that our model of distributed system is a generalization of the shared variable model of Lynch and Fischer [LF81]. In that model, the participants consist of shared variables and processors. Each action involves exactly one processor and one shared variable.

Similarly our model includes synchronous protocols in which every processor sends a message to every other during each round. One way to model this is to specify that the set of possible states is of the form $Q = M^n$, i.e. each processor's total configuration consists of an n-tuple. We can specify that the ith entry of j's state is the value of the message sent from i to j during the previous round. This can be done as follows: for all processors i, j, and for all global states

---

[2]Our definition of knowledge given in Section 3 will be that of inherent knowledge—those facts that a participant could deduce given arbitrary computational power. Thus, in a global state $p \in R_\mathcal{P}$, a participant i will know that we are in some $q \in R_\mathcal{P}$ with $q \overset{i}{\sim} p$, and its knowledge will consist exactly of those facts true in all such q. The problem of determining membership in $R_\mathcal{P}$ is not relevant to the notions considered in this paper. It certainly is relevant, however, when considering knowledge in cryptographic protocols when an explicit bound is given on the computational resources of the participants.

[3]This approach is different from most of the other formal specifications of protocols of which we are aware, e.g. [CM85], [HM85], [HF85], [PR85]. The more usual approach is to say that after a message is sent it may sometime later be received by the addressee, but a message in transit is not explicitly modeled.

p, q, r, s, if $\langle p,q \rangle$ and $\langle r,s \rangle$ are in τ and if processor i has the same state in p as in r, then the ith component of processor j's state is the same in q as in s.

The sense in which our model could be too general is that we allow any transition relation τ. Of course, for certain applications we can make appropriate restrictions. We have already seen that we can restrict our attention to processors which communicate with shared variables, or to synchronous message passing protocols. Similarly, instead of letting each processor's transitions be perfectly general, we can restrict our attention to processors with specified computing power, e.g. finite automata, polynomial time Turing machines, etc.

One interesting kind of restriction to place on the transition relation τ is locality.

Definition 2.2 *Let $T = \{i_1, \ldots, i_k\}$ be a set of participants, and let $E_T(p,q)$ hold if $(p)_i = (q)_i$ for all $i \in T$.*

- *We say that $\langle p,q \rangle$ affects only* participants in T *if $E_{\overline{T}}(p,q)$ holds, where $\overline{T}$ is the set of participants not in T.*

- *We say that $\langle p,q \rangle \in \tau$ is enabled by T if for all p' such that $E_T(p',p)$, then $\langle p',q' \rangle \in \tau$ for the (unique) q' such that $E_T(q',q)$ and $E_{\overline{T}}(q',p')$.*

- *We say $\langle p,q \rangle \in \tau$ is local to T if it affects only participants in T and is enabled by T.*

- *We say that a protocol is* pairwise local *if every transition in τ is local to some set T of size two.*

Thus, a transition is local to T if only coordinates belonging to T are changed during the transition and if the local states of the participants not in T have no effect on whether or not this transition can occur. Note that a transition local to T does not necessarily affect all of the members of T. Note also that the same transition can be local to two sets T_1 and T_2 but not be local to their intersection. Consider for example the transition $\alpha = \langle (0,1,1,1), (1,1,1,1) \rangle$, and suppose τ contains every transition of the form $\langle (0,x_2,x_3,x_4), (1,x_2,x_3,x_4) \rangle$ *except* for $\langle (0,0,0,0), (1,0,0,0) \rangle$. Let $T_i = \{1,i\}$, $i = 2,3,4$. Then α affects only T_i (since only the first component changes), and α is enabled by T_i (since no matter how the components outside of T_i are changed, participant 1 can still make the transition from state 0 to 1). Thus, α is local to T_i for each i, but clearly α is not local to $\bigcap_i T_i = \{1\}$.

2.2   Comparison with Other Models

The shared variable model [LF81] is pairwise local: each transition is local to one processor and one shared variable. On the other hand the synchronous protocol described above is not pairwise local: each transition in general affects all n participants. We believe that if one models a distributed system at a sufficiently fine level then it will be pairwise local simply because it is difficult to insure that distant events occur simultaneously. However it is sometimes convenient to discuss synchronous protocols when the finer analysis would only obscure what is going on.

The models described in [CM85], [HM85], [HF85], [PR85] are all asynchronous message passing systems and thus are pairwise local when translated to our protocols. For readers more familiar with these other models, we will now consider one of them in more detail. Chandy and Misra [CM85] consider systems of n processors in which there are three disjoint sets of transitions: sends, receives, and local events. The relation between sends and receives is that each receive must correspond to a unique earlier send. The Chandy and Misra model forces the processors to remember their entire local history. Furthermore, the ability to perform a transition depends only on the local history of the affected processor except in the case of a receive, which also requires that the message to be received has already been sent. We can characterize the Chandy and Misra model in terms of our protocol model as follows:

Proposition 2.3 *The Chandy and Misra model [CM85] is isomorphic to the protocol model* $P = \langle n+1, Q, I, \tau \rangle$:

1. *Participants 1 to n are the processors and participant $n+1$ is the message buffer.*

2. *There are sets E of local events and M of messages. A message triple $\langle i, j, m \rangle$ is a send from i and a receive by j of message m. The local state of processor i is a list of local events and message triples, each of which is a send from i or a receive by i. The local states of the buffer consist of any multiset of message triples.*

3. *The set of initial global states is the singleton $I = \langle \lambda, \ldots, \lambda, \emptyset \rangle$ in which all processors have the empty list λ as their local history and the buffer is empty.*

4. *Each transition is of one of the following three forms. Transition (a) only involves participant i, and transitions (b) and (c) only involve participants i and $n+1$.*

    (a) *Local event $e \in E$ at processor i: e is appended to i's local state.*

    (b) *Send of $m \in M$ from processor i to processor j: the message triple $\langle i, j, m \rangle$ is appended to i's local state and added to $n+1$'s local state.*

    (c) *Receive by processor i of the message $m \in M$ sent by processor k: a message triple $\langle k, i, m \rangle$ is deleted from $n+1$'s local state and appended to i's local state.*

2.3   Two Examples

We conclude this section with two nontrivial examples of protocols, one asynchronous and the other synchronous. These protocols will be frequently referred to in the remainder of the paper.

Both protocols model the situation of a completely connected network of n processors which operate in rounds. On each round, every processor i sends a message $m_{i,j}$ to each other processor j. After receiving all of the messages sent to it on the given round, processor i changes state and chooses a new set of messages to send out on the next round. The new state and message set depend on the old state and on the messages received during the round.

In protocol A, the messages are sent asynchronously, one at a time, via message buffers. A buffer either contains a message or is empty. A message can only be sent to an empty buffer and only received from a non-empty buffer. Sending a message makes the buffer non-empty, and receiving a message makes the buffer empty again. Thus, the execution of each round takes many steps.

In protocol $\mathcal{B}$, all messages are sent and received in one big synchronous step, that is, one step of $\mathcal{B}$ corresponds to an entire round of $\mathcal{A}$.

2.3.1   Protocol $\mathcal{A}$

Let $\mathcal{A} = \langle n^2, Q_{\mathcal{A}}, I_{\mathcal{A}}, \tau_{\mathcal{A}} \rangle$ be an asynchronous message passing protocol defined as follows: The first n participants of $\mathcal{A}$ are the processors $a_1, \ldots, a_n$; the remaining $(n-1)n$ participants are buffers. For a global state p, we abuse our previous notation slightly and write $(p)_{a_i}$ to denote the component corresponding to a_i and $(p)_{b_{i,j}}$ to denote the component corresponding to buffer $b_{i,j}$.

The set of possible local states of a buffer $b_{i,j}$, $i \neq j$, is $Q_{\mathcal{A}}^b = M \cup \{\lambda\}$, where M is a set of possible messages and λ is a special symbol denoting the null message. $(p)_{b_{i,j}} = m \in M$ indicates that the single message m was sent by i but not yet delivered to j in global state p, and $(p)_{b_{i,j}} = \lambda$ indicates that no message is waiting.

The set of possible local states of a processor a_i is $Q_{\mathcal{A}}^a = (D \times (M \cup \{\lambda\})^{n-1} \times \mathbf{N})$. State $\langle d, m_1, \ldots, m_{i-1}, m_{i+1}, \ldots, m_n, r \rangle$ indicates that the processor is in internal state d at round $\lfloor r/2 \rfloor$ with pending messages $m_1, \ldots, m_{i-1}, m_{i+1}, \ldots, m_n$. If r is even, then the processor is in a 'send' state, waiting to place each $m_j \neq \lambda$ into buffer $b_{i,j}$. If r is odd, then the processor is in a 'receive' state waiting to fetch a message from $b_{j,i}$ for each j such that $m_j = \lambda$.

Thus, the complete set of local states $Q_{\mathcal{A}}$ is $Q_{\mathcal{A}}^a \cup Q_{\mathcal{A}}^b$.

The transitions making up $\tau_{\mathcal{A}}$ are of four kinds:

1. $\langle p, q \rangle \in Send_{i,j}$ if

   - $p \stackrel{c}{\sim} q$ for all $c \notin \{a_i, b_{i,j}\}$;
   - $(p)_{b_{i,j}} = \lambda$;
   - $(q)_{b_{i,j}} = m_j \neq \lambda$;
   - $(p)_{a_i} = \langle d, \ldots, m_{j-1}, m_j, m_{j+1}, \ldots, 2k \rangle$;
   - $(q)_{a_i} = \langle d, \ldots, m_{j-1}, \lambda, m_{j+1}, \ldots, 2k \rangle$.

2. $\langle p, q \rangle \in End\_send_i$ if

   - $p \stackrel{c}{\sim} q$ for all $c \neq a_i$;
   - $(p)_{a_i} = \langle d, \lambda, \ldots, \lambda, 2k \rangle$;
   - $(q)_{a_i} = \langle d, \lambda, \ldots, \lambda, 2k+1 \rangle$.

3. $\langle p, q \rangle \in Receive_{i,j}$ if

   - $p \stackrel{c}{\sim} q$ for all $c \notin \{a_i, b_{j,i}\}$;
   - $(p)_{b_{j,i}} = m_j \neq \lambda$;
   - $(q)_{b_{j,i}} = \lambda$;
   - $(p)_{a_i} = \langle d, \ldots, m_{j-1}, \lambda, m_{j+1}, \ldots, 2k+1 \rangle$;

- $(q)_{a_i} = \langle d, \ldots, m_{j-1}, m_j, m_{j+1}, \ldots, 2k+1 \rangle$.

4. $\langle p, q \rangle \in End\_receive_i$ if

  - $p \overset{c}{\sim} q$ for all $c \neq a_i$;
  - $(p)_{a_i} = \langle d, m_1, \ldots, m_n, 2k+1 \rangle$, where $m_j \neq \lambda$ for all $j \neq i$;
  - $(q)_{a_i} = \langle d', m'_1, \ldots, m'_n, 2k+2 \rangle$, where $m'_j \neq \lambda$ for all $j \neq i$, and d' and m'_j are functions of $(p)_{a_i}$.

Now we let τ_A consist of all the above transitions:

$$\tau_A = \bigcup_{i,j} Send_{i,j} \cup End\_send_i \cup Receive_{i,j} \cup End\_receive_i.$$

Finally let I_A be some nonempty set of global states in which the state of every processor a_i has the form $(d, m_1, \ldots, m_n, 0)$ with $m_j \neq \lambda$ for all $j \neq i$, and all the buffers are empty.

2.3.2   Protocol B

Our second example of a protocol is a synchronous version of A. Let $B = \langle n^2, Q_B, I_B, \tau_B \rangle$, where

$$\begin{aligned} Q_B^a &= D \times M^{n-1} \times \{2r \mid r \in \mathbb{N}\}, \\ Q_B^b &= \{\lambda\}, \\ Q_B &= Q_B^a \cup Q_B^b. \end{aligned}$$

Let $\overline{Q}_B = (Q_B^a)^n \times (Q_B^b)^{n(n-1)}$. Let the transitions τ_B consist of all pairs $\langle p, q \rangle \in \tau_A^* \cap (\overline{Q}_B \times \overline{Q}_B)$ such that no τ_A path in A from p to q goes through intermediate global states in $\overline{Q}_B$. Finally let $I_B = I_A$.

We see that the reachable global states of B all belong to $\overline{Q}_B$. Thus, all buffers are always empty and the local states of the a_i's are the corresponding states from A at the beginning of a round. It is not hard to see that B is a synchronous version of A such that in each round all processors send $n-1$ messages and then receive $n-1$ messages.

3   Definitions of Knowledge and Common Knowledge

It is convenient to picture a protocol P as a graph with nodes consisting of all the elements of R_P. There is a directed edge labelled τ from p to q just if $\langle p, q \rangle \in \tau$. Furthermore there is an undirected edge labelled 'i' between p and q just if $p \overset{i}{\sim} q$.[4]

---

[4]The reader familiar with Kripke models will observe that an alternate description of a protocol P is as a Kripke model $K = \langle R_P, \tau, \overset{1}{\sim}, \ldots, \overset{n}{\sim} \rangle$ where the $\overset{.}{\sim}$'s are equivalence relations; and furthermore for all worlds $w, w' \in R_P$ if $w \overset{i}{\sim} w'$ for all i then $w = w'$. See [FI85] where this characterization of protocols is used to obtain a simple proof that propositional logic of knowledge and branching time is EXPTIME complete.

Let E be an equivalence relation on the reachable global states R_P with equivalence classes $[p]_E$, $p \in R_P$. Corresponding to E is a modal operator $\Box(E)$. For any sentence α,[5] it is natural to make the following definition of $\Box(E)\alpha$, which we read as "box E α":

$$\langle P, p \rangle \models \Box(E)\alpha \quad \equiv \quad \forall q \in [p]_E (\langle P, q \rangle \models \alpha).$$

Thus, $\Box(E)\alpha$ holds just if α is true in all the worlds E-equivalent to the current world.

Several equivalence relations will be of interest. $\overset{i}{\sim}$, the indistinguishability relation for participant i, has already been defined. We denote $\Box\left(\overset{i}{\sim}\right)$ by K_i, which we read "i knows." Thus, i knows α just if α is true in all worlds which are indistinguishable by i from the current world.

We generalize to a group of participants $G \subseteq \{1, \ldots, n\}$. Let

$$\overset{G}{\approx} = \left(\bigcup_{i \in G} \overset{i}{\sim}\right)^*,$$

that is, the transitive closure of the union of the $\overset{i}{\sim}$ relations for $i \in G$. Thus, we have

$$p \overset{G}{\approx} q \Leftrightarrow (\exists r \geq 0)(\exists i_1, \ldots, i_r \in G)(\exists p_1, \ldots, p_{r-1})[p \overset{i_1}{\sim} p_1 \overset{i_2}{\sim} p_2 \ldots p_{r-1} \overset{i_r}{\sim} q].$$

We denote $\Box\left(\overset{G}{\approx}\right)$ by C_G, which we read "it is common knowledge among the members of G". Note that $\overset{\{i\}}{\approx} = \overset{i}{\sim}$, so also $\mathsf{C}_{\{i\}} \equiv \mathsf{K}_i$. We write $\approx$ for $\overset{G}{\approx}$ and C for C_G in the special case that G includes all participants.

The next result shows that $\mathsf{C}\alpha$ coincides with the definition current in the literature. (See for example [HM84].)

Theorem 3.1 *The following two statements are equivalent:*

1. $\langle P, p \rangle \models \mathsf{C}_G \alpha$.

2. $(\forall r \geq 0)(\forall i_1, \ldots, i_r \in G)(\langle P, p \rangle \models \mathsf{K}_{i_1} \mathsf{K}_{i_2} \ldots \mathsf{K}_{i_r} \alpha)$.

Proof

$(1 \Rightarrow 2)$: For any β, we have $\mathsf{C}_G \beta \to \beta$ since $p \overset{G}{\approx} p$. Thus, it suffices to show that for any β, if $\langle P, p \rangle \models \mathsf{C}_G \beta$, then for all $i \in G$, $\langle P, p \rangle \models \mathsf{C}_G \mathsf{K}_i \beta$. This is clear because if $q \overset{G}{\approx} p$ and $q' \overset{i}{\sim} q$ then $q' \overset{G}{\approx} p$; hence $\langle P, q \rangle \models \mathsf{K}_i \beta$. Since $\mathsf{K}_i \beta$ holds for all $q \in [p]_{\overset{G}{\approx}}$, it is common knowledge in G at p, as desired.

---

[5]We have intentionally left the logical language unspecified from which the sentence α is drawn, for all that we require is that it be possible to interpret α at the pair $\langle P, p \rangle$ (and we weaken even that requirement in Section 5). Of course the strongest such language would have a way to express each possible subset of R_P. The languages we consider may be taken to be some unspecified subset of this strongest language.

$(2 \Rightarrow 1)$: Suppose that $\langle P, p \rangle \not\models C_G \alpha$. It follows that there is a $q \in [p]_{\underset{\approx}{G}}$ such that $\langle P, q \rangle \models \neg \alpha$. Let $i_1, \ldots, i_r \in G$ be such that there exists $p_1, \ldots, p_{r-1}$ with $p \overset{i_1}{\sim} p_1 \overset{i_2}{\sim} p_2 \ldots p_{r-1} \overset{i_r}{\sim} q$. It follows that $\langle P, p \rangle \models \neg K_{i_1} K_{i_2} \ldots K_{i_r} \alpha$.   ∎

As an example of the above concepts, the next proposition shows that for the synchronous protocol $\mathcal{B}$ described at the end of the last section, whenever a processor is in round r, it is common knowledge among all the processors that they are in round r. We will see in the next section that this assertion is false for the asynchronous protocol $\mathcal{A}$.

Proposition 3.2 *Let $P = \{1, \ldots, n\}$ be the set of processors in protocol $\mathcal{B}$ (omitting the buffers). Let $i, j \in P$, let $\alpha(i, r)$ be a formula meaning that processor i is in round r, and let $q \in R_\mathcal{B}$ be any reachable global state. Then*

$$\langle \mathcal{B}, q \rangle \models \alpha(i, r) \rightarrow C_P \alpha(j, r).$$

Proof   It is trivial to show by induction that for all $p \in R_\mathcal{B}$, all the processors are in the same round. Therefore suppose that $\langle \mathcal{B}, q \rangle \models \alpha(i, r)$. It follows that for all $p \in [q]_{\underset{\approx}{P}}$, $\langle \mathcal{B}, p \rangle \models \alpha(j, r)$.
∎

4   Common Knowledge in Asynchronous Systems

Informally, an "asynchronous system" has two kinds of participants, "active" and "passive". Typically, the active elements are processors and the passive elements are memory cells or message ports. Every step of such a system consists of an interaction between an active and a passive element, and whether or not a step can occur depends only on the states of the element pair involved.

In our more general model, we have only one kind of participant, so we define a protocol to be *asynchronous* if it is pairwise local as defined in Section 2. Thus, every interaction "involves" at most two participants, and two steps involving disjoint sets of participants can occur in either order with the same effect.

The theorem that follows depends on much less than full asynchrony. Thus, we define a very weak notion of an asynchronous protocol that we call "nonsimultaneous".

Definition 4.1 *Let $G \subseteq \{1, \ldots, n\}$ be a specified set of participants in a protocol $P = \langle n, Q, I, \tau \rangle$. We will call P nonsimultaneous with respect to G if for all $\langle p, q \rangle \in \tau$, there is a participant $i \in G$ not affected by the transition $\langle p, q \rangle$. We say that P is nonsimultaneous if it is nonsimultaneous with respect to the set of all participants.*

As an example, note that a message passing protocol such as in [CM85] is nonsimultaneous with respect to its set of processors provided it has at least two processors. Note also that any asynchronous protocol with at least three participants is nonsimultaneous.

The following theorem shows that in a nonsimultaneous protocol, no new common knowledge can be acheived. (Cf. [HM84], Theorem 3.)

Theorem 4.2 *Let P be a protocol and G a set of participants. Let p be any global state in R_P and let p_0 be an intial state from which p is reachable by a sequence of τ steps, all of which are nonsimultaneous with respect to G. Let α be any sentence in a logic for P. Then $\langle P, p \rangle \models C_G \alpha$ iff $\langle P, p_0 \rangle \models C_G \alpha$.*

Proof It suffices to show that $q \overset{G}{\approx} r$ for any step $\langle q, r \rangle \in \tau$ that is nonsimultaneous with respect to G, for then $p_0 \overset{G}{\approx} p$ follows by considering the path of steps from p_0 to p, and the theorem then follows from the definition of common knowledge in G. But if $\langle q, r \rangle \in \tau$ is nonsimultaneous with respect to G, then there must exist a participant $j \in G$ unaffected by the transition, i.e. such that $q \overset{j}{\sim} r$. It follows that $q \overset{G}{\approx} r$. ∎

Corollary 4.3 *Let G be a set of participants in a protocol P that is nonsimultaneous with respect to G. Then it is impossible to gain new common knowledge among the members of G.*

As an example, consider the protocol $\mathcal{A}$ discussed at the end of the last section. It is easy to check that $\mathcal{A}$ is nonsimultaneous with respect to any set of G participants including at least two processors or at least two buffers. Thus, no new common knowledge among the members of any such G can arise in $\mathcal{A}$. This is in sharp contrast to the situation for $\mathcal{A}$'s cousin $\mathcal{B}$ (cf. Proposition 3.2).

It would seem at first glance that the difficulty in achieving common knowledge has to do with the problem of reaching an arbitrary depth of K's with only finitely many messages. We conclude this section with a look at finite state protocols where common knowledge is equivalent to a *bounded* stack of K's.

Theorem 4.4 *Let $P = \langle n, Q, I, \tau \rangle$ be a finite state protocol, i.e. $|Q| < \infty$. For each i, let*

$$Q_i = \{(q)_i \mid q \in R_P\}.$$

Thus, each processor is a $|Q_i|$-state automaton. Let $r = \min\{|Q_i| \mid 1 \leq i \leq n\}$. Let p be any global state and let α be any formula. Then the following are equivalent:

1. $\langle P, p \rangle \models C\alpha$.

2. For all $i_1, i_2, \ldots, i_{2r-1}, (\langle P, p \rangle \models K_{i_1} \ldots K_{i_{2r-1}} \alpha)$.

Proof

$(1 \Rightarrow 2)$: By definition of C.

$(2 \Rightarrow 1)$: Suppose that $\langle P, p \rangle \not\models C\alpha$. Then there must exist $q \in [p]_{\approx}$ such that $\langle P, q \rangle \models \neg\alpha$. Consider a minimum length $\sim$ chain from p to q:

$$p = p_0 \overset{i_1}{\sim} p_1 \overset{i_2}{\sim} p_2 \ldots p_{s-1} \overset{i_s}{\sim} p_s = q$$

No nonconsecutive pair p_j, p_k of global states agree on any component because if they did the chain could be shortened. It follows that in any given component, each state appears at most twice. Therefore $s \leq 2r - 1$. It follows that

$$\langle P, p \rangle \models \neg K_{i_1} K_{i_2} \ldots K_{i_{2r-1}} \alpha.$$

∎

Example 4.5 *Consider the protocol* $P_r = \langle 2, \{1, \ldots, r+1\}, \{\langle 1, 1 \rangle\}, \tau_r \rangle$ *where,*

$$\tau_r = \{(\langle i, i \rangle, \langle i+1, i \rangle) \mid 1 \leq i \leq r\} \cup \{(\langle i+1, i \rangle, \langle i+1, i+1 \rangle) \mid 1 \leq i < r\}.$$

This protocol has the unique computation chain:

$$\langle 1, 1 \rangle, \ \langle 2, 1 \rangle, \ \langle 2, 2 \rangle, \ \langle 3, 2 \rangle, \ldots, \langle r, r-1 \rangle, \ \langle r, r \rangle, \ \langle r+1, r \rangle.$$

Furthermore, for all reachable global states p *and* q, *we have* $p \approx q$. *Thus, for any* α,

$$\langle P_r, p \rangle \models C\alpha \ \Leftrightarrow \ \text{for all } q \in R_{P_r}, \langle P_r, q \rangle \models \alpha.$$

Let α *say that processor 1 is not in state 1. Then* $\langle P_r, \langle 1, 1 \rangle \rangle \not\models \alpha$, *so* $\langle P_r, \langle r+1, r \rangle \rangle \not\models C\alpha$. *On the other hand, it is easily seen that*

$$\langle P_r, \langle r+1, r \rangle \rangle \models K_1 \underbrace{K_2 K_1 K_2 K_1 \ldots K_2 K_1}_{2r-2} \alpha.$$

It follows that for all $i_1, i_2, \ldots, i_{2r-2} \in \{1, 2\}$,

$$\langle P_r, \langle r+1, r \rangle \rangle \models K_{i_1} \ldots K_{i_{2r-2}} \alpha,$$

showing that the bound in Theorem 4.4 cannot be improved.

5   Alternate Definitions of Knowledge

Halpern and Moses argue that, "If Cp is to be attained, all processors must start supporting it simultaneously."[6] Their conclusion is that in the absence of perfect global clocks and guaranteed exact message delivery times, one must settle for weaker notions than common knowledge. They suggest alternative notions and discuss when these can be acheived.

---

[6][HM84], Lemma 2.

We draw a differenct conclusion from the same problem, namely we believe that there is not a best or most desirable common knowledge which one would acheive if one could; but rather that different notions of knowledge and common knowledge may be appropriate for different protocols.

It is useful to consider our example protocols $\mathcal{A}$ and $\mathcal{B}$. We hope the reader will agree that they are realistic instances of an asynchronous and a synchronous message passing protocol, respectively. Recall that new common knowledge among the n processors is attainable in $\mathcal{B}$ but not in $\mathcal{A}$. This is confusing because in a very strong sense $\mathcal{A}$ and $\mathcal{B}$ are isomorphic protocols (cf. [CM85]).[7]

The difference between protocols $\mathcal{A}$ and $\mathcal{B}$ concerns the granularity at which processors in the two protocols may introspect. In $\mathcal{B}$, processors are only allowed to think about what they know at the start of each round. The fact that two structures whose observable behaviors are equivalent should differ so dramatically in terms of their knowledge gives us cause to reexamine our definitions of knowledge and common knowledge.

Let $\mathcal{P}$ be any protocol and let $S \subseteq R_{\mathcal{P}}$ be any subset of reachable global states. For each i, let $\overset{i}{\sim}_S$ be the restriction of $\overset{i}{\sim}$ to $S \times S$. As before, let $G \subseteq \{1,\ldots,n\}$ be a group of the participants in a protocol. Let

$$\overset{G}{\approx}_S = \left(\bigcup_{i \in G} \overset{i}{\sim}_S \right)^*,$$

that is, the transitive closure of the union of the $\overset{i}{\sim}_S$ relations for $i \in G$. Thus, we have

$$p \overset{G}{\approx}_S q \quad \Leftrightarrow \quad p, q \in S \text{ and}$$
$$(\exists r \geq 0)(\exists i_1,\ldots,i_r \in G)(\exists p_1,\ldots,p_{r-1} \in S)[p \overset{i_1}{\sim}_S p_1 \overset{i_2}{\sim}_S p_2 \ldots p_{r-1} \overset{i_r}{\sim}_S q].$$

We generalize our previous definitions of knowledge by letting K_i^S denote the modal operator $\Box\left(\overset{i}{\sim}_S\right)$ and by letting C_G^S denote the modal operator $\Box\left(\overset{G}{\approx}_S\right)$. As before, we omit mention of G when G includes all participants.

The intuitive meaning of "$\mathsf{K}_i^S \alpha$" is, "Participant i knows that α holds, assuming we are in S," and the intuitive meaning of "$\mathsf{C}_G^S \alpha$" is, "It is common knowledge among the members of G that α holds, assuming we are in S." The following theorem makes this intuition precise.

Theorem 5.1 *Let $S \subseteq R_{\mathcal{P}}$, let $p \in S$, and let σ mean, "We are in S." Let $G \subseteq \{1,\ldots,n\}$. Then*

1. $\langle \mathcal{P}, p \rangle \models \mathsf{K}_i^S \alpha \Leftrightarrow \langle \mathcal{P}, p \rangle \models \mathsf{K}_i(\sigma \to \alpha)$

2. $\langle \mathcal{P}, p \rangle \models \mathsf{C}_G^S \alpha \Leftrightarrow (\forall r \geq 0)(\forall i_1,\ldots,i_r \in G)(\langle \mathcal{P}, p \rangle \models \mathsf{K}_{i_1}^S \mathsf{K}_{i_2}^S \ldots \mathsf{K}_{i_r}^S \alpha)$.

---

[7] We will call a pair of protocols such as $\mathcal{A}$ and $\mathcal{B}$, all of whose interactions are accomplished by a series of messages, *isomorphic* if the set of messages sequences they generate is identical up to permutations which do not switch the order of a send and a receive by the same participant, nor the order of a send and its corresponding receive.

Proof (1) is immediate from the definition of K_i^S. The proof of (2) is similar to the proof of Theorem 3.1. ∎

For any protocol P and any nonempty $S \subseteq R_P$, the operators K^S and C^S seem to satisfy all requirements stated in [HM84] for such knowledge operators. In particular we note that they satisfy Kripke's S5 axioms (cf. [La77]).

Proposition 5.2 *For any protocol P, any nonempty $S \subseteq R_P$, and $G \subseteq \{1,\ldots,n\}$, the operators K_i^S and C_G^S satisfy the S5 axioms for modal operators.*

Proof This is immediate from the fact that each $\overset{i}{\sim}_S$ and $\overset{G}{\approx}_S$ is an equivalence relation. ∎

Let us now consider the protocol A with $S = R_B$. The following proposition relates knowledge in B to knowledge with respect to S in A.

Proposition 5.3 *Let $S = R_B$ and $p \in S$. Let α be any knowledge formula all of whose K's and C's have the superscript S. Let α' be the formula resulting from α when we remove all of the superscripts S.[8] Then*

$$\langle A,p\rangle \models \alpha \Leftrightarrow \langle B,p\rangle \models \alpha'$$

Proof This is an easy induction on the length of α. The most interesting case is when $\alpha = \mathsf{K}_i^S\varphi$. In this case

$$\langle A,p\rangle \models \mathsf{K}_i^S\varphi$$
$$\Leftrightarrow \quad (\text{for all } q \in [p]_{\overset{i}{\sim}_S})\langle A,q\rangle \models \varphi$$
$$\Leftrightarrow \quad (\text{for all } q \in [p]_{\overset{i}{\sim}_S})\langle B,q\rangle \models \varphi'$$
$$\Leftrightarrow \quad \langle B,p\rangle \models \mathsf{K}_i\varphi'$$

∎

It follows from Propositions 5.2 and 5.3 that if we consider the protocol A with $S = R_B$, then we get a quite reasonable definition of knowledge and common knowledge. Furthermore, with these definitions new common knowledge is attained in an asynchronous protocol.

Joe Halpern [Ha85] points out that we are in a sense cheating because when we consider K^S, we evaluate formulas only at the global states in S. This form of 'cheating' may however be useful and appropriate. An example of a useful restriction of attention to a set of safe states occurs in databases. A database must maintain some integrity constraints which can be violated in the middle of certain transactions. It is useful to assert that the constraints are always satisfied and to evaluate such assertions only at the safe states in which no transactions are incomplete. Note that during a typical run of the database system, no such safe states need occur.

---

[8]Recall that we haven't specified the syntax of the knowledge-free formulas. Any such knowledge-free subformula γ of α specifies a certain subset $T \subseteq R_A$. We assume that γ is changed to γ' in α' where γ' specifies the same subset restricted to R_B, i.e. $T' = T \cap R_B$.

6   Conclusions

We have given precise formulations of distributed protocols. For any subset S of the reachable states, we have given a precise definition of knowledge and common knowledge with respect to S. We have presented theorems outlining some cases where new common knowledge can be attained and some cases where it cannot. Most strikingly, we have shown that in certain situations two plausible choices for S can give completely different results.

One can now ask the question, "For which sets of protocols is there a 'best' choice for S?" and thus a 'best' definition for knowledge and common knowledge. We suspect that in at least certain situations there may be such a best S, and that in this case knowledge and common knowledge with respect to S may be valuable tools.

Many arguments in distributed systems are first formulated at the intuitive level of what certain processors 'know' at certain points in the computation. With precise definitions for these concepts, it may be easier to formulate clear and correct proofs. We believe that considerable work is needed in order to develop logical tools and demonstrate their usefulness on problems of interest in distributed systems.

Acknowledgements

We are grateful to Dick Stearns for helpful comments on an earlier draft of this paper and to Joe Halpern, Yoram Moses, Albert Meyer, and Nancy Lynch for probing questions, constructive criticism, and valuable suggestions on this work.

References

[CM85]   K. Mani Chandy and Jayadev Misra, "How Processes Learn," *Fourth ACM Symp. on Principles of Distributed Computing* (1985), 204–214.

[DM86]   Cynthia Dwork and Yoram Moses, "Knowledge and Common Knowledge in a Byzantine Environment I: Crash Failures," *this volume*.

[FI85]   Michael J. Fischer and Neil Immerman, "Propositional Logic of Knowledge and Time is Exponential Time Complete," manuscript (1985).

[Ha85]   J. Y. Halpern, personal communication.

[HF85]   J. Y. Halpern and Ron Fagin, "A Formal Model of Knowledge, Action, and Communication," *Fourth ACM Symp. on Principles of Distributed Computing* (1985), 224-236.

[HM84]   J. Y. Halpern and Y. Moses, "Knowledge and Common Knowledge in a Distributed Environment," *Third ACM Symp. on Principles of Distributed Computing* (1984), 50–61.

[HM85]   J. Y. Halpern and Y. Moses, "Knowledge and Common Knowledge in a Distributed Environment," revised manuscript (October, 1985).

[La77]   Richard Ladner, "The Computational Complexity of Provability in Systems of Modal Propositional Logic," *SIAM J. Comput. 6,* 3 (1977), 467-480.

[LF81]   Nancy A. Lynch and Michael J. Fischer, "On Describing the Behavior and Implementation of Distributed Systems," *Theoretical Comp. Sci. 13* (1981), 17–43.

[PR85]   Rohit Parikh and R. Ramanujam, "Distributed Processes and the Logic of Knowledge (preliminary report)," *Proc. of Workshop on Logics of Programs,* Brooklyn (1985), 256-268.

Knowledge and implicit knowledge in a distributed environment: Preliminary Report

Ronald Fagin
Moshe Y. Vardi

IBM Almaden Research Center
650 Harry Road
San Jose, California 95120-6099

Abstract: We characterize the states of knowledge that are attainable in distributed systems, where communication is done by unreliable message exchange. The reason that certain states of knowledge are unattainable is a conservation principle which says that information about "nature" that can be obtained by combining all of the knowledge of the members of a closed system is preserved. We axiomatize the class of formulas in the propositional modal logic of knowledge that are valid in attainable knowledge states, and we determine the complexity of the decision problem.

1. Introduction

A recent and exciting paradigm in the area of distributed systems, first put forward by Halpern and Moses [HM1], is that the right way to understand distributed protocols is by considering how communication changes the state of *knowledge* of distributed processes. To quote from [HM1], "Many tasks in a distributed system directly involve the achievement of specific states of knowledge, and others crucially depend on a variety of constraints on the state of knowledge of the parties involved". This paradigm has inspired computer scientists (cf. [CM, FHV1, Leh, Pa, PR]) to study an area that has so far been in the realm of economics [Au], philosophy [Hi], and artificial intelligence [MH] - the *logic of knowledge*.

In order to formalize reasoning about knowledge, we need semantic models for knowledge. The most common approach to modelling knowledge, due to Hintikka [Hi], is based on the *possible worlds semantics*. In this approach, the information that a "player" (or "agent" or "process") has about the world may be incomplete; rather than knowing precisely what the actual state of the world is, the player may only know that the actual state of the world belongs to a given set of possible states (the so-called possible worlds). A player then *knows* a fact φ to be true if φ is true in all the states that the player thinks are possible. Possible world semantics has been formalized using either Kripke structures [Kr] or modal structures [FV]. When used to model knowledge, modal structures are called *knowledge structures* [FHV1].

We can use these semantic models for knowledge to interpret formulas in the logic of knowledge. These formulas are propositional modal formulas, where for every player i we have a modality K_i. Intuitively, the formula $K_i\varphi$ says "player i knows φ". In order to understand the nature of knowledge better, it is helpful to characterize knowledge by axiomatizing valid formulas (the formulas that are satisfied by all knowledge structures). It turns out that the well-known modal logic S5 (which is described in the body of the paper) is a sound and complete axiomatization for knowledge structures, which may suggest that S5 is an appropriate formalism for reasoning about knowledge in distributed systems.

Knowledge structures can be viewed as abstract models for knowledge. Namely, they model all possible states of knowledge with no concern as to how knowledge is acquired in the first place. To reason formally about knowledge in distributed systems, we need, however, to know which states of knowledge are attainable in such systems. In particular, since players in distributed systems communicate with each other exclusively by exchanging messages, we need to know what states of knowledge are attainable via such communication.

To this end we start with a concrete model of knowledge. The basic element in this model is a *run*. A run is a description of a distributed system over time; it consists of a description of the "real world" or "nature", which we assume does not change as a result of communication in the system, the players' initial information about nature, and the messages sent and received by the players. Two runs are *equivalent* with respect to a player i, or "i-equivalent", if they are indiscernible as far as player i is concerned. A player i is said to "know" φ in a run S if φ is true in all runs that are i-equivalent to S. (This concrete model of knowledge is suggested in [CM, DFIL, HF, HM1, PR, RP], and is also implicit in [Dw].) It is not hard to verify that under this interpretation of "know", the axiom system S5 that we have discussed is sound. That is, the axioms and rules of inference of S5 all hold under this interpretation.

We now consider the abstract counterpart of the above concrete model, i.e., the knowledge structures that correspond to the run-based model. It turns out that we do *not* get *all* knowledge structures. In other words, there are knowledge structures that describe knowledge states that are unattainable via message exchange. In particular, S5 is not complete for reasoning about knowledge in distributed systems! For example, if the only primitive proposition is p and if the only players are 1 and 2, then the formula

(1) $\quad K_1((p \wedge \sim K_1 p \wedge \sim K_2 p) \vee (\sim p \wedge \sim K_1 \sim p \wedge K_2 \sim p))$

is not satisfiable in distributed systems, even though it is S5-consistent. To get a complete axiomatization it is necessary to augment S5 with an additional axiom. (We shall see that if there is another primitive proposition besides p or if there is another player besides players 1 and 2, then (1) *is* satisfiable in distributed systems.)

To better understand this phenomenon, it is useful to consider the logic of knowledge and *implicit* knowledge. Implicit knowledge, introduced by Halpern and Moses [HM1], is the knowledge that can be obtained by pooling together the knowledge of a group. Put differently, the implicit knowledge of a group G is what someone could infer given complete knowledge of what each member of G knows. For example, if Alice knows φ_1 and Bob knows $\varphi_1 \Rightarrow \varphi_2$, then together they have implicit knowledge of φ_2, even though neither of them might individually know φ_2. The basic feature of message-based knowledge is *conservation* of implicit knowledge of nature: that is, communication among the players cannot increase the implicit knowledge of the group as a whole about nature. This conservation principle is *dynamic*, in that it deals with *changes* in knowledge. Surprisingly, this dynamic principle has consequences on *static* implicit knowledge. Even more surprisingly, this principle not only affects what (static) implicit knowledge the players can have as a group but also what (static) knowledge individual players can have.

The main point that we are trying to get across in this paper is that knowledge in a distributed systems depends in a crucial way on the way in which processes communicate with each other. Here we investigate one particular model of communication, but this model is not more basic than other prevalent models. For example, in our model communication is unreliable. As we shall point out in the paper, if we assume that communication is reliable, than the effect on the attainable knowledge states is drastic. We believe that the issue of how communication affects knowledge deserves a great deal of further study.

The outline of this paper is as follows. In Section 2, we give the syntax and semantics of runs. In Section 3, we state and prove the conservation principle for implicit knowledge. In Section 4 we describe a property of implicit knowledge that follows from the conservation principle, and we give an axiom that captures this property. In Section 5, we discuss a concrete example which shows that S5 is not a complete axiomatization for communication-based knowledge. Specifically, we show that the formula (1) above is not satisfiable under communication. In Section 6, we give two sound and complete axiomatizations for knowledge under message exchange; one axiomatization involves implicit knowledge, and the other does not. In Section 7 we show that if we assume that communication is reliable, then the set of attainable knowledge states is restricted drastically. In Section 8, we discuss the effect of changing the class of messages. Sections 9-11 study the model theory of our framework. Section 9 reviews the definitions of knowledge worlds from [FHV1], and Section 10 characterizes those knowledge worlds that can arise under message exchange, which are called *message-based knowledge worlds*. In Section 11, we show that implicit knowledge behaves badly in general but nicely in message-based knowledge worlds. We conclude with some remarks in Section 12.

2. Runs

We assume that there is a fixed finite set of primitive propositions, and a fixed finite set $\mathcal{P}$ of players. The class of *formulas* is the smallest set that contains the primitive propositions, is closed under the Boolean connectives $\sim$ and $\wedge$, and contains $K_i\varphi$ if it contains φ, for each player i. The class of *extended formulas* is defined similarly, except that also $I\varphi$ is an extended formula if φ is. Thus, extended formulas allow also the modal operator I ("It is implicit knowledge that").

We are about to give the syntax and semantics of runs. Throughout this paper, we assume that communication is *synchronous* and proceeds in "rounds". We assume that messages may be lost, that is, never received. (As we shall show later, if messages are guaranteed to be delivered, then the situation changes radically.) We also assume that if a message is ever received, then it is received in the round it was sent.

We assume that some fixed truth assignment to the primitive propositions is "the actual truth assignment", or "nature". An alternative viewpoint (which is useful, for example, in statistics [Sa]) is that instead of primitive propositions and truth assignments, there is a fixed finite set of *primitive states*, and that "nature" is one of these primitive states. To make it easier to pass back and forth between these two viewpoints, we shall usually refer to a truth assignment as a primitive state. Let $\mathcal{N}$ be the set of primitive states.

We begin with an intuitive description of the "initial information" of each player, and how communication takes place. At the beginning (or "in the 0th round"), each player i is "told" a set $T(i)$ of primitive states, one of which is nature. We view $T(i)$ as player i's initial information about nature. In particular, if $T(i) = \{t\}$, where t is nature, then player i knows completely about nature, and if $T(i)$ is the set of all primitive states, then player i knows nothing about nature. One intuitive way to think about what we have just said is that before there is any communication between the players, each player "studies nature", and player i "learns" $T(i)$ (that is, player i gains the information that nature is a member of the set $T(i)$). No player has any information about any other player's initial information about nature. After players obtain this initial information about nature, all information is gained by messages that are sent between the players. Intuitively, no one ever "studies nature" again (we also assume that nature never changes). We make this assumption, since we are interested in characterizing the knowledge of each player when new information is gained *only* by message exchange. We leave as a problem how to characterize the knowledge of each player when it is possible for a player to gain directly more information about nature at any time.

In each round, each player may send any number of messages to the other players. For example, in round 3, player 1 may send three messages to player 2, no messages to player 3, and one message to player 4.

We now discuss the class $\mathcal{M}$ of messages. As we shall see later, in order to get our completeness results, the class $\mathcal{M}$ must be sufficiently rich; for example, the class of formulas (or even the class of extended formulas) is not sufficiently rich to serve as the class of messages. It is technically convenient to distinguish two types of messages: *messages about the past*, and *messages about the future*. "Messages about the past" talk about previous rounds; for example, on round 7, one message about the past is "I sent message φ to player j in round 5". "Messages about the future" make certain promises about future messages; for example, on round 7, one message about the future is "If ψ holds in round 31, then in round 31 the only messages I will send to player j are in the set Φ". We shall assume that every message is *honest* [HF]. In the case of messages about the past, honesty means that the message is true (our semantics is such that this will automatically guarantee that the sender of the message *knew* that the message was true when he sent it). In the case of messages about the future, honesty means that every promise is fulfilled. It is convenient to consider messages about the future to be honest at the time they are sent; however, the promises made must be kept. Thus, at a later date, messages about the future may be rendered dishonest. Shortly, we shall discuss other reasons why we distinguish between messages about the past and messages about the future. The class $\mathcal{M}$ of messages consists of the following (where φ is a message and Φ is a finite set of messages):

1. Messages about the past:
    a. "I knew θ just after round r", where θ is an extended formula.
    b. "I sent message φ to player j in round r".
    c. "I sent precisely the set Φ of messages to player j in round r".
    d. "I received message φ from player j in round r".
    e. "I received precisely the set Φ of messages from player j in round r".
    f. "Every message that I sent in round r to player j I still know to be true".
    g. Each finite Boolean combination of messages about the past.

2. Messages about the future:
    "If ψ holds in round r, then in round r the only messages I will send to player j are in the set Φ", where ψ is a message about the past.

Note that, for example, the message "I sent message φ to player j in round r" is a message about the past, even if φ is a message about the future. Note also that messages about the future simply restrict the class of future messages. In particular, sending no more messages at all automatically makes a message about the future honest.

In our examples, we often find it convenient to allow extended formulas as messages. If θ is an extended formula, and if the message θ is sent in round $r+1$, then this message θ can be viewed as a shorthand for the message "I knew θ just after round r".

Why are we so restrictive as to which messages about the future that we allow? First, it is shown in [HF] that serious problems arise if too general messages about the future are allowed. In particular, with more general messages about the future it is hard to make sense out of "honesty", and there does not seem to be a reasonable and natural semantics. Second, the messages we have defined are all we need in order for our results (in particular, our complete axiomatizations) to go through. Third, we shall show later (in Section 8) that in a certain sense, our results still hold if more messages are allowed; however, adding more messages can considerably complicate the semantics. Finally, with the class of messages we have defined, runs have the following nice property: if S is a k-round run, and if in the $(k+1)$st round no messages are sent (and, of course, none are received), then the result is a $(k+1)$-round run. In particular, every run is the prefix of an arbitrarily long run. If we were to allow messages about the future to be closed under Boolean combinations, then we would lose this property. For example, if a player were to send both a message about the future and its negation, then clearly there is no way to fulfill both of these "promises".

Why did we not define a "message about the past" by player i in round r to be simply an arbitrary disjunction of histories of player i up to round r (where a "history of player i up to round r" is a complete description of the set T of primitive states that he learned from nature in round 0, along with a complete description of the messages sent and received by player i in each round s where $1 \leq s < r$)? The reason is that the above messages would have to be infinite disjunctions, since there are an infinite number of messages (specifically, messages about the future) that player i could potentially send in, say, round 1.

We need a few more definitions before we can give the formal definition of the syntax and semantics of runs. If a message φ about the past is a Boolean combination of messages $\varphi_1, ..., \varphi_t$, each of one of the types (a) - (f), then we say that each φ_m ($1 \le m \le t$) is a *direct submessage* of φ. If "I sent message ψ to player j in round r" is a direct submessage of φ, then let us say that φ *directly involves r*, and similarly for the other messages of types (a) - (f). For example, the message

"I knew θ just after round 2" $\vee$ "I sent message ψ to player j in round 5",

where ψ is the message "I sent message δ to player j in round 3", directly involves rounds 2 and 5 but does not directly involve round 3. Intuitively, φ directly involves r if round r is mentioned "at the top level" of φ. It is also convenient to say that the message about the future "If ψ holds in round r, then in round r the only messages I will send to player j are in the set Φ", *directly involves round r*.

We now begin the formal definition of the syntax and semantics of runs. A *k-round run* is a tuple $(\gamma, T, \text{sent}, \text{received})$, where (a) $\gamma \in \mathcal{W}$ (thus, γ is a primitive state); (b) T is a function $T: \mathcal{P} \rightarrow 2^{\mathcal{W}}$; and (c) sent is a function sent: $\mathcal{P} \times \mathcal{P} \times \{1, ..., k\} \rightarrow 2^{\mathcal{M}}$ (and similarly for **received**). Intuitively, γ is "nature"; $T(i)$ gives player i's "initial information about nature", as discussed earlier; sent(i, j, r) is the set of messages sent by player i to player j in round r, and received(i, j, r) is the set of messages received by player i from player j in round r. We assume that $\gamma \in T(i)$ for each player i (that is, nature is one of the possibilities that player i learns is possible in the 0th round). We also assume that sent$(i, j, 0) = \varnothing = $ received$(i, j, 0)$ for each i, j (that is, no messages are sent or received in the 0th round). Intuitively, in the 0th round, players learn their initial information about nature, and in rounds 1,2,..., players communicate with each other. We also make the following assumptions:

1. received$(i, j, k + 1) \subseteq $ sent$(j, i, k + 1)$ ("Each message is received in the round in which it was sent").
2. If φ is a message about the past that directly involves round r and $\varphi \in $ sent(i, j, k), then $r < k$ ("'Messages about the past' are really about the past").
3. If φ is a message about the future that directly involves round r, and if $\varphi \in $ sent(i, j, k), then $r > k$ ("'Messages about the future' are really about the future").

Finally, we wish to say that every message is honest. It is convenient for us to refer to an honest message sent by player i as *i-honest*. When we say that a message is *honest*, we mean that if it was sent by player i, then it is i-honest. To formally define what an i-honest message is, we assume inductively that we have completely defined k-round runs (in particular, we have defined honesty for k-round runs, and insisted that every message be honest in a k-round run). We then define what it means for a k-round run S to satisfy an extended formula φ (written $S \models \varphi$). We then define what it means for a message φ to be i-honest in a $(k + 1)$-round run S (written $S \models_i \varphi$), and we then insist that every message in a $(k + 1)$-round run be honest. The base case ($k = 0$) has been taken care of, since no messages are sent in the 0th round.

Let us say that the k-round runs $S = (\gamma, T, \text{sent}, \text{received})$ and $S' = (\gamma', T', \text{sent}', \text{received}')$ are *i-equivalent* (written $S \sim_i S'$) if the following conditions hold:

1. $T(i) = T'(i)$ ("player i receives the same information in the 0th round of both runs").
2. sent$(i, j, r) = $ sent$'(i, j, r)$ for each player j and each round r with $1 \le r \le k$ ("player i sends the same messages to each player in the same rounds of both runs").
3. received$(i, j, r) = $ received$'(i, j, r)$ for each player j and each round r with $1 \le r \le k$ ("player i receives the same messages from each player in the same rounds of both runs").

Thus, player i cannot distinguish between two i-equivalent k-round runs. We may say that in run S, player i thinks run S' is *possible* if $S \sim_i S'$.

We now define what it means for a k-round run S to satisfy an extended formula φ (written $S \models \varphi$).

1. $S \models p$, where p is a primitive proposition, if $S = (\gamma, T, \text{sent}, \text{received})$ and p is true under the truth assignment γ.

2. $S \models \sim\varphi$ if $S \not\models \varphi$.

3. $S \models \varphi_1 \wedge \varphi_2$ if $S \models \varphi_1$ and $S \models \varphi_2$.

4. $S \models K_i\varphi$ if $S' \models \varphi$ whenever $S' \sim_i S$.

5. $S \models I\varphi$ if $S' \models \varphi$ for each S' such that $S' \sim_i S$ for every $i \in \mathcal{P}$.

Intuitively, part (4) of the definition says that player i *knows* φ in a k-round run if φ is satisfied by every k-round run that player i thinks is possible. Part (5) of the definition says that φ is *implicit knowledge* in a k-round run if φ is satisfied by every k-round run that everyone thinks is possible (cf. [HM2]). It is useful to note for later use that the following formulas are valid (satisfied by every run): $K_i\varphi \Rightarrow I\varphi$ ("Anything known by player i is implicit knowledge"), and $K_i\varphi_1 \wedge K_i(\varphi_1 \Rightarrow \varphi_2) \Rightarrow K_i\varphi_2$ ("What player i knows is closed under modus ponens").

If $0 \leq k' \leq k$, then the k'-round prefix of a k-round run $(\gamma, T, \text{sent}, \text{received})$ is defined in the obvious way: the k'-round prefix is $(\gamma, T, \text{sent}', \text{received}')$, where $\text{sent}'(i,j,r) = \text{sent}(i,j,r)$ for each i,j and each $r \leq k'$, and similarly for $\text{received}'$.

Finally, we define what it means for a message $\varphi \in \text{sent}(i,j,s)$, where $1 \leq s \leq k+1$, to be *i-honest* in a $(k+1)$-round run $S = (\gamma, T, \text{sent}, \text{received})$ (written $S \models_i \varphi$).

1. $S \models_i$ "I knew θ just after round r" if $S' \models K_i\theta$, where S' is the r-round prefix of S.

2. $S \models_i$ "I sent message φ to player j in round r" if $\varphi \in \text{sent}(i,j,r)$.

3. $S \models_i$ "I sent precisely the set Φ of messages to player j in round r" if $\Phi = \text{sent}(i,j,r)$.

4. $S \models_i$ "I received message φ from player j in round r" if $\varphi \in \text{received}(i,j,r)$.

5. $S \models_i$ "I received precisely the set Φ of messages from player j in round r" if $\Phi = \text{received}(i,j,r)$.

6. $S \models_i$ "Every message that I sent in round r to player j I still know to be true" if $S \models_i \varphi$ whenever $\varphi \in \text{sent}(i,j,r)$.

7. $S \models_i \sim\varphi$ if $S \not\models_i \varphi$.

8. $S \models_i \varphi_1 \wedge \varphi_2$ if $S \models_i \varphi_1$ and $S \models_i \varphi_2$.

9. $S \models_i$ "If ψ holds in round r, then in round r, the only messages I will send to player j are in the set Φ", if either (a) $r > k+1$, (b) $S' \not\models_i \psi$, where S' is the r-round prefix of S, or (c) $\text{sent}(i,j,r) \subseteq \Phi$.

The reader should note that in part (9), we are defining what it means for a message φ about the future, *which may have been sent in an early round of S*, to be honest in S. Intuitively, clause (a) of part (9) has the effect that a message about the future directly involving, say, round 17, is always considered honest before round 17.

The following lemma, whose straightforward proof is omitted, will be used later.

Lemma 2.1. *Assume that $S \sim_i S'$. Then $S \models_i \varphi$ iff $S' \models_i \varphi$, for every message φ.*

3. Conservation of implicit knowledge

In this section, we give a fundamental principle of communication-based knowledge, which says that no amount of communication in a closed system can change the implicit knowledge about nature in the system. This principle is quite robust, and holds independent of our assumptions that communication is synchronous, that communication is unreliable, that if a message is received, then it is received in the round it was sent, etc.

If φ is a formula, S is a k-round run, and $r \leq k$, then we say that φ is *implicit knowledge after r rounds of S* if $S' \models I\varphi$, where S' is the r-round prefix of S.

The conservation principle for implicit knowledge: *Let φ be a propositional formula, and let S be a k-round run. Assume that $0 \le r \le k$ and $0 \le s \le k$. Then φ is implicit knowledge after r rounds of S if and only if φ is implicit knowledge after s rounds of S.*

Thus, implicit knowledge about nature never changes after the 0th round. The conservation principle is false if φ is not required to be a propositional formula, that is, if φ is not a formula about nature. For example, if φ is $K_1 p$, where p is a primitive proposition, and if player 1 learns nothing from nature (in round 0) but learns that p is true in round 1 because of a message from player 2, then φ is implicit knowledge after round 1 (it is even known by player 1 after round 1), but it is not implicit knowledge after round 0 (it is even false after round 0).

We now prove the conservation principle. It suffices to show that φ is implicit knowledge after r rounds of S if and only if φ is implicit knowledge after the 0th round of S. If φ is implicit knowledge after the 0th round of S, then it is easy to see that φ is implicit knowledge after r rounds of S (this is because nature never changes, and information about nature is never lost). Assume now that φ is not implicit knowledge after the 0th round of S. We shall show that φ is not implicit knowledge after r rounds of S. Let S be $(\gamma, T, \text{sent}, \text{received})$. Since φ is not implicit knowledge after the 0th round of S, it follows from our definition of satisfaction that there is some primitive state β such that (a) β does not satisfy φ, and (b) $\beta \in T(i)$ for every player i. Let S' be $(\beta, T, \text{sent}, \text{received})$. Thus, S' is just like S, except that the primitive state in S' is β instead of γ. It is straightforward to see that S' is a k-round run. The only nontrivial issue is to show that every message in S' is honest. But this follows from Lemma 2.1, since every message in S is honest, and S' is i-equivalent to S for every player i. Now S' does not satisfy φ, since β does not satisfy φ. Therefore, since S' is i-equivalent to S for every player i, it follows that φ is not implicit knowledge after r rounds of S. This was to be shown.

4. A new axiom

In this section, we present an interesting new axiom, which we shall show is sound. Like the conservation principle, this axiom is quite robust under a number of changes in our assumptions.

Define a *primitive state formula* to be a formula that completely describes a primitive state. For example, if there are exactly two primitive propositions, namely p and q, then up to equivalence, there are exactly four primitive state formulas, namely $p \wedge q$, $p \wedge \sim q$, $\sim p \wedge q$, and $\sim p \wedge \sim q$. The new axiom is:

$I \sim \alpha \Rightarrow (K_1 \sim \alpha \vee ... \vee K_n \sim \alpha),$

where α is a primitive state formula, and where $1, ..., n$ are all the players. Note that $K_j \sim \alpha$ appears within this new axiom for every player j. This axiom says that if it is implicit knowledge that a primitive state is impossible, then the stronger fact is true that some player knows that the primitive state is impossible. In other words, if by putting all of their information together the players could rule out the primitive state α, then some player, by himself, could have ruled out α. This is quite surprising, since we might imagine that it could happen that the reason it is implicit knowledge that a primitive state is impossible is because of some complicated combination of "high depth knowledge" of the various players (we shall define the depth of formulas shortly).

To prove the soundness of this axiom, let us consider the contrapositive. The contrapositive says that if all of the players individually think that the primitive state α is possible, then $\sim \alpha$ is not implicit knowledge. We now show that this is true about an arbitrary k-round run S. Assume that in S, all of the players think that the primitive state α is possible. So, all of the players think that α is possible after the 0th round of S. We now show that $\sim \alpha$ is not implicit knowledge after the 0th round. Let

S' be the 0-round prefix of S. Let S'' be a 0-round run in which α is the primitive state, and which is i-equivalent to S' for every player i. Thus, each player learns the same information from nature in (the 0th round of) S'' as in S'. Since all of the players think that α is possible after the 0th round of S, it is easy to see that S'' is indeed a run. Since $S'' \models \alpha$, and since $S'' \sim_i S'$ for every player i, it follows that $\sim\alpha$ is not implicit knowledge after the 0th round of S, which was to be shown. Hence, by the conservation principle for implicit knowledge, it follows that $\sim\alpha$ is not implicit knowledge after the kth round. Hence, $\sim\alpha$ is not implicit knowledge in S, which was to be shown.

Example 4.1. We now show that the formula that results by allowing α in our new axiom be a primitive proposition p, rather than a primitive state formula, is not sound if there are at least two primitive propositions. Assume that there are two primitive propositions p and q, and two players, Alice and Bob. Consider the 0-round run where both p and q are false, and where, in the 0th round, Alice learns that p and q are either both true or both false and Bob learns that q is false (but he learns nothing about p). Then $\sim p$ is implicit knowledge, since Alice and Bob could combine their information and learn that p is false. However, neither Alice nor Bob know that p is false. Thus, the new axiom does not hold if we were to let α be p. ∎

We just showed that one generalization of our new axiom is not sound. We now give a sound generalization. Let us say that player i is *indifferent* to the primitive proposition p if for each truth assignment t that player i thinks is possible, he also thinks that the truth assignment t' is possible, where t' is the same as t except that p is true in t if and only if p is false in t'. Let α be a *partial state formula*, that is, a formula which describes a truth assignment to a subset X of the primitive propositions (if X were the set of all primitive propositions, then we would have a primitive state formula). If every player is indifferent to every primitive proposition that is not in X, it is not hard to show that $I\sim\alpha \Rightarrow (K_1\sim\alpha \vee \dots \vee K_n^{\cdot}\sim\alpha)$, is still sound, even though α is only a partial state formula, and not a (full) primitive state formula. This may be important in practice, where there may be infinitely many primitive propositions, but where, except for those in a small set X, every player may be indifferent to all of them.

To help understand the new axiom, we now give a general principle of implicit knowledge which has the new axiom as a corollary. We begin with some definitions. If Σ is a set of extended formulas, and σ is a single extended formula, then we say that Σ *implies* σ, written $\Sigma \models \sigma$, if every run that satisfies every member of Σ also satisfies σ. Thus, $\Sigma \models \sigma$ if there is no "counterexample" run that satisfies every member of Σ but does not satisfy σ. We may write $\Sigma \not\models \sigma$ if it is not the case that $\Sigma \models \sigma$. If Σ is a singleton $\{\tau\}$, then we may write $\tau \models \sigma$ for $\{\tau\} \models \sigma$.

The *depth* of a formula φ, denoted depth(φ), is defined as follows:
1. depth(p) $= 0$ if p is a primitive proposition
2. depth($\sim\varphi$) $=$ depth(φ)
3. depth($\varphi_1 \wedge \varphi_2$) $=$ max$\big($depth(φ_1), depth(φ_2)$\big)$
4. depth($K_i\varphi$) $= 1 +$ depth(φ)

Note that we are only defining the depth for formulas, not for extended formulas.

As before, let the players be $1, \dots, n$. Let us say that an extended formula φ *follows from the depth k knowledge of the players in run S* if there are formulas $\varphi_1, \dots, \varphi_n$, each of depth at most k, such that $S \models K_i\varphi_i$ for each player i, and $\{\varphi_1, \dots, \varphi_n\} \models \varphi$.

The next theorem helps give us some insight about implicit knowledge in runs. We shall show that our new axiom follows easily from it.

Theorem 4.2. *Let φ be a depth k formula that is implicit knowledge in run S, that is, S ⊨ Iφ. Then φ follows from the depth k knowledge of the players in run S.*

This theorem follows easily from a result in Section 11. It is surprising for the same reasons we gave earlier that our new axiom is surprising: we might imagine that it could happen that the reason that φ is implicit knowledge is because of some complicated combination of high depth knowledge of the various players.

We now show that our new axiom follows directly from a special case of this theorem. We need the following simple lemma.

Lemma 4.3. *Let Σ be a set of propositional formulas, and let α be a primitive state formula. If $\Sigma \models {\sim}\alpha$, then $\sigma \models {\sim}\alpha$ for some $\sigma \in \Sigma$.*

Proof. Assume that $\sigma \not\models {\sim}\alpha$ for each $\sigma \in \Sigma$. It follows easily that the truth assignment represented by α makes σ true for every $\sigma \in \Sigma$. It again follows easily that $\Sigma \not\models {\sim}\alpha$. The lemma follows. ∎

We now show that the new axiom follows from Theorem 4.2 and Lemma 4.3. Assume that $I{\sim}\alpha$ holds in run S. We must show that $S \models K_i{\sim}\alpha$ for some player i. Since ${\sim}\alpha$ is a propositional formula, it follows from Theorem 4.2 that ${\sim}\alpha$ follows from the depth 0 knowledge of the players in run S. That is, there are propositional formulas $\varphi_1, \dots, \varphi_n$ such that $S \models K_i\varphi_i$ for each player i, and $\{\varphi_1, \dots, \varphi_n\} \models \varphi$. By Lemma 4.3, $\varphi_i \models {\sim}\alpha$ for some player i. Hence, $S \models K_i{\sim}\alpha$. This was to be shown.

5. An S5-consistent formula that is not satisfiable under communication

Assume that there is only one primitive proposition p, and only two players, Alice and Bob. Let φ be the formula

(2) $\qquad K_{Alice}((p \wedge {\sim}K_{Alice}p \wedge {\sim}K_{Bob}p) \vee ({\sim}p \wedge {\sim}K_{Alice}{\sim}p \wedge K_{Bob}{\sim}p))$

This is formula (1) from the introduction, where we have replaced players 1 and 2 by Alice and Bob. It is easy to verify that φ is S5-consistent (in the sense that there is a model of S5 which satisfies this formula). In this section, we show that no run satisfies φ. Thus, ${\sim}\varphi$ is valid in our system. In particular, this shows that S5 is not a complete axiomatization for knowledge under message exchange. In the next section, we give two sound and complete axiomatizations (one using implicit knowledge and one not using implicit knowledge).

Let φ_1 be the formula $p \wedge {\sim}K_{Alice}p \wedge {\sim}K_{Bob}p$, which says that p is true, and that neither Alice nor Bob knows that p is true. Let φ_2 be the formula ${\sim}p \wedge {\sim}K_{Alice}{\sim}p \wedge K_{Bob}{\sim}p$, which says that p is false, that Alice does not know that p is false, and that Bob knows that p is false. Then the formula φ that we wish to show is not satisfied by any run is $K_{Alice}(\varphi_1 \vee \varphi_2)$.

It is instructive to give two proofs that φ is not satisfiable. The first proof, which is somewhat informal, proceeds as follows.

Let S be a k-round run that satisfies φ. Since everything Alice knows is true, it follows that S satisfies $\varphi_1 \vee \varphi_2$. Therefore, Alice does not know whether p is true or false in S. Also, Alice can reason to herself as follows:

> *I know that either φ_1 or φ_2 holds. Assume that φ_1 holds. Then p would be true, and Bob would not know that p is true, just as I do not know that p is true. In particular, since we would both think that it is possible that p is false, we would not have implicit knowledge that p is true. This follows immediately from the axiom $Ip \Rightarrow (K_{Alice}p \vee K_{Bob}p)$ of Section 4, where the primitive state formula α is ${\sim}p$. In the next round, Bob could correctly send me a message saying that he does not know that p is false. This*

would tell me that φ_2 is false, since φ_2 implies that Bob knows that p is false. Since I already know that either φ_1 or φ_2 holds, I could then deduce that φ_1 holds. But φ_1 implies that p is true, and so I would deduce that p is true. In particular, after the next round, Bob and I would have implicit knowledge that p is true. This violates the conservation principle for implicit knowledge, since I already observed that p was not implicit knowledge. This contradiction shows that φ_1 is impossible. Therefore, φ_2 holds, and so p is false. I have just proven that p is false, and so I know that p is false in run S. But this contradicts the fact that I do not know whether p is true or false in run S!

The second proof shows directly, without appealing to the notion of implicit knowledge, that φ is unsatisfiable. Let S be a k-round run that satisfies φ. Now φ implies $\sim K_{Alice}\sim\varphi_1$, since if Alice knows that φ_1 is false, then she knows that φ_2 is true, although it is clear that the formula $K_{Alice}\varphi_2$ is inconsistent. We have shown that Alice thinks that φ_1 is possible. This means that there is some k-round run S_1 that is Alice-equivalent to S and that satisfies φ_1. In particular, p is true in S_1. Let S_2 be just like S_1, except that p is false in S_2. As in the proof of the conservation principle for implicit knowledge, it is easy to see that S_2 is a k-round run, which is both Alice-equivalent and Bob-equivalent to S_1. Now $S_1 \models \varphi_1$, and so $S_1 \models p$. Hence, $S_1 \models \sim K_{Bob}\sim p$. Therefore, since S_1 and S_2 are Bob-equivalent, it follows that $S_2 \models \sim K_{Bob}\sim p$. Now S_2 is Alice-equivalent to S, since S_2 is Alice-equivalent to S_1, which is Alice-equivalent to S. So, since $S \models \varphi$, it follows that $S_2 \models \varphi_1 \vee \varphi_2$. Clearly $S_2 \not\models \varphi_1$, since $S_2 \models \sim p$. Hence, $S_2 \models \varphi_2$. In particular, $S_2 \models K_{Bob}\sim p$. But we showed that $S_2 \models \sim K_{Bob}\sim p$. This is a contradiction.

We have just given two proofs that there is no run that satisfies φ when (a) there is exactly one primitive proposition p and (b) Alice and Bob are the only players. However, if either (a) or (b) is false, then there is a run that satisfies φ. We now exhibit a run that satisfies φ if (b) is false, and leave as an amusing exercise for the reader to find a run that satisfies φ if (a) is false.

Example 5.1.   Assume that there are three players (Alice, Bob, and Charlie), and one primitive proposition p. We now exhibit a 1-round run that satisfies φ. In fact, it is convenient to exhibit two such runs, S_1 and S_2. In S_1, the primitive proposition p is true; in the 0th round of run S_1, neither Alice nor Bob learn that p is true, but Charlie learns that p is true. In round 1 of S_1, Alice receives a message from Charlie saying: "In the next round, I will not send any messages to Bob" (it is easy to see that this can be viewed as one of our messages about the future). In round 2 of S_1, Alice receives a message from Bob saying: "I do not know that p is true", and a message from Charlie saying: "If p is false, then Bob knows that p is false". In S_2, the primitive proposition p is false; in the 0th round of run S_2, Alice does not learn that p is false, but both Bob and Charlie learn that p is false. In round 1 of S_2, Charlie receives a message from Bob saying: "I know that p is false". In round 1 of S_1, Alice receives a message from Charlie saying: "In the next round, I will not send any messages to Bob". In round 2 of S_1, Alice receives a message from Bob saying: "I do not know that p is true", and a message from Charlie saying: "If p is false, then Bob knows that p is false". No other messages are sent in either run. Note that the two runs are Alice-equivalent. In both runs, Alice still does not know whether p is true or false after the second round. This is because the two runs are Alice-equivalent, and in one run p is true, while in the other, p is false.

We now show that φ is satisfied by, say, run S_1. In S_1 (that is, at the end of round 2 of S_1), Alice knows that Bob does not know that p is true. This is because (a) Bob told her in round 2 that he (Bob) does not know that p is true, and (b) she knows that he did not learn that p is true in round 2, since she knows that no one sent him any messages in round 2 (Charlie promised Alice that he would not send Bob any messages, and she also knows that she certainly didn't send any messages).

Now Alice knows that there are two possibilities: (i) p is true, and (ii) p is false. In case (i), Alice knows (as we just saw) that Bob does not know that p is true, and she of course knows that she does not know that p is true; hence, Alice knows that if case (i) holds, then formula φ_1 holds. Alice also knows that if case (ii) holds, then Bob knows that p is false (since Charlie told her this, and since once Bob knows that p is false, Bob always knows that p is false.) In case (ii), she of course also knows that she does not know that p is false. Hence, Alice knows that if case (ii) holds, then formula φ_2 holds. So Alice knows that either φ_1 or φ_2 holds. Hence, run S_1 satisfies $K_{Alice}(\varphi_1 \vee \varphi_2)$; that is, run S_1 satisfies φ. ∎

6. Complete axiomatizations and decision problems

In this section we give a sound and complete axiomatization for the extended formulas that are valid in runs, that is, which are satisfied by every run. We also give a sound and complete axiomatization where only formulas, rather than extended formulas, are allowed in the axioms.

We begin by presenting the classical axiom system S5 (or actually, its generalization to multiple players). Following Halpern and Moses [HM2], we refer to the system as $S5_n$ when there are n players $1, ..., n$. The axioms are:

- All substitution instances of propositional tautologies.
- $K_i\varphi \Rightarrow \varphi$ ("Whatever player i knows is true").
- $K_i\varphi \Rightarrow K_iK_i\varphi$ ("Player i knows what he knows").
- $\sim K_i\varphi \Rightarrow K_i \sim K_i\varphi$ ("Player i knows what he does not know").
- $K_i\varphi_1 \wedge K_i(\varphi_1 \Rightarrow \varphi_2) \Rightarrow K_i\varphi_2$ ("What player i knows is closed under modus ponens").

There are two rules of inference: modus ponens ("from φ_1 and $\varphi_1 \Rightarrow \varphi_2$ infer φ_2") and knowledge generalization ("from φ infer $K_i\varphi$").

We now give Halpern and Moses' system $S5I_n$, which they show is a sound and complete axiomatization for knowledge and implicit knowledge in Kripke structures [HM2]. $S5I_n$ contains all of the axioms and rules of $S5_n$, along with some axioms for implicit knowledge. The first implicit knowledge axiom is:

- $K_i\varphi \Rightarrow I\varphi$ ("Whatever each individual player knows is implicit knowledge").

The remaining axioms of $S5I_n$ say that implicit knowledge behaves like individual knowledge.

- $I\varphi \Rightarrow \varphi$
- $I\varphi \Rightarrow II\varphi$
- $\sim I\varphi \Rightarrow I \sim I\varphi$
- $I\varphi_1 \wedge I(\varphi_1 \Rightarrow \varphi_2) \Rightarrow I\varphi_2$

Let ML_n (where ML stands for "Message Logic") be $S5I_n$, along with our new axiom from Section 4:

- $I \sim \alpha \Rightarrow (K_1 \sim \alpha \vee ... \vee K_n \sim \alpha)$,

where α is a primitive state formula. Note that $K_j \sim \alpha$ appears within this new axiom for every player j.

We are now ready to state our completeness theorem for extended formulas. Of course, since we are interested in communication, we only consider the case where there are at least two players. (We note that for the case of exactly one player, we would just add another axiom which says $I\varphi \Rightarrow K_1\varphi$, which the one player is player 1.)

Theorem 6.1. ML_n *is a sound and complete axiomatization for valid extended formulas in runs with $n \geq 2$ players.*

Theorem 6.1 is hard to prove. Details will appear in a later version [FHV2] of this paper.

It is natural to ask for a sound and complete axiomatization when only formulas, rather than extended formulas, are allowed in the axioms (that is, where the axioms do not mention implicit knowledge). We now give such an axiom system, which we call ML_n^- (where the superscripted minus sign refers to the fact that implicit knowledge is not part of the language). The system consists of $S5_n$, along with a new axiom, which we shall give shortly.

Define a *pure knowledge formula* to be Boolean combination of formulas of the form $K_i\varphi$, where φ is arbitrary. For example, $K_2p \vee (K_1 \sim K_3 p \wedge \sim K_2 \sim p)$ is a pure knowledge formula, but $p \wedge \sim K_i p$ is not. Assume that there are n players $1, ..., n$. Our new axiom is:

(3) $K_i(\varphi \Rightarrow \sim\alpha) \Rightarrow K_i(\varphi \Rightarrow (K_1 \sim \alpha \vee ... \vee K_n \sim \alpha))$,

for all players i, all pure knowledge formulas φ, and all primitive state formulas α.

Note that $K_j \sim \alpha$ appears within this new axiom for every player j. A loose translation of this axiom is "If player i knows that some 'pure knowledge' φ is incompatible with some primitive state α, then player i knows the stronger fact that the pure knowledge φ forces some player to know that the primitive state α is impossible". We now show that this somewhat unintuitive axiom (3) is sound. If not, then let S be a run that does not satisfy (3). So $S \models K_i(\varphi \Rightarrow \sim\alpha)$ and $S \not\models K_i(\varphi \Rightarrow \psi)$, where ψ is the formula $K_1 \sim \alpha \vee ... \vee K_n \sim \alpha$. Since $S \not\models K_i(\varphi \Rightarrow \psi)$, there is a run S' such that $S \sim_i S'$ where $S' \models \varphi$ and $S' \models \sim\psi$. Since $I \sim \alpha \Rightarrow \psi$ is valid (this is our new Message Logic axiom), it follows that $S' \not\models I \sim \alpha$. Therefore, there is a run S'' such that $S'' \sim_j S'$ for every player j, where $S'' \models \alpha$. Since $S'' \sim_j S'$ for every player j, it is straightforward to show that every pure knowledge formula satisfied by S' is satisfied by S''. Therefore, $S'' \models \varphi$. By transitivity of $\sim_i$, we know that $S'' \sim_i S$. Therefore, since $S \models K_i(\varphi \Rightarrow \sim\alpha)$, it follows that $S'' \models \varphi \Rightarrow \sim\alpha$. But we already showed that $S'' \models \varphi$ and $S'' \models \alpha$. This is a contradiction. Hence, (3) is sound.

The formula

(4) $K_{Alice}((\sim K_{Bob}p \wedge \sim K_{Bob}\sim p) \Rightarrow p) \Rightarrow K_{Alice}((\sim K_{Bob}p \wedge \sim K_{Bob}\sim p) \Rightarrow (K_{Alice}p \vee K_{Bob}p))$.

is an instance of the new axiom (3). It is straightforward to verify that (4) implies that formula (2) in Section 5 is unsatisfiable.

As before, if we allow α in the new axiom (3) to be a primitive proposition, rather than a primitive state formula, then the axiom does not remain sound, even if α is the only primitive proposition that appears in φ.

Theorem 6.2. ML_n^- *is a sound and complete axiomatization for valid formulas in runs.*

Theorem 6.2, like Theorem 6.1, is hard to prove. Details will appear in a later version [FHV2] of this paper.

It is interesting to consider what would happen if we were to allow only messages about the past (that is, if in our definition of the class of messages, we were to eliminate clause 2, which defines messages about the future).

Theorem 6.3.   *If only messages about the past are allowed, and if there are exactly two players, then our axiomatizations are still complete (that is, Theorem 6.1 and Theorem 6.2 still hold). However, our axiomatizations are not complete if there are at least three players.*

Proof.   The first part of the theorem holds, since our completeness proof in the case of two players does not require messages about the future. We now give an example that shows that if we were to restrict messages to be about the past, then our axiomatizations are not complete for at least three players. Assume that there are three players, say, Alice, Bob, and Charlie. Let p be a primitive proposition. If every message is about the past, then it is impossible to arrive at a situation where Alice knows that Bob knows p and that Charlie does not know p: this is because Alice never knows whether Bob has just told Charlie that p is true. It is instructive to see how, by allowing messages about the future, it is possible for Alice to know that Bob knows p and that Charlie does not know p (for pedagogical reasons, we shall use slightly more general "messages about the future" than we have already defined, although of course this is not essential). Bob sends a message to Alice, telling her that he knows p and that he has never sent a message to Charlie and never will; Charlie sends a message to Alice telling her that he does not know p; and Alice does not send any messages to Charlie. ■

We close this section by giving the complexity of the decision problems for ML_n and ML_n^-. It is known [HM2] that the decision problem for $S5_n$ (with $n \geq 2$) is PSPACE-complete. The next theorem says that ML_n and ML_n^- are no harder (and no easier) than $S5_n$. Of course, in ML_n and ML_n^-, we are interested only in the case when $n \geq 2$, that is, when there are at least two players.

Theorem 6.4. *The decision problems for ML_n and ML_n^- are PSPACE-complete (when $n \geq 2$).*

7. What if communication is reliable?

In this section, we briefly consider the situation where communication is reliable, that is, where messages can never be never lost. In this case, the set of states of knowledge that can arise is greatly restricted, as we shall show. Nevertheless, the conservation principle and our axioms are still sound, as the reader can verify.

Let us say that two runs are *equivalent* if they satisfy the same extended formulas.

Theorem 7.1. *Assume that there are only two players, and that communication is reliable. Then every run is equivalent to a 1-round run where both players send exactly one message.*

Proof. Assume that the two players are players 1 and 2. Let $S = (\gamma, T, \text{sent}, \text{received})$ be a run (where communication is reliable). Of course, received is now redundant, since $\text{received}(i, j, r) = \text{sent}(j, i, r)$ for every i, j, r. If V is a set of primitive states, then let us say that V is *possible initial information about nature for player 1* if there is some primitive state γ' such that $S' = (\gamma', T', \text{sent}, \text{received})$ is a run, where $T'(1) = V$ and $T'(2) = T(2)$. Intuitively, "V is possible initial information about nature for player 1" if as far as player 2 is concerned, all of player 1's messages would have been legal if V would have been player 1's initial information about nature. Similarly, we define what if means for a set V of primitive states to be *possible initial information about nature for player 2*.

If V is a set of primitive states, then let τ_V be the formula

(5) $(\bigwedge\{K_1 \sim \alpha: \alpha \notin V\}) \wedge (\bigwedge\{\sim K_1 \sim \alpha: \alpha \in V\}).$

Intuitively, τ_V says that player 1 thinks that precisely the primitive states in V are possible. Let φ_1 be the formula

(6) $\bigvee\{\tau_V: V \text{ is possible initial information about nature for player 1}\}$

Intuitively, φ_1 gives precisely the information that player 2 has about player 1 in S. Similarly, define φ_2. Let $S^\# = (\gamma, T, \text{sent}', \text{received}')$ be a 1-round run (with γ and T the same as in S), where the only message that player 1 sends is "I knew φ_1 just after round 0", and similarly for player 2. It is not hard to see that $S^\#$ is a 1-round run that fulfills the conditions of the theorem. ■

Corollary 7.2. *Assume that there are only two players, and that communication is reliable. Let the set of primitive states be fixed. Then there are only a finite number of distinct equivalence classes of runs (where two runs are in the same equivalence class if they satisfy the same extended formulas).*

Proof. Since there are only a finite number of distinct 1-round runs of the type $S^{\#}$ as defined in the proof of Theorem 7.1, the result follows immediately. ∎

Theorem 7.1 and Corollary 7.2 contrast with the situation in which communication is unreliable. For, let S_k be a k-round run in which Alice tells Bob in the first round that Alice knows that the primitive proposition p is true, where Bob acknowledges to Alice in the second round that he received this message from Alice, where Alice acknowledges to Bob in the third round that she received Bob's acknowledgment, and so on through the kth round. It is easy to see that S_k is not equivalent to any $(k-1)$-round run, and that no two of the runs S_k are equivalent.

We note that it follows from Corollary 7.2 that our axiomatizations in Section 6 are not complete (although, as we have noted, they are sound). In particular, it can be shown that if there are exactly two players and if α is a primitive state formula, then the formula $(K_1 K_2 \alpha \wedge K_2 K_1 \alpha) \Rightarrow K_1 K_2 K_1 \alpha$ is valid.

The reader should note that the results of this section apply only to the case of exactly two players. The case of three or more players is currently under investigation.

8. Changing the class of messages

In Theorem 6.3 and Section 7, we considered some effects of changing the class of messages. In this section, we briefly discuss the effect more generally. Most importantly, it turns out that our class of messages is rich enough that increasing the class in a reasonable way does not cause the set of axioms to change. We now discuss what we mean by this claim.

If all of the assumptions we have made hold, except that the class of messages is changed to $\mathcal{M}'$, then let $R(\mathcal{M}')$ be the set of all runs (involving these messages), and let $A(\mathcal{M}')$ be the resulting complete axiomatization for the valid extended formulas. Let $\mathcal{M}$ be the class of messages we have allowed in this paper, and assume that $\mathcal{M} \subseteq \mathcal{M}'$. Assume further that our axioms remain sound when $\mathcal{M}'$ is the class of messages (that is, assume that $A(\mathcal{M}) \subseteq A(\mathcal{M}')$. It turns out that the completeness proof then shows that $A(\mathcal{M}) = A(\mathcal{M}')$, that is, our axiomatization is still complete.

It is instructive to give a false "proof" of this fact. It is easy to convince oneself that if $\mathcal{M}_1 \subseteq \mathcal{M}_2$, then $A(\mathcal{M}_2) \subseteq A(\mathcal{M}_1)$. After all, if we have more possible runs, then there should be fewer valid formulas. Therefore, in our case, $A(\mathcal{M}') \subseteq A(\mathcal{M})$. Since by assumption $A(\mathcal{M}) \subseteq A(\mathcal{M}')$, it follows that $A(\mathcal{M}) = A(\mathcal{M}')$, as desired.

It is indeed true that if the class of models increases, then the set of axioms can only decrease (or stay the same). However, in our case, a "model" is *not* a run, but rather, a pair $(S, \mathcal{R})$, where S is a run and $\mathcal{R}$ is a set of runs. Namely, $\mathcal{R}$ is the set of runs that are conceivable; for us, $\mathcal{R}$ is $R(\mathcal{M}')$, where $\mathcal{M}'$ is the class of messages. So the set of models is not necessarily comparable, even if $\mathcal{M}_1 \subseteq \mathcal{M}_2$.

Example 8.1. Let p and q be primitive propositions. Let $\mathcal{M}_1$ contain exactly one message, namely, "I know p", and let $\mathcal{M}_2$ contain exactly two messages, namely, "I know p" and "I know q". Let σ be the formula $\sim K_1 K_2 q$, and let τ be the formula $\sim((K_1 K_2 p) \wedge K_1(q \wedge \sim K_3 K_2 q))$. It is easy to see that σ is in $A(\mathcal{M}_1)$ (since there are no messages involving q), but not in $A(\mathcal{M}_2)$. We now sketch a proof that τ is in $A(\mathcal{M}_2)$ but not in $A(\mathcal{M}_1)$. We first show that τ is in $A(\mathcal{M}_2)$. If not, then let S be a run in $R(\mathcal{M}_2)$ that satisfies $(K_1 K_2 p) \wedge K_1(q \wedge \sim K_3 K_2 q)$. Since S satisfies $K_1 K_2 p$, there has been at least one round of message exchange in S. Since player 1 knows q, for all player 1 knows, the following occurred: player 2 learned that q was true in the 0th round, and told player 3 in the next round that he (player 2) knows q. In this case, player 3 would know that player 2 knows q. Since as far as player 1 is concerned, this gives a possible run, it follows that player 1 does not know that player 3 does not know that player 2 knows q. This is a contradiction. We now show that τ is not in $A(\mathcal{M}_1)$. For, let S be a run where player 1 learns in round 0 that q is true, and where player 2 tells player 1 that player 2 knows that p is true. Then S satisfies $\sim\tau$, since player 1 knows that player 3 cannot know that player 2 knows q (since there are no messages involving q). Thus, $A(\mathcal{M}_1)$ and $A(\mathcal{M}_2)$ are incomparable, even though $\mathcal{M}_1 \subseteq \mathcal{M}_2$. ∎

9. Knowledge structures and knowledge worlds

In this section we briefly review the definition of *knowledge worlds* from [FHV1]. We first discuss them informally.

Example 9.1. Assume there are two players, Alice and Bob, and that there is only one primitive proposition p. There are various "levels" of knowledge. At the "0th level" ("nature"), assume that p is true. The 1st level tells each player's knowledge about nature. For example, Alice's knowledge at the 1st level could be "I (Alice) don't know whether p is true or false", and Bob's could be "I (Bob) know that p is true". The 2nd level tells each player's knowledge about the other player's knowledge about nature. For example, Alice's knowledge at the 2nd level could be "I know that Bob knows whether p is true or false", and Bob's could be "I don't know whether Alice knows p". Thus, Alice knows that either p is true and Bob knows it, or else p is false and Bob knows it. At the 3rd level, Alice's knowledge could be "I know that Bob does not know whether I know about p". This can continue for arbitrarily many levels. ∎

We now give the formal definition of a (knowledge) world. We assume a fixed finite set of primitive propositions, and a fixed finite set $\mathcal{P}$ of players. A *0th-order knowledge assignment*, f_0, is a truth assignment to the primitive propositions. We call $\langle f_0 \rangle$ a *1-ary world* (since its "length" is 1). Assume inductively that k-ary worlds $\langle f_0, \ldots, f_{k-1} \rangle$ have been defined. Let W_k be the set of all k-ary worlds. A *kth-order knowledge assignment* is a function $f_k: \mathcal{P} \to 2^{W_k}$. Intuitively, f_k associates with each player a set of "possible k-ary worlds". There are certain semantic restrictions on f_k, which we shall list shortly. These restrictions enforce the properties of knowledge mentioned above. We call $\langle f_0, \ldots, f_k \rangle$ a *$(k+1)$-ary world*. (Although we shall deal only with worlds, we note for completeness that an infinite sequence $\langle f_0, f_1, f_2, \ldots \rangle$ is called a *knowledge structure* if each prefix $\langle f_0, \ldots, f_{k-1} \rangle$ is a k-ary world for each k.)

Before we list the restrictions on f_k, let us reconsider Example 9.1. In that example, f_0 is the truth assignment that makes p true. Also, $f_1(\text{Alice}) = \{p, \bar{p}\}$ (where by p (respectively, $\bar{p}$) we mean the 1-ary world $\langle f_0 \rangle$, where f_0 is the truth assignment that makes p true (respectively, false)), and $f_1(\text{Bob}) = \{p\}$. Saying $f_1(\text{Alice}) = \{p, \bar{p}\}$ means that Alice does not know whether p is true or false. We can write the 2-ary world $\langle f_0, f_1 \rangle$ as $\langle p, (\text{Alice} \mapsto \{p, \bar{p}\}, \text{Bob} \mapsto \{p\}) \rangle$. Let us denote this 2-ary world by w_1. Let w_2 be the 2-ary world $\langle \bar{p}, (\text{Alice} \mapsto \{p, \bar{p}\}, \text{Bob} \mapsto \{\bar{p}\}) \rangle$, and let w_3 be $\langle p, (\text{Alice} \mapsto \{p\}, \text{Bob} \mapsto \{p\}) \rangle$. In Example 9.1, $f_2(\text{Alice}) = \{w_1, w_2\}$, since Alice thinks both w_1 (where p is true and Bob knows it) and w_2 (where p is false and Bob knows it) are possible worlds. Similarly, $f_2(\text{Bob}) = \{w_1, w_3\}$, since Bob thinks both w_1 (where p is true and Alice does not know it) and w_3 (where p is true and Alice knows it) are possible worlds.

A $(k+1)$-ary world $\langle f_0, \ldots, f_k \rangle$ must satisfy the following restrictions for each player i:

(K1) $<f_0,...,f_{k-1}> \in f_k(i)$, if $k \geq 1$ ("The real k-ary world is one of the possibilities, for each player"). In our example, we see that indeed $p \in f_1(\text{Alice})$ and $p \in f_1(\text{Bob})$. Furthermore, $w_1 \in f_2(\text{Alice})$ and $w_1 \in f_2(\text{Bob})$, where we recall that w_1 is the "real" 2-ary world $<f_0,f_1>$.

(K2)   If $<g_0,...,g_{k-1}> \in f_k(i)$, and $k > 1$, then $g_{k-1}(i) = f_{k-1}(i)$ ("Player i knows exactly what he knows"). Let us consider our example. Alice thinks there are two possible 2-ary worlds, namely w_1 and w_2, since $f_2(\text{Alice}) = \{w_1, w_2\}$. If we write w_2 as $<g_0,g_1>$, then indeed $g_1(\text{Alice}) = \{p, \bar{p}\} = f_1(\text{Alice})$, as required. Intuitively, although Alice has doubts about Bob's knowledge, she has no doubts about her own knowledge. Thus, in all 2-ary worlds she considers possible, her knowledge is identical, namely, she does not know whether p is true or false.

(K3) $<g_0,...,g_{k-2}> \in f_{k-1}(i)$ iff there is a $(k-1)$st-order knowledge assignment g_{k-1} such that $<g_0,...,g_{k-2},g_{k-1}> \in f_k(i)$, if $k > 1$ ("i's higher-order knowledge is an extension of i's lower-order knowledge"). In our example, since Alice thinks either p or $\bar{p}$ is possible, there is some 2-ary world she thinks possible (namely, w_1) in which p is true, and there is some 2-ary world she thinks possible (namely, w_2) in which p is false. Conversely, because she thinks w_1 and w_2 are both possible, it follows that she thinks either p or $\bar{p}$ is possible.

We now define what it means for an $(r+1)$-ary world $<f_0,...,f_r>$ to satisfy formula φ, written $<f_0,...,f_r> \models \varphi$, if $r \geq \text{depth}(\varphi)$, where $\text{depth}(\varphi)$ is defined as in Section 4.

1. $<f_0,...,f_r> \models p$, where p is a primitive proposition, if p is true under the truth assignment f_0.
2. $<f_0,...,f_r> \models \sim\varphi$ if $<f_0,...,f_r> \not\models \varphi$.
3. $<f_0,...,f_r> \models \varphi_1 \wedge \varphi_2$ if $<f_0,...,f_r> \models \varphi_1$ and $<f_0,...,f_r> \models \varphi_2$.
4. $<f_0,...,f_r> \models K_i\varphi$ if $<g_0,...,g_{r-1}> \models \varphi$ for each $<g_0,...,g_{r-1}> \in f_r(i)$.

Let us again consider Example 9.1. Let w_1 and w_2 be, as before, the two 2-ary worlds that Alice considers possible. Then $w_1 \models K_{\text{Bob}}p$, since according to w_1, the only 1-ary world Bob considers possible is $<p>$. Similarly, $w_2 \models K_{\text{Bob}}\sim p$. Hence, both w_1 and w_2 satisfy $(K_{\text{Bob}}p \vee K_{\text{Bob}}\sim p)$. Since both of the 2-ary worlds that Alice considers possible satisfy $(K_{\text{Bob}}p \vee K_{\text{Bob}}\sim p)$, it follows that in our example $<f_0,f_1,f_2> \models K_{\text{Alice}}(K_{\text{Bob}}p \vee K_{\text{Bob}}\sim p)$.

The following crucial lemma shows a certain robustness in the definition of the satisfaction of a formula in a world.

Lemma 9.2.   *Assume that* $\text{depth}(\varphi) = k$ *and* $r \geq k$. *Then* $<f_0,...,f_r> \models \varphi$ *iff* $<f_0,...,f_k> \models \varphi$.

10. Message-based knowledge worlds

In this section we define a restricted class of knowledge worlds, which we call "message-based knowledge worlds". The reason for the name is that these turn out to be precisely the worlds that arise under message exchange.

First, 1-ary (respectively, 2-ary) message-based knowledge worlds are exactly the same as 1-ary (respectively, 2-ary) knowledge worlds, as defined in Section 9. Then $(k+1)$-ary message-based knowledge worlds (for $k \geq 2$) are $(k+1)$-ary knowledge worlds $<f_0,...,f_k>$ that satisfy the following additional restrictions for each player i: (a) $f_k(i)$ is a set of k-ary message-based knowledge worlds, and (b) whenever $<g_0,g_1,...,g_{k-1}> \in f_k(i)$, and whenever $g_0' \in g_1(j)$ for every player j, then $<g_0',g_1,...,g_{k-1}> \in f_k(i)$. What condition (b) says is that whenever player i thinks that a world $w = <g_0, g_1, ..., g_{k-1}>$ is possible, then he also thinks that every world $<g_0',g_1,...,g_{k-1}>$ is also possible, for every truth assignment g_0' consistent with everyone's knowledge about nature in w, that is, consistent with g_1. Intuitively, a good way to think of this is that instead of players "imagining" possible worlds that look like $<g_0,g_1,...,g_{k-1}>$, every player imagines "worlds" $<g_1,...,g_{k-1}>$, where automatically for every truth assignment g_0 consistent with g_1, the player thinks that the world $<g_0,g_1,...,g_{k-1}>$ is possible.

The next theorem shows that message-based knowledge worlds correspond to the knowledge gained in runs.

Theorem 10.1. *For each k-round run S and each nonnegative integer r, there is an r-ary message-based knowledge world $w = <f_0,f_1,...,f_{r-1}>$ such that S and w satisfy precisely the same formulas of depth $r-1$ or less. Conversely, for each r-ary message-based knowledge world w, there is a k-round run S (for some k) such that S and w satisfy precisely the same formulas of depth $r-1$ or less.*

The difficult step of the proof consists of taking an arbitrary message-based knowledge world and producing a run, including a complete description of what messages each player sends in each round and which messages are lost, such that the world and the run satisfy the same formulas (of appropriate depth).

11. Implicit knowledge in message-based knowledge worlds

Implicit knowledge of a group of players is the knowledge that can be obtained by pooling together the group's knowledge. Let $<f_0,...,f_k>$ be a $(k+1)$-ary world. For each player i, the set $f_k(i)$ consists of all the k-ary worlds that player i thinks are possible. Thus, implicitly the players think that precisely the k-ary worlds in $\bigcap_{i \in \mathcal{G}} f_k(i)$ are the possible ones. If φ is a formula of depth r, where $r \leq k$, then we say that $<f_0,...,f_k>$ satisfies $I\varphi$ if φ is satisfied by all the k-ary worlds in $\bigcap_{i \in \mathcal{G}} f_k(i)$.

Consider now an extension $<f_0,...,f_k,f_{k+1}>$ of $<f_0,...,f_k>$. In view of Lemma 9.2, we might be tempted to believe that $<f_0,...,f_k,f_{k+1}>$ satisfies $I\varphi$ if and only if $<f_0,...,f_k>$ satisfies $I\varphi$. Unfortunately, this is not the case; instead, implication holds in only one direction. Thus, if $<f_0,...,f_k>$ satisfies $I\varphi$, then also $<f_0,...,f_k,f_{k+1}>$ satisfies $I\varphi$. But it is possible that $<f_0,...,f_k>$ does not satisfy $I\varphi$, while $<f_0,...,f_k,f_{k+1}>$ satisfies $I\varphi$. This can happen because a k-ary world w can be a member of $\bigcap_{i \in \mathcal{G}} f_k(i)$, even though no extension of it is a member of $\bigcap_{i \in \mathcal{G}} f_{k+1}(i)$. (Note, however, that if a world is in $f_k(i)$, then some extension of it is in $f_{k+1}(i)$, by restriction (K3) on knowledge worlds.)

Put differently, the extended formula $I\varphi$, where φ is a formula of depth k, is not a formula of depth $k+1$, but rather it is a formula of arbitrary depth. To understand this, recall our example of implicit knowledge from the introduction. If Alice knows ψ and Bob knows $\psi \Rightarrow \varphi$, then together they have implicit knowledge of φ, though neither of them might individually know φ. Now even though the formula φ is of depth k, the formula ψ can be of arbitrary depth, so the implicit knowledge of φ is essentially knowledge of arbitrary depth. Unfortunately, the framework of knowledge structures and knowledge worlds requires that formulas be assigned a well-defined depth, so this framework cannot handle implicit knowledge (in particular Lemma 9.2 would fail for extended formulas if we were to define depth($I\varphi$) = 1 + depth(φ)).

Surprisingly, in the context of message-based knowledge, implicit knowledge is quite "well behaved". The basis for this is the following property of message-based knowledge worlds.

Lemma 11.1. *In a message-based knowledge world, if $k > 1$, then $<g_0,...,g_{k-2}> \in \bigcap_{i \in \mathcal{G}} f_{k-1}(i)$ if and only if there is g_{k-1} such that $<g_0,...,g_{k-2},g_{k-1}> \in \bigcap_{i \in \mathcal{G}} f_k(i)$.*

Note the strong similarity between Lemma 11.1 and restriction (K3) on knowledge worlds. As we noted earlier, Theorem 4.2 follows from Lemma 11.1.

As we said before, Lemma 11.1 does not hold for arbitrary knowledge worlds. For message-based communication, it follows from Lemma 11.1 that if φ is a formula of depth k, then we can define $I\varphi$ to be of depth $k + 1$. We can then define the semantics of extended formulas in message-based knowledge structures in a straightforward way, and extend Theorem 10.1 to deal with extended formulas. Details will be given in a later version of this paper.

12. Concluding remarks

The main point of the paper is that we cannot reason about knowledge without taking into account how the knowledge is acquired in the first place. We have focused here on distributed systems where knowledge is acquired via unreliable message exchange. Certain knowledge states were shown to be unattainable in this model. We have characterized the attainable knowledge states and axiomatized the formulas that are valid in in such states. It turns out that the basic feature of message-based knowledge is conservation of implicit knowledge. Thus our results, as well as recent results in [DM, DM, PR, RP], indicate that implicit knowledge is a fundamental concept to the understanding and analysis of distributed systems.

In this paper we have focused on a particular model of communication. Our main assumptions are as follows.
1. Nature never changes.
2. Communication is synchronous, and proceeds in rounds.
3. Communication is unreliable.
4. If a message is received at all, then it is received in the round it was sent.
5. Messages are taken from a particular class of messages.
6. Players "receive information about nature", and then all information is obtained by communication, without any further input "from the outside".

Though these assumptions are quite natural, one may want to consider other models of communication, where the above assumptions are changed. We believe that the issue of how communication affects knowledge deserves a great deal of further study. Thus beyond its technical contributions, this paper opens up an interesting, and we hope fruitful, line of research.

13. Acknowledgments

The authors are grateful to Cynthia Dwork, Yoram Moses, and Larry Stockmeyer for helpful suggestions. We are especially grateful to Joe Halpern for making major simplifications to our completeness proofs, and for pointing out that increasing the class of messages might, in the general case, destroy completeness.

14. Bibliography

[Au]   R. J. Aumann, Agreeing to disagree, *Annals of Statistics* 4,6 (1976), pp. 1236-1239.

[CM]   M. Chandy and J. Misra, How processes learn, *Proc. 4th ACM Symp. on Principles of Distributed Computing*, 1985, pp. 204-214.

[Dw]   C. Dwork, Bounds on fundamental problems in parallel and distributed computation, Ph.D. thesis, Cornell University, 1984.

[DM]   C. Dwork and Y. Moses, Knowledge and common knowledge in a Byzantine environment I: crash failures, this proceedings, 1986.

[DFIL] C. Dwork, M.J. Fischer, N. Immerman, and N.A. Lynch, A theory of protocols, unpublished notes, 1984.

[FHV1]   R. Fagin, J. Y. Halpern, and M. Y. Vardi, A model-theoretic analysis of knowledge, *Proc. 25th IEEE Symp. on Foundations of Computer Science*, West Palm Beach, Florida, 1984, pp. 268-278.

[FHV2]   R. Fagin, J. Y. Halpern, and M. Y. Vardi, To appear.

[FV]   R. Fagin and M. Y. Vardi, An internal semantics for modal logic, *Proc. 17th ACM Symp. on Theory of Computing*, 1985, pp. 305-315.

[HF]   J. Y. Halpern and R. Fagin, A formal model of knowledge, action, and communication in distributed systems: preliminary report, *Proc. ACM Symp. on Principles of Distributed Computation*, 1985, pp. 224-236.

[HM1]   J. Y. Halpern and Y.O. Moses, Knowledge and common knowledge in a distributed environment, *Proc. 3rd ACM Symp. on Principles of Distributed Computing*, 1984, pp. 50-61.

[HM2]   J. Y. Halpern and Y.O. Moses, A guide to the modal logics of knowledge and belief, *Proc. International Joint Conference on Artificial Intelligence (IJCAI-85)*, 1985, pp. 480-490.

[Hi]   J. Hintikka, *Knowledge and belief*. Cornell University Press, 1962.

[Kr]   S. Kripke, Semantical analysis of modal logic, *Zeitschrift fur Mathematische Logik und Grundlagen der Mathematik* **9** (1963), pp. 67-96.

[Leh]   D. Lehman, Knowledge, common knowledge, and related puzzles, *Proc. 3rd ACM Symp. on Principles of Distributed Computing*, 1984, pp. 467-480.

[MH]   J. McCarthy and P. Hayes, Some philosophical problems from the standpoint of artificial intelligence, in *Machine Intelligence 4*, (ed. D. Michie), American Elsevier, 1969, pp. 463-502.

[Pa]   R. Parikh, Logics of knowledge, games, and nonmonotonic logic, *Proc. FST-TCS*, 1984, Lecture Notes in Computer Science - vol. 181, pp. 202-222.

[PR]   R. Parikh and R. Ramanujam, Distributed processing and the logic of knowledge, *Proc. Workshop on Logics of Programs*, Brooklyn, 1985.

[RP]   S. Rosenschein and F. Pereira, Knowledge and action in situated automata, unpublished manuscript, 1985.

[Sa]   L. J. Savage, *The Foundations of Statistics*, Wiley, New York, 1954.

The Logic of Distributed Protocols
(Preliminary Report)

Richard E. Ladner [1]
Department of Computer Science
University of Washington
Seattle, Washington 98195

John H. Reif [2]
Aiken Computation Laboratory
Harvard University
Cambridge, Massachusetts 02138

ABSTRACT

A propositional logic of distributed protocols is introduced which includes both the logic of knowledge and temporal logic. Phenomena in distributed computing systems such as asynchronous time, incomplete knowledge by the computing agents in the system, and game-like behavior among the computing agents are all modeled in the logic. Two versions of the logic, the *linear logic of protocols* (*LLP*) and the *tree logic of protocols* (*TLP*) are investigated. The main result is that the set of valid formulas in *LLP* is undecidable.

[1]Research supported by the National Science Foundation Grant No. DCR-8402565.

[2]Research supported by the Office of Naval Research Contract No. N00014-80-C-0647.

1   Introduction

Motivation and Background

Ever since the seminal work of Floyd [6], Naur [14], and Hoare [9] there has been an increasing interest in the development and analysis of formal tools to reason about program behavior. This interest has led to the creation of a large number of logical systems for handling various types of program behavior. Such logical systems are called *logics of programs*. Notable examples of logics of programs are dynamic logic originally defined by Pratt [19] and temporal logic of programs introduced by Pnueli [18]. The large body of literature in logics of programs has deepened our understanding about reasoning about program behavior, not only about how to reason, but also about what inherent limitations there are in our reasoning. Important results include the discovery of complete proof systems for some of the logics, computational upper and lower bounds for some of the logics, and the establishment of the relative expressive power of different logics.

More recently it has been recognized that the logics of programs developed so far are inadequate for reasoning about the behavior of distributed algorithms or, what we call *protocols*. Generally speaking, a protocol is an algorithm whose execution is shared by a number of independent participants or what we call *players*. Each player may be unaware of what the other players are exactly doing. Therefore, a key ingredient found in the behavior of many protocols (and not found in sequential or parallel algorithms) is the *lack of knowledge* about the complete state of the protocol by each of its players. A good example of this is found in the work on distributed agreement by Pease, Shostok, and Lamport [21]. They show that it is impossible for there to be a protocol such that the non-faulty players agree on a common value when there is a total of three players and at most one is faulty. The proof relies on the fact that, in the presence of inconsistent information coming from the other two players, it is possible for a non-faulty player to remain ignorant of which of the other two players is "lying". They also show that there is a protocol which allows the non-faulty players to agree on a common value when there are four players and at most one is faulty. The proof relies on the fact that in two rounds of exchanging information the non-faulty players can know enough to come to agreement. In one round they cannot know enough. Any logic of protocols must include as part of it a logic of knowledge. A number of researchers have begun the development of logics of distributed protocols which include the notion of knowledge [7] [8] [10] [12] [13] [16].

In this paper we present two new logics of distributed protocols and prove some basic theorems about them. The logics are basically logics of knowledge which incorporate a notion of global time. The logics are capable of implicitly modeling asynchronous time by allowing the players to be ignorant of global time. In addition, the logics are capable of implicitly modeling game-like behavior of distributed computation.

Any logic of protocols should also include a logic for time, or temporal logic. In particular, a key feature of time in a distributed computing setting is that it is asynchronous, that is, there is no global time that the independent computing agents know about. Asynchrony of time does not rule out the possibility of global time, only that if there is a global time then the individual computing participants have only limited knowledge of it. Temporal logics have been extensively studied in the context of both sequential and concurrent programs [1], [2], [3], [18], [25].

In addition, the behavior of distributed protocols exhibit game-like qualities which should be modeled in the logic of protocols. For example, the distributed agreement problems described above are "competitions" of a sort. Some of the players must come to agreement despite the potential maliciousness of lying opponents. Another example of game-like property in distributed computing is the definition of the guaranteed lockout problem [11], [17]. Several formal treatments of game-theoretic aspects of computing have been introduced [17], [22], [23]. An early attempt to include game-like properties into a logic of programs is found in the work of Reif and Peterson [24]. Games and game-like behavior can be mathematically formalized in what is called *game theory*. It is not surprising that game theory should play an important role in distributed computing, because it already plays a significant role in Economics and Ecology, where multiple independent, yet interacting, players co-exist, compete, and cooperate [15]. We propose a (Church/Turing-like) Thesis for distributed computing.

- *Distributed protocols are equivalent to (i.e., can be formally modeled as) games.*

The fact that a logic is capable of modeling game-like behavior is critical if it is claimed to accurately model properties of distributed protocols.

The work done so far on the logic of protocols which includes knowledge also includes, to varying degrees, time and to varying degrees is capable of implicitly modeling games [7] [8] [10] [12] [13] [16]. We feel, however, that the logics developed so far do not adequately model phenomena in protocols like asynchrony. In addition, they seem (with the possible exception of Parikh and Ramanujam's work [16]) to be capable of modeling only restricted classes of games. We feel that the logics of distributed protocols that we present go further than those of previous researchers in two ways:

- Our logics of protocols better model asynchronous time.

- Our logics better model the game-like behavior of protocols.

Indeed, the proof of our main theorem on the undecidability of one of the two logics relies heavily the fact that the logic is capable of modeling a certain three-player incomplete information game, where the players move asynchronously.

The Logic of Protocols

Informally, the logics we define are propositional logics with modal operators $\Box$, $\Box^*$, and K_i for $1 \leq i \leq t$ for some t. The number t refers to the number of players and $K_i p$ means that player i knows that p holds. The expression $\Box p$ means that in the next moment p must hold and $\Box^* p$ means that now and forever in the future p must hold. We can imagine that there is a global time which each of the players may or may not be knowledgeable of. This is akin to the common way of thinking about time in a distributed system where we imagine that the events taking place in the system are actually totally ordered but that each process in the system is unaware of the ordering except for those events that take place in its own process.

We will define two logics of protocols, the *linear logic of protocols* (*LLP*) and the *tree logic of protocols* (*TLP*). The semantics of *LLP* and *TLP* are related to but not the same as, respectively, the linear and branching time semantics for the temporal logic of programs [18] [1]. In the semantics of both *LLP* and *TLP* global time is allowed to branch, but in *LLP* from each player's point of view time is linear. This models the fact that in distributed systems, from one process' point of view there is only one visible history of events, but many system histories may be consistent with that one visible history. In *TLP* global time can branch and players can be aware of it. The distinction between *LLP* and *TLP* can best be understood game theoretically. In a certain sense a model in a semantics for the logic of protocols will define a game, what players do and do not know about the game, and a strategy for each of the players in the game. In *LLP* each player receives no direct knowledge of the states of the other players. Hence, whatever knowledge about the other players states can be, at best, inferred. In *LLP* each player's strategy must be a blindfold strategy, that is, what each player does in a play of the game is preordained and cannot be changed as the game progresses. In *TLP* there is no preordained strategy for each player. A player can react differently in different plays of the game. In a practical sense, *LLP* models a distributed computing situation where the actions of each computing participant are determined as locally as possible. In *TLP* the actions of each participant are dependent on the interaction between the participants.

Asynchrony of time is modeled in *LLP* and *TLP* by the fact that, although there is a global time, the individual players may not have full knowledge about it. So the combination of global time and lack of knowledge about it by the players models asynchronous time. Time can be passing, but an individual player may have no idea if time has progressed at all. Game-like behavior is modeled in *LLP* and *TLP* in a combination of ways. First, time can branch which models a choice of possible moves in a game. Second, players have lack of knowledge which models incomplete information in a game. Third, there may be a number of players which models multi-person games. To understand the semantics of *LLP* and *TLP* it is sometimes helpful to imagine an omniscient player, player 0, different from the players who may have lack of knowledge, players 1 to t. Player 0 knows all. It knows about the global time and every thing the other players know. In a distributed computing system, player 0 corresponds to the system taken as a whole, while players 1 to t model the individual computing agents in the system.

The Results

The main results of this paper are:

- The introduction of a logic of protocols that adequately models knowledge and time, including asynchrony and game-like behavior.

- Theorems that reveal the mathematical structure of the models for the logic of protocols.

- A proof that the set of valid formulas in *LLP* is undecidable.

The third result is surprising for a number of reasons. First, *LLP* is a propositional logic. Second, taken separately, each of the logic of knowledge and the logic of time are decidable. In particular, the propositional temporal logic is decidable, in fact decidable in deterministic exponential time. (The temporal logic with just $\square$ and $\square^*$ is a special case of dynamic logic which has deterministic exponential time upper and lower bound complexity [5], [20].) Further, the propositional logic of knowledge without time is also decidable. (The logic of knowledge is PSPACE complete and the logic of knowledge limited to one player is Co-NP complete [7].) But combining the two logics together in the way we suggest in this paper leads to an undecidable logic. This result adds more strong evidence to the thesis that reasoning about distributed systems is much more difficult than reasoning about sequential programs. Finally, the proof of the undecidability of *LLP* is interesting in its own right. The proof genuinely uses the asynchrony, lack of knowledge, and game-like behavior that are expressible in the logic of protocols.

There is still a lot that we do not know about the logics of protocols. For example, it is still an open question whether or not the set of valid formulas in TLP is decidable. It would seem that LLP is just a special case of TLP, but all we know at present is that every formula that is valid in TLP is also valid in LLP. There is no reason *prima facie* that the undecidability of LLP would imply the undecidability of TLP. Moreover, our proof of the undecidability of LLP relies heavily on the fact that we are using the linear semantics for the logic. Our proof of the undeciability of LLP also relies on there being more than one player. In the case there is just one player we have strong evidence that the logic of protocols with either the linear or tree semantics is decidable.

The paper is organized as follows: In Section 2 we give the formal definitions for the logics of protocols along with an example. In Section 3 we present some fundamental theorems which reveal the structure of models for the logics. In Section 4 we present the main result that the set of valid formulas in LLP is undecidable.

2 The Formal Syntax and Semantics

In this section we give the formal syntax and sematics for the logics of protocols with t players. We assume we have a set of propositional variables Φ, Boolean logical connectives, $\neg$, $\wedge$, Boolean constants 0 and 1, and modal operators $\square$, $\square^*$, and K_i for $1 \leq i \leq t$. The set of logic of protocols *formulas* are defined inductively:

1. If $P \in \Phi$ then P is a formula and 0 and 1 are formulas.

2. If p and q are formulas then so are $\neg p$, $p \wedge q$, $\square p$, $\square^* p$, and $K_i p$ for $1 \leq i \leq t$.

The set of formulas is the smallest set satisfying 1. and 2. above.

The additional boolean operators $\vee$, $\supset$, and $\equiv$ can be defined in the usual way from $\neg$, $\wedge$, 0, and 1. $(p \vee q = \neg(\neg p \wedge \neg q), p \supset q = \neg p \vee q, p \equiv q = (p \supset q) \wedge (q \supset p))$. In addition, we can define the dual modal operators for $\square$, $\square^*$, and K_i. Define $\Diamond p = \neg \square \neg p$, $\Diamond^* p = \neg \square^* \neg p$.

In the semantics we are about to define formally we imagine some underlying distributed system with global time and t players. The system can move from one state of the system to another and as the system moves sequences of states of the system form histories, the last state in the history being the current state. One history extends a second if the sequence of states that forms the first history has as a prefix the second history. A successor of a history is an extension by just one move of the system. In general the system is nondeterministic in that there may be more than one successor. The propositional variables represent primitive statements that hold or not in given states. In general a formula will hold for a given history or not. Let w be a history of the system. Informally, $\square p$ holds at w if p holds at every successor v of w, and $\square^* p$ holds at w if p holds at w and at every history v that extends w. Thus, $\Diamond p$ holds at w if p holds in some successor history v, and $\Diamond^* p$ holds at w if p holds at w or at some history v that extends w. The formula $K_i p$ holds at w if p holds at every history v indistinguishable from w from player i's point of view. Shortly, we will make precise the notion of "indistinguishable from player i's point of view."

Definition of Models

Let Φ be a set of propositional variables. A *model* or *tree model* for the logic of protocols with t players is a $(t+4)$-tuple

$$M = (W, W_0, \pi, \rho, \preceq_1, ..., \preceq_t)$$

where W is a set of states, $W_0 \subseteq W$ is a set of initial states, $\pi : W \to 2^\Phi$ is a mapping indicating which propositional variables hold at which states, $\rho \subseteq W \times W$ is a relation indicating the next move relation, and for each i, $\preceq_i \subseteq W^* \times W^*$ indicating what player i does and does not know, where W^* is the set of all finite sequences (strings) of members of W. In addition M must satisfy properties listed $A_1 - A_3$ below.

Given a nonempty sequence $w \in W^*$ define $last(w)$ to be the last member of the sequence. We define the set of *histories* of M, W^ρ, inductively as follows. If $w \in W_0$ then $w \in W^\rho$ and if $w \in W^\rho$, $(last(w), a) \in \rho$ then $wa \in W^\rho$, and there are no other members of W^ρ. If u and v are two histories then define $u \subseteq^\rho v$ if u is a prefix of v and $u \subset^\rho v$ if u is a proper prefix of v, that is $u \subset^\rho v$ if $u \subseteq^\rho v$ and $u \neq v$. In what follows we let i be arbitrary where $1 \leq i \leq t$. In general, u, v, w, x, y will range over W^ρ unless otherwise specified. The first additional property of M is:

A_1 : $\preceq_i$ is a reflexive and transitive relation on W^ρ.

This first property begins to express the meaning of the relation $\preceq_i$. Intuitively, $u \preceq_i v$ means that from player i's point of view the history v is an extension of the history u. Property A_1 expresses that player i's view of history is reflexive and transitive. We can now express the idea that two histories are indistinguishable from player i's point of view by defining the equivalence relation, $\approx_i$, on W^ρ:

$$u \approx_i v \text{ if and only if } u \preceq_i v \text{ and } v \preceq_i u.$$

The relation $\approx_i$ is an equivalence relation because $\preceq_i$ is reflexive and transitive. Precisely, $u \approx_i v$ means that histories the u and v are indistinguishable from player i's point of view. Further define: $u \prec_i v$ if and only if $u \preceq_i v$ and $u \not\approx_i v$.

The remaining properties are:

A_2 : If $u \subseteq^\rho v$ then $u \preceq_i v$,

A_3 : If $u \preceq_i v$ then $v' \approx_i u$, for some $v' \subseteq^\rho v$.

Properties A_2 and A_3 express more clearly how player i can come to view two histories to be indistinguishable. First, if one history extends another then player i's view is consistent with that extension. Second, if one history extends another from player i's point of view then there must be an earlier time in the first history when player i's view was the same as his view of the second history.

A *linear model* is a model which satisfies the following additional property:

A_4 : $u \preceq_i v$ or $v \preceq_i u$.

Some fundamental properties of models and linear models will be given in the next section.

Definition of Truth

Let $M = (W, W_0, \pi, \rho, \preceq_1, ..., \preceq_t)$ be a model and $w \in W^\rho$. If p is a formula then we define the relation $M, w \models p$ inductively on the structure of p.

1. $M, w \models 1$ and $M, w \not\models 0$,

2. $M, w \models P$ if and only if $P \in \pi(last(w))$, if $P \in \Phi$,

3. $M, w \models \neg p$ if and only if $M, w \not\models p$,

4. $M, w \models p \wedge q$ if and only if $M, w \models p$ and $M, w \models q$,

5. $M, w \models \Box p$ if and only if for all $a \in W$ such that $wa \in W^\rho$, $M, wa \models p$,

6. $M, w \models \Box^* p$ if and only if for all $v \in W^*$ such that $wv \in W^\rho$, $M, wv \models p$,

7. $M, w \models K_i p$ if and only if for all $v \in W^\rho$ such that $v \approx_i w$, $M, v \models p$.

Define TLP_t and LLP_t to be the logic of protocols with t players where the interpretation of formulas is made in, repectively, tree and linear models for the logic of protocols with t players. Define TLP and LLP to be the logic of protocols corresponding to TLP_t and LLP_t where the number of players t is unbounded.

We say that a formula p is *satisfiable in* TLP_t if there is a tree model $M = (W, W_0, \pi, \rho, \preceq_1, ..., \preceq_t)$ and a $w \in W_0$ such that $M, w \models p$. Further, p is *valid in* TLP_t if for every tree model $M = (W, W_0, \pi, \rho, \preceq_1, ..., \preceq_t)$ and every $w \in W_0$, $M, w \models p$. A formula is *satisfiable in* LLP_t if it is satisfiable in some linear model and *valid in* LLP_t if it is valid in all linear models. We say that a formula p is *valid (satisfiable) in* TLP (LLP) if it is *valid (satisfiable) in* TLP_t (LLP_t) for some t where the knowledge operators, K_i in p are such that $i \leq t$.

Example

For example, consider a model $M = (\{a, b, c\}, \{a\}, \pi, \rho, \preceq_1)$ where

1. $\pi(a) = \pi(b) = \{P\}$, $\pi(c) = \emptyset$,

2. $\rho = \{(a, b), (b, c), (c, c)\}$,

3. $\preceq_1 = \{(a, a), (a, abc^i), (abc^i, abc^j) : i, j \geq 0\}$.

Figure 1. graphically illustrates what this model looks like.

In the model M, player 1 can distinguish the history a from the history ab, but cannot distinguish the histories $ab, abc, abcc, ...$ Now consider the formula

$$p = K_1 \Box P \wedge \neg \Box K_1 P.$$

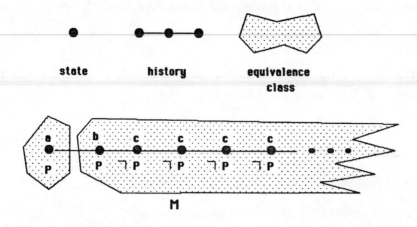

Figure 1: Illustration of the model M. Indistinguishable histories are enclosed.

We have $M, a \models p$. This formula is interesting because it is an instance of the negation of one of Lehman's axioms for his logic of knowledge and time [12]. This points out a fundamental difference between previous models and ours. Our models allow for asynchrony. Player 1 is aware of going from the history a to the history ab, but is totally unaware of going from history ab to abc. In history a he knows that in one step P will be true, but in one step he does not know that P will be true because in one step his knowledge of time suddenly becomes limited. On the other hand the slightly modified formula $K_1 \square^* P \wedge \neg \square^* K_1 P$ is not satisfiable which naturally implies that the formula $K_1 \square^* P \supset \square^* K_1 P$ is valid.

3   Structure of Models

The properties $A_1 - A_4$ by themselves do not give a clear picture of what tree and linear models look like. The goal of this section is to present by way of two theorems a concrete picture of tree and linear models. The following describes in word what models look like. In any model the histories, W^ρ, form a family of trees, where each non-initial history has a unique immediate predecessor history and every history has zero or more immediate successor histories. Consider each player i individually. The histories are partitioned into equivalence classes by the relation $\approx_i$. In the tree model case the equivalence classes themselves form a family of trees, where the predecessor and successors of an equivalence class are implicitly induced by the relation $\preceq_i$. In the linear model case the equivalence classes form a sequence where the linear order of the sequence is implicitly induced by the relation $\preceq_i$. Figure 3 describes the models graphically.

To lead to our two theorems we are required to pass through a sequence of lemmas. In what follows we let $M = (W, W_0, \pi, \rho, \preceq_1, ..., \preceq_t)$ be a model and let $1 \leq i \leq t$. Define $w \in W^\rho$ to be *i-minimal* if $v \preceq_i w$ implies $v \approx_i w$. The proofs of Lemmas 3.1 - 3.6 are omitted to save space.

Lemma 3.1 A member w of W^ρ is i-minimal if and only if $w \approx_i w_0$ for some $w_0 \in W_0$.

If $w \in W^\rho$ is not i-minimal define $pred_i(w)$ to be the unique w' such that for some $a \in W$, $w' \subseteq^\rho w'a \subseteq^\rho w$, and $w' \prec_i w'a \approx_i w$. Such a string exits by Lemma 3.1 and by property A_2.

Lemma 3.2 If $u, v \in W^\rho$ are such that $pred_i(u) \preceq_i v \preceq_i u$ then either $v \approx_i pred_i(u)$ or $v \approx_i u$.

The final lemma in this series shows that the $pred_i$ function is invariant under $\approx_i$.

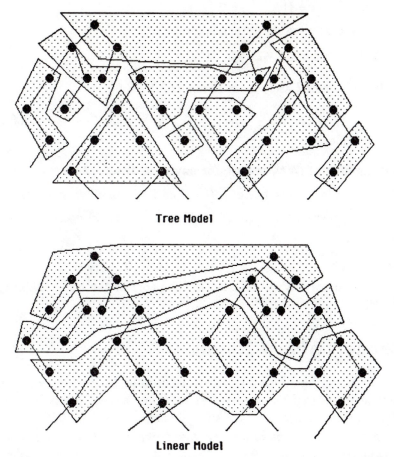

Tree Model

Linear Model

Figure 2: Graphical depiction of a tree model and a linear model.

Lemma 3.3 If $u, v \in W^\rho$ are such that $u \approx_i v$ and u is not i-minimal then $pred_i(u) \approx_i pred_i(v)$.

If $w \in W^\rho$ then define $succ_i(w)$ to be the set of all $wva \in W^\rho$ such that $v \in W^*$, $a \in W$, and $w \approx_i wv \prec_i wva$.

Lemma 3.4 If $u, v \in W^\rho$ are such that $v \in succ_i(u)$ then $pred_i(v) \approx_i u$.

Lemma 3.5 If $u, v, x \in W^\rho$ are such that $u \in succ_i(v)$ and $v \preceq_i x \preceq_i u$ then $x \approx_i v$ or $x \approx_i u$.

We also get a corresponding result to Lemma 3.3 if the model M is linear.

Lemma 3.6 Let M be a linear model. If $u, v, x, y \in W^\rho$ are such that $x \in succ_i(u)$, $y \in succ_i(v)$, and $u \approx_i v$ then $x \approx_i y$.

The properties listed in Lemmas 3.1 - 3.6 essentially give us the structure of the equivalence classes of W^ρ under the equivalence relation $\approx_i$. Let $[w]_i$ be the equivalence class of w under $\approx_i$. Define $[W^\rho]_i = \{[w]_i : w \in W^\rho\}$. The reflexive, transitive relation $\preceq_i$ induces a partial order $\leq_i$ on $[W^\rho]_i$ in a natural way. We say that $[u]_i \leq_i [v]_i$ if $u \preceq_i v$. The relation $\leq_i$ is reflexive, transitive, and antisymmetric on its domain $[W^\rho]_i$. We can further, define $[u]_i <_i [v]_i$ if $[u]_i \leq_i [v]_i$ and $[u]_i \neq [v]_i$.

Theorem 3.7 Let $M = (W, W_0, \pi, \rho, \preceq_1, ..., \preceq_t)$ be a tree model. The set $[W^\rho]_i$ ordered by $\leq_i$ is a family of trees. Specifically:

1. The roots of $[W^\rho]_i$ are $\{[w_0]_i : w_0 \in W_0\}$,

2. If $[w]_i$ is not a root then its parent is $[pred_i(w)]_i$,

3. The children or $[w]_i$ are $\{[v]_i : v \in succ_i(w)\}$.

The proof follows immediately from Lemmas 3.1 - 3.6.

Theorem 3.8 Let $M = (W, W_0, \pi, \rho, \preceq_1, ..., \preceq_t)$ be a linear model. The set $[W^\rho]_i$ is linearly ordered by $\leq_i$. Specifically:

1. The least member of $[W^\rho]_i$ is $[w_0]_i$ for any $w_0 \in W_0$,

2. If $[w]_i$ is not the least member of $[W^\rho]_i$ then its immediate predecessor is $[pred_i(w)]_i$,

3. If $[w]_i$ is not the greatest member of $[W^\rho]_i$ then its immediate successor is $[v]_i$ for any $v \in succ_i(w)$.

The proof follows from Lemmas 3.1 - 3.6.

The result of Theorem 3.8 will be used in the proof of the undecidability of the set of valid formulas in LLP.

4   The Undecidability Result

In this section we prove that the set of valid formulas in LLP is undecidable. More specifically we show that the set of satisfiable formulas in LLP_2 is not recursively enumerable. Since a formula p in the logic of protocols with two players is valid in LLP if and only if the formula $\neg p$ is not satisfiable in LLP_2, it follows that validity in LLP is undecidable if satisfiabilty in LLP_2 is undecidable.

Theorem 4.1 The set of satisfiable formulas in LLP_2 is not recursively enumerable.

Proof   Some of the ideas behind this proof come from a proof of the undecidability of a certain three-player game which is an instance of the guaranteed lockout problem defined by Peterson and Reif [17]. The motivation behind this proof is implicitly game theoretic. The general plan is to show that given a Turing machine T a formula f_T can be constructed with the property that T runs without halting with a blank input if and only if the formula f_T is satisfiable in some linear model. Since the set of Turing machines that do not halt on a blank tape is not a recursively enumerable set then the set of satisfiable formulas in LLP is not recursively enumerable.

Let M be a one tape Turing machine with states Q, tape symbols Γ, $Q \cap \Gamma = \emptyset$, blank symbol $B \in \Gamma$, start state $q_0 \in Q$, and transition partial funtion $\delta : Q \times \Gamma \to Q \times \Gamma \times \{R, L\}$. Let $\Delta = Q \cup \Gamma \cup \{\#, \cent\}$, where $\#$ and $\cent$ are new symbols. Define an ID to be a string of the form $\cent a_1 \cent a_2 \cent ... \cent a_m \cent$ where $a_1 a_2 ... a_m \in \Gamma^* Q \Gamma^*$. Define the *initial ID* to be $\cent q_0 \cent B \cent$. Finally, define an *infinite computation* to be an infinite string of the form

$$\#^{m_0} C_0 \#^{m_1} C_1 \#^{m_2} C_2 \#^{m_3} ...$$

where

1. C_i is an *ID* for all i,

2. C_0 is the initial *ID*,

3. C_{i+1} follows from C_i in one move of T for all i,

4. $|C_i| = 2i + 5$ for all i,

5. $m_i > 0$ for all i,

The reason why infinite computations have this unusual form will be clarified later. Let $q = \lceil log_2|\Delta| \rceil$. With each symbol $\sigma \in \Delta$ we assign a specific Boolean vector $(\sigma_1, ..., \sigma_q)$ of length q. When we talk about σ in the context of a formula we are referring to its representation as a Boolean vector. The formula we will construct will have propositional variables X, and S_{ij} for $i = 1, 2$ and $1 \le j \le q$. Let S_1 and S_2 be the vectors $(S_{11}, S_{12}, ..., S_{1q})$ and $(S_{21}, S_{22}, ..., S_{2q})$. In general, we will think of S_1 and S_2 as variables that take on values in Δ. If U and V are two Boolean vectors of the same length m. We use the abbreviation "$U = V$" to stand for $(U_1 \equiv V_1) \wedge ... \wedge (U_m \equiv V_m)$.

We define a function $collapse : \Delta^\omega \to \Delta^\omega \cup \Delta^*$ by $collapse(s)$ is the string obtained from s by collapsing multiple contiguous occurrences of the same symbol to one occurrence. That is, if a_i is a member of Δ for all i, $a_i \ne a_{i+1}$ for all i, and $m_i > 0$ for all i then

$$collapse(a_0^{m_0} a_1^{m_1} ...) = a_0 a_1 a_2 ....$$

Further, if a_i is a member of Δ for $0 \le i \le r$, $a_i \ne a_{i+1}$ for $0 \le i < r$ and $m_i > 0$ for $0 \le i < r$ then $collapse(a_0^{m_0} a_1^{m_1} ... a_r^\omega) = a_0 a_1 ... a_r$ Two members s_1 and s_2 of Δ^ω are *identical collapsed* if $collapse(s_1) = collapse(s_2)$.

Informally, the formula f_T describes a situation involving two players, player 1 and player 2. For all time player 1 knows the value of S_1 and player 2 knows the value of S_2. Neither player ever knows the value of X. As time passes the successive values of S_1 form an infinite string $s_1 \in \Delta^\omega$. Even though player 1 knows S_1 he is unaware of time passing if the value of S_1 does not change form one moment to the next. Intuitively, as time passes player 1 sees $collapse(s_1)$, not s_1 itself. Similarly, s_2 is the successive values of S_2 and player 2 only sees $collapse(s_2)$. Because neither player knows X it will turn out that if the formula f_T is satisfied in a linear model it will be satisfied in a linear model with two infinite histories, one corresponding to each of the possibilities $X = 0$ and $X = 1$.

Consider the case $X = 0$. As time progresses the successive values of S_1 form an infinite string $e_1 \in \Delta^\omega$. Similarly, successive values of S_2 form the infinite string e_2. The formula will force $e_1 = e_2$, $collapse(e_1) = e_1$, and $collapse(e_2) = e_2$.

If $X = 1$ then infinite strings m_1 and m_2 are formed from successive values of S_1 and S_2 respectively. The formula f_T forces the two strings to match in a way such that, when m_1 and m_2 are interpreted as infinite computations, the first *ID* of m_1 "matches" the second *ID* of m_2, the second *ID* of m_1 "matches" the third *ID* of m_2, and so on. This "matching" guarantees that if m_1 and m_2 are identical collapsed then each of m_1 and m_2 are infinite computations. In the linear model satisfying the formula it will be guaranteed that e_1 and m_1 are identical collapsed and that e_2 and m_2 are identical collapsed. Thus, in the linear model satisfying f_T all four strings e_1, m_1, e_2, and m_2 are identical collapsed and each is an infinite computation. The formula f_T guarantees that embedded in any linear model satisfying it is a "proof" that an infinite computation exists. The "proof" can be found by examining the two infinite histories arising from the lack of the players knowledge about the variable X. Thus T does not halt on the blank input if and only if f_T is satisfied in a linear model.

We now describe the "matching" that is forced by the formula f_T Consider the two infinite computations:

$$s = \#^5\#^3 C_0\#^3 C_1\#^3 C_2\#^3 C_3\#^3 \ldots$$
$$t = \#C_0\#C_1\#C_2\#C_3\#C_4\# \ldots$$

Because $|C_0| = 5$ and $|C_{i+1}| = |C_i| + 2$ then the i-th ID of s "lines up" with the $(i+1)$-st ID of t. The initial padding in s matches the initial ID of t the rest of the padding in s aligns the middle $\#$ of each $\#^3$ with a corresponding $\#$ in t. There is a function $F : \Delta^7 \to \Delta \cup \{\varepsilon\}$ which can be used to verify the matching after the 5-th character of s and the 6-th character of t. Let s_i and t_i be the $(i+1)$-st characters of s and t respectively, so that $s = s_0 s_1 s_2 \ldots$ and $t = t_0 t_1 t_2 \ldots$. The symbol ε, which is needed to make F a totally defined function, is a new symbol with its own representation as a Boolean vector. The function F can be defined in such a way that for all $i \geq 5$, $F(s_i, s_{i+1}, \ldots, s_{i+6}) = t_{i+1}$. We can define F as follows:

$$F(\sigma_0, \sigma_1, \ldots, \sigma_6) = \begin{cases} \# & \text{if } \sigma_0 = \sigma_1 = \sigma_2 = \#, \\ B & \text{if } \sigma_2 = \sigma_3 = \sigma_4 = \#, \\ \cent & \text{if } \sigma_0 = \cent \text{ or } \sigma_2 = \cent, \\ \sigma_2 & \text{if } \sigma_1 = \cent \text{ and } (\{\sigma_0, \sigma_2, \sigma_4\} \cap Q = \emptyset \text{ and } \sigma_2 \neq \# \text{ or} \\ & \quad \sigma_4 \in Q \text{ and } \delta(\sigma_4, \sigma_6) = (p, \tau, R)), \\ \sigma_1 & \text{if } \sigma_1 = \cent \text{ and } \sigma_2 \in Q \text{ and } \delta(\sigma_2, \sigma_4) = (p, \tau, L), \\ \tau & \text{if } \sigma_1 = \cent \text{ and } (\sigma_0 \in Q \text{ and } \delta(\sigma_0, \sigma_2) = (p, \tau, L) \text{ or} \\ & \quad \sigma_2 \in Q \text{ and } \delta(\sigma_2, \sigma_4) = (p, \tau, R)), \\ p & \text{if } \sigma_1 = \cent \text{ and } (\sigma_0 \in Q \text{ and } \delta(\sigma_0, \sigma_2) = (p, \tau, R) \text{ or} \\ & \quad \sigma_2 \in Q \text{ and } \delta(\sigma_4, \sigma_6) = (p, \tau, L)), \\ \varepsilon & \text{otherwise.} \end{cases}$$

The following Propostion describes completely the properties that F must possess.

Proposition 1. Let $s = s_0 s_1 s_2 \ldots$ and $t = t_0 t_1 t_2 \ldots$ be infinite strings in Δ^ω with the properties:

1. $s \in \#^8 \cent q_0 \cent B \cent ((\neg \cent\cent)^* \#^3 \cent)^\omega$,

2. $t \in \#(\cent \neg \cent)^\omega$,

3. For all $i \geq 5$, $F(s_i, s_{i+1}, \ldots, s_{i+6}) = t_{i+1}$,

4. $collapse(s) = collapse(t)$.

Then, s and t are infinite computations.

The proof of the Proposition is straightforward but tedious.

We are now ready to define f_T. We will specify eight formulas $f_1 - f_8$ in such a way that

$$f_T = \bigwedge_{m=1,2} K_m \left[\bigwedge_{n=1}^{8} f_n \right].$$

To simplify the formulas we make some abbreviations. We already mentioned the abbreviation "$S = T$" when S and T are Boolean vectors. We use the notation "$\Box^k p$" to stand for $\Box \Box \ldots \Box p$ where the number of $\Box$'s is k. So $\Box^0 p = p$. If $\sigma \in \Delta$ then we use "$\neg\sigma$" to abbreviate $\Delta - \{\sigma\}$. After each conjunct f_i we will provide some intuition about what the conjunct means. Intuitively we can imagine time as a sequence of *moments*, so that each conjunct must hold in the initial moment (moment 0). Conjuncts of the form $\Box^* p$ force p to hold for all moments. A subformula of a conjunct of the form $\Box^k p$ forces p to hold in the k-th moment from the time the whole subformula holds.

$$f_1 : \Box^* \bigwedge_{i=1,2} \bigvee_{\sigma\in\Delta} K_i(S_i = \sigma)$$

The formula f_1 states that at all time each player i knows the value of its variable S_i which is one of the symbols in Δ.

$$f_2 : \Box^* \bigwedge_{i=1,2} \bigwedge_{j=0,1} \neg K_i(X = j)$$

The formula f_2 states that for all time neither player knows the value of X.

$$f_3 : \Box^* \bigwedge_{j=0,1} (X = j \supset (\Diamond(X = j) \wedge \Box(X = j)))$$

The formula f_3 states that for all time, if X has a certain value then there is a next moment when it has the same value and in every next moment it has the same value. This formula guarantees that there is always a next moment. That is, time does not stop. This formula also guarantees that if initially X has a certain value then it has that value forever. This formula also guarantees that, as time passes, the successive values of S_i form an infinite string in the language Δ^ω.

$$f_4 : S_2 = \cent \wedge \Box^*((S_2 = \cent \supset \Box(S_2 \neq \cent)) \wedge (S_2 \neq \cent \supset \Box(S_2 = \cent)))$$

The formula f_4 states that initially S_2 has the value $\cent$ and for all time if the value of S_2 is $\cent$ then in the next moment the value is not $\cent$ and *vice versa*. Thus, as time passes the successive values of S_2 form an infinite string in the language $(\cent\neg\cent)^\omega$.

$$f_5 : X = 0 \supset \Box^*(S_1 = S_2)$$

The formula f_5 states that if at the beginning the value of X is 0 then for all time the value of S_1 equals the value of S_2. Thus, if the value of X is 1 then the infinite string formed by successive values of S_1 is identical to the infinite string formed by successive values of S_2.

$$f_6 : X = 1 \supset S_1 = \cent \wedge \bigwedge_{1 \leq k \leq 8} \Box^k(S_1 = \#) \wedge \Box^9(S_1 = \cent) \wedge$$
$$\Box^{10}(S_1 = q_0) \wedge \Box^{11}(S_1 = \cent) \wedge \Box^{12}(S_1 = B) \wedge \Box^{13}(S_1 = \cent)$$

$$f_7 : X = 1 \supset \Box^{13}\Box^*((S_1 = \cent \supset \Box(S_1 \neq \cent)) \wedge ((S_1 \neq \cent \wedge S_1 \neq \#) \supset \Box(S_1 = \cent)) \wedge$$
$$((S_1 = \cent \wedge \Box(S_1 = \#)) \supset (\Box^2(S_1 = \#) \wedge \Box^3(S_1 = \#) \wedge \Box^4(S_1 = \cent))))$$

The formulas f_6 and f_7 combined together state, if $X = 1$ then the successive values of S_1 form an infinite string in the language $\cent\#^8\cent q_0\cent B\cent((\neg\cent\cent)^*\#^3\cent)^\omega$.

The final formula in f_T is:

$$f_8: \; X = 1 \supset \square^6\square^* \bigvee_{\sigma_0,\ldots,\sigma_6,\tau\in\Delta} (\bigwedge_{0\le k\le 6} \square^k(S_1 = \sigma_k) \wedge \square(S_2 = \tau) \wedge F(\sigma_0,\ldots,\sigma_6) = \tau)$$

The formula f_8 states that if the value of X is 1 then the infinite strings formed by successive values of S_1 and S_2 must match in a nice way. For $i \ge 6$, i-th, $(i+1)$-st, ... , $(i+6)$-th characters of the infinite string formed by successive values of S_1 and the $(i+1)$-st character of the infinite string formed by successive values of S_2 must match according to the function F.

Claim I. If T does not halt on a blank input tape then f_T is satisfiable.

There is not enough space to include the details of the proof of this claim. Given an infinite computation of T on a blank tape a linear model satisfying f_T can be constructed.

Claim II. If f_T is satisfiable then T does not halt on a blank input tape.

Let $M = (W, W_0, \pi, \rho, \preceq_1, \preceq_2)$ be a linear model and let w_0 be a member of W_0 such that $M, w_0 \models f_T$. By Theorem 3.8 for each $i = 1, 2$ and for each $x_0 \in W_0$, $x_0 \approx_i w_0$. Hence, for all $x_0 \in W_0$ and for $1 \le n \le 8$, $M, x_0 \models f_n$. Choose $u_0, v_0 \in W_0$ such that $M, u_0 \models X = 0$ and $M, v_0 \models X = 1$. Such u_0 and v_0 exist because $M, w_0 \models f_2$. Because $M, u_0 \models f_4$ and $M, v_0 \models f_3$ there must exist two infinite sequences $u_0u_1u_2...$ and $v_0v_1v_2...$ in W^ω, each of which is an infinite history. Let $u[k] = u_0u_1...u_k$ and $v[k] = v_0v_1...v_k$. Again, by f_4 we have $M, u[k] \models X = 0$ and $M, v[k] \models X = 1$ for all $k \ge 0$.

Because $M, u[k] \models f_1$ and $M, v[k] \models f_1$, there exist infinite sequences $e_1 = e_{10}e_{11}e_{12}...$, $e_2 = e_{20}e_{21}e_{22}...$, $m_1 = m_{10}m_{11}m_{12}...$, and $m_2 = m_{20}m_{21}m_{22}... \in \Delta^\omega$ such that

$$M, u[k] \models S_1 = e_{1k} \quad M, u[k] \models S_2 = e_{2k}$$
$$M, v[k] \models S_1 = m_{1k} \quad M, v[k] \models S_2 = m_{2k}$$

Leaving out the details the formulas f_1, f_4, f_5 and the fact that M is a linear model guarantee the following:

$$collapse(m_2) = m_2 = e_2 = e_1 = collapse(m_1).$$

The formulas $f_4, f_6 - f_8$ guarantee the following:

- $m_2 \in (\cent\neg\cent)^\omega$ (f_4),

- $m_1 \in \cent\#^8\cent q_0\cent B\cent((\neg\cent\cent)^*\#^3\cent)^\omega$ (f_6, f_7),

- $F(m_{1i}, m_{1(i+1)}, ..., m_{1(i+6)}) = m_{2(1+1)}$ for all $i \ge 6$ (f_8).

If we let $s = m_{11}m_{12}m_{13}...$ and $t = m_{21}m_{22}m_{23}...$ then s and t satisfy Proposition 1. Hence, T does not halt on a blank tape. $\square$

5   Conclusion

Although we have introduced two logics of protocols, *TLP* and *LLP*, we have only been able to show undecidability for *LLP* which is arguably the less interesting of the two logics. *TLP* can model general games of incomplete information while *LLP* only can model blindfold games. It is our belief that *TLP* is also undecidable, but direct application of the techniques in this paper does not seem sufficient to prove it. Fischer and Immerman have recently developed a logic which seem to model Markov games, games where strategies do not depend on complete histories but only on the current position of the game [4]. The Fischer-Immerman logic is decidable.

It is not yet clear which logics which include knowledge and time will turn out to be the most useful. What is clear already is that the study of logics for distributed computation is enriching our understanding of what the foundations of distributed computation are.

References

[1] Ben-Ari, M., Manna, Z., and Pnueli, A. The Temporal Logic of Branching Time. Eighth ACM Symposium on Principles of Programming Languages, 1981, pp. 164-176.

[2] Emerson, E.A. and Halpern J.Y. Decision Procedures and Expressiveness in the Temporal Logic of Branching Time. Proceedings of the Fourteenth Annual ACM Symposium on Theory of Computing, 1982, pp. 169-180.

[3] Emerson, E.A. and Sistla, A.P. Deciding Branching Time Logic. Proceedings of the Sixteenth Annual ACM Symposium on Theory of Computing, 1984, 14-24.

[4] Fischer, M.J. and Immerman, N. Foundations of Knowledge in Distributed Systems. Conference on Theoretical Aspects of Reasoning About Knowledge, Asilomar, March 19-22, 1986.

[5] Fischer, M.J. and Ladner, R.E. Propositional Dynamic Logic of Regular Progams. *Journal of Computer and System Sciences, Vol. 18, No. 2*, 1979, pp. 194-211.

[6] Floyd, R.W. Assigning Meaning to Programs. In J.T. Schwartz (ed.) *Mathematical Aspects of Computer Science*, Proc. Symp. in Applied Math. 19. Providence, R.I. American Math. Soc., 1967, pp 19-32.

[7] Fagin, R., Halpern,J.Y., and Vardi, M.Y. A Model-Theoretic Analysis of Knowledge: Preliminary Report. 25th Annual Symposium on Foundations of Computer Science, 1984, pp. 268-287.

[8] Halpern, J.Y. and Fagin, R. A Formal Model of Knowledge, Action, and Communication in Distributed Systems. Proceedings of the Fourth Annual ACM Symposium on Principles of Distributed Computing, 1985, pp 224-236.

[9] Hoare, C.A.R. An Axiomatic Basis for Computer Programming. *Communications of the ACM, Vol. 12*, 1969, pp. 576-580.

[10] Halpern, J.Y. and Moses, Y. Knowledge and Common Knowledge in a Distributed Environment. Proceedings of the Third Annual ACM Conference on Principles of Distributed Computing, 1984.

[11] Ladner, Richard E. The Complexity of Problems in Systems of Communicating Processes. *Journal of Computer and System Sciences, Vol. 21, No. 2*, 1980, pp. 179-194.

[12] Lehman, Daniel. Knowledge, Common Knowledge and Related Puzzles. Proceedings of the Third Annual ACM Conference on Principles of Distributed Computing, 1984, pp. 62-67.

[13] Moses, Y., Dolev D., and Halpern, J.Y. Cheating Husbands and Other Stories: A Case Study of Knowledge, Action, and Communication. Proceedings of the Fourth Annual ACM Symposium on Principles of Distributed Computing, 1985, pp 215-223.

[14] Naur, P. Proof of Algorithms by General Snapshots. *BIT, Vol. 6*, 1966, pp 310-316.

[15] Owen, G., *Game Theory*, Academic Press, 1982.

[16] Parikh, Rohit and Ramanujam, R. Distributed Processes and the Logic of Knowledge. *Logic of Programs, Lecture Notes in Computer Science, No. 193*, Ed. by Rohit Parikh, Springer-Verlag, N.Y., 1985, pp 256-268.

[17] Peterson, Gary L. and Reif, John H. Multiple-Person Alternation. 20th Annual Symposium on Foundations of Computer Science. IEEE Computer Society, 1979, pp. 348-363.

[18] Pnueli, A, The Temporal Logic of Programs. 18th Annual Symposium on Foundations of Computer Science, 1977, pp 46-57.

[19] Pratt, V.R. Semantical Considerations on Floyd-Hoare Logic. 17th Annual Symposium on Foundations of Computer Science, 1976, pp.109-121.

[20] Pratt, V.R. A Near Optimal Method for Reasoning about Action. MIT Technical Report, LCS/TM-138, 1979.

[21] Pease, M., Shostak, R., and Lamport, L. Reaching Agreement in the Presence of Faults. *Journal of the ACM, Vol. 27, No. 2*, 1980. pp 228-234.

[22] Reif, John H. Universal Games of Incomplete Information. Proceedings of the Eleventh Annual ACM Symposium on Theory of Computing. ACM, 1979, pp. 288-308.

[23] Reif, John H. The Complexity of Two-Player Games of Incomplete Information. *Journal of Computer and System Sciences, Vol. 29, No. 2*, 1984, pp. 274-301.

[24] Reif. John H. and Peterson, Gary L. A Dynamic Logic of Multiprocessing with Incomplete Information. Seventh Annual ACM Symposium on Principles of Programming Languages, 1980, pp. 193-202.

[25] Sistla, A.P. and Clarke, E.M. The Complexity of Propositional Linear Temporal Logics. Ninth Annual ACM Symposium on Principles of Programming Languages, 1982, 159-168.

Panel: Objects of knowledge and belief: sentences vs. propositions?

Panel Chairman: Robert C. Stalnaker, Cornell University
Panelists: Hans Kamp, Univeristy of Texas, Austin
Kurt Konolige, SRI International
Hector J. Levesque, Univeristy of Toronto
Richmond H. Thomason, University of Pittsburgh

Abstract: It has been an object of much controversy in the literature whether knowledge should be taken to be a relation between agents and sentences (the *syntactic* or *sentential* approach) or a relation between agents and propositions (the *semantic* or *propositional attitude* approach). In this panel, we discuss the relative merits of the two approaches.

PARADOXES AND SEMANTIC REPRESENTATION

Richmond H. Thomason
Linguistics Department
University of Pittsburgh
Pittsburgh, PA 15260

ABSTRACT

Many researchers in Computer Science, Linguistics, Logic, and Philosophy have been discovering in various ways that analogues of the Liar paradox pose deep foundational problems for intensional semantics. In this survey paper I state my own view of what the problems are, and try to provide a broad perspective on the issues, with many references to the literature. Although the paper concentrates on developments in Philosophical Logic, I hope that the paper will help all researchers concerned with these problems to locate their concerns in a broad, interdisciplinary framework.

1. The Liar Paradox

The problematic traits of the Liar Paradox are hardy, and likely to survive transplanting. We have become interested in what can be learned from intensional variants of the Paradoxes, variants that apply to propositional attitudes in a computational setting. But it is worth beginning with problems posed by logical paradoxes in general, and in particular by the Liar.[1]

A paradox is a plausible argument leading to an implausible conclusion. Paradoxes have always intrigued logicians, and many of the most interesting results of modern symbolic logic have been obtained by showing how certain paradoxes, or near-paradoxes, can be precisely formalized.

When we reach an implausible conclusion, we feel compelled to revise our opinions; so paradoxes call out for explanatory solutions: a satisfactory account of what went wrong in the reasoning. In case the paradox can be formalized (say, in the form of an inconsistent theory), there will be a related technical project of making reasonably small changes in the formalization that issue in a consistent theory (or at least, in a theory not known to be inconsistent).

The Liar Paradox seems to have been designed to humble logicians. Tarski's theorem,[2] after all, is a theorem, and imposes constraints on attempts to solve the Liar, just as Gödel's theorem imposes constraints on programs aimed at providing foundations for mathematics. This forces a technically satisfactory solution to the Liar to adopt at least one of the following three strategies.

Strategy 1: Hold certain seemingly intelligible notions to be inexpressible. (A special case of this would be giving up classical logic—holding classical negation, for instance, to be inexpressible.)

Strategy 2: Give up plausible schematic principles on truthlike predicates, such as Convention T.

Strategy 3: Impose limits on the extent to which language can be used to talk about its own syntax.

---

[1]In keeping with modern treatments of the Liar, I am treating it as a phenomenon of *direct discourse;* the "what" in 'What I am saying is false' is a sentence. We are leading up to variations on the Liar in which the "what" is construed as a proposition, a belief or the like.

[2]See [Tarski 1956].

The classification is meant to divide approaches to the semantic paradoxes along lines corresponding to the pressures that will apply in attempting to make a case that the approach represents an explanatory solution. A language-limiting strategy, for instance, will have to argue that some seemingly sensible notions in fact are illusory; or at least, can't be expressed. A principle-limiting strategy must argue that the generality of the relevant principles is in fact less than it seems to be. And a self-reference-limiting strategy will have to argue that, for some reason, things that really are language-like can't be described as such—at least, not in full detail.

The language-limiting strategy includes solutions that introduce language-internal hierarchies, like the ramified theory of types,[3] as well as those, like Tarski's metalinguistic solution, that make the hierarchies language-external. Putting the hierarchy into linguistic context of utterance, as Burge[4] suggests, is an interesting compromise between the internal and external treatments. Still, like the other hierarchical solutions, it has the consequence of making many things unexpressible; in particular, there is no type-free way to say that a sentence is true. Thus, the *explanation* that is required in order to turn a technical solution of this sort into an explanatory solution of the paradox will be an argument that certain things that seem to be sayable in a type-free way in fact are not.

These hierarchies can all be extended naturally into the transfinite ordinals, and at successor ordinals seem to involve a process in which a process of reflection on a lower level somehow brings to light new truths.

With a certain amount of reluctance, I decided to include cases in which classical logic is given up under the first heading as well. This agrees well with solutions, like Kripke's,[5] that appeal to truth-value gaps and "choice negation." In explaining such theories, it is natural to fall into a turn of speech in which the sentences that are not true are divided into (i) those whose negations are true, and (ii) all the rest. This seems to create a usage of 'not true' that is not represented in the theory itself. So, if you want to show an approach of this sort to be explanatory, you'll have to argue that the sense of negation that seems to correspond to this usage is illusory.[6] These considerations would also apply plausibly to the type-free lambda calculus as an approach to the Liar. Here, in view of the Curry paradox,[7] a conditional satisfying *modus ponens* must be ruled out of linguistic bounds, as well as a classical negation.

---

[3][Whitehead & Russell 1910]

[4]See [Burge 1979].

[5]See [Kripke 1975].

[6]Kripke's paper makes it clear that he is well aware of this problem.

[7]See [Curry 1942].

The logical solution that seems to fit the language-limiting pattern least well is a paraconsistent approach, based on a version of relevance logic.[8] The tactic that enables theories to be nontrivial theories to be inconsistent seems to depend less on restricting the background language than on giving up the principle of (material) *modus ponens*:

$$[\phi \wedge (\sim\phi \vee \psi)] \rightarrow \psi$$

For this reason, it might be best to place paraconsistent approaches with principle-limiting strategies. But since—for reasons that are rooted fairly deep in the philosophy of language—it is always difficult to distinguish between giving up *principles of logic* and limiting ones language, I prefer to classify it under the first category, with the other logical solutions, while remembering that it is exceptional in some ways.

Gupta's approach[9] is a good example of the principles-limiting strategy. The application of jump operators and fixpoints to the technical analysis of truth derives from Kripke, but is placed in a setting that preserves classical logic. Something else has to give—and what gives is Convention T.

The self-reference-limiting strategy has at least the following technical interest: how much can be preserved of the apparatus of syntax if enough syntax is given up to block proofs of Tarski's theorem?[10] Gupta's results[11] show that a surprising amount can be done with a restricted syntax of this sort.

On the other hand, the explanatory potential of the self-reference-limiting strategy seems to be unpromising. An explanation would have to make it plausible that, although our theory uses genuine names of sentences, it will become inconsistent if it is made explicit that this is what they name. But it is very hard to see how merely adding more linguistic detail about things we are already describing in some dim fashion could create contradictions. Moreover, as many people have noticed and Kripke shows vividly in [Kripke 1975], it isn't necessary to use an indirect construction like Gödel's diagonal method to construct self-reference of the sort demanded by the Liar; the ability to baptise things with a proper name also serves the purpose.

Commentators on [Kripke 1975] have neglected what seems to me to be one of the most important contributions to the recent literature on the Liar. This is the point,

---

[8] See [Priest 1979], [Visser 1984], and [Woodruff 1984]

[9] See [Gupta 1982] and [Gupta 1984].

[10] We know from Gödel's work that if a syntactic theory is strong enough to enable every primitive recursive syntactic function to be characterized, then it will enable us to prove Tarski-like theorems, *via* Gödel's diagonalization technique.

[11] See [Gupta 1982].

which Kripke establishes by artful deploying of examples, that contingent, extralinguistic considerations can play a rôle in determining whether a sentence is used paradoxically. Any solution that does not show how this can occur is inadequate.

2. The Liar in an Intensional Setting

The Liar Paradox shows that truth is somehow *ineffable;* the relation between sentences and their truth values is problematic, and theories that enable this relation to be expressed are subject to various maladies.[12]

Intensionality has to do with semantic representations of sentences that are more full-blooded than mere truth-values, and which therefore are able to support interpretations of modal operators, or perhaps of propositional attitudes like 'know', 'believe', and 'be likely'. The general way of dealing with such constructions is to interpolate certain values between sentences and their truth-values; I will call these values *propositions,* without assuming anything about what propositions are.

Propositions are the middle-men between sentences and truth; sentences express propositions, and propositions have truth values. As long as there are enough propositions—so that, for instance, if one sentence is contingent and another necessary we don't have to associate the same proposition with the two—we have the materials to provide formally correct interpretations of intensional constructions.

Explanatory interpretations would require propositions to have more structure. In terms of this structure, for instance, if we could define operations of conjunction, necessitation, and belief on propositions we could then let the conjunction of ϕ with ψ be the conjunction of the proposition expressed by ϕ and the proposition expressed by ψ; the necessitation of ψ be the necessitation of the proposition associated with ψ; and the "belief" of ϕ be the "belief" of the proposition associated with ϕ.[13] The explanation, then, consists in establishing a semantic operation, like necessitation on propositions, and then using it to interpret a syntactic operation.

However, Tarski's theorem applies to languages with intensional operators; and truth will still be ineffable in such languages. And if truth is a composition of two relations, one of them must be ineffable. This means that either (i) the relation between sentences

---

[12] Anyone who is worried about my not taking into account the fact that this relation is sensitive to context of utterance should suppose that what I say is relative to a fixed context.

[13] The possible worlds approach to propositions accomplishes this by arranging things so that the propositions are members of a closure algebra. Boolean connectives map into boolean operations of the algebra; necessitation maps into the interior operation.

and the propositions they express or, (ii) the relation between propositions and their truth values, must be problematic.

Both alternatives are uncomfortable. On the first, we make the semantic interpretation of sentences mysterious; on the second, we lose the ability to deploy certain kinds of semantic explanations. The very simple explanations that truth-functions offer for boolean connectives like conjunction, for instance, would precipitate a hierarchy of metalanguages, because the notion of the truth of a proposition for a language L would not be expressible in L.

The difficulty is exacerbated by the Montague-Löb results,[14] which stand to the Knower Paradox as Tarski's theorem stands to the Liar Paradox. Tarski's theorem shows that a truth connective T, satisfying the scheme

$$T\phi \leftrightarrow \phi,$$

will produce inconsistency if it is construed as a syntactic predicate. Montague's results show that connectives satisfying very weak modal conditions will do the same.

Such results have the effect of enlarging the list of natural language constructions that will be mysterious or unexplainable if we follow alternative (ii) and make the relation between sentences and the propositions they express unproblematic. Not only words like 'necessarily' and 'possibly' satisfy these modal conditions, but also the modal auxiliaries, and words like 'provable'. Also, it is convenient to place modal conditions on epistemic attitudes like 'know'; either as an idealization, or as a formulation of "implicit knowledge."[15] Under these idealizations, semantic explanations of epistemic attitudes also will be threatened.[16]

Hilary Putnam argues that there is a tension between two common assumptions about meaning:[17]

(I)   To know the meaning of a term is to be in a certain psychological state.

(II) The meaning of a term determines its extension (and as a special case, the meaning of a sentence) determines its truth value.

The difficulty that I have been trying to develop can be put as a somewhat similar tension between assumptions.

---

[14]See [Löb 1955] and [Montague 1974].

[15]The crucial part of the modal idealization consists of conditions guaranteeing that $K\phi$ will hold for each logically valid first-order sentence ϕ.

[16][Thomason 1980] extends the Montague results to idealized belief-like connectives, which do not satisfy the scheme $B\phi \rightarrow \phi$.

[17]I paraphrase from pp. 135-6 of [Putnam 1975].

(I ′) The semantic representations of sentences are *graspable*, in a sense that implies that they can be calculated.

(II ′) The semantic representations of sentences are *alethic*, in a sense that implies that they yield relatively simple explanations of boolean connectives, modal operators, and the like.

This pair of conflicting assumptions is somewhat similar to Putnam's. But it seems to me that the second opposition raises deeper problems for semantic theory, because the considerations that fuel the conflict are grounded in logical limitations related to the semantic paradoxes, and because graspability is a clearer and more tractable concept than psychological representability.

Since a semantic theorist who stresses the desirability of (I ′) is likely to favor a view of semantic interpretation as translation or compiling, and one who stresses the desirability of (II ′) is likely to favor explanations having to do with truth and reference, the opposition is related to representationalist-realist debates in the foundations of cognitive psychology.[18]

But again, an opposition related to the paradoxes puts the matter in a different light. It suggests a less controversialist approach to the issues, since for technical reasons each of the two alternatives will be surrendering something desireable and a synthesis combining the merits of the two approaches will not be readily forthcoming.

Finally, the opposition between (I ′) and (II ′) is closely related to *Benacerraf's problem* in the philosophy of mathematics. Benacerraf's opposition is between finding a philosophical account of mathematics that is both epistemologically satisfactory, and capable of giving a plausible ontology to classical mathematics. Stressing the need to explain how we can have knowledge in mathematics leads to programs that cross the border from philosophy of mathematics to mathematics itself, since the need to provide such explanations is closely related to the revisionist programs in mathematics associated with constructivism. The need to be true to classical analysis makes it very hard to put mathematics in a reasonable relation to a knowing subject. It seems to me that Benacerraf's problem is best regarded not as distinct from my opposition between graspability and explicability in semantics, but as the special case of the difficulty where mathematical language is at stake.

This approach to foundational difficulties in semantics suggests that in coming to grips with the problems, we must look to work on technical solutions to the Liar Paradox. Since most of the recent outpouring of work on this topic has been motivated by a pure interest in the challenge of the semantic paradoxes, this seems to be another case of mathematics coming into being as it is needed, by a kind of preestablished harmony. Occasionally when

---

[18]See [Fodor 1975] and [Dennett 1978]; also, contrast [Fodor 1975] with [Stalnaker 1984] and [Barwise & Perry 1983].

I have been present at talks on the paradoxes, someone in the audience has asked what the wider relevance of the technical work is. Generally, the answer that I have heard is that the work is interesting, regardless of questions of relevance. This is true, but I believe that a much stronger case can be made for the usefulness of this work.

3. Ways out

Placing the Liar in an intensional setting does not seem to open many solution strategies that cannot be classified as modifications of approaches to the Liar. Each of the three general strategies canvassed in Section 1 could be applied to the Knower Paradox, and—depending on the extent to which the solution is explanatory—could be made into a foundation of a theory of intensional semantic representation, in natural language semantics or computational semantics.

There is still much work to be done in developing the details of the necessary theories. This is becoming an active area of research, judging from the projects that I'm aware of;[19] after the dust has settled a bit, it should be possible to make comparative judgments with more confidence; nevertheless, it looks as if the pattern of technical solutions that will emerge will be similar to ones that have been developed for the Liar.[20]

Against this background, the new approaches to the problem that an intensional setting affords stand out as particularly noteworthy. I see three such possibilities.

---

[19]See [Perlis 1985], [Asher & Kamp 1986], [des Rivières & Levesque 1986], [Kremer 1986], and [Morgenstern 1986]. Since time was short for preparing this paper, I have not said much about research on type-free programming languages, and work in natural language semantics inspired by this research. However, this research is very relevant, especially as a source of insights into the positive constraints that need to be placed on a successful theory. That is, we can see from this work what expressive limitations would be too severe to enable certain programming strategies to be implemented naturally, or to enable sense to be made of natural language constructions that seem perfectly sensible from an intuitive standpoint. See [Chierchia1982], [Stoy 1977], and [Reynolds 1983].

[20]In some cases, of course, the relation is explicit and intended; Asher and Kamp's approach, for instance, is a modification of Gupta's; Kremer and Morgenstern base their work on Kripke's construction.

Strategy 1′: Impose limits on the extent to which language can be used to talk about its propositions, while at the same time allowing it the full expressive power of quotation.

Strategy 2′: Do not require every sentence to express a proposition, and explicitly limit Convention T to sentences that express propositions.

Strategy 4: Claim that propositional attitudes are not alethic, do not satisfy modal conditions. Thus, though Liar-like puzzles may arise with truth and necessity, they could not arise with attitudes, like knowledge and belief.

Strategy 1′ depends on the fact that propositions—beliefs, claims, and the like—are somehow less tangible than sentences. Thus, the claim that their properties are problematic may be more defensible than the claim that syntactic properties are mysterious. I do not know of any official attempt to develop this strategy, but there is an intriguing relation to Benacerraf's solution of Lucas' puzzle about Gödel's incompleteness theorem. Essentially, Benacerraf's approach[21] is to say that the ideal mathematician can know *that* he is a Turing machine, but cannot know *which* Turing machine he is. The analogous strategy in resolving the conflict between the graspability and the alethic character of propositions would be to claim that propositions are in fact sentences of the "language of thought," but that we cannot—on pain of inconsistency—know which sentences they are. This strategy has not, as far as I know, been developed, or even proposed; but it strikes me as an intriguing idea, worth following up, especially since much of the necessary mathematical work has been done by logicians exploring the consistency of Benacerraf's proposal.[22]

Strategy 2′ is suggested in [Thomason 1982]. However, there is a price: because of variations on the usual paradoxical constructions, of the sort discussed in [Parsons 1974], it is possible in this variation to prove some things that can also be proven not to express a proposition. The resulting theories are problematic in some ways, even though they need not be formally inconsistent.

Strategy 4 is defended in [Cresswell 1985]. The approach is interesting, but I am not convinced that it is explanatory. The best way of motivating this approach would be by means of linguistic examples showing that the modalities and the attitudes take different objects. Unfortunately, the evidence is mixed: 'What he believes is true' is perfectly acceptable. However, as Cresswell points out in [Cresswell 1985], p. 40, 'Jeremy believed

---

[21]See [Benacerraf 1967].

[22]See [Reinhardt 1983] and [Flagg 1984].

that the sentence Miriam uttered and what Mary hinted were equally true' does not seem to be totally unintelligible, though it conflates a sentential and a propositional object.

What makes this strategy particularly difficult to defend, it seems to me, is that its proponent has not only to explain why the attitudes do not satisfy alethic conditions, but why it is a *logical* matter that they do not satisfy such conditions. It is easy enough for me to see that my own beliefs aren't closed under logical consequence. It is harder to see why if a rational agent's beliefs *were* closed under logical consequence, and other plausible conditions were met, a contradiction would ensue.

There remains one interesting strategy that I omitted from the list, because it is not new, and also is too complex to classify in a few words. This is Ramified Type Theory. This theory was developed with the intensional paradoxes in mind, and it provides a way of escaping not only the Knower Paradox, but other puzzles as well.[23] Russell and Whitehead gave the approach up in favor of the Simple Theory of Types, because of difficulties it raised for the Logicist program in the foundations of mathematics. This was an early stage in what became a vigorous extensionalist program in Symbolic Logic, with only a few holdouts: the constructivists, and some others such as Carnap, Church, and Fitch.

Now that intensional problems have become not only respectable but central, I think it might be rewarding to dust off the Ramified Theory of Types, and to reformulate it so that it can be compared with contemporary theories.

4. Consequences for Semantic Representation[24]

The cognitive expectation is that semantics will work out in much the same way as syntax; semantics will be a theory of semantic competence, describing the "knowledge" of the ideal speaker. One consequence of the Knower Paradox is a proof that the ideal speaker's theory will be inconsistent, given this approach to semantics and other plausible assumptions. For on this model of competence, propositions will be recursively generated, like syntactic structures—and the relation between sentences and propositions will be recursive. Thus, if the ideal speaker's theory contains arithmetic, the relation between sentences and propositions will be expressible in the language. The assumption that the ideal speaker's knowledge is logically closed, which seems exactly like other assumptions warranted by this sort of idealization, leads to a contradiction.

This is simply another way of restating the tension between the cognitive goal of graspability to which I alluded in Section 2. The correct reaction, I think, is that the

---

[23]See [Prior 1961] and [Thomason 1982].

[24]For the most part, this section summarizes points made in [Thomason 1979], which is still unpublished.

metaphor of the ideal speaker needs reappraisal when semantics is taken to be part of the ideal speaker's competence; it seems to me that the relation between theories of the language and speakers is more problematic than the metaphor suggests. In any case, I believe that if the consequences of adhering to the goal of graspability are worked out carefully, it will lead to strong forms of constructivism, or paraconsistent approaches, or other approaches that involve revision of logical foundations. Any assessment of strong forms of cognitivism should take these consequences into account.

As for the issue of semantic representation, my guess is that we are not going to find any theories that make everyone happy. Years of hard work by the best logical talents have not done this with the Liar, and it would be foolish to expect it to happen with the problems that the Knower poses for semantic representations. We can expect, though, that we will develop a variety of technical solutions, and that these will help to clarify the better alternatives. In seeking for *explanatory* solutions, I would hope that those who favor syntactic representations will be aware of the challenge for their approach posed by the modalities, and in general by the linguistic constructions favored by model-theoretic logicians; and equally, that those who favor nonsyntactic representations will be mindful of the need to say something about epistemological questions. This piece of advice is statesmanlike, and therefore boring. I'm sorry for that—but humility really seems to be the proper attitude when attempting to deal with the semantic paradoxes.

5. Consequences for Computer Science

In all cases in which these problems make contact with a nonphilosophical discipline, such as Computer Science, Linguistics, or Psychology, I am uncertain about how close the encounter is or ought to be. In each of these cases it seems that we have reached a pretty rarefied level of the discipline, at so great a distance from implementations, or linguistic evidence, or human experimentation, that the connection with the discipline is stretched near the breaking point. And maybe this is just as well; I would not want to bet on the future of a science if this depended on a definitive solution to the semantic paradoxes. We have to remember that foundational problems are not a sign of an unhealthy discipline; sciences like physics and mathematics have highly problematic foundations, which concern most practicing physicists and mathematicians very little, if at all.

One long-range approach to foundational difficulties, then, is to leave them to a few specialists—usually a small group of technically minded philosophers and reflective scientists—and to treat them as peripheral. The cognitive sciences, as they develop, could conceivably settle into this sort of relation to the paradoxes of representation. To a large extent, this will depend on how able we are to produce solutions that are explanatory and scientifically fruitful.

I don't want to close with the impression that foundational problems of representation are irrelevant to cognitive sciences. These problems certainly do constrain the theories that can be articulated in disciplines such as Computer Science. And there are plausible, well motivated trains of reflection leading from centrally placed material in the cognitive disciplines to these problems of semantic representation. Finally, in the present climate it would be especially unrewarding to draw hard boundaries between Computer Science and Philosophical Logic—though, as I say, one possible line of long-term development might draw these lines so that the job of worrying about an explanatory solution is left to the philosophers.

The point of all this is that I'm uncertain about the long-range prospects for the theory of representation in Computer Science. At this point I wouldn't recommend investing heavily in any particular solution to the paradoxes. And in a situation where different solutions will be pursued, and new ideas can count for so much, it's very difficult to make very reliable long-range predictions. On the other hand, I do have some short-range advice.

The more closely I have become acquainted with the theories of reasoning that are being presently developed in Computer Science, the more urgently I have felt the need for philosophers to become acquainted with these theories. Philosophers, for instance, seem to know little about knowledge representation, whereas Computer Scientists have learned the relevant philosophy. But in the case of the paradoxes, it seems to me that Computer Scientists still have as much to learn from Philosophers as Philosophers have to learn from Computer Scientists. One short-range consequence for Computer Science, then, is that familiarity with the philosophical literature on the paradoxes is important for research on paradox-related issues concerning semantic representation. Fortunately, [Martin 1984] is an excellent written source; and meetings such as this one provide a pleasant way to speed up the interdisciplinary interactions.

ACKNOWLEDGMENTS

I am grateful to Anil Gupta for comments on part of this paper. I would like to dedicate this paper to my teacher Frederic B. Fitch, who labored for many years on the foundations of semantics. Much of his work on the paradoxes is still being rediscovered.

REFERENCES

N. Asher and H. Kamp. The Knower's Paradox and Representational Theories of Attitudes. *This volume.*

J. Barwise and J. Perry. *Situations and Attitudes.* MIT Press, 1983.

P. Benacerraf. Mathematical Truth. *Journal of Philosophy 70* (1973), pp. 661-679.

P. Benacerraf. God, the Devil and Gödel. *The Monist 51* (1967), pp. 9-32.

T. Burge. Semantical Paradox. *Journal of Philosophy 76* (1979), pp. 169-98.

T. Burge. Epistemic Paradox. *Journal of Philosophy 81* (1984), pp. 5-28.

G. Chierchia. Nominalization and Montague Grammar: a Semantics without Types for Natural Languages. *Linguistics and Philosophy 5* (1982), pp. 303-354.

M. Cresswell. *Structured Meanings.* The MIT Press, 1985.

H. Curry. The Inconsistency of Certain Formal Logics. *Journal of Symbolic Logic 7* (1942), pp. 115-117.

D. Dennett A Cure for the Common Code? In *Brainstorms,* by D. Dennett. Bradford Books, 1978, pp. 90-108.

J. des Rivières and H. Levesque. The Consistency of Syntactical Treatments of Knowledge. *This volume.*

R. Flagg. Consistency of Church's Thesis with Epistemic Arithmetic. Abstract, *Journal of Symbolic Logic 49* (1984), pp. 679-680.

J. Fodor *The Language of Thought.* Thomas A. Crowell Co., New York, 1975.

A. Gupta. Truth and Paradox. *Journal of Philosophical Logic 11* (1982), pp. 1-60.

A. Gupta. The Meaning of Truth. Unpublished manuscript, University of Illinois at Chicago, 1984.

H. Herzberger. Naive Semantics and the Liar Paradox. *The Journal of Philosophy 79* (1982), pp. 479-497.

M. Kremer. *Logic and Truth.* Ph.D. Dissertation, University of Pittsburgh, 1986.

S. Kripke. Outline of a Theory of Truth. *Journal of Philosophy 72* (1975), pp. 690-716.

M. Löb. Solution of a Problem of Leon Henkin. *Journal of Symbolic Logic 20* (1955), pp. 115-118.

R. L. Martin, ed. *Recent Essays on Truth and The Liar Paradox.* Oxford University Press, 1984.

R. L. Martin, ed. *The Paradox of the Liar.* Yale University Press, 1970. (Second edition with supplementary bibliography, Ridgeview Press, 1978.)

R. Montague. Syntactical Treatments of Modality, with Corollaries on Reflexion Principles and Finite Axiomatizability. In *Formal Philosophy,* by R. Montague, Yale University Press, 1974.

L. Morgenstern. A First-Order Theory of Planning, Knowledge, and Action. *This volume.*

C. Parsons. The Liar Paradox. *Journal of Philosophical Logic 3* (1974), pp. 381-412.

D. Perlis. Languages with Self-Reference I: Foundations. *Artificial Intelligence 25* (1985), pp. 301-322.

G. Priest. The Logic of Paradox. *Journal of Philosophical Logic 8* (1979), pp. 219-241.

A. Prior. On a Family of Paradoxes. *Notre Dame Journal of Formal Logic 2* (1961), pp. 16-32.

H. Putnam The Meaning of Meaning. In *Language, Mind and Knowledge,* ed. Keith Gunderson. University of Minnesota Press, 1975, pp. 131-193.

W. Reinhardt. The Consistency of a Variant of Church's Thesis with an Axiomatic Theory of an Epistemic Notion. Unpublished Manuscript, University of Colorado, 1983.

J. Reynolds. Types, Abstraction and Parametric Polymorphism. In *Information Processing 83,* ed. R. Mason, Elsevier Science Publishers, 1983, pp. 513-523.

R. Stalnaker. *Inquiry.* MIT Press, 1984.

J. Stoy. *Denotational Semantics: the Scott-Strachey Approach to Programming Language Theory.* MIT Press, 1977.

A. Tarski. The Concept of Truth in Formalized Languages. in *Logic, Semantics, Metamathematics,* by A. Tarski, pp. 152-278, Oxford University Press, 1956.

R. Thomason. Indirect Discourse is not Quotational. *The Monist 60* (1977), pp. 340-354.

R. Thomason. A note on Syntactic Treatments of Modality. *Synthese 44* (1980), pp. 391-395.

R. Thomason. Some Limitations to the Psychological Orientation in Semantic Theory. Unpublished manuscript, University of Pittsburgh, 1979.

R. Thomason. Paradoxes of Intentionality? Unpublished manuscript, University of Pittsburgh, 1982.

A. Visser. Four Valued Semantics and the Liar. *Journal of Philosophical Logic 13* (1984), pp. 181-212.

A. Whitehead & B. Russell. *Principia Mathematica,* first edition, vol 1. Cambridge University Press, 1910.

P. Woodruff. Paradox, Truth and Logic. Part I: Paradox and Truth. *Journal of Philosophical Logic 13* (1984), pp. 181-212.

WHAT AWARENESS ISN'T:
A SENTENTIAL VIEW OF IMPLICIT AND EXPLICIT BELIEF

Kurt Konolige
Artificial Intelligence Center
SRI International
Center for the Study of Language and Information
Stanford University

ABSTRACT

In their attempt to model and reason about the beliefs of agents, artificial intelligence (AI) researchers have borrowed from two different philosophical traditions regarding the folk psychology of belief. In one tradition, belief is a relation between an agent and a proposition, that is, a *propositional attitude*. Formal analyses of propositional attitudes are often given in terms of a possible-worlds semantics. In the other tradition, belief is a relation between an agent and a sentence that expresses a proposition (the *sentential* approach). The arguments for and against these approaches are complicated, confusing, and often obscure and unintelligible (at least to this author). Nevertheless strong supporters exist for both sides, not only in the philosophical arena (where one would expect it), but also in AI.

In the latter field, some proponents of possible-worlds analysis have attempted to remedy what appears to be its biggest drawback, namely the assumption that an agent believes all the logical consequences of his or her beliefs. Drawing on initial work by Levesque, Fagin and Halpern define a *logic of general awareness* that superimposes elements of the sentential approach on a possible-worlds framework. The result, they claim, is an appropriate model for resource-limited believers.

We argue that this is a bad idea: it ends up being equivalent to a more complicated version of the sentential approach. In concluding we cannot refrain from adding to the debate about the utility of possible-worlds analyses of belief.

Introduction

Artificial Intelligence has borrowed from two different philosophical traditions for its formalizations of belief and knowledge. In one tradition, belief is a relation between an agent and a proposition, that is, belief is a *propositional attitude*. In the other tradition, belief is a relation between an agent and a sentence that expresses a proposition. We will call this the *sentential* approach.

The propositional attitude approach has an elegant formalization using in the possible-world semantics developed by Hintikka [4] and Kripke [8]. As is well known, as long as no "impossible" worlds are allowed, this semantics enforces the condition that an agent's beliefs are closed under logical consequence. It is appropriate only for agents who are perfect reasoners with infinite computational capabilities, something which is not realistic for either human or computer agents. Hintikka [5] called this undesirable property *logical omniscience*, a somewhat ambiguous term; here we will use the more precise expression *consequential closure*.

Although it is an idealization, the possible-worlds model is popular because it lends itself to logical analysis. By contrast, the formalization of sentential belief can be relatively complicated, as seen in the work of McCarthy [10], Perlis [12], Konolige [6], and others. Yet because it does not make the assumption of consequential closure, it comes closer to capturing the behavior of real agents.

In a recent paper, Fagin and Halpern [2] attempt to deal with the problem of resource-limited reasoning (among others) by combining features of the two approaches. They are motivated by an idea of Levesque's [9]: that there is a distinction between *explicit beliefs* (those beliefs an agent actually has or professes to) and *implicit beliefs* (all the logical consequences of his implicit beliefs). In their *logic of general awareness*, Fagin and Halpern represent implicit beliefs in the usual fashion with a possible-worlds semantics. To account for explicit belief in this model, they introduce a syntactic filter at each possible world, so that explicit beliefs are implicit beliefs restricted to those sentences allowed by the filter. In the language, they use an *awareness operator* to specify the filter; hence the name of the logic. Awareness is a *syntactic* concept, since its argument is interpreted as a sentence, rather than a proposition.

It seems clear that a logic of general awareness can indeed model resource-limited reasoning from beliefs. However, implicit in the paper is the notion that it is the marriage (unholy though it may be!) of sentential and propositional approaches that is responsible for this result, so that the "elegance and intuitive appeal of the semantic [i.e., possible-worlds] approach" is preserved. Here we take a critical view of this position, and argue that a logic of general awareness is essentially equivalent to the sentential approach, but the addition of possible-worlds elements adds unmotivated and unintuitive complications.

The Argument

A sentential view of explicit and implicit belief

In the sentential view, beliefs are represented as sets of statements or sentences. In its simplest form, the distinction between implicit and explicit belief can be represented by the following diagram:

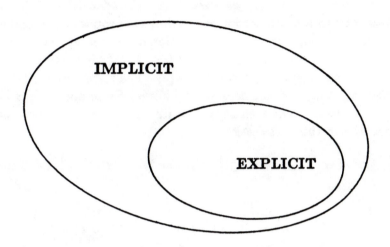

Figure 1.   Explicit and implicit belief.

The set of implicit beliefs is the set of logical consequences of the explicit beliefs. If the explicit beliefs are inconsistent, the implicit beliefs are every sentence of the language.

In the sentential approach, the explicit beliefs are normally considered to be primary, that is, they represent the beliefs of the agent, and the implicit beliefs are derived from them by closure under logical consequence. Generally, in giving a formal characterization of explicit beliefs, one attempts to capture how agents syntactically derive one belief from others. One example of this type of system is the *deduction model* (Konolige [7]). This model is based on the observation that AI knowledge bases usually consist of a core set of basic beliefs and a deductive mechanism for deriving some, but usually not all, logical consequences of the core set.

Unhappy with the syntactic characterization of explicit belief, Levesque [9] attempted to characterize explicit belief using a semantics similar to possible-worlds analyses of implicit belief. This analysis has some severe problems in modeling resource-limited reasoning, however, and Fagin and Halpern [2] present an alternative of their own, which we now review.

A logic of general awareness

For our purposes, we can restrict the logic to the simple case of a single believer, Ralph.

We assume a standard propositional language with negation and conjunction as the basic operators, together with a distinguished primitive proposition $\perp$, which is always interpreted as false. To this we add three unary modal operators: B (*explicit belief*), L (*implicit belief*), and A (*awareness*). All intermixtures are permitted, e.g., $BAL\phi$.

A *Kripke structure for general awareness* is a tuple $M = \langle S, \pi, \mathcal{A}, \mathcal{B} \rangle$, where S is a set of states, $\pi(s, p)$ is a truth-assignment for each primitive proposition p and state $s \in S$, and B is a transitive, euclidean, and serial binary relation on S (the *accessibility relation*). For each possible world s, $\mathcal{A}(s)$ is a set of sentences of the modal language such that $\perp \in \mathcal{A}(s)$. At least initiallly, this is the *only* restriction on $\mathcal{A}(s)$. The formulas in $\mathcal{A}(s)$ are those Ralph in state s is "aware of," but does not necessarily believe. Fagin and Halpern stress that various restrictions can be placed on awareness to capture a number of different meanings for "aware of." We discuss this in the next section.

The semantics of the language is given by the truth relation $\models$, defined as follows:

$$
\begin{aligned}
&M, s \not\models \perp \\
&M, s \models p, && \text{if } p \text{ is a primitive proposition and } \pi(s, p) = \textbf{true.} \\
&M, s \models \neg\phi && \text{if } M, s \not\models \phi. \\
&M, s \models \phi \wedge \psi && \text{if } M, s \models \phi \text{ and } M, s \models \psi. \\
&M, s \models L\phi && \text{if } M, t \models \phi \text{ for all } t \text{ such that } t\mathcal{B}s. \\
&M, s \models B\phi && \text{if } \phi \in \mathcal{A}(s) \text{ and } M, t \models \phi \text{ for all } t \text{ such that } t\mathcal{B}s. \\
&M, s \models A\phi && \text{if } \phi \in \mathcal{A}(s).
\end{aligned}
\tag{1}
$$

In this semantics, the implicit belief operator L has a standard possible-worlds semantics. It obeys both the positive introspection axiom $L\phi \supset LL\phi$, the negative introspection axioms $\neg L\phi \supset L\neg L\phi$, and the consistency axiom $\neg L\perp$. This is by virtue of the accessibility relation being transitive, euclidean, and serial, respectively. In short, if we restrict the language to just L, we have the belief logic of weak $S5$, plus the consistency axiom (see Halpern and Moses [3]).

As Fagin and Halpern note, explicit belief is defined by the semantics as implicit belief restricted to those sentences permitted by awareness. Thus $B\phi \equiv L\phi \wedge A\phi$. If Ralph is aware of all sentences, then $B\phi \equiv L\phi$ for all ϕ, and explicit and implicit belief are identical.

What is awareness?

Suppose we are trying to represent the behavior of a knowledge base (which we again call Ralph), which responds *yes* to some queries and *no* to others. $B\phi$ then means that the Ralph responds *yes* to the query ϕ, and $\neg B\phi$ is the *no* response. What can we interpret awareness as in this situation? The suggested meaning for $A\phi$ is "Ralph is able to determine whether or not ϕ follows from his initial premises in time T."[1] That is, the sentences Ralph is "aware of" are some class for which it is easy to do deductions, or to show that no deductions exist. We can draw this picture to represent the various sets of sentences and their relationships:

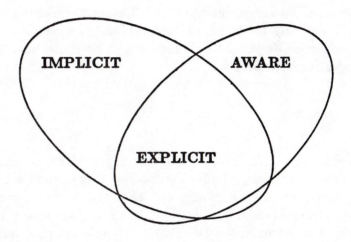

Figure 2.   Awareness and belief.

Note that this is the same as our previous picture, except that the intersection of awareness and implicit belief is what defines the explicit beliefs. Logical consequence has taken over the role of deduction from an initial set of beliefs; the awareness filter restricts explicit beliefs to a subset of the consequences. However, unlike Levesque's scheme, the awareness filter is a purely syntactic notion; the set of sentences in the aware set is arbitrary (with the exception of $\perp$).

The logic of general awareness thus characterizes agents as perfect reasoners, restricted in some way to considering a subset of possible sentences to reason about. Now we ask two

---

[1]The actual phrase that Fagin and Halpern use is "[Ralph] is able to compute the truth of ϕ within time T." However truth is not the appropriate notion for knowledge bases, since it certainly may be the case that they have incorrect or incomplete information about the world.

questions:

1. Does the possible-world semantics play an essential role in this approach?

2. How intuitive and useful is the general notion of an awareness-limited perfect reasoner for representing limited reasoning?

The role of possible-world semantics

In his original work on knowledge and belief, Hintikka [4] used a possible-worlds semantics to systematize various principles he proposed to govern the consistency ("defensibility") of sets of sentences about knowledge and belief. These principles were derived first, from various arguments; it was only fortuitous that conditions on accessibility, such as transitivity and reflexivity, would (as Kripke showed) turn out to be equivalent. For example, consider the axiom of "negative introspection:"

$$\neg B\phi \supset B\neg B\phi \tag{2}$$

This sentence states a condition on Ralph's introspective capabilities, namely, he knows when he doesn't belief something. In Kripke models, this condition is enforced by making the accessibility relation euclidean (if xBy and xBz, then yBz). The semantical analysis makes the negative introspection rule valid, but does not give us any insight into the nature of introspection. For example, the fact that B is *euclidean* does not help us to predict what other introspective capabilities Ralph should have, or how negative introspection might break down or degrade in certain situations. Kripke models do not give us the principles upon which we might build and defend a theory of belief, but they are a useful formal tool for analyzing the properties of various modal logical systems.

In the case of awareness, the formal correspondence between accessibility conditions and sets of awareness sentences breaks down; hence the connection between accessibility conditions and belief is ruptured. For example, suppose Ralph believes p; we conclude that all of Bp, Ap, and Lp are true. What is required for BBp to be true? We know $BBp \equiv (LBp \wedge ABp) \equiv (LLp \wedge LAp \wedge ABp)$, and by transitivity LLp is true. We need the further conditions:

1. $A\phi \supset LA\phi$ (semantically, if $\phi \in A(s)$ and tBs, then $\phi \in A(t)$), and

2. $B\phi \supset AB\phi$.[2]

---

[2]Fagin and Halpern suggest that a self-reflective Ralph will be aware what he is aware of, and suggest for this case the condition that if $\phi \in A(s)$, then $A\phi \in A(s)$. This makes the sentence BAp true, but says nothing about awareness of *beliefs*, that is, ABp.

Neither (1) nor (2) is affected by the structure of accessibility. Hence the nice formal analysis of introspective properties obtainable in Kripke semantics is not present in the logic of general awareness.

Finally, we note that the logic of general awareness has a natural sentential semantics. Recall that belief is defined as the intersection of those sentences Ralph is aware of with those sentences he implicitly believes:

$$M, s \models B\phi \quad \text{if } \phi \in \mathcal{A}(s) \text{ and } M, t \models \phi \text{ for all } t \text{ such that } t \mathcal{B} s$$

The first half of the conjunction refers explicitly to a set of sentences (those in $\mathcal{A}(s)$); the second half implicitly by the use of possible worlds. It is possible to give this second set a syntactic characterization also. As we have noted, L is axiomatized as weak $S5$ plus consistency. Moore [11] has shown that weak $S5$ characterizes *stable sets*. A set S is stable if it contains all tautologies, is closed under *modus ponens*, and obeys the following conditions:

1. If $\phi \in S$, $L\phi \in S$.

2. If $\phi \notin S$, $\neg L\phi \in S$.

So from a sentential point of view, models of general awareness consist of a stable set intersected with an arbitrary awareness set.

Resource-limited reasoning with awareness

How compelling is the picture of resource-limited reasoning presented by the logic of limited awareness (Figure 2)? What we are asking here is if there is any motivation from our intuitions about folk-psychological notions of belief. For example, the deduction model seems plausible in its general form, because agents learn facts about the world from their observations or from being told, and then go on to deduce further consequences. We might expect to characterize the beliefs of a resource-limited agent by noting what facts he learns, and what rules he uses to infer other facts. Such a model would be useful in predicting the behavior of the agent, given partial information about his beliefs.

On the other hand, the logic of general awareness represents agents as perfect reasoners, restricted to considering some syntactic class of sentences. There don't seem to be any clear intuitions that this is the case for human or computer agents. As an exercise, here are two possible psychological stories that would fit into the awareness framework:

1. Agents compute all logical consequences of their beliefs, throwing away those not in the awareness set, perhaps because of memory limitations. This is not a plausible story, because agents are also affected by time limitations.

2. Agents use a complete logical deduction system to compute consequences of beliefs, but do not pursue those lines of reasoning which require deriving sentences not in the awareness set. This is plausible, because incomplete derivations of this nature could be accomplished with limited space and time resources, given tight enough syntactic restrictions on the derivable sentences. However, this particular story is just the deduction model of belief.

Conclusion: propositional attitudes and possible worlds

It does not seem that there is much to be gained by considering a logic of general awareness, at least as far as modeling resource-limited reasoning from beliefs is concerned. It is no more powerful than current sentential logics, and can be re-expressed in these terms. The practice of mixing sentential and possible-world elements in the semantics does not preserve the elegance of the latter, or offer any essential insight into the psychological nature of explicit belief.

The lesson we should draw from this is not that propositional attitude and sentential views of belief are irreconcilable and should not be intermixed, but rather that the introduction of possible worlds bears rethinking. As Stalnaker [13] notes, in possible-world analyses of belief, possible worlds are simply a formal device for saying what a proposition *is*. If we *define* propositions as sets of possible worlds, then we can easily analyze their properties. However, ease does not mean accuracy: as we have noted, the undesirable property of consequential closure emerges from this analysis.

Yet the idea of possible worlds has a certain intuitive appeal — one speaks of *epistemic alternatives*, as if there were worlds that, for all Ralph knows, could be the actual world. The problem is that epistemic alternatives do not seem to be anything at all like possible worlds. For example, Ralph, being a good computer scientist, doesn't really know whether $P = NP$, so there should be some epistemic alternatives in which it is true, and some in which it is false. Yet because it is a question of mathematics, $P = NP$ is either true in all possible worlds, or false in all of them. Similarly, we might argue that although the laws of physics are obeyed in all possible worlds, Ralph may not have a very good idea of how physical systems behave, and so his epistemic alternatives include worlds that are clearly physically impossible.

If epistemic alternatives are not possible worlds, what are they? Perhaps they are something like the "notional worlds" of Dennett [1]. Whatever they are, it seems that Ralph's inferential capabilities will play a role in their definition. For suppose that Ralph can believe ϕ and $\phi \supset \psi$ without inferring ψ. Then there will be epistemic alternatives in which ϕ and $\phi \supset \psi$ are true, but ψ is not. On the other hand, if Ralph always infers ψ from ϕ and $\phi \supset \psi$, then all epistemic alternatives will be closed under this inference.

Well, this is obviously not a complete or very convincing story about propositional attitudes and belief. Still, fully fleshed out, it may be a reasonable alternative to the normal formalization using possible worlds.

Acknowledgements

I am grateful to David Israel and Joe Halpern for their comments on an earlier draft of this paper. This research was supported in part by Contract N00014-85-C-0251 from the Office of Naval Research, and in part by a gift from the Systems Development Foundation.

References

[1] Dennett, D. C. (1982). Beyond belief. In *Thought and Object*, A. Woodfield editor, Clarendon Press, Oxford, pp. 1–95.

B. Meltzer and D. Michie editors, Edinburgh University Press, Edinburgh, Scotland, pp. 120–147.

[2] Fagin, R. and Halpern, J. Y. (1985). Belief, awareness, and limited reasoning. In Proceedings of the Ninth International Joint Conference on AI, Los Angeles, California, pp. 491–501.

[3] Halpern, J. Y. and Moses, Y. (1985). A guide to the modal logics of knowledge and belief: preliminary draft. In Proceedings of the Ninth International Joint Conference on AI, Los Angeles, California, pp. 479–490.

[4] Hintikka, J. (1962). *Knowledge and Belief*. Cornell University Press, Ithaca, New York.

[5] Hintikka, J. (1975). Impossible possible worlds vindicated. *J. Philosophical Logic* 4, pp. 475–484.

[6] Konolige, K. (1980). A first-order formalization of knowledge and action for a multiagent planning system. Artificial Intelligence Center Tech Note 232, SRI International, Menlo Park, California.

[7] Konolige, K. (1984). *A Deduction Model of Belief and its Logics*. Doctoral thesis, Stanford University Computer Science Department Stanford, California.

[8] Kripke, S. A. (1963). Semantical considerations on modal logics. *Acta Philsophica Fennica* 16, pp. 83–94.

[9] Levesque, H. J. (1984). A logic of implicit and explicit belief. In Proceedings of the National Conference on Artificial Intelligence, Houston, Texas, pp. 198–202.

[10] McCarthy, J. (1979). First-order theories of individual concepts and propositions. In *Machine Intelligence 9*, B. Meltzer and D. Michie editors, Edinburgh University Press, Edinburgh, Scotland, pp. 120–147.

[11] Moore, R. C. (1983). Semantical Considerations on Nonmonotonic Logic. Artificial Intelligence Center Technical Note 284, SRI International, Menlo Park, California.

[12] Perlis, D. (1981). Language, computation, and reality. Department of Computer Science Technical Report 95, University of Rochester, Rochester, New York.

[13] Stalnaker, R. C. (1984). *Inquiry*. MIT Press, Cambridge, Massachusetts.

REASONING ABOUT KNOWLEDGE IN ECONOMICS

Robert J. Aumann
The Hebrew University of Jerusalem
Givat Ram, 91904 Jerusalem

SUMMARY

Reasoning about other people's reasoning and knowledge about other people's knowledge lie at the heart of game theory and economic theory. Each person affects everybody else. You cannot decide what to do without some knowledge or belief about what others will do; and this must be based on an estimate of their knowledge and beliefs, about substantive matters as well as about what they think about each others' beliefs and about your beliefs. A coherent framework for analyzing these interactions is thus of the essence for these disciplines.

This lecture will survey some of the aspects of game and economic theory that are particularly closely related to knowledge about knowledge. Topics that may be touched upon include common knowledge, the evolution of beliefs in repeated games, universal models for beliefs about beliefs, correlated and independent equilibrium, and games played by automata.

SUMMARY OF
"ON AUMANN'S NOTION OF COMMON KNOWLEDGE --
AN ALTERNATIVE APPROACH"

Tommy Chin-Chiu Tan
Graduate School of Business
University of Chicago
Chicago, IL 60637

Sérgio Ribeiro Da Costa Werlang
Department of Economics
Princeton University
Princeton, NJ 08544

ABSTRACT

We provide a bayesian model of knowledge which is based on the of infinite recursion of beliefs. The framework allows a direct formalisation of statements such as "everyone knows that (everyone knows)^m that an event A has occurred" and "A is common knowledge". An important and novel feature of our approach is that we explicitly formalise the statement "the information partitions are common knowledge" when we demonstrate the equivalence of our approach to the seminal contribution of Professor Aumann. This allows us to circumvent the self-reference which exists in that definition. The main theorem of the paper shows that given an Aumann structure, there exists a structure in the infinite recursion such that an event is common knowledge in the sense of Aumann if and only if it is common knowledge in our sense.

SUMMARY

[What follows is only a summary and description of results in Tan and Werlang(1985). Due to potential conflicts with journals,we regret not being able to submit the complete paper.]

Intuitively, an event is common knowledge if everyone knows it, everyone knows that everyone knows it, ... , and so on.

The notion of common knowledge is central (although frequently unstated) in economic modelling and game theory. The maintained hypothesis in most models is that the structure of the model and the rationality of the agents in the model are common knowledge. Indeed, it would be difficult to imagine how one should proceed in the analysis of a game if the rules of the game and the rationality of the other players were not common knowledge. Even Harsanyi's analysis of an incomplete information game, for instance, converts such a game into a larger bayesian game which is implicitly assumed to be common knowledge (at least by other writers using his framework).

However, a formal definition of common knowledge was not available to economists until the seminal paper of Aumann (1976). Aumann's framework is given formally in Section 2. As far as we know, it remains the most concise and elegant treatment of common knowledge in the literature.

The purpose of this paper is to offer an alternative definition of common knowledge which is less elegant and more cumbersome than Aumann's original framework. The framework offered here is based on the infinite recursion of beliefs introduced by Armbruster and Böge(1979), Böge and Eisele(1979) and Mertens and Zamir(1985). The definition of common knowledge given here is of course implicit in the three earlier contributions, however, the purpose of this paper is to make it explicit and to prove an equivalence theorem between the two, mathematically quite different, approaches.

Let us motivate the need for another definition of common knowledge, which by our own admission is less parsimonious than the original definition offered by Professor Aumann. Our interest in this alternative definition stems from both theoretical and practical considerations.

The first feature of the new definition is that the infinite recursion of beliefs offers a mathematical language which allows us to formalise the intuitive notion of common knowledge directly. As a result, the defintion which we give in Section 4, translates verbally into the intuitive notion given in the first paragraph of this paper. In contrast, Aumann's definition , which makes use of agents' information partitions and the meet of the information partitions, requires a moment of thought before its relation to the intuitive notion is transparent. The price we have to pay for the alternative definition is that we have to invoke the more complex structure of the infinite recursion.

A related feature of the alternative approach is that the language of the infinite recursion allows one to easily define levels of knowledge which are lower than common knowledge. For instance, a statement like "everyone knows (everyone knows)^m that the event has occurred" can be formalised directly, without further requiring that the event be common knowledge.

Aumann's framework, which relies on information partitions of individuals, contains a self-reference. One has to implicitly assume that the information partitions are common knowledge themselves before one is able to define an event being common knowledge. The self-reference occurs precisely during that moment of thought when the reader is converting Aumann's mathematical definition into the intuitive notion of common knowledge (see the discussion in Section 2).

The advantage of the infinite recursion is that the framework is well defined mathematically, and since the notion of common knowledge is directly formalised, it does not contain self-references. Professor Aumann was of course aware of this issue in his original contribution and suggested that expanding the underlying uncertainty space would circumvent this problem. The results reported here, as well as related work by Brandenburg and Dekel (1985), demonstrates that one has to begin with the infinite recursion to achieve this.

For the readers familiar with the Aumann definition, an important feature of our approach (and to our knowledge, a novel feature in the literature) is that in Section 5, we explicitly formalise the assumption "the private information partitions are common knowledge", which is implicit and self-referential in the original definition.

Our interest in this alternative definition of common knowledge has its beginnings in our efforts to formally define the statement "rationality is common knowledge in a game" and to derive the behavioural implications of such a hypothesis (see Tan and Werlang, 1985). We found that it was not always convenient to work with Aumann's framework when the events of interest were rather complex, like rationality or a class of games. For example, to apply Aumann's framework for rationality, the space of uncertainty would have to be the set of all possible behaviour in a game, in which rationality is an element. Furthermore, one would have to find information partitions for the agents in order to define the event rationality as being common knowledge. We found these two steps unintuitive and thought that the first step of defining the space of all behaviour would be mathematically intractible. Furthermore, we were also interested in investigating the implications of the limited knowledge of rationality, a task which Aumann's definition did not facilitate.

In our search for a framework more suitable for the questions which we were addressing, we found that once one has invested the fixed capital of understanding the infinite recursion, many of the questions became simple exercises in that framework and the proofs of theorems were simple inductive arguments once the correct definitions were obtained. Hence, the definitions of "knowledge up to level m" and "common knowledge" that we give below are ones which we found extremely useful in other contexts. They provide an algorithm for anyone who is interest in defining any given event as being common knowledge, without having to think about the appropriate information partitions. Moreover, it also facilitates the investigation of what such a hypothesis might imply.

The main result of this paper is the equivalence theorem in Section 5 between the definition given here and the original definition of Aumann. What we show is that given an Aumann structure (defined formally in Section 2), there is a structure in terms of the infinite recursion of beliefs such that an event is common knowledge in the sense of Aumann if and only if the event is common knowledge in the sense given in Section 4. A related result by Brandenburg and Dekel (1985) complements our result neatly. They show that given an infinite recursion structure, there is an Aumann structure (i.e. a apace of uncertainty and information partitions and an element of the space) such that an event is common knowledge in the infinite recursion sence if and only if it is common knowledge int he sense of Aumann. Hence, these two results demonstrate that the two approaches are entirely equivalent and the choice of one or the other depends on the problem of interest.

In Aumann (1976), there was a discussion of the notion of reachability which he suggested as a way of directly capturing the intuitive notion of common knowledge. In the proof of the main theorem in Section 5, we formalise and make extensive use of reachability. However, it should be clear from a reading of the proof that the notion is far from intuitive and somewhat more cumbersome than the infinite recursion.

Section 2 gives Aumann's definition and provides a more technical discussion of some of the points raised above. A simple example, which is used throughout the paper, is provided there. Section 3 provides a introduction to the infinite recursion of beliefs, the bayesian interpretation of the framework, and the main result in that area. Section 4 provides the alternative definition of common knowledge and finally Section 5 states and proves the main equivalience result of this paper.

References

Armbruster, W. and W. Böge (1979), "Bayesian Game Theory," in *Game Theory and Related Topics*, edited by O. Moeschlin and D. Pallaschke, Amsterdam: North-Hollland, 17-28.

Aumann, R. J. (1976), "Agreeing to Disagree," *The Annals of Statistics*, 4(6), 1236-1239.

Böge, W. and T. H. Eisele (1979), "On Solution of Bayesian Games," *International Journal of Game Theory*, 8(4), 193-215.

Brandenburg, A. and E. Dekel (1985), "Hierarchies of Beliefs and Common Knowledge," Research Paper, Graduate School of Business, Stanford University.

Geanakoplos, J. and H. Polemarcharkis (1982), "We Can't Disagree Forever," *Journal of Economic Theory*, 28(1), 192-200.

Mertens, J. F. and S. Zamir (1985), "Formalisation of Harsanyi's Notion of 'Type' and 'Consistency' in Games with Incomplete Information," *International Journal of Game Theory*, 14(1), 1-29.

Milgrom, P. (1981), "An Axiomatic Characterisation of Common knowledge," *Econometrica*, 49(1), 219-222.

Myerson, R. (1983), "Bayesian Equilibrium and Incentive Compatibility: An Introduction," J.L. Kellogg Graduate School of Management, Discussion Paper

No. 548, Northwestern University.

Tan, T.C.C. and S.R.C. Werlang (1984), "The Bayesian Foundations of Rationalisable Strategic Behaviour and Nash Equilibrium Behaviour," Mimeo.

Tan, T.C.C. and S.R.C. Werlang(1985), "On Aumann's Notion of Common Knowledge -- An Alternative Approach," Economics and Econometrics Working Paper No. 85-26, Graduate School of Business, University of Chicago.

ON PLAY BY MEANS OF COMPUTING MACHINES

(preliminary version)

Nimrod Megiddo[1]   and   Avi Wigderson

Mathematical Sciences Research Institute
Berkeley, California 94720

Abstract. This paper examines the "bounded rationality" inherent in play by means of computing machines. The main example is the finitely repeated prisoners' dilemma game which is discussed under different models. The game is played by Turing machines with restricted number of internal states using unlimited time and space. The observations in this paper strongly suggest that the cooperative outcome of the game can be approximated in equilibrium. Thus, the cooperative play can be approximated even if the machines memorize the entire history of the game and are capable of counting the number of stages.

---

[1] The IBM Almaden Research Center, 650 Harry Road San Jose, California 95120-6099, and Tel Aviv University, Tel Aviv, Israel.

1. Introduction

We consider here the famous prisoners' dilemma game, a version of which is stated below. The framework however applies to games in general. The prisoners' dilemma game was chosen since it focuses on the central issue raised in this paper.

Definition 1.1. By the (one-shot) *prisoners' dilemma game G* we refer to a game as follows. The game is played by two players with symmetric roles. Each player has to choose (independently of the other) between the action C ("cooperate") and the action D ("defect"). The payoffs to the two players, corresponding to the four possible combinations of choices of actions, are as follows. The players are each paid 3 units of utility if both play C. Both are paid 1 if both play D. If one plays C and the other one plays D then the one who plays C gets 0 and the other one gets 4.

Definition 1.2. The finitely repeated prisoners' dilemma consists of N rounds, where during each round the one-shot prisoners' dilemma game is played, and both players are then informed of each other's actions. The number N is common knowledge between the players, that is each knows N, each knows that each knows N, each knows that each knows that each knows N, and so on.

Definition 1.3. A Nash-equilibrium point in a 2-person game is a pair $\sigma = (\sigma^1, \sigma^2)$ of strategies (one for each player) such that, given that player i ($i = 1,2$) is playing σ^i, the other player, $3 - i$, cannot get a higher payoff for himself by playing any strategy other than σ^{3-i}.

The perplexing fact about the finitely repeated prisoners' dilemma is the following:

Proposition 1.4. *The only equilibrium payoffs in the finitely repeated prisoners' dilemma correspond to "defection" by both players throughout. Moreover, this equilibrium is obtained by iterated elimination of dominated strategies.*

Proof. It can easily be shown by induction on k that in any equilibrium the players must play (D,D) in round $N + 1 - k$, ($k = 1, ..., N$).

It has been said that the prisoners' dilemma may be "resolved" by "bounded rationality". One possibility of bounding rationality is to have the players play the game through computing machines. In this paper we discuss issues that can be dealt with under different models of play by means of computing machines. We do not attempt to present a formal theory of rationality and bounded rationality. Our work was inspired by the works of Neyman [N] and Rubinstein [Ru] where the prisoners' dilemma game was considered as being played by means of finite automata. Neyman's results are cited in Section 2. We consider two approaches: (i) Given the number of rounds, choose a machine for playing the game. (ii) Choose a machine that will be play any number of rounds, given as input at the start of the game. The only restriction is on the number of internal states of the machine. It should be emphasized that most of the results are nonconstructive and we do not believe that the approach taken in this paper will lead to a practical resolution of the prisoners' dilemma

2. Play by means of finite automata

In this section we cite results recently obtained by A. Neyman [N]. He has pointed out that finite automata [HU] of appropriate sizes may cooperate in the finitely repeated prisoners' dilemma game.

Definition 2.1. Let $G^N(s_1, s_2)$ denote a 2-person game as follows. Two ("human") players, 1 and 2, independently choose finite automata of sizes s_1 and s_2, respectively, which then play the prisoners' dilemma game for N rounds. The action of an automaton amounts to the combination of its play and the state it switches to. The action depends on its own state and on the play of the other automaton during the preceding round (except, of course, for the very first round).

A fairly simple result stated in [N] is the following:

Proposition 2.2. *(i) If $2 \leq s_1, s_2 \leq N - 1$ then in the game $G^N(s_1, s_2)$ there exist equilibria that result in the play of (C, C) in each round. (ii) If either s_1 or s_2 is at least N then there does not exist an equilibrium point that results in the play of (C, C) during every stage of the game.*

Intuitively, Proposition 2.2 can be traced to the fact that an automaton with less than N states cannot recognize that it is playing the last round of an N-round game, when the last round is being played. In this context, we can state another result that follows easily by a similar argument:

Proposition 2.3. *If both $s_1 \geq N$ and $s_2 \geq N$ then every pure strategy equilibrium (that is, a pair of deterministic choices of deterministic automata, which is in equilibrium) results in the play of (D, D) throughout.*

Interestingly, even when $s_1 \geq N$, if $s_2 < N$ then there exist other deterministic equilibria that approximate the cooperative play. For example, if s_1 is unbounded and $s_2 = 2$, the following automata are in equilibrium. Player 2 plays C in his START state, and stays in this state as long as player 1 plays C. In this state, if 1 played D then 2 switches to his second state END, at which he plays D and stays in END, regardless of what player 1 does. Player 1 uses N of his states to count to N. In his state q_i ($i = 1, ..., N - 1$) he plays C and switches to state q_{i+1}, if 2 played C; otherwise, if 2 played D then 1 plays D and switches to state q_N. In his state q_N he plays D and stays in q_N.

A much stronger result, with respect to equilibria in mixed strategies in $G^N(s_1, s_2)$, is stated in [N]. A mixed strategy amounts to a probability distribution over automata. Thus, the players in this case are allowed to randomize their choices of automata, and their probabilistic choices are considered to be in equilibrium if the *expected* payoffs satisfy the equilibrium conditions. The stronger result of [N] is as follows.

Proposition 2.4. *For any integer k, there is an N_0 with the following property: for every $N \geq N_0$ and every pair (s_1, s_2) such that $N^{1/k} < \min(s_1, s_2) < \max(s_1, s_2) < N^k$, there exists a mixed strategy equilibrium, where the payoffs to each player are at least $3 - 1/k$.*

3. Play by means of unrestricted Turing machines

Our purpose is to study Neyman-type models with more general computing machines. For the sake of completeness we include in the Appendix a description of how the game is actually played through Turing machines. We also include a brief definition of one type of a Turing machine. The unfamiliar reader is however advised to consult, for example, [HU] for more detail. Intuitively, one can think of computer programs instead of Turing machines. Thus, our model corresponds to a situation where real players write computer programs to play the game for them.

Our approach differs from Neyman's in several ways: (i) We consider machines with unlimited memory, whereas automata have no memory besides their states. (ii) We work with *uniform* machines, that is, our players write programs that can play *any* number of rounds, where the number of rounds is given to the program at the start of the game. (iii) We concentrate on deterministic choices of machines, whereas Neyman considers choices of probability distributions over the space of all possible deterministic machines.

Rationality in our model is bounded in the sense that, regardless of the number of rounds the game, choices of actions in the game are determined by a *finite* control, even though the entire history of the game may be held in memory. The implications of this restriction are discussed below. As we show later, finiteness in itself does not suffice for obtaining high payoffs in equilibrium. For high payoffs to be feasible in equilibrium, there has to be a specific bound on the size of the machine, that is, the number of internal states (or the length of the computer program, in the intuitive interpretation).

One may consider various definitions of the game, corresponding to different restrictions on the computational resources. In this paper we consider only restrictions on the number of internal states of the machine. In real computers this corresponds to restricting the length of the computer program, that is the space for storing the instructions, excluding the space for storing program variables. We start with the case where the number of internal states of the machine is not restricted. A more precise definition follows.

Definition 3.1. Let Γ denote a game as follows. Two players independently choose Turing machines for repeatedly playing the prisoners' dilemma game for some unknown *finite* number of rounds. The number of rounds, N, is chosen by "nature" and given to the *machines* as input before round 1.

A natural question here is whether the players are at all restricted (in the game Γ) when they have to play through Turing machines. The answer is *yes*:

Proposition 3.2. *There exist strategies for playing the game Γ that cannot be played through any Turing machine.*

Proof. The proof follows by a classical cardinality argument. Since a strategy for Γ amounts to choosing a strategy for each N-round game, it follows that there are $2^{\aleph_0}$ strategies for playing the game Γ. On the other, there are only $\aleph_0$ Turing machines.

Those strategies of Γ, which can be played by Turing machines, may be called *recursive strategies*. The "advantage" of the definition of Γ is that it allows for "bounded rationality" without imposing a strict limit. Rationality is bounded in the sense that players are restricted in their decision rules, even though they may have unlimited time and space for computation.

So far, we have not defined a payoff function for the game Γ. In other words, we have not specified how the number N is chosen by nature after the players have selected their machines. However, we show below that, regardless of the rule by which payoffs for different values of N are aggregated, there does not exist a "cooperative equilibrium". Given any pair of strategies (σ_1, σ_2), we say that player i has a profitable deviation if there is a strategy σ_i^* that yields him payoff higher than σ_i, given that the other player plays σ_{3-i}.

Proposition 3.3. *For any pair of machines (T_1, T_2) playing Γ and for each player i $(i = 1, 2)$, there exists a machine T_i^* with the following property: for every N, if in the N-round game there exists a profitable deviation for i (relative to the play of (T_1, T_2)), then T_i^* discovers such a possibility for a profitable deviation and executes it.*

Proof. The proof is based on a "simulation" argument. One Turing machine can simulate the execution of another, that is, compute the entire run of the other machine. Since the size of the machine is not restricted, player i can choose a machine that, given N, simulates the entire play of T_1 against T_2. This machine can thus find a profitable deviation (whenever there exists one) and then play the game, carrying out that deviation.

We thus conclude the case of unrestricted machines with the following theorem, which follows from Propositions 1.4 and 3.3:

Theorem 3.4. *If the players are restricted to recursive strategies, but the size of machine is not restricted, then every equilibrium results in the play of (D, D) throughout any N-round game.*

Remark 3.5. It can be shown that even when players are allowed to choose probabilistic machines, still every equilibrium pair of machines results in the steady play of (D, D).

4. On machines with limited numbers of internal states

It is important to note that in all our models we do *not* require the machines to halt after N rounds. Such a requirement would probably make most of the questions trivial. Of course, only the first N rounds are taken into the account of payoffs.

Henceforth, we consider only play through machines with restricted numbers of states, that is, each player must choose a machine whose size does not exceed some given upper bound. The simulation argument used in the preceding section does not hold anymore. A simulation may require a number of additional states which exceeds the limit. Thus, machines may be in a highly paying equilibrium if they use a number of states close to the limit. In the present section we study this aspect. We first consider (for a didactical purpose) the case where the number of rounds is *fixed* in advance, that is, "given N, choose a machine." We return later to the uniform case of "choose a machine, get N".

Definition 4.1. Let $\Gamma^N(s_1, s_2)$ denote the N-round game where players, knowing N, choose machines of no more than s_1 and s_2 states, respectively.

Consider any sequence $S = ((S_1^1, S_1^2), \ldots, (S_N^1, S_N^2))$, of pairs of choices in the N-round game, that is, $S_j^i \in \{C, D\}$, $(i = 1, 2, j = 1, \ldots, N)$. Obviously, there are many pairs of machines that together produce the same sequence S. Denote by $\mathcal{T}(S)$ the set of all such pairs of machines.

Proposition 4.2. *The set $\mathcal{T}(S)$ is a cartesian product, $\mathcal{T}(S) = \mathcal{T}^1(S) \times \mathcal{T}^2(S)$, of sets of machines for the individual players.*

Proof. It is easy to verify that if (T_1, T_2) and (T_1', T_2') produce S then so do (T_1, T_2') and (T_1', T_2).

Let us define more restricted sets $\mathcal{R}^1$ and $\mathcal{R}^2$ as follows.

Definition 4.3. For any S, let $\mathcal{R}^i = \mathcal{R}^i(S)$ be the set of all the machines for player i that do the following:
(i) Play S_1^i in round 1.
(ii) Keep playing according to S if the opponent does.
(iii) If during any round the opponent deviates from S then switch to playing D in all following rounds.

Let us examine the possibility of achieving (in equilibrium) payoffs higher than those of the steady play of (D, D), when the number of rounds N is fixed, while the number of states is restricted. The question is which sequences S can be realized in equilibrium, given the limits on the numbers of states. Player i is mostly limited with respect to S if he must use all of his states for playing according to S. Intuitively, sequences S, with respect to which the players are mostly limited, are good candidates to be realizable in equilibrium, since the machines have minimum freedom for deviating from such strategies.

Definition 4.4. For any sequence S, other than the steady play of (D, D), let the *critical round*, $j^* = j^*(S)$, be the last round where at least one of the players plays C.

Proposition 4.5. *Let S be any symmetric sequence of actions (that is, $S_j^1 = S_j^2$ for every j) other than the steady (D, D). Suppose player 2 chooses a machine $T_2 \in \mathcal{R}^2(S)$. Under these conditions, if T_1 is a machine for player 1, that yields him a payoff higher than the machines in $\mathcal{R}^1(S)$, then T_1 plays according to S in rounds $1, \ldots, j^*(S) - 1$ and then switches to playing D.*

Proof. The proof follows from the fact that if 1 deviates from S during some round $j < j^*$ then his payoff can increase only in round j. However, the local gain (getting 4 instead of 3) is washed off by the loss in round j^* (a drop from 3 to 1) which is caused by this deviation.

We are now led to the interesting problem of designing highly paying sequences S, which are feasible subject to the limit on the number of internal states, such that none of the players can deviate *precisely* in round $j^*(S)$. We first develop some concepts that suggest solutions to the problem. Recall that we do not require the machines to halt at any time after round N.

Definition 4.6. Consider a Turing machine T that "plays" either C or D (see the Appendix for a detailed description of how the game is played). We say that T can *count* if for *any* natural number N, starting with the number N written on the work tape (in binary), T plays C precisely N times in a row, and then plays D.

Proposition 4.7. *There exists a Turing machine with two states that can count.*

Proof. The construction is simple and is left as an exercise to the reader.

Denote by $f(s)$ the number of different Turing machines (as specified in the Appendix) with s internal states that work with three tape symbols: $\{0, 1, \#\}$. It is easy to see that there are integers β and γ such that $f(s) = (\beta s)^{\gamma s}$. Obviously, the number of different strings (of C's and D's) that such machines can generate is bounded by $f(s)$. This observation gives rise to the following definition, which is in the spirit of Kolmogorov complexity [K]:

Definition 4.8. For any $x \in \{C, D\}^k$ (that is, x is a string of of length k consisting of C's and D's) the *state-complexity of x*, denoted $s(x)$, is defined to be the minimum number of internal states in a Turing machine (as specified in the Appendix) that outputs the string x and then halts.

The configuration of two machines playing together may be thought of as a single "distributed" machine producing some output. However, if the machines send each other the same signals then this configuration is duplicating the work of each of them. Thus, $s(x)$ is also the minimum number of states in each member of a pair of Turing machines that (when playing together some finitely repeated prisoners' dilemma) produce the symmetric sequence corresponding to x and then *halt*.

We are interested in strings x that are hard to construct. The idea is that each machine would have to "waste" most of its power on the generation of the string x.

Remark 4.9. Suppose the machines also have to watch each other, that is, to switch to D as soon as the opponent has deviated from x. Here more states may be required. However, for symmetric play, only one more state suffices. We assume each machine can read in round $i > 1$ the moves of both machines during round $i - 1$ before it has to choose its move for round i. Alternately, it suffices to assume that each machine can read whether the moves in the preceding round were identical.

Thus, what the machine has to do is verify that in the preceding round both players made the same move; if not, it enters a special state NOMORE. Once in NOMORE, it always plays D. In fact, often there no additional state is required. Suppose the machine is not taking full advantage of the power of s states. For example, the machine never finds itself in a situation that it reads a blank on its work tape while its internal state is some q_i. This suggests a slot that can be used for watching the opponent. We can modify the machine as follows. Whenever the moves of the preceding round are not identical, the machine erases the contents of the current cell of its work tape, leaves the work-head in its place, and switches to internal state q_i. If the machine reads a blank while in state q_i then it plays D, and does not change anything else. Thus, in symmetric play at most one additional state may be required for watching the opponent and this may happen only when the full power of s states is used.

Definition 4.10. A string x is called *efficient* with respect to s if it exploits all the states, that is, $s(x) = s$.

Proposition 4.11. *For every s, there exists an string x, efficient with respect to s, whose length is not greater than* $\log_2 f(s)$.

Proof. There are precisely 2^k different strings of length k. On the other hand, there are at most $f(s)$ different strings that can be produced by s-state machines. Let $k = \lfloor \log_2 f(s) \rfloor$. It follows that there is a string y of length $k + 1$ that cannot be produced by any s-state machine. Let $y = y_1 y_2 ... y_{l+1}$ be such an infeasible string of *minimal* length (hence $l \leq k$). Consider the prefix $y' = y_1 ... y_l$. This latter string *is* feasible. Suppose, per absurdum, it is not efficient. Thus it can be produced by an $(s-1)$-machine T which halts after y' is produced. It is this halting property that allows us to modify T into an s-state machine T' that produces the string y. Specifically, instead of entering the halting state of T, the modified machine T' enters the additional state, prints y_{l+1}, and then halts. Thus, we have reached a contradiction and it follows that y' is efficient.

5. Fixed N, deterministic machines, unlimited space

In this section we consider the case of a fixed N, that is, the players may choose different machines for different numbers of rounds. For simplicity of the discussion, let us assume that these machines receive no input in this case.

We propose a machine that works as follows. It plays according to a string of the form xC^∞, where x is a certain string of length k, and C^∞ is an infinite string of C's. If during any round the opponent machine has not played the same way, our machine switches to playing D throughout. Recall that $f(s) = (\beta s)^{\gamma s}$ denotes the number of different Turing machines (as specified in the Appendix) with no more than s states. The following proposition is analogous to Proposition 4.11:

Proposition 5.1. *There exists a string x of length $O(s \log s)$ such that xC^{∞} is played by some s-state machine (when the opponent is doing the same) but not by any $(s-1)$-state machine.*

Proof. There are 2^k distinct infinite strings of the form xC^{∞} where x is of length k. Obviously, if $2^k > f(s)$ then there exists a string x of length k, such that xC^{∞} cannot be produced by any s-state machine. As in Proposition 4.11, let y' denote the *suffix* of length l of a string y of length $l+1$, where yC^{∞} cannot be produced by any s-state machine and, furthermore, y is of minimal length with respect to this property. It follows that $l \leq \log_2 f(s) = O(s \log s)$. Moreover, y' cannot be played by any $(s-1)$-state machine.

Obviously, we can also show that there exists a string xC^{∞}, where x is of length $O(s \log s)$, which can be played by an s-state machine that also *watches the opponent*, such that no $(s-1)$-state machine can do the same.

At this point it seems that we are close to proving the existence of a high-payoff equilibrium. Suppose both players use the same machine T^* that plays xC^{∞} and also watches the opponent, that is, switches to playing D as soon as the opponent deviates from the string xC^{∞}. Moreover, suppose x is so complex that no $(s-1)$-state machine can do the same. It is conceivable that there is an $(s-1)$-state machine that plays xC^{∞} without watching the opponent. But since one additional state always suffices for watching the opponent, it follows that there is no $(s-2)$-state machine that plays xC^{∞}. The resulting play is described by the string xC^{N-k}, where $k < N$ is the length of x, even though the machines keep on playing C ad infinitum. By Proposition 4.5, the only profitable deviation for either player is to play according to xC^{N-k-1} during the first $N-1$ rounds, and then play D. The key question is whether there exists an s-state machine that does it. In other words, the only way to deviate profitably is to use a machine that not only plays according to the string xC^{N-k-1} in the first $N-1$ rounds but also "counts" so as to play D in round N. Intuitively, this counting task seems to require (at least for *some* strings x obtained in this way) computational resources that are not available (for example, two more internal states). Of course, there may exist special strings x such that although xC^{∞} requires $s-1$ states, there is a machine that produces enough information on its work tape so that it can play D in round N with just one more state. However, this seems to imply some connection between the string x and the number N. It seems reasonable to conjecture that there is at least one string x of length $O(\log f(s))$ for which this does not happen.

Motivated by the previous discussion, we now state a specific conjecture and prove results implied by it. Note that we do not have any specific reason to insist on play of strings of the form xC^{N-k}. The only property we need from a string is that it be complex and contain sufficiently many C's. Recall that $f(s)$ is the number of Turing machines (as defined in this paper) with s states. We say that a Turing machine T *produces* a string x if the output of T starts with x. In particular, the machine is not required to halt or even to stop outputing.

The Hypothesis. *If N and s are given so that $\log f(s) = o(N)$ then there exists an N-string x with following properties: (i) x is produced by some s-state Turing machine T. (ii) x contains only $o(N)$ D's. (iii) If j is the largest index such that $x_j = C$ then the N-string x', where $x'_i = x_i$ for $i \neq j$ and $x'_j = D$, is not produced by any s-state machine.*

The hypothesis reflects our intuition that at least for some strings y, a string of the form yC^∞ contains less information than a string of the form yC^lD. If Kolmogorov complexity is a good measure of information contents then this difference should be reflected in the number of states in the machine. We are not aware of any result with respect to Kolmogorov complexity which does not follow by a counting argument. However, counting arguments do not seem to work here so we believe new techniques have to be developed for proving this hypothesis. We conjecture that a stronger assertion is true, namely, that in (iii) the string x' cannot be produced by any machine with $s + g(s)$ states for some slowly increasing function $g(s)$. However, for our purpose, it suffices to consider only one additional state for the difference between watching and not watching the opponent. Stated more directly, we rely on an extended hypothesis as follows.

The Extended Hypothesis. *Under the conditions of the Hypothesis, the string x (but not x') is produced by an s-state machine T^* that also watches the opponent.*

Recall that the payoff to both players when they play (C, C) in the one-shot game is 3 and the goal is to achieve (in equilibrium) an average payoff of approximately 3 per round.

Theorem 5.2. *Assuming the extended hypothesis, if $s = o(N / \log N)$ then for every $\epsilon > 0$, there is an N_0 such that for all $N \geq N_0$, an average payoff of at least $3 - \epsilon$ can be obtained in equilibrium in the N-round game, played by s-state Turing machines (with no limit on space).*

Proof. Obviously, $s = o(N / \log N)$ implies $\log f(s) = o(N)$. Let T^* be an s-state machine the produces a string x as stated in the extended hypothesis. Suppose both players use T^* for playing the game. Thus, in every stage they play either (C, C) or (D, D). But the number of D's is $o(N)$, hence the average payoff per stage tends to 3 when N tends to infinity. This pair of choices is in equilibrium since the only profitable deviation is to play according to x, except that the last C is replaced by a D (see Proposition 4.5). The extended hypothesis states that such a deviation cannot be implemented by an s-state machine.

Remark 5.3. It is interesting to compare Theorem 5.2 to Neyman's results (Propositions 2.2, 2.4). For the comparison, recall that automata have no memory, so in a certain sense they have to use some of their states as memory. Thus, they need at least N states just for counting to N. It is therefore not surprising that even $(N-1)$-state automata can play steady (C,C) in equilibrium. On the other hand, a Turing machine with only two internal states can count to any N, when given the number N in binary as input (Proposition 4.7). We note that the results of the present section can be easily adapted to a model in which the number N is also given to the machine as input. It is obvious that with N states, both automata and Turing machines can play only the steady (D,D) in equilibrium relative to deterministic choices of machines. The proof of this claim is as follows. Given any pair of machines (M_1, M_2), each player i can design an N-state machine M_i' that plays precisely what M_i would play against M_{3-i} (regardless of what $3-i$ actually plays) and yet deviate in the critical round if there is one. Consider a game where players have to choose specific machines rather than probability distributions over machines. If the machines are automata then a restriction to $N-1$ states allows steady (C,C) in equilibrium, but N states leave only the steady (D,D) in equilibrium. Thus, in the context of deterministic choice of automata, the issue is precisely the ability to count to N; this amounts to sufficient "memory" in the form of states. In the case of Turing machines, memory is not the issue. The equilibrium is based on complexity of computation. The machines have unlimited space but they play strategies that waste their computational power so that with the remaining power they cannot count. We have not yet pursued the case of probabilistic choices of (deterministic) machines.

6. Uniform deterministic machines with limited number of states

In the tradition of theoretical computer science a Turing machine is perceived as a "uniform" tool. Here this corresponds to machines that can play a game of *any* number of rounds N which is given to the machine as input. Thus we are now interested in a game as follows.

Definition 6.1. We denote by $\Gamma(s_1, s_2)$ a game where the players have to choose Turing machines T_1, T_2 with no more than s_1 and s_2 states, respectively. The machines then play an N-round prisoners' dilemma game, where the number N is written in binary on the input tapes of the machines.

We discuss here the symmetric case, that is, $s_1 = s_2 = s$. The asymmetric case is a trivial extension of the symmetric one (see the conclusion of this paper). Notice that neither have we defined a payoff function for the game $\Gamma(s_1, s_2)$ nor have we specified the mechanism by which the number of rounds N is selected. One can think of a strong notion of equilibrium as follows.

Definition 6.2. A pair of machines (T_1, T_2) for $\Gamma(s_1, s_2)$ is in *strong equilibrium* if for any other allowable machine T_i' for player i $(i = 1, 2)$ there does *not* exist a number N (or, more weakly, there is an N_o such that there does *not* exist a number $N > N_o$) such that in the N-round game i strictly prefers T_i' over T_i, given that the opponent plays T_{3-i}.

Unfortunately, as we see in the following proposition, the notion of strong equilibrium is "too strong". This is true because machines may interpret their inputs in various ways.

Proposition 6.3. *Suppose T_1 and T_2 are deterministic machines for playing the game $\Gamma(s,s)$ and suppose that, except possibly for finitely many values of N, the play of these machines in the N-round game is different from the steady (D,D). Under these conditions, for s sufficiently large, for at least one player i, there exists an s-state machine T_i' such that for infinitely many values of N, i prefers T_i' over T_i when his opponent plays T_{3-i}.*

Proof. Consider a "universal" machine T_i', for player i, that acts as follows. For input N sufficiently large, T_i' reads the 2k-bit prefix of the input string (where k is some sufficiently large constant whose construction by T_i' will be discussed later) and decodes it as a description of a pair of Turing machines. In most of the cases this would be meaningless and we allow T_i' to play arbitrarily. However, when the 2k-bit prefix describes a valid pair of machines, (T_1^*, T_2^*), T_i' then simulates the play of (T_1^*, T_2^*) on the input N and discovers a round (if one exists) in which player i can deviate profitably in the sense of the N-round game. When T_i' actually plays the game, it plays like T_i^* would have played against T_{3-i}^* but deviates in the critical round. We now discuss the choice of the number k. First, there are obvious ways to encode the description of a Turing machine in binary. Let us fix such an encoding. Obviously, the size of the code of a machine with s states is $O(s \log s)$. Given the number s, we would like to construct a number k such the length of code of any machine with s states does not exceed k. Obviously, we can construct a number k of the form $k = 2^j$ where $j = O(\log s)$ is an integer, and moreover, this effort does not require more than $O(\log s)$ states. Now, if $N \geq 2k$, all the pairs of s-states machines are encoded by some strings with less than 2k bits, so in some fixed fraction of the cases (at least 2^{-2k}), T_i' simulates precisely the pair (T_1, T_2). Obviously, for at least one of the players such a machine T_i' is preferred in infinitely many cases. Note that the universal machine needs a only constant number of states (that is, independent of s) for most of its work except for the construction of the number k.

Because of Proposition 6.3, we prefer to work with a weaker notion of equilibrium. We consider a *weighted average* of the payoffs of the N-round games. That is, if the play of the machines results in payoffs $u_i^N(T_1, T_2)$ (for player i) in the N-round game, then in the "grand game" we define payoffs $U_i(T_1, T_2) = \sum_N P_N u_i^N(T_1, T_2)$, where $P_N \geq 0$ and $\sum_N P_N = 1$[2]. We argue that under a certain assumption on the weighting sequence P_N and the extended hypothesis, there exists a pair of deterministic machines in equilibrium yielding high payoffs.

---

2   It should be noted that this weighting function does *not* turn our game into a kind of an infinitely repeated one. It is well-known that if a game is repeated indefinitely, but after each round there is a probability $\alpha > 0$ of stopping, then despite ending (with probability 1) after a finite number of rounds, this game is equivalent to an infinitely repeated game with discounted payoffs. In our case, the interpretation may be that the players play the N-round game with probability P_N but they always *know* the number of rounds *in advance*.

As argued before, the idea behind the equilibria in this paper is that the machines playing them are so busy with the implementation of the strategy, that they cannot do almost anything else. We now extend the ideas developed in the previous sections to the case of selecting uniform machines, given a *distribution* on the number of rounds. The strategy to be used by the machines is similar to the one described for the case of a fixed N.

In Section 5 we stated an hypothesis about machines with no input. Here we discuss machines with input and we believe an analogous assertion is also true.

The Extended Hypothesis (for machines with input). *For every s, there exist numbers $L = L(s)$ and $N_0 = N_0(s)$, and a monotone increasing function $\mu_s(N)$, such that for every $N \geq N_0$, there exists an N-string x with following properties: (i) x is produced by some s-state Turing machine T when given the number in N in binary as input, and T also watches the opponent. (ii) x has the form yC^{N-k} where the length of y less than $L(s)$. (iii) For every $N' \geq N - \mu_s(N)$, a string x' that begins with $yC^{N'-k-1}D$ is not produced by any s-state machine when given the number N as input.*

The intuition here is that there has to be a string y that can be produced only by machines with at least s states and there is one which produces yC^∞. Since N is considerably larger than k, it seems there is a y with the following property: if y is produced as a prefix of a string $z \neq yC^\infty$ then z and yC^∞ must disagree on some index less than $N - \mu_s(N)$, for some slowly increasing function $\mu_s(N)$.

Let $H(s)$ denote the set of s-state machines T such that for any input N, while watching the opponent, the machine T plays according to a string of the form yC^{N-k}, where the length of y is less than $L(s)$. Denote the number of such machines by $h(s)$.

Proposition 6.4. *Suppose the input N is drawn from a probability distribution $P = \{P_N : N = 1, 2, ...\}$ and denote $P'(s) = \sum_{N \geq N_0(s)} P_N$. Then, under the extended hypothesis for machines with input, for any s, there exists an s-state machine $T \in H(s)$ that satisfies the following: (i) T plays a string of the form yC^{N-k}, watching the opponent. (ii) The probability (induced by the distribution P), that any string $yC^{N'-k-1}D$, where $N' \geq N - \mu_s(N)$ can be played by some s-state machine (given N, not necessarily watching the opponent) is less than $1 - P'(s)/h(s)$.*

Proof. Let us say that machine T is "defeated" by machine T' on the number N if, given N, T produces a string yC^{N-k} (watching the opponent) while T' produces the string $yC^{N'-k-1}D$ with $N' \geq N - \mu_s(N)$. Notice that only the case $N' = N$ corresponds to a profitable deviation. For any $T \in H(s)$ and any input N, let $a(T, N) = 1$ if T is not defeated on N by any s-state machine; otherwise, let $a(T, N) = 0$. By the extended hypothesis for machines with input, for every $N \geq N_0(s)$,

$$\sum_{T \in H(s)} a(T, N) \geq 1.$$

It follows that

$$\sum_N P_N \sum_{T \epsilon H(s)} a(T,N) \geq P'(s),$$

so that

$$\frac{1}{h(s)} \sum_{T \epsilon H(s)} \sum_N P_N \, a(T,N) \geq \frac{P'(s)}{h(s)}.$$

The left-hand side of the latter inequality is the average, taken over all $T \epsilon H(s)$, of the probability that the output of T is not defeated on N by any s-state machine. It follows that there is at least one such machine for which this probability is at least $P'(s)/h(s)$.

Proposition 6.4 suggests conditions on the distribution P and the number of states s, under which good equilibria exist. The idea is as follows. Suppose both players "agree" to use the machine T described in Proposition 6.4 but one of them is unfaithful and uses another s-state machine T' instead. Consider a distribution P that does not converge too fast to zero. For a deviation in a certain N-round game (against a faithful player) to be profitable, it must occur in the *last* round. The profit then is only 1. However, if the deviation occurs before round $N - \mu_s(N)$ then the unfaithful player incurs a *loss* of at least $2\mu_s(N) - 1$, since for at least $\mu_s(N)$ rounds the faithful player would then play D instead of C. The assumption is that $\mu_s(N)$ is increasing. If the probability for large values of N is sufficiently large, the expected profit is negative. For simplicity, we state the result as follows. We first determine the scope of our probability distributions. Given a natural number n and a positive ϵ, let $\mathscr{P}_{n,\epsilon}$ denote the set of probability distributions $P = (P_1, P_2, ...)$ ($P_i \geq 0$, $\Sigma P_i = 1$), over the naturals, for which $P(\{N \leq n\}) \leq \epsilon$.

Theorem 6.5. *Under the extended hypothesis for machines with input, for any number of states s, there exist a natural number $n = n(s)$ and an $\epsilon = \epsilon(s) > 0$, such that for any probability distribution $P \epsilon \mathscr{P}_{n,\epsilon}$, there exists a pair of s-state deterministic machines that are in equilibrium in $\Gamma(s,s)$ relative to the distribution P, whose average payoffs per round in the N-round game tend to that of (C,C), as N tends to infinity.*

7. Conclusion

We have discussed mainly the symmetric case of the the prisoners' dilemma game, that is, players have to use machines under the same restrictions. Similar ideas can be used in a more general situation, that is, asymmetric restrictions (not necessarily on numbers of states) and more general games.

Consider first the asymmetric prisoners' dilemma game. More precisely, suppose the players are restricted to s_1 and s_2 states in their machines, respectively, where s_1 and s_2 are not necessarily equal.

The extension is easy. Suppose $s_1 < s_2$. Player 1 uses the same strategy as in the symmetric case, that is, he plays xC^∞ where x is chosen appropriately and also watches player 2. Player 2's strategy depends on the value of s_2. Let q denote the minimum number of states, with which player 2 could play according to xC^∞, except that in the last round he would play D. The high-payoff equilibrium depends on the the value of q. The extended hypothesis essentially states that $q > s_1$. If $s_2 \geq q + 1$ then player 2 plays this way and also watches player 1; this is possible since only one additional state is required for watching. If $s_2 \leq q - 1$ then player 2 plays exactly as in the symmetric case. The difficult case is $s_2 = q$. Here player 2 can profitably deviate from the strategy of the symmetric case. However, he may have to do that at the expense of not watching player 1. On the other hand, if player 1 is not being watched then he can deviate profitably.

In a general repeated game situation the long sequence of (C, C) of the prisoners' dilemma game should be replaced by a sequence of payoff pairs that yield high average payoff. For sufficiently large s and N (but s must be small relative to N), any individually rational payoff pair can be approximated by the average payoff in some equilibrium. The players choose a sequence of pairs of moves which is, on the one hand, complex (so that it requires all the states of the machine), and on the other hand yields approximately the desirable payoff. The equilibrium is achieved by prescribing "punishments" to a deviator. These ideas seem fairly standard in the context of repeated games.

We have discussed here restrictions only on the numbers of states, or alternately, lengths of programs. It seems that similar ideas should work when other computational resources are limited. For example, one might consider a game where players can use any number of machines of a fixed type where the total number of machine operations between rounds is limited. Then an equilibrium is likely to exist, based on a string whose computation requires the maximum number allowed. However, even if such equilibria can be shown to exist, it would probably be very hard to construct one and prove that it is an equilibrium.

References

[HU]   J. E. Hopcroft and J. D. Ullman, *Introduction to automata theory, languages, and computation*, Addison-Wesley, Reading, Mass., 1979

[K]   A. N. Kolmogorov, "Three approaches for defining the information quantity", *Prob. Inform. Trans.*, **1** (1965) 1-7.

[N]   A. Neyman, "Bounded complexity justifies cooperation in the finitely repeated prisoners' dilemma", manuscript, February 1985.

[Ru]   A. Rubinstein, "Finite automata play -- The repeated prisoner's dilemma", Research Report No. 149, Department of Economics, The Hebrew University, Jerusalem, Israel, 1985.

Appendix: The mechanism

In this appendix we specify the mechanism by which our machines play the game. Our machines are standard Turing machines with the following features: (i) a read/write *work tape*, (ii) a read-only *input tape*, (iii) a *play* device which can be set to either C or D and also can be read, and (iv) an *eye* which can read either C, D or #. Before round 1 the eye sees #. The game is administered by a "referee". The referee first writes into the input tapes of the participating machines the number N of rounds to be played (in binary encoding). After round i the "referee" shows each "eye" what was "played" by the other machine. The machine then has to specify its choice of C or D for the following round. The machine can be in one of a *finite* number of internal states including two special states: PAUSE and GO. The work of each machine is determined by a "next move" function δ. The arguments of the function δ are the following: (i) the current state (except for PAUSE), (ii) the symbols currently being scanned on the work and input tapes, the symbol currently seen by the eye, and the symbol shown on the play device (before round 1 this play device shows #). The function δ then gives the next state (possibly PAUSE), a direction command (left, right, or stay) for moving the head of the work tape or reading the next symbol on the input tape, a symbol to be written on the work tape and a "play" (i.e., C or D). After the state of the machine is changed to GO, the latter is supposed to enter the state PAUSE, with either C or D on the play device, after a finite number of steps. The "referee" acts as follows. When both machines are in their respective PAUSE states, the referee reads the play devices and shows the contents to each other's eye. He then changes the states of both machines to their respective GO states.

A probabilistic machine is almost the same as a deterministic one with the addition of a "coin". This is another device that at any time reads either 0 or 1 with probability ½ each, independently of other parts of the system and the history of the run. This reading is also an argument of the next-move function of the machine.

Note that we do not assume any time limit. So, if a player uses a machine that may not enter its PAUSE state is a certain situation, it may be impossible to prove that he is using an illegal machine even though the game will not proceed.

A THEORY OF HIGHER ORDER PROBABILITIES[1]

Haim Gaifman
Mathematics Department The Hebrew University Jerusalem, Israel
Currently Visitor at SRI

ABSTRACT

We set up a general framework for higher order probabilities. A simple HOP (Higher Order Probability space) consists of a probability space and an operation *PR*, such that, for every event *A* and every real closed interval Δ, *PR(A ,Δ)* is the event that *A*'s "true" probability lies in Δ. (The "true" probability can be construed here either as the objective probability, or the probability assigned by an expert, or the one assigned eventually in a fuller state of knowledge.) In a general HOP the operation *PR* has also an additional argument ranging over an ordered set of time-points, or, more generally, over a partially ordered set of stages; *PR(A,t,Δ)* is the event that *A*'s probability at stage *t* lies in Δ. First we investigate simple HOPs and then the general ones. Assuming some intuitively justified axioms, we derive the most general structure of such a space. We also indicate various connections with modal logic.

---

[1]A part of this paper has been included in a talk given in a NSF symposium on foundations of probability and causality, organized by W. Harper and B. Skyrms at UC Irvine, July 1985. I wish to thank the organizers for the opportunity to discuss and clarify some of these ideas.

Introduction

The assignment of probabilties is the most established way of measuring uncertainties on a quantitative scale. In the framework of subjective probability, the probabilities are interpreted as someone's (the agent's) degrees of belief. Since justified belief amounts to knowledge, the assignment of probabilities, in as much as it can be justified, expresses knowledge. Indeed, knowledge of probabilities, appears to be the basic kind of knowledge that is provided by the experimental sciences today.

This is knowledge of a partial, or incomplete, nature, but not in the usual sense of "partial". Usually we mean by "partial knowledge" knowledge of some, but not all, of the facts in a certain domain. But knowing that a given coin is unbiased does not enable one to deduce any non-tautological Boolean combination of propositions which describe outcomes in the next, say fifty tosses. And yet it constitutes very valuable knowledge about these very same outcomes. What is the objective content of this knowledge ? What kind of fact is the fact that the true probability of "heads" is 0.5, i.e., that the coin is unbiased ? I shall not enter here into these classical problems[2]. I take it for granted that, among probability assignments, some are more successful, or better tuned to the actual world, than others. Consequently probability assignments are themselves subject to judgement and evaluation. Having, for example, to estimate the possibility of rain I might give it, going by the sky's appearance, 70%. But I shall be highly uncertain about my estimate and will adopt the different value given, five minutes later, in the weather forecast.

Thus we have two levels of uncertainty:

1. Uncertainty concerning the occurence of a certain event - expressed through the assignment of probabilities.

2. Uncertainty concerning the probability values assigned in 1.

---

[2]My Salzburg paper [1983] has been devoted to these questions. The upshot of the analysis there has been that even a "purely subjective" probability implies a kind of factual claim, for one can asses its success in the actual world. Rather than two different kinds, subjective and objective probabilties are better to be regarded as two extremes of a spectrum.

When this second level is itself expressed by assigning probabilities we get <u>second order</u> probabilities. An example of a second order probability is furnished by a cartoon in "The New Yorker" showing a forecaster making the following announcement:

"There is now 60% chance of rain tomorrow, but, there is 70% chance that later this evening the chance of rain tomorrow will be 80%."

Just as we can iterate modal or epistemic operators, so in the system to be presented here we can iterate the probability-assignment operator to any depth. The goal of this paper is to present a general and adequate semantics for higher order probabilities and to obtain, via representaton theorems, nice easily understood structures which give us a handle on the situation.

The basic structure to be defined here is a **HOP** (Higher Order Probability space). A *simple* HOP is based on a field of events, F, and on a binary operator $PR(\ ,\ )$ which associates with every event A and every real closed interval Δ an event $PR(A,\Delta)$ in F. The intended meaning is that $PR(A,\Delta)$ is the event that A's true probability lies in the interval Δ.

"True probability" can be understood here as the probability assigned by an ideal expert or by someone fully informed. <u>It is however up to us (or to the agent) to decide what in the given context constitutes an "ideal expert" or "someone fully informed"</u>. If "full information" means knowing *all* the facts then, of course, the true (unknown to us) probability has only two values 0 and 1; this will make the HOP trivial in a certain sense. In the other extreme, the agent may regard himself as being already fully informed and this leads to the "opposite" trivialization of the HOP. Generally, the agent will regard the expert as being more knowledgeable than himself, but not omniscient; e.g., the expert might know the true bias of a coin but not the outcomes of future tossings, or he might have statistical information for estimating the bias, which the agent lacks.

The agent himself at some future time can be cast in the role of being "fully informed". Thus, if P is the forecaster's present probability function and if PR represents his state of knowledge later in the evening, then his announcement in "The New Yorker" cartoon can be summed up as follows, where $A =$ 'tomorrow it will rain':

$$P(A)=.6 \qquad P(PR(A\ ,\ [.8,.8]))=.7$$

In order to represent knowledge at different stages, we make PR into a 3-place operator: $\underline{PR(A,\ t\ ,\ \Delta)}$ is the event that the probability of A at stage t lies in Δ. The stages can be time-points, in which case t ranges over some ordered set. More generally, the set of stages is only partially ordered, where $s \leq t$ if the knowledge at stage t includes the knowledge at stage s. (Different agents may thus be represented in the structure.) This is how a HOP is defined in general. We shall first establish the properties of simple HOPs, then use them to derive those of the more general spaces.

We shall also define, in a seperate section, a formal logical calculus, to be called *probability logic*, which is naturally associated with simple HOPs. Various modalities can be reconstructed within this calculus. The general HOPs give rise to stage-dependent modalities whose calculus will be outlined at the end of the paper.

The import of the subject for various branches of philosophy and for the foundations of probability is obvious. Also obvious should be its bearing upon applied probabilistic reasoning in distributed networks, or upon efforts to incorporate such reasoning in AI systems. Mathematically, most of this paper is rather easy. Our goal has not been to prove difficult theorems, but to clarify some basic concepts and to outline a general, conceptually "clean", framework within which one can use freely and to good effect statements such as: 'With probability 0.7 Adam will know at stage 3 Bob's probability for the event *A*, with error $\leq$ 0.01' (where Adam and Bob are either people or processors). Statements of this form express intuitive thinking which may underly involved technical proofs; to use them openly and precisely can help us as a guide for finding and organizing our arguments.

A theoretic framework for higher order probabilities may also yield insights into systems of reasoning which employ non-probabilistic certainty measures. For when probability is itself treated like a random variable, we can use various methods of "safe" estimation which do not necessarily yield a probability measure. For example, define the *certainty measure* of an event A to be the largest α such that, with probability 1, the probability of A is $\geq \alpha$. This is only one, apparently the most conservative, measure among various measures that can be used.

Higher order probabilities have been considered by De-Finetti, but rejected by him owing to his extreme subjectivist views. Savage considered the possibility but did not take it up, fearing that the higher order probabilities will reflect back on the ground level, leading to inconsistencies. Instances of higher order probabilities figure in works of Good [1965] and Jaynes [1958]. More recent philosophical works are by Domotor [1985], Gardenfors [1975] (for qualitative probabilities), Miller [1966], Skyrms [1980 A], [1980 B] - who did much to clarify matters, van-Frassen [1984], and others.

Due to limitations of space and deadline I have not entered into details of various proofs. Some of the material has been abridged; I have included some illustrative examples of simple HOPs, but not the more interesting ones of general HOPs (which arise naturally in distributed systems). Also the bibliography is far from complete.

Simple HOPs

Definition and Basic Properties

As in Kolmogoroff's framework [1933] we interpret propositions as <u>subsets</u> of some universal set, say W, and we refer to them as <u>events</u>. We can regard W as the set of all possible worlds. Thus we have $X =$ set of all worlds in which X is true and we get the following standard correspondence:

$\lor$ (disjunction) $\mapsto$ $\cup$ (union)
$\land$ (conjunction) $\mapsto$ $\cap$ (intersection)
$\neg$ (negation) $\mapsto$ - (complementation)

Terminology: A <u>Boolean Algebra</u> (of sets) is a class of sets closed under finite unions (and intersections) and under complementation (with respect to some presupposed universal set, in our case - W). A <u>field</u> is a Boolean algebra closed under countable unions (what is known also as a σ-algebra). The field (Boolean algebra) <u>generated by</u> a class S of sets is the smallest field (Boolean algebra) which contains S as a subclass. Note that in generating a Boolean algebra we apply finitary operations only, whereas in generating a field infinitary countable operations are used. A field is <u>countably generated</u> if it has a countable set of generators. All probabilities are assumed here to be countably additive.

A **HOP** is a 4-tuple *(W, F, P, PR)*, where F is a field of subsets of W, to be called <u>events</u>, P is a probability over F and PR is a mapping associating with every $A \in F$ and every real closed interval Δ an event *PR(A,Δ)*,

$PR:$ $F \times$ *set of closed intervals* $\rightarrow$ F

As explained in the introduction *PR(A,Δ)* is the event that the true (or the eventual, or the expert-assigned) probability of A lies in Δ. P is the agent's current subjective probability.

Among the closed intervals, we include also the empty interval, $\emptyset$. The minimal and maximal elements of F are, respectively, **0** and **1**; that is: **0** = empty subset of W = False, **1** = W = True.

In the explanations I shall use "probability" both for the agent's current subjective probability as well as for the true, or eventual one; the contexts indicate the intended reading.

The following axioms are postulated for a HOP:

(I) *PR(A , [0,1])* = **1** (For every A, the event that A's probability lies in *[0,1]* is W, i.e., true.)

(II) *PR[A,∅]* = **0** (That A's probability lies in the empty interval is the empty event, i.e., false.)

(III) *If $\Delta_1 \cup \Delta_2$ is an interval then $PR(A, \Delta_1 \cup \Delta_2) = PR(A, \Delta_1) \cup PR(A, \Delta_2)$* ($A$'s probability lies in the interval $\Delta_1 \cup \Delta_2$ iff it lies either in Δ_1 or in Δ_2)

In the follwing two axioms "n" is a running index ranging over $\{1, 2, \dots\}$.

(IV) $\cap_n PR(A, \Delta_n) = PR(A, \cap_n \Delta_n)$ (A's probability lies in every Δ_n iff it lies in their intersecton).

(V) *If, for all $n \neq m$, $A_n \cap A_m = \emptyset$, then* $\cap_n PR(A, [\alpha_n, \beta_n]) \subset PR(\cup_n A_n, [\Sigma_n \alpha_n, \Sigma_n \beta_n])$ (For pairwise disjoint A_ns, if A_n's probability lies in $[\alpha_n, \beta_n]$, $n = 1, 2, \dots$, then the probability of $\cup_n(A_n)$ lies in $[\Sigma_n \alpha_n, \Sigma_n \beta_n]$).)

Note that axioms **(I)**-**(V)** involve only W, F and PR. The crucial axiom which connects PR with P will be stated later.

THEOREM 1 *For every HOP, $H = (W, F, P, PR)$ there is a mapping p which associates with every x in W a probability, p_x, over F such that*

(1) $PR(A, \Delta) = \{x : p_x(A) \in \Delta\}$

The mapping p is uniquely determined by **(1)** *and can be defined by:*

(2) $p_x(A) = inf\{\alpha : x \in PR(A, [0, \alpha])\}$

as well as by:

(2') $p_x(A) = sup\{\alpha : x \in PR(A, [\alpha, 1])\}$.

Vice versa, if, for every $x \in W$, p_x is a probability over F such that $\{x : p_x(A) \in \Delta\}$ is in F for all $A \in F$ and all real closed Δ, and if we use **(1)** *as a definition of PR then Axioms* **(I)**-**(V)** *are satisfied.*

We call p the <u>kernel</u> of the HOP.

The proof of Theorem 1 is nothing more than a straight-forward derivation of all the required details from the axioms, using **(2)** as the definition of p_x. (The "vice versa" part is even more immediate than the first part.)

We can now extend PR and define $PR(A, \Xi)$, for arbitrary subsets Ξ of reals, as $\{x : p_x(A) \in \Xi\}$. If Ξ is a Borel set then $PR(A, \Xi)$ is in F.

The meaning of p_x is obvious: <u>it is the probability which corresponds to the maximal state of</u>

knowledge in world x - the distribution chosen by the expert of that world.

Notation: For $\alpha \in [0,1]$, $PR(A,\alpha) =_{df} PR(A, [\alpha,\alpha])$.

The picture is considerably simpler in the discrete case, where W is countable. Assuming with no loss of generality that $\{x\} \in F$ for every $x \in W$, the probability of some $A \subset W$ is simply the sum of the probabilities of the worlds in A. In that case, we can eliminate the closed intervals and consider only the special cases $PR(A,\alpha)$ where α ranges over $[0,1]$; also our 5 axioms can be replaced by 3 simpler ones. Discrete cases arise in many situations and are very useful as illustrative examples. But to consider only the discrete case is highly restrictive.

Notation: For $x,y \in W$, $A \in F$, put: $p(x,A) =_{df} p_x(A)$ and (assuming $\{y\} \in F$) $p(x,y) =_{df} p(x,\{y\})$ and $P(y) =_{df} P(\{y\})$.

In the discrete case P is obviously determined by the values $P(x)$, $x \in W$. Thus, ordering W, we can represent P as a probability vector (a countable vector of non-negative entries which sum up to 1). Similarly the kernel p becomes a probabilty matrix (a countable square matrix in which every row is a probability vector). Examples (i) and (ii) in the **Examples** subsection can serve to illustrate the situation (the discussion there presupposes however the next subsection).

Mathematically, what we have got is a Markov process (with initial probability P and transition probabilities $p(x,)$, $x \in W$). But the interpretation is altogether different from the usual interpretation of such a structure. The connection between P and the kernel p is established in the sixth axiom.

Axiom (VI) And Its Consequences

Let $P(A|B)$ be the conditional probability of A, given B. It is defined in the case that $P(B) \neq 0$ as $P(A \cap B)/P(B)$. It is what the agent's probability for A should be had he known B.

Axiom (VI_w)   If $P(PR(A , [\alpha,\beta])) \neq 0$ then $\alpha \leq P(A \mid PR(A , [\alpha,\beta])) \leq \beta$.

Axiom (VI_w) (the weak form of the forthcoming Axiom (VI)) is a generalization of Miller's Principle to the case of interval-based events. Rewritten in our notation, Miller's Principle is: $P(A \mid PR(A,\alpha)) = \alpha$. Axiom ($VI_w$) appears to be the following rule: My probability for A should be no less than α and no more than β, were I to know that in a more informed state my probability for A will be within these bounds. Plausible as it sounds, the use of the hypothetical "were I to know that..." needs in this context some clarification. Now a well-known way of explicating conditional probabilties is through conditional bets. Using such bets van-Frassen [1984] gives a Dutch-book argument for the Principle: Its violation makes possible a system of bets (with odds in accordance with the agent's probabilities) in which the agent will incur a net loss in all circumstances. In this argument $PR(A,\alpha)$ is interpreted as the event that the agent's probability for A at a certain future time will be α, in which case he should accept at that time bets with odds α. The same kind of Dutch-book can be constructed if Axiom $(\mathbf{VI_w})$ is violated. (Here it is crucial that we use an <u>interval</u>, the argument fails if we replace $[\alpha,\beta]$ by a non-convex Borel set.)

Axiom $(\mathbf{VI})$ is the interval-based form of the stronger version of Miller's Principle which was suggested by Skyrms [1980 A].

Axiom (VI)   *If C is a finite intersection of events of the form $PR(B,\Delta)$, and if $P(C \cap PR(A,[\alpha,\beta])) \neq 0$, then*

$$\alpha \leq P(A \mid C \cap PR(A,[\alpha,\beta])) \leq \beta$$

The same intuition which prescribes $(\mathbf{VI_w})$ prescribes $(\mathbf{VI})$; also here the violation of the axiom makes possible a Dutch-book against the agent. What is essntial is that events of the form $PR(B,\Delta)$ be, in principle, <u>knowable to the agent</u>, i.e., be known (if true) in the maximal states of knowledge as defined by our structure.[3]

In what follows integrating a function $f(t)$ with respect to a probability m is written as $\int f(t) \cdot m(dt)$.

Lemma 1   *Axiom $(\mathbf{VI_w})$ implies that the following holds for all $A \in F$:*

(3) $P(A) = \int p(x,A) \cdot P(dx)$

The proof consists in applying the formula $P(A) = \Sigma_i P(A \mid B_i) \cdot P(B_i)$, where the B_i's form a partition, passing to the limit and using the definition of an integral.

The implication $(\mathbf{3}) \Rightarrow (\mathbf{VI_w})$ is not true in general. Note that in the discrete case $(\mathbf{3})$ becomes:

(3$_d$) $P(x) = \Sigma_y p(x,y) \cdot P(y)$

which means that the probability vector is an eigen-vector of the kernel.

Definition   Call two worlds $x,y \in W$ <u>epistimically equivalent</u>, (or, for short, <u>equivalent</u>) and denote it by $x \simeq y$, if $p_x = p_y$. For S - a class of events, define $K[S]$ to be the field generated by all events of the form $PR(A,\Delta)$, $A \in S$, Δ - a real closed interval.

---

[3] It is important to restrict C in Axiom $(\mathbf{VI})$ to an intersection of such events. The removal of this restriction will cause the p_x's to be two-valued functions, meaning that all facts are known in the maximal knowledge states.

Epistemic equivalence means having the same maximal knowledge. Evidently $x \simeq y$ iff, for all A and all Δ, $x \in PR(A, \Delta) \leftrightarrow y \in PR(A, \Delta)$; this is equivalent to: for all $C \in K[F]$, $x \in C \leftrightarrow y \in C$. If $K[F]$ is generated by the countably many generators X_n, $n = 0, 1, \ldots$ then the equivalence classes are exactly all non-empty intersections $\cap_n X_n{'}$ where each $X_n{'}$ is either X_n or its complement. Hence the equivalence classes are themselves in $K[F]$, they are exactly the <u>atoms</u> of this field. The next lemma shows that the condition that $K[F]$ be countably generated is rather mild, for it holds whenever F itself is countably generated (which is the common state of affairs):

Lemma 2 *If S is either countable or a countably generated field, then $K[S]$ is countably generated.*

(As generators for $K[S]$ one can take all $PR(A, \Delta)$, $A \in S$, Δ - a rational closed interval; the second claim is proved by showing that if S' is a Boolean algebra that generates the field S then $K[S'] = K[S]$.)

Terminology: A <u>0-set</u> is a set of probability 0. Something is said to hold for <u>almost all x</u> if it holds for all x except for a 0-set. The probability in question is P, unless specified otherwise.

Theorem 2 *If F is countably generated then axiom* **(VI)** *is equivalent to each of the following conditions:*

(A)   **(3)** *holds (for all A) and the following is true: Let C_x be the epistemic equivalence class to which x belongs, then*

$$p_x(C_x) = 1 \quad \text{for almost all } x.$$

(B)   **(3)** *holds and, for almost all x, for all A:*

(4) $p_x(A) = \int p_y(A) \cdot p_x(dy)$

The proof that axiom **(VI)** is equivalent to **(A)** and implies **(B)** uses only basic measure theory. The present proof of **(B)** $\Rightarrow$ **(A)** relies on advanced ergodic theory[4] and I do not know if this can be avoided. Fortunately the rest of this paper does not rely on this implication (except the corresponding implication in Theorem 3). Note that in the discrete case **(4)** is equivalent to:

(4$_d$) $p(x,z) = \Sigma_y p(x,y) \cdot p(y,z)$

(4$_d$) means that the kernel, as a matrix, is equal to its square.

Let $\{E_u : u \in U\}$ be the family of epistemic equivalence classes, with different indices attached to

---

[4] I am thankful to my colleagues at the Hebrew University H. Furstenberg, I. Katzenelson and B. Weiss for their help in this item. Needless to say that errors, if any, are my sole responsibility.

different classes. Let P_u be the common p_x for $x \in E_u$; let m be the probability, defined for all $V \subset U$ such that $\cup_{u \in U} E_u \in F$, by:

$$m(V) = P(\cup_{u \in V} E_u)$$

Then **(A)** is equivalent to the following condition:

(C)   *For all A in F*

$$P(A) = \int_U P_u(A) \cdot m(du)$$

and for almost all (with respect to m) u

$$P_u(E_u) = 1$$

The first equality in **(C)** is a recasting of **(3)**; it can be equivalently described by saying that <u>P is a mixture of the P_u's with weight function m</u>. Altogether **(C)** means that we have here what is known as the <u>disintegration of the probability space</u>. It makes for a rather transparent structure.

For W - countable the disintegration means the following: After deleting from the kernel-matrix rows and columns which correspond to some set of probability 0, the rest decomposes into submatrices around the main diagonal in each of which all rows are equal, with 0's in all other places; P itself is a mixture of these rows. Such HOPs are exactly those that can be constructed as follows (hence this is the method for setting up higher order probabilities which avoid a Dutch book):

- *Chose a partition $\{E_u : u \in U\}$ of W into non-empty disjoint sets, with different u's marking different sets.*

- *Chose for each u in U a probability, P_u, on W such that $P_u(E_u) = 1$ for all $u \in U'$, where U' is some non-empty susbset of U.*

- *Chose a probability, m, on U such that m(U')=1, and let P be the mixture of the P_u's with weight function m.*

- *For each $u \in U$ and each $x \in E_u$ put $p_x = P_u$ and define $PR(A,\Delta)$ to be $\{x : p_x(A) \in \Delta\}$.*

The construction is essentially the same for a general W (with a countably generated F); some additional stipulations of measurability should be included in order to make possible the formation of the mixture and to ensure that the $PR(A,\Delta)$'s are in F.

Definition   Call P_u and its corresponding equivalence class, E_u, <u>ontological</u> if $P_u(E_u) = 1$, call it and its corresponding class <u>coherent</u> if P_u is a mixture of ontological P_v's. Call a world <u>ontological (coherent)</u> if it belongs to an ontological (coherent) equivalence class.

An ontological class is of course coherent. A coherent class which is not ontological must get the value 0 under its own P_u. It represents a state of knowledge in which the agent knows for sure that his eventual probability function will be different from his current one (and that it will be an ontological one).

The set of ontological worlds gets the value 1 under P and under each p_x where x is coherent. It is refered to as the ontological part of the HOP. Together with the structure induced by the original HOP it forms by itself a simple HOP. Similarly we define the coherent part of the HOP as the set of all coherent worlds (together with the induced structure). As far as calculating probabilities goes, only the ontological part matters. Coherent non-ontological worlds are useful as representatives of transitory states of knowledge.

Examples

Example 1: $W = \{w1, w2, w3\}$ $P = (1/3, 1/3, 1/3)$ and the kernel matrix is:

$$
\begin{array}{ccc}
.5 & .5 & 0 \\
0 & .5 & .5 \\
.5 & 0 & .5
\end{array}
$$

The agent's current probability assigns each world the value 1/3. Eventually, in world $w1$ he will know that he is not in $w3$ and he will assign each of the worlds $w1$, $w2$ the value 0.5. This is the meaning of the first row. The other rows are similarly interpreted.

By direct checking one can verify that $(\mathbf{VI_w})$ is satisfied. (The checking of all cases in this example is easy because $PR(A,\alpha) \neq \emptyset$ only for $\alpha = 0.5, 1$.) However the matrix is not equal to its square, hence Axiom $(\mathbf{VI})$ is violated, as indeed the following case shows: Put $A = \{w1\}$, $C = PR(\{w2\}, 0.5)$. Then $C = \{x : p(x,w2) = 0.5\} = \{w1, w2\}$ and similarly $PR(A, 0.5) = \{w1, w3\}$. Hence $A = PR(A, 0.5) \cap C$ implying $P(A \mid PR(A, 0.5) \cap C) = 1 \neq 0.5$. This can be used to construct a Dutch book against the agent.

Note also that the epistemic equivalence classes are $\{w1\}, \{w2\}$ and $\{w3\}$ and that non is ontological; hence also there are no coherent worlds here.

Example 2 $W = \{w1, w2, ..., w8\}$, P is: $(.1, .2, .2, .1, .4, 0, 0, 0)$ and the kernel matrix is:

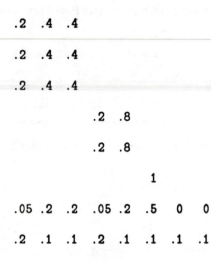

```
             .2   .4   .4

             .2   .4   .4

             .2   .4   .4

                      .2   .8

                      .2   .8

                          1

        .05  .2   .2  .05  .2   .5   0    0

         .2  .1   .1   .2  .1   .1   .1   .1
```

where all undisplayed entries are 0. The sets {w1,w2,w3}, {w4,w5} and {w6} are equivalence classes which are ontological. P is a mixture of these 3 types of rows, with weights 0.5, 0.5, 0, respectively. Hence condition (C) is satisfied, therefore also Axiom (VI). $w7$ is a coherent non-ontological world, because the 7th row is a mixture of the first three types (with weights .25, .25, .5) $w8$ is not coherent. The ontological part consists of the upper left 6×6 matrix and the coherent part of the 7×7 one.

The example can be made more concrete by the following scenario. A number is to be chosen from {1,2,3}. For $i=1,2,3$, the number chosen in wi is i, but in each of these 3 worlds the maximal knowledge consists in assigning probabilities 0.2, 0.4, 0.4 to the 3 possibilities. In $w4$ the number chosen is 1 and in $w5$ it is 2; in either of these worlds the maximal knowledge consists in assigning the probabilities 0.2, 0.8. In $w6$ the number is 2 and it is also assigned probability 1. In the agent's current state he assigns probability 0 to finding himself eventually in the third state of maximal knowledge, and equal probabilities to the first and second states. World $w7$ represent a similar situation but with different weights. We can imagine 3 lotteries for chosing the number; in each equivalence class the maximal knowledge is knowledge of the chosen lottery.

Example 3:   Let H be the probability of "heads" of some given coin of unknown bias. Treat H as a random variable. The agent's knowledge is represented by a probability distribution for H. Say it is the uniform distribution over [0,1]. The expert does not know the value of H but he has some additional information. Say his additional information is the value of N - the number of "heads" in 50 independent tosses. Then our worlds can be regarded as pairs (h,n), such that in (h,n) the event $H=h \cap N=n$ is true; here h is a real number in [0,1] and n an integer between 0 and 50. The field F is generated by the sets $[\alpha,\beta] \times \{n\}$, $0 \leq \alpha \leq \beta \leq 1$, $n=0,...,50$.

Given $H=h$, we get the binomial distribution $b_{h,50}$ for N. This fact, together with the agent's uniform distribution for H, determines his probability P over F. The expert's probability in world (h,n) is obtained by conditioning on his information, it is $P(|N=n)$. There are 51 equivalence classes which correspond to the 51 possible values of N and all worlds are ontological.

As is well known, different values of N give rise to different conditional distributions of H. Therefore the events $N=n$ are in the field generated by the events[5] $PR(H\in[\alpha,\beta], \Delta)$. The whole field F is therefore generated by events which are either of the form $H\in[\alpha,\beta]$ or obtained from these by applying the operator PR. Consequently we can give an abstract description of this HOP which does not mention the fifty tosses. The only function of the tosses is to affect the distribution of H; in our framework such changes in distribution constitute themselves events which can be treated directly, without having to bring in their causes.

The Case of a General Field

The restriction that F be countably generated is a mild one. The probability spaces which commonly appear in theory, or in applications, are essntially of this nature[6]. Usually we are interested in properties that involve only countably many generators. We will first show that for studying such properties we can always restrict ourselves to the case where the underlying field is countably generated.

Definition Given a simple HOP (W, F, P, PR) and given $S\subset F$, define $H[S]$ as the smallest field containing S and closed under PR (i.e., $A \in H[S] \Rightarrow PR(A,\Delta) \in H[S]$ for every real closed interval Δ).

$H[S]$, together with the restrictions of P and PR to it, forms a subHOP, where this notion is defined in the obvious way.

Lemma 3 *If S is a Boolean algebra and, for every A in S and every rational closed interval Δ, $PR(A,\Delta)$ is in S, then $H[S]$ is the field generated by S.*

This means that, once we have a Boolean algebra closed under $PR(,\Delta)$ for all Δ with rational endpoints, we get all the rest by countable Boolean operations without using PR.

Corollary *If S is either countable, or a countably generated field, then $H[S]$ is countably generated.*

---

[5]Actually there are 51 real numbers α_n such that the event $N=n$ is the same as $PR(H\le 1/2, \alpha_n)$.

[6]They are *seperable*, i.e., for some countably generated field every event in the space differs from a set in the field by a 0-set.

Using this we can derive from Theorem 2 an analogous result for general fields:

Theorem 3   *Axiom* **(VI)** *is equivalent to each of the following conditions:*

(A')   **(3)** *holds and for every C in K[F], for almost all x:* $p_x(C)=1$ *if* $x \in C$, $p_x(C)=0$ *otherwise.*

(B')   **(3)** *holds and for every A in F* **(4)** *is true for almost all x.*

(B') differs from the analogous **(B)** of Theorem 2 in that the exceptional 0-set for **(4)** can depend on A.

Say that *A is equal a.e. to B* if $A-B$ and $B-A$ are 0-sets. Say that two classes of sets are *equal modulo 0-sets* if every member of one is equal a.e. to some member of the other.

Assuming Axiom **(VI)** we get:

Corollary *If* $S \subset F$, *then:* (i) *The fields* $K[S]$, $K[K[S]]$ *and* $K[H[S]]$ *are equal modulo 0-sets.* (ii) *If S is a boolean algebra then* $H[S]$ *is equal modulo 0-sets to the field generated by* $S \cup K[S]$.

(To show, for example, that $K[S]=K[K[S]]$ modulo 0-sets, consider $C \in K[S]$; by Theorem 3, $\{x : p_x(C) \in \Delta\}$ is equal a.e. to C if $\Delta=[1,1]$, is equal a.e. to $W-C$ if $\Delta=[0,0]$, and is a 0-set if $0,1 \notin \Delta$. Hence, for all Δ, $PR(C,\Delta)$ is equal a.e. to one of: C, $W-C$, W, $\emptyset$. Since $K[K[S]]$ is generated by such sets, the claim follows.)

Roughly speaking, (ii) means that, modulo 0-sets, nested applications of PR reduce to non-nested applications. A stronger, syntactical version of this is given in the next section.

Probability Logic

Let Ξ be a set of reals such that $0,1 \in \Xi$. Call an interval with end-points in Ξ a Ξ-*interval*.

Let $\mathbf{PRL}_\Xi$ be the calculus obtained by adjoining sentential operants, $PR(\ ,\Delta)$, to the propositional calculus, where Δ ranges over all closed Ξ-intervals. Here, for the sake of convenience, I use 'PR' for the syntactical operant, as well as for the operation in HOPs. Given some class $\{X_i : i \in I\}$ of sentential variables, the class of all wffs (well formed formulas) of $\mathbf{PRL}_\Xi$ is the smallest such that:

- Every sentential variable is a wff

- If ϕ and ψ are wffs, so are $\neg\phi$ and $\phi*\psi$ where $*$ is any of the standard binary connectives.

- If ϕ is a wff and Δ is a closed Ξ-interval then $PR(\phi,\Delta)$ is a wff.

Let $H = (W,F,P,PR)$ be a simple HOP and let τ be a mapping which maps each sentential variable to a member of F. Then the value $|\phi|_{H,\tau}$ of the wff ϕ is defined by interpreting the sentential connectives as the corresponding Boolean operations and each syntactic operant $PR(\,,\Delta)$ as the operation $PR(\,,\Delta)$ of the HOP.

Definition A wff ϕ is *p-valid*, to be denoted $\models_p \phi$, if, for every simple HOP H which satisfies Axiom **(VI)** and every τ, the probability of $|\phi|_{H,\tau}$ is 1. Two wffs ϕ,ψ are *p-equivalent* if $\phi \leftrightarrow \psi$ is p-valid.

Call ϕ a *PC-formula* if it is a wff of the propositional calculus, i.e., does not contain any PR.

Theorem 4 *Every wff of* $\mathbf{PRL}_{\Xi}$ *is p-equivalent to a Boolean combination of PC-formulas and formulas of the form* $PR(\sigma,\Delta)$ *in which σ ranges over PC-formulas.*

This means that as far as probabilities are concerned (i.e., if we disregard 0-sets) we need not use nested PR's.

Theorem 5 *Translate into* $\mathbf{PRL}_{\Xi}$ *the wffs of propositional modal logic with the necessity operant N, by replacing each $N(\psi)$ by $PR(\psi, [1,1])$. Let ϕ^* be the translation of ϕ. Then*
$$S5 \vdash \phi \quad iff \quad \models_p \phi^*$$

Thus S5 becomes a fragment of $\mathbf{PRL}_{\Xi}$. This relation becomes more explicit if we rewrite '$PR(\psi,\Delta)$' as '$N_\Delta(\psi)$'.

It can be shown that for $\Xi =$ set of rationals the set of p-valid wffs is recursive. Also $\mathbf{PRL}_{\Xi}$ can be provided with a natural set of formal axioms so that, with modus ponens as derivation rule, p-validity coincides with provability.

Some Questions

Other validity notions can be considered (e.g., that $|\phi|_{H,\tau}$ always contains all coherent worlds in the HOP), as well as other interpretations of the necessity operant (e.g., as $\phi \wedge PR(\phi,[1,1])$). What modal logics are thereby obtained?

General HOPs

In general, a HOP is a stucture of the form:

$$(W, F, P, T, PR)$$

where, as before, (W, F, P) is a probability space, $T = (T, <)$ is a partially ordered set and where

$$PR : F \times T \times set\ of\ closed\ intervals \; \rightarrow \; F$$

$PR(A,t,\Delta)$ is the event that the probability of A at stage t lies in Δ. If the stages coincide with time points then the partial ordering of T is total. As before, P is the current subjective probability; here "current" is earlier (i.e., less than or equally informative) than the stages in T. Put:

$$PR_t(A,\Delta) =_{df} PR(A,t,\Delta)$$

The first five axioms (I^*) - (V^*) in this setting are the obvious generalizations of our previous axioms (I) -(V). Namely, we replace 'PR' by 'PR_t and require that the condition hold for all t in T.

Theorem 1 generalizes in the obvious way and we get, for each $t \in T$ and each $x \in W$, a probability $p_{t,x}$ which detemrines PR_t; it represents <u>the maximal state of knowledge at stage t in world x</u>.

The "correct" generalization of Axiom (VI) is not as obvious, but is not difficult to find:

Axiom (VI^*) *For each $t \in T$ the following holds: If C is a finite intersection of events of the form $PR_s(B,\Delta)$ where every s is $\leq t$, and $P(C \cap PR_t(A,[\alpha,\beta])) \neq 0$, then*

$$\alpha \; \leq \; P(A \mid C \cap PR_t(A,[\alpha,\beta])) \; \leq \; \beta$$

The argument for this axiom is the same as the argument for Axiom (VI). The essential point is that if $s \leq t$ then true events of the form $PR_s(B,\Delta)$ are known at stage t. The same Dutch book argument works for Axiom (VI^*).

As before, we consider fields generated by knowable events and define epistemic equivalence; but now these concepts depend on the stage parameter, to be displayed here as an additional subscript. Thus we put:

$$x \simeq_t y \; \leftrightarrow_{df} \; p_{t,x} = p_{t,y}$$

Then $x \simeq_t y$ iff $x \in A \leftrightarrow y \in A$, for all $A \in K_t[F]$.

Theorem 6   *Assume F to be countably generated, then Axiom (VI^*) is equivalent to the conjunction of:*

(D)   *For each $t \in T$ the simple HOP (W, F, P, PR_t) satisfies Axiom (VI).*

and

(E)   *For each $s \leq t$, $x \simeq_t y \Rightarrow x \simeq_s y$, for almost all x,y (i.e., for all $x,y \in W'$ where $P(W') = 1$).*

(E) means that, as we pass to more progressive stages, almost everywhere epistemic equivalence is the same or becomes stronger; the partition into equivalence classes can change only by becoming more refined.

Like Theorem 2 the last theorem has a version that applies to general fields but I shall not enter here into it. In the following theorem F is assumed to be countably generated.

Theorem 7   *Assume Axiom* (VI*). *Let $s \leq t$. Then, for almost all x, $p_{s,x}$ is a mixture of $p_{t,y}$'s (where y ranges over W).   Consequently, for almost all x, $(W, F, p_{s,x}, PR_t)$ is a simple HOP satisfying Axiom* (VI).

Logic of HOPs and Stage Dependent Modalities

Fix a partially ordered set $T = (T,<)$. The logic $\mathbf{PRL}_{\mathbf{g},T}$ (which corresponds to HOPs with set of stages T) is defined in the same way as $\mathbf{PRL}_{\mathbf{g}}$, except that PR has an additional argument ranging over T. As before we employ a systematically ambiguous notation. Define ϕ to be p-valid if it gets probability 1 in all HOPs in which the set of stages is T.

Now consider a propositional modal language, $\mathbf{M}_T$, in which we have, instead of a single necessity operant, an indexed family N_t, $t \in T$. $N_t\phi$ states that ϕ is necessary at stage t, i.e., necessary by virtue of the maximal knowledge available at that stage.

For $\phi \in \mathbf{M}_T$, let ϕ^* be the wff obtained by replacing each $N_t\psi$ by $PR_t(\psi, [1,1])$. It can be shown that the set of all ϕ in $\mathbf{M}_T$ such that ϕ^* is p-valid is exactly the set of wffs derivable, by modus ponens and the rule: if $\vdash\phi$ then $\vdash N_t\phi$, from the following axioms:

(i) All tautologies.   (ii) For each $t \in T$, the axiom schemas of S5, with N replaced by N_t, and

(iii) $N_s\phi \rightarrow N_t\phi$,   for each $s \leq t$.

Note that (iii) accords well with the intended meaning of the N_t's: If something is necessary at stage s it is also nesessary at later stages. On the other hand, something not necessary at stage s can be necessary later.

REFERENCES

Domotor, Z 1981   *Higher Order Probabilities* (Manuscript).

Gaifman, H. 1983   *Towards a Unified Concept of Probability* Manuscript of invited lecture to the 1983 International Congress for Logic Philosophy and Methodology of Science, Salzburg. To appear in the proceedings of the congress, North Holland.

Gardenfors, P. 1975
    Qualitative Probability as Intentional Logic Journal of Philosophical Logic 4, pp.171-185.

Good, I.J. 1965   The Estimation of Probabilities, Cambridge Massachusets.

Jaynes, E.T. 1958   Probability Theory in Science and Engineering, Dallas.

Kolmogoroff, A.N. 1933
    Grundbegriffe der Wahrscheinlichkeit Ergebnisse der Mathematik und ihrer Grenzgebitte, No 2, Berlin.

Miller, D. 1966   *A Paradox of Information* British Journal for the Philosophy of Science 17.

Skyrms, B. 1980A   *Higher Order Degrees of Belief* in "Prospects for Pragmatism" Essays in honor of F.P. Ramsey, ed. D.H. Mellor.

Skyrms, B. 1980B   Causal Necessity (Appendix 2), Yale New-Haven Conn.

van Frassen, B. 1984
    Belief and the Will Journal of Philosophy, No 81 pp. 235-256.

The list is far from being complete. Some important papers not mentioned in the abstract are to be found in Ifs, W. Harper ed. Boston Reidel,1981. Material related in a less direct way: non-probabilistic measures of certainty (e.g., the Dempster-Shafer measure), expert systems involving reasoning with uncertainties, probabilistic protocols and distributed systems, has not been included, but should be included in a fuller exposition.

ON EPISTEMIC LOGIC AND LOGICAL OMNISCIENCE

Moshe Y. Vardi

IBM Almaden Research Center
650 Harry Road
San Jose, CA 95120-6099

Abstract

We consider the logical omniscience problem of epistemic logic. We argue that the problem is due to the way in which knowledge and belief are captured in Hintikka's possible worlds semantics. We describe an alternative approach in which propositions are sets of worlds, and knowledge and belief are simply a list of propositions for each agent. The problem of the circularity in the definition is solved by giving a constructive definition of belief and knowledge worlds. We show how to incorporate notions such as reasoning and context of use in our model. We also demonstrate the power of our approach by showing how we can emulate in it other epistemic models.

> *"Do I contradict myself?*
> *Very well, then, I contradict myself.*
> *(I am large, I contain multitudes.)"*
>   Walt Whitman

1. Introduction

Epistemic logic, the logic of epistemic notions such as *knowledge* and *belief*, is a major area of research in artificial intelligence (cf. [FH85, Ko80, Le84, MH69, Mo85, XW83]). The major existing formal model of knowledge and belief, originated by Hintikka [Hi62], is based on the *possible worlds* approach. The basic notion of this approach is a set W of alternative worlds. Knowledge and belief of an agent, who is situated in the actual world w, consist of the agent distinguishing a subset W' of W as the set of worlds that are possible alternatives to w. Thus the agent knows or believes p in w if p is true in all the worlds in W'

A fundamental problem with this model is the so called *logical omniscience* problem [Hi75]. Essentially, the problem is that an agent always knows all the logical consequences of her knowledge. That is, if agent a knows p and if p logically implies q, then a also knows q. In particular, a knows all valid sentences. (The problem with belief is analogous.) This situation is, of course, unintuitive and unrealistic.

One can accept this situation by endowing the epistemic notions with new pre-systematic interpretations. For example, one can restrict oneself to idealized agent with unbounded reasoning power [Mo85], or one can reinterpret knowledge and belief to be *implicit* rather then *explicit*, i.e., a believes p if p follows from a's explicit beliefs [HM84, Le84, RP85]. But this leaves us in want of a precise treatment of knowledge and belief in the customary senses.

As was pointed out by Cresswell [Cr70, Cr72, Cr73], the problem of logical omniscience can be dealt with by allowing *non-classical* worlds in our semantics, that is, worlds in which not all valid (in the standard sense of valid) formulas need be true, or in which inconsistent formulas may be true. (A weaker notion of a similar kind is contained in Kripke's notion of non-normal worlds [Kr65].) Such worlds are called *impossible* in [Hi75] and *nonstandard* in [RB79]. This approach was pursued further by Levesque [Le84], where the non-classical worlds are called, following [BP83], "situations". (Levesque claims that his approach is different from the possible worlds approach. A closer examination, however, shows that Levesque is actually pursuing the nonclassical possible worlds approach advocated by Cresswell.)

The non-classical worlds approach fails, however, to supply a satisfying solution to the logical omniscience problem for two reasons. First, the intuition behind the non-classical worlds, and in particular the inconsistent ones (called in [Le84] "incoherent situations"), is not clear at all. Thus it is far from obvious how to define the semantics of logical connectives in such worlds. Secondly, and worse, it turns out that the addition of non-classical worlds does not make the agents any less logically omniscient, but rather it just changes the logic in which the agents reason. That is, the agents still believe in all the "logical consequences" of their beliefs, where these are not the standard logical consequences but rather the logical consequences in some nonstandard logical system. For example, the agents in Levesque's model [Le84] turn out to be perfect reasoners in Anderson's and Belnap's *relevance logic* [AB75]. Unfortunately, it does not seem that agents can reason perfectly in relevance logic any more than in classical logic.

We believe that the roots of the logical omniscience problem lie not only in the structure of the worlds (i.e., whether they are classical or non-classical) but also in the very fundamental way in which epistemic notions are captured in Hintikka's possible worlds approach [Hi62]. Let us have a closer look at the role played by the worlds.

At the most fundamental level, possible worlds theory is a theory that takes alternative possibilities as its basic primitive notion. While this theory is controversial in some circles (see [Ma73, St76, St85] for arguments pro and con), we are willing to accept it. The only assumption that this theory makes is that there are many *conceivable* states of affairs. Hintikka in [Hi62] went further to model knowledge and belief as a a relation between these conceivable states. According to this approach, at any state an agent has in mind a set of states that are *possible* relative to that state (the set of possible states is a subset of the set of all conceivable states). It is this set of possible states that captures the agent's knowledge or belief. Unfortunately, this way of capturing epistemic notions is far from being intuitive, and goes a long way beyond the basic assumption underlying the possible worlds theory. Thus by modelling knowledge and belief the way he did, Hintikka made a dubious metaphysical commitment, whose side-effect is the logical omniscience problem.

In the rest of this paper we study another approach that still has possible worlds as its basic notion, but does not make the metaphysical commitment made by Hintikka. The outline of the paper is as follows. In §2 we describe Montague's approach to modelling epistemic notions (since we wish to make as few metaphysical assumptions as possible we consider belief rather than knowledge), and we describe the shortcomings of that approach. In §3 we describe our approach, and we investigate its properties. In §4 we show how to model different modes of reasoning in our approach. §5 compares our approach with other approaches for modelling belief that have been suggested in the literature. We conclude with some comments in §6.

2. Belief in Propositions

The most simplistic way to model belief is by *belief sets*. Let L be the assertion language. Then a belief set for an agent a is a set of sentences of L. Intuitively, a believes that ϕ, where ϕ is a sentence of L, if and only if ϕ is in the belief set of a. This model makes no assumptions on the nature of belief. In fact not only can a have contradictory beliefs, but also a can even believe in inconsistent sentences such as $p \wedge \neg p$. Representing an agent's beliefs by a set of sentences in the basic idea underlying the models in [Eb74], [Ko83], [Ko85], and [MH79]. This approach, in which "a believes that" is viewed as a predicate on sentences rather than a sentential connective, is called in [Le84] the *syntactic* approach. Let us look now at the semantic analogue of this approach.

Let W be the set of all possible worlds, and suppose that the notion of *satisfaction* of a sentence ϕ in a world w, denoted $w \models \phi$, is defined. For the moment let us not worry about how worlds and satisfaction are defined. The *intension* of a sentence ϕ is the set of worlds in which it is satisfied, i.e., $I(\phi) = \{w : w \models \phi\}$. In this framework, the semantics of ϕ is fully determined by its intension. Thus if two sentences ϕ and ψ have the same intension, i.e., $I(\phi) = I(\psi)$, then they are *semantically equivalent*; in fact, they are *semantically synonymous*. Thus in a semantical model of belief, i.e., a model where agents believe in semantical objects and not in syntactical objects, agents cannot discern between synonymous sentences. So if a believes that ϕ, then she also believes that ψ.

Does such a model solve the logical omniscience problem? It does and it does not. It does because it is no longer the case that if a believes that ϕ and if ϕ semantically implies ψ, then a believes that ψ. In particular, an agent does not have to believe in all valid sentences, and it can believe in contradictory sentences. Nevertheless, if a believes that ϕ and if ϕ is semantically equivalent to ψ, then a believes that ψ. The latter phenomenon is, however, unavoidable as long as one wishes to keep the basic framework of the possible worlds approach and view "a believes that" as a sentential connective that applies to intensions. We refer the reader to [Cr85,Th80] where different approaches to propositional attitudes are taken, and we continue with the study of the possible worlds approach.

In trying to formalize the model, we encounter the difficulty that our informal definitions are in some sense circular. In order to define worlds, we have to define belief, in order to define belief, we have to define semantical equivalence, and in order to define semantical equivalence, we have to define worlds. To get around that difficulty we make the following observation. The relation of semantical equivalence partitions the set of all sentences of L into equivalence classes. Rather than saying that a believes that ϕ, we can say that a believes that $[\phi]$, where $[\phi]$ is the equivalence class of ϕ. Since all sentences in an equivalence class have the same intension, there is a natural correspondence between subsets of W and equivalence classes. Thus rather than list all the equivalence classes in which a believes, we can list the corresponding subsets of W (which are the intensions of the equivalence classes). That is, we can say that an agent's belief is a set of *propositions*, where a proposition is a set of worlds.

This motivates the following definition. We assume a set $\mathbf{P}$ of atomic propositions and a set $\mathbf{A}$ of agents. A *belief structure* is a triple $M=(W,N,\Pi)$, where W is a nonempty set, which we take to be the set of possible worlds, $\Pi:\mathbf{P}\rightarrow 2^W$ gives the intensions of the atomic propositions, and $N:\mathbf{A}\times W\rightarrow 2^{2^W}$ assigns to every agent the set of propositions in which the agent believes in any world.[1]

The language L is the smallest set that contains $\mathbf{P}$, is closed under Boolean connectives and contains $B_a\phi$ ("a believes that ϕ") if ϕ is in L and a is in $\mathbf{A}$. We now can define what it means for a world w in M to satisfy formulas.

- $M,w\models p$, where $p\in\mathbf{P}$, if $w\in\Pi(p)$.
- $M,w\models\neg\phi$ if $M,w\not\models\phi$.
- $M,w\models\phi\wedge\psi$ if $M,w\models\phi$ and $M,w\models\psi$.
- $M,w\models B_a\phi$ if $\{u:M,u\models\phi\}\in N(a,w)$ (that is, $B_a\phi$ is satisfied in w if the intension of ϕ is among the propositions that a believes in w).

What we have described so far is essentially Montague's *intensional logic* of belief [Mo70]. We find it, however, quite unsatisfying, for two reasons. First, this approach leaves the notion of a possible world as a primitive notion, and it does not gives us any intuition about the nature of these worlds. While this might be

---

[1] If there is only one agent then N can be taken as a function $N:W\rightarrow 2^{2^W}$. Such structures are called in the literature *neighborhood structures* [Se72] or *minimal structures* [Ch80]. They were introduced for technical reasons, which are unrelated to epistemic logic, by Montague [Mo68], who used them to interpret his *pragmatic* language, and Scott [Sc70].

seen as an advantage by the logician whose interest is in epistemic logic, it is a disadvantage for the "user" of epistemic logic whose interest is mostly in using the framework to model belief states. One might say that belief structure are models for epistemic logic and not for epistemic notions. For a further elaboration of this point see [FHV84,FV85]. Secondly, since the above approach does not elaborate on the issue of the nature of the possible worlds, it also leaves open the question of where one gets the set W of possible worlds in the first place. Note that the choice of W is quite significant, since it determines the relation of semantical equivalence, which we want to make as weak as possible. In the next section we describe another approach towards modelling belief in propositions.

3. Belief Worlds

In this section we define belief worlds constructively. This enables us to take W to be the set of *all* possible worlds. As a result, the relation of semantical equivalence will be as weak as it can be, i.e., it will be the relation of logical equivalence.

Basically, a world consists of a truth assignment to the atomic propositions and a collection of sets of worlds. This is, of course, a circular definition, and to make it meaningful we follow the methodology used in [FHV84, FV84, Va85], and define worlds inductively according to their *depth*.[2] A world of depth 0 is a truth assignment to the atomic propositions; a world of depth 1 is essentially a collection of sets of worlds of depth 0; a world of depth 2 is essentially a collection of sets of worlds of depth 1; etc. This process can be carried out to the limit, giving us worlds of infinite depth.

Formally, we define a *0th-order assignment*, f_0, to be a truth assignment $f_0 : P \rightarrow \{0,1\}$ to the atomic propositions. We call $<f_0>$ a *1–ary world* (since its "length" is 1). Assume inductively that k-ary worlds $<f_0, \ldots, f_{k-1}>$ have been defined. Let W_k be the set of all k-ary worlds. A *kth-order assignment* is a function $f_k : A \rightarrow 2^{2^{W_k}}$. Intuitively, f_k associates with each agent a set of propositions, where each proposition is a set of k-ary worlds. There is a "compatibility" restriction on f_k's, which we shall discuss shortly. We call $<f_0, \ldots, f_k>$ a *(k+1)-ary world*. An infinite sequence $<f_0, f_1, f_2, \ldots>$, where each *prefix* $<f_0, \ldots, f_{k-1}>$ is a k-ary world, is called an *infinitary* world, to distinguish it from *finitary* worlds. W_ω is the set of infinitary worlds (there are uncountably many of them), and $\mathbf{W}$ is the set of all worlds.

The restriction that we mentioned earlier ensures that each level extends the preceding levels. That is, if we take the propositions in the $(k+1)$st level, and chop off their kth level, we should get the propositions of the kth level. To define this restriction formally, we need the following definition. Let $X \subseteq W_k$. Then $chop(X)$ is the set of worlds obtained by chopping off the last level in the worlds in X, that is,

$$chop(X) = \{<f_0, \ldots, f_{k-2}> \; : \; <f_0, \ldots, f_{k-2}, f_{k-1}> \in X\}.$$

We can now state the restriction as:

$$f_{k-1}(a) = \{chop(X) \; : \; X \in f_k(a)\}$$

---

[2] In [FHV84, FV84, Va85] this methodology is used to model epistemic notions in the aforementioned Hintikka style.

The reader might be annoyed by the fact that we can carry our construction to the limit, assuming somehow an infinite amount of information. Nevertheless, in the next section we shall see that infinitary worlds can arise naturally.

We now define what it means for a finitary belief world to *satisfy* a formula of L.

- $<f_0, \ldots, f_r> \models p$, where p is a atomic proposition, if $f_0(p)=1$.

- $<f_0, \ldots, f_r> \models \neg\phi$ if $<f_0, \ldots, f_r> \not\models \phi$.

- $<f_0, \ldots, f_r> \models \phi/\backslash\psi$ if $<f_0, \ldots, f_r> \models \phi$ and $<f_0, \ldots, f_r> \models \psi$.

- $<f_0, \ldots, f_r> \models B_a\phi$ if $r \geq 1$ and $\{w : w \in W_r$ and $w \models \phi\} \in f_r(a)$ (in particular, $<f_0> \not\models B_a\phi$.)

Since in our belief worlds higher levels always extend lower levels, to determine satisfaction it suffices to consider a long enough prefix. To formalize this statement we need to define *depth* of formulas, which is intuitively the depth of nesting of belief modalities.

- $depth(p)=0$, if p is atomic propositions.

- $depth(\neg\phi)=depth(\phi)$.

- $depth(\phi/\backslash\psi)=max\{depth(\phi), depth(\psi)\}$.

- $depth(B_a(\phi))=1+depth(\phi)$.

Lemma 1: Assume that $depth(\phi)=k$ and $r \geq k$. Then $<f_0, \ldots, f_r> \models \phi$ iff $<f_0, \ldots, f_k> \models \phi$. []

Note, however, that the satisfaction relation is defined between all worlds and all formulas, regardless of the arity of the worlds and the depth of the formulas. The reader who is familiar with [FHV84, FV85, Va85] should note the difference in the methodology here and in those papers. Here we consider both finitary worlds and infinitary worlds to be full-fledged objects, while in the aforementioned papers finitary worlds are merely building blocks of infinitary worlds.

We can now define satisfaction for infinitary worlds. We say that the infinitary world $w=<f_0, f_1, \cdots>$ satisfies ϕ, written $w \models \phi$, if $<f_0, \ldots, f_k> \models \phi$, where $k=depth(\phi)$. This is a reasonable definition, since if $w' = <f_0, \ldots, f_r>$ is an arbitrary prefix of w such that $r \geq k$, it then follows from Lemma 1 that $w \models \phi$ iff $w' \models \phi$.

We now want to show that worlds can be extended *conservatively*, i.e., without changing the agents' beliefs. Let us say that two worlds w_1 and w_2 are *equivalent*, denoted $w_1 \equiv w_2$, if they satisfy exactly the same formulas, i.e., if $w_1 \models \phi$ if and only if $w_2 \models \phi$, for all formulas ϕ in L.

Theorem 2: For every k-ary world $w=<f_0, \ldots, f_{k-1}>$ there is a $(k+1)$-ary world $w' = <f_0, \ldots, f_{k-1}, f_k>$, such that $w \equiv w'$. Furthermore, for every k-ary world $w=<f_0, \ldots, f_{k-1}>$ there is an infinitary world $w' = <f_0, \ldots, f_{k-1}, f_k, \cdots>$, such that $w \equiv w'$. []

(This theorem does not have an analogue in [FHV84, FV85, Va85], since there the satisfaction relation between worlds and formulas is a partial relation.)

A formula ϕ is *valid* if it is satisfied by all belief worlds. Clearly if $depth(\phi)=k$, then it suffices to consider $(k+1)$-ary worlds. Since only finitely many worlds need be considered, we get:

Theorem 3: The validity problem for belief worlds is decidable. []

We can also axiomatize validity in the following way:

Theorem 4: The following formal system is sound and complete for validity in belief worlds:

(A1) All substitution instances of propositional tautologies.

(R1) From $\phi \equiv \psi$ infer $B_a \phi \equiv B_a \psi$. []

Thus validity is fully characterized by propositional reasoning plus substitutivity of equivalents. It follows that the logic of belief worlds is the generalization of the modal logic E [Ch80] to include multiple modalities.

We can now relate belief worlds, as defined in this section, to belief structures, as defined in the previous section. Intuitively, what we want to do is to construct a belief structure M so that the worlds in that structure will correspond to belief worlds. The natural choice for the set of possible worlds in M is, of course, the set $\mathbf{W}$ of all belief worlds. By Theorem 2, we can restrict ourselves, without loss of generality, to W_ω, the set of infinitary worlds. Also, it is easy to define the interpretation for atomic propositions. The nontrivial part is to define N. To do this we need some definitions.

Let $X \subseteq W_\omega$ be a set of infinitary worlds. Then $prefix_k(X)$ is the set of k-ary worlds that are prefixes of worlds in X. That is, $prefix_k(X)$ is the set

$$\{<f_0, \ldots, f_{k-1}> : <f_0, \ldots, f_{k-1}, f_k, \cdots > \in X\}$$

Let $w = <f_0, f_1, \ldots> \in W_\omega$, and $a \in \mathbf{A}$. We define $N_a(w)$ as the collection

$$\{X : X \subseteq W_\omega \text{ and } prefix_k(X) \in f_k(a), \text{for all } k \geq 0\}.$$

We can now define the desired belief structure.

Theorem 5: Let $M_b = (W_\omega, N, \Pi)$ be a belief structure, where W_ω is the set of all infinitary worlds, $\Pi(p) = \{w : w \models p\}$ for $p \in \mathbf{P}$, and $N(a, w) = N_a(w)$. Then $M, \mathbf{f} \models \phi$ if and only if $\mathbf{f} \models \phi$, for all formulas ϕ of L. []

Thus our approach has lead us to select a particular belief structure as the standard one, in the sense that for this structure semantical equivalence and logical equivalence are identical.

Theorem 5 claims that there is a belief structure that model the collection of all belief worlds. Thus belief structures are as expressive as belief worlds. One may suspect, however, that belief worlds are not as expressive as belief structures. The reason for this suspicion is as follows. The semantics of a possible world w in a belief structure $M = (W, N, \Pi)$ depends on three parameters: (a) the atomic propositions that are true in w, (b) $N(a, w)$ for each agent a, and (c) the set W. The set W is the *context* in which the agents operate [Cr73, Mo70, St80]; it is the set of possibilities that it is the point of the discourse to distinguish between; it is the set of possibilities that are compatible with the agents' *constraints* [BP83]. The presence of context is what makes belief structure adequate to interpret *pragmatic* languages [Mo68].[3] Belief worlds, on the other hand, seem not to have any notion of variable context. Put differently, belief worlds have a standard fixed context -

---

[3] According to Morris [Mo38], *pragmatics* is concerned with relations between linguistic expressions, the objects to which they refer, and the contexts of use of the expressions. The other two branches in the study of language are *syntax*, which is concerned with relations among linguistic expressions, and *semantics*, which is concerned with relations between expressions and the object to which they refer.

the set W. Thus it seems that in our effort to find a standard context we have lost the ability to model all other contexts. Surprisingly, this is not the case!

Theorem 6. Let $M=(W,N,\Pi)$ be a belief structure, and let $w\in W$. Then there is a belief world $\mathbf{f}_w$ such that $M,w\models\phi$ if and only if $\mathbf{f}_w\models\phi$, for all formulas ϕ of L. []

Theorem 6 is superficially similar to certain theorems in [FHV84, FV85, Va85], but its proof is quite different. The difference stems from the fact that the theorems in those papers deal with Kripke semantics that does not have the context component that Montague semantics (or rather pragmatics) has.

4. Reasoning

The agents in our model have very little reasoning power. This is clearly demonstrated by the fact that the formulas $B_a\phi/\backslash B_a\psi$ and $B_a(\phi/\backslash\psi)$ are incomparable, i.e., either of them can be satisfied in some belief world w, while the other is not satisfied in w. Suppose now that we do want to endow the agents with some reasoning power (which is probably the case if the agents we have in mind are supposed to have some intelligence). Here is a sample of formulas that we may want to be valid in our models:

(B1) $\neg B_a\mathbf{false}$

(B2) $B_a\mathbf{true}$.

(B3) $B_a(\phi/\backslash\psi)\supset B_a\phi$.

(B4) $B_a\phi/\backslash B_a\psi\supset B_a(\phi/\backslash\psi)$.

Let us see now what conditions we have to put on belief structures to capture these modes of reasoning. It turns out that B1-B4 can be captured by imposing certain algebraic restrictions on belief worlds $<f_0,\ldots,f_k\cdots>$.

Consider first B1 and B2. The intension of **false** is the empty set, so to ensure that agents do not have false beliefs, we require that $\emptyset\notin f_k(a)$, for all $k\geq 1$. The intension of **true** is the set of all worlds, so to ensure that agents believe in true things, we require that $W_{k-1}\in f_k(a)$, for all $k\geq 1$. Note though that if a does not believe that **false**, then she does not believe any contradictory formula. Similarly, if a believes that **true**, then she believes all valid formulas.

Consider now B3 and B4. We know that the intension of $\phi/\backslash\psi$ is the intersection of the intensions of ϕ and ψ. Thus to capture B3 we require that if $X\subseteq Y\subseteq W_k$ and $X\in f_k(a)$, then also $Y\in f_k(a)$, for all $k\geq 1$, and to capture B4 we require that whenever $X,Y\in f_k(a)$ then also $(X\cap Y)\in f_k(a)$, for all $k\geq 1$.

Note that B3 and B4 characterize completely different modes of reasoning. B3 characterizes drawing conclusion from individual facts one believes in, while B4 characterizes putting these facts together. If a believes that p when she thinks that the probability that p is true is very high, then a may employ B3 but not B4. The rationale for that is that if $\phi/\backslash\psi$ is very probable, then so are ϕ and ψ, but if ϕ and ψ are very probable, it does not necessarily entail that $\phi/\backslash\psi$ is very probable. (This explains the *lottery paradox* [Ky61]. One can believe for every particular lottery ticket holder x that x will not win the lottery, while still believing that someone will win the lottery.) We come back to this mode of reasoning in the next section.

Consider now reasoning that agents can do that involves introspection rather than deduction. Introspection about one's own beliefs can take two forms:

(B5) $B_a\phi \supset B_a B_a \phi$

(B6) $\neg B_a\phi \supset B_a \neg B_a \phi$.

In B5 agents are aware of their beliefs and in B6 they are aware of their doubts. For a discussion of epistemic introspection see [Le78]. The conditions needed to capture B5 and B6 are less intuitive than the restriction needed to capture B1-B4. To capture B5 we require that for all $k \geq 1$ if $X \in f_k(a)$, then $\{<g_0, \ldots, g_k> : X \in g_k(a)\} \in f_{k+1}(a)$. To capture B6 we require that for all $k \geq 1$ if $X \notin f_k(a)$, then $\{<g_0, \ldots, g_k> : X \notin g_k(a)\} \in f_{k+1}(a)$.

The restrictions that capture B5 and B6 have the significant consequence that they force the worlds to be infinitary. In other words, in finitary worlds agents do not have unlimited introspection, since introspection, by its reflexive nature, generates arbitrarily deep beliefs.

Finally, we mention how to modify belief worlds to obtain *knowledge* worlds. There is a general agreement that one property that distinguishes knowledge from belief is that the former is by definition correct. That is, if an agent knows that ϕ, then ϕ must be true; otherwise we would not have said that the agents know that ϕ, but rather we would have said that the agent believes that ϕ. It is not hard to see that in order to capture this property we have to require that $<f_0, \ldots, f_{k-1}> \in X$ for all $X \in f_k(a)$.

5. Models for Local Reasoning

It is well known that neighborhood semantics is more expressive than Kripke semantics. To further demonstrate the power of our approach we compare it here to models for belief with a particular mode of reasoning. We show that belief worlds can emulate two variants of Kripke structures.

In the previous section we saw different modes of reasoning that agents may employ. Let us consider again the reasoning characterized by B1, B2, and B3. The interpretation that we gave to that mode of reasoning was that a believe that ϕ if she thinks the the probability that ϕ is true is very high. Another possible interpretation is that agents have multiple "frame of minds" or "dispositions". Thus, a may believe that ϕ in one frame of mind, and she may believe that ψ in another frame of mind, but she never puts ϕ and ψ together to infer that $\phi /\backslash \psi$. This mode of reasoning, which we call *local reasoning* following [FH85], has been considered by several authors [FH85, Le85, RB79, St85, Za85], who modelled it by different variants of Hintikka semantics. Our aim in this section is to show that our models and the models studied in the aforementioned papers are essentially equivalent.

The model that we have for local reasoning is belief worlds $<f_0, \ldots, f_k \cdots >$ that satisfy the following constraints, for all $a \in A$ and $k \geq 1$:

- $\emptyset \notin f_k(a)$.

- $W_{k-1} \in f_k(a)$.

- If $X \subseteq Y \subseteq W_{k-1}$ and $X \in f_k(a)$, then $Y \in f_k(a)$.

We call these worlds *belief worlds for local reasoning* or, for short, *LR belief worlds*. We now describe two other approaches to modelling local reasoning that have been suggested in the literature.

Several authors have suggested modelling local reasoning by the following variant of Hintikka semantics. In Hintikka semantics each agents has a set of worlds that are thought as possible alternative. In the suggested variant, each agent has a collection of sets of worlds, where each set constitutes the alternatives in one frame of mind [FH85, Le85, St85, Za85]. An agent a believes that ϕ if ϕ is true in all alternatives in some frame of mind of A. Formally, an *FHLSZ belief structure* is a belief structure, i.e, it is a triple $M=(W,N,\Pi)$, where W is a nonempty set of worlds, $\Pi:\mathbf{P}\to 2^W$, and $N:\mathbf{A}\times W\to 2^{2^W}$. Here we interpret N an an assignment to agents of collection of sets of alternatives. Because we interpret N differently from before, the definition of satisfaction is also different.

- $M,w\models p$, where $p\in\mathbf{P}$, if $w\in\Pi(P)$.

- $M,w\models\neg\phi$ if $M,w\not\models\phi$.

- $M,w\models\phi/\backslash\psi$ if $M,w\models\phi$ and $M,w\models\psi$.

- $M,w\models B_a\phi$ if for some $U\in N(a,w)$ we have that $M,u\models\phi$ for all $u\in U$.

Note that, even though FHLSZ belief structures look like belief structures, their semantics is closer to Kripke semantics than to Montague semantics.

Rescher and Brandon have suggested using *non-standard* possible worlds to model local reasoning [RB79]. Non-standard worlds are built from other worlds by two operations: *schematization* and *superposition*. The schematization operation combines worlds conjunctively. Thus, p holds in the schematization of u and v, denoted $u\cap v$, if p holds both in u and v. The superposition operation combines worlds disjunctively. Thus, p holds in the superposition of u and v, denoted $u\cup v$, if p holds in either u or v. Note that conjunctive worlds can be fuzzy, we can have that neither p nor $\neg p$ holds in $u\cap v$, while disjunctive worlds can be over determined, we can have that both p and $\neg p$ hold in $u\cup v$. We now proceed with formal definitions.

Let W be a set of worlds. We define the class of *non-standard possible worlds expressions* (expressions, for short) as the smallest class $\mathbf{E}$ that is closed under the following closure conditions:

- $W\subseteq\mathbf{E}$.

- If $w_i\in\mathbf{E}$ for all i in an index set I, then $\underset{i\in I}{\cap}w_i\in\mathbf{E}$.

- If $w_i\in\mathbf{E}$ for all i in an index set I, then $\underset{i\in I}{\cup}w_i\in\mathbf{E}$.

We now define *non-standard* (NS) belief structures. (Note: NS belief structures have not been defined in [RB79]. Our treatment, however, is based on ideas from [RB79].) An NS belief structure is a triple $M=(W,N,\Pi)$, where W is a nonempty set, $\Pi:\mathbf{P}\to 2^W$, and $N:\mathbf{A}\times W\to\mathbf{E}$. Here N assigns to each agent a non-standard world that the agent believes is the actual world. The divergence from Hintikka semantics is that there are no alternative worlds here. Rather, the agent believes that she exists in some particular world, albeit a non-standard one.

Satisfaction of formulas in worlds is defined as follows.

- $M,w\models p$, where $p\in\mathbf{P}$, if $w\in\Pi(P)$.

- $M,w\models\neg\phi$ if $M,w\not\models\phi$.

- $M,w\models\phi/\backslash\psi$ if $M,w\models\phi$ and $M,w\models\psi$.

- If $N(a,w)=\underset{i\in I}{\cap}w_i$, then $M,w\models B_a\phi$ if $M,w_i\models\phi$ for all $i\in I$.

- If $N(a,w)= \bigcup_{i\in I} w_i$, then $M,w\models B_a\phi$ if $M,w_i\models\phi$ for some $i\in I$.

Our main result in this section is that the three approaches to local reasoning that we have described above, which seem on the surface to be rather different, are essentially equivalent.

Theorem 7.

(1)   Let $\mathbf{f}$ be an LR belief world. Then there is an FHLSZ belief structure M and a world w in M such that $\mathbf{f}\models\phi$ if and only if $M,w\models\phi$ for all formulas ϕ of L.

(2)   Let M be an FHLSZ belief structure, and let w be a world in M. Then there is an NS belief world N and a world u in N such that such that $M,w\models\phi$ if and only if $N,u\models\phi$ for all formulas ϕ of L.

(3)   Let M be an NS belief structure, and let w be a world in M. Then there is an LR belief world $\mathbf{f}$ such that such that $M,w\models\phi$ if and only if $\mathbf{f}\models\phi$ for all formulas ϕ of L.   []

6. Concluding Remarks

We have presented a framework in which epistemic notions are modelled by sets of propositions, where propositions are sets of possible worlds, and have shown how notions such as reasoning and context of use can be incorporated in the framework. We have also demonstrated the power of our approach by showing how we can emulate in it other epistemic models. Our framework alleviates the logical omniscience problem, but does not solve it completely - we still have substitutivity of equivalents in epistemic contexts. We now suggest two lines of possible attack on the problem.

First, one can try to incorporate the nonclassical worlds approach with our approach (cf. [Cr70, Cr72, RB79]). As we have argued before, this cannot solve the problem, but merely changes the standard logical system into a nonstandard one. An weakening of the logical system might, however, be desirable.

Alternatively, one can accept the fact the epistemic notions are not purely intensional. Rather than discard all semantics and embrace fully the aforementioned syntactic approach, one can try to inject small doses of syntax into the semantics (cf. [Cr75, FH85, Ra82]).

Acknowledgements.   Part of this research was done while I was visiting the Center for Study of Language and Information at Stanford University with support from the System Development Foundation. I was inspired to investigate the model described in this paper by stimulating discussions with Ron Fagin and Joe Halpern about their model for limited reasoning [FH85]. I'd also like to thank Ron Fagin, Joe Halpern, Yoram Moses, and Ed Wimmers for their helpful comments on previous drafts of this paper.

REFERENCES

[BP83]   Barwise, J., Perry, J.: *Situations and Attitudes*, Bradford Books, Cambridge, 1983.

[Ch80]   Chellas, B.F.: *Modal logic.* Cambridge Univ. Press, 1980.

[Cr70]   Cresswell, M.J.: Classical intensional logics. *Theoria* 36(1970), pp. 347-372.

[Cr72]   Cresswell, M.J.: Intensional logics and logical truth. *J. Philosophical Logic* 1(1972), pp. 2-15.

[Cr73]   Cresswell, M.J.: *Logic and Languages*, Methuen, London, 1873.

[Cr75]   Cresswell, M.J.: Hyperintensional logic. *Studia Logica* 34(1975), pp. 25-38.

[Cr85]   Cresswell, M.J.: *Structured Meanings.* MIT Press, 1985.

[Eb74]   Eberle, R.A: The logic of believing, knowing, and inferring. *Synthese* 26(1974), pp. 356-382.

[FH85]   Fagin, R., Halpern, J.Y.: Belief, awareness, and limited reasoning. *Proc. 9th Int'l Joint Conf. on Artificial Intelligence*, Los Angeles, 1985, pp. 491-501.

[FHV84]   Fagin, R., Halpern, J.Y., Vardi, M.Y.: A model-theoretic analysis of knowledge. *Proc. 25th IEEE Symp. on Foundations of Computer Science*, West Palm Beach, 1984, pp. 268-278.

[FV84]   Fagin, R., Vardi, M.Y.: An internal semantics for modal logic. *Proc. 17th ACM Symp. on Theory of Computing* Providence, 1985, pp. 305-315.

[Hi62]   Hintikka, J.: *Knowledge and belief.* Cornell Univ. Press, 1962.

[Hi75]   Hintikka, J.: Impossible possible worlds vindicated. *J. Philosophy* 4(1975), pp. 475-484.

[HM84]   Halpern, J.Y., Moses, Y.: Knowledge and common knowledge in distributed environments. *Proc. 3rd ACM Symp. on Distributed Computing*, 1984, pp. 50-61.

[Ko80]   Konolige, K.: A first-order formalization of knowledge and action for a multi-agent planning system. In *Machine Intelligence* 10 (J.E.Hayes, K.Michie, and Y-H. Pao, eds.), Ellis Howrood Limited, Chichester, England, 1982.

[Ko83]   Konolige, K.: A deductive model of belief. *Proc. 8th Int'l Joint Conf. on AI*, 1983, pp. 377-381.

[Ko80]   Konolige, K.: Belief and incompleteness. In *Formal Theories of the Commonsense World* (J.R. Hobbs and R.C. Moore, eds.), Ablex Publishing Company, 1985, pp. 359-404.

[Kr75]   Kripke, S.A.: Semantical analysis of modal logic II : Non-normal propositional calculi. In *The theory of models* (L. Henkin and A. Tarski, eds.), North-Holland, 1965, pp. 206-220.

[Ky61]   Kyburg, H.: *Probability and the logic of rational belief.* Wesleyan Univ. Press, 1961.

[Le78]   Lenzen, W.: Recent work in epistemic logic. *Acta Phil. Fenn.* 30(1978), pp. 1-219.

[Le84]   Levesque, H.J.: A logic of implicit and explicit belief. Proc. National Conf. on Artificial Intelligence, 1984, pp. 198-202.

[Le85]   Levesque, H.J.: *Global and local consistency and completeness of beliefs.* Unpublished manuscript, 1985.

[Ma73]   Mackie, J.L.: *Truth, probability, and paradox.* Clarendon Press, 1973.

[MH69]   McCarthy, J., Hayes, P.J.: Some philosophical problems from the standpoint of artificial intelligence. In *Machine Intelligence* 4 (B. Meltzer and D. Michie, eds.), Edinburgh Univ. Press 1969, pp. 463-502.

[MH79]   Moore, R.C., Hendrix, G.: Computational models of beliefs and the semantics of belief-sentences. Technical Note 187, SRI International, AI Center, 1979.

[Mo38]   Morris, C.: *Foundations of the theory of signs.* Univ. of Chicago Press, 1938.

[Mo68]   Montague, R.: Pragmatics. In *Contemporary Philosophy* (R. Kalibansky, ed.), La Nuova Italia Editrice, Florence, 1968, pp. 102-121.

[Mo70]   Montague, R.: Universal grammar. *Theoria* 36(1970), pp. 373-398.

[Mo85]   Moore, R.C.: A formal theory of knowledge and action. In *Formal Theories of the Commonsense World* (J.R. Hobbs and R.C. Moore, eds.), Ablex Publishing Company, 1985, pp. 319-358.

[Pu70]   Purtill, R.L.: Believing the impossible. *Ajatus* 32(1970), pp. 18-24.

[Ra82]   Rantala, V.: Impossible worlds semantics and logical omniscience. *Acta Phil. Fenn.* 35(1982), pp. 106-115.

[RB79]   Rescher, N., Brandon, R.: *The logic of inconsistency.* Rowman and Littlefield, 1979.

[RP85]   Rosenschein, S.J., Pereira, C.N.: *Knowledge and action in situated automata.* Forthcoming.

[Sa82]   Saarinen, E.: Propositional attitudes are not attitudes towards propositions. *Acta Phil. Fenn.* 35(1982), pp. 131-162.

[Sc70]   Scott, D.: Advice on modal logic. In *Philosophical problems in logic* (K. Lambert, ed.), Reidel, 1970, pp. 143-173.

[Se72]   Segerberg, K.: *An essay on classical modal logic.* Uppsala, Philosophical Studies, 1972.

[St76]   Stalnaker, R.C.: Possible worlds. *Nous* 10(1976), pp. 65-75.

[St80]   Stalnaker, R.C.: Logical semiotics. In *Modern logic - A survey* (E. Agazzi, ed.), Reidel, 1980, pp. 439-456.

[St85]   Stalnaker, R.C.: *Inquiry.* MIT Press, 1985.

[Th80]   Thomason, R.H.: A model theory for propositional attitudes. *Linguistics and Philosophy* 4(1980), pp. 47-70.

[Va85]   Vardi, M.Y.: A model-theoretic analysis of monotonic knowledge. *Proc. 9th Int'l Joint Conf. on Artificial Intelligence*, Los Angeles, 1985, pp. 509-512.

[XW83]   Xiwen, M., Weide, G.: W-JS: A model logic of knowledge. *Proc. 8th Int'l Joint Conf. on AI*, 1983, pp. 398-401.

[Za85]   Zadrozny, W.: *Explicit and implicit beliefs - a solution of a problem of H. Levesque.* Unpublished manuscript, 1985.

MENTAL SITUATION CALCULUS

John C. McCarthy
Department of Computer Science
Stanford University
Stanford, CA 94305

ABSTRACT

The situation calculus of (McCarthy and Hayes 1969)[1] has mainly been used to reason about states of the physical world, taking into account the locations and physical properties of objects and admitting such events as moving them. Analogously we can consider a mental situation calculus (MSC) in which the situations include beliefs, goals, intentions and other mental qualities, and the events include inferring, observing, establishing goals and discharging them.

MSC has several motivations:

1. MSC involves reifying beliefs, and one of its basic forms will be believes(<proposition>, ss) standing for the assertion that the proposition is believed in mental situation ss. The formalism allows for belief not to be closed under inference. In fact one of the possible mental actions is to make an inference. Therefore, we can describe in detail the circumstances under which we want our system to make inferences.

2. Non-monotonic reasoning requires closer control over inference than deduction, because of its tentative character. Some problems that have recently arisen with blocks world axiomatizations may require that circumscription be controlled in accordance with the pedigree of the system's objective beliefs and not merely being determined by what the beliefs are.

3. It looks like several useful methods of control of reasoning can be accomplished by hill-climbing in mental situation space.

Besides reifying beliefs, MSC involves reifying goals and partial plans for achieving them. Depending on progress the paper to be presented will include both general discussion of MSC and specific formalizations.

---

[1] McCarthy, John and P.J. Hayes. 1969: "Some Philosophical Problems from the Standpoint of Artificial Intelligence." In Machine Intelligence 4, edited by D. Michie. American Elsevier, New York, NY.

A RESOLUTION METHOD FOR QUANTIFIED MODAL LOGICS OF KNOWLEDGE AND BELIEF

Christophe Geissler
École Nationale Superieure
des Telecommunications
Paris, France

Kurt Konolige
Artificial Intelligence Center
SRI International
Center for the Study of
Language and Information
Stanford University

ABSTRACT

B-resolution is a sound and complete resolution rule for quantified modal logics of knowledge and belief with a standard Kripke semantics. It differs from ordinary first-order binary resolution in that it can have an arbitrary (but finite) number of inputs, is not necessarily effective, and does not have a most general unifier covering every instance of an application. These properties present obvious obstacles to implementation in an automatic theorem-proving system. By using a technique similar to *semantic attachment*, we obtain a very natural expression of *B*-resolution that is potentially efficient, and easily understood and controlled. We have implemented the method and used it to solve the Wise Man Puzzle.

Introduction

Modal logics with a possible-world semantics have been widely used to formalize various accounts of belief and knowledge in Artificial Intelligence (AI) (Moore [17], Levesque [14], and McCarthy [15]) and more recently in Computer Science in general (Halpern and Moses [7]). These logics are important both as an analytic tool in analyzing systems, and as a means of endowing artificial agents with the ability to reason about the knowledge and belief of other agents. In this latter category we include query answering (Levesque [14]), dialogue understanding (Appelt [2], Cohen and Perrault [3], and Grosz [6]), and multiagent planning systems (Konolige [9], Rosenschein and Genesereth [19]). It is widely recognized (see, for example, Moore [17]) that efficient and conceptually transparent proof methods are needed for these systems. By *efficient* we mean that computer automation of the methods produces those proofs needed for reasoning about belief within allowable time and space limitations; by *conceptually transparent* we mean that the action of the theorem prover is readily understandable, and the proofs clear and direct, so that it is easy to check and modify the behavior of the system.

While there has been a good deal of useful work on decision procedures for propositional modal logics (see Halpern and Moses [8]), fewer results have been obtained for quantified modal logics. Hilbert-style and natural deduction axiomatizations (Kuo [13]) exist, but there are no serious proposals to automate them. As an alternative, McCarthy [15] proved theorems about a modal system by axiomatizing its possible-worlds semantics in a first-order system; subsequently Moore [17] used this technique to efficiently automate proofs. However, this is not a direct proof technique, because it involves reasoning about possible worlds and other objects of the semantic domain, rather than manipulating beliefs directly.

In this paper we present an efficient, direct proof method for a modal logic of belief that is based on Robinson's resolution principle ([18]). First we briefly review the modifications to first-order resolution that are necessary to establish the B-resolution rule. This rule has several properties which present problems for implementation in an automatic theorem-prover: it is non-effective, so we must find a way to apply it incrementally; and we must also develop techniques for controlling the size of the search space it generates.

The key idea we use to solve both problems is the concept of *semantic attachment* (Weyhrauch [22]). To illustrate this technique, consider the statements "A believes P" and "A doesn't believe $P \vee Q$." These are inconsistent in possible-worlds semantics, because there is no world compatible with A's beliefs in which P is true and $P \vee Q$ is false. We can show this inconsistency by deducing a contradiction from P and $\neg(P \vee Q)$. Thus we can prove facts about belief statements by attaching to their meaning and performing a computation (in this case, deduction). The structure of reasoning is clear, and it is easy to understand and control the often confusing embedding of agents reasoning about other agents' beliefs.

The Resolution Method

Language preliminaries

We assume a modal language L built on a first-order language with function symbols. The modal atoms are of the form $[S]\phi$, where S is a term denoting an agent and ϕ is a formula denoting a proposition. The intending meaning is that a believes or knows ϕ.

The semantics of L are the standard Kripke possible-world models with an accessiblity relation for each agent. It is well-known that various properties of knowledge and belief can be expressed by placing conditions on the accessibility relations (Halpern and Moses [8]). For simplicity of exposition we will limit ourselves to the system K, which has no restrictions, although versions of the resolution method have been derived for all the important systems (T, $K4$, $S4$, $K5$, $K45$, $S5$, etc.).

For technical reasons we make one further assumption: the domain of each possible world is a subset of the domain of any accessible world. Rescinding this restriction is possible, but introduces further complications in the resolution method that we do not wish to address here.

Herbrand's Theorem

One version of Herbrand's Theorem is: *a set of universal sentences is unsatisfiable if and only if a finite subset of its instances are.* Stated in this form, it sanctions the "lifting" of proofs over ground sentences to those with universal variables. Unfortunately, Herbrand's Theorem is not true for modal logics with Kripke semantics, as we can see from the following counterexample:

$$P(m(c))$$
$$\neg[S]P(m(c)) \tag{1}$$
$$\forall x.Px \supset [S]Px$$

We can construct a model as follows. Let P be the property of being non-Italian, let $m(x)$ denote the mayor of the city x, and c denote New York. Suppose S believes the mayor of New York is Fiorello LaGuardia (and not Ed Koch, the actual mayor); it is easy to confirm that all the sentences are satisfied.

Now if we substitute $m(c)$ for x in the third sentence, the resulting set is unsatisfiable. The reason is that, although x must refer to the same individual in all possible worlds, the substituted expression $m(c)$ need not. So even if a universal sentence is true in a model, some of its instances can be false.

Our solution to this problem is to redefine the meaning of "instance" by introducing a *bullet operator* (•) whenever there is a substitution for variables inside the context of modal operators. $\bullet t$ always refers to whatever t denotes in the actual world, no matter what the context of interpretation; the bullet operator thus acts like a rigid designation operator for terms. In the above example, substituting $m(c)$ for x yields

$$P(m(c)) \supset [S]P(\bullet m(c)), \tag{2}$$

which is still satisfied by the original model, since $\bullet m(c)$ refers to Ed Koch even in the context of S's beliefs.

With this revised definition of substitution (and instance), Herbrand's Theorem is once more valid (see Konolige [11]).

Clause form

Converting to clause form is the same as for first-order logic, with modal atoms having different argument structures treated as if they were different predicate symbols. Thus $[S]\forall x.Px$, $[S]Pa$, and $[S]\exists x.Px$ are all considered to be different nilary predicates. Modal atoms with n free variables are n-ary predicates, e.g., $[S](Px \land \exists y.Py)$ and $[S](\exists y.Py \land Px)$ are different unary predicates with the free variable x. Note that variables quantified under the scope of the modal operator remain unanalyzed or inert in B-resolution, and do not interact with variables quantified outside the operators. An example:

$$\forall x \exists y Rxy \supset [S]\exists z.Rxyz \quad \Rightarrow \quad \neg R(x, f(x)) \lor [S]\exists z.R(\bullet x, \bullet f(x), z) \tag{3}$$

Note that substitution of $f(x)$ for y in the modal context is done with $\bullet f(x)$. Also, in clause form we automatically insert a bullet operator before quantified-in variables (like x), to distinguish them from variables whose quantifiers are inside the scope of modal operators (like z).

B_K-resolution

Our resolution method is based on Stickel's *total narrow theory resolution* rule [21], which has the following form. Let L be a language that embeds a theory T, that is, the axioms of T contain a set of predicates P of L (but not necessarily all predicates of L). Suppose there is a decision procedure for determining a set of ground literals W in P to be unsatisfiable (according to T). Then

A resolution method for QML

$$
\begin{array}{c}
L_1 \vee A_1 \\
L_2 \vee A_2 \\
\vdots \\
L_n \vee A_n \\
\hline
A_1 \vee A_2 \vee \ldots \vee A_n
\end{array}
, \quad \text{when } \{L_1, L_2, \ldots L_n\} \text{ is } T\text{-unsatisfiable}
\tag{4}
$$

is a resolution rule that is sound and complete for the theory T. This rule includes binary resolution as a special case, where L_1 and L_2 are complementary literals.

For the modal logic K, this rule is rephrased as follows. Let Γ be a set of formulas of L; by $\Gamma^\bullet$ we mean the same formulas with the bullet operator uniformly replaced by a unary function not appearing in Γ. Then, in the case of ground clauses,

$$
\begin{array}{c}
[S]\phi_1 \vee A_1 \\
[S]\phi_2 \vee A_2 \\
\vdots \\
[S]\phi_n \vee A_n \\
\neg[S]\delta \vee A \\
\hline
A_1 \vee A_2 \vee \ldots \vee A_n \vee A
\end{array}
, \quad \text{when } \{\phi_1, \phi_2, \ldots \phi_n, \neg\delta\}^\bullet \text{ is } K\text{-unsatisfiable.}
\tag{5}
$$

is a sound resolution rule for K. If we are allowed to infer instances of any clause, then by Herbrand's Theorem for L it is also a complete rule. Because it is a rule for the logic K, we call this the B_K-resolution rule.

Implementation problems

The following problems must be solved to obtain an efficient implementation of B_K-resolution.

1. There is no decision procedure for unsatisfiability in quantified K.

2. Although we have given the resolution rule for the ground case, to be useful it must also be able to handle free variables in the arguments of the modal atoms. In this respect, B_K-resolution is more complicated than ordinary binary resolution, because in general there is no most general unifier covering all possible ground resolutions. For example, consider the following two clauses:

$$
\begin{array}{l}
[S](P\bullet a \wedge P\bullet b) \\
\neg[S]P\bullet x
\end{array}
\tag{6}
$$

There are two substitutions for x which yield a resolvent (a/x and b/x), but no "most general" unifier.

3. The search space is exponential in the number of modal literals. Consider the following example:

$$[S]r \vee A_1$$
$$[S]p \vee A_2$$
$$[S](p \supset q) \vee A_3 \tag{7}$$
$$\underline{\neg[S]q}$$
$$A_1 \vee A_2 \vee A_3$$

Only the last three clauses are needed for the resolution; indeed, including the first clause will not lead to a proof if A_1 cannot eventually be resolved away. In order to be complete in general theory resolution rules must be applied to a *minimal* set of unsatisfiable literals. If there are n clauses containing one modal literal each, there are 2^n possible B_K-resolutions that must be tried.

4. The above search space problem is compounded by the presence of variables, since a given clause may have to be used twice. For example, there is a resolution of the clauses

$$Px \vee [S]P{\bullet}x$$
$$\neg[S](P{\bullet}a \wedge P{\bullet}b) \tag{8}$$

yielding the resolvent $Pa \vee Pb$. However, this requires the first clause to be used twice in the belief resolution rule (5), as follows:

$$Pa \vee [S]P{\bullet}a$$
$$Pb \vee [S]P{\bullet}b$$
$$\underline{\neg[S](P{\bullet}a \wedge {\bullet}b)}$$
$$Pa \vee Pb$$

5. If there are several clauses with negative belief literals for the same agent, we may duplicate our efforts in deciding unsatisfiability each time. Consider again example (7), and suppose there is another clause with the negative belief literal $\neg[S](q \wedge p)$. A resolution using this clause and the positive belief clauses exists; however, in finding it we duplicate the work involved in deciding that $\{p, p \supset q, q\}$ is unsatisfiable.

A proof procedure for B_K-resolution

Semantic attachment

We now give a version of B_K-resolution which treats the problems just mentioned. The key idea is to replace the unsatisfiability condition of (5) with a recursive call to the theorem-prover, using as input the arguments of the modal atoms. If the recursive call is successful, then the resolution rule can be applied. Because it is not certain that the call will terminate, processing of the call must be interspersed with other activities of the theorem-proving process. At any given time, the theorem prover must "time-share" its attention between ordinary binary resolution and multiple invocations of the semi-decision procedure.

In addition, we structure the semi-decision procedure so that it accepts free variables in formulas, and eventually returns substitutions covering all proofs that can be found with instantiations of these variables.

The idea of showing validity or unsatisfiability of a predication by means of a computation that reflects the intended meaning of the predicate is called *semantic attachment* (Weyhrauch [22]). In belief resolution, we compute the unsatisfiability of a set of modal literals by performing deductions on their arguments. This process is a generalization of semantic attachment in two ways. First, we show the unsatisfiability of a *set* of modal literals, rather than a single atom. Second, by allowing variables, we are able to perform many different instances of semantic attachment at once. Without this ability, belief resolution would not be efficient in the presence of variables, because we would have to first chose an instantiation of the modal literals without knowing whether it would lead to a resolution or not.

An example

Our implementation of (5) has much in common with Kripke's [12] device of auxiliary tableaux. We define a structure called a *view*, which is an annotated instantiation of the theorem-proving process. Here is a short example to illustrate the basic idea. Assume initial clauses:

1. $[S]Pa$
2. $\neg Pb$
3. $Qx \vee Px \vee [S]P{\bullet}x$
4. $\neg[S](Pa \wedge P{\bullet}y) \vee Qy$
5. $\neg Qb$

Note that we have added a bullet operator to each variable under the scope of a belief atom. Ordinary resolution work as usual, for example, 2 and 3 can be resolved to yield:

6. $Qb \lor [S]P \bullet b$ 2,3

Clause 4 contains a negative belief literal, and we open a new view in an attempt to resolve it:

view S, rems $(0, Qy)$
1. $\neg Pa \lor \neg Pn(y) \lor Ans(0, y)$

This is view *for* S, the agent of the belief. The clause is derived from $\neg(Pa \land P \bullet y)$; note the substitution of the function n for the bullet operator. The *Ans* predicate keeps track of the input free variable y; it also contains the additional argument "0" to indicate that it is connected to the remainder (*rems*) indexed by 0. If a proof is found in the view, the remainder Qy will be returned with an appropriate binding for y as a deduced clause of the original proof.

We can add the arguments of positive belief atoms to the view, as in clause 1 (of the original clause set). The view now contains:

view S, rems $(0, Qy)$
1. $\neg Pa \lor \neg Pn(y) \lor Ans(0, y)$
2. Pa

These two clauses can be resolved, yielding:

view S, rems $(0, Qy)$
1. $\neg Pa \lor \neg Pn(y) \lor Ans(0, y)$
2. Pa
3. $\neg Pn(y) \lor Ans(0, y)$ 1, 2

Clause 6 has a positive belief literal, so we add its argument also:

view S, rems $(0, Qy)$ $(1, Qb)$
1. $\neg Pa \lor \neg Pn(y) \lor Ans(0, y)$
2. Pa
3. $\neg Pn(y) \lor Ans(0, y)$ 1, 2
4. $Pn(b) \lor Ans(1)$

Clause 4 contains an answer predicate with a new index. The remainder of the original clause containing the positive belief atom (6) is inserted into the indexed remainder list. Note that the bullet operator was replaced with the same function n as in clause 1.

Clauses 3 and 4 resolve, yielding a clause containing just answer predicates:

view S, rems $(0, Qy)$ $(1, Qb)$

1.	$\neg Pa \vee \neg Pn(y) \vee Ans(0, y)$	
2.	Pa	
3.	$\neg Pn(y) \vee Ans(0, y)$	$1, 2$
4.	$Pn(b) \vee Ans(1)$	
5.	$Ans(0, b) \vee Ans(1)$	$3, 4$

Now we gather up the remainders indexed by the answer predicates in the answer clause, namely, Qb (index 1) and Qy (index 0). Using the substitution b/y generated by the Ans-predicate, we return $Qb \vee Qb$ $(= Qb)$ as the result.

1.	$[S]Pa$	
2.	$\neg Pb$	
3.	$Qx \vee Px \vee [S]P \bullet x$	
4.	$\neg [S](Pa \wedge P \bullet y) \vee Qy$	
5.	$\neg Qb$	
6.	$Qb \vee [S]P \bullet b$	$2, 3$
7.	Qb	$1, 4, 6$

Clauses 5 and 7 resolve to give the null clause, completing the proof.

Views

Formally, a view is an annotated, finite set of clauses. The annotation is a list of remainders to be used in returning a result from the view. We perform four operations on views.

Opening a view. Let C be a clause of the form $\neg [S]\phi \vee A$. A view for S may be created. Into it we insert clauses formed from ϕ as follows. Let W be the set of clauses resulting from putting $(\neg \phi)^{\bullet}$ into clause form, and let $\mathbf{x}$ be the free variables of ϕ. We insert each member of W into the view, disjoining the answer predicate $Ans(0, \mathbf{x})$. We also add the annotation $(0, A)$ to the remainder list.

Adding a positive belief literal. Let C be a clause of the form $[S]\phi \vee A$, and let $\mathbf{x}$ be the free variables of ϕ. To any existing view for S we may add the clauses formed by converting $\phi^{\bullet}$ to clause form and disjoining $Ans(n, \mathbf{x})$, where n is a new index. (n, A) is added to the remainder list.

Stepping a view. A resolution step may be performed in any view. This includes using one of the four operations described here to create and manipulate embedded views.

Returning an answer. If a clause containing only answer literals is deduced in a view, we may assert a new clause in the proof containing the view. Let

$$
\begin{aligned}
&Ans(0,\mathbf{a})\vee \\
&Ans(n_1,\mathbf{a}_1^1)\vee \quad \cdots \quad \vee Ans(n_1,\mathbf{a}_{i_1}^1)\vee \\
&\quad\quad\vdots \\
&Ans(n_k,\mathbf{a}_1^k)\vee \quad \cdots \quad \vee Ans(n_k,\mathbf{a}_{i_k}^k)
\end{aligned}
$$

be the answer clause, and let $A_n(\mathbf{a})$ be n^{th} remainder with $\mathbf{a}$ substituted for its free variables ($\mathbf{a}$ may itself contain variables). The returned clause is:

$$
\begin{aligned}
&A_0(\mathbf{a})\vee \\
&A_{n_1}(\mathbf{a}_1^1)\vee \quad \cdots \quad \vee A_{n_1}(\mathbf{a}_{i_1}^1) \\
&\quad\quad\vdots \\
&A_{n_k}(\mathbf{a}_1^k)\vee \quad \cdots \quad \vee A_{n_k}(\mathbf{a}_{i_k}^1)
\end{aligned}
$$

Note that only one $Ans(0,\mathbf{a})$-predicate is allowed in the answer clause. Multiple answer predicates are allowed for positive belief atoms, because more than one instance of these atoms may participate in B_K-resolution.

The use of the *Ans*-predicate allows us to perform a schematic proof, where the input sentences can have free variables. At the end of a proof, the answer predicates give the necessary instantiations of the free variables. Thus we have "lifted" B_K-resolution from the ground case.

If these rules are added to a refutation system using ordinary resolution, we can prove the following result. Let W be a set of clauses of L, and suppose there is a set of ground instances $W\theta$ such that B_K-resolution derives the ground clause C. Then there is a sequence of applications of the view rules on W that returns a clause C' having a ground instance C. Thus these rules faithfully implement B_K-resolution, and together with ordinary resolution form a sound and complete system for K.

Agent terms

We have implicitly assumed that in modal atoms of the form $[S]\phi$, S is a ground term. However, we may easily lift to the more general case of variables, because the agent term is not in a modal context. There are two modifications to the rules. First, in opening a view, $\mathbf{x}$ is a list of all variables in both ϕ and S. Second, we may add a positive belief literal $[S']\psi$ to any view for S, if S and S' have a most general unifier θ. When adding clauses obtained from ψ, we must also disjoin the answer predicate $Ans(0, \mathbf{x}\theta)$. This is to assure that a result is returned only if all the participating clauses have unifiable agent terms.

Controlling the search space

Avoiding redundancies

We now address the implementation problems mentioned in the previous section. All of the methods mentioned here maintain the soundness and completeness of B_K-resolution.

1. The view rules split each possible B_K-resolution into a sequence of effective steps. These steps may be interspersed with other activities of the theorem-prover, including ordinary resolution.

2. The use of answer predicates allows a schematic proof within views, so that free variables in the input can be tolerated. Separate proofs are found whenever there is no unifying instance of the input variables that allows a single schematic proof. Consider again example (6). If we open a view for the negative belief atom, and add the positive one, we get:

   view S, rems (0,x)
   1. $\neg Pn(x) \vee Ans(0, x)$
   2. $Pn(a)$
   3. $Pn(b)$

   There are two proofs, one with a/x and one with b/x. Note that if there are no free variables or remainders when we add a clause, we can forgo the answer predicate.

3. We do not need to separately consider all possible combinations of modal literals that could lead to B_K-resolvents. The proof structure of the view takes care of this: only the remainders of those clauses that participated in the proof are returned in the result. Consider again example (7). We open a view for the negative belief literal, and add the arguments of all three positive belief literals. The view looks like this:

   view S, rems $(1, A_1)$ $(2, A_2)$ $(3, A_3)$
   1. $\neg q$
   2. $r \vee Ans(1)$
   3. $p \vee Ans(2)$
   4. $\neg p \vee q \vee Ans(3)$

Two resolutions yield $Ans(2) \lor Ans(3)$, returning the result $A_2 \lor A_3$. Although the clause $[S]r \lor A_1$ was added to the view, it was never used in the proof.

4. Although several instances of the same clause may be needed to form a B_K-resolvent, we need only add its belief literal *once* to the view. Consider again example (8). We open a view for the negative belief literal, and add the positive one, obtaining:

> view S, rems $(1, Px)$
> _____
> 1. $\neg Pn(a) \lor \neg Pn(b)$
> 2. $Pn(x) \lor Ans(1, x)$

By two resolutions of the second clause, we get:

> view S, rems $(1, Px)$
> _____
> 3. $\neg Pn(b) \lor Ans(1, a)$ 1, 2
> 4. $Ans(1, b) \lor Ans(1, a)$ 2, 3

This is a particularly nice result, since the necessity of using multiple copies of a clause in resolution gives rise to nasty control problems.

5. With a little care in indexing the *Ans*-predicates, we can eliminate the redundancies caused by performing the same deductions on the arguments of positive belief literals in different views. Suppose we create only one view for each agent S, but we allow any negative belief literal $\neg[S]\phi$ to be added to this view, in the same way as positive literals are added. We keep track of the answer index so that that we can identify it as arising from a negative belief literal. Resolution are performed as usual within the view. However, to return an answer, we apply the following condition: exactly one *Ans*-predicate arising from a negative belief literal must appear in the answer clause. For example, consider the following clause set:

> 1. $[S]\forall x.Px$
> 2. $[S](\forall x.Px \supset Qx)$
> 3. $A_0 \lor \neg[S]Qa$
> 4. $A_1 \lor \neg[S]Qb$

We open a single view, inserting all belief literals:

> view S rems $(0, A_0)$ $(1, A_1)$
> _____
> 1. Px
> 2. $\neg Px \lor Qx$
> 3. $\neg Qa \lor Ans(0)$
> 4. $\neg Qb \lor Ans(1)$

Resolving 1 and 2 yields Qx, which can be resolved separately against 3 and 4, returning A_0 and A_1, respectively. However, any resolutions which contain *both* 3 and 4 as ancestors will have $Ans(0)$ and $Ans(1)$ predicates, and so will not generate any result clauses.

The interesting point to note here is that we need open only a single view for each agent, instead of each negative belief literal. The view acts as a deductive testbed in which we try to show different combinations of belief and nonbelief are inconsistent for the agent.

It is possible to generalize this strategy to different agents sharing a set of common beliefs: a single view is created for all the agents. This is particularly useful when one has to deal with agent terms having variables, as in the following clause set:

1. $\neg Px \vee [x]q_1$
2. $\neg Px \vee [x](q_1 \supset q_2)$
    $\vdots$
n. $\neg Px \vee [x](q_{n-1} \supset q_n)$
$n+1.$ Pa
$n+2.$ Pb
$n+3.$ $\neg[a]q_n \vee \neg[b]q_n$

It is clear that a and b share many of the same beliefs, and that a great deal of effort will be saved if we assert these beliefs in the same view.

Heuristic control

We have investigated several refinements of the view rules that do not maintain completeness, but may be useful heuristic methods for controlling the size of the search space.

The first is to limit the depth of recursion of views. In a particular problem domain we can often judge whether or not it is useful to reason about agents reasoning about agents reasoning about agents ... and so on. By refusing to open views that are embedded beyond a certain depth, we can control inferences about nested reasoning. More fine-grained control is also possible, if we know that certain types of nested reasoning will be more useful than others. For example, if introspective reasoning is not required (an agent reasoning about his or her own beliefs) then we can refuse to open a view for S if it is embedded in a view for S.

A second method of control is to integrate the view rules into a set-of-support strategy. The most obvious method is to open a view only for negative belief literals in the set of support. The rationale is that we often have a large number of facts about an agent's beliefs, and we are trying to prove from these that the agent has some other belief. A negative literal $\neg[S]\phi$ will appear in the set of support when we are trying to prove that S has the belief ϕ.

Unlike in ordinary resolution, this set-of-support strategy is not complete because it does not permit inferences about lack of belief. For example, we cannot infer $\neg[S]p$ from $[S](p \supset q)$ and $\neg[S]q$, because there are no negative belief literals in the set of support.

Implementation

The view rules for quantified modal K have been implemented using a nonclausal connection-graph theorem prover developed by Stickel [20]. The implementation itself is of interest, especially the method of sharing the attention of the theorem-proving process between views (see Geissler and Konolige [5]).

In addition, we have incorporated theories of common belief, and a simple modal form of the situation calculus (McCarthy and Hayes [16]) as a logic of time. We have derived an automatic proof of the Wise Man puzzle that illustrates these ideas, showing the interaction between belief, action, and time. The proof is conceptually simple and easy to follow.

Other resolution systems for modal logics

Currently there are at least two other approaches to using resolution in a quantified modal logic, both for temporal logics. Fariñas-del-Cerro [4] describes a resolution method for restricted languages in which there are no quantifiers in modal contexts. Such languages are not suitable for knowledge and belief, because it is impossible to express, for example, the statement "Ralph knows that someone is a spy."

Abadi and Manna [1] derive sound and complete nonclausal resolution rules for propositional temporal logics, and are working on extending their techniques to the quantified case.

This work is interesting because it incorporates induction rules, a necessity for completeness in temporal logics containing both *next state* and *always* operators. When belief logics are extended to contain common belief operators, a similar problem surfaces (see Halpern and Moses [7]). We may be able to adopt a solution analogous to those found for temporal logics; currently we have only incomplete resolution rules for common belief.

A major difference between temporal logic resolution and the methods presented here is the use of semantic attachment. The temporal resolution rules are binary rules that transfer arguments in and out of the scope of modal operators; eventually a form results that can be resolved away. This type of resolution does not seem to result in perspicuous, easily-controlled proof methods.

Acknowledgements

We are grateful to Mark Stickel for his help in modifying the connection-graph theorem prover. This research was supported in part by Contract N00014–85–C–0251 from the Office of Naval Research, and in part by a gift from the Systems Development Foundation.

References

[1] Abadi, M. and Manna, Z. (1985). Nonclausal temporal deduction. Report No. STAN-CS–85–1056, Computer Science Department, Stanford University, Stanford, California.

[2] Appelt, D. (1985). *Planning English sentences.* Cambridge University Press, Cambridge, U. K.

[3] Cohen, P. R. and Perrault, C. R. (1979). Elements of a plan-based theory of speech acts. *Cognitive Science* **3**, pp. 177–212.

[4] Fariñas-del-Cerro, L. (1983). Temporal reasoning and termination of programs. In Proceedings of the Eighth International Joint Conference on Artificial Intelligence, Karlsruhe, West Germany, pp. 926-929.

[5] Geissler, C. and Konolige, K. (1986). Implementation of a resolution system for modal logic. Forthcoming Artificial Intelligence Center Tech Note, SRI International, Menlo Park, California.

[6] Grosz, B. J. (1981). Focusing and description in natural language dialogues. In *Elements of Discourse Understanding,* Cambridge University Press, Joshi, A. K., Webber. B, and Sag, I., Eds.

[7] Halpern, J. Y. and Moses, Y. (1984). Knowledge and common knowledge in a distributed environment. In Proceedings of the 3rd ACM Conference on Principles of Distributed Computing, pp. 50–61.

[8] Halpern, J. Y. and Moses, Y. (1985). A guide to the modal logics of knowledge and belief: preliminary draft. In Proceedings of the Ninth International Joint Conference on AI, Los Angeles, California, pp. 479–490.

[9] Konolige, K. (1980). A first-order formalization of knowledge and action for a multiagent planning system. Artificial Intelligence Center Tech Note 232, SRI International, Menlo Park, California.

[10] Konolige, K. (1984). A deduction model of belief and its Logics. Doctoral dissertation, Stanford University, Stanford, California.

[11] Konolige, K. (1986). Resolution methods for quantified modal logics. Forthcoming Artificial Intelligence Center Tech Note, SRI International, Menlo Park, California.

[12] Kripke, S. A. (1959). A Completeness Theorem in Modal Logic. *Journal of Symbolic Logic* **24**, pp. 1–14.

[13] Kuo, V. (1984). A formal natural deduction system about knowledge: modal logic W-JS. Unpublished manuscript, Stanford University.

[14] Levesque, H. J. (1982). A Formal Treatment of Incomplete Knowledge Bases. FLAIR Technical Report No. 614, Fairchild Laboratories, Palo Alto, California.

[15] McCarthy, J. *et. al.* (1978). On the model theory of knowledge. Memo AIM–312, Stanford University, Stanford.

[16] McCarthy, J. and Hayes, P. J. (1969). Some philosophical problems from the standpoint of Artificial Intelligence. In *Machine Intelligence 4*, B. Meltzer and D. Michie editors, Edinburgh University Press, Edinburgh, Scotland, pp. 120–147.

[17] Moore, R. C. (1980). Reasoning about knowledge and action. Artificial Intelligence Center Technical Note 191, SRI International, Menlo Park, California.

[18] Robinson, J. A. (1965). A machine-oriented logic based on the resolution principle. *J. Assoc. Comput. Mach. 12*, pp. 23–41.

[19] Rosenschein, J. S., and Genersereth, M. R. (1984). Communication and cooperation. Heuristic Programming Project Report 84–5, Stanford University, Stanford, California.

[20] Stickel, M. E. (1982). A nonclausal connection-graph resolution theorem-proving program. Proceedings of the AAAI-82 National Conference on Artificial Intelligence, Pittsburgh, Pennsylvania, pp. 229–233.

[21] Stickel, M. E. (1985). Automated deduction by theory resolution. *Proceedings of the Ninth International Joint Conference on Artificial Intelligence,* Los Angeles, California.

[22] Weyhrauch, R. (1980). Prolegomena to a theory of mechanized formal reasoning. *Artificial Intelligence 13*, no. 1–2.

Steps Towards a First-Order Logic of Explicit and Implicit Belief

Gerhard Lakemeyer
Department of Computer Science
University of Toronto
Toronto, Ontario
Canada, M5S 1A4

Abstract

Modelling the beliefs of an agent who lacks logical omniscience has been a major concern recently. While most of the work has concentrated on propositional logics of belief, this paper primarily addresses issues raised by adding quantifiers to such logics. In particular, we are focusing on *quantifying in* and the distinction between "knowing what" and "knowing that". After arguing why a model of limited reasoning should preserve this distinction, we show how this can be accomplished by a semantics based on a restricted form of tautological entailment.

Introduction

Ever since *possible-worlds semantics* was first proposed for models of knowledge and belief, [Hint62][1] it has been argued that this semantics is not a realistic model for reasoning, mainly because it requires the reasoner to be *logically omniscient*, that is, beliefs are closed under logical implication. Clearly, the assumption that, among other things, an agent knows *all* valid sentences is quite unnatural and it also leads to serious computational problems. We adopt the view of [Leve84b] and [FaHa85] that possible-worlds semantics is good for expressing what is *implicit* in an agent's knowledge, but more restricted models should be used to characterize what is believed *explicitly*. As a formal tool in the study of belief, these authors use modal logics, an approach followed also in this work.

An interesting application of belief logics is the study of knowledge bases (KBs) that are part of larger systems requiring quick responses from their KBs, as in robots. If the KB is characterized as a finite set of sentences in a language like first-order logic, fast limited reasoning may be favored over full theorem proving. The efficiency versus completeness trade-offs are only some of many issues which can be studied very elegantly using belief logics, as demonstrated in [Leve84b] and [FaHa85].

The literature on limited reasoning reveals that there are at least two major approaches to avoiding logical omniscience. One is syntactic in nature; the other tries to give a semantic account. An example of the former is to limit the set of inferences by describing models of belief as explicit sets of sentences, as is done in [Eber74] and [MoHe79]. Alternatively, [Kono84] models beliefs using a base set of sentences together with a possibly incomplete set of deduction rules. One fundamental problem with this syntactic approach is that the answer to the question of which sentences should be believed can be quite arbitrary and lacks an intuitive semantic account.

Levesque[Leve84b] is among the first who attempt to address exactly this issue and give a plausible semantics for explicit beliefs. He restricts himself to a propositional logic of explicit and implicit belief. He uses two modal operators B and L to capture this distinction, a convention we will also follow in this paper. A sentence $B\alpha$ is then said to be true if α is explicitly believed by the agent. Similarly, $L\alpha$ expresses that α is believed implicitly. The key idea for his semantics of explicit belief is that worlds (or *situations*, as he calls them) may be incompletely specified or even contradictory. This is realized in the following way: for any situation s and propositional letter p, s will support the truth of p, its falsity, both or none, which amounts to assigning p one of four truth values $\{\}, \{t\}, \{f\}, \{t, f\}$ instead of the usual two. A sentence α is then said to be explicitly believed if the truth of α is supported in all situations the agent thinks possible (the *belief set*). This avoids logical omniscience in that the truth of a sentence no longer bears any relationship to its negation, which is crucial for *modus ponens*. At the same time, contradictory beliefs like $B(p \wedge \neg p)$ are possible. Levesque shows that his semantics for explicit beliefs coincides with that of tautological entailment in relevance logic (as in [AnBe75] and [Beln77]).

---

[1]Originally, Hintikka developed his semantics using so-called *model sets*, but he later [Hint71] recast the theory in terms of the now standard notions of possible-worlds semantics.

In the same spirit, Fagin and Halpern [FaHa85] propose several propositional logics for belief that try to give plausible accounts of why people are not logically omniscient. Examples are lack of awareness, resource-boundedness, not knowing the relevant rules, and focus of attention. In contrast to Levesque, the authors stick to two-valued logics and allow for multiple agents. Being two-valued means that contradictory beliefs of the form $B(p \wedge \neg p)$ can no longer be satisfied. However, their "society of minds" logic allows sentences of the form $Bp \wedge B\neg p$ to be satisfiable (see also [Leve] for a similar proposal). Finally, Fagin and Halpern suggest treatments for nested beliefs, which Levesque did not consider in his original paper.

Given that all of the above was based on propositional logic, the obvious question arises as to whether we can find similar quantified versions. That is a non-trivial matter. A major stumbling block is that first-order logic by itself is undecidable. Patel-Schneider [Pate85] proves that an existing model of limited reasoning, namely the first-order version of tautological entailment, is also undecidable. By modifying this model, however, he arrives at a decidable version. (See also [Fris85], who uses quite different methods with surprisingly similar results). While this seems to be a good starting point for investigating models of explicit belief — and in fact, that is exactly what we are going to propose — by itself it is not entirely satisfactory. Since Patel-Schneider's language is that of classical first-order logic, it lacks the primitives to talk about beliefs (such as the B or L operator). Thus it cannot address important issues like nested beliefs or quantifying in.

In this paper we will concentrate on the problem of *quantifying in* with respect to a first-order logic with modal operators B and L assuming a single agent. We start with a brief discussion of the distinctions between "knowing that" and "knowing what". We give reasons why we think those distinctions should not be given up in the context of explicit belief. After introducing Patel-Schneider's model of limited reasoning, we show that its obvious extension to a belief logic has some rather undesirable properties. We then develop a model that solves these problems and maintains the key features of quantifying in.

"Knowing What" and "Knowing That"

Since Frege, the phenomenon that Leibniz' principle of substituting equals for equals seems to break down in propositional attitudes like *knowing* has been of considerable concern among philosophers (for example, [Freg92] and [Lins71]). One manifestation of the problem is the distinction between "knowing what" and "knowing that".[2] For example, I may know that the current President of the US lives in the White House without knowing who he (or she!) is.

Belief logics that want to be able to distinguish between the two cases usually allow two ways of denoting individuals. One uses *standard names* or *rigid designators*, where there can be no doubt about the identity of the referred object; e.g., "7" always denotes one particular number. The other uses *non-rigid designators*, where the individual referred to may vary from interpretation to interpretation like the term "President of the US".

---

[2]The main distinction made in logic between knowledge and belief is that knowledge must be true in the actual world, while beliefs may not. Although we favor the latter, this distinction is of no consequence for this work and we sometimes even use "know" instead of "believe".

These two classes of names plus the distinction between quantifiers outside and inside the scope of belief operators make it possible to capture some of the intuition behind "knowing what" and "knowing that". In logics of implicit beliefs that are based on classical modal logics like S5 or weak S5 (as in [Moor80] or [Leve82]), the following sentences come out valid ($\models$) or not valid ($\not\models$) in a possible worlds semantics with a fixed universe of discourse over all worlds: Let P be a unary predicate, x a variable, a a non-rigid designator, and n a standard name.

1) $\models \exists x L P x \supset L \exists x P x$

2) $\not\models L \exists x P x \supset \exists x L P x$

3) $\models L P a \supset L \exists x P x$

4) $\not\models L P a \supset \exists x L P x$

5) $\models L P n \supset \exists x L P x$

6) $\models L \forall x P x \supset \forall x L P x$

7) $\models \forall x L P x \supset L \forall x P x$

As an example, if we read L as "is known" and P as "is a teacher", the first two statements reflect the distinction between "knowing what" and "knowing that" as follows: The first says that whenever some particular individual (identified by his standard name) is known to be a teacher, then it is known that there exists a teacher. The second, on the other hand, states that knowing that there is a teacher does not imply that there is a particular individual who is known to be a teacher.

Assuming that the above seven statements are reasonable choices for implicit beliefs, the question arises whether a model of explicit belief can or should have a different view. To us, tampering with 1 or 3 does not make much sense. Falsifying 1, for example, amounts to allowing for an agent who believes P for a known individual, but fails to acknowledge the existence of one!

The most important point we want to make, however, is that 2 and 4 should not come out valid under explicit belief. Doing so would essentially collapse the distinction between "knowing that" and "knowing what", which has a grave consequence for the expressiveness of the representation language. There would be no way of telling a knowledge base that somebody is a P without telling it who it is! At best, incomplete knowledge of this kind could be approximated by finite disjunctions, but there would be no existential quantification.

Finally, let us take a look at the last sentence, $\forall x L P x \supset L \forall x P x$. Essentially, it expresses that the rule of *universal generalization* applies to implicit belief. We feel that this may not necessarily be the case in explicit beliefs.[3] Since in propositional models of explicit belief *modus ponens* had to be given up as a valid inference rule within beliefs, it should not be too surprising if universal generalization fails when adding quantifiers.

---

[3]Even in possible worlds semantics this sentence, the controversial *Barcan Formula*, can fail, if worlds are allowed to have differing universes of discourse [HuCr68].

The main goal of the rest of the paper is to develop a suitable semantics for explicit belief. It will have the properties 1-6 concerning quantifying in, but not 7 (universal generalization fails). Implicit beliefs, which will be modelled in the standard possible worlds fashion, will of course exhibit all seven properties.

The Language $\mathcal{L}$

The language we use is basically a straightforward extension of Levesque's propositional logic of explicit and implicit beliefs [Leve84b] to the first-order case. The only non-standard feature is the explicit representation of standard names, which are called *parameters* in the language.

$\mathcal{L}$ consists of countably infinite sets of *variables* V, *parameters* N, and *function* and *predicate* symbols. Function symbols with no arguments are also called *constants*, but note that they are non-rigid designators and not to be confused with parameters, the rigid designators of our language. A *term* is either a variable, a parameter, or a function symbol whose arguments are themselves terms. A *closed* term is a term not containing any variables. $\mathcal{T}$ denotes the set of all closed terms. An *atomic formula* (or simply *atom*) is a predicate symbol with terms as arguments. Given the atomic formulas, the logical connectives $\neg$ and $\vee$, the existential quantifier $\exists$, and modal operator symbols B and L, we can generate all well-formed formulas of $\mathcal{L}$ using the standard formation rules.[4] Given the usual meaning of *bound* and *free* variables, we say $\alpha^{x/t}$ is that formula obtained from α, where all occurrences of the free variable x are replaced by the term t. The same convention is used if α is a term instead of a formula. Finally, a formula with no free variables is called a *sentence*.

As noted at the beginning of this section, parameters serve as standard names or rigid designators in our language. We refer to them as numerals $1, 2, 3 \dots$. They are needed, as pointed out in the previous section, so that we can distinguish "knowing what" from "knowing that". In order to give them their intended meaning, we will simply use the parameters themselves as the fixed universe of discourse in all models. For a more thorough discussion of why this trick is sound, and for more reasons why the use of standard names comes in handy in modal belief logics, see [Leve82].

Since we are not concerned with nested beliefs in this discussion, we restrict $\mathcal{L}$ to that set of formulas that have no nested occurrences of B or L. Furthermore, we write $\mathcal{L}_1$ for the subset of $\mathcal{L}$ with *no* occurrences of B or L.

t-Entailment

The notion of explicit belief that we will put forward in this paper has a strong resemblance to Patel-Schneider's notion of *t-entailment*, a variant of tautological entailment in first-order relevance logic. The semantics for this decidable form of entailment uses world descriptions that are straightforward generalizations of situations introduced in [Leve84b]: for any predicate symbol P with parameters $(\vec{n})$ as arguments, a situation s supports either the truth of $P\vec{n}$,

---

[4]Other connectives like $\wedge$, $\supset$, and the universal quantifier $\forall$ are defined in the usual way from $\neg$, $\vee$, and $\exists$.

its falsity, both, or none. In addition, every closed term is mapped into a standard name (its meaning with respect to s) using a *coreference relation* as in [Leve84a]. A coreference relation $\equiv$ can be characterized as follows:

a) $\equiv$ is an equivalence relation.

b) No two standard names corefer.

c) Every closed term has a coreferring standard name.

d) If t_1 and t_2 corefer, so do t^{x/t_1} and t^{x/t_2}, where t contains one free variable x.

It is easy to see that every closed term has a unique coreferring standard name. A situation s is a triple

$$s \;=\; <T^s, F^s, \equiv_s> \,.$$

T^s and F^s map every k-ary predicate symbol into a k-place relation over N. Truth- and false-support of atomic formulas containing parameters corresponds to membership in either T^s or F^s. $\equiv_s$ denotes the coreference relation of s.

We call the set of all situations S. We also use the following shorthand: given a situation s, a k-ary predicate symbol P and a vector of closed terms $\vec{t} = t_1, \ldots, t_k$, we say $(\vec{t}) \in T^s(P)$ if $(n_1, \ldots, n_k) \in T^s(P)$, where $n_i \equiv_s t_i$ (similarly for $(\vec{t}) \in F^s(P)$).

Finally, in order to interpret formulas with variables, we introduce *variable maps* ν from V into N. $\mathcal{V}$ is the set of all such variable maps. We notate ν_n^x as that variable map identical to ν except that x gets mapped into n. For convenience we take the liberty of applying variable maps also to terms and sequences of terms with the intent that all occurrences of variables in a term become replaced by the standard name called for by the variable map (e.g., $\nu(f(x), g(y, x)) = f(3), g(6, 3)$ if $\nu(x) = 3$ and $\nu(y) = 6$).

We are now just about ready to present Patel-Schneider's semantics. A pivotal role in attaining a decidable form of entailment is played by his very restricted interpretation of existential quantification. Formulas are interpreted with respect to a *set* of situations that share a common coreference relation (called a *compatible* set of situations). Such a set S supports the truth of a formula $\exists x \alpha$ only if there is a standard name n so that $\alpha^{x/n}$ has true support in *every* element of S. We will refer to this way of interpreting $\exists$ as *global existential quantification*. The semantics from [Pate85], with adaptations to our notation,[5] is: let S be a compatible set of situations, ν a variable map. The language is $\mathcal{L}_1$, since this semantics does not account for belief operators.

1. $S, \nu \models_T P\vec{t} \iff$ *for all $s \in S$* $\nu(\vec{t}) \in T^s(P)$

   $S, \nu \models_F P\vec{t} \iff$ *for all $s \in S$* $\nu(\vec{t}) \in F^s(P)$

2. $S, \nu \models_T \neg \alpha \iff S, \nu \models_F \alpha$

---

[5]Actually, it is a little more than just a notational change, since the language Patel-Schneider uses has no parameters. Adding them, however, is of no consequence for his results.

$$S, \nu \models_F \neg \alpha \iff S, \nu \models_T \alpha$$

3. $S, \nu \models_T \alpha \vee \beta \iff \exists S_1 S_2 \; S = S_1 \cup S_2 \; s.t. \; S_1, \nu \models_T \alpha \; and \; S_2, \nu \models_T \beta$

   $S, \nu \models_F \alpha \vee \beta \iff S, \nu \models_F \alpha \; and \; S, \nu \models_F \beta$

4. $S, \nu \models_T \exists x \alpha \iff for \; some \; n \in N \; S, \nu_n^x \models_T \alpha$

   $S, \nu \models_F \exists x \alpha \iff for \; all \; n \in N \; S, \nu_n^x \models_F \alpha$

t-entailment($\longrightarrow_t$) is then defined as: $\alpha \longrightarrow_t \beta$ if and only if for all compatible sets of situations S and variable maps ν, if $S, \nu \models_T \alpha$ then $S, \nu \models_T \beta$.

At first glance it seems that it is not $\exists$ but rather $\vee$ that gets a special treatment in this semantics. On closer inspection, however, it becomes clear that it is the special way of looking at existential quantification that causes the somewhat odd interpretation of $\vee$. Let's look at the example $S, \nu \models_T (\exists x Px \vee \exists y Qy)$. According to the semantics, we can partition S into S_1 and S_2 such that all of S_1 supports Pn and all of S_2 supports Qm for some fixed n and m. But that is just another way of saying: for some fixed parameters n and m, $Pn \vee Qm$ is supported in all situations of S, where $\vee$ is now interpreted in the usual way.

One important property of t-entailment that seems to be crucial for it being decidable is the fact that $(Pa \vee Pb) \not\longrightarrow_t \exists x Px$. This is caused exactly by the special treatment of $\exists$ we have just discussed. We feel that this is not an unreasonable limitation, since it reflects a certain constructive or intuistionistic mode of reasoning. Applying this feature to a logic of explicit and implicit belief would mean: while the existential is clearly *implicit* in the disjunction, we may not want to require that any agent who believes the disjunction explicitly automatically be able to reason by cases and come up with the existential.

From t-entailment to Explicit Belief

Levesque based his semantics for a propositional belief logic on world descriptions that are situations, belief sets that are sets of situations, and tautological entailment. An analogous and probably the simplest extension to Patel-Schneider's semantics would have us view world descriptions as compatible sets of situations and a belief set as a set of compatible sets of situations. With this picture in mind, we get the following definition for explicit belief:

Let Γ be a set of compatible sets of situations, and let S and ν be as before.

5. $S, \nu \models_T B\alpha \iff \forall S' \in \Gamma \; S', \nu \models_T \alpha$

   $S, \nu \models_F B\alpha \iff S, \nu \not\models_T B\alpha$

Very soon one discovers that this approach has some rather undesirable properties, one of them being that for all S, ν, and Γ,

if $S, \nu \models_T B\alpha \vee B\beta$, then $S, \nu \models_T B\alpha \wedge B\beta$!

This follows directly from the peculiar semantics of disjunctions and the fact that, if S supports $B\alpha$, so does any $S \subseteq S$. One of the consequences is that there are no S and Γ that support the truth of $\exists x B\alpha \lor \neg \exists x B\alpha$, a sentence that should come out valid given a suitable semantics.

Intuitively, the problem seems to be the following. If we interpret S as the actual situation and Γ as the set of situations that are believed possible, then the semantics of $\lor$ leads us to assume that the truth of any sentence α containing a disjunction is somehow dependent on the structure of S. This seems rather counterintuitive in case α talks about beliefs, since the truth about beliefs (in contrast to knowledge) does not depend on what the world is really like. And certain sentences like $B\alpha \lor \neg B\alpha$ should come out true no matter what the world and the belief set look like.

We feel that these problems can be overcome if we go back to the more intuitive notions of belief logics, where we have a single situation representing the "actual" situation and a set of situations, which are meant to be those the agent thinks possible. The ideas of t-entailment and, in particular, the notion of global existential quantification should be restricted to this belief set, i.e., only when interpreting a sentence starting with a B.

In more concrete terms, our aim is a semantics that has as little effect as possible on the standard way of interpreting modal logics in order to retain most of their intuitive appeal. The interpretation of B should look like:

$$...S, s, ... \models_T B\alpha \iff \langle \text{ condition enabling global exist. quant. } \rangle \text{ and}$$
$$\forall s' \in S \ ...S, s'... \models_T \alpha$$

The desire to achieve global existential quantification through a condition that is *local* to the interpretation of the B operator is guided by the intuition that whatever is done to limit the set of explicit beliefs of the system should have only a minimal effect on the interpretation of logical connectives other than the belief operators. In our case it will result only in a slight twist to the interpretation of $\exists$. This will avoid the problems encountered with the non-solution discussed at the beginning of this section.

Before going into the details about how global existential quantification is realized, it should be noted that the sets of situations as used in t-entailment are too restrictive if viewed as belief sets. All members of the set have the same coreference relation, which destroys the difference between non-rigid and rigid designators, a key feature in distinguishing "knowing what" from "knowing that". For example, if *brother(john)* corefers with the standard name *jim* in all possible situations, then one should conclude that the system knows who he is. Therefore, we allow members of belief sets to have different coreference relations from now on.

In order to get an idea of how to achieve global existential quantification on those sets, assume we are given a situation s (the "actual" situation), a belief set S, and a variable map ν. Interpreting $S, s, \nu \models_T B(\exists x Px \lor \exists y Qy)$ should have the effect of picking two individuals a and b global to the entire belief set and replacing the expression by

$$\forall s' \in S \ \ S, s', \nu_a^x \models_T Px \ \text{ or } \ S, s', \nu_b^y \models_T Qy \ (*).$$

It turns out that these global choices can be realized via a function C (called the *choice function*) that takes as arguments the variable map, which takes care of dependencies on leading universal quantifiers, and the variable name. (*) can then be replaced by

$$\exists C \forall s' \in S \;\; S, C, s', \nu_{C(\nu,x)}^{x} \models_T Px \;\; \text{or} \;\; S, C, s', \nu_{C(\nu,y)}^{x} \models_T Qy,$$

where $C(\nu, x) = a$ and $C(\nu, y) = b$. (Note that the original expression should also carry a choice function for the interpretation of $\exists$ outside the belief context.)

Therefore, the condition enabling global existential quantification simply amounts to the selection of a choice function before quantifying over the belief set.

So far we have not mentioned what kind of values choice functions range over. From our discussion on quantifying in, it should be clear that the range cannot be standard names, since for a sentence like $B\exists x Px$ to be true Pn would have to be true in every element of the belief set, where n is some standard name. Then, of course, we can choose exactly the same n to make $\exists x BPx$ true. The idea is to give a substitutional account of global existential quantification, allowing also non-rigid terms to be substituted. Under that view, $B\exists x Teacher\, x$ can be true if $brother(john)$ is a teacher in all situations, even though this name may refer to different individuals. In a sense, we are saying that the system believes the existence of a teacher if it can *name* one.

Note that, outside the belief context, using terms instead of parameters is redundant, since there the interpretation is done with respect to a *single* situation, and every term corefers with a parameter. This property also allows us to represent "knowing who" properly. All we have to do is to make sure that variables that are used both to talk about the actual situation s and the beliefs S as in $\exists x (Teacher\, x \wedge BTeacher\, x)$ have as a value a standard name (provided by s), when a belief is interpreted. Technically, this can be done locally when encountering a B by converting the variable map ν that is active at that moment into a map ν_s whose values are just the coreferring standard names (from s) of the values of ν.

Before presenting the formal semantics, we summarize the major technical changes necessary that allow the transition from t-entailment to explicit beliefs.

a) The belief set consists of arbitrary first-order situations.

b) The range of variable maps is extended from N to T to allow variables to be replaced by arbitrary closed terms.

c) A choice function C is introduced, mapping pairs of variable maps and variable names into the set of closed terms:
$$C : \mathcal{V} \times V \longrightarrow \mathcal{T}.$$
The set of all choice functions is called $\mathcal{C}$.

d) The conversion of all values of variables into standard names (in the context of explicit or implicit belief). Let s be a situation, ν a variable map. ν_s is the variable map s.t. $\nu_s(x) = n$, where $n \in N$ and $n \equiv_s \nu(x)$.

Finally, since implicit beliefs are to be interpreted as in a regular possible-worlds semantics, we need the concept of possible worlds compatible with a situation (a straightforward adaptation from [Leve84b]).

$$\mathcal{W}(s) = \{s' \in S \mid \text{ for every k-tuple } \vec{n} \in N^k \text{ and every k-ary predicate P}$$

$\quad$ a) $\vec{n}$ is in exactly one of $T^{s'}(P)$ and $F^{s'}(P)$

$\quad$ b) if $\vec{n} \in T^s(P)$ then $\vec{n} \in T^{s'}(P)$

$\quad$ c) if $\vec{n} \in F^s(P)$ then $\vec{n} \in F^{s'}(P)$

$\quad$ d) $\equiv_{s'} \; = \; \equiv_s \}$

$\mathcal{W}(S)$, the set of all possible worlds compatible with S, is then the union of all $\mathcal{W}(s)$ for $s \in S$. We can now give the full semantics for the language $\mathcal{L}$:

Let $s \in S$, $S \subseteq \mathcal{S}$, $\nu \in \mathcal{V}$, then

1. $S, s, \nu \models_T \alpha \iff \exists C \in \mathcal{C} \; S, C, s, \nu \models_T \alpha'$ [6]

   $S, s, \nu \models_F \alpha \iff \exists C \in \mathcal{C} \; S, C, s, \nu \models_F \alpha'$

2. $S, C, s, \nu \models_T P\vec{t} \iff \nu(\vec{t}) \in T^s(P)$

   $S, C, s, \nu \models_F P\vec{t} \iff \nu(\vec{t}) \in F^s(P)$

3. $S, C, s, \nu \models_T \neg\alpha \iff S, C, s, \nu \models_F \alpha$

   $S, C, s, \nu \models_F \neg\alpha \iff S, C, s, \nu \models_T \alpha$

4. $S, C, s, \nu \models_T \alpha \vee \beta \iff S, C, s, \nu \models_T \alpha \text{ or } S, C, s, \nu \models_T \beta$

   $S, C, s, \nu \models_F \alpha \vee \beta \iff S, C, s, \nu \models_F \alpha \text{ and } S, C, s, \nu \models_F \beta$

5. $S, C, s, \nu \models_T \exists x \alpha \iff S, C, s, \nu^x_{C(\nu, x)} \models_T \alpha$

   $S, C, s, \nu \models_F \exists x \alpha \iff \forall t \in \mathcal{T} \; S, C, s, \nu^x_t \models_F \alpha$

6. $S, C, s, \nu \models_T B\alpha \iff \exists C' \in \mathcal{C} \; \forall s' \in S \; S, C', s', \nu_s \models_T \alpha$

   $S, C, s, \nu \models_F B\alpha \iff S, C, s, \nu \not\models_T B\alpha$

7. $S, C, s, \nu \models_T L\alpha \iff \forall s' \in \mathcal{W}(S) \; \exists C' \in \mathcal{C} \; S, C', s', \nu_s \models_T \alpha$

   $S, C, s, \nu \models_F L\alpha \iff S, C, s, \nu \not\models_T L\alpha$

In the remainder of this section, we discuss how this semantics relates to classical Tarskian semantics and look at some of the properties of explicit and implicit belief. We start by defining *validity* for a formula $\alpha \in \mathcal{L}$ as

$$\models \alpha \iff \text{ for all } S, s \in \mathcal{W}(S), \nu \in \mathcal{V} \; S, s, \nu \models_T \alpha$$

---

[6] α' is the same as α except that all variable names are distinct. This condition is needed, since the choice functions depend on variable names. Note that in subsequent proofs we ignore the renaming step in order to preserve clarity.

Given that the semantics uses a non-standard way of interpreting $\exists$, one should feel somewhat uncomfortable with this definition of validity. Namely, does it have anything to do with what we normally call a valid sentence? The first task will therefore be to show that this notion of validity does in fact reduce to standard Tarskian validity if a sentence contains no modal operator. Furthermore, we will show that the same holds for truths about beliefs, something we found missing in our first extension to t-entailment.

Given a Tarskian world $w = <T^w, F^w, \equiv_w>$ $(\in \mathcal{W}(S))$, we define a Tarskian style interpretation function $I_w : \mathcal{L}_1 \longrightarrow \{T, F\}$ as follows:

$$I_w(P\vec{n}) = T \iff \vec{n} \in T^w(P)$$

$$I_w(\neg\alpha) = T \iff I_w(\alpha) = F$$

$$I_w(\alpha \vee \beta) = T \iff I_w(\alpha) = T \text{ or } I_w(\beta) = T$$

$$I_w(\exists x\alpha) = T \iff \text{ for some } n \in N \ I_w(\alpha^{x/n}) = T$$

$$I_w(\alpha^{x/t_1}) = I_w(\alpha^{x/t_2}), \text{ where } t_1 \equiv_w t_2 \text{ and } x \text{ is the only free variable in } \alpha.$$

Tarskian validity for a sentence $\alpha \in \mathcal{L}_1$ is then defined as

$$\models^\tau \alpha \text{ if and only if for all } w \in \mathcal{W}(S) \ I_w(\alpha) = T.$$

The following lemma states a strong correspondence between our semantics and Tarskian semantics.

Lemma 1 *For any sentence* $\alpha \in \mathcal{L}_1, w \in \mathcal{W}(S), S, \text{ and } \nu$

$$I_w(\alpha) = T \iff S, w, \nu \models_T \alpha$$
$$I_w(\alpha) = F \iff S, w, \nu \models_F \alpha$$

Proof : By induction on α. Since both model theories coincide in their definitions for atoms, negations, and disjunctions, the only interesting case is existential quantification. We show the only if direction for both statements, where α starts with a $\exists$.

Let $I_w(\exists x\alpha) = T$, then $I_w(\alpha^{x/n}) = T$ for some $n \in N$, implying $\exists C \ S, C, w, \nu \models_T \alpha^{x/n}$. From lemma 9 in the appendix we get $\exists C' \ S, C', w, \nu^x_n \models_T \beta$, but then $\exists C'' \ S, C'', w, \nu^x_{C''(\nu,x)} \models_T \beta$ (choose $C'' = C'$ except $C''(\nu, x) = n$) implying $\exists C'' \ S, C'', w, \nu \models_T \exists x\alpha$, from which $S, s, \nu \models_T \exists x\alpha$ follows.

Now let $I_w(\exists x\alpha) = F$, then $\forall n \in N \ I_w(\alpha^{x/n}) = F$, which implies $\forall n \in N \ \exists C \ S, C, s, \nu \models_F \alpha^{x/n}$. From lemma 9 it follows that $\forall n \in N \ \exists C' \ S, C', s, \nu^x_n \models_F \alpha$ and by lemma 8 of the appendix, $\forall t \in \mathcal{T} \ \exists C'' \ S, C'', s, \nu^x_t \models_F \alpha$. Finally, with lemma 10 of the app. we obtain $\exists C^* \forall t \in \mathcal{T} \ S, C^*, s, \nu^x_t \models_F \alpha$, which implies $S, s, \nu \models_F \exists x\alpha$. ∎

From the previous lemma it follows immediately that the two notions of validity coincide for sentences not containing modal operators.

Theorem 2 *For any* $\alpha \in \mathcal{L}_1, \models^\tau \alpha \iff \models \alpha$

From theorem 2 we derive immediately that, for example, $(Pa \vee Pb) \supset \exists x Px$ is valid in our logic, that is, existential quantification outside modal operators behaves normally.

For sentences that do contain modal operators, we proceed as follows. A formula α' is called a *first-order substitution* of α, if it is obtained from α by substituting all occurrences of $B\beta$ ($L\beta$) in α by a new predicate $P_{B\beta}\vec{x}$ ($P_{L\beta}\vec{x}$), where $\vec{x}$ is the vector of all free variables in β.

Lemma 3 *For any $\alpha \in \mathcal{L}$, its first-order substitution α', and for any $S, C, s \in \mathcal{W}(S)$, and ν*

$$S, C, s, \nu \models_{\mathbf{T}} \alpha \iff S, C, s', \nu \models_{\mathbf{T}} \alpha'$$
$$S, C, s, \nu \models_{\mathbf{F}} \alpha \iff S, C, s', \nu \models_{\mathbf{F}} \alpha',$$

where $s = s'$ except for all $P_{B\beta}$ in α' we define (and similarly for $P_{L\beta}$)

$$T^{s'}(P_{B\beta}) = \{\vec{n} \mid S, C, s, \nu_{\vec{n}}^{\vec{x}} \models_{\mathbf{T}} B\beta\}$$
$$F^{s'}(P_{B\beta}) = \{\vec{n} \mid S, C, s, \nu_{\vec{n}}^{\vec{x}} \models_{\mathbf{F}} B\beta\}$$

Proof : Trivial. Note that s' itself is a possible world, since exactly one of $S, C, s, \nu_{\vec{n}}^{\vec{x}} \models_{\mathbf{T}} B\beta$ or $S, C, s, \nu_{\vec{n}}^{\vec{x}} \models_{\mathbf{F}} B\beta$ is true for all $\vec{n}$. ∎

Theorem 4 *Let α' be a first-order substitution of a sentence $\alpha \in \mathcal{L}$.*
If $\models^{\tau} \alpha'$, then $\models \alpha$.

Proof : Assume $\models^{\tau} \alpha'$ and $\not\models \alpha$. Then there are S, s, and ν s.t. for all C, $S, C, s, \nu \not\models_{\mathbf{T}} \alpha$, but then $S, C, s', \nu \not\models_{\mathbf{T}} \alpha'$. From lemma 1 it follows that $I_{s'}(\alpha') \neq T$, and therefore $\not\models^{\tau} \alpha'$ contradicting our assumption. ∎

As a corollary, for example, we get immediately that $\forall x B\alpha \vee \neg \forall x B\alpha$ is valid. Overall, then, $\mathcal{L}$ is "upward compatible" with classical first-order logic.

We can now turn to results concerning implicit and explicit beliefs and, of course, quantifying in. First of all, implicit beliefs are modelled according to possible worlds semantics. In particular, the operator L behaves much like the K operator in Levesque's logic $\mathcal{KL}$ (without equality)[Leve82]. Logical omniscience of implicit beliefs is captured in the following theorem.

Theorem 5

a) If $\models \alpha$ then $\models L\alpha$ for $\alpha \in \mathcal{L}_1$ *Implicit belief of first-order valid formulas*

b) $\models L\alpha \wedge L(\alpha \supset \beta) \supset L\beta$ *Modus Ponens*

c) $\models \forall x L\alpha \supset L\forall x\alpha$ *Universal Generalization*

Proof : We prove only (a) here. If $\models \alpha$, then for all $S, s \in \mathcal{W}(S)$, and ν there is a C s.t. $S, C, s, \nu \models_{\mathbf{T}} \alpha$. Since $\mathcal{W}(S) \subseteq \mathcal{W}(S)$, we get immediately $\forall s' \in \mathcal{W}(S) \exists C$ s.t. $S, C, s', \nu \models_{\mathbf{T}} \alpha$. With $\nu_s(x) \equiv_s \nu(x)$ the result follows from lemma 8 (appendix).

The idea to keep in mind is that in any interpretation of L we can choose a different choice function for every possible world, which reduces to a Tarskian interpretation as we have seen in theorem 2. ∎

Explicit and implicit beliefs have the proper connection, i.e., every explicit belief is also implicitly believed.

EXPLICIT AND IMPLICIT BELIEF   337

Theorem 6 $\models B\alpha \supset L\alpha$

Proof : It is easy to see that whenever a situation s supports the truth (falsity) of α, so does every possible world compatible with s (even with the same choice function). Also, having a choice function ranging over all elements of the belief set (as for $B\alpha$) is a much stronger requirement than being able to choose a different C for every element of the set (as for $L\alpha$). ∎

Finally, we have the following properties for explicit and implicit beliefs with respect to quantifying in:

Theorem 7 *For any α in $\mathcal{L}_1$ and any parameter n and closed term a*

a) $\models \exists x B\alpha \supset B\exists x\alpha$ *and* $\models \exists x L\alpha \supset L\exists x\alpha$
b) $\models B\alpha^{x/a} \supset B\exists x\alpha$ *and* $\models L\alpha^{x/a} \supset L\exists x\alpha$
c) $\models B\alpha^{x/n} \supset \exists x B\alpha$ *and* $\models L\alpha^{x/n} \supset \exists x L\alpha$
d) $\models B\forall x\alpha \supset \forall x B\alpha$ *and* $\models L\forall x\alpha \supset \forall x L\alpha$

Proof : We only look at explicit beliefs here.
     a) $\models \exists x B\alpha \supset B\exists x\alpha$
It suffices to show that, if $S,C,s,\nu \models_T \exists x B\alpha$, then $S,C,s,\nu \models_T B\exists x\alpha$ for any $S,C,s,$ and ν. Let $S,C,s,\nu \models_T \exists x B\alpha$, then $S,C,s,\nu^x_{C(\nu,x)} \models_T B\alpha$ and therefore $\exists C'$ s.t. $\forall s' \in S$
$S,C',s',(\nu^x_{C(\nu,x)})_s \models_T \alpha$. Let $C(\nu,x) \equiv_s n$ for some $n \in N$, then define C'' as C' except $C''(\nu,x) = n$, from which the result follows.
     b) $\models B\alpha^{x/a} \supset B\exists x\alpha$
As before, let $S,C,s,\nu \models_T B\alpha^{x/a}$, then $\exists C'$ s.t. $\forall s' \in S$ $S,C',s',\nu_s \models_T \alpha^{x/a}$, and therefore (by lemma 9 of the appendix) $\exists C''$ s.t. $\forall s' \in S$ $S,C'',s,(\nu_s)^x_a \models_T \alpha$. Define C^* as C'' except that $C^*(\nu_s,x) = a$, from which the result follows.
     c) $\models B\alpha^{x/n} \supset \exists x B\alpha$
It suffices to show that for all C s.t. $C(\nu,x) = n$, if $S,C,s,\nu \models_T B\alpha^{x/n}$, then $S,C,s,\nu \models_T \exists x B\alpha$. Let $S,C,s,\nu \models_T B\alpha^{x/n}$, then $\exists C' \forall s' \in S$ $S,C',s',\nu_s \models_T \alpha^{x/n}$, and therefore (by lemma 9) $\exists C'' \forall s' \in S$ $S,C'',s',(\nu_s)^x_n \models_T \alpha$. Since $(\nu_s)^x_n = (\nu^x_n)_s$, we get $S,C,s,\nu^x_n \models_T B\alpha$. Then, since we assumed that $C(\nu,x) = n$, it follows that $S,C,s,\nu \models_T \exists x B\alpha$.
     d) $\models B\forall x\alpha \supset \forall x B\alpha$
Again, the proof is not hard. On the left hand side, the quantifier ranges over all closed terms, whereas the right hand side essentially restricts the quantification to parameters. ∎

In addition, it is easy to show that "knowing that" is strictly weaker than "knowing what" for both implicit and explicit beliefs: There are $\alpha \in \mathcal{L}_1$ and non-rigid terms a s.t.

a) $\not\models B\exists x\alpha \supset \exists x B\alpha$ and $\not\models L\exists x\alpha \supset \exists x L\alpha$
b) $\not\models B\alpha^{x/a} \supset \exists x B\alpha$ and $\not\models L\alpha^{x/a} \supset \exists x L\alpha$

As an example for explicit belief, let $\alpha = Px$ and $S = \{s_1,s_2\}$, where $s_1 \models_T P1$ and $s_2 \models_T P2$, and $a \equiv_{s_1} 1$ and $a \equiv_{s_2} 2$ for some constant a. In addition, let no other term corefer with 1 or 2 in either situation.

     The limited reasoning power on explicit beliefs can be summarized as follows: There are α and $\beta \in \mathcal{L}$ such that

a) $\not\models\ B\alpha \wedge B(\alpha \supset \beta) \supset B\beta$ No Modus Ponens

b) $\not\models\ \forall x B\alpha \supset B\forall x\alpha$ No Universal Generalization

The failure of modus ponens follows directly from the fact that the propositional subset of our logic reduces to Levesque's logic in [Leve84b].

An example why universal generalization fails is the following: Let $\alpha = \exists y P x y$ and $S = \{s_1, s_2\}$. Both s_1 and s_2 support the truth of $P12, P23, P34, \ldots$, and for some constant a, $a \equiv_{s_1} 1$ and $a \equiv_{s_2} 2$. All other terms corefer with parameter 1 in both situations. Then certainly S supports $\forall x B\alpha$, since only parameters are relevant here. However, there is no term we could substitute for y s.t. S supports $B\exists y \alpha^{x/a}$.

As a concluding remark we note that the notion of explicit belief we have put forward in this paper allows an agent to hold beliefs with varying degrees of strength.

A very weak kind is the belief of a disjunction, since, for example, $B(Pa \vee Pb) \supset B\exists x Px$ is not valid. (As in t-entailment, it is easy to construct a belief set, where this sentence fails. Simply let $S = \{s_1, s_2\}$, where s_1 supports only the truth of Pn and s_2 the truth of Pm for distinct parameters n and m.) On the other hand, note that $B(Pa \vee Pb) \supset L\exists x Px$ is valid.

Although explicit beliefs of type "knowing that" are stronger than disjunctive beliefs, they are strictly weaker than those of type "knowing what":

$$\not\models\ B\exists x\alpha \supset \exists x B\alpha \quad vs. \quad \models\ \exists x B\alpha \supset B\exists x\alpha$$

Finally, a belief about the existence of someone having some property α is strongest, if the system can pinpoint a particular individual with that property: $\models\ B\alpha^{x/n} \supset \exists x B\alpha$, where n is a parameter.

Conclusion

A major focus of this paper has been the problem of quantifying in as it relates to logics of explicit and implicit belief. We have presented a semantics for explicit belief that preserves the ability to distinguish between "knowing what" and "knowing that", but is otherwise much weaker than implicit belief.

Work on the semantics and its properties is still in progress. Recently, we have obtained a decidability result that closely mirrors that of Patel-Schneider's t-entailment for formulas of the form $B\alpha \supset B\beta$, where α and β are in prenex normal form (that is, all quantifiers are moved to the front). We hope to report on these issues and present a complete axiomatization in a later paper.

An interesting phenomenon of our semantics that needs further study is the fact that not all logically equivalent forms of a formula are believed explicitly. For example, $B(\forall x \exists y (Px \vee Qy)) \supset B(\exists y \forall x (Px \vee Qy))$ is not valid.

Finally, two further areas of investigation are nested beliefs and a belief logic with equality. For example, it seems reasonable to expect $\models B(n = n)$ to hold for any parameter n. On the other hand, it is not clear whether $\models B(t_1 = n) \wedge B(t_2 = n) \supset B(t_1 = t_2)$ should come out true for arbitrary terms t_1 and t_2.

Acknowledgements

I am indebted to Hector Levesque for many enlightening discussions on this topic and his comments on earlier drafts of this paper. I would also like to thank Alan Frisch, Jim des Rivières, Murray Mazer, Greg McArthur, and Martin Stanley. Their comments have led to numerous improvements of the paper. Financial support was gratefully received from the World University Service of Canada.

References

[AnBe75] Anderson, A. R. and Belnap, N. D., *Entailment, The Logic of Relevance and Necessity*, Princeton University Press, 1975.

[Beln77] Belnap, N. D., A Useful Four-Valued Logic, in G. Epstein and J. M. Dunn (eds.), *Modern Uses of Multiple-Valued Logic*, Reidel, 1977.

[Eber74] Eberle, R. A., A Logic of Believing, Knowing and Inferring, *Synthese* 26, 1974, pp. 356-382.

[FaHa85] Fagin, R. and Halpern, J. Y., Belief, Awareness, and Limited Reasoning: Preliminary Report, *Proc. Int. Joint Conf. on AI*, August 1985, pp. 491-501.

[Freg92] Frege, G., Über Sinn und Bedeutung, *Zeitschrift für Philosophie und philosophische Kritik*, Vol. 100, 1892, pp. 25-50.

[Fris85] Frisch, A. M., Using Model Theory to Specify AI Programs, *Proc. Int. Joint Conf. on AI*, August 1985, pp. 148-154.

[Hint62] Hintikka, J., *Knowledge and Belief: An Introduction to the Logic of the Two Notions*, Cornell University Press, 1962.

[Hint71] Hintikka, J., Semantics for Propositional Attitudes, in L. Linsky (ed.), *Reference and Modality*, Oxford University Press, Oxford, 1971.

[HuCr68] Hughes, G. E. and Cresswell, M. J., *An Introduction to Modal Logic*, Methuen and Company Ltd., London, England, 1968.

[Kono84] Konolige, K., Belief and Incompleteness, SRI Artificial Intelligence Note 319, SRI International, Menlo Park, 1984.

[Leve82] Levesque, H. J., A Formal Treatment of Incomplete Knowledge Bases, Tech. Report No. 3, Fairchild Lab. for AI Research, Palo Alto, 1982.

[Leve84a] Levesque, H. J., Foundations of a Functional Approach to Knowledge Representation, *Artificial Intelligence*, Vol. 23, 1984, pp. 155-212.

[Leve84b] Levesque, H. J., A Logic of Implicit and Explicit Belief, Tech. Rep. No. 32, Fairchild Lab. for AI Research, Palo Alto, 1984.

[Leve] Levesque, H. J., Global and Local Consistency and Completeness of Belief, in preparation.

[Lins71] Linsky, L. (ed.), *Reference and Modality*, Oxford University Press, Oxford, 1971.

[Moor80] Moore, R. C., Reasoning about Knowledge and Action, Technical Note 181, SRI International, Menlo Park, 1980.

[MoHe79] Moore, R. C. and Hendrix, G., Computational Models of Beliefs and the Semantics of Belief-Sentences, Technical Note 187, SRI International, Menlo Park, 1979.

[Pate85] Patel-Schneider, P. F., A Decidable First-Order Logic for Knowledge Representation, *Proc. Int. Joint Conf. on AI*, August 1985, pp. 455-458, (an extended version is in preparation as: AI Tech. Report No. 45, Schlumberger Palo Alto Research).

Appendix

We state three technical lemmas about choice functions, which we used in previous proofs. Loosely speaking, these lemmas express that choice functions are very flexible with respect to variable maps. The first lemma says that choice functions are basically equivalent modulo the substitution of coreferring terms in a variable map.

Lemma 8 *Given a situation s, a variable x, and a closed term u, define choice functions C_1 and C_2 s.t. for all $v \in \mathcal{T}$, where $u \equiv_s v$, $C_1(\nu_u^x, y) = C_2(\nu_v^x, y)$ for all ν and y. Then, for all S, ν, v with $u \equiv_s v$ and α:*

$$S, C_1, s, \nu_u^x \models_T \alpha \iff S, C_2, s, \nu_v^x \models_T \alpha$$
$$S, C_1, s, \nu_u^x \models_F \alpha \iff S, C_2, s, \nu_v^x \models_F \alpha$$

Lemma 9 tells us that using a variable map is equivalent to direct substitution of values into a formula, provided no substitutions occur within beliefs.

Lemma 9 *For closed terms u and v define two choice functions C_u and C_v s.t. $C_u(\nu_u^x, y) = C_v(\nu_v^x, y)$ for all y and ν and some x. Then, for any $\alpha \in \mathcal{L}$ with x free in α, but not in the scope of a B or L, and any S, s and ν with $\nu(x) = v$:*

$$S, C_u, s, \nu_u^x \models_T \alpha \iff S, C_v, s, \nu \models_T \alpha^{x/u}$$
$$S, C_u, s, \nu_u^x \models_F \alpha \iff S, C_v, s, \nu \models_F \alpha^{x/u}$$

The next lemma shows an important case of merging a set of choice functions with respect to a partitioning of variable maps over one variable.

Lemma 10 *For any closed term t let C_t be some choice function. Then, for any x and α there is a C s.t. for all $u \in \mathcal{T}$:*

$$S, C_u, s, \nu_u^x \models_T \alpha \iff S, C, s, \nu_u^x \models_T \alpha$$
$$S, C_u, s, \nu_u^x \models_F \alpha \iff S, C, s, \nu_u^x \models_F \alpha$$

Proof : Let $C(\nu, y) = C_t(\nu, y)$ for $\nu(x) = t$. The rest follows by a simple induction argument on $|\alpha|$. ∎

LOGICIANS WHO REASON ABOUT THEMSELVES

Raymond M. Smullyan
Department of Philosophy
Indiana University
Bloomington, IN 47405

ABSTRACT

By treating belief as a modality and combining this with problems about constant truth tellers and constant liars (knights and knaves) we obtain some curious epistemic counterparts of undecidability results in metamathematics. Gödel's second theorem gets reflected in a logician who cannot believe in his own consistency without becoming inconsistent. Löb's theorem reflects itself in a variety of beliefs which of their own nature are necessarily self-fulfilling.

We shall consider some "epistemic" problems related to undecidability results in metamathematics.

Our action shall take place on an island in which each native is classified as either a <u>knight</u> or a <u>knave</u>. Knights make only true statements and knaves make only false ones. Any such island will be called a <u>knight-knave</u> island. On such an island, no native can claim to be a knave, since no knight would falsely claim to be a knave and no knave would correctly claim to be one.

Our two main characters are a logician L who visits the island and meets a native N who makes a statement to L.

FOREVER UNDECIDED

We will say that L is (always) <u>accurate</u> if he never believes any false proposition.

Problem 1

An accurate logician L visits the island and meets a native N who makes a certain statement. Once the native has made this statement, it becomes logically impossible for L to ever decide whether N is a knight or a knave (if L should ever decide either way, he will lose his accuracy). What statement could N make to ensure this?

Solution

One solution is that N says: "You will never believe that I am a knight." If L ever believes that N is a knight, this will falsify N's statement, making N a knave and hence making L inaccurate in believing that N is a knight. Therefore, since L is accurate, he will never believe that N is a knight. Hence N's statement was true, so N really is a knight. It further follows that N will never have the false belief that N is a knave. And so L must remain forever undecided as to whether N is a knight or a knave.

Discussion

The character N (as well as L) will be constant throughout this article. We shall let k be the proposition that N is a knight. Now, whenever N asserts a proposition p, the reality of the situation is that $k \equiv p$ is true (N is a knight if and only if p). For any proposition p, we shall let Bp be the proposition that L does or will believe p. The native

N has asserted ~Bk (you will never believe I'm a knight) and so k≡~Bk is true. From this we concluded that k must be true, but L can never believe k (assuming that L is always accurate).

More generally, given <u>any</u> proposition p such that p≡~Bp is true, if L is accurate, then p is true, but L will never believe p (nor will he believe ~p).

There is a complete parallelism between logicians who <u>believe</u> propositions and mathematical systems that <u>prove</u> propositions. When dealing with the latter, we will let Bp be the proposition that p is <u>provable</u> in the system.* In the system dealt with by Gödel, there is a proposition p such that p≡~Bp is true (even provable) in the system. Under the assumption that all provable propositions of the system are true (under a standard interpretation), it then follows (by the argument of Problem 1) that p, though true, is not provable in the system--nor is the false proposition ~p.

AN ACCURACY PREDICAMENT

For the problems that now follow, we must say more about the logician's reasoning abilities: We will say that he is of <u>type 1</u> if he has a complete knowledge of propositional logic--i.e. he sooner or later believes every tautology (any proposition provable by truth-tables) and his beliefs (past, present and future) are closed under modus ponens--i.e. if he ever believes p and believes p⊃q (p implies q) then he will (sooner or later) believe q.

Of course these assumptions are highly idealized, since there are infinitely many tautologies, but we can assume that the logician is immortal.

We henceforth assume that L is of type 1. From this it follows that given any propositions that L believes, he will sooner or later believe every proposition that can be derived from them by propositional logic. We shall also make the inessential assumption that if L can derive a conclusion q from a proposition p taken as a premise, he will then believe p⊃q. [This assumption adds nothing to the set of L's beliefs, but it makes many of the arguments shorter and more transparent.]

It is to be understood in all the problems that follow, that when L visits the knight-knave island that he <u>believes</u> it is a knight-knave island, and so when he hears N assert a proposition p, then L <u>believes</u> the proposition k≡p (N is a knight if and only if p).

---

*More precisely, we have a formula Bew(x) (read: "x is the Gödel number of a provable sentence") and for any proposition (sentence) p we let Bp be the sentence Bew(n̄), where n is the Gödel number of p.

We shall say that L believes he is (always) accurate if for every proposition p, L believes B̄p⊃p (he believes: "If I should ever believe p, then p must be true.") A reasoner (logician) who believes he is always accurate might aptly be called conceited.

Problem 2

A reasoner L of type 1 visits the island and N says to him: "You will never believe that I'm a knight." The interesting thing now is that if L believes that he is always accurate, then he will become inaccurate. Why is this?

Solution

Suppose L believes that he is always accurate. Then he will reason: "If N is a knave, his statement is false, which means that I will believe he's a knight and hence be inaccurate. This is impossible, since I am always accurate. Therefore he can't be a knave; he must be a knight."

At this point L believes that N is a knight, which makes N's statement false, hence N is really a knave. Thus L is inaccurate in believing that N is a knight. [We might remark that if L hadn't assumed his own accuracy, he would never have lapsed into an inaccuracy. He has been justly punished for his conceit!]

Peculiarity

We will call a reasoner peculiar if there is some proposition p such that he believes p and also believes that he doesn't believe p. [This strange condition doesn't necessarily involve a logical inconsistency, but it is certainly a psychological peculiarity!]

Problem 2A

Show that under the hypotheses of Problem 2, L will become not only inaccurate, but peculiar!

Solution

We have seen that L will believe that N is a knight. Then L will believe what N said and hence believe that he doesn't believe that N is a knight.

Remark. Even if the island that L visits is not a really a knight-knave island, but L only _believes_ that it is (he believes k≡~Bk) the above argument goes through (though the argument of Problem 2 does not).

THE GÖDEL CONSISTENCY PREDICAMENT

We shall say that L is of _type 2_ if he is of type 1 and also _knows_ that his beliefs are closed under modus ponens--i.e. for every p and q he (correctly) believes: "If I should ever believe both p and p⊃q, then I will believe q." And so he believes (Bp&B(p⊃q))⊃Bq [and being of type 1, he also believes the logically equivalent proposition: B(p⊃q) ⊃ (Bp⊃Bq)].

We shall call a reasoner _normal_ if whenever he believes p, he also believes that he believes p. We shall say that he _believes_ he is normal if he believes all propositions of the form Bp⊃BBp (he believes: "If I should ever believe p, then I will believe that I believe p.") We define a reasoner to be of _type 3_ if he is a normal reasoner of type 2. If he also _believes_ that he is normal, then we define him to be of type 4. Our main concern will be with reasoners of type 4. [They are the counterparts of mathematical systems of type 4--defined analogously, only reading "provable" for "B".]

A reasoner of type 4 (or even type 3) who believes p⊃q will also believe B(p⊃q) (by normality), hence will believe Bp⊃Bq (since he believes B(p⊃q)⊃(Bp⊃Bq)). This means that if a reasoner L of type 4 visits a knight-knave island (or even one that he _believes_ is a knight-knave island) and hears a native N assert a proposition p, then he will not only believe k⊃p (which he will, since he will believe k≡p), but will also believe Bk⊃Bp (he will believe: "If I should ever believe he's a knight, then I will believe what he said."). He will also believe B~k⊃B~p.

We shall define a reasoner to be _consistent_ if he never believes any proposition and its negation. [An inconsistent reasoner of even type 1 will sooner or later believe _every_ proposition q, since p⊃(~p⊃q) is a tautology. Also, if we take some fixed contradictory proposition f (for logical _falsehood_), a type 1 reasoner is consistent if and only if he never believes f, since for every p, the proposition f⊃p is logically true, hence if the reasoner believes f, he will believe p).

We will say that a reasoner _believes_ he is consistent if for every proposition p he believes ~(Bp&B~p) (he believes: "I will never believe both p and ~p"). [For a reasoner of type 4--or even of type 3,--this is equivalent to his believing that he will never believe f. This is not hard to show.]

Now we come to our first "big" problem.

Problem 3

[After Gödel's Second Theorem] - A logician L of type 4 visits a knight-knave island (or at least he <u>believes</u> it to be one) and meets N who says: "You will never believe that I'm a knight."   Prove that if L is consistent, he can never know that he is--or put another way, if L ever believes that he is consistent, he will become inconsistent.

Solution

Suppose L is confident of his consistency.   Then he will reason: "Suppose I never believe he's a knight.   Then I'll believe what he said-- I'll believe that I don't believe he's a knight.   But if I ever believe he's a knight, I'll also believe that I <u>do</u> believe he's a knight (since I am normal).   This means I would be inconsistent, which isn't possible (sic!).   Therefore, I never will believe he's a knight.   He said I never would, hence he's a knight."

At this point, L believes that N is a knight.   Being normal, he then continues: "Now I believe he's a knight.   He said I never would, so he's a knave."

At this point L is inconsistent (a while ago he believed N was a knight).

Discussion

Isn't it possible for a consistent reasoner of type 4 to know that he is consistent?   Yes, but only if he believes no proposition of the form p≡~Bp. [In the above problem, for example, L should have had the good sense to doubt that he was really on a knight-knave island!] However, with the type of mathematical system investigated by Gödel, the analogous option is not open--there really <u>is</u> a proposition p such that p≡~Bp is provable in the system (and the system is of type 4).   And so, by an analogous argument, the system, if consistent, cannot prove its own consistency (say in the form that ~Bf is not provable).

Henkin's Problem

For the same system, there is also a proposition p such that p ≡ Bp is provable in the system.   [This is like a native of the island who says: "You <u>will</u> believe that I'm a knight."] On the fact of it, p could be true and provable, or false and unprovable; is there any way to tell which? This problem remained open for some years and was finally solved by Löb, who showed the stronger fact that if Bp⊃p is provable in the system, so is p.   [His proof utilized the fact that there is also another proposition q such that q≡(Bp⊃q) is provable in the system.]   We now turn to a striking epistemic version of this.

SELF-FULFILLING BELIEFS AND LÖB'S THEOREM

We now have a change of scenario. A logician L of type 4 is <u>thinking</u> of visiting the island of knights and knaves because he has heard a rumor that the sulphur baths and mineral waters there might cure his rheumatism. He is home discussing this with his family physician and asks: "Does the cure really work?" The doctor replies: "The cure is largely psychological; the belief that it works is self-fulfilling. If you <u>believe</u> that the cure will work, then it will."

The logician fully trusts his doctor and so he goes to the island with the prior belief that if he should believe that the cure will work, then it will. He takes the cure, which lasts a day, and which is supposed to work in a few weeks (if it works at all). But the next day, he starts worrying: He thinks: "I know that if I should believe that the cure will work, then it will, but what evidence do I have that I will ever <u>believe</u> that the cure works? And so how do I know that it will?"

A native N passes by and asks L why he looks so disconsolate. L explains the situation and concludes: "--and so how do I know that the cure will work?" N then draws himself up in a dignified manner and says: "If you ever believe I'm a knight, then the cure will work."

Problem 4

Amazingly enough, the logician <u>will</u> believe that the cure will work, and, if his doctor was right, it will. How is this proved?

Solution

We let c be the proposition that the cure will work. L has the prior belief that Bc⊃c. Also, since N said that Bk⊃c, L believes k≡(Bk⊃c). And so L reasons: "Suppose I ever believe that he's a knight (suppose I believe k). Then I'll believe what he said--I'll believe Bk⊃c. But if I believe k, I'll also believe Bk (since I am normal). Once I believe Bk and believe Bk⊃c, I'll believe c.   Thus, if I ever believe he's a knight, then I'll <u>believe</u> that the cure will work. But if I believe that the cure will work, then it will (as my doctor told me). Therefore, if I ever believe he's a knight, then the cure will work. Well, that's exactly what he said, hence he's a knight!"

At this point, L believes that N is a knight. Since L is normal, he continues: "Now I believe he's a knight. And I have already proved that if I believe he's a knight, then the cure will work. Therefore the cure will work."

The logician now believes that the cure will work. Then (if his doctor was right), it will.

Reflexive Reasoners (and Systems)

Generalizing the above problem, for any proposition p, if a reasoner of type 4 believes Bp⊃p, and if there is a proposition q such that he believes q≡(Bq⊃q), then he will believe p.

We will call a reasoner reflexive if for every proposition p there is some q such that the reasoner believes q≡(Bq⊃p). And so if a reflexive reasoner of type 4 believes Bp⊃p, he will believe p. This is Löb's theorem (for reasoners).

For systems, we define reflexivity to mean that for any p (in the language of the system) there is some q such that q≡(Bq⊃p) is provable in the system. Löb's theorem (in a general form) is that for any reflexive system of type 4, if Bp⊃p is provable in the system, so is p.

Remarks

Here are some variants of Problem 4 that the reader might like to try as exercises: Suppose N had instead said: "The cure doesn't work and you will believe that I'm a knave." Prove that L will believe that the cure works.

Here are some other things that N could have said to ensure that L will believe that the cure works:

(1) If you believe that I'm a knight, then you will believe that the cure will work.

(2) You will believe that if I am a knight then the cure will work.

(3) You will believe I'm a knave, but you will never believe that the cure will work.

(4) You will never believe either that I'm a knight or that the cure will work.

THE STABILITY PREDICAMENT

We will call a reasoner unstable if there is some proposition p such that he believes that he believes p, but doesn't really believe p. [This is just as strange a psychological phenomenon as peculiarity!]

We will call him stable if he is not unstable--i.e. for every p, if he believes Bp then he believes p. [Note that stability is the converse of normality.] We will say that a reasoner believes that he is stable if for every proposition p, he believes BBp⊃Bp (he believes: "If I should ever believe that I believe p, then I really will believe p).

Problem 5

If a consistent reflexive reasoner of type 4 believes that he is stable, then he will become unstable. Stated otherwise, if a stable reflexive reasoner of type 4 believes that he is stable, then he will become inconsistent. Why is this?

Solution

Suppose that a stable reflexive reasoner of type 4 believes that he is stable. We will show that he will (sooner or later) believe every proposition p (and hence be inconsistent).

Take any proposition p. The reasoner believes BBp⊃Bp, hence by Löb's theorem he will believe Bp (because he believes Br⊃r, where r is the proposition Bp, and so he will believe r, which is the proposition Bp). Being stable, he will then believe p.

A QUESTION OF TIMIDITY

The following problem affords another (and rather simple) illustration of how a belief can be self-fulfilling.

Problem 6

A certain country is ruled by a tyrant who owns a brain-reading machine with which he can read the thoughts of all the inhabitants. Each inhabitant is a normal, stable reasoner of type 1.

There is one particular proposition E which all the inhabitants are forbidden to believe--any inhabitant who believes E gets executed! Now, given any proposition p, we will say that it is dangerous for a given inhabitant to believe p if his believing p will lead him to believing E.

The problem is to prove that for any proposition p, if a given inhabitant believes that it is dangerous for him to believe p, then it really is dangerous for him to believe p.

Solution

Suppose an inhabitant does believe that it is dangerous for him to believe p. He thus believes the proposition Bp⊃BE. We will show that Bp⊃BE is therefore true--i.e. if he should ever believe p, then he really will believe E.

Suppose he believes p. Being normal, he will then believe Bp. And since he also believes Bp⊃BE and is of type 1, he will believe BE. Then, since he is stable, he will believe E.

A GRAND INDECISION

We again consider a reflexive, stable reasoner of type 4. There is a proposition p such that he can never believe p and can never believe ~p without becoming inconsistent in either case. [And so if he is consistent, he will never believe either one.] Can you find such a proposition p? [Note: Unlike Problem 1, we are **not** assuming that the reasoner is always accurate.]

Solution

We let f be any tautologically contradictory proposition--any proposition such that ~f is a tautology. Then for any proposition q, the proposition ~q≡(q⊃f) is a tautology, and so any reasoner--even of type 1--who believes ~q will believe q⊃f.

We now take for p the proposition Bf--the proposition that the reasoner believes (or will believe) f. [Of course if a reasoner of type 1 believes f, he will be inconsistent, since f⊃p is a tautology for every p].

If the reasoner should believe Bf, he will believe f (since he is stable) and hence will be inconsistent. On the other hand, if he should ever believe ~Bf, he will believe Bf⊃f, and so by Löb's theorem, he will believe f and again be inconsistent. [This last observation is due to Georg Kreisel.]

MODEST REASONERS

We have called a reasoner conceited if he believes all propositions of the form Bp⊃p. At the other extreme, let us call a reasoner modest if he never believes Bp⊃p unless he believes p. [If he believes p and is of type 1, he will, of course, <u>have</u> to believe Bp⊃p--in fact q⊃p for any q whatsoever]. Löb's theorem (for reasoners) can be succinctly stated: Any reflexive reasoner of type 4 is modest.

The theory of modest reasoners of type 4 (or rather the analogous theory for systems) is today an elaborate one, of which we can say here but a little. For one thing, it can be shown that any modest reasoner of type 4 must be reflexive (a sort of converse of Löb's theorem). Another thing: Let us say that a reasoner <u>believes</u> he is modest if for every p, he believes the proposition B(Bp⊃p)⊃Bp. [Of course, all these propositions are <u>true</u> if the reasoner really is modest.] It is not difficult to show that any reasoner of type 4 (or even any normal reasoner of type 1) who believes he is modest really is modest. [The reader might try this as an exercise.] It can also be shown (but this is a bit more tricky) that every modest reasoner of type 4 believes that he is modest. A surprising result (due to Kripke, deJongh and Sambin) is that every reasoner of type 3 who believes he is modest will also believe he is normal--and thus is of type 4! And so for any reasoner, the following 4 conditions are equivalent: (1) He is a reflexive reasoner of type 4; (2) He is a modest reasoner of type 4; (3) He is a reasoner of type 4 who believes he is modest; (4) He is a reasoner of type 3 who believes he is modest. [Proofs of these equivalences can be found in [2], or in a more formal version, in [1].]

Reasoners satisfying any of the above equivalent conditions correspond to an important system of modal logic known as G--accordingly, they are called (in [2]) <u>reasoners of type G</u>. Boolos [1] has devoted an excellent book to this modal system and [2] contains a host of epistemic problems about reasoners of this and other types. [A particularly curious reasoner to be met in [2] is the <u>queer</u> reasoner--he is of type G and believes that he is inconsistent. But he is wrong in this belief!]

I wish to conclude with another epistemic puzzle which I think you might enjoy trying as an exercise.

A reasoner of type 4 (not necessarily reflexive) goes to an island which is and which he believes to be a knight-knave island. He visits it because of a rumor that there is gold buried there. He meets a native and asks: "Is there really gold here?" The native then makes two statements: (1) If you ever believe I'm a knight, then you will believe that there is gold here; (2) If you ever believe I'm a knight, then there <u>is</u> gold here.

Is there gold on this island or not? Why?

References

G. Boolos. The Unprovability of Consistency.   Cambridge University Press
    (1979).

R. Smullyan.   Forever Undecided: A Puzzle Guide to Gödel.   Knopf (In
    Press).

Knowledge and Efficient Computation

by
Silvio Micali
Computer Science Department
MIT
545 Technology Square
Cambridge, MA 02139

Abstract

We informally discuss "knowledge complexity": a measure for the amount of knowledge that can be feasibly extracted from a communication. Our measure provides an answer to the following two questions:

1) How much knowledge should be communicated for proving a theorem?

2) How to prove correctness of cryptographic protocols?

We sympathize with the readers who are distressed by the level of informality of this short abstract. Most of the material is contained in the reference [GMR]. We encourage the readers to consult it for precise definitions.

1. Knowledge Complexity

Everyone would agree that communication is *the* tool for transfering or exchanging knowledge. This, however, does not answer basic questions like

Which communications convey knowledge?

How much knowledge is contained in a communication?

knowledge Complexity, a notion introduced in [GMR], provides an answer to these questions in a framework where computation is bounded. In sections 2 and 3 we indicate how these ideas can be applied to two contexts in which knowledge is particularly relevant: theorem proving and cryptographic protocols.

1.1 The Basic Scenario

In our framework communications that convey knowledge are those transmitting the result of an <u>infeasible</u> computation, therefore a computation that we cannot perform by ourselves. Before proceding any further, we have to settle the question of which computations should be considered infeasible. Theoretical computer science regards as "feasible" those computations that can be performed in polynomial time (i.e. in time polynomial in the length of the input) and as "infeasible" those requiring, say, exponential time. [1]

Recently, coin tossing has been proved useful for efficient computation (see for example the probabilistic primality tests of Solovay and Strassen [SS], Rabin [R] and Goldwasser and Killian [GK]). Since the ability of flipping a coin is common to anyone, we will consider infeasible those computations that cannot be performed in probabilistic polynomial time (i.e. in polynomial time and making random choices as well).

Our scenario consists of two "agents" (read Turing machines) A and B and an input x known to both of them. We think of A as the "communicator" and of B as the "receiver". They "talk" back and forth about x. (In a more restricted scenario, as in the case of radio broadcasting, A will be the only one to speak and B will only listen.) As we are interested in quantifying how much knowledge can be "efficiently extracted" from a communication, B is bound to compute in probabilistic polynomial time, while A has no restrictions on its computational power. In many relevant cases, however, A may also be bound to feasible computations, but happens to possess more "insights" about x. One such case is discussed in the next sub-section and more natural examples arise in the context of section 3.

Our scenario is deceivingly resemblant the one of Information Theory. There A is the *only* witness of some event, the occurrence of which it communicates to B. More precisely, B knows the probability of the possible events,

---

(1) It is apparent that the computation time necessary for solving a problem depends on the size of the problem, i.e. the number of bits necessary for describing it. For instance, multiplying two integers will require more time for longer integers than for shorter ones. The running time is thus considered as a function of the input length, usually denoted by k. A problem is solvable in polynomial time if there is a constant c and an algorithm (Turing machine) that solves of its instances of size k within time (number of steps) k^c. It may seem arbitrary to equate "feasibility" with polynomial time, as k needs to be pretty big before k^{50} (that is a particular polynomial running time) becomes less than, say, $k^{\log(\log k)}$ (that is a non-polynomial running time). However, there are many reasons justifying the choice of polynomial time as "efficient time". For example, polynomial time is a robust notion in that it appears to be independent of the particular computational model (computer) used. Another advantage is that the composition of two feasible computations is itself a feasible computation. This is so as "polynomial of polynomial is polynomial", very much the same way as the finite union of finite sets is finite.

but is totally unaware of which specific event actually occurred.

One fundamental difference between other models and ours is that x is a <u>common</u> input. Another difference is that B is only capable of feasible computations and cannot, for instance, derive all the logical consequences of the information in its hand. [2]

Let, for instance, B be a scientist (bound, as a human, to feasible computation only). Let the common input x be Nature (that indeed is under everybody's eyes) and A be an "angel" willing to reveal some of nature's best kept secrets. The angel and the scientist will discuss about x. It is in this scenario that we address the question of how much knowledge has the scientist gained by this conversation. Given what we said above, answering is easy in at least two cases. If A sends to B n random bits, for example, though this will be n bits of information, it would be no *knowledge* because B could easily generate random bits by himself. Similarly, the result of any probabilistic polynomial-time computation will not contain any knowledge.

We do not present here a formal and general upper bound (expressed in bits) for the amount of knowledge that can be communicated to a polynomial time receiver. A precise formulation of the new measure relies on many technical details and is unsuitable for such a short abstract. We will, however, present the motivation behind it and mention the notions necessary to its formalization. This is best done by discussing an example.

1.2 An Example

Assume that a crime x has happened, that B is a reporter and A a police officer. A understands the rights of the press but, for obvious reasons, also tries not to release too much knowledge about x. Should reporter B call the police officer A to know more about x? It depends. If he has probability essentially equal to 1 of efficiently generating, alone at home, in front of his typewriter, the "same" conversations (about this <u>specific</u> crime x) that he might have with A, he should not bother to call: A will give him zero knowledge about x. Assume, instead, that B may, efficiently and by himself (i.e. without A's intervention), generate four conversations about x, one of which (but is not clear which one) is guaranteed to be the one actually occuring if talking to A. In this case, the knowledge that B may receive from A about x cannot exceed two bits. Moreover, this is an absolute upper bound for any kind of knowledge B may receive. Possibly, the knowledge B is interested in is even less. Still, it may pay off to call. If, finally, B has <u>only</u> chance 1 in 2^{100} of generating the possible conversations about x with the police officer by an efficient procedure, then the officer is a real gossiper and B should rush to the telephone!

Let us stress once more that it is crucial that B should be able to "simulate" A efficiently. The ability of generating the conversations in question with probability 1 but in exponential time would be totally useless. Essentially, because B would not live long enough to see the result of his computations! It is the probability of quickly imitating A that essentially measures the "amount of knowledge that A may give to our <u>specific</u> reporter B".

Much more important, however, is the notion of an agent (police officer) that only gives away *at most* a certain amount of knowledge, *no matter with whom it talks.* An honest reporter will not try to get out of A knowledge that is

(2) This will in general make the analysis particularly delicate as polynomial time is a notion easy to define but difficult to use. In fact though progress has been made towards estimating the computational difficulty of problems still very fundamental questions remain open.

not supposed to receive. However, nobody guarantees the officer that he is talking to an honest reporter. Indeed a dishonest and news-hungry B', though still bound to feasible computation, may be able to find out more about x. Despite this capability, if the officer is so skillful to be one who communicates, say, at most 2 bits of knowledge, no matter how tricky questions B' asks and how much he cheats, he will not get out of him more than two bits about x.

Proving that some communicator A, that is programmed to answer certain type of questions, releases at most two bits of knowledge is certainly more difficult. Essentially because a proof must consider all possible polynomial-time strategies for B'. Still, as we point out is section 2 and 3, such proofs have been found in some cases. First, we need to refine the concepts of the previous example.

1.3 Our Example Revisited

In the example above, we talked about the probability with which B, by himself and efficiently, may generate the discussion that it and A may have on input x. However, everyone knows that some randomness is present in every conversation. Let our communicator be the most predictable police officer you can imagine. Still, for no crime the set of his relative possible comments will consist of a single element. Rather, to any possible crime will be associated an *ensemble* of possible trivialities. Guessing exactly which comment will be actually said will be almost impossible, but nevertheless inessential as these comments are all "equivalent". Insisting in predicting individual strings would mislead us toward a wrong definition of knowledge, one in which essentially all communicators would appear releasing enormous amounts of knowledge. Consider a communicator T that, no matter what the input is, always transmits a randomly chosen 100-bit string. It will be pretty hard to correctly guess which string it will send us, but it will be extremely easy to dispose of T and replace it by flipping a 100-bit string ourselves whenever we want its opinion. This leads to the following point of view.

The probabilistic programs (agents) A and B, together with the input x specify a *probability distribution AB_x*, namely the set of all possible conversations of A and B about x. These probability distributions may be extremely complex. What is relevant to our analysis is the computational difficulty of *sampling AB_x*, i.e. picking elements with exactly the probabilities they are assigned in AB_x. Let us revise in this light some of the cases discussed in our example of section 1.3.

Reaching a more appropriate level of generality, we will say that A gives zero knowledge to B if, on input x, B will be able, by himself, to sample AB_x in polynomial time. That is, if B can efficiently select conversations c with exactly the probability distribution with which A and B talking together would select it.

Let us consider the next case. One way in which A gives B at most 2 bits of knowledge is the following: on input x, B can efficiently select 4 conversations, one of which will be selected exactly according to AB_x, though B does not necessarily know which one.

1.4 A Pinch of Operationism (or: One More Visit To Our Example)

To reach a powerful level of generality, we have to further refine the notion of "efficient samplability" of AB_x given in the previous sub-section. There we insisted that B, alone and reasonably quickly, is able to select elements with exactly the same probability they are assigned in AB_x. Why do we need these probabilities to be *exact?* There is no compelling reason. For example, let D_1 be the uniform probability distribution over the set of the 1000-bit strings and let the distribution D_2 assign equal probability to all 1000-bit string except the string 000...0 (one thousand times) which will be assigned probability 0. Then it will be humanly impossible to distinguish D_1 from D_2 by randomly drawing elements from them. Only after the Universe has ended will we find out that the string 000...0 does not come up with the same frequency when sampling D_2 as when sampling D_1. For all practical considerations, D_1 is equal to D_2.

Above we only discussed a particular way in which two probability distributions appear equal: the two probability distributions assign equal probability to equal strings except for a set whose total probability is negligibly small. However, as the following example suggests, this may not be the only way in which two probability distributions may appear equal. Consider a particular Turing machine M. let S_1^k be the set of the k-bit inputs on which M halts after $2^{\sqrt{k}}$ steps and S_2^k the set of k-bit inputs on which M does not halt. Now choose a particular k with the constraints that it is bigger than a million and that S_1^k and S_2^k contain, say, more than 2^{100} elements. Then, let us consider the uniform probability distribution for S_1^k and for S_2^k. This time the two distributions cannot be close as they are defined on totally disjoint sets. Nevertheless, it is conceivable that, by cleverly choosing M, the two distributions may appear equal from all practical points of view!

The notion that naturally includes all "plausible" ways of two distributions appearing equal (including of course the ones suggested above) is that of *Polynomial Time Undistinguishable Probability Distributions*. The precise definition is given in [GMR]. Here we only intend to outline the point of view behind the definition.

In essence, two objects X and Y can be called distinct only if there is an explicit procedure that tells them apart. At a second glance, what we really need is a procedure that is reasonably fast. If all polynomial time procedures fail to distinguish X from Y, then X and Y are either equal or distinguishable only by "angels". But, for us humans, it is an act of intellectual honesty to consider them equal.

We should rivisit once more our example armed with this new level of generality. In essence, the reporter receives 0 knowledge from the police officer if can efficiently generate a set of conversations that cannot be feasibly distinguished from the text of the conversations that he might have with the officer. In this case, experiencing the "real" conversations with the officer is useless as no other human (somebody who is bound to polynomial time) can find any difference with the fake ones. Whatever the reporter may find in the real conversations or UL "whatever" he can succeed doing with the real conversations, he may also find or succeed in doing with the fake ones.

One may ask at this point why further generalizations are not necessary. The best reassurance that the right formalization has been achieved can be derived from the successful application of these concepts to other fields of interest. Indeed, knowledge complexity enabled us to study some fundamental questions relative to the proving process (see next section) and to prove the correctness of cryptographic protocols, an extremely puzzling and difficult task.

2. The Knowledge Complexity of Theorem Proving Procedures

How much knowledge should be communicated for proving a theorem T?

Certainly enough to verify that T is true. Usually, much more. For example, to prove that a certain a is a quadratic residue mod m (i.e. a square mod m), it is sufficient to communicate an x such that $a \equiv x^2 \bmod m$. This communication, however, contains more knowledge than just the fact that a is a quadratic residue. It communicates a <u>square root</u> of a. We intend to measure the additional knowledge that a prover gives to a verifier during a proof, and investigate whether this additional knowledge may be essentially 0.

To be able to contain the amount of knowledge released during a proof we need to consider a natural generalization of efficient theorem-proving procedures.

2.1 Interactive Proof Systems

Much effort has been previously devoted to make precise the notion of an efficient theorem-proving procedure. *NP* constitutes a very successful formalization of this notion. Loosely speaking, a theorem is in provable in NP if its proof is easy to verify once it has been found. Let us recall Cook's [C] (and independently Levin's [L]) influential definition of *NP* in this light.

The *NP* proof-system consists of two communicating Turing machines A and B: respectively, the *prover* and the *verifier*. The prover is exponential-time, the verifier is polynomial-time. Both A and B are deterministic, read a common input and interact in a very elementary way. On input a string x, belonging to an *NP* language L, A computes a string y (whose length is bounded by a polynomial in the length of x) and writes y on a special tape that B can read. B then checks that $f_L(y) = x$ (where f_L is a polynomial-time computable function relative to the language L) and, if so, halts and accepts. This process is illustrated in figure 1.

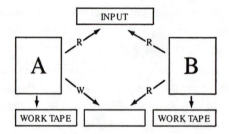

Fig. 1: The *NP* proof-system[*]

The notion of a proof, like the notion of a computation, is an intuitive one. Intuition, however, may and must be formalized. Computability by (deterministic) Turing machines is an elegant example of formalization of the intuitive concept of a computation. Each formalization, however, cannot entirely capture our original and intuitive notions,

[*] (By $----\!>$ we denote a read/write head, by $---R->$ a read-only head and by $---W->$ a write-only head)

exactly because they are intuitive. Following our intuition, probabilistic algorithms [R] [SS] [GK] are means of computing, though they are not in the previous formal model. Similarly, NP is an elegant formalization of the intuitive notion of a theorem-proving procedure. However, NP only captures a particular way of communicating a proof. It deals with those proofs that can be "written down in a book".

We want to introduce interactive proof-systems to capture a more general way of communicating a proof. We deal with those proofs that can be "explained in class". Informally, in a classroom, the lecturer can take full advantage of the possibility of interacting with the "recipients" of the proof. They may ask questions at crucial points of the argument and receive answers. This makes life much easier. Writing down a proof that can be checked by everybody without interaction is a much harder task. In some sense, because one has to answer in advance all possible questions.

Before arguing that our interactive proof systems capture the intuitive notion of a proof we need to ask: what is intuitively required from a theorem-proving procedure? First, that it is possible to "prove" a true theorem. Second, that it is impossible to "prove" a false theorem. Third, that communicating a proof should be efficient in the following sense. It does not matter how long must the prover compute during the proving process, but it is essential that the computation required from the verifier is easy.

The theorem-proving procedures we consider are

1) *efficient*: the "recipient" of a proof must be quickly convinced of its correctness.

2) *probabilistic*: on input a false n-bit long statement, the recipient may erroneously be convinced that it is correct with very small probability, say $\frac{1}{2^n}$. On input a true n-bit long statement, the recipient should rightfully be convinced of its correctness with very high probability, say $1 - \frac{1}{2^n}$.

3) *interactive*: to verify the correctness of a statement, the "recipient" of the proof may actively ask questions and receive answers from the "prover".

Rather than giving a formal definition of our interactive proof-systems let us present an example.

Example 1: Let Z_m^* denote the set of integers between 1 and m that are relatively prime with m. An element $a \in Z_m^*$ is a *quadratic residue* mod n if $a = x^2$ mod m for some $x \in Z_m^*$, else it is a *quadratic nonresidue*. Now let $L = \{(m,x) \mid x \in Z_m^* \text{ is a quadratic nonresidue}\}$. Notice that $L \in$ NP: a prover needs only to compute the factorization of m and send it to the verifier without any further interaction. But looking ahead to zero knowledge proof-systems, we will consider a more interesting interactive proof-system for L. The verifier B begins by choosing $n = |m|$ random members of Z_m^*, $\{r_1, r_2, ..., r_n\}$. For each i, $1 \leq i \leq n$, he flips a coin, and if it comes up heads he forms $t_i = r_i^2$ mod m, and if it comes up tails he forms $t_i = x \cdot r_i^2$ mod m. Then B sends $t_1, t_2, ..., t_n$ to A. The prover, having unrestricted computing power, finds which of the t_i are quadratic residues, and uses this information to tell B the results of his last n coin tosses. If this information is correct, B accepts.

Why does this work? If $(m,x) \in L$, then A correctly predicts all last n coin tosses of B who will definitely accept. If (m,x) not in L, then the $\{t_i\}$ are just random quadratic residues, and the prover will respond correctly in the last part of the computation with probability $1/2^n$. In fact, for each of the last n coin tosses of B, A has probability exactly $1/2$ of guessing it correctly.

We may view our interactive proof-systems as a special service offered by ATT. "Dial 144 for mathematical theorem proving". Some user may want to know whether x belongs to language L and dials 144. Immediatly he is connected with a Super Expert able to solve all problems. The trouble is that the user does not trust him. He may not be as expert as he claims or he may be a cheater ready to tell the user false information. Therefore the user will not take his word about what is true. He trusts however the coin he flips and, if at the end of the conversation he has been convinced, than he believes that $x \in L$. In fact he knows that if this was not the case, the probability of being convinced (taken over his own coin tosses) was exponentially vanishing.

We now address our next question.

2.2 The Knowledge Complexity of a Language

To prove that a formula is satisfiable it suffices to exhibit a satisfying assignment. This proof, however, appears to contain more knowledge than the single bit "satisfiable/non-satisfiable" ! Using knowledge complexity, we give a measure for the amount of additional knowledge that must be transfered during a theorem-proving procedure and show that, in some cases it may essentially be 0.

Let us view the case in which the additional knowledge is 0 in our ATT scenario. ATT charges a dollar for each call to 144. During a call the expert can be asked about only one theorem. Assume that the question is whether $x \in L$, i.e. whether x belongs to the set of true theorems. (Here we will assume that x does belong to L.) It is the purpose of the caller checking the validity of the received proof and, it must be admitted, getting at least two theorems at the price of one. ATT does not know whether the caller is a cheater and wants to insure that he only gets that $x \in L$ is true theorem. Can ATT succeed in this? Yes if membership in L can be shown releasing 0 additional knowledge. Rather than dealing with the general notion, we confine ourselves to discuss a restricted scenario.

The particular prover-recipient pair of example 1 possesses the following interesting property. When $x \in L$, A can show to B that indeed x belongs to L and *nothing else*. What is a way of expressing this? When $x \in L$, what B possesses at the end of the proof. First, knowledge of the fact that indeed x is in L, which was the main goal of the proof anyway. Second the actual *text* of the proof, that is an element e randomly selected from AB_x. However, in this example; once B has been convinced that $x \in L$, e becomes totally useless to it. In fact B can generate such e's alone and with the right probability distribution; he can efficiently sample AB_x without A's help. B may perfectly imitate A by looking at his own coin tosses. When B sends t_i computed by squaring r_i, it will imitate A by answering "quadratic residue". When B sends t_i computed by squaring r_i and then multiplying it by x, it will imitate A by answering "quadratic nonresidue". In other words, once B sees that A is able to predict its secret coin tosses, which "prooves" that x is a non-square mod n, it can predict its own coin tosses by himself as they are not secret to him!

Notice however, that, in example 1, A <u>is not</u> proving quadratic non-residuosity without releasing 0 additional knowledge. Rather, A is releasing 0 additional knowledge to the specific B of example 1. In fact, some other B' that interacts with A may decide to create the t_i's in a different way. For instance, such a B may send the sequence of integers $t_i = i$ and therefore receive an answer about their quadratic residuosity that it may not be able to compute by itself if deciding quadratic residuosity is not in probabilistic polynomial time.

However, a (more complex!) interactive proof system for proving quadratic non-residuosity that releases 0 knowledge (to anybody!) can be found in [GMR]. Recently we found a similar proof system for proving quadratic residuosity as well. This is surprising as no efficient algorithm for deciding quadratic residuosity mod m is known when m's factorization is not given. Moreover, all known NP proofs for this problem exhibit the prime factorization of m. This indicates that adding interaction to the proving process, may decrease the amount of knowledge that must be communicated in order to prove a theorem.

Zero-knowledge proof systems are a surprise and we believe that they cannot prove membership in every language. We actually intend to classify languages according to the amount of additional knowledge that must be released for proving membership in them.

We believe that knowledge complexity is one of the fundamental parameters of a language or, equivalently, of a theorem-proving procedure. Theorem-proving procedures are in fact intended to communicate knowledge and it is very natural to classify them according to the amount of knowledge they must communicate.

3. Applications of Knowledge Complexity to Cryptographic Protocols

In traditional computational complexity or communication complexity, the goal is to communicate as much knowledge as possible as efficiently as possible. Since all participants are considered good friends, no one cares if more knowledge than necessary is communicated. The situation with respect to cryptographic protocols is very different. In this case there is generally no problem at all communicating the knowledge efficiently, but the whole problem is making sure not *too much* knowledge has been communicated.

Model theoretic knowledge has been used to analyze protocols. For example, in [HR] it has been used to prove Rabin's "Oblivious Transfer" correct in some setting. However, as pointed out in [FMR], Rabin's oblivious transfer still lacks a proof of correctness in a complexity theoretic framework.

We believe that knowledge complexity provides the right framework to discuss the correctness of crytographic protocols. For example, applying these ideas [FMR] modified Rabin's oblivious transfer so that it can be proved correct.

Knowledge complexity helps in proving or disproving the correctness of cryptographic protocols as these are based on the secrecy of some private information and should preserve this secrecy. The privacy of some information is what gives us an advantage over our adversaries. Let A(lice) possess the prime factorization of an integer n (say $n = p_1 \cdot p_2$), while B(ob) only knows n. During a protocol with B, A must protect the privacy of her information. Assume that A can perform each step of the protocol without having even to look at the value of p_1 and p_2. Then it is easy to show that the protocol did not compromise the privacy of n's factorization. It is also easy to see, however, that the protocol could not have accomplished any interesting task. In fact A has not made use of her "advantage"! The protocol may accomplish a non-trivial task if, in at least one step of it, A performs a computation c that depends on p_1 and p_2. This raises the question:

Will $c(p_1, p_2)$ betray to much information about p_1 and p_2?

Classical information theory does not provide an answer to this question. Knowledge complexity can. In particular,

1)   We can quantify the amount of knowledge about p_1 and p_2 that c conveys and

2)   We can design protocols so to minimize this amount of knowledge.

We use this to give an upper bound on the number of times a single protocol or a combination of protocols can be played, using a common secret key, without giving away too much information about the secret key. In addition, trying to measure the amount of knowledge revealed during the execution of a protocol about the secret, may pin point weaknesses in the design of the protocol.

A most important application of these ideas is that it allows us to prove correctness of protocols in a *modular* way. Complex protocols are usually composed of sub-protocols. For instance, many protocols use a sub-protocol for "coin tossing over a telephone" (Blum [Bl1]). However, it is not clear how to use a "normal" definition of correctness of "coin tossing" to prove the correctness of the main protocol. In general, it appears that much stronger definitions for these sub-protocols are needed in order to fit them modularly and cleanly inside larger protocols. Full details will be given in the forthcoming paper on the applications of Knowledge Complexity to the theory of cryptographical protocol.

Acknowlededgement

Many thanks to Oded Goldreich for his many helpful suggestions.

References

[Bl1] M. Blum, *Coin flipping by telephone*, IEEE COMPCON 1982.

[C]   S.Cook, *The Complexity of Theorem-Proving Procedures"*, Proc. of 3rd STOC, 1971.

[FMR]M. Fischer, S. Micali and C. Rackoff, *A Secure Protocol for the Oblivious Transfer*, Lecture Eurocrypt 1984.

[GM]S. Goldwasser, and S. Micali, *Probabilistic Encryption*, JCSS Vol. 28, No. 2, April 1984.

[GM]S. Goldwasser, and S. MIcali ,*Proofs with Untrusted Oracles*, Unpublished Manuscript 1983.

[GGM]O. Goldreich, S. Goldwasser, and S. Micali, *How to Construct Random Function*, 25th FOCS, 1984.

[GMR]S. Goldwasser, S. Micali and C. Rackoff, *The Knowledge Complexity of Interactive Proof-Systems* 17th Annual ACM Symp. on Theory of Computing, pp 291-304. Better version to appear on the Journal of ACM.

[GK] S. Goldwasser and J. Killian, *A provably Correct and Provably Fast Primality Test*, to appear 18th STOC

[HR] J. Halpern and M.O. Rabin, *A Logic to reason about likelihood*, Proc. of 15th STOC, 1983.

[L] L.A.Levin, *Universal Sequential Search Problems*, Probl. Inform. Transm. 9/3 (1973), pp. 265-266.

[R] M. Rabin,

[SS] R. Solovay and V. Strassen *A fast Monte-Carlo test for primality*, SIAM J. on Comp., 1977, pp. 84-85.

Realizability Semantics
for Error-Tolerant Logics
(preliminary version)

John C. Mitchell
AT&T Bell Labs

Michael J. O'Donnell
The University of Chicago

December 19, 1985

Abstract

Classical and constructive logics have shortcomings as foundations for sophisticated automated reasoning from large amounts of data because a single error in the data could produce a contradiction, logically implying all possible conclusions. Relevance logics have the potential to support sensible reasoning from data that contains a few errors, limiting the impact of those errors to assertions that are naturally related to the erroneous information. There are a number of competing formal systems for relevance logic in the literature, with different sets of theorems. Applications of relevance logics, and particularly choices between formalisms, are hampered by the lack of clear intuitive semantic treatment of relevance.

This paper proposes plausible semantic treatments of relevance logic based on intuitive restrictions on the behavior of realizability functions. We examine two versions of realizability semantics. The first uses models which consist entirely of realizability functions that preserve *independence* of evidence, while the second semantics requires functions to be *strictly monotone* with respect to strength of evidence. We show soundness for the first semantics, and soundness and completeness theorems over a "nonstandard" set of models for the second. The second approach also yields completeness over "nonstandard" models for intuitionistic implication.

1. Introduction

Many computer systems, such as database query systems and "expert" systems, are designed to answer questions based on a given body of information:

> Mr./Ms. X provides the computer with a body of information (or refers implicitly to information already stored) and asks a question.
>
> The computer derives an answer and responds.

It is also natural to view programming in logic programming languages [Kow79], [ODo85] in this way. A formal framework for defining the correct behavior of these systems is well-known: the body of information is assumed to be in a particular logical language, the question gives rise to a set of *syntactically appropriate* answers, and the response is *correct* if it is both syntactically appropriate to the question and logically implied by the given information. (Often questions are of the form *"For what x is P(x)?,"* in which case the syntactically appropriate answers are all formulas of the form P(y); see [BS76] for further discussion.) Assuming the notion of syntactic appropriateness to be rather straightforward, we see that correctness reduces to logical implication. Classical logic, in which assumptions $p_1, \ldots, p_n$ imply a conclusion c if every possible situation (world, model or interpretation) with all of the p_i true also has c true, is typically considered an appropriate basis for establishing correctness.

In relational database systems, the logical language expressing the information is a small subset of the first order predicate calculus. The only formulas are *tuples* such as *Manages(Joe,Fred)*, i.e., predicate symbols applied to sequences of constant symbols. Questions are of the form

$$\text{For what } x_1, \ldots, x_n \text{ is } p[x_1, \ldots, x_n]?,$$

where p is a first-order formula over the constant and predicate symbols occurring in tuples. Since the form of the question is always the same, only the predicate p need be given; actual database systems provide some syntactic sugar for expressing predicates. The syntactically appropriate answers to such a relational question are the ground formulas of the form $p[c_{1,1}, \ldots, c_{1,n}]$. A query processor is expected to find all correct answers. As with questions, the common structure of answers is omitted, and only the relevant tuples are generally given. Relational database query systems are designed to yield precisely the tuples representing formulae of the form described above which are logically implied by the information in the database. The semantics used to determine logical implication are classical first-order semantics, which seems to work quite well for simple query and answer. See [GMN84] for a survey of logical deduction as a database concept.

Relational database systems may be used as a paradigm for more sophisticated systems merely by allowing more and more generality in the formulae in the database. For example, the formula

$$\forall x, y, z \, . \, (Manages(x, z) \wedge Manages(y, z)) \rightarrow x = y$$

asserts the important fact that an employee may have only one manager. Such assertions are studied in the literature on relational databases under the name of *functional dependencies*, but they are treated as assertions *about* the contents of a database, and are not allowed to be *in* a database themselves.

Unfortunately, classical first-order predicate calculus has some shortcomings as a foundation for deriving the logical consequences of *unrestricted* first-order formula in a database. For example, suppose the formula asserting that no employee has more than one manager is stored in a database along with the two formulas *Manages(Fred,Joe)* and *Manages(Alice,Joe)* and the intuitively obvious formula *Fred ≠ Alice*. Since these four formulae are mutually contradictory, there is no interpretation in which they are simultaneously true. Therefore, in classical first-order logic, *every* formula is a logical consequence of these four. So, according to a correctness criteria based on classical logic, a database systems answering

$$\text{For what } x \text{ is Bonus(Mary,x)?}$$

with \$1,000,000,000 is considered correct. Since this does not really seem intuitively correct, the classical correctness condition is too permissive. Without rejecting logic *per se* as a basis for correctness, we would like to be more restrictive. Since the erroneous inference above is based on irrelevant erroneous postulates (the uniqueness of managers is not relevant to Mary's bonus), a formal analysis of relevance seems to be required. Notice that the relational database model avoids the problems associated with logical contradiction by restricting the contents of databases in a way that makes it is impossible to express logical contradiction (although information in a database may certainly be wrong, and may contradict other known information not included in the database).

The problem of reasoning in the presence of error is a problem of generating *knowledge* from other knowledge. Two considerations lead to a very different treatment of knowledge here than in the more usual approach through modal logic [Hin62]. The purpose of the modal approach is to provide a language for *discussing* knowledge. Thus, a special modal operator K is introduced, and Ka asserts that a is *known*. Assertions not preceded by K are taken as assertions of absolute truth. So Ka may be read as, *it is absolutely true that a is known*. In the database reasoning problem outlined above, *all* assertions are taken to be assertions of knowledge, based on the best available information, rather than of absolute truth, so an explicit modal operator is superfluous. Also, the usual modal definition of knowledge requires that knowledge is a refinement of truth. That is, $Ka \longrightarrow a$ (if a is known, then a is true) is a postulate. Such a definition of knowledge as realized truth is interesting theoretically, but has restricted application, since there is no general way in practice to distinguish true knowledge from rationally supported belief. So, we will define a logic in which the assertion a is taken to mean that a is known, or believed, on the basis of rational consideration of evidence from reliable (but not infallible) sources. We submit that this sort of assertion is the one normally intended by the phrase "it is known." The reader who is offended by such an interpretation is encouraged to substitute *rational belief* for *knowledge*, and to consider the following proposals accordingly.

Before discussing solutions to the problem of reasoning in the presence of contradictions and other errors, we would like to rule out two tempting but flawed approaches. First, we might try to detect and eliminate contradictions before answering any questions. Detection of contradiction is as hard as every other inference problem, and seems to require processing the whole database. There is no reason to hope for a tractable detection strategy except at the cost of very strong restrictions on a database. Once a contradiction is detected, it must be removed. Fagin, Ullman and Vardi discussed ways of removing contradictions by making syntactically minimal changes to a database [FUV83]. This work was intended as a foundation for *updates* to databases, but there is no evidence that syntactically minimal changes can be determined efficiently, nor that they are intuitively appropriate. If automated reasoning is to be applied to complex formulae, it appears unavoidable that we must survive contradictory and erroneous data until it is detected and corrected. In the meantime, we cannot avoid giving erroneous answers to questions that depend on the erroneous data, but we should answer other questions correctly.

Another natural approach to error is to quantify it through probability theory or some other numerical theory of uncertainty. It may be feasible to quantify some possibilities for error in such a way, but never all of them. No matter how thoroughly we have analyzed known uncertainties, we must accept the possibility of errors arising in totally unforeseen ways. Typographical errors alone (particularly errors in typing in probabilities of error) may be deadly. So, the quantification of error presupposes a foundation that can survive unquantified errors. We will not even introduce a nonnumerical modal operator to point out uncertainty (informally, a phrase of the form, "it is likely, but not certain, that . . .") since *all* assertions are to be taken as potentially erroneous.

In order to reason safely in the presence of errors, we must change the basic attitude of classical logic toward logical implication. Classically, the postulate p implies the conclusion c if, whenever p is *absolutely, unquestionably true*, then so is c. In practical reasoning, we are never absolutely sure of postulates, and must be ready to abandon the classical viewpoint when necessary. In the past, this change of viewpoint has been accomplished by abandoning temporarily the formal system in which reasoning has been going on, and switching to a more conservative informal system. For example, when set theory was discovered to be inconsistent, mathematicians were able to distinguish informally those inferences that depended on the contradiction from those that did not (even though most of these mathematicians professed classical ideology). [1] For automated reasoning, the more conservative viewpoint that survives contradictions must itself be formalized. Notice that intuitionistic, or constructive, reasoning does not by itself solve the problem. To an intuitionist, p implies c if, whenever p may be *absolutely, unquestionably demonstrated* by some effective procedure, then so may c. Intuitionistic logic rejects certain classically accepted formulae, such as $a \lor \neg a$, but still allows a contradiction to imply all possible conclusions. The new sort of implication required lets p imply c if, whenever the best available information includes p, it is reasonable to believe c as well. It is not immediately obvious how to formalize such a concept, but the example of uniqueness of managers implying Mary's large bonus shows that neither classical nor intuitionistic formal logic suffices. Apparently, the new implication must enforce some sort of *relevance* of p to c when p implies c.

Logicians of a philosophical bent have studied several formal systems enforcing relevance of postulates to implied conclusions. Such systems are collectively called *relevance logics*, and are best explained by Anderson and Belnap [AB75]. Proponents of relevance logic from the philosophical community often claim that some sort of relevance logic represents the only true idea of logical implication. For our purposes, it is only important that a relevance logic may provide a useful definition of logical implication in the presence of error. Shapiro and Wand [SW76], and Belnap [Bel76] [Bel75], have already advocated the usefulness of relevance logics to automatic reasoning.

The application of relevance logics has been hindered by a lack of intuitively satisfying semantics for such logics. Routley and Meyer [RM73] and, independently, Fine [Fin74], defined Kripke-like semantics for certain relevance logics, and proved soundness and completeness. Their semantics involves a *trinary* relation between possible worlds, and that relation seems very difficult to understand intuitively.

This paper proposes new semantic treatments of relevant implication, based on the intuitionistic concept of realizability [Kle45, KV65, Lau70]. Soundness and completeness theorems are proved for relevant implication, motivated by similar theorems for intuitionistic implication. The new semantics may provide a plausible foundation for the formal analysis of error-tolerant reasoning. Avron recently and independently proposed a totally different semantic explanation of another relevance logic. His approach divides the universe into domains of relevance; classical logic is valid within, but not between, domains. For Avron, p relevantly implies c if $\neg p \lor c$, and p is in the same domain of relevance as c. By contrast, our semantics define the relation p relevantly implies c, but not any symmetric relation of relevance between predicates. There is not enough technical information about applications of the two semantic treatments yet to allow a rational choice between them.

Section 2 sketches the concepts behind realizability semantics for relevance logics. Section 3 introduces a well-known formal system for intuitionistic implication, based on the lambda-K calculus, and two formal systems for relevant implication, derived from the intuitionistic system by restricting the use of variables in terms (equivalently, the use of assumptions in proofs). Section 4 presents realizability semantics for intuitionistic implication, with soundness and completeness. Section 5 extends the semantics, soundness results, and a completeness result, to relevance logics.

2. Intuitive Foundations for Relevance Logic

Although intuitionistic logic does not allow meaningful reasoning in the presence of contradictions, intuitionistic semantics seems to provide a useful starting point for developing relevant semantics. A constructive proof of $a \longrightarrow b$ is an effective function mapping constructive proofs of a to constructive proofs of b. In the presence of errors, such a function must map not only proofs of a, but seemingly reliable *evidence* for a to at least as reliable evidence for b. See Helman [Hel77b] for a discussion of the philosophical aspects of proofs as functions on evidence. This view of proofs as functions leads naturally to a consideration of types: if we regard the collection of evidence for a as the "type" a, and

---

[1] However, at least one false theorem was published by Burali-Forti [Bur67], who did *not* recognize his derivation as a paradox, but thought that it proved that the ordinals are not well ordered. (Set theorists today uniformly agree that the ordinals are well ordered.)

similarly for b, then a proof of $a \longrightarrow b$ is a function from type a to type b. Serendipitously, the type of functions from a to b is commonly written $a \longrightarrow b$.

The interpretation of proofs as functions certainly supports *modus ponens*, from a and $a \longrightarrow b$ to infer b, since the function proving $a \longrightarrow b$ can be applied to the evidence for a, producing evidence for b. Problems may arise when evidence *against b* is taken as evidence against a. Suppose that the function proving $a \longrightarrow b$ ignores its input, and produces a fixed piece of seemingly reliable, but erroneous, evidence for b. Suppose that evidence against b is also available. It makes no sense to take this evidence against b as evidence against a, since the proof that $a \longrightarrow b$ did not actually establish any connection between a and b.

The standard intuitionistic development of negation (also valid classically) provides a concrete illustration of the problem of negative evidence. $\neg a$ is defined to be $a \longrightarrow \Lambda$, where Λ is a manifest falsehood, and $\Lambda \longrightarrow b$ for all b. As discussed in Section 1, a contradiction $a \wedge \neg a$ with such a negation implies all formulae b. Furthermore, the constructive interpretation of implication, in the presence of errors, does not support *modus tollens*. *Modus tollens*, or contrapositive reasoning, allows $\neg a$ to be inferred from $a \longrightarrow b$ and $\neg b$. *Modus tollens* may be derived from *modus ponens*, and the definitions of $\neg$ and Λ above. But, as argued before, if the constructive proof of $a \longrightarrow b$ is a constant function, evidence against b does not yield evidence against a. Intuitionistic logic is normally interpreted over a universe containing only correct constructive proofs. In that universe, modus tollens presents no problem. We seek a modified interpretation of implication over a universe containing both correct and incorrect evidence, that still supports modus tollens.

In addition to expanding the domains of functions to include evidence as well as proof, we must require a function proving $a \longrightarrow b$ to establish a real connection between a and b. The stronger concept of implication, with an appropriate definition of negation, should support *modus tollens* as well as *modus ponens* in spite of errors. In particular, a relevant proof that $a \longrightarrow b$ must be a function that, given more and more evidence for a, produces more and more evidence for b. With such an increasing property, any reason for distrusting evidence for b gives a legitimate reason to distrust evidence for a as well. Constant functions must certainly be ruled out, but many nonconstant functions, for instance those that are constant over large subsets of their domains, must be ruled out as well. We formalize these intuitive concerns in two ways by imposing a relation of *independence* between pieces of evidence, or by imposing an anti-symmetric ordering relation, and insisting in each case that proofs of relevant implication preserve the relation.

3.   Proof Systems for Intuitionistic and Relevance Logics

Type-theoretic foundations for constructive logic originated in [Kre56], and may also be found in [How80, Ste72, FLO83, Mar75]. We will take a type-theoretic approach to both proofs and semantics of formulas, using the notation of [Ste72, FLO83]. The basic syntactic idea is to adopt the *typed lambda calculus*, a notation for describing typed functions, as a proof system. The usual typed lambda calculus (lambda-K calculus) serves as a proof system for intuitionistic logic. Proof systems for various relevance logics may be derived from lambda-K calculus by imposing restrictions which insure that all arguments to a function are relevant to the value of the function. The most obvious relevance restriction is that the argument of a function must appear in the body of the function definition. This restriction yields the *lambda-I calculus* and the relevance system **R**. Additional restrictions, motivated by semantic definitions for relevant functions, yield other relevance logics.

It is helpful to think of lambda terms as natural deduction proofs since lambda calculus is actually a notational variant of natural deduction [How80, Mar75, MP85]. Natural deduction proofs are intended to formalize the common "blackboard-style" arguments in which we assume α, derive β from α, and then conclude from this derivation that α must imply β. Thus natural deduction proof involve introducing assumptions into proofs and later discharging assumptions to obtain proofs of implications. In lambda calculus expressions, which we will call *testimony terms*, assumptions are represented by variables and discharged assumptions by lambda-bound variables. Since we will consider a formula a proved only when we have a proof of a with all assumptions discharged, our proof system will involve some machinery for keeping track of free variables in terms.

In the following definitions, $\vdash$ and $\rightarrow$ are intended as formal symbols, while $\in$, $\Longrightarrow$, and $\longrightarrow$ are metasymbols denoting the usual mathematical concepts of set membership, implication, and sets of functions.

Definition 3.1

Let $\mathbf{P}_0$ be a set of symbols called *primitive types* or *propositions*. Members of $\mathbf{P}_0$ (and later $\mathbf{P}$) are denoted $a, b, c, \ldots$.

The set $\mathbf{P}$ of *types* or *propositions* is defined inductively as follows:

P1. $a \in \mathbf{P}_0 \Longrightarrow a \in \mathbf{P}$

P2. $a, b \in \mathbf{P} \Longrightarrow (a \rightarrow b) \in \mathbf{P}$ ∎

Definition 3.2

For each $a \in \mathbf{P}$, we choose an infinite set $\mathbf{V}^a$ of *variables of type* a, written $u^a, v^a, \ldots$, and let $\mathbf{V}$ be the set of all variables $\mathbf{V} = \bigcup\{\mathbf{V}^a \mid a \in \mathbf{P}\}$.

The set $\mathbf{T}$ of *testimony terms*, together with their types, are defined inductively below. Members of $\mathbf{T}$ are denoted $\alpha, \beta, \gamma, \ldots$. We write $\alpha \vdash a$ to mean that the testimony term α has type a or, equivalently, α is a proof of a.

T1. $x^a \in \mathbf{V}^a \Longrightarrow x^a \in \mathbf{T} \bigwedge x^a \vdash a$

T2. $\alpha, \beta \in \mathbf{T} \bigwedge \alpha \vdash a \bigwedge \beta \vdash (a \rightarrow b) \Longrightarrow (\beta\alpha) \in \mathbf{T} \bigwedge (\beta\alpha) \vdash b$

T3. $\beta \in \mathbf{T} \bigwedge \beta \vdash b \bigwedge x^a \in \mathbf{V}^a \Longrightarrow (\lambda x^a \beta) \in \mathbf{T} \bigwedge (\lambda x^a \beta) \vdash (a \rightarrow b)$

The set $\mathcal{A}(\alpha)$ of assumptions, or free variables, in term α is defined as follows.

F1. $\mathcal{A}(x^a) = \{x^a\}$

F2. $\mathcal{A}(\beta\alpha) = \mathcal{A}(\beta) \cup \mathcal{A}(\alpha)$

F3. $\mathcal{A}(\lambda y^b \beta) = \mathcal{A}(\beta) - \{y^b\}$ ∎

The testimony terms above are the terms of the conventional typed lambda-K calculus. It is easy to see that if $\alpha \in \mathbf{T}$, then there is a unique a such that $\alpha \vdash a$. If $\mathcal{A}(\alpha) = \emptyset$, we say α is *closed*. An occurrence of variable x^a within a subterm $\lambda x^a \alpha$ is said to be *bound*.

For one plausible definition of relevance, a more subtle analysis of the occurrence of variables is required.

Definition 3.3

Let $X \subseteq \mathbf{V}$ be a set of variables. The set $\mathcal{R}_X(\alpha)$ of variables occurring *relevantly in α with respect to X* is defined as follows.

RR1. $\mathcal{R}_X(x^a) = \{x^a\}$

RR2. $\mathcal{R}_X(\beta\alpha) = \mathcal{R}_X(\beta) \cup (\mathcal{R}_X(\alpha) - \mathcal{A}(\beta))$

RR3. $\mathcal{R}_X(\lambda y^b \beta) = \mathcal{R}_{X \cup \{y^b\}}(\beta) - \{y^b\}$ ∎

The condition α *is relevant in x^a with respect to X* is equivalent to α *is free in x^a, and no bound variable or variable in X appears to the left of all occurrences of x^a*. Notice that if α is relevant in x^a with respect to X and $Y \subseteq X$, then α is relevant in x^a with respect to Y. In particular, α is relevant in x^a with respect to $\emptyset$ if and only if α is *free* in x^a, and no bound variable of α appears to the left of all occurrences of x^a. Two interesting classes of relevant terms may be defined by restricting abstractions $(\lambda x^a \beta)$ so that x^a must be free (alternatively, relevant) in β.

Definition 3.4

The restricted testimony set $\mathbf{T}_R$ is defined as $\mathbf{T}$, except that the last clause is changed to

T3′. $\beta \in \mathbf{T} \bigwedge \beta \vdash b \bigwedge x^a \in \mathcal{A}(\beta) \Longrightarrow (\lambda x^a \beta) \in \mathbf{T} \bigwedge (\lambda x^a \beta) \vdash (a \rightarrow b)$

Similarly, $\mathbf{T}_{RR}$ is defined as $\mathbf{T}$, except that the last clause is changed to

T3″. $\beta \in \mathbf{T} \bigwedge \beta \vdash b \bigwedge x^a \in \mathcal{R}_{\emptyset}(\beta) \Longrightarrow (\lambda x^a \beta) \in \mathbf{T} \bigwedge (\lambda x^a \beta) \vdash (a \rightarrow b)$

We use $\alpha \vdash_R b$ as an abbreviation for $\alpha \vdash b \bigwedge \alpha \in \mathbf{T}_R$, and similarly for $\vdash_{RR}$.   ∎

The lambda terms in the testimony set $\mathbf{T}_R$ defined above are precisely the terms of the *simply typed lambda-I calculus* [FLO83], [Ste72], [Chu41]. The set $\mathbf{T}_{RR}$ has the additional restriction that the left-to-right order of variables abstracted by nested λ's must be the same as the left-to-right order of their leftmost occurrences. For example, $xy(x(zy))$ may only be abstracted as $\lambda x \lambda y \lambda z(xy(x(zy)))$, not as $\lambda y \lambda x \lambda z(xy(x(zy)))$, etc.

Lambda terms are usually intended to be read as function definitions, with $(\beta \alpha)$ representing the function β applied to the argument α, and $\lambda x^a \alpha$ representing the function of x^a whose values are described by the term α. We follow the usual conventions for the lambda calculus [Chu41]: parentheses are omitted with the convention that application associates to the left and $\rightarrow$ associates to the right. Superscripts are omitted from variables when the type is clear from context, or not important. Since the functional nature of lambda terms is reflected in the computation rules of β- and η-reduction, restricted class of lambda terms are unlikely to semantically define restricted classes of functions unless they are closed under these reduction rules. It is easy to show that R and RR are closed under β- and η-reduction.

Theorem 3.5

Let Q be R, RR, or null.

If $\alpha[((\lambda x^a \beta[x^a])\gamma)] \vdash_Q b$, then $\alpha[\beta[\gamma]] \vdash_Q b$.

If $\alpha[(\lambda x^a(\beta x^a))] \vdash_Q b$, and $x^a \notin \mathcal{A}(\beta)$, then $\alpha[\beta] \vdash_Q b$.

Proof sketch: elementary induction on the structure of β.   ∎

Notice that $\mathbf{T}_R$ and $\mathbf{T}_{RR}$ are *not* closed under the reverse of β- and η-reduction.

Having defined the syntax of testimony terms, we may gain some intuition for lambda calculus as a proof system by informally translating testimony terms into natural deduction proofs (see [How80, FLO83, MP85, Ste72] for further discussion). If $\beta \vdash a \rightarrow b$ and $\alpha \vdash a$, then $(\beta \alpha)$ denotes the proof

> *the proof denoted by β, ending in*
> $i_1 : a \rightarrow b$

> *the proof denoted by α, ending in*
> $i_2 : a$

b by Modus Ponens, i_1, i_2

Similarly, if $\beta \vdash b$, then $\lambda x^a \beta$ denotes the proof

Assume a

> *the proof denoted by β, ending in*
> $i : b$

end assumption

$a \rightarrow b$ by discharging assumption a

For example, the lambda term for the identity function, $(\lambda x^a x^a)$, may be read as a proof that a implies a:

1 : Assume a

2 : *a* by 1

end assumption

3 : $a \to a$ by Deduction Rule, 2

Since terms with free variables correspond to partial proofs with undischarged assumptions, the theorems of the systems $\mathbf{I}_\to$, $\mathbf{R}_\to$, and $\mathbf{RR}_\to$ are those types a for which there exists a closed term with $\alpha \vdash a$, $\alpha \vdash_R a$, and $\alpha \vdash_{RR} a$, respectively:

Definition 3.6
$\vdash_Q a \iff \exists \alpha \in \mathbf{T}_Q . \alpha \vdash_Q a \wedge \mathcal{A}(\alpha) = \emptyset$, where Q is R, RR, or null
$\mathbf{I}_\to = \{ a \mid \vdash a \}, \mathbf{R}_\to = \{ a \mid \vdash_R a \}, \mathbf{RR}_\to = \{ a \mid \vdash_{RR} a \},$ ∎

$\mathbf{I}_\to$ is the positive intuitionistic theory of implication. $\mathbf{R}_\to$ is the theory of relevant implication from [AB75], syntactically the most natural logic of relevant implication. Clearly, $\mathbf{RR}_\to \subseteq \mathbf{R}_\to \subseteq \mathbf{I}_\to$. Both containments are strict, the first since $(\lambda x^a \lambda y^{a \to b}(yx)) \vdash_R a \to (a \to b) \to b$, but not $\vdash_{RR} a \to (a \to b) \to b$, (although $(\lambda y^{a \to b} \lambda x^a (yx)) \vdash_{RR} (a \to b) \to a \to b$). The second containment is strict because $(\lambda x^a \lambda y^b x) \vdash a \to b \to a$, but not $\vdash_R a \to b \to a$. The intuitionistic theory of implication, $\mathbf{I}_\to$, is itself a strict subtheory of the classical theory of implication since $((a \to b) \to a) \to a$ holds classically, but not $\vdash ((a \to b) \to a) \to a$. The restricted relevance system $\mathbf{RR}_\to$, motivated by semantic considerations discussed in Section 5.1, seems to be new. The restriction on binding order is similar to, but more stringent than, that of *ticket entailment* ($\mathbf{T}_\to$ of [AB75]). Proofs of ticket entailments are usually defined by restricting application (*modus ponens*), rather than lambda-abstraction (*the deduction rule*). Each of $\mathbf{RR}_\to$ and $\mathbf{T}_\to$ may be presented either way. The difference does not affect the theorems, but does change the proofs from postulates.

The basic idea of connecting relevance logics to the lambda-I calculus has been noticed before. In particular, Helman [Hel77a] gave an insightful treatment of a lambda-I calculus, extended to handle conjunction, and showed a restricted soundness and completeness of the typing mechanism for a particular semantic interpretation. Helman's definitions of soundness and completeness were *not* intended to provide thorough foundations for reasoning. Helman's semantics depend on the inclusion in each functional domain of a special element representing undefinedness. Helman's relevant functions are the strict functions – those that preserve undefinedness – including functions that are constant on the well-defined elements of their domains. Since the undefined elements are not denotable by lambda terms, undefined values may only be produced by returning an undefined argument, so strict constant functions, and many other conceivable functions with undefined elements, are not lambda-definable. Helman did not try to analyze the behavior of the definable strict functions on well-defined arguments, which we believe is crucial to the intuitive impact of such semantics. Rather than perform such an analysis, we have sought a direct characterization of the extensional character of relevant functions, without adding any intensional structure such as undefined elements. Helman's completeness depends critically on the impossibility of producing an undefined value except by copying out an undefined argument, and also on the *a priori* assumption that all functions of interest as potential proofs are lambda-definable. Pottinger [Pot74] also defined relevant implication in an intuitionistic setting, and investigated the interaction of the two implications. He did not attempt to provide semantics.

4. Evidence Semantics for Intuitionistic Logic

4.1. Evidence

Let a particular language be fixed for the rest of the paper, *i.e.*, fix $\mathbf{P}_0$. Also fix an infinite set $\mathcal{U}_0$ to be the universe of primitive objects. All of the subsequent discussion holds independently of these choices. A model for any of the logics of this paper consists of a set of evidence for each formula. The definition of model uses the preliminary definition of frame [Hen50].

Definition 4.1
A *frame* $\mathcal{F}$ over $\mathcal{U}_0$ is a family of sets $\{\,\mathcal{F}_a \mid a \in \mathbf{P}\,\}$ indexed by types such that for all $a \in \mathbf{P}_0$, $\mathcal{F}_a \subseteq \mathcal{U}_0$, and for all $a, b \in \mathbf{P}$, $\mathcal{F}_{a \to b}$ is a set of functions from $\mathcal{F}_a$ to $\mathcal{F}_b$.
The *full frame* $\{\,\mathcal{U}_a \mid a \in \mathbf{P}\,\}$ *over* $\mathcal{U}_0$ is defined by

> U1. $a \in \mathbf{P}_0 \Longrightarrow \mathcal{U}_a = \mathcal{U}_0$
>
> U2. $a, b \in \mathbf{T} \Longrightarrow \mathcal{U}_{a \to b} = \{f \mid f : \mathcal{U}_a \longrightarrow \mathcal{U}_b\}$

We use $f, g, h, \alpha, \beta, \ldots$ to denote members of a frame $\mathcal{F}$.   ∎

While an arbitrary frame may have an arbitrary selection of functions in $\mathcal{F}_{a \to b}$, a model must at least contain all functions defined by testimony terms.

Definition 4.2
A *lambda-K* model is a frame $\mathcal{F}$ such that, for all $a, b, c \in \mathbf{P}$, there are elements $K_{a,b} \in \mathcal{F}_{a \to b \to a}$ and $S_{a,b,c} \in \mathcal{F}_{(a \to b \to c) \to (a \to b) \to a \to c}$ with

> $K_{a,b}(\alpha)(\beta) = \alpha$
>
> $S_{a,b,c}(\alpha)(\beta)(\gamma) = \alpha(\gamma)(\beta(\gamma))$

A *fully inhabited model* is a frame $\mathcal{F}$ with $\mathcal{F}_a \neq \emptyset$ for all $a \in \mathbf{P}$.
The full frame $\mathcal{U}$ over $\mathcal{U}_0$ is also called the *standard model over* $\mathcal{U}_0$.   ∎

The lambda-K models are precisely the frames that are closed under lambda definability [Bar84, Mey82]. Note that the standard model is a lambda-K model. It seems worthwhile to mention an alternative to the above definitions. At first glance, a frame $\mathcal{F}$ over $\mathcal{U}_0$ might appear to be substructure of the full frame $\mathcal{U}$. This is not true because, although $\mathcal{F}_{a \to b}$ is a subset of $\mathcal{U}_{a \to b}$ for $a, b \in \mathbf{P}_0$, $\mathcal{F}_{a \to b \to b}$ is not a subset of $\mathcal{U}_{a \to b \to b}$ since the functionals in $\mathcal{U}_{a \to b \to b}$ are defined on a larger domain. However, as shown in the equational completeness proof of [Fri75], there is a partial homomorphism from the full frame $\mathcal{U}$ over $\mathcal{U}_0$ to any frame $\mathcal{F}$ over $\mathcal{U}_0$. Since, for the purposes of obtaining completeness theorems for logics we are not specifically concerned with equations between testimony terms, we could have defined models as "substructures" of the full frame which contain K and S instead of as homomorphic images of substructures. This would make some technical arguments simpler, but complicates the interpretation of testimony terms as elements of models. Specifically, since extensionality fails on "substructures," it is not clear which function to assign to a testimony term $\lambda x^a.\alpha$ (see [Mey82] for further discussion). Furthermore, η-reduction fails on "substructures." Läuchli proves completeness using substructures of the standard model [Lau70] and, in the final paper, we intend to use partial homomorphisms to compare his results with ours.

We associate semantic evidence with proofs according to the usual semantics of the typed lambda calculus.

Definition 4.3
An *environment* η for frame $\mathcal{F}$ is a function from $\mathbf{V}$ to $\bigcup \mathcal{F}$, such that $\forall x^a \in \mathbf{V}^a . \eta(x^a) \in \mathcal{F}_a$.
$\mathbf{Env}(\mathcal{F})$ denotes the set of all environments for frame $\mathcal{F}$.
If $\eta \in \mathbf{Env}(\mathcal{F})$, then $\eta[\alpha/x^a]$ is the environment with $\eta[\alpha/x^a](x^a) = \alpha$ and $\eta[\alpha/x^a](y^b) = \eta(y^b)$ when $x^a \neq y^b$
The *meaning* of a term $\alpha \in \mathbf{T}$ *in* environment η, written $[\![\alpha]\!]\eta$, is defined by

> $[\![x^a]\!]\eta = \eta(x^a)$
>
> $[\![(\beta\alpha)]\!]\eta = [\![\beta]\!]\eta([\![\alpha]\!]\eta)$
>
> $([\![(\lambda x^a \beta)]\!]\eta)(f) = [\![\beta]\!]\eta[f/x^a]$ for all $f \in \mathcal{F}_a$.   ∎

It can be shown that for every testimony term (lambda-term) α and environment η in lambda-K model $\mathcal{F}$, the meaning $[\![\alpha]\!]\eta$ is well-defined [Bar84, Mey82]. In addition, if $\alpha \vdash a$, then $[\![\alpha]\!]\eta \in \mathcal{F}_a$. If α is closed, then $[\![\alpha]\!]\eta$ is independent of η, so we often write $[\![\alpha]\!]$ for the meaning of α.

One important model is the *term model* for an equational theory $\mathcal{E}$.

Definition 4.4

Let $\mathcal{E}$ be an equational theory over $\mathbf{T}$, with $=_\mathcal{E}$ the provable equality relation on terms.
The *term model* is the fully inhabited lambda-K model $T^\mathcal{E} = \{T_a^\mathcal{E}\}$, where $T_a^\mathcal{E} = \{[\alpha] \mid \alpha \vdash a\}$, with

$$\alpha \vdash a \in \mathbf{P}_0 \implies [\alpha] = \{\beta \mid \alpha =_\mathcal{E} \beta\}$$
$$\beta \vdash a \to b \implies [\beta] \text{ is the function defined by } \forall \alpha \vdash a \,.\, [\beta]([\alpha]) = [\beta\alpha]$$

$T^{\beta\eta}$ denotes the term model for β, η-equality [Bar84, Fri75, Mey82, Sta82a].   ∎

In the term model $T^\mathcal{E}$, we have $\alpha =_\mathcal{E} \beta$ iff $[\alpha] = [\beta]$. It is important to note that a term model $T^\mathcal{E}$ has elements $[\alpha]$ defined by *open* terms as well as closed terms. In fact, since $[x^a] \in \mathbf{T}_a$, $T^\mathcal{E}$ contains evidence for every formula. However, as we shall see, only certain formulas will have evidence in all beliefs. There is a lambda-K model derived from the *closed* terms, in which each type with a closed term contains exactly one function, and each type without a closed term is empty. However, this model is not fully inhabited.

4.2. Intuitionistic Belief and Validity

We define semantic validity using the subsidiary notion of belief. Beliefs are sets of evidence (from some model) which satisfy some closure conditions and the valid formulas in a model are taken to be those that are supported by all beliefs. Thus the the validity of formulas is determined by the closure conditions used to define beliefs. The simplest notion of belief is a set of evidence that is closed under *modus ponens*.

Definition 4.5

A *belief* $\mathcal{G}$ over frame $\mathcal{F}$ is a family of sets $\{\mathcal{G}_a\}$ such that

$$\mathcal{G}_a \subseteq \mathcal{F}_a$$
$$\forall a, b \in \mathbf{T}, \beta \in \mathcal{G}_{a \to b}, \alpha \in \mathcal{G}_a \,.\, \beta(\alpha) \in \mathcal{G}_b$$ ∎

This seems a minimal requirement on beliefs: if anyone believes evidence $\beta \in \mathcal{F}_{a \to b}$ for the implication $a \to b$, and evidence $\alpha \in \mathcal{F}_a$ for a, we assume that he or she will believe evidence $\beta(\alpha)$ for b.

A reasonable belief for a particular logic should contain only functions that provide acceptable evidence for the logic in question, and a standard belief should include all such evidence. Different choices of sets of beliefs, as well as different choices of classes of models, will support different logical theories. For intuitionistic logic, we would like for beliefs to contain all of the *uniformly constructible functions*.

Pseudodefinition 4.6

A *standard intuitionistic belief* is a subframe of a frame $\mathcal{F}$ containing exactly the uniformly constructible functions in $\mathcal{F}$.
A *full intuitionistic belief* is a subframe of a frame $\mathcal{F}$ containing all of the uniformly constructible functions in $\mathcal{F}$, and perhaps more.   ∎

The pseudodefinition above *cannot* be formalized satisfactorily, since there is no proper formal characterization of the uniformly constructible functions. Fortunately, we can formally characterize classes of beliefs in such a way that the fullness of the beliefs is intuitively apparent, and the implicational theory of the formal classes of beliefs is the same as that of the standard beliefs. In particular, if a function is *uniformly* constructible, it cannot refer to the internal structure of the primitive objects that it operates on. Therefore, the function must be invariant under substitutions of one primitive object for another of the same type.

Definition 4.7

A *functionally closed belief* is a belief $\mathcal{G}$ over frame $\mathcal{F}$ such that

$$\mathcal{G}_{a \to b} = \{ \beta \in \mathcal{F}_{a \to b} \mid \forall \alpha \in \mathcal{G}_a \, . \, \beta(\alpha) \in \mathcal{G}_b \}$$

The *classical belief* over frame $\mathcal{F}$ is $\mathcal{F}$ itself.

A *hereditary permutation* π over frame $\mathcal{F}$ is a family $\{\pi_a\}$ of permutations defined as follows.

$\pi 1.$ $a \in \mathbf{P}_0 \implies \pi_a(\alpha)$ is some permutation of $\mathcal{F}_a$

$\pi 2.$ $\pi_{a \to b} : \mathcal{F}_{a \to b} \to \mathcal{F}_{a \to b}$ is the permutation defined by $\pi_{a \to b}(\alpha) = \pi_b \circ \alpha \circ \pi_a^{-1}$

The *invariant belief* over a frame $\mathcal{F}$ is the belief containing $\alpha \in \mathcal{F}_a$ iff $\pi_a(\alpha) = \alpha$ for every hereditary permutation π. ∎

Classical beliefs are always functionally closed, but invariant beliefs may not be. Invariant beliefs seem to be full intuitionistic beliefs over some models (see discussion of "P-structures" in [Sta82a]), but this is not susceptible to formal statement and proof. In lambda calculus parlance, a functionally-closed belief is called a *logical predicate*; see [Plo80, Sta82c].

The semantics for intuitionistic and relevance logics hinge on distinguishing certain evidence as *logical evidence*. We define a formula (type) to be *valid* in a model if the model contains logical evidence for the formula (logical evidence of that type). *Logical evidence* in a model is defined to be the evidence occurring in every legitimate belief. Several different definitions of legitimate belief can be considered, based on Definition 4.7 above. The intent is that a formula should be valid if there exists ideal abstract evidence for it in every model. Every proof is a construction of evidence, and we can ask whether the formally constructible evidence corresponds appropriately to the ideal evidence.

Definition 4.8

If $\mathcal{F}$ is a model, and $\mathcal{G}$ a belief, $\mathcal{F}, \alpha, \mathcal{G} \models a$ is intended to mean that α is evidence for a in $\mathcal{F}$ and believed by $\mathcal{G}$. Formally,

$\mathcal{F}, \alpha, \mathcal{G} \models a$ if $\alpha \in \mathcal{G}_a$

$\mathcal{F}, \alpha \models_F a$ if $\mathcal{F}, \alpha, \mathcal{G} \models a$ for every functionally closed belief $\mathcal{G}$

$\mathcal{F}, \alpha \models_C a$ if $\mathcal{F}, \alpha, \mathcal{G} \models a$ for the classical belief $\mathcal{G}$

$\mathcal{F}, \alpha \models_I a$ if $\mathcal{F}, \alpha, \mathcal{G} \models a$ for the invariant belief $\mathcal{G}$

$\mathcal{F} \models_Q a$ if there exists an α with $\mathcal{F}, \alpha \models_Q a$, where Q is either F, C, or I

$\models_{S,Q} a$ if $\mathcal{F} \models_Q a$ for every standard model $\mathcal{F}$, where Q is either F, C, or I

Similarly, $\models_{\lambda K, Q}$ denotes validity in all lambda-K models, $\models_{F \lambda K, Q}$ denotes validity in all fully inhabited lambda-K models. ∎

Notice that the existential quantification over evidence comes before the universal quantification over beliefs. A set of beliefs in a model is used to distinguish the "logical evidence," the evidence occurring in all belief, from arbitrary evidence. In general, the valid formulae are determined by the intersection of a set of beliefs. It is interesting to note that $\models_{S,C}$ is classical validity [Lau65, Lau70]. Intuitionistic logic $\mathbf{L}_{\to}$ is sound for every combination, but we prove completeness only for $\models_{\lambda K, F}$, $\models_{F \lambda K, F}$. Läuchli has proved completeness for $\models_{\lambda K, I}$ (modulo the technical distinction between his "proof assignments" and our "models", which are images of proof assignments under partial homomorphisms) [Lau70].

4.3. Soundness and Completeness

We show that if $\vdash a$, then $\models a$ by demonstrating that if α is a closed testimony term, i.e., $\mathcal{A}(\alpha) = \emptyset$, then $[\![\alpha]\!]$ belongs to every belief. We prove this using the following lemmas about open terms.

Lemma 4.9

Let $\mathcal{F}$ be a lambda-K model and $\mathcal{G}$ a functionally closed belief over $\mathcal{F}$. Let $\eta \in \mathbf{Env}(\mathcal{G})$ be any environment such that $\eta(x^a) \in \mathcal{G}^a$ for all x^a. Then,

$$\forall \alpha \in \mathbf{T} . \; \alpha \vdash a \Longrightarrow \mathcal{F}, [\![\alpha]\!]\eta, \mathcal{G} \models a$$

Proof: Straightforward induction on the structure of α. See [Plo80, Sta82c]. ∎

Lemma 4.10
Let $\mathcal{F}$ be a lambda-K model and π a hereditary permutation over $\mathcal{F}$. Let $\eta \in \mathbf{Env}(\mathcal{G})$. Then,

$$\forall \alpha \in \mathbf{T} . \; \pi([\![\alpha]\!]\eta) = [\![\alpha]\!](\pi\eta),$$

where $(\pi\eta)$ is the environment defined by $(\pi\eta)(x) = \pi(\eta(x))$.

Proof: Straightforward induction on the structure of α, using the definition of π to show that $\pi(\alpha\beta) = (\pi\alpha)(\pi\beta)$. See [Plo80, Sta82a] for some related discussion. ∎

Theorem 4.11
Let $\mathcal{F}$ be a lambda-K model and $\mathcal{G}$ a functionally closed or invariant belief over $\mathcal{F}$. For any closed $\alpha \in \mathbf{T}$ with $\alpha \vdash a$, we have

$$\mathcal{F}, [\![\alpha]\!], \mathcal{G} \models a$$

Proof: From the two previous lemmas. ∎

Corollary 4.12
$\forall a \in \mathbf{P} . \; \vdash a \Longrightarrow \models_{P,Q} a$, where P is either S, λK, or $F\lambda K$, and Q is either F, C, or I. ∎

The converse, *completeness*, for $\models_{F\lambda K,S}$, relies on the following lemma about term models.

Lemma 4.13
[Sta82b, Sta82c] Let α be a testimony term with $\alpha \vdash a$. In any term model $\mathcal{T}^\mathcal{E}$, the following are equivalent:

1. $\exists \beta . \; \alpha =_\mathcal{E} \beta \bigwedge \mathcal{A}(\beta) = \emptyset$

2. For all functionally closed beliefs $\mathcal{G}$ over $\mathcal{T}^\mathcal{E}$, $[\alpha] \in \mathcal{G}_a$ ∎

The proof of Lemma 4.13 given in [Sta82b] relies on the assumption that there is only one primitive proposition (propositional variable). The more general lemma stated here may be proved using an argument similar to the completeness proof for type inference given in [Hin83].

Theorem 4.14
$\models_{\lambda K,F} a \Longleftrightarrow \models_{F\lambda K,F} a \Longleftrightarrow \vdash a$

Proof: Show that $\models_{\lambda K,F} a \Longrightarrow \models_{F\lambda K,F} a \Longrightarrow \vdash a \Longrightarrow \models_{\lambda K,F} a$. The first implication is trivial. For the second, assume that $\models_{F\lambda K,F} a$. In particular, $\mathcal{T}_{\beta\eta} \models_{F\lambda K} a$; equivalently, for all functionally closed beliefs $\mathcal{G}$ over $\mathcal{T}_{\beta\eta}$, we have $\mathcal{T}_{\beta\eta}, \mathcal{G} \models a$. So, by Lemma 4.13, $\vdash a$. The third implication is Corollary 4.12. ∎

The completeness of $\vdash$ for $\models_{F\lambda K,F}$ is rather weak since we have used the term model instead of the standard model. Completeness for $\models_{F\lambda K,F}$ is not vacuous, however, because it holds for the *fully inhabited* lambda-K models. Allowing small lambda-K models leaves open the question of whether functions in all beliefs over larger models prove additional theorems. A proof of completeness for $\models_{S,F}$ would be much more satisfying, but might involve strengthening the difficult theorem of [Plo80] [2]. Läuchli [Lau70] essentially proves completeness for $\models_{\lambda K,I}$ using a correspondence between evidence models and Kripke models. Based on a result similar to Lemma 4.13 proved in [Sta82a], we conjecture that there is a direct proof of completeness for $\models_{F\lambda K,I}$.

---

[2]Essentially, Plotkin's lambda-definability theorem implies completeness for the standard model when each belief is replaced by a family of beliefs indexed by "possible worlds" of Kripke model.

5. Evidence Semantics for Relevant Implication

Our basic semantic idea for relevance logics is to restrict the functions in the beliefs of intuitionistic logic so that each function must always use its argument in some way. Certainly, constant functions must be ruled out, since they lead to the forbidden theorem $a \rightarrow b \rightarrow a$, and subsequent irrelevant consequences. Nonconstancy is not enough: because a nonconstant function may be constant over a large part of its domain, the nonconstant functions are not closed under composition. In general, we augment the structure of models or beliefs to include a binary relation on evidence, and require that every function in a belief preserve that relation. Many variations may be produced by choosing different sorts of relations, by choosing to preserve only positive instances of the relations, or negative ones as well, and by choosing to incorporate the relations in beliefs, where each function must preserve many different relations, or in models, where each function need preserve only one relation to qualify as evidence. We explore two sets of choices, differing in several of these parameters. Although we do not claim to give the definitive treatment of relevance, and are not even sure that there is a unique one, we believe that our analysis through relation-preserving functions gives a useful basis for understanding the semantics of relevance logics intuitively, and for comparing different logics.

5.1. Relevance Semantics Using Models Containing Independence-Preserving Functions

Our first semantics for relevance defines relevant functions to be those that preserve *independence* of evidence, and uses these independence relations as components of models. This approach is appropriate for $\mathbf{RR}_{\rightarrow}$. The intuition behind relevant functions in $a \rightarrow b$ is that completely different evidence for a, given as input, must always yield completely different evidence for b as output. Perhaps the most obvious candidates for relevant functions are the *injective*, or *one-to-one*, functions. A closer inspection shows that injectivity is not enough. If β is injective, and $\alpha_1 \neq \alpha_2$, then $\beta(\alpha_1) \neq \beta(\alpha_2)$. But, suppose that $\beta(\alpha_1)$ and $\beta(\alpha_2)$ are of type $a \rightarrow b$, and that they differ at only one point in the domain associated with a. Such functions could hardly be taken as giving completely different evidence that a implies b. Even the stronger requirement that $\forall \gamma \, . \, \beta(\alpha_1)(\gamma) \neq \beta(\alpha_2)(\gamma)$ is not enough, since it may be satisfied by merely permuting the range of the function β. Use of this pointwise definition of independent functions yields a logic, not explored here, in which an assumption may be used only once, so $(a \rightarrow a \rightarrow b) \rightarrow a \rightarrow b$ fails to hold.

In order to guarantee that two pieces of functional evidence are completely different, we need to require that their ranges are completely different. For functions whose ranges contain structureless, independent, primitive objects, rather than other functions, the appropriate requirement is $\forall \gamma, \delta \, . \, \beta(\alpha)(\gamma) \neq \beta(\alpha_2)(\delta)$, that is, the ranges of $\beta(\alpha_1)$ and $\beta(\alpha_2)$ are disjoint. In general, the appropriate definition of a *relevant function* is that it preserves a *relevant independence* relation, as defined inductively below.

Definition 5.1

A *relevant independence relation* is a hierarchy $\mathcal{R}$ of binary relations $\mathcal{R}_a \subseteq \mathcal{U}_a \times \mathcal{U}_a$ such that:

1. $\forall a \in \mathbf{P}_0 \, . \, \alpha \mathcal{R}_a \beta \Longrightarrow \alpha \neq \beta$
2. $\forall a, b \in \mathbf{P}, \beta_1, \beta_2 \in \mathcal{U}_{a \rightarrow b} \, . \, (\beta_1 \mathcal{R}_{(a \rightarrow b)} \beta_2 \iff \forall \alpha_1, \alpha_2 \in \mathcal{U}_a \, . \, \beta(\alpha_1) \mathcal{R}_b \beta(\alpha_2))$ ∎

Technically, it seems to make no difference whether or not $\mathcal{R}_a$ is required to be symmetric, as well as irreflexive.

To develop some intuition for relevant independence and relevant functions, consider the case where, for $a \in \mathbf{P}_0$, $\alpha_1 \mathcal{R}_a \alpha_2 \iff \alpha_1 \neq \alpha_2$. In this case, two functions are relevant independent if and only if their *primitive ranges* (the sets of primitive testimony generated by applying the functions to all possible sequences of arguments) are disjoint. Relevant functions might also be called *hereditarily injective* functions. Let $a_1, \ldots, a_n, b \in \mathbf{P}_0$. A function $\gamma \in \mathcal{U}_{a_1 \rightarrow \cdots \rightarrow a_n \rightarrow b}$ preserves such an $\mathcal{R}$ iff

$$\forall \langle \alpha_1, \ldots, \alpha_n \rangle, \langle \beta_1, \ldots, \beta_n \rangle \in \mathcal{U}_{a_1} \times \cdots \times \mathcal{U}_{a_n} \, .$$
$$\langle \alpha_1, \ldots, \alpha_n \rangle \neq \langle \beta_1, \cdots, \beta_n \rangle \Longrightarrow \gamma(\alpha_1) \cdots (\alpha_n) \neq \gamma(\beta_1) \cdots (\beta_n)$$

In other words, such a relevant function γ is injective from $\mathcal{U}_{a_1} \times \cdots \times \mathcal{U}_{a_n}$ to $\mathcal{U}_b$. In general, when the a_is may not be primitive, then γ preserves $\mathcal{R}$ whenever

$$\forall \langle \alpha_1, \ldots, \alpha_n \rangle, \langle \beta_1, \ldots, \beta_n \rangle \in \mathcal{U}_{a_1} \times \cdots \times \mathcal{U}_{a_n}.$$
$$(\exists i \in [1, n] \,.\, \alpha_i \mathbf{R}_{a_i} \beta_i) \Longrightarrow \gamma(\alpha_1) \cdots (\alpha_n) \neq \gamma(\beta_1) \cdots (\beta_n)$$

a condition somewhat weaker than injectivity. The converse does *not* hold. A function $\gamma \in \mathcal{U}_a {\longrightarrow} \mathcal{U}_b {\longrightarrow} \mathcal{U}_c$ may be relevant, yet $\gamma(\alpha_1)(\beta_1) = \gamma(\alpha_2)(\beta_2)$, where $\alpha_1 \mathcal{R}_a \alpha_1$, and $\beta_1 \neq \beta_2$, but $\neg \beta_1 \mathcal{R}_b \beta_2$.

Models for this relevance semantics are the same as those for intuitionistic semantics, but with an independence relation that all functions must preserve.

Definition 5.2
A *relational frame* is a pair $\langle \mathcal{F}, \mathcal{R} \rangle$, where $\mathcal{F}$ is a frame, and $\mathcal{R}$ is hierarchy of binary relations $\mathcal{R}_a \in \mathcal{U}_a \times \mathcal{U}_a$ for each $a \in \mathbf{P}$

An *independence model* is a relational frame $\langle \mathcal{F}, \mathcal{R} \rangle$, such that $\mathcal{R}$ is a relevant independence relation, and

$$\forall a, b \in \mathbf{P}, \beta \in \mathcal{F}_{a \to b}, \alpha_1, \alpha_2 \in \mathcal{U}_a \,.\, \alpha_1 \mathcal{R}_a \alpha_2 \Longrightarrow \beta(\alpha_1) \mathcal{R}_b \beta(\alpha_2)$$

A *standard* independence model is a $\langle \mathcal{F}, \mathcal{R} \rangle$ with

$$\forall a, b \in \mathbf{P} \,.\, \mathcal{F}_{a \to b} = \{ \beta \in \mathcal{U}_{a \to b} \mid \forall \alpha_1, \alpha_2 \in \mathcal{U}_a \,.\, \alpha_1 \mathcal{R}_a \alpha_2 \Longrightarrow \beta(\alpha_1) \mathcal{R}_b \beta(\alpha_2) \}$$

A *belief* over $\langle \mathcal{F}, \mathcal{R} \rangle$ is just a belief over $\mathcal{F}$

Standard intuitionistic, full intuitionistic, functionally closed, classical, and *invariant* beliefs may be considered over relational frames, just as over frames.

A belief is *independence-invariant* if it contains all of the functions in $\mathcal{F}$ that are invariant under all hereditary permutations that preserve $\mathcal{R}$

$\langle \mathcal{F}, \mathcal{R} \rangle, \mathcal{G}, \alpha \models a$ if $a \in \mathcal{G}_a$

The subscripts F, C, T, I on $\models$ refer to classes of beliefs, as before

Similarly, RI refers to the independence-invariant beliefs, and R to the independence models   ∎

The soundness of $\vdash_{RR}$ with respect to various $\models_Q$ follows from a slightly stronger result dealing with the behavior of relevant variables.

Theorem 5.3
For all independence models $\langle \mathcal{F}, \mathcal{R} \rangle$, $\eta \in \mathbf{Env}(\mathcal{F})$, $a \in \mathbf{P}$, $\alpha \vdash a$, $x^b \in \mathbf{V}^b$, and $\beta, \gamma \in \mathcal{F}_b$, the following two properties hold:

1. $[\![\alpha]\!]\eta \in \mathcal{F}_a$
2. $x^b \in \mathcal{R}_{\{y_1^{b_1}, \ldots, y_n^{b_n}\}}(\alpha) \bigwedge \beta \mathcal{R}_b \gamma \bigwedge \delta_1, \epsilon_1 \in \mathcal{F}_{b_1} \bigwedge \cdots \bigwedge \delta_n, \epsilon_n \in \mathcal{F}_{b_n}$
   $\Longrightarrow [\![\alpha]\!]\eta[\beta/x, \delta_1/y_1, \ldots, \delta_n/y_n] \mathcal{R}_a [\![\alpha]\!]\eta[\gamma/x, \epsilon_1/y_1, \ldots, \epsilon_n/y_n]$

Proof sketch: By induction on the structure of α. The steps are tedious but straightforward.   ∎

Corollary 5.4
$\vdash_{RR} a \Longrightarrow \models_{P,Q} a$, where P is either S or R, and Q is either $F, C, I,$ or RI ∎

We conjecture that $\mathbf{RR}_{\to}$ is complete for $\models_{S,I}$, and possibly for $\models_{S,RI}$. No completeness results for $\mathbf{RR}_{\to}$ have been proved yet.

In responding to a very perceptive question from Mitchell Wand, we found an apparent paradox in the association of relevant functions with the lambda-*I* calculus. The lambda-*I* calculus is sufficiently powerful to compute many arithmetic functions, including addition and multiplication, using an encoding of positive integers into lambda-terms. But, addition and multiplication are not one-to-one, since, for example, $1 + 2 = 2 + 1$. There is really no paradox here, because the representations of integers in the lambda-*I* calculus do not denote independent functions, so there are no particular restrictions on the behavior of relevant functions applied to integers.

5.2. Relevance Semantics Using Beliefs Containing Monotone Functions

The second semantic treatment of relevance is appropriate for the theory $\mathbf{R}_\rightarrow$. It is based on the idea that a relevant function β is one such that, if α_2 is strictly stronger evidence than α_1, then $\beta(\alpha_2)$ is strictly stronger than $\beta(\alpha_1)$. In this case, the ordering of evidence is incorporated into *beliefs*, rather than models.

Definition 5.5

A *lambda-I* model is a frame $\mathcal{F}$ such that for all $a, b, c \in \mathbf{T}$, there exist elements

$$I_a \in \mathcal{F}_a$$
$$B_{a,b,c} \in \mathcal{F}_{(b\rightarrow c)\rightarrow(a\rightarrow b)\rightarrow a\rightarrow c}$$
$$C_{a,b,c} \in \mathcal{F}_{(a\rightarrow b\rightarrow c)\rightarrow b\rightarrow a\rightarrow c}$$
$$S_{a,b,c} \in \mathcal{F}_{(a\rightarrow b\rightarrow c)\rightarrow(a\rightarrow b)\rightarrow a\rightarrow c}$$

such that

$$I_a(\alpha) = \alpha$$
$$B_{a,b,c}(\alpha)(\beta)(\gamma) = \alpha(\beta(\gamma))$$
$$C_{a,b,c}(\alpha)(\beta)(\gamma) = \alpha(\gamma)(\beta)$$
$$S_{a,b,c}(\alpha)(\beta)(\gamma) = (\alpha\gamma)(\beta\gamma)$$
■

Equivalently, the lambda-*I* models are those that are closed under lambda-*I* definability [Bar84]. Note that every standard or lambda-*K* model is a lambda-*I* model.

Definition 5.6

Let $\mathcal{G}$ be a frame. A *hereditary strict partial ordering* of $\mathcal{G}$ is a family of binary relations $<_a$ such that

For $a \in \mathbf{P}_0$, $<_a$ is a strict partial ordering of $\mathcal{G}_a$

$$\forall a, b \in \mathbf{P}, \beta_1, \beta_2 \in \mathcal{G}_{a\rightarrow b} \ . \ \beta_1 <_{a\rightarrow b} \beta_2 \iff (\forall \alpha \in \mathcal{G}_a \ . \ \beta_1(\alpha) <_b \beta_2(\alpha))$$

A *monotone belief* over frame $\mathcal{F}$ is a pair $\langle \mathcal{G}, < \rangle$, where $\mathcal{G}$ is a belief over $\mathcal{F}$, $<$ is a hereditary strict partial ordering of $\mathcal{G}$, and for all $\beta \in \mathcal{G}_{a\rightarrow b}$, $\alpha_1, \alpha_2 \in \mathcal{G}_a$ we have $\alpha_1 <\alpha_2 \implies \beta(\alpha_1) < \beta(\alpha_2)$
A monotone belief $\langle \mathcal{G}, < \rangle$ over $\mathcal{F}$ is *monotone functionally closed* if

$$\mathcal{G}_{a\rightarrow b} = \{ \beta \in \mathcal{F}_{a\rightarrow b} \mid \forall \alpha_1, \alpha_2 \in \mathcal{G}_a \ . \ \beta(\alpha_1) \in \mathcal{G}_b \bigwedge \alpha_1 <_a \alpha_2 \implies \beta(\alpha_1) <_b \beta(\alpha_2) \}$$

■

See [Gan80] for related discussion. Note that $<_{a\rightarrow b}$ is defined *pointwise* on functions in $\mathcal{G}_{a\rightarrow b}$, while $\mathcal{R}_{a\rightarrow b}$ is defined *globally* over the whole domains of such functions. For partial ordering relations, the pointwise definition allows repeated use of assumptions, and the objection raised for pointwise definition of independence relations is not compelling.

We say that $\alpha \in \mathcal{F}_a$ is *monotone relevant evidence for a* if $\alpha \in \mathcal{G}_a$ for every monotone belief $\langle \mathcal{G}, < \rangle$ over $\mathcal{F}$. Relevant satisfaction and validity are defined as for intuitionistic logic:

Definition 5.7

$\mathcal{F}, \alpha, \langle \mathcal{G}, < \rangle \models a$ if $\alpha \in \mathcal{G}_a$
$\mathcal{F}, \alpha \models_M a$ if $\mathcal{F}, \alpha, \langle \mathcal{G}, < \rangle \models a$ for every monotone functionally closed belief $\langle \mathcal{G}, < \rangle$ over $\mathcal{F}$
Additional subscripts may be used to indicate sets of models as before
$\models_{\lambda I, M} a$ ($\models_{F\lambda I, M} a$) if $\mathcal{F} \models_M a$ for every (fully inhabited) lambda-*I* model $\mathcal{F}$
■

5.3.   *Soundness and Completeness*

Theorem 5.8
Let $\mathcal{F}$ be a lambda-I model, $\langle \mathcal{G}, < \rangle$ a monotone functionally closed belief over $\mathcal{F}$ and $\eta \in \mathbf{Env}(\mathcal{G})$ an environment with $\eta(x^a) \in \mathcal{G}_a$ for all x^a. Then,

$$\forall \alpha \in \mathbf{T} . \, \alpha \vdash a \Longrightarrow \mathcal{F}, [\![\alpha]\!]\eta, \langle \mathcal{G}, < \rangle \models a$$

Proof: Straightforward induction on the structure of α; see [Gan80].   ∎

Corollary 5.9
$\forall a \in \mathbf{P} . \vdash a \Longrightarrow \models_{P,Q} a$, where P is either S, λI, or $F\lambda I$, and Q is either F, M, C, or I.   ∎

The converse, *completeness*, for $\models_{F\lambda I,M}$, relies on the following lemma about term models. Let $\mathcal{T}_{I-\beta\eta}$ be the term model $\mathcal{T}_{\beta\eta}$ restricted to lambda-I terms.

Lemma 5.10
Let α be a testimony term with $\alpha \vdash_R a$. In the term model $\mathcal{T}_{I-\beta\eta}$, the following are equivalent:

1. $\mathcal{A}(\alpha) = \emptyset$

2. For all monotone functionally closed beliefs $\langle \mathcal{G}, < \rangle$ over $\mathcal{T}_{I-\beta\eta}$, we have $[\alpha] \in \mathcal{G}_a$ ∎

The proof of Lemma 5.10 is similar in outline to that of 4.13, but involves some additional complications. Completeness is proved as for intuitionistic implication.

Theorem 5.11
$\models_{\lambda I,M} a \iff \models_{F\lambda I,M} a \iff \vdash_R a$ ∎

We believe that this completeness theorem can be strengthened in two ways. By essentially the same proof techniques, we conjecture that completeness for both $\models_{F\lambda K,M}$ and $\models_{F\lambda I,F}$ can be proved, but we have not checked all the details. Thus it seems that we can either allow more functions in the model (completeness for $\models_{F\lambda K,M}$), or remove the restriction of monotonicity (completeness for $\models_{F\lambda I,F}$). Of the two, completeness for $\models_{F\lambda K,M}$ is by far the more interesting, since it suggests that monotonicity distinguishes relevant evidence from intuitionistic evidence, a result similar to Helman's [Hel77a]. We conjecture that $\vdash_R$ is complete for $\models_{S,M}$ as well, although there is less technical evidence for this conjecture.

6.   Negation and Other Connectives

The usual constructive type-theoretic interpretation of $\neg a$ is $a \longrightarrow \Lambda$, where Λ is "absurdity" and $\rightarrow$ is interpreted intuitionistically. Absurdity is axiomatized by $\Lambda \longrightarrow b$ for all b. Prawitz [Pra65] gives the two changes to this interpretation that are required for the fault-tolerant logic of this paper. First, as argued in the introduction, a derivation of Λ from a does not provide evidence against a if the derivation of Λ does not really use the assumption a. So, the implication in the definition of negation should be *relevant*. Second, a Λ that implies everything is too strong. Therefore the axiom $\Lambda \longrightarrow b$ for absurdity is dropped. To avoid confusing this "relevant" absurdity with the usual intuitionistic notion of absurdity, we may replace the symbol Λ with a symbol Σ, representing great surprise, but not implying anything else. Thus, $\neg a$ is interpreted as $a \rightarrow \Sigma$ (with $\rightarrow$ *relevant*), indicating evidence against a that will cause surprise if positive evidence for a is discovered. Surprises should be rare, but they do happen occasionally, so we do not have $\Sigma \rightarrow b$ for all b. Notice that both changes are needed: if $\neg a$ is interpreted as $a \longrightarrow \Sigma$, with the intuitionistic $\rightarrow$, then $(a \wedge \neg a) \longrightarrow \neg b$ would hold for all b, although positive statements would not necessarily follow. In summary, no new rules are required for relevant reasoning about negation, merely the extension of $\mathbf{P}_0$ by

P0. $\Sigma \in \mathbf{P}_0$

and the convention that $\neg a$ is an abbreviation for $a \rightarrow \Sigma$.

All of the usual logical connectives, including conjunction, disjunction, and universal and existential quantification, have been given type-theoretic interpretations for intuitionistic logic. See [Ste72] for a thorough treatment or [How80] for a brief, readable account of the main ideas. Essentially, conjunction corresponds to Cartesian product, disjunction to marked union, and quantification to dependent functional types, where the type of one component, or of the value returned by a function, may depend on another component, or on the argument to a function. Completeness for second-order quantification follows from the results of [MM85].

The extension of these interpretations to relevance logics is not immediate, because there are several plausible choices of definitions for relevant independence and ordering of evidence over these structures. Each choice leads to a different theory. It is tempting to start by introducing multiple conjunctions and disjunctions into a combined theory, to test by experience the usefulness of each. If we take the realizability interpretation of relevance logic totally seriously, however, we should attach the responsibility for defining independence to the implication sign, not to conjunction and disjunction. The resulting system of multiple implications appears to be quite clumsy, so an appeal to semantic principles could be useful.

In the syntactic analysis of proofs involving conjunctions and disjunctions, the appropriate definition of relevant occurrence of a variable is unlikely to coincide perfectly with that of free variable, even for the monotone semantics. Notice also that conventional representation techniques, such as the representation of a pair $\langle a, b \rangle$ by a function mapping 0 to a and 1 to b, may not respect a given definition of independence. Careful study is required to determine which representations should be preserved in relevance logics, and whether such preservation requires additional restrictions on proofs of conjunctions and disjunctions corresponding to relevance restrictions on their functional representations. It would be particularly helpful to settle on an interpretation of second-order universal quantification early in the study, since many other connectives may be defined from that one (see [Pra65, Ste72]).

7. Conclusion and Directions for Further Investigation

The most commonly used models for intuitionistic and relevance logics are Kripke models involving "possible worlds." We have examined an alternative in which models comprise sets of "evidence" for each proposition. Evidence models seem likely to be useful for studying a variety of logics, and we have proved some completeness theorems for intuitionistic propositional implications and relevant propositional implications. Since we have used the standard model theory for typed lambda calculus, the completeness theorems also yield characterizations of λK-definable and λI-definable functions over certain models. The characterization of λI-definable functions seems to be new, and interesting apart from the application to relevance logic.

The evidence models discussed in this paper vary according to two parameters: the class of functions included in the models, and the class of beliefs used in the definition of validity. To be precise, a formula a is valid with respect to a class $\mathcal{M}$ of models and class Q of beliefs if, for every model $\mathcal{F}$ from $\mathcal{M}$, there is evidence $\alpha \in \mathcal{F}_a$ belonging to every belief $\mathcal{G} \subset \mathcal{F}$ from class Q. Thus, to preserve completeness for a given set of formulas, varying the class $\mathcal{M}$ of models must be balanced against changes in the class Q of beliefs. Ideally, we would like to work with "standard" models consisting of all functions over chosen ground sets and with classes of beliefs that have simple mathematical characterizations. In fact, we have only proved completeness theorems with respect to classes of models which include models constructed from open and closed lambda terms. Perhaps, by altering the classes of beliefs we consider, we may be able to achieve completeness for more natural classes of models. In evaluating various choices, it is important to see how easy it is to give counterexamples to intuitionistic and relevant implications.

While the technical results to date are far from definitive, and the range of choices is larger than we would like, we believe that evidence models provide a basis for discussing those choices that allows direct application of intuition and experience. Questions such as, *"how is the strength of functional evidence related to the strengths of the function's values at different points"* and, *"must relevant evidence always map dependent pieces of evidence to dependent ones, as well as independent to independent"* are not easy, but they are susceptible to intuitive discussion. Our evidence semantics provide a way to determine the impact of such discussion on formal systems of proof.

References

[AB75]   A.R. Anderson and N.D. Belnap. *Entailment: the Logic of Relevance and Necessity.* Volume **I**, Princeton University Press, Princeton, New Jersey, 1975.

[Bar84]   H.P. Barendregt. *The Lambda Calculus: Its Syntax and Semantics.* North Holland, (revised edition) 1984.

[Bel75]   N.D. Belnap. How a computer should think. In G. Ryle, editor, *Contemporary Aspects of Philosophy*, Oriel Press, Stocksfield England, 1975. pages 30-56.

[Bel76]   N.D. Belnap. A useful four-valued logic. In *Modern Uses of Multiple-Valued Logic*, D. Reidel, Dordrecht, Netherlands, 1976.

[BS76]   N.D. Belnap and T.B. Steel. *The Logic of Questions and Answers.* Yale University Press, 1976.

[Bur67]   C. Burali-Forti. A question on transfinite numbers. In J. van Heijenoort, editor, *From Frege to Gödel – a Source Book in Mathematical Logic, 1879-1931*, pages 104–112, Harvard University Press, Cambridge, Massachusetts, 1967. Translation from Italian of Una Questione Sui Numeri Transfiniti, *Rendiconti del Circolo Matematico di Palermo 11* (1897) pp. 154-164.

[Chu41]   A. Church. *The Calculi of Lambda-Conversion.* Princeton University Press, Princeton, New Jersey, 1941.

[Fin74]   K. Fine. Models for entailment. *J. Philosophical Logic*, 3:347–372, 1974.

[FLO83]   S. Fortune, D. Leivant, and M. J. O'Donnell. The expressiveness of simple and second-order type structures. *Journal of the ACM*, 30(1):151–185, 1983.

[Fri75]   H. Friedman. Equality between functionals. In R. Parikh, editor, *Logic Colloquium*, pages 22–37, Springer-Verlag, 1975.

[FUV83]   R. Fagin, J. D. Ullman, and M. Y. Vardi. On the semantics of updates in databases. In *Second ACM SIGACT-SIGMOD Symposium on Principles of Database Systems*, pages 352–365, Atlanta, Georgia, 1983.

[Gan80]   R.O. Gandy. Proofs of strong normalization. In *To H.B. Curry: Essays on Combinatory Logic, Lambda-Calculus and Formalism*, pages 457–477, Academic Press, 1980.

[GMN84] H. Gallaire, J. Minker, and J.-M. Nicolas. Logic and databases: a deductive approach. *Computing surveys*, 16(2):153–185, 1984.

[Hel77a] G. Helman. Completeness of normal typed fragment of λ-system *u*. *J. Philosophical Logic*, 6(1):33–46, 1977.

[Hel77b] G. Helman. *Restricted Lambda Abstraction and the Interpretation of Some Non-Classical Logics.* PhD thesis, University of Pittsburgh, 1977.

[Hen50]   L. Henkin. Completeness in the theory of types. *Journal of Symbolic Logic*, 15(2), June 1950. pages 81-91.

[Hin62]   J. Hintikka. *Knowledge and Belief.* Cornell University Press, 1962.

[Hin83]   R. Hindley. The completeness theorem for typing lambda terms. *Theor. Comp. Sci.*, 22, 1983. pages 1-17.

[How80]   W. Howard. The formulas-as-types notion of construction. In *To H.B. Curry: Essays on Combinatory Logic, Lambda-Calculus and Formalism*, pages 479–490, Academic Press, 1980.

[Kle45]   S.C. Kleene. On the interpretation of intuitionistic number theory. *J. Symbolic Logic*, 10, 1945. pages 109–124.

[Kow79]   R. Kowalski. *Logic for Problem Solving*. Elsevier North-Holland, New York, 1979.

[Kre56]   G. Kreisel. Interpretation of analysis by means of constructive functionals of finite type. In A. Heyting, editor, *Constructivity in Mathematics*, pages 101–128, North-Holland, Amsterdam, 1956.

[KV65]   S.C. Kleene and R.E. Vesley. *The foundations of intuitionistic mathematics*. North-Holland, 1965.

[Lau65]   H. Läuchli. Intuitionistic propositional calculus and definably non-empty terms (abstract). *Journal of Symbolic Logic*, 30, 1965. pages 263.

[Lau70]   H. Läuchli. An abstract notion of realizability for which intuitionistic predicte calculus is complete. In Kino Myhill and Vesley, editors, *Intuitionism and Proof Theory: Proc. of the Summer Conference at Buffalo N.Y.*, North Holland, 1970. pages 227-234.

[Mar75]   P. Martin-Löf. An intuitionistic theory of types: predicative part. In *Logic Colloquium, 1973*, pages 73–118, North-Holland, Amsterdam, 1975.

[Mey82]   A.R. Meyer. What is a model of the lambda calculus ? *Information and Control*, 52(1), 1982. pages 87-122.

[MM85]   J.C. Mitchell and A.R. Meyer. Second-order logical relations. In *Logics of Programs*, June 1985. pages 225-236.

[MP85]   J.C. Mitchell and G.D. Plotkin. Abstract types have existential types. In *Proc. 12-th ACM Symp. on Principles of Programming Languages*, pages 37–51, January 1985.

[ODo85]   M. J. O'Donnell. *Equational Logic as a Programming Language*. M.I.T. Press, 1985.

[Plo80]   G.D. Plotkin. Lambda definability in the full type hierarchy. In *To H.B. Curry: Essays on Combinatory Logic, Lambda Calculus and Formalism*, pages 363–373, Academic Press, 1980.

[Pot74]   G. Pottinger. *Constructive Relevance Logics*. Technical Report, Carnegie-Mellon University, 1974. Earlier version: A Theory of Implications, Ph.D. dissertation, University of Pittsburgh (1972).

[Pra65]   D. Prawitz. *Natural Deduction*. Almquist and Wiksell, Stockholm, 1965.

[RM73]   R. Routley and R. K. Meyer. The semantics of entailment (i). In H. Leblanc, editor, *Truth, Syntax, Modality*, pages 199–243, North-Holland, Amsterdam, 1973. (II), *Journal of Philosophical Logic* 1 (1972) pp. 53-73. (III), *Journal of Philosophical Logic*, 1 (1972) pp. 192-208.

[Sta82a] R. Statman. Completeness, invariance and lambda-definability. *J. Symbolic Logic*, 47:17–26, 1982.

[Sta82b] R. Statman. Embeddings, homomorphisms and lambda-definability. (Manuscript.), 1982.

[Sta82c] R. Statman. Logical relations and the typed lambda calculus. (Manuscript.), 1982. To appear in Information and Control.

[Ste72]   S. Stenlund. *Combinators, Lambda Terms and Proof Theory*. Reidel, Dordrecht-Holland, 1972.

[SW76]   S. Shapiro and M. Wand. *The relevance of relevance*. Technical Report CSD 46, Indiana University, 1976.

THEORETICAL FOUNDATIONS FOR BELIEF REVISION

João P. Martins
Dep. Eng. Mecânica
Inst. Superior Técnico
Av. Rovisco Pais
1000 Lisboa
Portugal

Stuart C. Shapiro
Dep. Computer Sci.
University at Buffalo
226 Bell Hall
Buffalo, N.Y. 14260
USA

ABSTRACT

Belief revision systems are AI programs that deal with contradictions. They work with a knowledge base, performing reasoning from the propositions in the knowledge base, "filtering" those propositions so that only part of the knowledge base is perceived - the set of propositions that are under consideration. This set of propositions is called the set of believed propositions. Typically, belief revision systems explore alternatives, make choices, explore the consequences of their choices, and compare results obtained when using different choices. If during this process a contradiction is detected, then the belief revision system will revise the knowledge base, "erasing" some propositions so that it gets rid of the contradiction.

In this paper, we present a logic suitable to support belief revision systems and discuss the properties that a belief revision system based on this logic will exhibit. The system we present, SWM, differs from most of the systems developed so far in two respects: First, it is based on a logic which was developed to support belief revision systems. Second, its implementation relies on the manipulation of sets of assumptions, not justifications. The first feature allows the study of the formal properties of the system independently of its implementation, and the second one enables the system to work effectively and efficiently with inconsistent information, to switch reasoning contexts without processing overhead, and to avoid most backtracking.

INTRODUCTION

The ability to reason about and adapt to a changing environment is an important aspect of intelligent behavior. Most computer programs constructed by researchers in AI maintain a model of their environment (external and/or internal), which is updated to reflect the perceived changes in the environment. The model of the environment is typically stored in a knowledge-base (containing propositions about the state of the environment) and the program manipulates the information in this knowledge base. Most of the manipulation consists of drawing inferences from information in the knowledge base. All the inferences drawn are added to the knowledge base. One reason for model updating (and thus knowledge base updating) is the detection of contradictory information about the environment. In this case the updating should be preceded by the decision of what proposition in the knowledge base is the culprit for the contradiction, its removal from the knowledge base*, and the subsequent removal from the knowledge base of every proposition that depends on the selected culprit.

Belief revision systems are AI programs that deal with contradictions. They work with a knowledge base, performing reasoning from the propositions in the knowledge base and "filtering" the propositions in the knowledge base so that only part of the knowledge base is perceived - the set of propositions that are under consideration. This set of propositions is called the set of believed propositions. When the belief revision system considers another of these sets, we say that it changes its beliefs. Typically, belief revision systems explore alternatives, make choices, explore the consequences of its choices, and compare results obtained when using different choices. If during this process a contradiction is detected (i.e., both a proposition and its negation belong to the set of believed propositions), then the belief revision system will revise the knowledge base, "erasing" some propositions so that it gets rid of the contradiction. The Truth-Maintenance System (TMS) [Doyle 79], was the first domain-independent belief revision system. TMS maintains a knowledge base in which propositions are explicitly marked as believed or disbelieved. When a contradiction is found, TMS revises its beliefs so that no inconsistent propositions are believed. Doyle's research triggered the development of several belief revision systems [Goodwin 82, 84; McAllester 78, 80; McDermott 82, 83; Thompson 79]. These systems share two characteristics: (1) they are mainly concerned with implementation issues, paying no special attention to the logic underlying the system; (2) each proposition is justified with the propositions that directly originated it. The first aspect does not allow the formal study of the properties of the systems independently of their implementations: in those systems, it is very difficult to define and study the properties

---

* Or making it inaccessible to the program.

of the underlying logic except by repeatedly running the program*.   The
second aspect originates systems that can only deal with one situation at
a time, are not able to perform inferences in a state where a
contradiction was derived, and present a large computing overhead both
when switching between situations and in computing the culprit for a
contradiction.

As a reaction against these problems, the early 80's saw the
development of new kinds of belief revision systems, characterized by:
(1) an explicit concern about the foundations of the systems,
independently of their implementations [Doyle 82, 83; Martins 83; Martins
and Shapiro 83] and (2) the use of a new type of justifications [Martins
83; Martins and Shapiro 83; deKleer 84, 86a, 86b].

JUSTIFICATION-BASED VS. ASSUMPTION-BASED SYSTEMS

A fundamental issue in belief revision systems is to be able to
identify every proposition that may have contributed to a contradiction.
This is important since, on the one hand, we don't want to blame some
assumption irrelevant to the contradiction as the culprit, and, on the
other hand, when searching for the assumption responsible for the
contradiction we don't want to leave out any assumption possibly
responsible for the contradiction. In order to do this, belief revision
systems have to to keep a record of where each proposition in the
knowledge base came from. These records are inspected while searching for
the culprit of a contradiction. Thus, associated with every proposition
in the knowledge base, there will be a set, called the support of the
proposition, that tells where that proposition came from.

After selecting the culprit for a contradiction, the belief revision
system typically "changes its beliefs", i.e., considers another set of the
propositions in the knowledge base that does not contain the culprit of
the contradiction nor any proposition derived from it. Furthermore, when
considering a given set of propositions, the belief revision system
ignores all the other propositions that may exist in the knowledge base.

There are two different ways of recording the origin of propositions;
corresponding to justification-based and assumption-based systems [deKleer
84]. In justification-based systems, the support of each proposition
contains the propositions that directly originated it. This approach was
taken by [Doyle 79; Goodwin 82, 84; McAllester 80; McDermott 82; Thompson

---

* Although there are techniques to prove properties about programs, and
thus one may be tempted to use them to prove properties about these
programs, without the statement of the underlying logic one does not have
a clear idea of what properties to prove.

79].   In <u>assumption-based</u> systems, the support of each proposition
contains the hypotheses (non-derived propositions) that originated it.
This approach was taken by [Martins 83; deKleer 84, 86a, 86b].

Assumptions-based systems present advantages over justification-based
systems, with respect to: (1) Identifying the possible culprits for a
contradiction, (2) changing sets of beliefs, and (3) comparing sets of
beliefs.   The main advantage that justification-based systems present over
assumption-based ones concerns the explanation of their reasoning.   In
fact, since these systems maintain a record of the history of the
derivation of each proposition in the knowledge base they can explain how
a given proposition was obtained.   DeKleer [deKleer 84] presents an
excellent discussion on these issues.

There is, however, a hidden assumption behind assumption-based
systems, which is that it is possible to compute <u>exactly</u> which hypotheses
underlie a given proposition.   The obvious solution of unioning the
hypotheses underlying each of the parent propositions to compute the
hypotheses underlying a derived proposition won't do.*   Another important
issue is how to "remember" the contradictions that were derived and to
avoid getting into the same contradiction twice.

In the next section we present a logic, the SWM system, that addresses
these two problems.   Each proposition in SWM is associated with a set (the
origin set) that contains those, and only those, hypotheses used in its
derivation.   Each proposition in SWM is also associated with another set
(the restriction set) containing the sets of hypotheses which are
incompatible (produce inconsistencies) with the proposition's origin set.
The SWM system defines how these sets are formed and propagated through
the application of the rules of inference.   Based on SWM, we define an
abstract model for an assumption-based belief revision system.

THE SWM SYSTEM

In this section we introduce a logic, the SWM system (after <u>S</u>hapiro,
<u>W</u>and and <u>M</u>artins) that was developed to support belief revision systems.
When discussing a logic, there are two aspects to consider, its syntax and
its semantics.

The <u>syntax</u> of a logic includes a set of formation rules and a set of
rules of inference.   The set of <u>formation</u> <u>rules</u> determines which formulas
are legal in the logic.   These formulas are called well-formed formulas,
<u>wffs</u> for short.   We will assume standard formation rules for wffs with ~,

---

* This is implicitly done in some justification-based systems, e.g., with
the SL-justifications of TMS [Doyle 79].

v, &, -> as connectives and ∀, E as quantifiers. See, for example, [Lemmon 78, pp.44 and 104]. The set of <u>rules</u> <u>of</u> <u>inference</u> (the deductive system) specifies which conclusions may be inferred from which premises. Given an argument (P,c),* we say that c is <u>deducible</u> from P, written P|-c, if there is a sequence of rules of inference which when applied to P produces c.

The <u>semantics</u> of a logic concerns the study of the conditions under which sentences are true or false. The semantics are completely determined by the specification of two things, the interpretations of the language (every possible assignment of a particular object to each particular member of the language) and the truth conditions for it (what it means for a given sentence to have a given truth value in a given interpretation). We say that the argument (P,c) is <u>valid</u> if there is no interpretation in which each sentence in P is true and in which c is false. If (P,c) is valid, we write P|=c.

There is nothing about validity in the deductive system, and there is nothing about deducibility in the semantics. Although syntax and semantics are separate parts of a logical system, and thus deducibility and validity are intensionally distinct, they must fit together properly in order for the system to make any sense. A logic is said to be <u>sound</u> if and only if every argument deducible in its deductive system is valid according to its semantics. A logic is said to be <u>complete</u> if and only if every argument valid according to its semantics is deducible in its deductive system. Given a "reasonable" semantics, a logic can be unsound due to "wrong" rules of inference; and a logic can be incomplete due to the lack of necessary rules of inference or due to rules of inference that are too constraining. The SWM system is an incomplete logic, since several arguments valid according to its semantics are not deducible in its deduction system. This fact should not be regarded as a drawback of the logic but rather as a feature that makes it attractive for its intended applications.

The first step towards formally analyzing arguments consists of providing precise meaning for everyday terms like "and", "or", "if", "if...then...", "every", "some", etc. In the process of translating an informal argument into a formal one, some of the features of the informal argument are lost. The important point is to keep in the model those features that are of interest to the modeler. Therefore, when assigning meaning to the logical terms, one should bear in mind which features of the informal arguments one wants to preserve in their formal counterparts. In our case, our main goal is to keep a record of propositional

---

* A premisse-conclusion argument is an ordered pair (P,c) in which P is a set of propositions, called <u>premisses</u> and c is a single proposition, called <u>conclusion</u>.

dependencies, and our approach adopts the meaning of the logical connectives used in classical logic and builds a deductive system that blocks some unwanted deductions (resulting in an incomplete system). Most of the blocked deductions involve the introduction of irrelevancies.

One of the fundamental problems that any logic underlying a belief revision system has to address is how to keep track of and propagate propositional dependencies. This is important, because, in the event of detection of a contradiction, one should be able to identify exactly which assumptions were used in the derivation of the contradictory propositions: We don't want to blame some assumption irrelevant to the occurrence of the contradiction as the culprit for the contradiction, and, when looking for the possible culprits for a contradiction, we don't want to leave out any assumption possibly responsible for the contradiction. In logic, the relevance logicians also want to keep track of what propositions were used to derive any given proposition. Relevance logicians have developed mechanisms to keep track of what assumptions were used in the derivation of a given proposition and to prevent the introduction of irrelevancies. One way of doing this (used in the FR system of [Anderson and Belnap 75, pp.346-348] and in the system of [Shapiro and Wand 76]) consists of associating each wff with a set, called the origin set, which references every hypothesis used its derivation. The rules of inference are stated so that all the wffs derived using a particular hypothesis will reference this hypothesis in their origin sets. Whenever a rule of inference is applied, the origin set of the resulting wff is computed from the origin sets of the parent wffs.* In order to guarantee that the origin set only contains the hypotheses actually used in the derivation of the wff, and no more hypotheses, some of the applications of the rules of inference allowed in classical logic are blocked. Most of this mechanism was adopted in the SWM system.

Besides the dependency-propagation mechanism, there is another advantage in using relevance logic, to support belief revision systems. In classical logic a contradiction implies anything; thus, in a belief revision system based on classical logic, whenever a contradiction is derived it should be discarded immediately. In a relevance-logic-based belief revision system, we may allow the existence of a contradiction in the knowledge base without the danger of filling the knowledge base with unwanted deductions. In a relevance logic-based belief revision system all a contradiction indicates is that any inference depending on every hypothesis underlying the contradiction is of no value. In this type of systems we can even perform reasoning in a knowledge base known to be inconsistent. See, for example, [Martins 83], and [Martins and Shapiro

---

* The resulting origin set can either be the union of the origin sets of the parent wffs or the set difference of the origin sets of the parent wffs.

86].

Another important issue in belief revision systems which will be reflected in our logic consists in the recording of the conditions under which contradictions may occur. This is important because once we discover that a given set is inconsistent,* we may not want to consider it again, and even if we do want to consider it, we want to keep in mind that we are dealing with an inconsistent set. In the SWM system, contradictions are recorded by associating each wff with a set, called the restriction set, that contains information about which sets unioned with the wff's origin set produce an inconsistent set. When new wffs are derived, their restriction sets are computed directly from the restriction sets of the parent wffs, and when contradictions are detected all the wffs whose origin set references any of the contradictory hypotheses has its restriction set updated in order to record the newly discovered contradictory set. Similarly to what happens with origin sets, we will make sure that restriction sets don't have any more information than they should.

In addition, for the proper application of some rules of inference, it is important to know whether a given wff was introduced as a hypothesis or was derived from other wffs. In order to do this, we associate each wff with an identifier, called the origin tag that tells whether the wff is a hypothesis, a normally derived proposition, or a special proposition, that if treated regularly, would introduce irrelevancies into the knowledge base.**

Formally, the SWM system deals with objects called supported wffs. A supported wff consists of a wff and an associated triple containing an origin tag (OT), an origin set (OS), and a restriction set (RS). The set of all supported wffs is called the knowledge base. We write $A|t,a,r$ to denote that A is a wff with OT t, OS a, and RS r, and we define the functions $ot(A)=t$, $os(A)=a$ and $rs(A)=r$.

The problem of multiple derivations of the same wff is not directly addressed by the SWM system: if a proposition is derived in several different ways then it is added to the knowledge base with different OTs, OSs, and RSs. It is the computer system that interprets the knowledge base that worries about the problem of multiple derivations (see [Martins 83], and [Martins and Shapiro 84]).

---

* A set is inconsistent if a contradiction may be derived from it. A set is consistent just in case it is not inconsistent. We represent a contradiction by $-><-$, thus A is inconsistent if $A |- -><-$
** For a discussion of this latter case and the reasons that lead us to introduce this additional value for origin tags, refer to [Martins 83] or [Martins and Shapiro forthcoming].

The OS is a set of hypotheses. The OS of a supported wff contains those (and only those) hypotheses that were <u>actually</u> <u>used</u> in the derivation of that wff. The OTs range over the set {hyp, der, ext}: <u>hyp</u> identifies hypotheses, <u>der</u> identifies normally derived wffs within SWM, and <u>ext</u> identifies special wffs whose OS was extended. An RS is a set of sets of wffs. A wff, say A, whose RS is {R1, ... ,Rn} means that the hypotheses in <u>os</u>(A) added to any of the sets R1, ... ,Rn produce an <u>inconsistent</u> <u>set</u>. The RS of an extended wff will contain <u>every</u> set which unioned with the wff's OS will produce a set that is known to be inconsistent. Our rules of inference guarantee that the information contained in the RS is carried over to the new wffs whenever a new proposition is derived. Furthermore, the rules of inference guarantee that RSs do not contain any redundant information; i.e., given $A|t,a,\{R1,...,Rn\}$, the following types of redundancy do not arise:

1. There is no $r\in\{R1,...,Rn\}$ such that $r\cap a\neq\emptyset$.*

2. There are no $r\in\{R1,...,Rn\}$ and $s\in\{R1,...,Rn\}$, such that $r\subset s$.**

We say that the supported wff $A|t,a,\{R1, ... ,Rn\}$ has a <u>minimal</u> RS if the following two conditions are met:

     1. $\forall r\in\{R1, ... ,Rn\}$ $(r\cap a)=\emptyset$;

     2. $\forall r,s\in\{R1, ... ,Rn\}$ $r\not\subset s$.

In [Martins 83], we prove that all the supported wffs in the knowledge base resulting from the application of the rules of inference of the SWM system have minimal RS.

To compute the RS of a wff resulting from the application rule of inference, we define the functions μ and $\int$. The function μ is used whenever a rule of inference which generates a supported wff whose OS is the union of the OSs of the parent wffs is applied. It generates the RS of the resulting wff by unioning the RSs of the parent wffs and removing from the resulting set some sets which would be redundant, namely that would violate one of the two conditions listed above. The function $\int$ is used by the rules of inference which generate a supported wff with a

---

* Otherwise, the set would r contain extra information, namely, all the wffs in r a.

** Otherwise, the set s could be discarded from the restriction set without any loss of information: Since r belongs to the RS of $A|t,a,\{R1,...,Rn\}$, we know that that $a\cup r|- \to<-$. Also, since any set containing an inconsistent set is itself inconsistent, we could infer that $a\cup s$ is inconsistent, since $(a\cup r)\subset(a\cup s)$.

smaller OS than the parent wffs. It takes the RS of the several hypotheses in the resulting OS and computes a minimal RS from those RSs. The functions μ and $\int$ are defined as follows:

$$\mu(\{r1, \ldots ,rm\},\{o1, \ldots ,on\}) = \sigma'(\Psi(r1 \cup \ldots \cup rm, o1 \cup \ldots \cup on)),$$

where

$$\Psi(R,O) = \{a \mid (a \in R \ \& \ a \cap O = \emptyset) \ v \ (Eb)[b \in R \ \& \ b \cap O \neq \emptyset \ \& \ a=b-O]\}$$

and

$$\sigma'(R) = \{a \mid a \in R \ \& \ \sim(Eb)(b \neq a \ \& \ b \in R \ \& \ b \subset a)\}$$

and

$$\int(O)=\mu(\{r \mid EH \in O:r=\underline{rs}(H)\} \ , \ \{o \mid EH \in O:o=\underline{os}(H)\})$$

To compute the OT of a wff resulting from the application of the rules of inference, we define the function $\uparrow$ as follows:

$$\uparrow(a,b) \ = \ \begin{cases} \text{ext} & \text{if a=ext ot b=ext} \\ \\ \text{der} & \text{otherwise} \end{cases}$$

$$\uparrow(a,b,\ldots,c) = \uparrow(a,\uparrow(b,\ldots,c))$$

Two supported wffs are said to be <u>combinable</u> by some rule of inference if the supported wff resulting from the application of the rule of inference has an OS that is not known to be inconsistent. We define the predicate <u>Combine</u>, which decides the combinability of the supported wffs A and B:

$$\text{Combine}(A,B) = \begin{cases} \text{false} & \text{if } Er \in \underline{rs}(A) : r \subset \underline{os}(B) \\ \text{false} & \text{if } Er \in \underline{rs}(B) : r \subset \underline{os}(A) \\ \text{true} & \text{otherwise} \end{cases}$$

The rules of inference of the SWM system, guarantee that:

1. The OS of a supported wff contains <u>every</u> hypothesis that was used in its derivation.

2. The OS of a supported wff <u>only</u> contains the hypotheses that were used in its derivation.

3. The RS of a supported wff records <u>every</u> set known to be inconsistent with the wff's OS.

4. The application of rules of inference is blocked if the resulting wff
    would have an OS known to be inconsistent.

It is important to distinguish between a set <u>being</u> inconsistent and a
set <u>being known to be</u> inconsistent. An inconsistent set is one from which
a contradiction <u>can be</u> derived; a set known to be inconsistent is an
inconsistent set from which a contradiction <u>has been</u> derived. The goal of
adding RSs is to avoid re-considering known inconsistent sets of
hypotheses.

The OT and OS of a proposition reflect the way the proposition was
derived: the OS contains the hypotheses underlying that proposition, and
the OT represents the relation between the proposition and its OS. The RS
of a proposition reflects our current knowledge about how the hypotheses
underlying that proposition relate to the other hypotheses in the
knowledge base. Once a proposition is derived, its OT and OS remain
constant; however, its RS changes as the knowledge about all the
propositions in the knowledge base does. Again we do not address here the
problem of multiple derivations of the same proposition, a fundamental
problem in belief revision. In the SWM system, if the same wff is derived
in several different ways, then several supported wffs are added to the
knowledge base (all of them with the same wff) and thus the reason we say
that the OT and OS of a wff remain constant. The program that uses the
knowledge base generated by SWM treats these wffs appropriately.

The following are the rules of inference of the SWM system.*

<u>Hypothesis</u> (Hyp): For any wff A and sets of wffs R1...Rn (n>0), such that
$\forall r \in \{R1, \ldots , Rn\}$: $r \cap \{A\} = \emptyset$ and $\forall r, s \in \{R1, \ldots , Rn\}: r \not\subseteq s$, we may add
the supported wff A|hyp,{A},{R1, ... ,Rn} to the knowledge base,
provided that A has not already been introduced as a hypothesis.

<u>Implication Introduction</u> (->I): From B|der,o,r and any hypothesis H-o,
infer H->B|der,o$\in${H}, $\int$ (o-{H}).

<u>Modus Ponens - Implication Elimination, Part 1</u> (MP): From A|t1,o1,r1,
A->B|t2,o2,r2,   and   Combine(A,A->B),   infer
B|↑(t1,t2),o1 ∪ o2,μ({r1,r2},{o1,o2}).

<u>Modus Tollens - Implication Elimination, Part 2</u> (MT): From A->B|t1,o1,r1,
~B|t2,o2,r2,   and   Combine(A->B,~B),   infer

---

* There is an extra connective in the SWM system, the <u>truth-functional</u>
<u>or</u>, which will not be discussed in this paper. For a detailed
description of this connective, refer to [Martins 83], and [Martins and
Shapiro 84].

~A|↑(t1,t2),o1 ∪ o2,μ({r1,r2},{o1,o2}).

Negation Introduction (~I):

From A|t1,o,r, ~A|t2,o,r, and any set {H1, ... ,Hn}⊂o, infer
~(H1&...&Hn) | ↑(t1,t2), o-{H1, ... ,Hn}, ∫ (o-{H1, ... ,Hn}).
From A|t1,o1,r1, ~A|t2,o2,r2, o1≠o2, Combine(A,~A), and any set
{H1, ... ,Hn} ⊂ (o1 o2),   infer   ~(H1&...&Hn) | ext,
(o1 ∪ o2)-{H1, ... ,Hn}, ∫ ((o1 o2)-{H1, ... ,Hn}).

Negation Elimination (~E): From ~~A|t,o,r, infer A|↑(t,t),o,r.

Updating of Restriction Sets (URS): From A|t1,o1,r1, and ~A|t2,o2,r2, we
<u>must</u> replace each hypothesis H|hyp,{H},R such that H∈(o1 ∪ o2) by
H|hyp,{H}, σ'(R ∪ {(o1 ∪ o2)-{H}}). Furthermore, we <u>must</u> also replace
every supported wff F|t,o,r (t=der or t=ext) such that o ∩ (o1 ∪ o2)≠∅
by F|t,o, σ'(r ∪ {(o1 ∪ o2)-o}).

And Introduction (&I):

From A|t1,o,r and B|t2,o,r, infer A&B|↑(t1,t2),o,r.
From A|t1,o1,r1, B|t2,o2,r2, o1≠o2, and Combine(A,B), infer
A&B|ext,o1 o2,u({r1,r2},{o1,o2}).

And Elimination (&E): From A&B|t,o,r, and t≠ext, infer either A|der,o,r
or B|der,o,r or both.

Or Introduction (vI): From ~A->B|t1,o,r and ~B->A|t2,o,r, infer
AvB|↑(t1,t2),o,r.

Or Elimination (vE):

From AvB|t1,o1,r1, ~A|t2,o2,r2, and Combine(AvB,~A), infer
B|↑(t1,t2),o1 ∪ o2,μ({r1,r2},{o1,o2}).
From AvB|t1,o1,r1, ~B|t2,o2,r2, and Combine(AvB,~B), infer
A|↑(t1,t2),o1 ∪ o2,μ({r1,r2},{o1,o2}).
From   AvB|t1,o1,r1,   A->C|t2,o2,r2,   B->C|t3,o2,r2,   and
Combine(AvB,A->C), infer C | ↑(t1,t2,t3),o1 ∪ o2,μ({r1,r2},{o1,o2}).

∀ introduction (∀I): From B(t) | der,o ∪ {A(t)},r, in which A(t) is a
hypothesis which uses a term (t) never used in the system prior to
A's introduction, infer ∀(x)[A(x)->B(x)] | der,o, ∫ (o).*

---

* According to this rule of inference, the universal quantifier can only
be introduced in the context of an implication. This is not a drawback,
as may seem at first, since the role of the antecedent of the implication
(A(x)) is to define the type of object that are being quantified. This
is sometimes called relativized quantification.

<u>∀</u> <u>elimination</u> - <u>Universal</u> <u>Instantiation</u> (∀E):
From the supported wffs ∀(x)[A(x)->B(x)]|t1,o1,r1, A(c)|t2,o2,r2 and Combine(∀(x)[A(x)->B(x)], A(c)), in which c is any individual symbol, infer A(c)->B(c) | ↑(t1,t2),o1 ∪o2,μ({r1,r2},{o1,o2});

<u>E</u> <u>introduction</u> (EI): From A(c) | t,o,r in which c is an individual constant, infer E(x)[A(x)] | ↑(t,t),o,r;

<u>E</u> <u>elimination</u> (EE): From E(x)[A(x)] | t,o,r and any individual constant c which was never used before, infer A(c) | ↑(t,t),o,r.

Among others, the following theorems hold for SWM (their proof can be found in [Martins 83]):

<u>Theorem</u>: All the supported wffs in the knowledge base resulting from the application of the rules of inference of SWM have minimal RS.

<u>Theorem</u>: In the knowledge base resulting from the application of the rules of inference of SWM, if two supported wffs have the same OS, then they have the same RS as well.

<u>Theorem</u>: Every OS has recorded with it <u>every</u> known inconsistent set.

<u>A</u> <u>CONTEXTUAL</u> <u>INTERPRETATION</u> <u>FOR</u> <u>SWM</u>

We now discuss how a program using SWM should interpret SWM's wffs. We provide a <u>contextual</u> <u>interpretation</u> for SWM.   We use the word "contextual interpretation" instead of just "interpretation" for the following two reasons: On the one hand, we want to stress that we are not providing an interpretation for SWM in the logician's sense of the word; on the other hand, we want to emphasize that our definition of truth depends on the notion of context. This contextual interpretation defines the behavior of an abstract revision system (i.e., not tied to any particular implementation), which we call MBR (<u>M</u>ultiple <u>B</u>elief <u>R</u>easoner).

MBR works with a knowledge base containing propositions that are associated with an OT, OS, and RS (in SWM's sense). Propositions are added to the knowledge base according to the rules of inference of SWM. We define a <u>context</u> to be a set of hypotheses. A context determines a <u>Belief</u> <u>Space</u> (BS), which is the set of all the hypotheses defining the context and all the propositions that were derived exclusively from them. Within the SWM formalism, the wffs in a given BS are characterized by having an OS that is contained in the context. The set of contexts represented in the knowledge base is the power set of the set of hypotheses existing in the knowledge base.

Any operation performed within the knowledge base (query, addition, deletion, etc.) will be associated with a context. We will refer to this context as the <u>current</u> <u>context</u>. While the operation is being carried out, the only propositions that will be considered are the propositions in the BS defined by the current context. This BS will be called the <u>current</u> <u>BS</u>. A proposition is said to be <u>believed</u> if it belongs to the current BS. We can look at contexts as delimiting smaller knowledge bases (the Belief Spaces) within the knowledge base. The only propositions that are retrievable are those propositions that belong to the current BS.

A common goal of belief revision systems is to stay away from contradictions. Taking this into account, it would seem natural to constrain contexts to be consistent sets of hypotheses, not just any sets of hypotheses. However, it may be the case that one desires to perform reasoning within the BS defined by an inconsistent context (in SWM, the existence of contradictions is not as damaging as in classical logic, in which anything can be derived from a contradiction) and thus the condition that a context is not known to be inconsistent will not be compulsory but rather advisable if one doesn't explicitly want to perform reasoning in a BS that is known to be inconsistent. The reason why it is advisable is that within a BS defined by a context not known to be inconsistent some simplification can be considered during the application of the rules of inference (for details refer to [Martins 83]).

Let us now consider how MBR acts when a contradiction is detected. SWM has two rules of inference to handle contradictions: negation introduction and updating of restriction sets. When a contradiction is detected, one of two things will happen:

1. <u>Only</u> <u>one</u> <u>of</u> <u>the</u> <u>contradictory</u> <u>wffs</u> <u>belongs</u> <u>to</u> <u>the</u> <u>current</u> <u>BS</u>:* the contradiction is recorded (through the application of URS), but nothing more happens. The effect of doing so is to record that some set of hypotheses, properly containing the current context, is now known to be inconsistent. This results in what we call <u>belief</u> <u>revision</u> <u>within</u> <u>a</u> <u>context</u> <u>properly</u> <u>containing</u> <u>the</u> <u>current</u> <u>context</u>.

2. <u>Both</u> <u>contradictory</u> <u>wffs</u> <u>belong</u> <u>to</u> <u>the</u> <u>current</u> <u>BS</u>: URS is applied, resulting in the updating of the RSs of the propositions in the knowledge base, and, in addition, the rule of ~I may also be applied. This results in what we call <u>belief</u> <u>revision</u> <u>within</u> <u>the</u> <u>current</u> <u>context</u>, normally originating the disbelief (removal from the current context) of some of its hypotheses.

Examples of these types of belief revision can be found in [Martins 83].

---

* Note that at least one of the contradictory wffs belongs to the current BS, since a contradiction is detected whenever some newly derived wff contradicts some existing one, and newly derived wffs always belong to the current BS.

CONCLUDING REMARKS

In this paper, we discussed an important class of AI programs, belief revision systems. Belief revision is important whenever reasoning is performed with a knowledge base that may contain contradictory information. Belief revision systems are capable of considering only part of the knowledge base (the set of believed propositions), perform inferences from this set, and, if a contradiction is detected, replace this set by another one (change their beliefs), and afterwards disregards every proposition that does not belong to the new set. To obtain this behavior, belief revision systems have to maintain a record of where each proposition in the knowledge base came from. We discussed two ways of keeping these records, corresponding to assumption-based and justification-based systems.

In order to build an assumption-based belief revision system, we developed a formalism that associates each proposition in the knowledge base with the set of hypotheses used in its derivation. We presented a logic (SWM) loosely based on relevance logic that captures the notion of propositional dependency and is able to deal with contradictions. SWM associates two sets with each proposition: the origin set contains every hypothesis used in the derivation of the proposition; the restriction set contains those sets of hypotheses that are incompatible with the proposition's origin set.

Each proposition generated by the rules of inference of SWM has a minimal restriction set, in the sense that restriction sets are free from some kinds of redundancies. Each such proposition has a maximal restriction set in the sense that its restriction set records all inconsistent sets known so far. Every proposition with the same origin set has the same restriction set, reflecting the fact that restriction sets are both minimal and maximal.

We defined the behavior of an abstract program based on SWM, the Multiple Belief Reasoner (MBR). In MBR, a context is any set of hypotheses. A context determines a belief space (BS), which is the set of all propositions whose origin set is contained in the context. A BS contains all the propositions that depend exclusively on the hypotheses defining the context. Given any context, the only propositions whose truth value is known are those propositions that belong to the BS defined by the context. The truth value of all the other propositions is unknown. By a proposition having an unknown truth value, we mean that in order to compute its truth value one has to carry out further deduction, and it may even be possible that its truth value is not computable from the hypotheses under consideration. At any moment, the only propositions that are believed (and thus retrievable from the knowledge base) are the ones that belong to the BS under consideration.

MBR only considers the propositions in the BS under consideration and thus, when a contradiction is detected and, after selecting some hypotheses as the culprit for the contradiction, in order to make inaccessible to the belief revision system all the propositions that were previously derived from such hypotheses, all one has to do in MBR is remove the selected hypotheses from the context under consideration. Afterwards, all the propositions derived from the selected hypotheses are no longer in the BS under consideration and consequently are not retrievable by the deduction system.

Aknowledgements

Many thanks to John Corcoran, Jon Doyle, Donald McKay, Ernesto Morgado, J. Terry Nutter, William J. Rapaport and members of the SNePS Research Group for their criticisms and suggestions.

This work was partially supported by the National Science Foundation under Grant MCS80-06314 and by the Instituto Nacional de Investigação Científica (Portugal), under Grant No. 20536; Preparation of this paper was supported in part by the Air Force Systems Command, Rome Air Development Center, Griffiss Air Force Base, New York 13441-5700, and the Air Force Office of Scientific Research, Bolling AFB DC 20332 under contract No. F30602-85-C-0008.

References

Anderson A. and Belnap N., Entailment: The Logic of Relevance and Necessity, Vol.1, Princeton University Press, 1975.

de Kleer J., "Choices without Backtracking", Proc. AAAI-84, pp. 79-85.

de Kleer J., "An Assumption-Based Truth Maintenance System", Artificial Intelligence, Vol.28, No.1, 1986a.

de Kleer J., "Problem Solving with the ATMS", Artificial Intelligence, Vol.28, No.1, 1986b.

Doyle J., "A Truth Maintenance System", Artificial Intelligence, Vol.12 No.3, pp.231-272, 1979.

Doyle J., "Some Theories of Reasoned Assumptions: An Essay in Rational Psychology", Department of Computer Science, Carnegie-Mellon University, 1982.

Doyle J., "The Ins and Outs of Reason Maintenance", Proc. IJCAI-83, pp.349-351.

Goodwin J. W., "A Improved Algorithm for Non-Monotonic Dependency Net Update", Research Report LiTH-MAT-R-82-23, Software Systems Research Center, Linkoping Institute of Technology, Sweden, August 1982.

Goodwin J.W., "WATSON: A Dependency Directed Inference System", Proc. Non-Monotonic Reasoning Workshop, pp.103-114, 1984.

Lemmon E.J., Beginning Logic, Hackett Publishing Company, 178.

Martins J., "Reasoning in Multiple Belief Spaces", Ph.D. Dissertation, Technical Report 203, Department of Computer Science, State University of New York at Buffalo, 1983.

Martins J. and Shapiro S., "Reasoning in Multiple Belief Spaces", Proc. IJCAI-83, pp.370-373.

Martins J. and Shapiro S., "A Model for Belief Revision", Proc. Non-Monotonic Reasoning Workshop, pp.241-294, American Association for Artificial Intelligence, 1984.

Martins J. and Shapiro S., "Hypothetical Reasoning", Proc. Applications of Artificial Intelligence to Engineering Problems, 1986.

Martins J. and Shapiro S., "A Logic for Belief Revision", forthcoming.

McAllester D., "A Three-valued Truth Maintenance System", Technical Report Memo 473, Massachussets Institute of Technology, AI Lab., 1978.

McAllester D., "An Outlook on Truth-Maintenance", AI Memo 551, Massachussets Institute of Technology, AI Lab., 1980.

McDermott D., "Contexts and Data Dependencies: A Synthesis", Department of Computer Science, Yale University, 1982.

McDermott D., "Data Dependencies on Inequalities", Proc. AAAI-83, pp.266-269.

Shapiro S. and Wand M., "The Relevance of Relevance", Technical Report No.46, Computer Science Department, Indiana University, 1976.

Thompson A., "Network Truth-Maintenance for Deduction and Modelling", Proc. IJCAI-79, pp.877-879.

A Framework for Intuitionistic Modal Logics

(Extended Abstract)

Gordon Plotkin   Colin Stirling
Department of Computer Science
Edinburgh University

Introduction

This abstract presents work on a Kripkean analysis of intuitionistic
modal logic. As remarked in [BS] there ought to be such a subject, but
in fact there is very little literature [B1,B2,F1,F2,V1,V2,V3].
One possible explanation is simply that it is hardly obvious what the
applications would be. It seems to us however that there is a wide range of
computational applications and indeed so many are the possibilities that it is
worth beginning by sorting out the basic theory.

What we have in mind is to tie up Scott's theory of domains with the
logic of programs where one wants to know whether or not

$$p \models A$$

holds. Here p is a computational entity (state, function, process, trace
or whatever) taken from a type P of such entities and A is an assertion
(of dynamic logic, epistemic logic, temporal logic or whatever). If one
wanted to know whether A held of a program one would take p to be its
denotation. Now suppose P is a Scott domain (say a complete partial
order with least element $\perp$) and consider the assertion H, for "halts", or,
"is defined". Then it seems natural that

$$\perp \models H \vee \neg H$$

does __not__ hold as we would like the "truth value" of A above, viz $\{p \mid p \models A\}$,
to be upper closed. Indeed one of us has proposed, see [AS], following
Smyth's work [Sm] that for a __liveness__ property (generalization of total
correctness) one ought to take here as truth values all upper closed sets
(rather than the G_δ sets proposed by Smyth for specifications - we want

all intersections of opens and not just countable ones) and for safety
properties (generalization of partial correctness) one would take the Scott
closed sets.   Hence one expects to look at intuitionistic logics.

As a concrete example we tried linear time temporal logic, taking P
to be the set of total and partially defined execution sequences (or traces)
from a given set S of states so that:

$$P = S* \cup (S* \times \{\bot\}) \cup S^{\omega}$$

with the ordering $w \sqsubseteq w'$ iff $w = w'$ or there are v,v' such that $w = v\bot$
and $w' = vv'$, using an obvious notation.   However we soon became lost in
the details and realized we first needed an understanding of intuitionistic
modal logic before worrying about the more complex temporal connectives (or
epistemic, or whatever).

Previous work is mainly concerned with relating intuitionistic modal
logics either to fragments of first-order intuitionistic logic or to
classical modal logics using translations.   What is not presented is a general
framework similar to the Kripkean framework for classical modal logic.   There
have been other proposals to apply intuitionistic logic to Computer Science
[Ma,Mc] but these have concerned ideas centering around the realizability interpretation.   The present proposal to look at the uses of the Kripkean (or more
general such as topological) ones seems novel.

1.   'Minimal' Intuitionistic Modal Logic

The simplest version of a Kripkean intuitionistic modal frame consists
of a set of worlds W and two relations on it, $\langle W, \sqsubseteq, R \rangle$: the relation $\sqsubseteq$
is the intuitionistic information partial ordering whereas R is the modal
accessibility relation.   Questions then arise as to the interrelationships
between these two relations (compare the discussion of frames for combinations
of different modalities [T]).   Four possible conditions spring to mind:

1.   if w ⊑ w' and wRv   then ∃v'. w'Rv' and v ⊑ v'.
2.   if w ⊑ w' and w'Rv' then ∃v. wRv   and v ⊑ v'
3.   if v ⊑ v' and wRv   then ∃w'. w'Rv' and w ⊑ w'
4.   if v ⊑ v' and w'Rv' then ∃w. wRv   and w ⊑ w'

These can be represented as conditions for completing diagrams.   For
instance, 1 and 3 become:

     Which of these conditions, if any, should be imposed on the frame
depends to a large extent on the semantic clauses for the modal operators
and their expected interrelation.   Guided by the clauses for the
intuitionistic quantifiers we might suggest the following pair:

$$w \models \Diamond A \quad \text{iff} \quad \exists u. \; wRu \; \text{and} \; u \models A$$

$$w \models \Box A \quad \text{iff} \quad \forall w' \sqsupseteq w \; \forall u. \; \text{if} \; w'Ru \; \text{then} \; u \models A$$

Further, the following two schemata seem very natural:

$$\Diamond A \;\rightarrow\; \neg \Box \neg A$$

$$\neg \Diamond A \;\rightarrow\; \Box \neg A$$

Frame condition 1 guarantees the first of these: for a counterexample
would be (for some A);

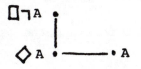

More generally, frame condition 1 guarantees that if $w \models \Diamond A$ and $w \sqsubseteq w'$
then $w' \models \Diamond A$.   In contrast it is frame condition 3 that guarantees the
second schema: for a counterexample would be (for some A):

Therefore it is these two conditions which we here impose on the definition of an intuitionistic modal frame. We believe that condition 1 is natural whereas the other condition is less so. For example, when R is a monotonic function, the first condition holds, but the second, in general, will not.

The sentential modal language $\mathcal{L}$ is given by the set of formulas A, where q ranges over a set of atomic sentences Q and ff is the false sentence:

$$A ::= ff \mid q \mid A \wedge A \mid A \vee A \mid A \rightarrow A \mid \Diamond A \mid \Box A$$

Negation is defined as usual: $\neg A$ is $A \rightarrow ff$. An intuitionistic modal model for $\mathcal{L}$ is a pair $\langle \mathcal{J}, V \rangle$ where $\mathcal{J}$ is an intuitionistic modal frame and V is a mapping from W into subsets of Q with the property:

if $w \sqsubseteq w'$ then $V(w) \subset V(w')$

We define the satisfaction relation $w \models_{\mathcal{M}} A$. The index $\mathcal{M}$ is dropped:

$w \not\models ff$

$w \models q$ iff $q \in V(w)$

$w \models A \wedge B$ iff $w \models A$ and $w \models B$

$w \models A \vee B$ iff $w \models A$ or $w \models B$

$w \models A \rightarrow B$ iff $\forall w' \sqsupseteq w$ if $w' \models A$ then $w' \models B$

$w \models \Diamond A$ iff $\exists u.\ wRu$ and $u \models A$

$w \models \Box A$ iff $\forall w' \sqsupseteq w\ \forall u.$ if $w'Ru$ then $u \models A$

The clauses for $\Diamond$ and $\Box$ are as discussed before and the others are standard.

The following lemma depends on the frame condition 1.

<u>Lemma 1.1</u>   If $w \sqsubseteq w'$ and $w \models A$ then $w' \models A$

The system below, IK, is an axiomatization of validity relative to arbitrary intuitionistic modal frames.

Axioms   1. Any intuitionistic sentential theorem instance

2. $\Box (A \rightarrow B) \rightarrow (\Box A \rightarrow \Box B)$

3. $\Box (A \rightarrow B) \rightarrow (\Diamond A \rightarrow \Diamond B)$

4. $\neg \Diamond ff$

5. $\Diamond (A \vee B) \rightarrow \Diamond A \vee \Diamond B$

6. $(\Diamond A \rightarrow \Box B) \rightarrow \Box (A \rightarrow B)$

Rules   MP   If $\vdash A$ and $\vdash A \rightarrow B$ then $\vdash B$

Nec   If $\vdash A$ then $\vdash \Box A$

Axiom A6 corresponds (see below) to the frame condition 2.   Some derived
theorems and rules are:

$$\Box \neg A \rightarrow \neg \Diamond A \qquad\qquad \Diamond \neg A \rightarrow \neg \Box A$$

$$\Box (A \wedge B) \longleftrightarrow \Box A \wedge \Box B \qquad\qquad \Box A \wedge \Diamond B \rightarrow \Diamond (A \wedge B)$$

$$\text{If } \vdash A \rightarrow B \text{ then } \vdash \Diamond A \rightarrow \Diamond B$$

IK has the disjunction property and is also both sound and complete:

Theorem 1.2 i. If $\vdash A \vee B$ then $\vdash A$ or $\vdash B$

ii. $\vdash A$ iff $\vDash A$

If $A \vee \neg A$ is added as an axiom to IK then the resulting system is
just minimal classical normal modal logic, the system K in [C].

2.   Further Modal Logics

The variety of standard classical modal logics, extensions of K, arise
by relating extra conditions on the modal accessibility relation to extra
axioms.   The result is correspondence theorems [VB]: for instance, the
axiom $\Box A \rightarrow \Box \Box A$ (or, equivalently, $\Diamond \Diamond A \rightarrow \Diamond A$)   corresponds to transitivity
of the accessibility relation.   The situation is more intricate for
intuitionistic modal logics.   There are two related features.

First, because of the breakdown in duality between $\Box$ and $\Diamond$, axioms like $\Box A \rightarrow A$ and $A \rightarrow \Diamond A$ are not equivalent (and are therefore unlikely to correspond to the same frame condition). This increases the variety of intuitionistic modal logics: for instance, there will be an 'S4' logic with axiom $\Diamond\Diamond A \rightarrow \Diamond A$ but without $\Box A \rightarrow \Box\Box A$. Secondly, the correspondence theorems do not involve just conditions on R but also include some interaction between it and $\sqsubseteq$. The general correspondence theorem below, the intuitionistic version of the $G^{k,l,m,n}$ schema [C], gives rise to a family of completeness results. Let R^n for $n \geq 0$ be defined as:

$$wR^0v \quad \text{iff} \quad w = v$$
$$wR^{n+1}v \quad \text{iff} \quad \exists u.\ wRu \ \text{ and } \ uR^n v$$

Let $G^{k,l,m,n}$ be the schema, for $k,l,m,n \geq 0$:

$$\Diamond^k \Box^l A \rightarrow \Box^m \Diamond^n A$$

Theorem 2.1   An intuitionistic modal frame validates $G^{k,l,m,n}$ iff the frame satisfies:

$$\text{if } wR^k u \ \text{ and } \ wR^m v \ \text{ then } \ \exists u' \sqsupseteq u \ \exists x (u'R^l x \ \text{ and } \ vR^n x)$$

Diagrammatically, the frame condition is:

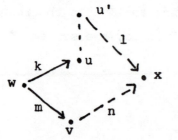

Note the presence of $\sqsubseteq$ between u and u'. Consider standard instances of the schema:

$$T\Box : \quad \Box A \rightarrow A \qquad\qquad T\Diamond : \quad A \rightarrow \Diamond A$$
$$S4\Box : \quad \Box A \rightarrow \Box\Box A \qquad\qquad S4\Diamond : \quad \Diamond\Diamond A \rightarrow \Diamond A$$
$$B\Box : \quad A \rightarrow \Box\Diamond A \qquad\qquad B\Diamond : \quad \Diamond\Box A \rightarrow A$$

$$D : \quad \Box A \rightarrow \Diamond A$$
$$S4.2 : \quad \Diamond\Box A \rightarrow \Box\Diamond A$$

T□(S4□,B□) corresponds to a different frame condition than T◊(S4◊,B◊).
For instance, S4□ and S4◊ are:

Addition of the axiom A∨¬A (which corresponds to the frame condition:
if w⊑w' then w = w') means that S4□ and S4◊ correspond to the
same frame condition, transitivity of R   (similarly, for T and B.)
Thus, theorem 2.1 appears to capture the intuitionistic correlate of the
classical correspondence theorem.

   Of particular interest, given the computational motivation, are
intuitionistic versions of the Diodorean modal systems [HC], S4.3 and
S4.3.1.   Classically, these correspond to linear time modal frames.
Recall a standard classical connectedness axiom H (which when added to
the modal system S4 results in S4.3):

$$◊A ∧ ◊B \longrightarrow ◊(A ∧ ◊B) ∨ ◊(B ∧ ◊A)$$

Theorem 2.2   An intuitionistic modal frame validates H iff the frame
               satisfies:
               if wRv and wRu then ∃v'⊒v ∃u'⊒u (wRv'Ru' or wRu'Rv')

Diagrammatically:

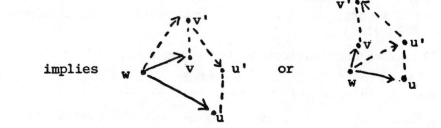

Again, note that addition of A ∨ ¬ A collapses the frame condition to
connectedness.   Work is still in progress to find correspondence theorems
for the variety of classically equivalent version of H and for the discreteness
axiom (and its classical equivalents) of S4.3.1.

Work is also in progress generalizing theorem 2.1 in a way analogous to [Sa]. Also we are working on finite model properties (and complexity): standard filtration techniques do not easily work because of the existential nature of the frame conditions. Finally, we would like to obtain results without imposing the conditions on frames, especially the second.

References

[AS]   B. Alpern and F. Schneider 'Defining liveness'. To appear in Information Processing Letters.

[B1]   R. Bull 'A modal extension of intuitionistic logic' Notre Dame Journal of Formal Logic pp. 142-146 (1965).

[B2]   R. Bull 'MIPC as the formalization of an intuitionist concept of modality' Journal of Symbolic Logic, pp. 609-616 (1966).

[B5]   R. Bull and K. Segerberg 'Basic modal logic' in [GG] pp.1-88 (1984).

[C]   B. Chellas 'Modal Logic' Cambridge University Press (1980).

[F1]   G. Fischer Servi 'On modal logic with an intuitionist base' Studia Logica , pp.141-149 (1977).

[F2]   G. Fischer Servi 'Semantics for a class of intuitionist modal calculi' in ed. M. Chiara 'Italian Studies in the Philosophy of Science' Reidel, Dordrecht, pp 59-72 (1981).

[GG]   ed. D. Gabbay and F. Guenthner 'Handbook of Philosophical Logic Vol II' Reidel, Dordrecht, (1984).

[HC]   G. Hughes and M. Cresswell 'An Introduction to Modal Logic' Methuen (1968).

[Ma]   P. Martin-Löf 'Constructive mathematics and computer programming', in 'Logic, Methodology and Philosophy of Science VI' North Holland (1982).

[Mc]   D. McCarty 'Realizability and recursive mathematics' Report CMU-CS-84-131, Dept. of Computer Science, Carnegie-Mellon (1984).

[Sa]   H. Sahlqvist 'Completeness and correspondence in the first and second order semantics for modal logic' in ed. S. Kanger 'Procs. of 3rd Scandinavian Logic Symposium' pp 110-143, North-Holland (1975).

[Sm]   M. Smyth 'Powerdomains and predicate transformers: a topological view' Research Report, Dept. of Computer Science, Edinburgh University SR-126-83 (1983).

[T]   R. Thomason 'Combinations of tense and modality' in [GG] pp 135-166 (1984).

[V1]   D.I. Vakarelov 'Simple Examples of Incomplete Logics' Comptes rendus de l'Academie Bulgare des Sciences, Tome 33, No. 5 (1980).

[V2]   D.I. Vakarelov 'Intuitionistic Modal Logics Incompatible With the Law of the Excluded Middle' Studia Logica XL, 2 pp 103, 111, (1981).

[V3]   D.I. Vakarelov 'An Application of Rieger-Nishimura Formulas to the Intuitionistic Modal Logics' Studia Logica, XLIV, 7 pp 79, 85 (1985).

[VB]   J. Van Bentham 'Correspondence theory' in [GG] pp 167-248 (1984).

AUTHOR INDEX